The Economics of Friendship

Mnemosyne Supplements

MONOGRAPHS ON GREEK AND LATIN LANGUAGE AND LITERATURE

VOLUME 429

The titles published in this series are listed at *brill.com/mns*

The Economics of Friendship

Conceptions of Reciprocity in Classical Greece

By

Tazuko Angela van Berkel

TUTA SUB AEGIDE PALLAS · 1683 ·

BRILL

LEIDEN | BOSTON

Library of Congress Cataloging-in-Publication Data

Names: Berkel, Tazuko Angela van, 1979- author.
Title: The economics of friendship : conceptions of reciprocity in classical Greece / by Tazuko Angela van Berkel.
Other titles: Mnemosyne, bibliotheca classica Batava. Supplementum ; 429.
Description: Leiden ; Boston : Brill, [2020] | Series: Mnemosyne supplements, 0169-8958 ; volume 429 | Includes bibliographical references and index.
Identifiers: LCCN 2019039751 (print) | LCCN 2019039752 (ebook) | ISBN 9789004416130 (hardback) | ISBN 9789004416147 (ebook)
Subjects: LCSH: Friendship–Greece. | Friendship in literature. | Values–Greece. | Exchange–Greece. | Interpersonal relations–Greece. | Greece–Civilization–To 146 B.C.
Classification: LCC DF78 .B397 2020 GN486.3 (print) | LCC DF78 GN486.3 (ebook) | DDC 938–dc23
LC record available at https://lccn.loc.gov/2019039751
LC ebook record available at https://lccn.loc.gov/2019039752

Typeface for the Latin, Greek, and Cyrillic scripts: "Brill". See and download: brill.com/brill-typeface.

ISSN 0169-8958
ISBN 978-90-04-41613-0 (hardback)
ISBN 978-90-04-41614-7 (e-book)

This book is printed on acid-free paper and produced in a sustainable manner.

Contents

Preface

What do we owe to others? And what does it mean to owe somebody? This book is about the many ways in which the Greeks of the Classical Period, ranging from the Athenian attending lawsuits to the elite philosopher of the 4th century, made sense of these questions. Meaningful relations have two important characteristics: first, they are all about the long haul, they fit into the long-term order of things, they are premised on patience, trust and accepting the many insecurities that human flesh is heir to; secondly, they revolve around partners who are prepared to see actions and gestures for what they are, as acts of kindness above and beyond the call of duty, who are prepared to understand themselves as part of a larger whole and to realize that life is not about getting even but about paying it forward.

This book is no stranger to the long haul. It was originally a doctoral thesis, which I defended at Leiden University in the fall of 2012. After enjoying the privileges of being a PhD-student at the Leiden University Centre for the Arts in Society, it was an idyllic six-month stay at the Netherlands Institute of Advanced Studies in Wassenaar (2012) and an appointment at Leiden University, funded from Ineke Sluiter's Spinoza prize, that allowed me to finish my dissertation and, after years of working on other projects, to return to it and revise it. A two-week period in 2017 of legitimized monomaniacism at the wonderful library of the Fondation Hardt in Geneva allowed me to return to the book and start to revise it: it was there that I laid the groundwork for chapters 3, 4 and 7.

In this book I argue that the specific ways of understanding what we owe to others are culturally specific. Nevertheless, I think I have come to understand a thing or two about gratitude. Gratitude means acknowledging that the things bestowed upon you are not so much the result of merit as they are the fruit of generosity. Ineke Sluiter and Josine Blok have been the best supervisors and role models I could have wished for. Thank you for paying it forward. And thank you, Ineke, for having my back in all the ways an aspiring academic can hope for.

Gratitude means acknowledging that achievements are rarely individual exploits, and that we are all part of a larger whole. I have benefited much from discussing my work and ideas with my colleagues at the Classics Department at Leiden, especially Marlein van Raalte, and within OIKOS, the Dutch National Research School for Classical Studies. Now is a wonderful time to be a classicist in the Netherlands. It is also a good time to be an interdisciplinary scholar. Memorable conversations with great scholars, such as David Konstan,

Josh Ober, Carla Risseeuw, Erik Bähre, Arjo Klamer and the late Allan Silver, have helped me to develop my own approach and to find my own voice.

Many thanks to both anonymous referees of Brill who have taken the time to provide me with incisive feedback and fair criticism; to Nina King, Helen Kuyper and Jan van Ophuijsen for proofreading and correcting my English; to Olivia Monster and Charlotte van der Voort for proofreading and updating my bibliography. Needless to say, all remaining mistakes are my own.

Finally, gratitude means kicking the habit that many academics crippled by impostor syndrome are prone to: saying sorry all the time. Often, "sorry" seems to be the easiest word for discharging a debt, a quick redemption. I am learning to convert these sorries into thank-yous, my "sorry I'm so so very late" into "thank you so much for your patience", "sorry I haven't been much fun lately" into "thank you for bearing with me". It is in this spirit that I wish to thank my friends, Anne, Kathleen, my beloved parents, brothers and sisters-in-law, Yuna, Vince, and Cas who is saving to buy his aunt's first book.

Yes, it does take a village. This is why I wish to dedicate this book to Mathilde, Jan, and Helen, my weird and wonderful family.

CHAPTER 1

Introduction: The Economics of Friendship

Friendship is the greatest boon.[1] Life is not worth living if you do not have at least one friend.[2] A worthy friend is a physician to your pain[3] and there is no possession lovelier than a friend.[4] A friend is another self.[5] Friends share everything.[6]

Classical Greek literature abounds in maxims, aphorisms and moral guidelines about friendship. Friendship, φιλία, was high on the philosophical agenda, repeatedly discussed in Socratic dialogues by both Xenophon and Plato; it was the topic of substantial parts of Aristotle's ethical work.[7] In popular discourse too, friendship was extensively talked about: it ranked alongside one's relationship with the gods,[8] and it was a matter one could consult the gods and oracles about.[9] This prominent place of φιλία in moral discourse can mean two things: (1) φιλία is of central importance in social life and its moral value is beyond doubt; (2) φιλία is being talked about because it is a problem: its function, value and meaning are contested. This book will argue that both statements can be true at the same time.

It has been noted that in the classical period the concept of φιλία is "characterized by unresolved tensions and contradictions."[10] One specific source of such tensions and contradictions was the role and meaning of money, trade and detached exchanges in social life. The sources reflect an abundance of questions, views and dilemmas among the Greeks of the Classical Period. There was cynicism about the capacity of money to "buy friends",[11] moral censure towards

---

1 E.g. Xen. *Mem.* II.iv.2: μέγιστον ἀγαθόν; cf. *Hiero* III.1: μέγα ἀγαθόν, III.3: μέγιστον ἀγαθόν.

2 Democr. DK 68b22: ζῆν οὐκ ἄξιος, ὅτῳ μηδὲ εἷς ἐστι χρηστὸς φίλος. Cf. Ar. *EN* 1155a5 ff.

3 Men. *Sent.* 456 (Jäkel): Λύπης ἰατρός ἐστιν ὁ χρηστὸς φίλος.

4 Men. *Sent.* 575 (Jäkel): Οὐκ ἔστιν οὐδὲν κτῆμα κάλλιον φίλου.

5 Ar. *EN* 1166a31–32; cf. *EE* 1245a29–30, *MM* 1213a11–13.

6 Eur. *Or.* 735. Cf. Eur. *Andr.* 376–377: φίλων γὰρ οὐδὲν ἴδιον, οἵτινες φίλοι | ὀρθῶς πεφύκασ', ἀλλὰ κοινὰ χρήματα; Aristoph. *Plut.* 234; Plato, *Rep.* IV.424a1–2; V.449c5.

7 E.g. Xen. *Mem.* II, III.xi; Pl. *Lysis*, *Rep.* 1; Ar. *EN* VIII and IX, *EE* VII. Fürst (1996).

8 Is. 1.16.

9 The gods: e.g. Xen. *Mem.* II.vi.8; on oracles see Parker (1967), 272–273. Friendship could also be the subject of magic spells and curses; e.g. Soph. *OC* 1192–1194. Cf. Winkler (1990), 77–78.

10 Gonzalez (2000), 386. Cf. Gonzalez (1995), 70: "aporia is rooted in the very nature of friendship."

11 Soph. Fr. 88 (Radt): τὰ χρήματ' ἀνθρώποισιν εὑρίσκει φίλους, (…) | ἔπειτα δ' οὐδεὶς ἐχθρὸς οὔτε

 | DOI:10.1163/9789004416147_002

relatives who appeared to be putting money above family,[12] jokes about daughters who affectionately kiss their fathers only to fish out the triobolus from under his tongue.[13] There were expressions of despair over the fact that, unlike gold and silver, friends have no mark of validity impressed on them,[14] analogies of testing friends by circumstances just like gold is tested by fire,[15] claims that in times of need a friend is better than money,[16] and that the exchange value of a genuine friend is incalculable.[17] There were thought experiments with the idea that friends may have a price,[18] be treasures,[19] commodities,[20] possessions,[21] profitable,[22] or objects of purchase.[23]

This book is about Classical Greek conceptualizations of "relationships", the bonds that the Greeks in the world of the classical polis called φιλία. It is not so much about the relationships themselves, the social fabric of ties that people were born into and that they developed, expanded and adapted in the course of their lives[24] but more about the ways the Greeks of the Classical Period *thought* they related to each other: about how they preferred to express the nature of their bonds and the expectations that go with them, how they preferred to represent the to and fro of obligations, how they talked about relationships that

---

φύεται | πρὸς χρήμαθ' οἵ τε φύντες ἀρνοῦνται στυγεῖν. Cf. Aristoph. *Plut.* 829–839; Pind. *Pyth.* 5,5; Bias DK 73a, Eur. *Med.* 561, *El.* 1131.

12 Lys. 32.17; Isae. 9.25.

13 Aristoph. *Wasps* 605–612.

14 Eur. *Med.* 516–519: ὦ Ζεῦ, τί δὴ χρυσοῦ μὲν ὃς κίβδηλος ᾖι | τεκμήρι' ἀνθρώποισιν ὤπασας σαφῆ, | ἀνδρῶν δ' ὅτωι χρὴ τὸν κακὸν διειδέναι | οὐδεὶς χαρακτὴρ ἐμπέφυκε σώματι. Cf. n. 257 below.

15 Is. 1.25.

16 Men. *Sent.* 214. (Jäkel)

17 Eur. *Or.* 1156–1157: ἀλόγιστον δέ τοι |τὸ πλῆθος ἀντάλλαγμα γενναίου φίλου.

18 Xen. *Mem.* II.v.

19 φίλοι as θησαυρός: Eur. *El.* 565, Xen., *Cyr.* VIII.ii.19; as deposits of wealth: Soph. *OT* 232; Men. *Sent.* 810 (Jäkel), Is. 1.29; φίλοι as more secure investments than hoards of money: Men. *Dysc.* 805–812.

20 Φίλοι as χρήματα: Xen. *Mem.* II.iii. Cf. Anaximenes 1.10.4: φίλοι χρήματα κτήματα. τὰ δὲ ἐπίκτητα φίλοι χρήματα κτήματα.

21 Φίλοι as κτήματα: Xen. *Mem.* II.iv.1: the φίλος as πάντων κτημάτων κράτιστον; Men. *Sent.* 575: Οὐκ ἔστιν οὐδὲν κτῆμα κάλλιον φίλου; Hdt. 5.24.3: κτημάτων πάντων ἐστὶ τιμιώτατον ἀνὴρ φίλος συνετός τε καὶ εὔνοος. Cf. Xen. *Oec.* I.14. Cf. Dirlmeier (1931), 50.

22 Φίλοι as κέρδος: Xen. *Mem.* I.ii.7: μέγιστον κέρδος. Cf. Xen. *Ag.* XI.v: τούς γε μὴν διαβόλους μᾶλλον ἢ τοὺς κλέπτας ἐμίσει, μείζω ζημίαν ἡγούμενος φίλων ἢ χρημάτων στερίσκεσθαι.

23 Xen. *Mem.* II.x; Eur. fr. 934: νοῦν ἔχοντος ⟨ἦν ἄρα⟩ | φίλον πρίασθαι χρημάτων πολλῶν σαφῆ. Eur. *Or.* 1155–1157: οὐκ ἔστιν οὐδὲν κρεῖσσον ἢ φίλος σαφής, | οὐ πλοῦτος, οὐ τυραννίς· ἀλόγιστον δέ τοι | τὸ πλῆθος ἀντάλλαγμα γενναίου φίλου.

24 For historical surveys of φιλία in Classical Athens, see Konstan (1997), 53–91, Millett (1991), 109–126, Blundell (1989), introduction, Foxhall (1998).

had turned sour, how they motivated changes in the terms or conditions of relationships or the termination of these. It is about **folk theory** of social relations.[25]

This book is also about the **conceptual tools** that shape Classical Greek thinking about relationships. Thinking and talking about abstractions such as relatedness, obligations and expectations requires tools, such as concepts, metaphors, models and contrastive oppositions. It requires principles of organization and demarcation: what counts as φιλία and what does not? Are there differences within the range of "relations"? How do we describe the difference between the relation a lover has to his beloved and a client to a prostitute? Are teachers our friends, because they give us wisdom, or are they our slaves because they work for us? Is ritual sacrifice the same as bribing the gods? Are parents creditors who have given us life as a kind of cash advance?

Statements about φιλία, positive and negative, reflect and constitute ideals. Statements about social norms ("how does it work in our society") are almost always closely bound up with normative statements ("how *should* it work", "how I *wish* it worked"). Reconstructions of the Greek attitude towards personal relations are reconstructions of their wishful thinking. Does this mean that we, as practitioners of the history of mentalities, are stuck with fair-weather reports, hypocrisy and political correctness? Not quite. A lot can be learned about people's convictions, sensitivities, worries and fears if one listens to what they wish for. In fact, the frequent problematization of φιλία in the Classical Age is telling in itself, since one of the main issues that people were preoccupied with was the nature of **reciprocity** in φιλία. In 5th- and 4th-century Athens, the prevailing norm was the dual principle of Helping Friends and Harming Enemies.[26] The underlying idea is that friendship is a form of solidarity and that solidarity is "a mutual thing": friendship consists in a continuous process of give and take. "Friends make gifts, gifts make friends."[27] This idea of reciprocity was not only central in philosophical works; reciprocity in φιλία (or the breach and lack of it) was also essential to many tragedy plots[28] and served to characterize opponents (anyone who mistreats his φίλοι) and speakers (anyone who has

25 Cf. Section 4 below on the EMIC/ETIC-distinction in the social sciences.

26 E.g. Pl. *Rep.* 331e–332a; Lys. 9.20; Eur. *Ion.* 1045–1047; Aristoph. *Birds* 420 ff.; Soph. *Ant.* 643 ff.; Xen. *Anab.* I.iii.6, *Cyr.* I.iv.25, *Hiero* II.2; Xen. *Mem.* II.vi.35. See below in Section 2. The Helping Friends Harming Enemies slogan is coined in the influential study by Blundell (1989) who demonstrates the importance of φιλία in Sophocles' plays. See Belfiore (2000) on Harming Friends as the most important plot pattern in Athenian drama.

27 Sahlins (1972), 186.

28 See Belfiore (2000) for a study on φιλία in the characterization, imagery, and plot structure of fifth-century Athenian drama. Cf. Blundell (1989).

always treated his φίλοι well) in legal or political speeches.[29] In several sources we find the norm of reciprocity propagated and repeated,[30] to the point where we may seriously question how self-evident this norm was. Why does something that goes without saying have to be said so often?

The motif of reciprocity persists into Hellenistic and Roman literature.[31] However, the importance of reciprocity in φιλία bonds seems to be a focus that is peculiar to the Classical era.[32] One of the factors that may be at play here is that conceptually speaking the norm of reciprocity is not entirely self-evident and unambiguous. Although proper adherence to the norms of φιλία belongs to the core skills of forming a society,[33] these norms are felt to be less than self-evident: people start to talk about the norms that they live by out of a perceived need to formulate them explicitly. There is much that can be said about the historical causes behind this phenomenon; the scale and complexity of polis life, for instance, may have contributed to an increased interest in the topic.[34] However, part of the interest in the norms of φιλία is catalyzed by a related but distinct development: the increasing monetization, scaling-up and complexity of the Athenian economy.

It is here that the phenomenon of commercial exchange comes in. In the literature of Classical Athens, the conceptual apparatus of the market provides

29 Aristotle lists τὸ φιλεῖν as one of the effects that a speaker should aim at in his audience. *Rhet.* II.iv. Cf. Konstan (2007), 169–184.

30 See section 2.1 below.

31 E.g. Sen. *De Beneficiis*. Although the theme of reciprocity persists, it is supplemented with other preoccupations, such as frankness (παρρησία, as opposed to flattery). E.g. Plut. *Quomodo*, Themistios, Or. 22.276c, Philodemus, *Peri parrhêsias*. Cf. Konstan (1998), (1997), 93–148. On παρρησία in friendship, see the introduction in Sluiter & Rosen (2004); Van Raalte (2004) for παρρησία and philosophical friendship in Plato's dialogues; Fitzgerald (1996) and (1997) for an account of the centrality of παρρησία in friendship in Plutarch and Philodemus.

32 Seaford (1993), (1994) points out that the theme of violence between φίλοι does not have the central role in Homeric epics that it has in Attic tragedy. Belfiore (2000) xvi: "The predominance in tragedy of violation of *philia* may reflect a period and social context (fifth-century democratic Athens) in which reciprocal relationships between family members and other kinds of *philoi* had become problematic, in a way that they were not in Homer, because of the emergence of new modes of social and economic life." Foxhall (1998), 67: "In short, philosophers focused on "friendship" because it was a problem for them." Konstan (1998), 280 for the idea that the theme of reciprocity between equals is specific for the Classical Age.

33 Φιλία as a cohesive tie: e.g. Pl. *Prot.* 322c: δεσμοὶ φιλίας συναγωγοί; friendship as concord: Pl. *Rep.* 351d; Pl. *Leg.* VI.757a1–758a2; *Rep.* 311B9–C1; 127C; *Epistula* 6.323b, *Rep.* I.315D; *Alc.* 1.126bc; *Clit.* 409e, *Leg.* III.693b1–5.

34 Belfiore (2000), introduction; Seaford (1994).

the **models and metaphors** that help in shaping ideas about relationships. At the same time, this conceptual apparatus represents a way of dealing with persons and objects that the Greeks felt was at odds with the norms of φιλία, of friendship, kinship and ruler-ship. In these situations, monetary economy and the market provide a **contrastive model** from which other relationships can be demarcated. Conversely, the conceptual apparatus of the market itself finds its articulation in its contrast to φιλία-reciprocity. The rapid developments in the Athenian economy prompted economic reflection, discourse about money, debt and trade, and such reflection was high on the intellectual agenda. One of the issues on this agenda was whether there is a meaningful difference between "economic relations" and "personal relations".

The economic developments of the Classical Period have sometimes been described as a process of "disembedding", i.e. an emancipation of the economic realm from social and political structures.[35] This claim, pertaining to the economic performance and the system as a whole, is not part of the argument in this book. What will be argued is that the Classical Period witnesses the emergence of a new type of interpersonal relationship: the disembedded exchange, i.e. the instantaneous transaction of equivalent goods that takes place outside the norms of a durable relationship. It is against the foil of this disembedded type of exchange relationship that ideals of φιλία-reciprocity are articulated in this period. This book is about both sides of the coin: about the way in which φιλία-reciprocity and commercial exchange have come to define each other in a mutually dependent way.

1 Friendship: Money Can't Buy It?

Our modern everyday language is imbued with "money talk". We use economic metaphors, the idea of money, and metaphors of banks and markets to express our ideas about relationships with particular persons or relationships in general. Friendships require personal "investments", for "time is money", but there is a "payoff" and it will "cost you" if you do not; you may feel deeply "indebted" to some of your friends, but when it is "payback time" you will "square your account" with a friend who has lost all "credit" with you: he has turned out to be a "counterfeit" friend.

Of course, these are only metaphors. But metaphors create realities. They are among our main vehicles for comprehending abstract concepts and perform-

35 See Section 3 below.

ing abstract reasoning,[36] and organize a world of unstructured experiences into concepts we can deal with and make us capable of dealing with them, incorporating them in our world view and drawing inferences from them.[37] In our cultural discourses, money provides a powerful system of metaphors that enable us to shape abstract concepts such as value, to comprehend obligations and commitments and to conceive of, approach and handle the world around us as instrumental to our goals.[38]

At the same time, most economic metaphors have a negative ring when applied to personal relationships. They usually refer to problematic relationships, and when applied to healthy relations they may strike us as "cynical" in that they appear to violate the "friendly" nature of the relationship in question. In modern Anglo-American and European culture, there is a tension between economic paradigms and the notion that anything "personal" is "not for sale"—"Money can't buy me love", after all, for that would be "pricing the invaluable".

Moreover, as recent psychological research has demonstrated, in Anglo-American culture merely activating the *concept* of money suffices to change interpersonal behavior. Test subjects primed with bank notes typically switch to an "every man for himself"-attitude: not only are they less helpful and generous towards others; they are also less inclined to ask for help from others.[39] Representations of money appear to trigger a sense of autonomy and self-sufficiency and to evoke an atomistic individualistic world-view. This is revealing for the place of money in the conceptual architecture of our culture: in our

---

36 In this book the term "metaphor" will be used in the sense of a conceptual metaphor, as defined by Lakoff & Johnson (1980). A conceptual metaphor is a cross-domain mapping in the conceptual system, i.e., the phenomenon of understanding one idea or conceptual domain in terms of another.

37 Cf. Lakoff (1993). Metaphors function as framing devices, i.e. as "makers of meaning" (R.T. Lakoff (2000), 47–48) and "structures of expectation" (Tannen (1979)).

38 Simmel (1978 [1900]) for a conception of money as both the means and the symbol of processes of atomization in modern society. E.g. Lakoff & Johnson (1980) on the "Time is Money"-metaphor; Mirowski (2002) on the metaphor of science as a commodity; Gramm (1996) on the danger of (more technical) economic metaphors (such as "the invisible hand", "trickle down"), Hoey (1988) on money as a metaphor for metaphor itself, Gray (1996) on monetary value as metaphor for linguistic significance; Voss e.a. (1992), 205 on monetary metaphors for the "costs" of warfare; Strathern (1972), 99–120 and (1996), 517–519 on monetary metaphors in the context of marriage and bridewealth in Melanesia. Conversely, there is growing attention for the importance of metaphors in economic modeling, e.g. McCloskey (1983) & (1985), ch. 5; Klamer & Leonard (1994) for a distinction between "pedagogical", "heuristic" and "constitutive" economic metaphors.

39 Vohs (2006); cf. Lea e.a. (2006). Skinner (1953), 79 for an early behaviorist theory of money as a "generalized token reinforcement": the incentive power of money derives from the mere association with what it can buy.

part of the world, there is a tension between other-regarding behavior or sentiments and the set of ideas, norms and expectations evoked by the concept of money.

At first sight, this tension between the conceptual domain of money and the domain of other-regarding sentiments seems to fit into a series of oppositions that figure prominently in our ideologies of friendship and other relations. We tend to distinguish between instrumental relationships and elective affinities, and accordingly call some "formal" and others "personal": we think we enter some relations predominantly because of ulterior ends (with our colleagues, doctors, cleaning ladies, up to the end of the scale where we may hesitate to speak of "relations" at all, such as nameless plumbers, shopkeepers and bank employees), and enter other relations because we are committed to the unique and irreplaceable person that the other is (our friends, lovers and life-long partners). Correspondingly, we feel that within instrumental relationships it is acceptable to be overtly motivated by self-interest (we make contracts and deals to negotiate and harmonize our respective interests), whereas in other relations we are expected to be motivated by a regard for the interest of the other (we help friends and care for our loved ones because of *them*, not because of ourselves).[40] We also tend to think that some relations revolve around objective obligations towards one another and others around subjective favors and the sincere intention to benefit the other: we legally or contractually owe a fee to doctors and cleaning ladies, whereas we "feel" that we should help a friend in need. We distinguish between coerced or enforceable duties and good turns that are done above and beyond the call of duty and that are, in the terminology of moral theology, "supererogatory".[41]

These oppositions reflect distinctions and categorizations that are good for *us* to work with. However, we need to be aware that these oppositions may not be universal or self-evident.[42] When making cross-cultural comparisons between the ways people conceptualize relationships, most of these oppositions are not so much useful analytical tools, but rather are themselves objects

40 Between instrumentalism and other-directed concern: Blum (1980), Stocker (1976), Badhwar (1991), Hurka (2006); Berger (1986). Between instrumentalism and valuing the intrinsic worth of a friend: Scanlon (1998). Between appreciating the other as a unique self and regarding the other as a particular instance of a general class: Suttles (1970), Wiseman (1986).

41 E.g. Titmuss (1970) in an argument for preferring a completely voluntary system of blood donation over commercialized "enforced" systems. Cf. Kawall (2005) and Heyd (2005) for the ambiguous nature of promising as an act of supererogatory self-enforcement.

42 Cf. Bourdieu (1990 [1980]) on the "debilitating" dualisms, such as subject/object, agency/structure, private/public, nature/culture.

of inquiry:[43] under what circumstances are these oppositions created, in what contexts are they used, how are they manipulated?

This book is about Classical Greek conceptualizations of relationships in response to the increasing monetization of the Athenian economy. In Classical Athens, the idea of money represents a cluster of concepts that are related to a type of economic actions, events and processes that economic theory calls "**disembedded**" economic transactions.[44] Disembedded transactions are economic phenomena that are not embedded in social, religious and political relations. For instance, the instantaneous exchange of equivalent goods that takes place in a market economy (and that we would call "commercial") does not have repercussions for the social or political status of either partner, the relation between them or the religious order in which they participate: the transactors may have been strangers before the exchange and may revert to being so once they each have got what they wanted out of the transaction.

We may feel that this is a very minimalistic account of a "relationship", as something that can be confined to the short time frame formed by the cooperative endeavor between buyer and seller. At the same time, these minimalistic relationships are easy to deal with conceptually: the obligations to and fro are clear and objectifiable (the seller needs to deliver goods, the buyer needs to furnish the price agreed to), there are straightforward procedures for reaching consensus about the terms of the exchange (buyer and seller can negotiate, perhaps while referring to something like a "market price"), and the expectations to and fro are relatively transparent. Inhabitants of Classical Greece occasionally felt that, if one gave it a thought, these minimalistic transactions resembled interactions with parents, friends and gods that were also about "give and take" (there seemed to be **isomorphism**), whereas at the same time they often objected to a notion that they were exactly the same (they resisted **reductionism**).

The sophist Antiphon, for instance, reproaches Socrates with not charging his students a fee in return for the wisdom he allegedly claims to offer them:[45]

---

43 An example is the current pervasive ideological distinction between relations based on formal obligations and relations that are labeled "personal" because they are supposedly based on a "subjective definition of the situation". See Silver (1990) and (1997). Cf. Heller (1979) and Lasch (1977) on the emergence of the ideological split between the notions of emotion and interest, expressiveness and instrumentality, and its relation with historical change in social structure as a consequence of capitalism. See Chapter Four.

44 The terminology of "embedded" and "disembedded" economies are coined by Polanyi (1968). See Section 3 below.

45 Xen. *Mem.* I.vi.11–12. See Chapter Five on this episode.

in terms of market rationality, not charging a fee is sheer stupidity. Socrates' reply is that selling wisdom and virtue to any bidder would make him a prostitute; *giving* wisdom makes him a friend.[46] Knowledge economy comes to be reframed as knowledge prostitution. This vignette only works with an audience capable of following Antiphon's line of reasoning and acknowledging the formal isomorphism between a market situation and Socrates conversing with young Athenians. Conversely, Socrates' reaction too makes sense to the audience: prostitution is an example of a market situation and the implication that the exchange of wisdom and virtue is a kind of prostitution is repulsive. The same exchange can be interpreted as a disembedded market exchange and as taking place within the context of friendship, and the two interpretations are felt to be irreducibly different.

Xenophon's Socrates articulates and defends his model of education and wisdom by exploiting and exploring the twilight zone where the conceptual domain of friendship and that of monetary economics overlap. It is in this overlap between two conceptual domains, each with its own norms and rationality, that many of the negotiations and conceptualizations of values and social norms that plague the notion of φιλία with unresolved tension and contradictions emerge.

2 Φιλία

2.1 *Forms and Norms of φιλία-reciprocity*

In the world of the Classical Greek polis, the repertory of socially important durable relationships contains heterogeneous, and therefore sometimes overlapping, relationship types. There are the relations within the οἶκος: between husband and wife, master and slave, parents and children; the relations with deities; those with the other members of the group one belongs to: one's army unit, deme, village, city-state; those with members of a different social group: guest friends and international relations.

Each of these relationship types allows for more than one **conceptualization**. An οἶκος and a polis, for instance, can be understood as a group that pools resources and responsibilities and distributes them, with individuals as a "member".[47] Alternatively, it is possible to view such a group in relational

46 Xen. *Mem.* I.vi.13.

47 For the phrase μετέχειν τῆς πολέως and the terminology of "sharing" and "participating" in the conception of Athenian citizenship, see Blok (2009), (2017). For the notion of household as functional unities wherein members share, see Foxhall (1989) and (1998). For the

terms as a system of **exchanges**, i.e. relations between two or more parties who cooperate with one another by exchanging things (not necessarily material): marriage itself can be conceptualized as an exchange between families and as consisting in a series of exchanges between husband and wife.[48] Similarly, it was a popular conception in the ancient world that the parent-child bond was shaped as a reciprocal exchange extended over a long period of time: children *owe* filial care to their ageing parents *because* of the antecedent care and sustenance they have been provided with in their infancy by their parents.[49] Along the same lines, relationships within the polis, e.g. between a wealthy liturgist and the *demos*, can be represented as a dyadic relation of give and take.[50]

In the world of the classical Greek polis, many of these relations that allow for a conceptualization in terms of give and take were understood as φιλία-relations. Relations ranging from bonds between parents and children,[51] husband and wife,[52] between members of the same οἶκος (οἰκεῖοι), blood kin (συγγενεῖς), in-laws (κηδεσταί), neighbors, lovers,[53] king and servants,[54] ξένοι,[55] members of political factions,[56] mortals and gods,[57] or even supra-individual entities

---

οἶκος as a "common stock" to which both husband and wife contribute, see e.g. Xen. *Oec.* VII.13.

48 Marriage as an exchange and solidification of bonds between men: Ormand (1999), 14–18, Rabinowitz (1993), 21–22; Wohl (1998), 18–22, 128–131, 178–179; Lyons (2003); Von Reden (1995a), 49–51, 151–158. Marriage as φιλία between men and women: e.g. Ar. *EN* VIII (1162a16–33), Men. *Sent.* 809 (Jäkel). Cf. Blundell (1989), 46, Mueller (2001); on χάρις in marriage, see Redfield (1982), 196–198, Dover (1974), 210, Halperin (1985), 162.

49 Hom. *Il.* 4.447–448 (= 17.301–302), Hes. *O&D* 187–188; Ar. *Pol.* 1332b35–41, [Dem.] 10.40, Eur. *Supp.* 361–364, Eur. *Alc.* 681–684, Eur. fr. 1064. For conceptions of filial duty, see Chapter Three. For reciprocity ("generalized reciprocity", see Section 4 below, and Chapter Two Section 3.2, Chapter Three Section 1.2, Chapter Four Sections 1.2 and 3.2) within the *oikos*, see Foxhall (1989). Cf. Schaps (1979), 55ff. For comparable values in modern Greece, Du Boulay (1974), 15–17.

50 Ober (1989), 192–247, Christ (2006).

51 E.g. Lys. 6.23. See Dirlmeier (1931), 7–21 on φιλία between kin. Cf. Blundell (1989), 39–45.

52 E.g. Xen. *Hiero* III.7; Ar. *EN* 1162a20–24, Eur. *Med.* 549.

53 E.g. Xen. *Mem.* II.vi. See Halperin (1985). Occasionally, our sources seem to suggest a tension between conceptualizing a relation in terms of φιλία and in terms of ἔρως. See Chapter Six (also on the Pohlenz-Von Arnim-controversy).

54 E.g. Xen. *Cyr.* VIII.ii. On this passage see Gray (2011), 319ff., Nadon (2011), 118ff., Due (1989), 215ff.

55 See n. 131 below.

56 E.g. Lys. 31.13.

57 E.g. Pl. *Euth.* 14c–15b, *Rep.* 390c; Cf. Dodds (1951), 35; Parker (1998), 122–125; Osborne & Alcock (1994) cf. the popular address to Zeus as φίλος (Cook 2.2.1167). Aristotle objects against conceiving relations with deities as φιλία because they are too unequal. *NE* 1158b33–59a5. Cf. *MM* 1208b27–35.

such as allied poleis,[58] all of these could be designated as φιλία-bonds and referred to with ΦΙΛ-terminology.

The terminology of φιλία signifies first and foremost a long-term bond of mutual solidarity:[59] two or more φίλοι are well-disposed to each other and have a certain way of expressing this solidarity towards each other. In the specific cultural and social circumstances of the world of the 5th- and 4th-century classical Greek polis, this solidarity is manifested in mutually treating each other well:[60] φίλοι are supposed to help one another and to do good towards one another on a basis of mutuality[61] that goes beyond the show of good intentions.[62] Forensic speeches are rife with invocations and expressions of the norm of φιλία:

[Text 1]

> τούτων συμπάντων κεφάλαιόν ἐστιν ἐννέα τάλαντα καὶ δισχίλιαι δραχμαί. ἔτι τοίνυν καὶ ἰδίᾳ τισὶ τῶν πολιτῶν ἀποροῦσι συνεξέδωκε θυγατέρας καὶ ἀδελφάς, τοὺς δ' ἐλύσατο ἐκ τῶν πολεμίων, τοῖς δ' εἰς ταφὴν παρεῖχεν ἀργύριον. καὶ ταῦτ' ἐποίει ἡγούμενος εἶναι ἀνδρὸς ἀγαθοῦ ὠφελεῖν τοὺς φίλους, καὶ εἰ μηδεὶς μέλλοι εἴσεσθαι·
>
> The total of all these benefactions is nine talents and two thousand drachmas. In addition to this, he privately helped some of the poorer citizens by contributing to their daughters' and sisters' dowries, ransomed others from the enemy, and provided money for others for their burial. He did

58 E.g. Lys. 2.21, 2.36, 2.73. See Panessa (1990), Bolmarcich (2010).

59 E.g. Soph. *Aj.* 680; Isoc. 1.1.

60 In other historical periods, the emphasis is different. E.g. Hellenistic friendship literature is preoccupied with frankness and free speech (Konstan (1997), 93–103); in modern Western societies, intimacy is a decisive criterion for real friendships. Silver (1990) (1997).

61 βοηθεῖν: e.g. Eur. *Or.* 671, Aristoph. *Eq.* 92–94, Xen. *Mem.* III.xii.4; εὐ ποιεῖν: e.g. Xen. *Mem.* IV.iv.24; Lys. 3.5 (a lover about his *eromenos*); εὖ ἔρδειν: e.g. Thgn. 573–574; εὖ δρᾶν: e.g. Soph. *Phil.* 672; εὐεργετεῖν: e.g. Xen. *Mem.* II.ix.8; Men. *Sent.* 219 (Jäkel). ὠφελεῖν: Aristoph. *Eq.* 92–94, Xen. *Mem.* III.vi.2. From the side of the receiver: εὖ πάσχειν: Eur. *Or.* 719; Thuc. 3.54.2. See Blundell (1989), esp. 26–59, on the twin principle of Helping Friends/Harming Enemies. Cf. Konstan (1997), 56–59; Millett (1991), 109–126; Dover (1974), 180–181; Bolkestein (1939), 159.

62 E.g. Soph. *Ant.* 543. Cf. Dirlmeier (1931), 28. Anthropologists have observed that in cultures where people are more dependent upon reciprocal relations than in ours, people rarely render thanks for gifts *verbally*: verbal displays of gratitude (reciprocating on the spot) are seen as shallow substitutes for a deeper sense of obligation to reciprocate with a real gift or favor. Pitt-Rivers (1992), 218, 244 n. 3; Malinowski (1922), 190, 270–273; Van Wees (1998), 26.

> this in the belief *that an honorable man should help his friends*, even if nobody would know about it.[63]

This quotation is part of the speaker's attempt to rehabilitate the reputation of his father and to exonerate him from the charge of embezzling large parts of the property of his relative Aristophanes (the property was confiscated after Aristophanes' ignominious execution, but the yields did not meet popular expectations). The speaker's defense strategy is to demonstrate the implausibility of his father stealing public property, given the man's habit of "spending fortunes voluntarily" (ἄνευ ἀνάγκης (…) πολλὰ ἀναλίσκειν)[64] on the city and on his friends (ἃ ἀνήλωσεν εἰς τὴν πόλιν καὶ εἰς τοὺς φίλους).[65] It is in this context that the speaker lists all the public benefactions (λειτουργίαι)[66] taken on by his father (totaling nine talents and two thousand drachmas!) and his private favors to fellow-citizens (financing dowries, ransoms and burials). Through all this, the speaker emphasizes, his father was not driven by ulterior motives, but solely by a wish to do the right thing and to do what a decent man ought to do: to help his friends (ὠφελεῖν τοὺς φίλους), with help that was manifested in a pattern of public spending and concrete material support. As is common in forensic speeches, the speaker takes care to show that his father both adhered to common and popular norms (he helped his friends) *and* that his father's support was above and beyond the call of duty (he helped his friends, but did so on an exceptional scale, even if nobody knew about it).

Friendly support need not be restricted to the providing of material means. Assistance may range from material help to immaterial favors such as speaking well of a friend,[67] but regardless of the precise content, it is structured as a **reciprocal** endeavor.[68] Friends are imagined and supposed to do each other good on a basis of mutuality; hence the repeated norm of returning a favor, giving a counter-gift and reacting to care and attention by offering care and

---

63 Lys. 19.59; *transl.* Todd (2000).

64 Lys. 19.56.

65 Lys. 19.56.

66 Lys. 19.57.

67 Helping one's φίλοι in court: Isae. 1.7, Hyp. I.10, Lyc. fr. XI, Lys. 5.1, 7.18, 21.22. Cf. Dirlmeier (1931), 36–38; friends as indispensable for political career: Xen. *Cyr.* VIII.vii.13, Pl. *Ep.* 7.325cd, Ar. *Pol.* 1284a20 ff., Plut. *Ar.* 1.2.4, *Mor.* 807d. Cf. Connor (1971). Cf. Dover (1974), 177; Bolkestein (1939), 133–148.

68 "Reciprocal" need not imply "equal": the respective parties may have different obligations and expectations, as is for instance the case in the φιλία between parents and children (Eur. *IA* 12–56; *Alc.* 302–304) or between mortals and gods (e.g. Soph. *Aj.* 680).

attention in return.[69] Often this norm of reciprocity is expressed in the vocabulary of "give and take", i.e. of giving (διδόναι), receiving (λαμβάνειν, δέχεσθαι) and returning (ἀποδιδόναι) or exchanging (ἀμείβειν, (ἐξ)αλλάττειν),[70] the good turns exchanged being "gifts" (a δῶρον, or a δωρεά),[71] or instances of χάρις, i.e. manifestations of generosity and gratitude.[72]

This structure of reciprocity typically extends over a longer time frame:[73] one receives help and is expected to help the other in return should the occasion arise. This time frame is what cements a bond into a φιλία-relation that

69 E.g. Dem. 20.6: οἱ δὲ τοὺς ἀγαθόν τι ποιοῦντας ἑαυτοὺς μὴ τοῖς ὁμοίοις ἀμειβόμενοι …; Xen. *Mem.* IV.iv.24: εὖ ποιεῖν … ἀντευεργετεῖν; Aristoph., *Plutus* 1029: τὸν εὖ παθόντα ἀντευποιεῖν; Thgn. 573–574: εὖ ἔρδων εὖ πάσχε; Soph. *Phil.* 672: εὖ δρᾶν εὖ παθών; Xen. *Mem.* II.ix.8: εὐρεγετεῖν … ἀντευεργετεῖν; Xen. *Mem.* II.viii.3: ὠφελεῖν … ἀντωφελεῖν; Xen. *Cyr.* VIII.iii.49: θεραπεύειν … ἀντιθεραπεύειν; Xen. *Mem.* I.iv.18: χαρίζεσθαι … ἀντιχαρίζεσθαι. Cf. Bolkestein (1939), 159; Blundell (1989), 26–59; Millett (1991), 109–126. Bolkestein (1939), 158: "[D]as Prinzip der Gegenseitigkeit [hat] eine der Grundlagen des sozialen Verkehrs der Griechen gebildet." On the central role of reciprocity in φιλία, see Millett (1991), 109–159, Mitchell (1997), 8–9. On the ideology of reciprocity from the Dark Age to the late-Archaic period, see Gallant (1991), 146 ff., Qviller (1981), Donlan 1981, 1985, Morris 1986a, Walcot (1970), Gallant (1982), Millett (1984), Morris 1986b. More abstract accounts of reciprocity are found in the philosophical writers: Pl. *Lys.* 212c–d; Ar. *EN* 1155b27–56a5, 1156b33–57a6, *Rhet.* 1381a7–10 Cf. Annas (1977).

70 E.g. Hes. *O&D* 354 ff.: καὶ δόμεν ὅς κεν δῶι καὶ μὴδόμεν, ὅς κεν μὴ δῶι | δώτῃ μέν τις ἔδωκεν, ἀδώτῃ δ' οὔτις ἔδωκεν. Dem. 20.64: ὅσους εὖ ποιήσαντας ἡ πόλις ἀντ' εὖ πεποίηκε. Epicharmus fr. 30 (Diels): ἁ δὲ ξεὶρ τὰν ξεῖρα νίζει. δός τι καὶ λάβοις τί κα. Men. *Sent.* 317, 322 (Meineke): λαβὼν ἀπόδος, ἄνθρωπε, καὶ λήψῃ πάλιν, | λυποῦντα λύπει, καὶ φιλοῦνθ' ὑπερφίλει; Hes. *O&D* 349 ff.: εὖ μὲν μετρεῖσθαι παρὰ γείτονος, εὖ δ' ἀποδοῦναι. Dem. 20.6: τοῖς ὁμοίοις ἀμειβόμενοι. Cf. Blundell (1989), 32–33.

71 Blundell (1989), 33: "Any kind of favour or service can be given and repaid like a gift." E.g. [Arist.] *Rhet. ad. Alex.* 1447: δωροῦνται πάντες ἐλπίζοντες ὠφεληθήσεσθαι, ἢ τῶν προτέρων εὐεργεσιῶν χάριν ἀποδιδόντες; [Pl.] *Def.* 414a: δωρεὰ ἀλλαγὴ χάριτος.

72 E.g. Eur. *HF* 1134–1137: καλὸς γὰρ ἀστοῖς στέφανος Ἑλλήνων ὕπο | ἄνδρ' ἐσθλὸν ὠφελοῦντας εὐκλείας τυχεῖν. | κἀγὼ χάριν σοι τῆς ἐμῆς σωτηρίας| τήνδ' ἀντιδώσω· νῦν γὰρ εἶ χρεῖος φίλων. The reciprocal nature of χάρις is brought out by the proverbial expression that "χάρις breeds χάρις" (Soph. *Aj.* 522; cf. *OC* 779, Eur. *Hel.* 1234, Ar. *Rhet.* 1385a16) and Aristotle's remark that the central position of the temple of the *Charites* in Athens signifies the importance of reciprocal χάρις in polis life (*EN* 1133a3–5); See Chapter Two Section 1 and Chapter Seven Section 1; Chapter Seven Section 1. Good turns in a marriage ("sexual χάρις"): see Chapter Six. Cf. Redfield (1982), 196–198; Halperin (1985), 162; good turns in politics, e.g. Lyc. *Leocr.* 100–101, Lys. 21.22–25; good turns in relations with gods: e.g. *CEG* 275, Aristoph. *Thesm.* 275–276 (with Fraenkel (1962), 118–119 and Parker (1998), 111); the term χαρίεσσα ἀμοιβή ("graceful return") occurs frequently on votive inscriptions; e.g. CEG 326. See Versnel (1981), 47 ff.; Van Straten (1981). See Chapter Two.

73 Often even preferably so: e.g. Dem. 23.134. Cf. Isoc. 1.30, Pl. *Phdr.* 233b–c, Crates 1.5 (Diels). Cf. Pearson (1962), 151 ff. Blundell (1989), 36: "[L]ong-term mutual benefit must take priority over immediate gratification." On the importance of time, see Chapter Two.

will extend into the future: φιλία requires and *presupposes* trust and reliability (both of them aspects of πίστις) and hence it *implies* trust.[74] The return of favors and the exchange of benefits are believed to create lasting ties of gratitude, goodwill and trust,[75] and to secure justice and cohesion in society.[76] In the world of the 5th- and 4th-century Greek polis, the popular name for such ties was φιλία.

2.2 *Semantic Preliminaries*

2.2.1 φιλία is Not a Feeling …

In the short overview above on φιλία and χάρις, two key terms in the ancient Greek conceptualization of relatedness, the elements of **emotions** and **affection** are conspicuous by their absence.[77] The terminology of φιλία first and foremost signifies a lasting bond of mutual solidarity structured along the lines of reciprocity.[78] This is obscured by the convention in Anglo-Saxon literature to translate the noun φίλος as "friend", the verb φιλεῖν as "to love" and the abstract noun φιλία as "friendship" and/or "love". This convention is justifiable for purposes of translation; in this book there will be much talk about "friendship"

74 E.g. Men. *Sent.* 100 (Jäkel). Absence of trust is one of the greatest sources of worry and lamentation for Theognis, because it makes friendship impossible: Thgn. 65–68, 73 f., 77–92, 95 ff., 115–128, 415 f., 811–814, 857–860. See Foxhall (1998), Blundell (1989), 34–36; for the close association of the language of friendship and of trust, see Taillardat (1982); Hummel (1987) argues for metrical complementarity between φίλος and πιστός in Homeric epic. Cf. Eisenstadt & Roniger (1984), 27 on the importance of trust in φιλία-relations outside the οἶκος, ranging from patron-client bonds, ξενία-relations to neighbors.

75 Trust (πίστις): e.g. Aesch. 1.132, 142, 147, Hes. *O&D* 708 f., Xen. *Hiero* IV.1. Goodwill (εὔνοια): Dem. 18.5, 21.282; Xen. *Anab.* VII.vii.46. Cf. Goldhill (1986), 79–107; Herman (1987), introduction, Konstan (1997), pp. 53–92, (1998); Millett (1991), 109–126, 218 ff. Gratitude (χάρις): see n. 76 above, and Chapters Two, Three and Four.

76 Cf. the popular conception of justice in Pl. *Rep.* 332a of "owing (ὀφειλεῖν) good to one's φίλοι and evil to one's ἐχθροί". See Chapter Four Section 2. Cf. Pl. *Euth.* 14b: gratifying the gods brings salvation to the *oikos* and the *polis* alike. See on this passage Chapter Two Section 1. Conversely, failed reciprocation is a serious offense and a breach of justice, and the absence of reciprocity is seen as corrosive for the solidarity and coherence within society. E.g. Thgn. 1.1135–1155 (with Levine (1985), 193): the departure of Pistis, Sophrosyne and the Kharites are symptomatic for an age of social disintegration; Hes. *O&D* 190 (with West (1978), ad loc.): in the Iron Age, there will be no more χάρις ("no appreciation") for those who keep their oath—one of the symptoms of a crisis for humanity. Xen. *Mem.* II.ii.13–14: failure to observe χάρις to one's parents excludes one from all realms of human life.

77 On the emotional aspects of χάρις, see Chapter Two.

78 My account of φιλία is heavily indebted to the unpublished work of Adriaan Rademaker, Christiaan Caspers, Evelyn van 't Wout and Casper de Jonge on the semantics of the verbs φιλεῖν, ἀγαπᾶν and στέργειν.

and "friends" where in the Greek texts the generic terms φιλία and φίλος have a larger extension than the specific bonds of elective affinities that are referred to by our modern friendship-vocabulary.

For purposes of analysis, it is instructive to realize that these translation conventions obscure aspects that are important for an understanding of Classical Greek reflection on human relations. The first is the place of emotions, affection and personal valuation in the conceptualization of human bonds. The argument is *not* that φιλία is fundamentally incompatible with affection and emotions. If anything, given the ubiquitously highly valued nature of φιλία, it is extremely unlikely that positive emotions are *absent* in a φιλία bond. The claim is different: the term φιλία *does not in itself denote* introspective phenomena. φιλία is first and foremost a **relational** term.[79]

I restrict myself to a (more or less) **synchronic** claim: both the social-historical and the semantic outlines offered here apply to the Greek world of the 5th- and 4th-century.[80] Within this historical context, φιλία primarily denotes the bond that persists between two φίλοι.[81] This is not to say that emotions and affects are altogether absent or irrelevant in a φιλία-relation;[82] it only indicates that their presence is not a decisive criterion for calling a relation one of φιλία. In some φιλία-bonds (e.g. between mother and child or between lovers) it is highly implausible that affection and emotions are absent; in other φιλία-bonds the relevance of emotions and affection become more questionable (e.g. neighbors, ξένοι), and in some cases it is downright far-fetched to presume the pres-

79 Aristotle, however, lists τὸ φιλεῖν as one of the πάθη in *Rhet.* II.vii.

80 I will therefore not elaborate on the semantics of the Homeric adjective φίλος which is subject to debate. Because the adjective is often construed in agreement with impersonal entities such as one's limbs, life, clothes and gifts, it is generally taken as roughly equivalent to a reflexive possessive pronoun ("one's own"). Adkins (1963), followed by Von Reden (1995) 45 and Scott (1984), argues that the adjective φίλος serves to demarcate those persons and things an individual can rely upon. Cf. Kretschmer (1927) who traces back the Indo-European reflexive pronoun to the Lydian *bilis* ("his own"). The discussion is reopened by Hooker (1989) and Robinson (1990), followed by Konstan (1997), who maintain that φίλος means "dear/beloved" and "loving" and that Homeric heroes "loved" their limbs, clothes and weapons dearly because they were fully aware that they depended on them for survival. Benveniste (1973), 273–288 interprets the Homeric use of the adjective φίλος in terms of reciprocity: all objects and persons involved in rituals and processes of "institutionalized reciprocity" are labeled metonymically φίλος. The question of Homeric φίλος is beyond the scope of this study.

81 Goldhill (1986), 79–83.

82 The reappraisal of emotions in ancient accounts of friendship is the most important contribution (and qualification of existing scholarship) of Konstan (1997) and Konstan (2000).

ence of emotions (e.g. between fellow citizens or cities).[83] Just as the English word "mother" may evoke strong feelings of affection and care without having the *meaning* of "loved one", the vocabulary of φιλία may, in some contexts, also evoke these positive emotions without denoting them.

This is somewhat easier to grasp for the nouns than for the transitive verb φιλεῖν. Although the past decades have seen a shift in the understanding of the nouns φίλος and φιλία, LSJ's description of the verb φιλεῖν has remained largely unchallenged: the semantic core of φιλεῖν is a notion of love or affection.[84] Still, the verb φιλεῖν, although compatible with φίλοι having warm emotions, good intentions and positive affects towards one another,[85] does not in itself denote an emotional disposition comparable to modern English "loving".[86] That is to say: a translation of "A φιλεῖ B" as "A loves B" may be defensible in many contexts, but the two phrases *say* different things.[87] Rather, the verb φιλεῖν is used to mark different aspects of a reciprocal φιλία bond, expressing that the subject of the verb is related to someone or something, with senses ranging from

83 E.g. Eur. *Heracl.* 975: φιλῶ τὴν πόλιν; Isoc. 8.121, 12.141 (τὸν δῆμον).

84 LSJ s.v. φιλέω: "A1) love, regard with affection; 2) treat affectionately or kindly, *esp.* welcome; 3) (opp. ἐρᾶν) regard with affection; 4) show outward signs of love, *esp.* kiss; 5) *of things as objects of love,* like, approve; B) (+ inf.) love *to do,* be fond *of doing, and so* to be wont *or* used *to do.*" Chadwick (1996), 21: "It must be observed that LSJ rarely attempts to give a real definition; it is more often content to pile up English words which will serve as translation-equivalents, and then when other examples require a different translation to add this, even if the new quotation does not in fact fall under the definition to be deduced from the earlier ones."

85 The fact that the verb φιλεῖν sometimes refers to "kissing" should not be taken to imply that it is primarily an emotion word. Kissing may be an expression of a φιλία-bond, but not necessarily of romantic or erotic love. Cf. Hdt. 1.134.1 where kissing is among the Persian ways of greeting a person equal in status.

86 Apart from φιλεῖν, there are several other verbs that are conventionally translated with the English verb "to love", notably ἀγαπᾶν, ἐρᾶν/ἔρασθαι and στέργειν. Schmidt (1969 [1879]), 474–491 and Cope & Sandys (1877) treat the vocabulary of φιλεῖν/φίλησις/φίλημα/φιλότης *en bloc* with ἐρᾶν/ἔρασθαι/ἔρως, στέργειν/στοργή and ἀγαπᾶν/ἀγάπη/ἀγάπησις. A shorthand introduction to the differences between the verbs would suggest that: the verb ἐρᾶν/ἔραμαι (+ gen.) signify desire rather than love (e.g. Soph. *El.* 360, Eur. *Hipp.* 688; Halperin (1985), cf. Chapter Six); the verb ἀγαπᾶν indicates a subject's positive response (i.e. "appreciation") of a person, thing or situation (Cope & Sandys (1877), 296, cf. Chapter Four); the verb στέργειν is the marked term in relation to φιλεῖν, as "unreserved commitment" in relation to "connection" (cf. Soph. *El.* 1102 where Clytaemnestra reproaches Electra that she "πέφυκας πατέρα σὸν στέργειν ἀεί", i.e. she "has the proclivity to *choose* her father's side.").

87 For the dangers and limitations of sentence-to-sentence translations that preserve truth conditions, Lakoff (1987), 313–317.

a vague "belonging to",[88] to a stronger sense of "being committed to", "showing loyalty"[89] or "depending on".[90]

The moral imperative of φιλία is made explicit by the Theban herald in Euripides' *Suppliant Women*:

[Text 2]

> φιλεῖν μὲν οὖν χρὴ τοὺς σοφοὺς πρῶτον τέκνα,
> ἔπειτα τοκέας πατρίδα θ', ἣν αὔξειν χρεὼν
> καὶ μὴ κατᾶξαι.
>
> Wise men *should be loyal to* their children first, then to their parents, then to their country, which they should make great and not destroy.[91]

For present purposes, three points deserve to be made. First of all, the normative thrust (χρή) of this piece of gnomic wisdom is not so much that there is a "feeling rule" (*one ought to love* ...);[92] rather it addresses matters of loyalty, loyalty that is to be expressed in concrete action—in this case: not to yield to the supplications of the women of Argos. Theseus, the addressee, must realize which loyalties ought to have priority: first those towards one's children, then towards one's parents and country. These essential loyalties towards oikos

---

88 When the verb φιλεῖν is not used to signify a bond between two animate parties, the elements of loyalty and reciprocity are absent. The verb φιλεῖν can also be used of direct objects that are inanimate to mark a repeated or repeatable connection between a subject and a concrete substantive (S φιλεῖ + *acc. rei*: S *is accompanied by*). E.g. Aeschyl. *Ag.* 642 (διπλῇ μάστιγι, τὴν Ἄρης φιλεῖ): Ares "goes with" the double *mastix*; Soph. *Ant.* 1059 (τἀδικεῖν φιλῶν): Creon accuses Teiresias of being bribed and *to have a tendency* towards ἀδικία. This use is ridiculed *ad absurdum* by Aristotle in *EN* VIII.2 (1155b29–31) where he makes the observation that although we say that we φιλεῖν wine we are not benevolent towards it. As such the construction S φιλεῖ + *acc. rei* may be roughly equivalent to compounds with prefix φιλο- or suffix –φιλος. The verb φιλεῖν can furthermore be used in a construction with an infinitive to signify a repeated or repeatable (S φιλεῖ + inf.: S *tends to, is prone to*). E.g. Soph. *El.* 320 (φιλεῖ γὰρ ὀκνεῖν πρᾶγμ' ἀνὴρ πράσσων μέγα): a man who is about to do something great will always recoil.

89 E.g. in Eur. *Suppl.* 506 and *Or.* 669 φιλεῖν is used with χρή (one is obliged to *show solidarity to*) resp. the suppliants or kin who are one's φίλοι.

90 This typically works both ways: adjective φίλος indicates both that someone "is on your side" *and* that he "is someone you are committed to."

91 Eur. *Supp.* 506–508; *transl.* Kovacs (2015), *adapted.*

92 Gnomic statements have a traditional ring to them, but can be created on the spot by a speaker with the help of traditional elements, such as the formula (οὐ) χρή + infinitive. Lardinois (1995), 215–216.

and polis unassailably override the suppliants' claim to Theseus' loyalty, all the more so, because the suppliants, themselves embedded in a network of loyalties and enmities, are a diplomatic can of worms for an Athens that has a vested interest in staying out of the conflict between Argos and Thebes. The herald's statement is not about affection but about loyalty.

Secondly, the relative clause ἣν αὔξειν χρεὼν καὶ μὴ κατᾶξαι, "[the native country] that one ought to make great and not destroy", should be read as exegetical for φιλεῖν: this is what loyalty, φιλία, towards one's πατρίς should consist in. Note that the imperative of loyalty is expressed in terms of actions, i.e. of "helping, not harming". The statement is not an imperative to *feel* things, but an imperative to *act* in accordance with the order of loyalty.

And, finally, gnomic statements are rarely mere reflections of commonly accepted moral truths.[93] Even though the moral of φιλία is presented as self-evident, it is invoked in support of a highly debatable point: to pressure Theseus to turn down the desperate pleas of a group of suppliant women and hence, in the eyes of the audience, to shatter the self-image of Athens "as savior of suppliants, bulwark of Greece and enforcers of Panhellenic nomoi".[94] In other words: it is the herald who opposes loyalty towards one's kin and native city with the solidarity pleas of the Argive suppliants—to thereby undermine any lingering solidarity that Theseus might have towards the suppliants. Normative statements about φιλία are like any kind of rule: only made explicit when there is a problem, when the situation is ambiguous and yielding conflicting claims.

[Text 3]

τίς γάρ ποτ' ἀστῶν ἢ ξένων ἡμᾶς ἰδὼν
τοιοῖσδ' ἐπαίνοις οὐχὶ δεξιώσεται,
"Ἴδεσθε τώδε τὼ κασιγνήτω, φίλοι,
ὣ τὸν πατρῷον οἶκον ἐξεσωσάτην,
ὣ τοῖσιν ἐχθροῖς εὖ βεβηκόσιν ποτὲ
ψυχῆς ἀφειδήσαντε προὐστήτην φόνου.
τούτω φιλεῖν χρή, τώδε χρὴ πάντας σέβειν·
τώδ' ἔν θ' ἑορταῖς ἔν τε πανδήμῳ πόλει
τιμᾶν ἅπαντας οὕνεκ' ἀνδρείας χρεών."

93 Van Emde Boas (2017), 40–41, on the communicative functions of γνῶμαι.

94 Hanink (2013).

> Which of the citizens or strangers when he sees us will not greet us with praise? "Look on these sisters, friends, who preserved their father's house, who when their enemies were firmly based took no thought of their lives, but stood forth to avenge murder! All should φιλεῖν them, all should revere them; all should honor them at feasts and among the assembled citizens for their courage!"[95]

Convinced by a false message, Electra presumes Orestes is dead and decides to assume the role of avenger of her father. Here we see Electra's attempt to win her sister Chrysothemis' support. Her plea takes the shape of a Homeric *tis*-speech ("someone (τις) will say"),[96] which forces an external focalization on the situation: she imagines citizens and strangers evaluating her deeds and treating her and her sister as public heroes.[97] In this fantasy, Electra imagines that people will say that the sisters have done exactly what may be expected of a true φίλος: to stand up for their οἶκος and to harm their ἐχθροί. The proper reaction to such ἀνδρεία, such "manly courage",[98] to treat these sisters as φίλοι (τούτω φιλεῖν χρή), or even: to *have* them as φίλοι, to take them on as φίλοι, to try to make them one's φίλοι. Electra's sense of reality set aside, what she imagines here is not that the sisters' courage will make them more lovable, but that it qualifies them as loyal and desirable φίλοι—as suitable marriage candidates.[99]

Here again, there is a strong normative thrust: unprecedented courage *calls for* a treatment as φίλοι (φιλεῖν), with respect (σέβειν) and with social valuation (τιμᾶν).[100] And there is a clear performative aspect to these imperatives: they do not represent feeling rules, but rules of engagement, of treatment to which a hero is entitled.

95 Soph. *El.* 975–984; *transl.* Lloyd-Jones (1990), *adapted*.

96 On the adaptation of Homeric *tis*-speeches by female Sophoclean characters, see Mossman (2012).

97 For the idea that Electra is figuring herself and Chrysothemis as tyrannicides like Harmodius and Aristogeiton, Juffras (1991). For the "fantastic" nature of this *tis*-speech and the way it characterizes Electra as transgressive (and losing touch), see Mossman (2012).

98 On the paradoxical, and alarming, application of masculine vocabulary of valuation on a woman, see Bassi (2003). Electra's transgressive masculinity echoes that of Clytaemnestra in Aeschyl. *Ag.* 351, where the chorus remarks that Clytaemnestra speaks like a man (γύναι, κατ' ἄνδρα σώφρον' εὐφρόνως λέγεις).

99 Cf. Soph. *El.* 970–971.

100 On the discourse of public honor in Sophocles, see Osborne (2012).

2.2.2 … but of Course, φίλοι Do Have Emotions

φιλία denotes a durable and long-term bond of mutual solidarity. It is a relation word, not an emotion term: the vocabulary of φιλία does not in itself denote emotions or "affectionate bonds" (in the sense of bonds that are formed *on the basis* of the presence of particular emotional inclinations), although emotions are obviously often present in such durable bonds of solidarity. Still, such an understanding of φιλία may seem counter-intuitive to many of us who have grown accustomed to translating ΦΙΛ-terms with a repertory of English expressions of love. Let me briefly single out one specific use of ΦΙΛ-terms, the so-called first person "expressions of love" (φιλῶ), and suggest that even these expressions, often used in contexts that are unmistakably charged with emotions and in speech acts that are evidently affectionate in nature, can be understood in relational terms.

In a survey of the uses of first person singular φιλῶ from the eighth through the third centuries BCE, David Konstan points out that, once we exclude the auxiliary uses of the verbs ("to be wont to") and the negatives ("I don't like that"), many uses occur in reference to the speaker's family (often children).[101] The first example adduced by Konstan is an exclamation in what is probably a fragment from Euripides' *Erechtheus*:[102]

[Text 4]

> φιλῶ τέκν᾽, ἀλλὰ πατρίδ᾽ ἐμὴν μᾶλλον φιλῶ.
>
> I φιλῶ my children, but I φιλῶ my homeland more.[103]

Admittedly, not much harm is done in a conventional translation: "I love my children, but I love my country more." There is, however, a problem when we use statements like these to make direct inferences about the presence or absence of emotions within the Greek οἶκος (as Konstan, albeit in a qualified sense, does). The shocking statement is about solidarity, about the speaker prioritizing her commitment to her country over her bond with her children. If Snell is right in identifying the fragment as belonging to the *Erechtheus*, what we see here is Praxithea justifying her decision to sacrifice her daughter for the sake of the city. Her long justification speech in Fr. 360 takes the form of

---

101 Konstan (2000), 107–111. Konstan counts 63 occurrences in total. Other frequent uses of first person expressions are with reference to one's city and oneself.

102 According to Snell's supplement to Nauck's edition.

103 Eur. *Erechth.* Fr. 360a (Nauck).

a rational calculation that strikes us as cold and inhuman,[104] but which is also rife with the vocabulary of reciprocal obligation—i.e. the reciprocal obligation between citizen and country.[105] Echoing the war-time rhetoric of dispensability of human lives and sacrifices for the greater good, Praxithea's deliberation inverses the priorities expressed by the Theban herald in T 2: yes, she is committed to her children, but her commitment to the country is of a higher order. Her φιλῶ-statements are not about love, but about obligations.

One of Konstan's more convincing examples of the affectionate use of φιλῶ-expressions is the soldier begging for Krateia's hand in Menander's *Misoumenos*:

[Text 5]

> παρθένον σ' εἴληφ' ἐγώ,
> ἀνὴρ ἐκλήθην πρῶτος, ἠγάπησά σε,
> ἀγαπῶ, φιλῶ, Κράτεια φιλτάτη·
>
> I took you as a virgin still. I was the first to be called your man. I cherished you, I still cherish you, I φιλῶ you, my φιλτάτη Krateia.[106]

Here we certainly have an emotionally charged and affectionate context, with both erotic and domestic overtones. In this context, where the soldier is unambiguously expressing a strong commitment to one particular woman, the first-person expression φιλῶ certainly has an emotional force: an utterance describing commitment may be expressive of deeply felt emotions—without *linguistically* denoting these emotions.

Compare the English "I would do anything for you": in locutionary terms, this phrase of course *does not denote* an emotion of love (linguistically speaking, it is a hypothetical promise of quite an open-ended nature). However, the utterance may in a given context *do* things beyond its linguistic form; *pragmatically* speaking (or: in illocutionary terms), the utterance may be a functional equivalent to "I love you".[107] This functional equivalence justifies in many contexts a translation of φιλῶ-phrases as "I love you". But when we are interested in cul-

---

104 Literally a calculation in Fr. 360.19–21: εἴπερ γὰρ ἀριθμὸν οἶδα καὶ τοὐλάσσονος | τὸ μεῖζον, οὑνὸς οἶκος οὐ πλέον σθένει | πταίσας ἁπάσης πόλεος οὐδ' ἴσον φέρει.

105 Fr. 360.1–4: τὰς χάριτας ὅστις εὐγενῶς χαρίζεται, | ἥδιον ἐν βροτοῖσιν· οἳ δὲ δρῶσι μέν, | χρόνῳ δὲ δρῶσι, δυσγενέστερον … | ἐγὼ δὲ δώσω παῖδα τὴν ἐμὴν κτανεῖν.

106 Men. *Mis.* 306–308 (Sandbach).

107 Austin (1962), Searle (1969).

turally specific cognitions and attitudes, it is crucial that we bear in mind that first-person expressions too depart from a relational understanding of φιλία.[108]

The fact that the vocabulary of φιλία does not in itself semantically refer to emotions or affection does not mean that such emotions are absent in a φιλία bond. What is more, many authors and characters who reflect on φιλία do find the presence of emotions and affects desirable, or even crucial, in a φιλία-bond. To Xenophon's Socrates the fact that family members can "rejoice" (χαίρειν) again in each other's presence is an indication that a disturbed φιλία-reciprocity is restored:

[Text 6]

> ἐὰν δὲ προστατήσῃς ὅπως ἐνεργοὶ ὦσι, σὺ μὲν ἐκείνας **φιλήσεις**, ὁρῶν ὠφελίμους σεαυτῷ οὔσας, ἐκεῖναι δὲ σὲ **ἀγαπήσουσιν**, αἰσθόμεναι **χαίροντά** σε αὐταῖς, τῶν δὲ προγεγονυιῶν εὐεργεσιῶν **ἥδιον μεμνημένοι** τὴν ἀπ' ἐκείνων **χάριν αὐξήσετε**, καὶ ἐκ τούτων **φιλικώτερόν** τε καὶ **οἰκειότερον** ἀλλήλοις ἕξετε.
>
> But if you encourage them to work, *you will φιλεῖν them, when you see that they are doing something for you*, and they will like you *when they realize that you are pleased with them*; and as you both *remember former acts of kindness with greater pleasure*, you will *increase the χάρις* aroused by these acts with the result that the *solidarity and closeness amongst you will increase.*[109]

Restoring the flow of reciprocal care (of doing good to each other and being beneficial to one another) will restore φιλία, the sense of mutual commitment. The addressee Aristarchus will "feel committed" (φιλήσεις) to his family members again, which will arouse positive feelings of appreciation (ἀγαπήσουσιν) in the objects of his φιλία, because they will see *his* positive emotional response to them (χαίροντα). Both parties will remember previous acts of reciprocity again, which increases mutual χάρις, and which will restore and foster the solidarity and cohesion in Aristarchus' οἶκος.[110]

---

108 A similar argument can be made for "affectionate forms of address" (φίλε, φίλτατε). Eleanor Dickey's study of ancient Greek terms of address establishes that most occurrences of φίλε and φίλτατε genuinely express affection and politeness. Dickey (1996), 107–145. A notable exception is Plato who uses friendship forms of address to "show the dominance of the speaker" (117).

109 Xen. *Mem.* II.vii.9.5; *transl.* Tredennick & Waterfield (1990), *adapted.*

110 On this passage, see Chapter Two Section 4.1.

This will be part of the argument in this book: emotions are not seen as the causal basis but as a natural consequence of a φιλία-bond. They are not spontaneous givens but emerge out of a well-functioning relationship of mutual solidarity and of a mutual understanding of such a relationship. Another illustration of this mechanism can be seen in Aristotle's discussion of the difference between benefactor and beneficiary. Aristotle objects to an understanding of this relationship as a kind of credit relationship:

[Text 7]

> οὐδ' ὅμοιον τὸ περὶ τοὺς δανείσαντας· οὐ γάρ ἐστι φίλησις περὶ ἐκείνους, ἀλλὰ τοῦ σῴζεσθαι βούλησις τῆς κομιδῆς ἕνεκα· οἱ δ' εὖ πεποιηκότες φιλοῦσι καὶ ἀγαπῶσι τοὺς πεπονθότας κἂν μηδὲν ὦσι χρήσιμοι μηδ' εἰς ὕστερον γένοιντ' ἄν.
>
> [T]he case of the lender does not even resemble this one. For with the lender there is *no attachment* involved, only wishing for the other's preservation for the sake of what is to be got from him; by contrast those who have bestowed benefits *are committed and appreciative towards* the recipients even if the latter are of no use and will not become useful in the future.[111]

The Debtor Paradigm of Obligation, that assimilates benefaction to credit, yields an understanding too cold for the situation, for such an understanding fails to take into account that friends positively value each other (ἀγαπᾶν). It leaves the elements of commitment (φίλησις, φιλεῖν) and appreciation (ἀγαπᾶν) out of the analysis.[112]

In both T 6 and T 7, a healthy φιλία-relationship is expected to bring certain emotions, affects and judgments along with it, without semantically implying these.[113] Emotions are produced by, shaped and interpreted in terms of relations, rather than the other way around. You don't make φίλοι because you feel a certain way towards them, but you feel this way because they are your φίλοι, because you share a φιλία-bond with them.

In this book it will be argued that although neither φιλία nor χάρις refers exclusively and specifically to emotions, in situations of isomorphism, where a reciprocal bond may be mistaken for an exchange on different terms, the sub-

---

111 Ar. *EN* IX.vii (1167b30–32); *transl.* Broadie & Rowe (2002), *adapted.*

112 On this passage and on the Debtor Paradigm, see Chapter Four Section 3.1.

113 Foxhall (1998), 66 for affection as both a lubricant that "smooths and soothes" φιλία-bonds, and as a quality which evolves with the relationship itself.

jective features of φιλία-reciprocity become distinctive for φιλία. Signaling and recognizing the emotions, dispositions and affection that go with successful and satisfying reciprocity become part of one's social competence—the competence of reading and conducting an exchange properly.

2.2.3 φιλία is Not a Relationship Type

A second controversial point is the noun φίλος. Is a φίλος a "friend"? In modern Western societies "friends" constitute a distinct category of individuals that we are not related to on other grounds such as the "stronger" ties of kinship or marriage.[114] In this modern conception, "friends" are imagined to be chosen rather than assigned; moreover, friends may have intimate feelings towards one another that are distinct from erotic attraction and romantic love. "My partner is my best friend" is not a tautology but an informative statement.

It has been debated whether there was such a "friend zone" in classical Greece. In a groundbreaking study David Konstan has argued that "the nouns *philos* and *philia* do not apply to the same relationship".[115] Whereas the nouns φιλία and the verb φιλεῖν can be applied to kin-relations, the noun ὁ φίλος refers to someone related to one according to a specific relationship type: "*philoi*, then, occupy an intermediate zone between kin and country. The relationship between *philoi* is voluntary or achieved as opposed to an ascribed connection grounded in status such as common membership in a family or community."[116] Therefore, the noun ὁ φίλος (not to be mistaken with the attributive adjective φίλος) "normally excludes (...) close kin".[117]

In response, Elizabeth Belfiore has argued that in the context of Attic tragedy, as Mary Whitlock Blundell has observed earlier, many plot structures revolve around φίλοι harming φίλοι.[118] The prototypical φιλία-bond that is sub-

---

114 Cf. Ramsøy (1968), 12 on present-day conceptions: "[M]ost other important social relationships exclude friendship. (...) [Friendship] tends to be incompatible with such relationships as those of mother and child, lovers, and employer and employee." Konstan (1997) uses the opposition "achieved" vs. "ascribed" relationship to classify ancient friendships (as "achieved").

115 Konstan (1996), 71. This dissociation of the noun φίλος from the rest of the ΦΙΛ-wordfield works best for the Aristotelian account of φιλία in *EE* (esp. VII.iv (1239a1–7), but is contradicted in cases as T9 below and numerous places in Attic drama (cf. n. 127 below) Cf. Eur. *Phoen.* 1446, Aristoph. *Nub.* 82–87, 1488, Aeschyl. *Sept.* 971, *Eum.* 354–359, Eur. *El.* 1230) and in almost every occurrence of the contrast between ἐχθροί and φίλοι. Cf. Blundell (1989). Belfiore (2000), referring to Ar. *Poet.* 1453b14–23, regards kin (siblings, parents-children) as the most prototypical sort of φίλοι. Cf. Dirlmeier (1931), Ebeling (1963).

116 Konstan (1997), 55.

117 Konstan (1997), 53.

118 Belfiore (1998), 3–20; Blundell (1989).

ject to such violation is kinship φιλία, and the φίλοι who are offenders and victims of such destructive events (πάθη) are typically blood kin: parent to children, child to parent and sibling to sibling. These are, as Belfiore argues, designated as each other's φίλοι. An important passage that Belfiore adduces against Konstan is Aristotle, *Poetics* 14:[119]

[Text 8]

> ἀνάγκη δὴ ἢ φίλων εἶναι πρὸς ἀλλήλους τὰς τοιαύτας πράξεις ἢ ἐχθρῶν ἢ μηδετέρων. ἂν μὲν οὖν ἐχθρὸς ἐχθρόν, οὐδὲν ἐλεεινὸν οὔτε ποιῶν οὔτε μέλλων, πλὴν κατ' αὐτὸ τὸ πάθος· οὐδ' ἂν μηδετέρως ἔχοντες· ὅταν δ' ἐν ταῖς φιλίαις ἐγγένηται τὰ πάθη, οἷον ἢ ἀδελφὸς ἀδελφὸν ἢ υἱὸς πατέρα ἢ μήτηρ υἱὸν ἢ υἱὸς μητέρα ἀποκτείνη ἢ μέλλη ἤ τι ἄλλο τοιοῦτον δρᾷ, ταῦτα ζητητέον. (…) ἔστιν δὲ πρᾶξαι μέν, ἀγνοοῦντας δὲ πρᾶξαι τὸ δεινόν, εἶθ' ὕστερον ἀναγνωρίσαι τὴν φιλίαν, ὥσπερ ὁ Σοφοκλέους Οἰδίπους.
>
> The interactions in question must necessarily occur either between *friends and relations*, or between enemies, or strangers. If an enemy takes on an enemy, there is nothing in his acting or planning to arouse pity, only the actual suffering of the victim. So too when the characters are strangers. What should be looked for are cases where the sufferings occur within *relational bonds*, as between brother and brother, son and father, mother and son, son and mother—where one kills, or is on the point of killing, the other, or is doing something else horrible. (…) It is also possible for the terrible deed to be done in ignorance, and the *relationship* to be discovered only later, as with Sophocles' Oedipus.[120]

In this passage, where Aristotle discusses the most effective tragedy plots, Aristotle first lists the logically thinkable ways (ἀνάγκη + infinitive) in which human beings can relate to one another: as φίλοι, as ἐχθροί and as μηδετέροι, "neither", "neutral". Here, the noun φίλος is used. We move on to the abstract noun φιλία: as acts of destruction between enemies or strangers are dramatically not very effective, Aristotle quickly decides that a good plot consists in the πάθη that take place within φιλία-bonds (ἐν ταῖς φιλίαις). The examples (οἷον) listed next by Aristotle are, undeniably, blood kin—who sometimes only too late "recognize their φιλία", as did Sophocles' Oedipus. Now admittedly, syntactically speaking, the examples of brother harming brother, son harming father etc. are

119 Belfiore (1998), 19–20.

120 Ar. *Poet.* 14 (1453b15–31); *transl.* Kenny (2013).

only listed as cases of φιλία violated by acts of destruction. But given that Aristotle starts his discussion with an exclusive categorization of logically conceivable relations in terms of φίλοι, ἐχθροί and μηδετέροι, it requires a lot of reading against the grain and the flow of argument to forge a distinction between φιλία (exemplified by blood kin) and φίλοι as non-kin friends.

While Belfiore's argument is persuasive, her conclusion is not: she speaks of clear indications that "the word (*sc.* the noun φίλος) must mean 'kin'" and of situations in which "it is very difficult not to give *philos* (with or without the article) the sense of 'kin'".[121] To my judgment, both Belfiore and Konstan fall victim to the same fallacy of confusing reference with sense (or denotation).[122] The wealth of evidence amassed by Konstan indeed seems to suggest that the noun φίλος is more often applied to non-kin than to kin; however, this does not necessarily imply that the noun *means* "non-kin friend". Similarly, the evidence adduced by Belfiore suggests that sometimes the noun φίλος quite markedly *is* applied to kin members; this fact in itself is equally insufficient to back up the claim that φίλος *means* kin.

How to get out of this conundrum? First of all, it is misguided to try to map φίλος and φιλία onto specific relationship types on a par with "kinship", "family", "lovers" and "companions". φιλία is a general relation term, signaling *a* reciprocal relationship between two or more people without specifying a relationship type or the specific nature of the relationship. The same relationship can be designated in more than one way: as a parent-child bond *and* as a case of φιλία, as a sexual interaction *and* as a long-term reciprocal φιλία, as a political dependency *and* as a mutually beneficial φιλία. Part of the argument in this book is that the vocabulary of φιλία and χάρις is often chosen to bring out the reciprocal aspects of a relationship. A mother is a φίλος *par excellence* because she initiates reciprocity with her unborn child.[123] A brother can patch up a quarrel with his brother by reinstating their φιλία, i.e.: by restoring the benevolent reciprocity that is normative between good brothers.[124] It goes without saying that such highlighting of the reciprocal elements in a relationship often serves specific rhetorical purposes.

This also has implications for the way we read conjunctions such as "kin and φίλοι". The prevailing reflex is to read such conjunctions "exclusively". A case in point is a passage from Lysias' speech *Against Andocides*, also adduced by Konstan:

121 Belfiore (1998), 20.
122 Lyons (1995), 74–79, 293.
123 Chapter Three Section 4.
124 Chapter Six Section 5.

[Text 9]

> ἐκ δ' οὖν τούτου τοῦ τιμήματος ἐδέδετο ἐγγὺς ἐνιαυτόν, καὶ ἐμήνυσε δεδεμένος **κατὰ τῶν αὑτοῦ συγγενῶν καὶ φίλων**, ἀδείας δοθείσης αὐτῷ, εἰ δόξειε τἀληθῆ μηνῦσαι. καὶ τίνα αὐτὸν δοκεῖτε ψυχὴν ἔχειν, ὁπότε τὰ μὲν ἔσχατα καὶ τὰ αἴσχιστα ἐποίει μηνύων **κατὰ τῶν ἑαυτοῦ φίλων**, ἡ δὲ σωτηρία ἀφανὴς αὐτῷ;
>
> As a result of this proposal, he was imprisoned for nearly a year. While in prison, he informed *against his own relatives and friends*, because he had been granted immunity if he were found to be telling the truth. What sort of a character do you think he has, given that he behaved in the most terrible and shameful way by denouncing *his own friends*, and his own chance of rescue was very unclear?[125]

Konstan quotes this passage in support of his thesis that the noun φίλοι normally excludes kin:[126] Andocides is reproached for giving testimony against his relatives (συγγενεῖς) and his φίλοι. This seems to suggest two distinct categories of victims of Andocides' treacherous character. However, there is also another possible reading for the disjunction: not so much "relatives and friends", but "relatives *and other* (*not-specified*) φίλοι". That the second reading is justifiable becomes evident when we read the subsequent sentence with a second, more inclusive, occurrence of φίλων.

In other words: the nouns φίλος and φιλία *can* in certain contexts be used "exclusively" for persons other than kinsmen, in-laws and other more specialized designations of interpersonal bonds (e.g. πατήρ, συγγενής, κηδεστής, σύμμαχος, ξένος), but they can also be used "inclusively" to cover the full range of interpersonal solidarities.[127] Phrases such as "φίλοι and kin"[128] or "φίλοι and

125 Lys. 19.23; *transl.* Todd (2000).

126 Konstan (1996), 53.

127 E.g. Is. 1.4: the speakers defend their claims to Cleonymus' inheritance, because they are his closest relatives (γένει ἐγγυτάτω προσήκοντες) and Cleonymus had given them the right of succession διὰ τὴν φιλίαν. Often persons are referred to as συγγενής *and* φίλος: Hdt. 2.90.2, 7.39.15, Thuc. 1.71.4, Xen. *Mem.* I.ii.48, I.ii.53, IV.iv.17, *Hiero* XI.14, *Oec.* V.10, *Cyr.* I.ii.7, VIII.v.21, Pl. *Phdr.* 233d, 239e, *Rep.* 487a, *Lys.* 210d, *Leg.* 718a, 730b, Lys. 21.6, Is. 5.35, Andoc. 1.56, Antiph. 1.29. Cf. Dirlmeier (1931), 7–21 on what he calls the "Doppelinhalt von φίλος". Adkins (1963), 33 for the idea that (Homeric) φίλος refers to anyone and anything that an ἀγαθός depends upon for his survival.

128 E.g. in Is. 4.18, the contrast between συγγενεῖς and ὀθνεῖοι φίλοι ("strange friends", i.e. φίλοι from outside the οἶκος) does not imply that συγγενεῖς are not φίλοι, but that kinship is a more relevant criterion (recognized by law) in inheritance cases than other types of relatedness (φιλία); in this context ὀθνεῖοι serves to disambiguate the non-kin φίλοι from φίλοι

one's household"[129] are not expressions of polarity[130] between φίλοι and non-φίλοι; rather, "kin" and "*oikos*" are specifications of φιλία that yield stronger claims in the rhetorical context at hand than non-specific φίλος—but they *are* φιλία-bonds.[131] The modern pedagogic wisdom that "parents should not aspire to be their children's friends" would probably have been incomprehensible in ancient Greek.[132]

This does not preclude the fact that φίλοι were sometimes chosen, nor does it restrict φιλία to ties of blood or other fixed criteria. The kinds of φιλία that dominate our sources, between citizen men of equal status, are constituted by choice and imagined as very volatile and uncertain relations,[133] precisely because they are a matter of constant and repeated choice. Conversely, someone related to one by blood can fail as a φίλος too if he does not meet the imposed norms:

[Text 10]

> Κρ. οὔτοι ποθ' οὑχθρός, οὐδ' ὅταν θάνῃ, φίλος.
> Αν. οὔτοι συνέχθειν, ἀλλὰ συμφιλεῖν ἔφυν.

---

by kinship. Ar. *EN* VIII.xii (1162a6–9) contrasts the φιλία between parents and children (ἡ τοιαύτη φιλία) with "that with unrelated persons" (τῶν ὀθνείων)—both are subcategories of φιλία.

129 E.g. Isoc. 15.99.

130 Konstan (1997), 54.

131 Similarly, ξενία is a specific subcategory of φιλία, although in *some* contexts "ξένος" and "φίλος" can be framed as opposites or distinct categories. φίλοι and ξένοι are not necessarily mutually exclusive categories: a ξένος, i.e. someone from a social or political unit different than one's own, can be one's φίλος, someone with whom one engages in a relation of reciprocal help and dependence. E.g. in Lys. 19.19–20 (Διονυσίου φίλου ὄντος καὶ ξένου), ξένος serves as a specification of φίλος; in Xen. *Hell.* IV.i.34, Agesilaus refers to the same people first as ξένοι and next as φίλοι. Cf. Konstan (1997), 83ff. Herman (1987) (1996a, b, c) regards φίλος as an antonym of ξεῖνος ("strange"), interpreting the Homeric occurrences of adjective φίλος as reflexive possessive pronouns ("own"), following Adkins (1963) and Chantraine (1968), ad loc. Cf. Bolkestein (1939), 214–231; Benveniste (1973), 273–288. Adkins (1963) is also followed by Von Reden (1995), 45 and Scott (1984). Cf. Kretschmer (1927) who traces back the Indo-European reflexive pronoun to the Lydian *bilis* ("his own"). Benveniste (1973) assimilates φιλέω to ξενίζω and φίλος to ξεῖνος. According to Belfiore (2000) φιλία is distinct from ξενία because ξενία is based on reciprocity, whereas φιλία is an ascribed relationship.

132 Although in Eur. *El.* 265, Electra's cry that women are the *philai* of their husbands, not of their children (γυναῖκες ἀνδρῶν, ὦ ξέν', οὐ παίδων φίλαι), seems to approach this sentiment, the point is that Electra expresses disappointment and bitterness over her mother's loyalty to Aegisthus overruling the loyalty to her children. *Pace* Konstan (1997), 59.

133 Foxhall (1998), 56.

Κρ. κάτω νυν ἐλθοῦσ', εἰ φιλητέον, φίλει
κείνους· ἐμοῦ δὲ ζῶντος οὐκ ἄρξει γυνή.

Creon: An enemy is never a friend, even when he is dead.
Antigone: I have no enemies by birth, but I have friends by birth.
Creon: Then go below and love those friends, if you must love them! But while I live a woman shall not rule![134]

A central issue in Sophocles' *Antigone* is the status of Polyneices, who, being a member of the Theban royal house, has undertaken an expedition against his own fatherland.[135] In the eyes of Creon, this very act has disqualified Polyneices as a φίλος and turned him into an ἐχθρός.[136] To Creon φιλία and ἔχθρα are achieved categories, reflecting one's merits *vis-à-vis* the country. Prior claims to φιλία are overruled by recent acts of enmity. To Antigone, φιλία is an inalienable category: Polyneices is her φίλος by birth and retains his claim on her loyalty.[137] What is more, the phrase ἔφυν, "it is my nature to", seems a downright invalidation of achieved solidarity claims: Antigone seems to recognize only the claims ascribed by birth.[138]

The contestation of Polyneices' status (φίλος or ἐχθρός) is played out as a conflict between two coexisting models of φιλία: φιλία as a bond that can be initiated by doing good to someone (and that engenders mutual obligations from that point on), and φιλία as a bond that one is born into (and that, also, engenders the obligation to treat the other well). Both are models that an inhabitant of the classical Greek polis lives by, and the ensuing paradox is real and understandable as well (albeit somewhat marginal in the realities of everyday life). It should be clear by now that the "problem of Polyneices" loses its dramatic pith and marrow if we follow either Konstan and Belfiore and only credit one horn of the dilemma with reality.

134 Soph. *Ant.* 522–525; *transl.* Lloyd-Jones (1994).

135 See Goldhill (1986), 90–106 for an analysis of φιλία-terminology in the *Antigone*. Cf. Nussbaum (1986), 51–84; Blundell (1989), 106–148.

136 It is significant (and it adds to Creon's characterization) that to Creon it is the fact that Polyneices has failed to live up to his obligation as a citizen of Thebes that turns him into an ἐχθρός—not the fact that he has violated the φιλία within his οἶκος.

137 This is Antigone's *professed* take on φιλία. In the reality of the play as it unfolds, Antigone rejects her φίλη Ismene on the grounds that Ismene's loyalty is confined to words.

138 The exceptional, and problematic, status of Polyneices is also thematized in Euripides' *Phoenician Women*, where Eteocles expresses a sentiment close to Antigone's: φίλος γὰρ ἐχθρὸς ἐγένετ', ἀλλ' ὅμως φίλος. (1446).

2.3 *Objective and Subjective Ties*

Both semantic issues, the scope of φιλία (are parents φίλοι?) and its contents (does it presuppose affectionate bonds?), raise questions about the importance of choice and the nature of obligation. If φιλία-bonds include relations you are born into, does this mean that you cannot choose your φίλοι? And if so, how does one acquire those φίλοι who are not related by blood? Should we see φιλία in the Classical Period as a semi-formal institution with objective rules and obligations? This has been suggested by several scholars who hold that φιλία "is not, at root, a subjective bond of affection and emotional warmth, but the entirely objective bond of reciprocal obligation."[139]

This objective duty-driven account of φιλία appears to be confirmed by our sources. There were recognized codes of conduct, including the swearing of oaths,[140] and some of the obligations owed by φίλοι could be passed on from father to son.[141] The principle that one should harm one's enemies and help one's friends is presented as something "ordained" (τετάχθαι) by the speaker of Lysias 9,[142] as a definition of justice by Polemarchus in Plato's *Republic*,[143] and as an unwritten divine law by Socrates and Hippias the sophist in Xenophon's *Memorabilia*.[144]

However, we also find examples that stress the **voluntary nature** of φιλία-obligations. Aristotle includes the principle Helping Friends/Harming Enemies amongst the things "deliberately chosen" by people,[145] drawing a distinction between reciprocating on the basis of law (νομική) and on the basis of character (ἠθική).[146] Adherence to the Helping Friends/Harming Enemies-principle is understood as a defining mark of a man's ἀρετή by Socrates in Plato's *Meno* as well as his namesake in Xenophon's *Memorabilia*—which presupposes that adhering to the principle is a meaningful action or choice, not merely a mechanical principle.[147] In addition, as we have seen, some sources emphasize

---

139 Heath (1987), 3–4. Cf. Donlan (1980), 15; Goldhill (1986), 82; Raccanelli (1998), 20. Cf. Springborg (1986), 198–199: "Modern classicists (…) have emphasized the extent to which concepts of friendship in antiquity describe quasi-juridical relations between individuals, and only secondarily as a consequence of mutual interaction, bonds of affection."

140 E.g. Xen. *Hell.* 1.3.12; Antiphon 6.39, with Fisher (1976), 18–19.

141 E.g. Lys. 18.26–27, Is. 2.19, [Dem.] 50.56.

142 Lys. 9.20.

143 Pl. *Rep.* I.332. Cf. *Clit.* 410a.

144 Xen. *Mem.* IV.iv.24.

145 Ar. *Rhet.* 1363a19–21.

146 Ar. *EN* VIII.xiii (1162b22–31). See Chapter Three Section 3.

147 Pl. *Meno* 71e, Xen. *Mem.* II.vi.35.

the critical importance of emotions in *real* φιλία-bonds.[148] Moreover, in various sources resembling T1 above, it is stressed that the principle of Helping Friends is not based on self-gratification or promotion of self-interest: proper acts of φιλία-support require certain dispositions and intentions.[149] This all suggests that performing one's obligations as a φίλος is understood as *more* than the mechanical allocation of goods and services (material or immaterial): there are all kinds of dispositions, intentions, emotions and moral orientations that matter, that make up the quality of the give-and-take underlying φιλία. Here we see a tendency *not* to conflate φιλία-obligations with legal duties: φιλία-bonds, even when they are realized and manifested in reciprocal behavior, are not to be entirely reduced to objective exchanges and the to and fro of obligations.

The argument of this book will be that this tension, between the objectifying definition of φιλία and the insistence on the critical importance of the subjective elements or aspects of φιλία-reciprocity, does not represent a contradiction or a paradox. The two aspects represent two sides of the same coin, two distinct perspectives on reciprocity.[150] In cases of perceived crisis, when a speaker feels that his φίλος has violated expectations, the speaker automatically adopts an external perspective on the situation: his φίλος has broken a Law of Friendship and *ought* to compensate him or to be punished according to some Objective Rule. The external perspective is the perspective of the detached observer who does not have access to the qualitative dimension of friendly reciprocity. The external perspective favors the concrete and the objectifiable, the catalogue of good turns back and forth, the hard bare bones of the skeleton of a φιλία dead and gone.

When, on the other hand, a φιλία-bond is healthy and functioning well, the sight of the skeleton is ghastly and repelling: φίλοι are absolutely certain that the meaning of their bond cannot be reduced to the mechanics of reciprocity. There is more to the friendship than give and take, for in a *real* friendship, φίλοι are helping each other "for free", and just for the sake of the other, without wishing the other to be aware, without counting and keeping track. In a functional φιλία-bond, φίλοι try as much as possible to see things from an internal perspective, the perspective that lends access to the qualitative dimension of an

148 Foxhall (1998); e.g. Dem. 25.52: kindness, courtesy and compassion in personal relations. See Section 2.2.2 above.

149 Cf. O'Brien (1967), 30–38. Contrast Adkins (1963) on φιλότης in Homeric society.

150 Cf. Konstan (1998), 283 with a somewhat different tack: "In place of the polar opposition between the purely voluntary actions of the private individual and the objectively constrained behavior enforced by the market and the law, there is a universe of informal interactions and transactions conceived simultaneously as voluntary and enjoined, spontaneous and socially regulated."

exchange: to the dispositions, intentions, emotions and moral orientations that make up the flesh of a living and moving φιλία-reciprocity.

As we have seen in Section 2.2, neither the subjective dimension nor the internal perspective is anchored in the semantics of ΦΙΛ-terminology. However, I will argue that in situations of isomorphism, when there is a perceived resemblance between φιλία-reciprocity and commercial exchange, the subjective dimension and the internal perspective become critical and distinctive for *real* φιλία—as opposed to its pale imitation: disembedded commercial exchange.

3 An Economic Mentality

3.1 *Great Transformations*

The 5th and 4th centuries BCE witness a spectacular transformation of Athenian economy and society[151] characterized by a rationalization of agriculture,[152] an increase in the division of labor,[153] the institution of paid labor,[154] the development of credit systems and banking practice,[155] the simplification and scaling up of retail trade[156] and foreign trade,[157] the monetization of politics[158] and warfare,[159] and an advance of commodification and commercialization.[160]

---

151 Kallet (2007); Schaps (2004), 1–17. Bresson (2016) locates the great changes in ancient Greece in "at least the end of the Archaic period" (14).

152 Osborne (1991); Schaps (2004), 163–174; Bresson (2016), 119–174.

153 Loomis (1998), 155; Harris (2002), 88–99 for a list of occupations attested in the period 500–250 BCE in Classical Athens (with the sensible words of caution and reservations made on pp. 68–71). Bresson (2016), 107–108, 110, 187–188.

154 Loomis (1998); Schaps (2004), 150–162.

155 Bresson (2016), 278–285; Shipton (1997), Cohen (1992) and Millett (1991).

156 Bresson (2016), 225–260; Schaps (2004), 111–123. Retail trade itself can be seen as a symptom of a process of economical scaling up, caused by the rise and development of the polis, a process of urbanization and the emergence of, somehow, an agricultural surplus. Whatever part coined money played *historically* in the complex process of disembedding or re-embedding of the economy, it is uncontroversial that at least from the mid-5th century BCE on, one of its prime functions was to facilitate commercial exchange, as a medium of exchange.

157 Bresson (2016), 286–338; 381–413. In ancient Greek culture there is a distinction between retail trade, καπηλεία, and long distance (usually overseas) trade, ἐμπορία. Cf. Pl. *Rep.* 371d5–7. Von Reden (2015), 161–169.

158 Schaps (2004), 124–137.

159 Schaps (2004), 138–149.

160 On the complex commercialization of 4th-century Athenian economy, see Shipton (1997).

Amidst these booming advancements, there is one more development that especially deserves our attention: the conceptual articulation of a new sort of relationship, the instantaneous transaction of equivalent goods that does not necessarily yield nor presuppose a long-lasting relationship between the exchange partners. The new relation is one disembedded from political, religious or social structures: a commercial exchange can take place between partners who are neither hostile nor acquainted and who cooperate to reach harmonization of needs on the spot. They may never see one another again. In fact, this new relationship is perhaps more aptly characterized as a "non-relation". Nevertheless, this non-relation, the disembedded transaction, is one of the central concepts in this book.

Economic historians may object to my use of the term "disembedded" for individual relations. The term "disembedded" was first coined by Karl Polanyi in his grand historical account of the emergence of market capitalism in the late eighteenth and early nineteenth century.[161] The unique feature of this new economy was the fact that it was disembedded from the social matrix, i.e., "in ideal form, at least, it commercialized and commoditized all goods and services in terms of a single standard, money, and set their prices through the self-adjusting mechanism of supply and demand."[162] The disembedded economy was defined in contrast to previous economies, that were "submerged (...) social relationships".[163] Although many embedded economies did have physical marketplaces, exchanges on such marketplaces did not take place in accordance with market principles (e.g., self-regulating rules of supply and demand).[164]

Initially, the terminology of "embedded" and "disembedded" economies applied to entire economic systems. Polanyi himself, for instance, classified historical economic systems by their mode of "integration", or embedding: some economies were integrated through reciprocity ("movements between correlative points or symmetrical groupings"), others through redistribution ("appropriational movements toward a center and out of it again"), and others through exchange ("vice-versa movements (...) between 'hands' under a market system"), some through a combination.[165] Capitalist market economies typically display all three types of integration, non-capitalist centralized states (such as

161 Polanyi (1944).

162 Isaac (2005), 14.

163 Polanyi (1944), 46. Other characteristics of "embedded economies" are that factors of production are not monetized or commoditized; access to land and labor was organized through ties of kinship and community.

164 Polanyi (1944), 46ff. Cf. Bohannon & Dalton (1962), 1–20, for the distinction between marketplaces and market principles.

165 Polanyi (1944), 250.

chiefdoms) a combination of redistribution and reciprocity, "primitive societies" only through reciprocity. The case of ancient Greece posed challenges for Polanyi. To his own surprise, he observed characteristics of market-based activity in fourth-century Athens: a market system undergoing fluctuations in prices created by the forces of supply and demand.[166] As Alain Bresson has pointed out, the logic of "embedding" and "disembedding" is rooted in an evolutionist theory of history.[167] Athens did not fit the evolutionist narrative.[168]

As capitalist economies are characterized by their combining of modes of integration, the notions of "embeddedness" and "disembeddedness" can also be applied to parts, or aspects, of an economic system. They can be used for economic activities. "Embeddedness" then comes to refer to the degree to which the relevant activity is constrained or informed by social, political or religious factors and considerations.

In this book, the term "disembedded" will be stripped of its evolutionists and systemic assumptions. The term "disembedded" will be primarily used for specific economic activities: the transaction of equivalent goods between individuals who choose to remain unrelated or to perceive the transaction as

166 Polanyi (1968), 78–115; Love (1991). Cf. Polanyi (1977), 238–251, on what he saw as the emergence of market-economic principles in Athens in the 320. See Bresson (2016), 12–15, for a concise and fair discussion of the significance of Polanyi's work for the study of the ancient economy. Xenophon in *De Vect.* IV.6 famously articulates economic phenomena that come close to laws of supply and demand. Bresson (2016), 432; Figueira (2012).

167 Bresson (2016), 14. Silver (1995), 196, for the warning that it is misguided to understand developments in economic history in terms of a unidirectional movement along a scale from embeddedness towards disembeddedness.

168 Polanyi's work, together with Finley (1985a), has given rise to the "substantivism vs. formalism"-debate, which revolves around the question whether the ancient economy can be analysed with the conceptual apparatus of modern economic theories that is developed for modern market economies. The substantivists argue that the ancient economy was so incommensurably different from ours that it cannot be understood with modern economic concepts and they attribute a limited role to money in the ancient economy. (Finley (1985a), 115, 132–135, 166–169). Recent defenders of the formalist position acknowledge the significant differences between ancient economy and the large-scale industrialized capitalist economies of the 19th and 20th century, but nevertheless maintain that the ancient economy too was subject to the market forces of supply, demand, quality and price, and thereby characterized by market economical transactions. E.g. Cohen (1991) on Athenian credit mechanisms regulated by market processes; Loomis (1998) who argues that at least from 432 BCE on, the economic forces of supply and demand were operative in ancient Athens, as well as monetary phenomena such as inflation and deflation; Harris (2002) who argues that the exchange of commodities on the agora was subject to forces of supply and demand. The discussions are summarized in Schaps (2004), 18–26, Cartledge (2002), Andreau (2002), Von Reden (2010), 9–12; Engen (2010), 6–9, 20–35, Bresson (2016), 1–30.

occurring "outside" of their relationship. It will be argued that the processes of "disembedding" and "embedding" can be understood as **discursive processes**, reflecting thinking about economic and social relations. In its most extreme and detached forms, this newly invented relation of the "disembedded transaction" is, in an important sense, a **fiction**. However, it is against the foil of this disembedded transaction that ideals of φιλία-reciprocity are articulated in 5th- and 4th-century discourse both popular and intellectual. And, conversely, it is in contexts where φιλία is compared to socially weaker exchange bonds that the notional disembedded transaction finds its articulation. This book is about this double-faced trend: about the way in which φιλία-reciprocity and commercial exchange have come to define each other in a mutually dependent way.

3.2 *Tangled up in Cause and Effect*

The transformation of the Athenian economy is an extremely complex historical event, intertwined with other transformative events, such as the settling of polis authority, the emergence of a public sphere and administrative apparatus,[169] the discovery and exploitation of the Laureion silver mines,[170] the institution of the Delian League, the explosive growth of the population of Attica, the urbanization of Attica, the growth of interregional trade and increased exchange with the colonies and processes of urbanization.[171] However complex the exact mechanisms of historical causation may be, one factor stands out in its implications for the way people think about interpersonal relations and interactions: the monetization of the Greek economy.

In Athens, coinage burst on the scene in the mid-6th century.[172] From the last quarter of the 6th century on low-value coins were in circulation, which is sug-

169 From c. 450 BCE pay for jurors and attendance at the council was instituted; from 399 BCE also for attendance in the Assembly.

170 Samons (2000), 202–204.

171 See Osborne (2007) on the transformation of the Athenian economy. Money itself is a sign of surplus wealth—wealth that does not require immediate conversion into subsistence goods, cattle or land. Increase of circulating money, even from external resources such as the allies of the Delian League, must at some point imply an increase of natural produce in Attica. Cartledge (1998), 20.

172 Electrum coinage was invented in Lydia, probably towards the end of the 7th century BCE. Von Reden (2010), 28 ff., Seaford (2004), 127 ff.; Bammer (1990), (1991), and Le Rider (2001), on the dating of the Artemision hoard between 590 and 560. Somewhere in the 550s electrum coinage was replaced by coins in silver and gold, spreading from Ephesos to Miletos, Teos and Phokaea, and next, with mediation of the Eastern Greek diaspora taken over by the city-states on the Greek mainland in the last quarter of the 6th century. Kim (2002), Howgego (1995), 4. By 480 BCE nearly 100 mints were operative on the Greek

gestive of the use of coinage for small transactions on a daily basis: regular retail trade conducted with silver coinage can be dated back to the late-6th/early-5th century BCE.[173] From at least the mid-5th century BCE on, we find signs of a thoroughly moneyed economy in Athens.[174] Intertwined with the development of early coinage, but not entirely reducible to it, there was a process of monetization in Greek culture.[175] This monetization of Greek culture not only affected the Athenian economy; it also had profound effects on Greek intellectual life[176] and on popular culture and morality. One of the areas in which monetization had **conceptual consequences** was the discourse about φιλία. The gradual monetization of Greek society produced a new notion of exchange that became increasingly prevalent in popular thought as a model to think with: the commercial transaction, i.e., the simultaneous exchange of equivalent goods that does not necessarily yield a lasting relationship between the participants.

With the monetization of the Mediterranean world, the development of retail trade and the transformation of the Athenian economy at large, and the development of judicial institutions, emerges a different articulation of the social domain: there are increasing opportunities to exchange "goods" and "services" on a basis that is increasingly independent of political and social considerations. Exchange need no longer be confined to φίλοι (good for good) and ἐχθροί (harm for harm), but may also take place in a regulated and neutral

---

mainland. This exceptional rapid spread throughout the Greek world (and its slowness to take root elsewhere) has led scholars to interpret coinage as a Greek phenomenon, tied to the development of the polis as a political entity and on the Greek world's political division. Mooring *et. al.* (2018). On the introduction of coinage in Athens and the first issues of Athenian coins, see Kraay (1966), Kroll (1981), Von Reden (1995a), 180–182, Schaps (2004), 105, Kraay (1964), 80–82, Kroll (1981), 13–17.

173 The introduction of low-value *bronze* coinage for small change is recorded in Athens from the 5th century BCE on. Kim (2001), (2002) has discovered that from the early days of coinage on, fractional silver coins of low denomination were minted. Even the first issues of the *Wappenmünzen* included coins of small denominations.

174 Von Reden (1997); Kraay (1964).

175 See Schaps (2004) for the argument that "the invention of coinage was the invention of money" (15): with the monetization of the Greek world, money first became equivalent with wealth. But see Von Reden (2010) (1997) who dissociates money and coinage and argues that there was a considerable amount of monetization in late Archaic Greece preceding coinage, as the conditions for the universality of conventions and a universal medium of exchanges were prepared in the 6th-century. Within the confines of this definition, it can be argued that Solon played a pivotal role, not in coinage, but in the monetization of Athens.

176 Cf. Seaford (2004) for an argument that the monetization of Greece created the preconditions for the monistic and reductionistic philosophical systems of the Presocratics.

sphere, the market, between partners who are neither hostile nor acquainted and who cooperate to reach harmonization of needs on the spot. These transactors do not operate on the basis of a preexisting relationship nor do they aim to establish one. Monetization provides the partners with a tool to objectify value, to compare values, and to quantify with unprecedented precision.[177] The development of judicial institutions provides partners with the means to enforce obligations upon others or to apply sanctions, even to exchange partners who live outside one's social field of influence. Together, these historical developments make a relatively new form of exchange prevalent in Greek thought: the instantaneous disembedded transaction. This new relation, the disembedded transaction, is sometimes **isomorphous** with the reciprocal exchange of care, favors, and gifts in the contexts of φιλία-relations. This means that exchanges are potentially ambivalent,[178] allowing for multiple interpretations of the same exchange events and yielding conflicting understandings of the relationships based on these.[179]

There is something counter-intuitive about the idea that the disembedded transaction is a new phenomenon. How new can it be? *Isn't it just the same as barter*? And has not barter, the exchange of the butcher's meat for the baker's bread, always been part of life?

3.3 *The Myth of Barter*

The classical exposition of monetary theory is the one by Carl Menger, who lists the following functions:[180]

(1) money is a unit of account, a measure of value;
(2) money is a means of payment;

---

177 In the Homeric poems, cattle are occasionally used as a measure of value, e.g. *Il.* 6.234–236 (a comparison of the value of the armor of Diomedes and Glaucus), 2.459 (a golden tassel on Athena's aegis), 21.79 (Lycaon as slave), 23.702–705, 885 (prizes in games), *Od.* 1.430–431 (Eurycleia sold as slave), 22.56–58 (compensation proposed by a suitor to Odysseus). Two fundamental differences with the use of coined money as a measure of value are: (1) Homeric cattle rarely combine the functions of measure of value *and* means of exchange; (2) by their very nature, cattle can only express relatively high values; they cannot offer precise quantification of low-value objects.

178 I follow Appadurai (1986), 3–16 and Kopytoff (1986), 64 in approaching the distinction between commodity and gift not as a material one but one that inheres in a distinction in modes of exchange. This model allows for the same thing to be both gift and commodity, its meaning shifting with the ideology attached to the situation of exchange. See Section 4 below.

179 See Chapter Two Section 1, Chapter Three Section 2, Chapter Four Section 3, Chapter Five Section 1, on conceptual analyses of and reactions on perceived isomorphism.

180 Menger (1909).

(3) money is a store of value;
(4) money is a medium of exchange.

These functions mutually support one other: to be a means of payment, money probably needs to be regarded as worthy of being a store of wealth, which means that at some point it must be used as a medium of exchange, which in turn requires a degree of commensurability. Objects that perform *some* of these functions (e.g., measure or store of value, or means of payment), or whose acceptability *within* a single function is restricted (utensil being exchangeable for some objects but not for all), can be called "special purpose money" as opposed to "all-purpose money".

It is essential to appreciate that Menger's monetary theory revolves around the assumption that money evolved organically from barter and that all monetary functions can be reduced to its primary function as "a medium of exchange".[181] As such, Menger's conception of money is part of a large-scale cultural genealogical discourse called the Myth of Barter by its detractors.[182] The most famous proponent of this myth is Adam Smith with his account of the evolution of complex society as driven by the universally human "propensity to truck, barter, and exchange one thing for another."[183] Smith sketches a scenario of society before the invention of money, where a baker would have wanted a butcher's meat at a moment when he had nothing to offer the butcher. "No

181 Polanyi (1977) takes the "medium of exchange" function to be the *least* basic one: it is only with the introduction of market exchange that payment comes to be envisaged in terms of the obligation to pay on the spot in exchange. (99, 104–105, 107, 109). Menger and Polanyi represent the two approaches to money that originate in Enlightenment thought: the Anglo-Saxon tradition adheres to a "commodity theory" (or "metallism") of money according to which money is in essence a commodity, a market phenomenon, an instrument of trade with a value independent of the context of transaction and only measurable against other objects. E.g. Ricardo (1817), Mill (1848). The German romantic "chartalist" (or anti-metallist) tradition approaches money as debt, i.e. a value "made by law" (Barbon 1690) that derives its value from the trust within a community (Müller 1816). The value of money is independent of the medium used to represent it, for money is not a commodity but a token; money is not a market phenomenon but a creation of centralized power that issues money as an IOU. E.g. Simmel (1978). The relative weight of money's different functions is still subject to debate. See e.g. Robbins & Akin (1999) for emphasis on means of exchange (cf. Lapavitsas 2005 for a refinement of the Marxist tradition on money as the Ur-commodity); Ingham (2004) for money as measure of value/unit of account.

182 Menger (1909), 8–9, 47–49, 67–69. This view on money as a pure instrument and commodity still lies at the heart of Keynesian monetary theory. Dowd (2000); Klein & Selgin (2000). For a definitive dismantlement of the myth of barter, see Graeber (2011), 21–42. Cf. Seaford (2004), 292 n. 1: "It is easy to be misled by the creation-myth of money (out of barter) into believing that pre-monetary society was based on barter."

183 Adam Smith, *Wealth of Nations* 1.2.1–2.

exchange can, in this case, be made between them," because without money, there is no simultaneous availability of barter material.

The myth of barter, or the "market hypothesis", consists in the interrelated claims that money developed from barter, that money was invented to facilitate trade and that money functioned primarily as a medium of exchange. Within this view on money, money is only instrumental and hence value-neutral: it merely is the one commodity singled out as a universal equivalent—a privileged commodity, but not a phenomenon with its own dynamics or with a capacity to transform the world.

Commonsensical though the market view may be, it fails to do justice to two remarkable facts: (1) the marginality of barter in pre-monetary Greece,[184] where most exchanges (lending, borrowing, and sharing) are conducted with neighbors and other φίλοι along the lines of long-term reciprocity;[185] (2) the **fiduciarity** of Greek coinage, i.e. the excess of the fixed conventional value of pieces of money over their intrinsic value.[186] The exchange-value is enabled to

---

184 Seaford (2004), 23–47. Osborne (2007), 294; Millett (1984); Donlan (1985b); Tandy (1997), 19–111; Snodgrass (1971). There is little archaeological evidence for retail trade or cash-crop markets before the mid-6th century. Schaps (2004), 111–123; there is archaeological evidence for trade overseas, not of subsistence goods, but luxury objects. Tandy (1997), 114. As to literary evidence, there are only three instances in Homer of exchanges of *things* (as opposed to people) that are not to create interpersonal links but for the sake of the things themselves: Euneus' ships from Lemnos that bring wine to the Greek camp (*Il.* 7.467–475), "Mentes"' cargo of gleaming iron to be exchanged with bronze from Temese (*Od.* 1.183–184), the Phoenician cargo, including a gold necklace, that Eumaeus tells about (*Od.* 15.416, 445, 452, 460–463). Exchanges of persons for goods (distinct from ransom) occur more frequently. E.g. *Il.*21.41, 23.746–747, 21.102, 22.44–45, 24.752, 21.454, *Od.* 1.430–431, 14.115, 15.429, 20.382–383. The evidential value of the absence of retail trade in Homeric epic is of course limited and problematic. In ancient Mesopotamia markets (in the sense of fixed places of retail trade) did exist already in the Old Babylonian period. Schaps (2004), 46–47. Polanyi's denial (1957 and 1963) of the existence of markets in the Near East is untenable. Cf. Jursa (2010), esp. 13–25.

185 Millett (1984); Donlan (1985b); Tandy (1997), 19–111; Snodgrass (1971).

186 Both points are forcefully made by Seaford (2004). Peacock (2006), 643: "Evidence of this 'fiduciarity' includes: (1) that it was rarely melted down to create bullion (such a change of form would have meant a loss in conventional value); (2) that it circulated at its bullion value only outside Greece, that is, outside the jurisdiction of the states whose authority conferred coin with fiduciary value." According to Seaford (2004), 6, fiduciarity is what is unprecedented about Greek coinage. Kroll (1998) argues that from 700 BCE onwards (almost a century before the invention of electrum coinage in the Eastern Greek colonies), silver in the form of weighed lumps or ingots has served a significant number of the functions that would later be performed by coined money: e.g. in the Solonic laws (early 6th century) several forms of payment (payment to victors in games, handling of private debts, the naucrary) were conducted in bullion payment (in "drachmas", i.e. a weight unit later to

exceed intrinsic value when money, in some form or another, bears a sign that guarantees future acceptability of the conventional value of money. Its degree of circulation depends on a general belief in this future acceptability and presupposes that it circulates among a group of individuals tied by a moral or legal framework.[187]

As such, monetary exchanges are conducted on premises radically different from barter: like theft and plunder, barter is typically conducted by individuals who are *not* tied together by any social framework,[188] performed in mutual distrust, without any investment in integration—a very unlikely subsoil for exchange based on fiduciarity. There is no recorded case of money developing out of barter in the anthropological field.[189] Barter, i.e., international trade,

become a value unit). This is supported by finds of uncoined silver, including low-weight silver fragments and by the formalization of weighing standards that have preceded the invention of coinage. Osborne (1996), 253–255; Horsmann (2000), with the interesting thesis that the introduction of coinage went hand in hand with metrological reforms. The high level of precision that is characteristic of coin money seems to be prepared for by the precise weighing of silver bullion; coinage, by having the advantage that coins can be counted instead of weighed, makes exchange easier. Kroll's hypothesis that the issuing authority profits from the slight overvaluation of coin in relation to its intrinsic value is speculative as Kurke (1999) points out (11–12). Seaford (2004) notes that the fiduciarity of ancient Greek coins never reaches the level of modern money (coins are predominantly struck from high-value metals in antiquity). The first mass-produced coins were struck in Britain around 1800; national paper money only appeared in the second half of the nineteenth century (as a substitute for specie and promissory notes); base metal coinage was introduced after the second world war. Cf. Hart (1986).

187 Seaford (2004), 7: "A group of individuals who know nothing of each other, or who have no shared symbol, have no basis on which the general belief can construct itself."

188 Sahlins (1972), 196–204. Not only was barter historically a marginal phenomenon; it is also commonly conceptualized as hostile exchange. Sahlins categorizes barter as negative reciprocity: "Persons stand in a relationship of 'negative' reciprocity where each strives to outdo the other and acquire as much profit as he can. Such relationships range from situations of 'barter' or 'haggling' to situations characterized by a succession of reprisals." (1965: 148–149); cf. (1972), 195: [Negative reciprocity is] "the most impersonal sort of exchange. In guises such as 'barter' it is from our own point of view the 'most economic'." Cf. Humphrey (1985) on the problematic concept of barter that has been classified both as "balanced" and as "negative" reciprocity in anthropology. The fundamental difference between barter and market exchange is that market exchange takes place in a regulated sphere under controlled circumstances between partners who share a political, legal or social framework; barter is socially far less integrated. For a discussion of the place of barter in the development of exchange see Humphreys (1985) and Davis (1992). But see Dodd (1994), xxii: "In barter the key requirement for transactors is information. This mostly concerns the location and trustworthiness of co-transactors. Money dispenses with this." Cf. Humphrey & Hugh-Jones (1992), 6–8, 61, 95, 107–141.

189 There is no historical evidence for a "barter → commodity → money"-transition. Ingham

in the ancient Mediterranean world both predated money[190] *and* effectively continued to be conducted without money; conversely, circulation-patterns of early coinage show that money was not used in international trade.[191]

As will be argued in Chapter Four, the Myth of Barter is best read as expressive of a particular anthropology rather than as historical fact. It is an instance of what I would like to call the Flintstones Effect:[192] a way of imagining a historical era with a stone age patina while keeping the modern-day furniture intact—exemplified by the stone fridge and the dino-driven lawn mower in the Flintstones' household. In Adam Smith's case, the stone fridge is the life in the 18th-century village society featuring bakers and butchers desperate to engage

---

(2000); Wray (2000) (2004); Crump 1981, 88–90; Humphrey (1985). Dalton (1982), 185: "[B]arter, in the strict sense of moneyless market exchange, has never been a quantitatively important or dominant model or transaction in any past or present economic system about which we have hard information." But note Howgego (1995), 14: "Economic theory is able to demonstrate how money might in principle have evolved out of barter, and it would be unwise to discard the possibility, especially given the ubiquity of barter." Cf. Anderlini & Sabourian (1992).

190 International trade in the Mediterranean world had existed for thousands of years before money. Schaps (1997), 95. Trade in the Near Eastern World continued to be conducted without money for thousands of years after the monetization of the Greek mainland. Schaps (1997), 95. Greek poleis too conducted predominantly barter in international trade: foreign trade did not require money (because of the great amounts of costly goods that could be easily bartered for other costly commodities, such as bullion and kind) and was not essentially facilitated by use of money, since to the trading partners, foreigners, a coin would be no better than its bullion value.

191 Kraay (1964). Kraay sees archaic coinage as limited-purpose money, i.e. primarily as a means of administrative payment (instituted for the standardization of payment), not used immediately as a widespread form of money, but predominantly received by the *polis* in the form of taxes (e.g. harbour dues), fines and penalties, and divided among citizens on occasions of surplus, paid to mercenaries or soldiers and experts, and spent on public works—but not used as a means of exchange in retail trade. See Price (1983) for the objection that Kraay's thesis leaves the problem of fiduciarity unadressed: the thesis assumes "that payment for service was acceptable and this in turn would suggest at least in part that coins were suitable for retail trade." (6). Cf. Tullock (1975), 491. Price's solution is to postulate a two-phase development of coinage: the first involves the minting of electrum coinage, in Lydia and Eastern Greece, which conceptually may have been more akin to gifts or medals, issued by states, monarchs or private individuals as some kind of bonus payment (in addition to everyday livelihood during their service) for e.g. mercenaries; in the second stage, about fifty years later, the city-states of the Greek mainland, started to mint silver currency, which circulated more widely from their sites of origin and which could be used as a *means of payment* for rewarding political, military and juridical office, because the earlier electrum coinage had already habituated the receivers to the concept of metallic payment.

192 This term is inspired by Jan Sleutels' "Flintstones Fallacy", the fallacy, often made in evolutionary psychology and philosophy of mind, of projecting modern self-conceptions onto earlier minds. Sleutels (2013).

in exchanges, retrojected into an undefined pre-monetary era and stripped of the one phenomenon that the thought experiment intends to explain: money. The resulting society is as fictitious as the Flintstones' household.

3.4 *Reversing the Order of Explanation*

What precisely makes the Athenian economy of the 5th and 4th century so qualitatively different from the economy we see in Homeric epic or in Hesiod's depiction of peasant life? Many of the economic activities, metaphors and models that we will see in the chapter to come did exist before the great transformation: paid labor (Homer's Poseidon),[193] lending and borrowing (Hesiod's peasants),[194] commercial exchanges (Homer's Phoenicians, conducting barter),[195] measuring wealth (Glaucus and Diomedes, with cattle).[196]

And they all did so without money. Several sorts of "proto-money", i.e., goods that perform some of the functions of later money, were in use long before coinage was invented: cattle functioned as a measure of value, grain as a store of wealth, utensils such as tripods or cauldrons as a means of payment in retributive contexts, iron spits as a medium of exchange in cultic and religious contexts,[197] metallic bullion as a store of wealth and medium of exchange in foreign trade.[198] The very terminology for money transactions and credit operations predate the invention of coin money: for instance, the term for "paying", ἀποτίνειν or τίνειν, originates in the sphere of revenge and compensation.[199]

---

193 Hom. *Il.* 21.445; cf. Hes. *O&D* 371.

194 E.g. Hes. *O&D* 342–363. Cf. Millett (1991), 27–35 and 44–52 on the terminology and development of early credit mechanism.

195 E.g. Hom. *Od.* 15.416, 445, 452, 460–463.

196 Hom. *Il.* 6.234–236.

197 For a long time, the idea that iron spits were used as a form of pre-coin currency was primarily based on etymology (*obelos* > *obolos*) and later literary stories of dubious reliability. It has been disputed whether iron spits were used as proto-money. Courbin (1983), Furtwängler (1980) Von Reden (1997). More recently there have been some archaeological finds to support the thesis. Strøm (1992), Seaford (2004), 109–114, Schaps (2004), 82–88.

198 There is evidence for the use of gold, silver and electrum bars adjusted to weight standards from c. 700 BCE on. Furtwängler (1986), 156.

199 Seaford (2004), 23–26; Wilson (2002). The noun ἀποτίμημα is also used in the context of dowries in late Archaic Athens. Cf. Von Reden (1997). The terminology of τίνειν is also related to ποινή (requital) and ἄποινα (compensation). In 7th- and early 6th-century Crete, cauldrons (λέβητες), were used as ἐπιτίμια or ἄποινα (compensation) in retributive contexts. Von Reden (1997), 157. There is some discussion about the relation of the field of τίνειν/ποινή to τιμή. According to Pokorny (1959), I.637 τιμή, τίω and ποινή all derive from the common root *$k^{u}eh_{1}$ ("respect, punishment, expiation"); so too Frisk (1970), II.901. Benveniste (1973), 334–345 and Beekes (2010), II.1490 separate τιμή, τίω with long ῑ (<*$k^{u}eh_{1}i$) from τίνω, τίσις with short ῐ (<*$k^{u}h_{1}i$). Wilson (2002), 20–26 argues for a single root.

As for terminology, there is no ancient Greek equivalent for our term "money". As money is an historically embedded phenomenon,[200] its conceptualization is differently organized and articulated in different cultures. Ancient Greek had a term for currency, τὸ νόμισμα, a term that reflects the fiduciary nature of coins—although the term applies to anything sanctioned by established usage, hence including custom and legal measures alike. There is also a term that refers to the material aspect of money, τὸ ἀργύριον, "piece of silver", a term for wealth, πλοῦτος, which included non-monetary forms of wealth, as well as a term for money in its capacity as a resource, a stand-incommodity, in the generalized plural τὰ χρήματα—a term applicable to any commodity.

This all seems to suggest that money as we know it did not enter the Greek world as a unified phenomenon nor as something completely novel that enabled the Greeks to do things they were not capable of before.[201] If there was no significant expansion of the repertory of economic actions, what exactly did change in the newly monetized economy of ancient Athens?

On the level of **history of mentalities**, however, two points need to be made. First of all, whereas there may not be one distinct operation or action (such as "paying", "borrowing" or "measuring") that the Greeks were not capable of before the invention of coinage, with the introduction of coined money there came to be **one means** that performed all functions that were previously performed by disparate means (cattle as a measure of value, grain as a store of wealth, tripods as blood-money, metallic bullion as a medium of exchange in foreign trade). Exchanges that were previously experienced as disparate and distinct (the administration of justice, the payment of mercenaries, the redistribution of resources, the exchange of goods) came to be interconnected in an unprecedented way.[202]

---

200 Von Reden (2010), 6ff.; (1995), 171–194. For the embeddedness of money as a phenomenon, cf. Parry & Bloch (1989), 21: "[T]he meanings with which money is invested are quite as much a product of the cultural matrix into which it is incorporated as of the economic functions it performs as a means of exchange, unit of account, store of value, and so on. It is therefore impossible to predict its symbolic meanings from these functions alone."

201 Von Reden (1995a), 175: "The absence of a name for the phenomenon of money in Greece suggests that it gradually emerged rather than being imposed from outside."

202 Cf. Seaford (2004). Osborne (2007), 292: "The utility of coinage rests in the way in which it can serve a number of functions which previously had not been served by a single medium."

Secondly, although money did not evolve from international trade and barter,[203] it did facilitate trade,[204] i.e. **retail trade**, trade within the polis.[205] Coinage, the agora and retail trade developed simultaneously in 6th-century Athens.[206] The exact causal mechanisms are notoriously hard to disentangle,[207] but within a short time span after its invention, coinage was used not as a specialist currency, but as a generally accepted means to meet social obligations in everyday retail trade used by a significant segment of the population.[208] The Athenian agora was not a periodic market (cash crop market) serving the needs

203 Alternative reconstructions of the origins of money include, next to the hypotheses of Kraay (1964) and Price (1983) (quoted above), hypotheses about the judicial and sacred origins of money that hold that the primary function of early money was its role as standard of value in early penal law. E.g. Laum (1924), followed by Seaford (1994), 191–234 and (2004), 9–15, 48–59, 102–104, for the thesis that coinage develops out of egalitarian sacrificial distribution (*obeloi*, iron spits, as the forerunner of *oboloi*, metallic coins); Will (1954), (1955), Grierson (1977) and Picard (1–15) who stress the etymological connection between νομίσμα and νόμος. Will is followed by Von Reden (1995a), 171–194, (1997), (2002), (2010). Kurke (1999), 22 ff. reverses the priorities by viewing money not so much as the cause but rather as a symptom of a conceptual revolution and a manifestation of systems of social evaluation in flux.

204 The adoption of silver coinage by the Greek *poleis* was in principle a market-exogenous act. Although Greek coinage may have been prepared for by various forms of proto-money (cattle, utensils, grain, bullion—each fulfilling *some* but not *all* of the functions that Greek coinage came to perform), the bestowing of fiduciary, conventional, value on silver coins was an important watershed.

205 In Greek there is a distinction between retail trade, καπηλεία, and long distance (usually overseas) trade, ἐμπορία. Cf. Pl. *Rep.* 371d5–7. See Finkelstein (= Finley) (1935), Hopper (1979), 47–67. In Classical Athens, ἐμπορία was presumably a viable activity for (aristocratic) landholders to export their own produce (Bravo (1977) 1–59); καπηλεία was most probably a full-time profession. Von Reden (1995), 171–194 warns against the fallacy of identifying money unproblematically with trade, commodification and a "disembedded" economy and opposing it with a traditional non-market gift economy.

206 Schaps (2004). This is the period in which the agora (presumably after being relocated to the more central position it had in the classical period) developed commercial functions in addition to its older political, social, judicial and religious roles. Von Reden (1995), 147 ff.; Morris (1991), Snodgrass (1991). The receptive ground for the emergence of a commercial market and the spread of coinage was probably provided by the radical transformation of the *polis*. The development and growth of a marketplace should not without qualification be taken to imply the emergence of a full-blown disembedded market economy (Von Reden 1995, 105–123; Möller (2007), 371–373). See n. 190 below.

207 Howgego (1995), 16: "The interaction of economic, social, and political changes was complex. The spread of coinage may itself be seen both as caused by such changes, and also as an agent in the process."

208 Seaford (2004), 18. This is supported by recent finds containing large numbers of fractional silver coins (1/10 gr.), from the first quarter of the 5th century, reported by Kim (2001). Fractional silver coins behave differently from large-denomination coins: small coins tend to

of a subsistence economy, but a permanent market functioning in a society of specialization.[209] By the 4th century, agricultural products were increasingly being raised for cash sale.[210] This is the context where our new relationship type, the disembedded transaction, finds its articulation.

With all due qualifications, it can be argued, that in late-6th and early-5th century BCE certain parts and aspects of the Athenian economy underwent a transformation that can be described as a process of disembedding. This is not to imply that the Athenian economy as a system was fully disembedded. We may even question whether such a thing exists: market exchange is *always* embedded in political structures—a construct such as fiduciary money could not possibly operate otherwise.[211] However, the historical record presents us with an economy that, within the life span of two generations, has transformed to such an extent that an entire population came to use money in everyday contexts of retail trade and other small-scale transactions. However much or little embedded in the public political life of the polis this economy as a system may be, it does consist in individual activities that often take the shape of immediate transactions between privately unrelated individuals, between people who do not necessarily have to be each other's φίλοι.[212]

One final, somewhat paradoxical, point deserves to be made. Although coin money in itself may not have been the only or ultimate cause of the development of trade and commerce, the Greeks did think it was. However complex the exact mechanisms of historical causation may be, to the 5th- and 4th-century Athenian, money was one of the most visible symptoms, and one of the most potent symbols, of these rapid and pervasive changes in political and socio-economic life. The place of money and monetary activities in the cultural imaginatary of Ancient Greece is part of the history of the disembedded transaction.

---

travel less far and are found in hoards only with similarly small coins. These archaic fractional coins were very likely used in everyday transactions.

209 Harris (2002).

210 Osborne (1991) for the role of *leitourgia* that forced the wealthy landowner to raise large amounts of cash, which made them dependent on selling agricultural produce in town markets. Public status came to depend on cash income.

211 Cf. the notion that *money* is always embedded and integrative ("money is always personal and impersonal"), see Hart (2007). Johnstone (2011), 2: "Money did not exert a depersonalizing effect, but *re*personalized relationships along different lines."

212 Cf. Seaford (1998), 3: "Commercial exchange embodies a relationship between the items exchanged rather than between the parties to the exchange, and generally involves a mutual absolute egoism that is by definition incompatible with (beneficial) reciprocity."

3.5 *Thinking about Money*

There is a tradition in European thought that maintains that money is a revolutionary force and that credits money with the rise of individualism or the "Western subject",[213] the emergence of abstract thought and rational calculation,[214] the emergence of symbolic thought,[215] the development of the market and the concept of the commodity,[216] the transition from *Gemeinschaft* to *Gesellschaft*,[217] the corrosion of society,[218] with being the root of all evil,[219] or the end of evil.[220]

The Greeks had a tradition of their own. Money is the measure of all things.[221] Money is the source of all evils.[222] Money is the man.[223] Money is power.[224] Classical Greek literature abounds in statements, provocative and trivial, positive and negative, about the nature and power of money. The Greeks of the Classical Age were fascinated by the phenomenon of money and what it brought about in the world around them.

The Myth of Barter had a precursor in the monetary theories of Plato and Aristotle: both assumed that money developed from barter and was invented

---

213 Money and individualism: Simmel (1978), Farenga (1985); money and the articulation of the Western subject: Seaford (2012).

214 Marx (1962) [1867], 104–108, Thomson 1955: 175–207, 251–270, 302–347; Shell 1978; Seaford 1994: 220–232; Crump (1978). For a problematization of the conception of money as the "most quantifiable expression of commodity" and as the "expression of index, and measure of commensurability", see LiPuma (1999), 198; cf. Strathern (1992), 191, Maurer (2003). Maurer (2005) on money as *resacralizing* exchanges and conversions.

215 Shell (1992): money as a metaphor for and exemplar of the problem of the relationship between sign and substance. Cf. De Saussure (1966), 115.

216 Polanyi (1944). Cf. Kelly (1992): uniscalar valuation as a hallmark of modern capitalist money; Taussig (1980): universal commodification (and erosion of other systems of value) as consequence of monetization.

217 Simmel (1907). Money as cause and consequence of the transformation from *Gemeinschaft* to *Gesellschaft*: Keister (2002), 40.

218 Simmel (1907) for the "money as acid"-hypothesis.

219 Macfarlane (1985).

220 Hirschman (1977) on seventeenth- and eighteenth-century capitalist ideology that held that capitalism was capable of accomplishing the repression of the passions in favor of "harmless" interests of commercial life.

221 Ar. *EN* IX.vii (1167b24–32). See Chapter Seven.

222 Soph. *Ant.* 295–301.

223 Pind. *Isthm.* 2.11.

224 E.g. Eur. *Phoen.* 438–442; Aristoph. *Plut.* 131: Zeus rules the gods because he has the most money; Thuc. 6.34.2: money makes war and other things thrive. See Kallet-Marx (1993), (1994) on the role of this equation in Thucydides' conception of Athens' military history.

to facilitate trade.[225] Although historically this is not correct, such theories are interesting precisely *because of* the Flintstones Effects that they exhibit: sources like these tell us that Greek intellectuals in the 4th-century had come to see money predominantly as a medium of exchange and an important instrument for trade. Plato credited the man who invented money as a benefactor who made retail trading (καπηλεία) possible by providing a medium that makes goods "even and commensurable" (ὁμαλήν τε καὶ σύμμετρον).[226] But Herodotus too, in ascribing paratactically the invention of both coinage and retail trade to the Lydians (they were the first κάπηλοι)[227] closely associates money with retail trade.[228] Money and trade were interrelated phenomena in Greek popular thinking.[229]

Moreover, the function of money as a measure of value and a unit of account established an association between money and a distinct kind of mentality: a calculating attitude attuned to economic advantages. Already in early 6th-century inscriptions, we find that χρήματα, resources or commodities, are totaled in monetary terms: the total value of rewards, even if they were in kind (e.g. "public maintenance plus exemption from taxes plus fifty jars of wine plus some other goods"), is expressed in monetary terms, even if no coined money has changed hands.[230] A scene in Aristophanes' *Wasps* presupposes a calculating economic mentality in the audience: characters count and calculate influxes of taxes and dues.[231] Numerous references to money (pay, cost, bribes) figure in the *Acharnians* where the market is a metaphor for democracy, presupposing monetary numeracy in the audience.[232] Thucydides' *History* is written for an audience capable of understanding the equation "money = power":[233] "money both fuels the polis and becomes the engine of its destruc-

225 Pl. *Rep*. 371d; Ar. *Pol*. 1257a19–40; *NE* 1133a17–20.

226 Pl. *Leg*. 918b–c.

227 Hdt. 1.94.1.

228 Kurke (1999); Osborne (2007), 294: "The way in which Herodotus links the Lydians being the first to mint coins with their being the first retail traders is very suggestive of the implications of coinage as he saw it in the late fifth century."

229 Aristoph. *Plut*. 147: Carion treats wealth and money as synonymous (cf. 131, 194–197).

230 Von Reden (2010), 36–41. Cf. Schaps (2004) for an argument that the monetization of the Greek world provided the preconditions for the conceptual equation of wealth with money.

231 E.g. Aristoph. *Wasps* 655–660. Kallet (2007).

232 Kallet (2007); Goldhill (1991) for an argument that the commercial imagery reveals the perversions of political exchange; Von Reden (1995a), 132–135 for an understanding of the market imagery as a parody on the interconnectedness of market exchange and politics. Cf. Möller (2007), 371–373 on the *agora*.

233 Kallet-Marx (1993), (1994).

tion."[234] Aristotle expresses ethical concern about what money does to one's mentality, as it facilitates an unlimited desire for wealth.[235]

People living in 5th- and 4th-century Athens displayed a form of economic rationality: they were calculating citizens living in a complex economy that was much reflected upon. The phenomena of money, trade, credit, pay, and calculation were closely associated and represented an economic cluster of ideas and norms, of a way of dealing with resources and the people controlling those resources. The *agora* was imagined to have a rationality of its own and to impose its own norms:[236] it was the place of weighing and calculating,[237] bargaining,[238] trickery[239] and fast information (how's the price of grain?).[240] In a market situation, the overt pursuit of self-interest is not only accepted but normative:[241] giving something away for free is considered

234 Kallet (2007), 71.

235 E.g. Ar. *Pol.* 1256b40; Aristoph. *Plut.* 189–197: whereas of everything else (sex, food, honor, etc.) there is satiety, of money we always want more. Cf. Hdt. 1.187: Darius "insatiable desire for money" makes him reopen a tomb; Xen. *Por.* IV.6–7: of silver nobody can ever have enough.

236 E.g. Aristotle's low opinion of the "market mob" (ἀγοραῖος ὄχλος) (Ar. *Pol.* 1328b40). The Athenian agora was a "hybrid place" (a notion from Stallybrass & White (1986), 27), where commercial activities were blended with and subordinated to civic exchanges. Millett (1998b), Von Reden (1995), 105–123. Cf. Möller (2007), 371: "Neither spatial nor linguistic boundaries separated commercial from political activities." On the symbolic value of the market as a locus of decision-making ("the marketplace of ideas"), see Sluiter (2011). Cf. the reactions of Plato and Aristotle on this blending: restricting commercial interactions on the agora (Pl. *Leg.* 849b–850a) or dissociating commerce from politics by creating two separate agoras (Ar. *Pol.* 1131a30–b14).

237 On the *metronomoi* (market officials), Camp (1986), 122–126; Stanley (1976), 36–45. On the use of standardized measures (only mandatory in retail trade), Johnstone (2011), 54. See Finley (1985b) 110–111, 116–117 for the influential view that the average Athenian lacked bookkeeping methods (e.g. double-entry bookkeeping) and skills to compare the profitability of different enterprises. Cf. Ste. Croix (1956). Macve (1985), 257–258 argues that double-entry bookkeeping is not the only way of calculating profit. Cf. Dem. 36.11. Cf. Faraguna (1994), 567–572 for the use of accounts and the importance of ἀκρίβεια in being a good οἰκόνομος, estate manager. Written accounts and documents were predominantly used to regulate *external* relationships. Johnstone (2011), 62–80.

238 Cf. the bargaining scenes in Aristophanes' comedies: e.g. *Pax* 1197–1264, *Ach.* 867–958. Cf. Johnstone (2011), 12–34, on haggling.

239 Cf. the trick of placing ripe figs on top of a basket to mask the bad ones: Alexis *PCG* 133.

240 E.g. Aristoph. *Ach.* 758–759; Theophr. *Char.* 4.15. Cf. Pl. *Leg.* 917b–c. Harris (2002), 76–77 on price fluctuations on the agora. Lewis (1996), 13–19 on the agora as "the public appearance par excellence" where information is most visibly circulated.

241 Van Wees (1998), 19–20. See Morris (2002) for a useful survey of different approaches (liberal humanism, new humanities, economics, sociology, new institutional economics) to the ancient concept of κέρδος, "gain, profit, advantage, desire for gain".

stupid[242]—a mentality that could be constructed as hostile in other areas of life.[243]

The ubiquity of money in society was also a controversial and contested issue. It raised the question of whether the market was a fitting metaphor for political administration (as parodied in the *Acharnians*), by insisting that politics is not the same as accountancy,[244] or by ridiculing a Persian king for running the Empire like a shop.[245] Another link that was readily available in the Greek mind was between money and commodification, i.e. approaching objects as things that can be exchanged in a single transaction (the Greek term χρήματα refers to both money and commodities).[246] The question concerning what items could be treated as a commodity (Labor? Education? Sex?) was subject to discursive negotiation;[247] popular discourse reflected on questions such as: "is *everything* for sale?",[248] "can we value art, physical health, patriotism, and love in the same way as we can value shoes and cheese?"[249] On a more meta-

242 Cf. Hdt. 3.140.1: Syloson resents his own stupidity for giving away a beautiful cloak, regarding the gift as a "loss" (cf. Chapter Two Section 3); Xen. *Mem*. I.vi.11–12: Antiphon regards Socrates' conversations with young Athenians as "free gifts", indicative for his market irrationality. Cf. Chapter Four Section 1. On the ideology of "business" that propagates norms to seek "value for money" and ridicule the "sucker" who overpays or undercharges, see Davis (1992), 7–8, 56–58. Cf. Polanyi (1968), 69, Van Wees (1998), 19–20.

243 E.g. Aristoph. *Ach*. 28 ff.: Dicaeopolis loathes the Athenian market where everybody shouts and praises his commodities for sale and wishes to be back home where they have never heard the words "for sale". Harris (2002), 76: "An Athenian might think about politics in the Assembly, cultivate friendships in the gymnasia and at symposia, and at home try to avoid quarrels with family and neighbours. But when he set foot in the agora, the main thing he thought about was *kerdos*, getting a bargain."

244 Dem. 18.227–229 with Cuomo (2001), 23 and Yunis (2001), 236.

245 Hdt. 3.89: Darius as a κάπηλος.

246 Commodities are commonly defined as entities that have use value and that can be exchanged in a "discrete transaction" (i.e.) for a counterpart that has, in the immediate context, an equivalent value. Discrete transactions have as their primary and immediate purpose to obtain the counterpart value; in contrast, "partial transactions" can only be understood in the context of a long-chain of transactions (favors, gifts), containing reference to the relationship between the exchange partners. Appadurai (1986), 3–16 and Kopytoff (1986), 68 for this definition of commodity; Kopytoff (1986), 69 for the terminology of "discrete" and "partial" transactions.

247 The conservative reactions of Plato, Xenophon and Aristotle on the sophistic movement reflect this question. See Chapters Six and Seven.

248 E.g. Aristoph. *Pax* 375: eternal bliss costs three drachmas; Aeschyl. *Ag*. 437: Ares is a trader (χρυσαμοιβός) of lives. Eur. *HF* 643–648: youth is not for sale. Eur. fr. 527: virtue cannot be bought. Cf. Eur. *El*. 253, 372.

249 E.g. Aristoph. *Frogs* 1368–1410. Cf. Von Reden (1995), 114 on this scene. On money as a universal means, see Seaford (2004), 162–165.

physical level, questions were raised as to what extent money as a measure is capable of quantifying everything.[250]

On a political level, market transactions and the use of coin money could be associated with egalitarianism and an affirmation of the polis as an authority;[251] market-transactions could be framed as deceit,[252] coinage as counterfeit metal (a hostile framing of its fiduciarity).[253] Fiduciarity was the subject and target of metaphysical questions about the nature of value: how does conventional value work?[254] What is the value of money if one can starve amidst one's gold like King Midas?[255]

It is within this larger cultural discussion about money that statements and problematizations of φιλία can be better understood. The statement that money is the measure of all things occurs in a philosophical treatment of friendship.[256] The theme of the counterfeit friend touches on thinking about

250 E.g. Ar. *EN* IX.i. (1164a1–2). Cf. Aristoph. *Pax* 1201. See Chapter Three on Aristotle's account of commensurability; Seaford (2004), 283–291 for an interpretation of Protagoras Man/Measure-statement as informed by monetization. Cf. Carruthers & Espeland (1998), 1400: money "commensurates incommensurabilities"; Marx (1844), 110: "makes impossibilities fraternize."

251 Which is the gist of Kurke (1989), (1999) and (2002).

252 E.g. Hdt. 1.153.1 where the Greek *agora* is misrepresented by the Persian king Cyrus as the scene of double-dealing; cf. the Scythian Anarchasis who defines the agora as the place for τὸ ἀλλήλους ἀπατᾶν καὶ πλεονεκτεῖν (D.L. 1.105) Xen. *Mem.* III.vii.6 were κάπηλοι are represented as suspicious deceitful individuals who buy cheap and sell dear. Cf. the new ἀγαθοί who deceive each other in Thgn. 59–60. See Kurke (1989) for an argument that they are not only to be identified with κάπηλοι (trade as mutual cheating), but more specifically with users of money; in Thgn. 183–192, the "new" circulation of women (cross-class marriages) is compared to the circulation of coins, as opposed to the closed system of aristocratic gift-exchange. Cf. Möller (2007). Kurke (2002) understands the association of coinage with καπηλεία (petty huckstering), deceit and profit as a hostile misrepresentation by an elitist tradition. The cluster of associations recurs in Anacreon fr. 358 (*PMG*). Cf. Kurke (1999), 187–191.

253 Kurke (1995), (1999), 41–100, (2009).

254 E.g. Ar. *EN* 1133a–b: as coinage (νόμισμα) has value not by nature but by convention (νόμος), it is in our power to make it useless. Cf. *MM* 1194a. Pl. *Rep.* 371b: coinage as a "symbol" for the sake of exchange; [Pl.] *Eryx.* 399e–400c: the currency of one society is useless in another. Cf. Hdt. 3.23: Ethiopians value bronze above gold; Plut. *Lys.* 17.1: The Spartans make iron deliberately useless and use it as money because it has no value elsewhere; D.L. 6.20–21, 71: Diogenes the Cynic defaces the currency because he gave no authority to convention as to natural law. Dem. 24.212–214: law is like currency and the man who debases law must be punished, as civic law must remain purely silver. See Seaford (2004), 136–146 on Greek thinking about fiduciarity; Kurke (1999), 299–331 on money as civic image.

255 E.g. Ar. *Pol.* 1257a–b.

256 See Chapter Three.

fiduciarity.[257] The idea that avarice and φιλία are incompatible[258] is related to both the concern that money has no limit and the norm that friends need to constrain their greed in order to share it with others. The idea that friends can be bought reflects the norm that you can make friends by means of assistance that will have a pay-off as it will be reciprocated. The idea of selling friends is a shorthand for neglecting a friendship by not reciprocating a good turn.

At first sight, the theme of friendship may seem to be a marginal phenomenon of limited importance for an understanding of ancient conceptions of money, trade, and economics. However, Greek reflections about the nature of φιλία-reciprocity can tell us something about the conceptual preconditions that enabled the Athenians of the 5th and 4th century to articulate a realm of disembedded commercial exchanges.

This is a conceptual matter. In reality, market exchanges in Athens were guided by and embedded in social and political values and norms: in practice, instead of balanced prices, social proximity or distance remained determining factors in pricing.[259] In the market too, φίλοι tend to get a better deal than total strangers, because friendship reduces the dangers of deceit, excessive pricing, and violence (i.e. friendship reduces "transaction costs").[260] Nevertheless, ancient sources tend to treat retail sellers and shopkeepers as men acting outside the norms of φιλία, with a distinct mentality—especially so in situations of perceived isomorphism between φιλία-reciprocity and disembedded exchanges.

---

257 See Seaford (1998) on the tragic metaphors of the χαρακτήρ (the inscribed mark) and the κίβδηλος φίλος (the counterfeit friend); Kurke (2009) on the χρησμὸς κίβδηλος (the counterfeit oracle) in Herodotus. Cf. Xen. *Oec.* XIX.16 (on the quality of flute-players), X.3 (ἀργύριον κίβδηλον as one of the instruments of trickery to make one appear to be ἀξιοφίλητος, worthy of φιλία); Eur. *El.* 572 (the χαρακτήρ of the stranger who turns out to be Orestes). Falsely stamped coin is a moral image at Aeschyl. *Ag.* 780. The image of the κίβδηλος φίλος occurs as early as Theognis, e.g. 117–124. It is contested whether the image in Theognis already refers to counterfeit coinage (Van Groningen (1966), 50–51, Hangard (1963), 62–66; Levine (1984), 128–133); see Kurke (1999), 54–55 and (2009) for an argument that the line of thought and other images reveal that the implicit image is that of coinage and not simply about corrupted metallic alloy. On the κίβδηλος-metaphor in general, see Hangard (1963), Alessandri (1998).

258 E.g. Pl. *Gorg.* 508a.

259 Möller (2007), 370. Cf. Millett (1991) on credit mechanisms among friends.

260 The term "transaction cost" was originally coined by Coase (1988 [1937]). Cost-free transactions are imaginary: market transactions always cost something in terms of time and effort to find and evaluate the relevant information and to effectuate the deal. These costs can efficiently be lowered by bringing transactions into a rule-bounded system where participants can trust procedures. Cf. Ober (2008) for an application of the concept to institutions and procedures in democratic Athens.

It is in such contexts of isomorphism that Greek intellectual and *folk* discourse experimented not only with different conceptualizations of friendship but also with the idea of disembedded transactions. What does it mean to interact on asocial terms? Does it imply a form of alienation or detachment—detachment between exchange object and transactor, knowledge and knower, beauty and bearer? This book is about these thought experiments.

4 Apparatus and Argument

To wrap up: the thesis of this book is that 5th- and 4th-century ancient Greek thought, both popular and intellectual, witnessed a double-faced trend in thinking about interpersonal relationships. On the one hand, it will be argued, potential isomorphism of φιλία-reciprocity with commercial disembedded exchange has prompted a conception of φιλία that puts a premium on displaying "subjectifying elements", such as dispositions, intentions, emotions and moral orientations: these subjective, internalized, phenomena that come with the give and take of friendship, come to be seen as distinctive features of φιλία—i.e. distinct from disembedded transactions that lack such subjective traits. On the other hand, this very same isomorphism has also prompted the emergence of the "non-relation", the "disembedded transaction", the "purely economic" exchange. Both φιλία and commerce come to be articulated by each other in a mutually dependent way.

To analyze this trend with a descriptive language that is consistent and explanatory is intrinsically problematic. It involves applying ETIC categories on EMIC concepts, i.e. projecting scholarly definitions and constructs formulated in a metalanguage distinct from the language and culture it studies onto phenomena emerging from an insiders' perspective.[261] However, many of the ETIC concepts that are used in studies on the ancient economy, economics, conceptions of friendship and ethics are part of our own modern conceptual landscape that is in itself the product of certain cultural preoccupations. Many of the concepts discussed as conceptual tools below will themselves be problematized in the remainder of the book.

261 On the ETIC/EMIC distinction, Harris (1976). On the need for etic definitions and categories, see Snoek (1987); on the anthropologist's task to articulate emic concepts in connection with etic experience-distance concepts of scholarship, see Geertz (1976). Both are followed by Blok (2002), Naerebout (e.g. 2006) and Versnel (1991) who apply the etic/emic distinction to some of the core issues in ancient history of mentality.

4.1 *Reciprocity: Definitions and Types*

Central to the argument is the concept of reciprocity.[262] In its broadest application, reciprocity is "the principle and practice of voluntary requital, of benefit for benefit (positive reciprocity) or harm for harm (negative reciprocity)".[263] Because such reciprocity is considered a cultural universal,[264] it would seem a useful concept with which to describe the dynamics of social lives and systems. On the other hand, it might be objected, it is a definition too broad, is vague and general, and lacks substance:[265] "[T]he description of all types of exchange as reciprocal easily leads to an obscuring of the significant differences between them."[266]

This is, however, exactly the point. It is the differences that are at stake, negotiated, denied and created in Classical Athens. Thinkers such as Socrates and Aristotle, but also voices in popular discourse as we see reflected in oratory and drama, were articulating conceptions of the relatively new phenomenon of the market, were negotiating and revising existing conceptions of φιλία, and were developing ideas about the demarcation of different types of reciprocal exchange. They did not have the conceptual apparatus of economic anthropology at their disposal; they did not have a concept of "reciprocity" apart from some non-specific idea of trading, swapping, of mutuality (ἀλληλο-compounds), and of giving things in exchange for (ἀντί + genitive case) other things. In some cases, as we will see, there was a propensity towards **reductionism**: to understand the give and take within a durable φιλία bond as roughly similar to the instantaneous give and take of the market or the extended give and take of credit.[267] In such cases, many distinctions that have been drawn up in theoretical literature, such as the distinction between "formal" and "personal" reciprocity,[268] or the distinction between "balanced" and "generalized"

262 For a useful overview of the vast amount of literature on this topic, see Van Wees (1998); for a lucid account of the history of scholarship on reciprocity, see Wagner-Hasel (2003). Often the term "reciprocity" is used in a more restricted sense as the performance and requital of gratuitous action.

263 Seaford (1998).

264 Gouldner (1960), 171.

265 Narotzky (2002). MacCormack (1976), 10, Parry (1986), 466.

266 MacCormack (1976), 101; cf. Davis (1992), 10–11; Van Wees (1998), 15–20.

267 This is reflected in the origin of our term "reciprocity". "Reciprocity" is a neo-Latin translation of the Aristotelian neologism ἀντιπεπονθός. Aristotle uses the term to describe the monetary exchange between shoemaker and builder. See Chapter Seven. The translation originates with Guilielmo du Val (1629) who renders it as *perpessio mutua et reciproca*. Initially, the term was translated with the calque *contrapassum* (Robert Grosseteste), *repassio, retaliatio* (Feliciano, Averroès). Cf. Theocarakis (2008), Kaye (1998).

268 Gouldner (1960).

reciprocity,[269] collapse. In other cases, analytical effort was put into distinguishing parent-child reciprocity from a creditor-debtor exchange, making all kinds of conceptual distinctions relevant again.

Therefore, working with the modern analytical term "reciprocity" requires a constant renegotiation of terminology, because our object of analysis, the changing conceptions of φιλία-interactions and market transactions, is itself discursive in nature, a shifting ground in itself. Hence, the term reciprocity as I will use it covers both "positive" and "negative" kinds of exchange, i.e. both the exchange of gifts or favors (*quid pro quo*) and the exchange of injuries (*tit for tat*, an eye for an eye) that is revenge.[270] The reason why both positive and negative exchange are relevant is that we are discussing the ways in which exchange is presented and perceived. The problem with market exchange is that its conceptualization and valuation is contested and varying depending on the context. Sometimes a market transaction can be seen as a positive exchange as both partners get out of it what they need. Sometimes a market transaction is framed as a negative exchange ("daylight robbery"): traders deceive each other, and they attempt to "get something for nothing", i.e. to get as much out of the deal as possible.[271]

Moreover, the term reciprocity will cover both "balanced" exchanges in which things are traded with the expectation of a return within a limited time frame, as well as "generalized" forms of reciprocity where the time lapse between gift and counter-gift, favor and return, is so long and undefined that exchanges are no longer experienced as exchanges, but rather as a generalized form of sharing.[272] As we will see in Chapter Three, φιλία-reciprocity can be

---

269 Sahlins (1972).

270 Moreover, in Greek conception, both positive and negative reciprocity could be expressed in terminology of "giving back" (ἀποδίδωμι) and "paying back" (ἀποτίνομαι). Cf. Blundell (1989), 29, 37. E.g. Democr. DK 93: χαριζόμενος προσκέπτεο τὸν λαμβάνοντα, μὴ κακὸν ἀντ' ἀγαθοῦ κίβδηλος ἐὼν ἀποδῶι. "When you do a favor, study the recipient first, in case he prove a scoundrel and repay evil for good."

271 Sahlins (1972), 195: "[Negative reciprocity is] the attempt to get something for nothing with impunity (...). The participants [overtly] confront each other as opposed interests, each looking to maximize utility at the other's expense." But Van Wees (1998), 24: "[I]t is necessary to distinguish two kinds of negative reciprocity: in the first, it is the attitude of the participants which is negative, insofar as they are openly 'selfish' and 'mean' with positively valued objects of exchange; in the second, it is the objects of exchange, the insults and injuries traded, which are negatively valued." Van Wees' distinction makes sense. However, in Greek conceptualization this distinction is often not made: not only do aristocratic sources frame retail trade as deceit and robbery, also the terminology of "paying" originates from negative retributive contexts.

272 Sahlins (1972) poses a "spectrum of reciprocities" based on different degrees of social dis-

conceptualized as both. An οἶκος that functions well is bounded by so-called "limits of trust",[273] i.e. notional boundaries of the household. Within these boundaries, reciprocity is generalized: husbands and wives, parents and children, normally do not experience the to and fro of doing good turns as discrete exchanges. Beyond the boundaries of the household, trust diminishes, and a more balanced kind of reciprocity emerges. When all is going well, the parent-child bond could be imagined as selfless and generalized where nobody needs to keep track. However, in situations of imminent conflict, the language of give and take, of discrete turns, i.e. of balanced reciprocity, creeps in. Moreover, the development of credit mechanisms enabled the Greeks to analyze these relations as balanced transactions: the parents' selfless gift of life and sustenance turns into a balanced, or even a commercial, loan.[274]

The term "reciprocity" also covers both "formal" exchanges, i.e. exchanges according to a set of definite rights and duties (e.g. laws), and "personal" exchanges, i.e. exchanges that are regulated by personal status and relations.[275] Whereas one would expect to find such a distinction between formalized and personalized reciprocal obligations in any society, the concept of "obligation" and "norm" (the "ought" in "one ought to respect one's parents") is itself under construction and negotiation in our Greek sources. As we will see in Chapter, Four, Aristotle distinguishes between reciprocities that are "legal" (i.e. with the backup of legal sanctions) and "character-based" (being a matter of character and morality); however, we also find a tendency to represent what we would call personal obligations as legal prescriptions: reciprocating good treatment by φίλοι is imagined to be an Unwritten Divine Law.[276] Moreover, failure to perform one's filial obligation to take care of one's parents is a formally recognized crime in Athenian legislation.[277]

---

tance (196–204): all forms of exchange are reciprocal, but the looser the bonds between the exchanging partners become, the less generously or voluntarily equivalence is calculated. The spectrum ranges from the pure gift in "generalized reciprocity" (putatively altruistic, no overt expectation of direct material return), to "balanced reciprocity" (returns of commensurate worth or utility are stipulated) to "negative reciprocity" (the attempt to get something for nothing).

273 Foxhall (1998), 55.

274 See Chapter Three. Whereas modern classifications of reciprocity tend to use (overt) intentions as a criterion, the Greeks of the Classical Period reflected upon (and questioned) the sincerity and reality of these intentions.

275 Gouldner (1960), 170, 175 distinguishes along the same lines between "specific and complementary" duties and "generalized and indeterminate" ones.

276 Xen. *Mem.* IV.iv.24.

277 E.g. Arist. *Ath.Pol.* LV.3; Rhodes (1981) ad loc. Cf. DL 1.55; Andoc. 1.74. Cf. Glotz (1904) for legal details.

Hence, in Classical Athens (as, arguably, in any culture) the boundaries between different types of exchange and reciprocity are open to debate and context dependent. The terminology of "formal", "personal", "generalized", "balanced", "positive" and "negative" reciprocity is essentially question-begging. And questioned it will be. Each of the chapters shall, in a distinct way, engage with one or more of the conceptual issues in the academic debate about reciprocity: about the functional vagueness in Marshall Sahlins' account of generalized reciprocity (Chapter Two), about David Graeber's reductionist approach to reciprocity (Chapter Three), about Pierre Bourdieu's insistence on the importance of time, improvisation and perspective in reciprocity (Chapter Two and Chapter Four), the putative altruism of reciprocity (Chapter Five), the language games and symbolic violence engendered by reciprocity (Chapter Six) and Aristotle's notion of proportional reciprocity (Chapter Seven). Each of these case studies requires some flexibility in the concept of reciprocity. Therefore, for purposes of analytical consistency, the distinctions that will be used to refer to different types of relations described in the source texts themselves are (i) between embedded and disembedded exchanges (see above), and (ii) between long-term and short-term exchanges.

4.2 *Long-Term vs. Short-Term*

The distinction between long-term and short-term (instantaneous) exchanges often remains a category projected by us on the source material. Ancient discussions of φιλία or market exchange do not always explicitly designate the reciprocity at hand as a long-term or short-term encounter. However, the use of this opposition is justifiable because it refers to an overtly visible characteristic of an exchange: are objects simultaneously exchanged or is there a time lapse between the two allocations?[278]

The long/short term nature of a particular exchange interacts with what in anthropological literature has been identified as two "transactional orders".[279] Many societies distinguish between two related but separate orders: some exchanges (e.g. marriage, sacrifice, agriculture) are imagined to contribute to the reproduction of the supra-individual "long-term" social, political or religious order;[280] other exchanges serve the pursuit of short-term individual self-interest. The relation between the two orders is not necessarily one of oppo-

278 See Chapter Two Section 3 for the role of time in the opposition between commerce and φιλία.

279 Parry & Bloch (1989), 24, applied by Kurke (1999), 6, 15, Von Reden (1995a), 6–7, Seaford (2004), 95.

280 Reciprocity in its restricted sense is often treated as a subcategory of "reproduction", i.e.

sition. Whereas the long-term order is always valued positively, exchanges belonging to the short-term order are morally underdetermined; pursuit of self-interest is often socially accepted unless it is felt to violate and interfere with the reproduction of the long-term order. Moral conflict arises when individuals are perceived to divert the resources of the long-term order for their short-term interest (prostituting yourself to collect your owndowry!)[281] or when there is no consensus over what counts as the long-term order (the polis?).[282] Bloch & Parry's model has become commonplace in economic anthropology as well as in studies on the ancient economy.[283] The specifics will be discussed in Chapter Five.

φιλία-bonds and χάρις-exchanges typically belong to the long-term order of things. The breakdown of φιλία-ties is treated as symptomatic of social and religious disintegration in general,[284] respect for φίλοι is on a par with reverence for gods,[285] and the Charites have an altar in a location that is of symbolic significance for the life in the polis.[286] Market-exchanges belong to the short-term order (they are imagined to be aiming at the overt pursuit of self-interest), and their valuation is ambiguous. When market trade is framed as deceit, individuals are represented as abusing the long-term order. Moreover, several sources contrast long-term φιλία-obligations with one-off transactions between strangers. However, we will see in Chapter Seven that Aristotle offers an interesting alternative conception of retail trade, as he understands the exchange between shoemaker and builder to be an instance of πολιτική φιλία, "friendship of the polis".[287] Friendships of the polis are, in Aristotle's system, all those ties that underwrite the aims of the polis (living, living together, living the good life). Retail trade serves to complement the individual's lack of autarky and enables a society to operate on division of labor and specializa-

---

all transactions aimed at reproducing the structure of a group or community over time. E.g. Weiner (1980), Gregory (1982), 29–35.

281 Hdt. 1.93–94.2 on the daughters of the Lydians, with Kurke (1999), 169–171.

282 See e.g. Kurke (2002) and (1999) for an argument that 5th-century literary representations of coinage reflect a conflict between "elitist" positions (that denies the authority of the public sphere represented by the agora) and "middling" positions over what constitutes the long- and short-term transactional orders. Cf. Morris (1994); Von Reden (1995a), 2–3, 96–97; Seaford (2004), 95 for a different application.

283 Von Reden (1995), 3, 96, 172; Kurke (1999), 14–15, 126–127, 168–170; Seaford (2004), 13–15, 95.

284 E.g. Thgn. 1.1135–1155 (with Levine (1985), 193): Hes. *O&D* 190 (with West (1978), ad loc.).

285 Is. 1.16.

286 Ar. *EN* v (1133a3–5). See Chapter Two Section 1.

287 Chapter Seven Section 4.

tion. On an individual level, market transactions are short-lived and ephemeral. On a systemic level, they have a cohesive force for society as a whole, and they underwrite the aims of the long-term transactional order. Hence, to Aristotle these short-term transactions are instances of φιλία, embedded in the life and aims of the polis.

4.3 *Gifts vs. Commodities*

The distinction between two transactional orders is related to the distinction between an embedded and a disembedded sphere of economy, embedded exchanges occurring in the context of pre-existing relations or aiming at establishing relations (e.g. with φίλοι), and disembedded exchanges featuring partners who overtly agree to be each aiming at providing for their own material wants.

This distinction is often symbolized by the distinction between commodities and gifts.[288] Commodities are commonly defined as alienable objects exchanged between two exchange partners in a state of mutual independence;[289] they have use value and can be exchanged in a discrete transaction for a counterpart that has, in the immediate context, an equivalent value.[290] Gifts, on the other hand, are often seen as inalienable things exchanged between two reciprocally dependent transactors;[291] a gift exchange is "partial", in the sense that it can only be understood in the context of the "entire transaction", i.e. the long-term chain of favors and obligations, containing reference to the relationship between the transactors.[292] Commodity exchange is all about the relation between objects; gift exchange is about the relation between subjects.[293]

288 A useful overview of anthropological theories of the gift can be found in Yan (2005) and in Carlà & Gori (2014).

289 Marx (1976 [1867]), 178. Cf. Gregory (1982), 12.

290 Cf. Kopytoff (1986), 68.

291 Mauss (1954 [1925]), 8–10: the gift is ultimately inalienable and inseparable from the person of the donor; Lévi-Strauss (1969 [1949]); Gregory (1982), 121: the gift "refers to the *personal relations* between people that the exchange of things in certain social contexts creates."

292 Kopytoff (1986), 69 for the terminology of "discrete" and "partial" transactions.

293 On a more systemic level, the terms "gift" and "commodity" are often used to refer to the organization of societies. In "commodity-oriented economies" people experience their interest in commodities as a desire to accumulate goods; a "gift economy" revolves around a desire to expand social relations, being "a shorthand for describing a relationship between production and consumption in which consumptive production shapes people's motivations and the form in which they recognize productive activities". Strathern (1990), 143–144. Cf. Gregory (1982), 41.

However, this polar opposition between gifts and commodities is problematic in several ways.[294] First of all, in reality, the boundaries between commodities and gifts are less fixed than one may think. In some societies, as was also the case in Classical Athens, the same object could be understood as a commodity in some contexts, and as a gift in others. Even money, the quintessential stand-in commodity, could be given and understood as a gift. Secondly, the same object could overtly be presented as a gift while covertly be understood as an alienable commodity with a calculable value.

Moreover, the transformation of the Athenian economy provoked a discussion about the repertory of objects that could be exchanged as a commodity in a disembedded transaction, and about the limits of commodification. In terms of the sociologist Arlie Hochschild, Classical Athenian discourse about gifts and commodities reveals a moving "market frontier", a notional frontier between goods and services available for rent on the one side and gifts and favors on the other.[295] Chapters Five and Six discuss the market frontier in the domains of education and sexuality.

Commodities and gifts are best understood as cultural constructs.[296] As Arjun Appadurai and Igor Kopytoff have argued, the difference between commodity and gift does not inhere in the nature of the object, but in the mode and the qualitative aspects of the exchange, the conditions under which an item is understood and presented to be exchanged.[297] If the exchange is presented as embedded because the transactors sense that there will be social or political repercussions, the allocation may be a gift. If the exchange is felt to be free of consequences, with transactors both openly aiming at providing for their own material wants, the allocation is a disembedded commodity exchange. Hence, deciding whether an item is to be understood as a commodity or a gift is a discursive and potentially ideological process.[298] A poet may resent an under-

294 Carlà & Gori (2014).

295 Hochschild (2004).

296 Of course, as in any society, in Classical Athens too there are boundaries to the repertory of objects that can be exchanged as a commodity. These boundaries are best conceptualized in terms of the "commodity candidacy" of a thing, i.e. the exchangeability of things in a particular social and historical context defined by symbolic, moral and classificatory standards and criteria. See Appadurai (1986), 13.

297 Appadurai (1986), 3–16, Kopytoff (1986), 64. Bourdieu (1990 [1980]), 126: "The 'way of giving', the manner, the forms, are what separate a gift from straight exchange, moral obligation from economic obligation."

298 Here, and in the rest of this book, I use "ideology" and "ideological" as referring to a "set of principles that delimits the boundaries of values and integrity and informs the patterns of behavior of most people within a society, and which is an ever-evolving and complex

standing of his poems as commodities or commission work by emphatically representing his work as gifts imbued with a cultural value that is irreducible to commercial value. A teacher like Antiphon may be in favor of understanding his teachings in political skills as a market commodity because it would enhance the dissemination of knowledge and power beyond the barriers of aristocracy.

But the most serious objection against a too naïve take on the gift/commodity opposition is that in 4th-century analytical discourse, the question was not only what allocations could be counted as a gift, but also what it was that **defined** the gift. If a gift elicits the obligation to reciprocate, how is this different from the obligation to repay a debt? Is a "pure" gift possible? We shall see in Chapter Four, how Aristotle develops a concept of "pure" gift, defined by the selfless intention of the donor—a concept that can only be understood as "an attempt to transcend the system of value" predicated on money.[299] 4th-century analyses of the gift should not be read as an attempt to preserve a pre-monetary notion of gifts; rather, they provide brand new articulations of the gift in opposition to the exchange of commodities. Here we see the emergence of a Hostile Worlds Thesis.

4.4 *Hostile Worlds and "Nothing But"*

In her groundbreaking analysis of "the purchase of intimacy", sociologist Viviane Zelizer describes the notional separation of economics and intimacy in modern culture.[300] She describes two common frameworks that people apply when thinking about the relation between economics and intimate relations. On the one hand, there is the Hostile Worlds approach, a set of "ideas and practices [that] emerge from the effort to mark and defend boundaries between categories of relations that contain some common elements, [that] could be confused, and would threaten existing relations of trust if confused."[301] A Hostile Worlds approach insists on, and thereby effectuates, a separation of domains; it holds that contamination, disorder, and disintegration will result when the two domains come into contact with each other: when we put a price on emotional or moral aspects of intimacy, or, conversely, when we corrupt economic transactions with intimacy. The other dominant framework is the Nothing-But approach: the reductionist argument that ostensibly separate domains, such as

---

matrix of ideas and beliefs which grows out of a society's experience and is colored by its history." Mitchell (1997), 179. Cf. Ober (1989), 38–40, Goldhill (1990), 97.

299 Mirowski (2001), 45–46. Carlà & Gori (2014), 10–11.

300 Zelizer (2005).

301 Zelizer (2005), 35–36.

economics and intimate relations, are not Hostile Worlds at all, but, in the final analysis, the same.[302]

Both the Hostile World thesis and the Nothing-But approach are ways of dealing with situations of isomorphism. We will find Nothing-But claims in comical, cynical or rude expressions of shocking reductionism: children are nothing but credit instruments.[303] We will also see that the response to such Nothing-But claims often takes the form of a Hostile World approach: the sophist is an anti-philosopher, the businessman a failed estate-manager.[304]

4.5 *Norms, Rules, and Sources*

Being a good friend and maintaining φιλία-bonds according to the social norms of reciprocity is, of course, lived practice. Being a competent participant in the economic life of the polis is so too. In Classical Athens, the capacity to observe the obligations of reciprocity in a socially acceptable way was believed to be indicative of one's social competences at large: it is shameful not to have friends.[305] As a proper dealing with one's φίλοι belongs to the core skills of social life, there are always normative stakes in talk about φιλία, however implicit those stakes may be. To see how this works, let us elaborate on a well-known analogy between talk about social rules and talk about language rules. The analogy works on several levels

First of all, social **competence**, like linguistic competence, is typically practical knowledge: know-how about things that everybody knows how to handle, but only few can express in a knowing-*that*.[306] Almost every native speaker of English is capable of forming intelligible sentences that meet with the criteria of the lexicon, of syntax, morphology, and pragmatics etc. and of understanding whether a sentence is formulated in a felicitous way. However, the number of people who are capable of formulating the rules of grammar in an articulate and coherent manner is considerably smaller. Practical knowledge, or know-*how*, is a kind of tacit knowledge that manifests itself in competent behavior (analogous to linguistic competence) and hence is distinct from theoretical knowledge that manifests itself in the form of propositions (analogous to grammatical knowledge).

302 Zelizer (2005), 29. In her own analysis, Zelizer rejects both these models, in favor of a Connected Lives perspective in which "relational work" takes place, i.e. the constant re-creation, reinforcement and renegotiation of boundaries between different kinds of ties.

303 Chapters Two, Three and Four.

304 Chapters Two, Three, Four, Five, Six, Seven.

305 Is. 1.24; Ar. *Rhet.* 1373a5.

306 On the notion of practical knowledge: Bourdieu (1977), 27, Gerrans (2005).

Secondly, just like the grammatical knowledge that we acquire at school is, in essence, prescriptive (it helps us to see whether we are formulating a sentence that is "correct"), generalizing statements about φιλία and reciprocity are always, in one way or another, **normative**. Even seemingly neutral or self-evident statements such as "your mother is your best φίλος" serve to create, enhance and perpetuate consensus over the norm that one should care for one's mother.

Thirdly, as one does not need to have theoretical knowledge to be a competent speaker of English, grammar rules usually only come in when somebody is perceived as having made a mistake: rules are only made explicit in contexts where competence is, for some reason, problematized. The same goes for social competence: most of the time, there is no need to talk about the norms we live by, as the very functioning of social norms is premised on their self-evident appeal: what goes without saying need not be said. Conversely, the fact that in the literature of 5th- and 4th-century Athens, the norm of reciprocity is so frequently propagated and repeated, reflects that the norms are not always felt to be self-evident.

Finally, grammar rules are a schoolteacher's tool to assess a pupil's competence, to control the norms of what counts as good English and to control the transmission of these norms. They are a vehicle for reproducing the standards of proper English, and they are the basis for the teacher's authority. Similarly, social norms are always *someone*'s norms. Aristotle's understanding of virtue as an activity to be shared in a selective circle of friends instead of a commodity for sale is an attempt to withdraw philosophy from the open market and to control its distribution by marginalizing the teachings by the sophists.

The core of the source material discussed in this book consists of the treatment of φιλία by Xenophon, Plato, and Aristotle. The justification for this choice lies in the fact that these intellectuals offer longer, sustained and explicit analyses of the social workings of exchange. The ancient discussions about the norms of reciprocity that are detected best by the modern eye are also the most explicit and sustained treatments of φιλία and of economic morality—and often also the most polarizing accounts. They have articulated ideas about friendship, market economy, commodification and value and both show persistent attempts to demarcate seemingly isomorphous exchanges from each other.

This obviously has a downside. As with many studies on *histoire des mentalités* of Classical Antiquity the views offered by the available literary sources have several biases. For one, they tend to represent views and debates that were prevalent in male-dominated and economically as well as culturally privileged circles.[307] These sources can be expected to favor particular understandings of φιλία-reciprocity as well as market transaction: they tend to be conservative in ideas about the proper allocation of economic, social and cultural resources because they have an interest in reproducing existing structures.

Xenophon, Plato, and Aristotle are like grammar teachers: by articulating the rules, they attempt to control rather than merely reflect the norms of what counts as socially desirable behavior and what not. They have been influential, not only as very problematic sources on the ancient Greek economy but also in articulating conceptions of money and the market. They have also been influential for Western philosophical conceptions of friendship. These two topics are not unrelated. These thinkers have been influential in conceptualizing the many ways in which people value the things they exchange and the people with whom they exchange.

4.6 *The Argument*

This book is about ancient social theory, about Classical Greek conceptualizations of relationships in response to the transformation of the Athenian economy. In studying conceptions of exchange relationships, it includes both implicit *folk theory* and explicit analytical discourse. In a series of case studies, it will trace a double-faced trend in ancient social theory, from which emerges a conception of φιλία-reciprocity as normatively subjective and a conception of market exchanges as notionally disembedded and "purely economic".

Ancient social theory, i.e. reflection on reciprocity, φιλία and exchange, occurs in different forms and scopes. Sometimes reflection is contained in isolated linguistic expressions: a maxim, a joke in comedy, an exclamation of despair in tragedy, a reproach in a speech. Sometimes reflection takes the form of a more sustained discussion, ranging from small (a vignette, a strophe from a poem, a short dialogue or a chapter in a philosophical treatise) to larger compositional units (a book, a work, an ethical system). We will deal with these different scales and scopes.

Chapter Two revolves around one **concept**: the concept of χάρις, the term that most markedly evoked ideals of reciprocity. Dealing properly with χάρις is a core social competence and, therefore, belongs to the realm of tacit knowledge. However, it will be argued that in our late-5th and 4th-century sources, there is a proliferation of explicitly formulated norms about the proper way of

307 On φιλία and women, see Foxhall (1998), 62–65.

understanding χάρις, expressive of both a Nothing-But worldview and a Hostile Worlds thesis. In other words: χάρις gets to be defined by comparison with isomorphous phenomena, such as disembedded exchanges. It is in these contexts of isomorphism that the grammar of χάρις-exchange is made explicit, in an analytical language that in itself has distorting effects because of the external perspective it assumes. Using Pierre Bourdieu's notion of *méconnaissance* as an analytical tool, I will argue that this external perspective is at odds with the workings of χάρις in a fully functional relation, where participants interpret χάρις from the inside and as an ongoing process. It is this internal perspective that lends access to the qualitative dimension of an exchange (dispositions, intentions, emotions and moral orientations) that comes to be a defining feature of χάρις in the new Age of Grace of 4th-century social theory.

Chapter Three focuses on one **relation**: the parent-child bond. In 5th- and 4th-century Athens, the idea that children owe their parents support was commonplace. Taking Marshall Sahlins' tripartite classification of reciprocity and its contestation by David Graeber as a point of departure, the chapter will inquire into the nature of this obligation. It will be argued that 5th- and 4th-century discourse about parents and children could have recourse to two conceptions of filial duty: the Gratitude Theory, according to which filial duty was understood as a reciprocal obligation, and the Debtor Paradigm that assimilated filial duty to the obligation to repay a debt. In its pure form, the Debtor Paradigm is rare in 5th- and 4th-century discourse. However, it will be argued that the Debtor Paradigm (a variant of the Nothing-But approach) provided the foil against which the Gratitude Theory could articulate a morally thicker account of obligation by integrating affects, emotions, and intentions.

Chapter Four elaborates on one **model** or **theory** for understanding obligation: the Debtor Paradigm of Obligation, a paradigm that assimilates obligations to outstanding debts. It will be argued that classical Greek thinking about moral obligations is informed by the phenomenon of monetary debt. Does this mean that debt is at the root of morality? It will be argued that the notion of debt itself is also under construction: to know what we *owe*, we must first understand how we *ought* to act. Moreover, ancient social theory was divided over the status of the Debtor Paradigm: does it provide an analogy (a moral obligation is *like* an outstanding debt) or is a reductionistic explanation of the Nothing-But kind (a moral obligation *fundamentally is* an outstanding debt)? Challenging both Pierre Bourdieu's and David Graeber's reductionism, I will argue that instead of wholesale assimilation of moral obligations to financial ones, 4th-century moral discourse actually witnesses a reverse tendency: to define gifts, benefactions and other social interactions in opposition to commercial disembedded exchanges. It is here that we see the birth of the twin theoretical fictions of the "pure gift" and the "pure commodity".

Chapter Five starts with an analysis of one **exchange object**: Socratic wisdom. The confrontation between Antiphon (who exchanges wisdom for money) and Socrates (who insists on the distinct value structure of wisdom) serves as a springboard for an analysis of the ways in which single exchanges are part of "total patterns", the totality of transactions that, in the terminology of Maurice Bloch and Jonathan Parry, belong to different spheres of exchange. The specific focus of the argument will be the role of philosophical discourse in marking off distinct transactional spheres. At stake is both the **demarcation** between the sphere of short-term acquisitive self-indulgent gratification and the long-term order of philosophy, friendship and virtue, *and* the proper **conversion** of the potentially sordid terminology of money and utility into ethical notions that sustain and legitimate the long-term order of the philosopher, the friend, and the estate-manager.

Chapter Six offers an interpretation of one **compositional unit**, the encounter of Socrates and the hetaera Theodote in Xenophon's *Memorabilia* II.xi, and the language games that are played in this short dialogue. Using Arlie Hochschild's notion of the Market Frontier, it will be argued that both Socrates and Theodote use the language of long-term reciprocity, of φιλία and χάρις, to position themselves at the right side of the frontier. Complementing the dialectics of the short-term and long-term of Chapter Five, Chapter Six elaborates on a different central opposition: the active/passive dichotomy. It will be argued that in order to position oneself on the right side of the Market Frontier, one has to exercise Active Partnership and take initiatives in benefiting the other. Active Partnership is both a precondition for and the substance of the philosophical ethics that Xenophon's Socrates has on offer. Moreover, it will be argued that the dialogue is as much about reciprocity and philosophy as it is about the power and proper use of language: the proper application of terms, the use of euphemisms, the power of metaphors and the value of dialogue itself.

Chapter Seven is an attempt to make sense of the **system of economic thought** and the **theory of value** behind Aristotle's *Nicomachean Ethics*. It will take Aristotle's famous shoemaker/builder-ratio in *NE* V.v as point of departure: the proposition that has been both hailed as a starting point of Western economic reflection and dismissed as trivial or metaphysically defective. It will be argued that the shoemaker/builder-ratio does *not* represent a disembedded exchange, nor does the proposition express a mechanism for price-formation. I will argue that Aristotelian "economics" too is best understood in relational terms. Rather than articulating a notion of economic value, the chapter on reciprocal justice invested in analyzing a specific type of interpersonal relationship: not the disembedded exchange relation, but the elusive category of "political friendship". The exchange of shoemaker and builder is therefore deeply embedded in the long-term order of the polis.

4.7 *A Note on Theory, Method and Discipline*

This is a foxy book. That is to say: this book self-identifies more as a fox who, asked what kind of hedgehog he aspires to be, has a hard time coming up with a compelling answer. It does not align itself easily within a particular subdisciplinary field of scholarship and its concomitant methodology. Which game are we playing: the philologist's, the historian's, philosopher's or the anthropologist's? What language is this book speaking? "All languages and none"?[308]

The answer is twofold. First: this book is about Classical Greek conceptualizations of relationships and the conceptual tools that shape these implicit and explicit ideas about the diverse forms of relationality. In other words, it purports to write a chapter in the history of mentalities in that its interest is not confined to individual attitudes or ideas, but also in articulating the historical and cultural conditions of their existence and the collective attitudes that are presupposed by the individual: not only in explicit theories and conscious thoughts, but also in the implicit assumptions and the logic of practice; not only in the substance or content of beliefs, but also in their structures.[309]

The primary access to this kind of conceptual architecture is predominantly linguistic in nature.[310] There is no way of doing History of Mentalities for ancient Greece properly without doing the philological handwork, without linguistics and semantic analysis, without discourse analysis or narratology, with-

308 Quotation from the transcript of Andrew Birkin's 1986 screenplay *The Name of the Rose*, based on Umberto Eco's novel. The proverbial fox and hedgehog find their origin in a fragment of Archilochus: πόλλ' οἶδ' ἀλώπηξ ἀλλ' ἐχῖνος ἓν μέγα (Fr. 103 Diehl) but were made famous as symbols for "types of thinkers" by Isaiah Berlin's 1967 essay on Tolstoy: the hedgehog is tenacious and centripetal in sticking to one style, idea or theory; the fox is agile and centrifugal, "moving on many levels" (1) and leaving things open-ended. The tragedy of Tolstoy was that he "was by nature a fox, but believed in being a hedgehog". The types were revived by Stephen Jay Gould (2003) as representing "humanistic" (the fox) and "scientific" (the hedgehog) thinking.

309 I here follow Burke (1986) demarcation and definition of History of Mentalities.

310 Even in sources that are more material and visual in nature, one could argue that the assumptions and values that they embody are *mediated by* a linguistic organization of concepts and a linguistic articulation of values.

out asking ourselves questions such as: how does the language of give and take work? How are statements about φιλία positioned within the structure and drift of the broader discourse they are part of? How can we best describe the mechanisms of perspective and temporal orientation that play such a crucial role in the use of χάρις-terminology?

At the same time, this book makes a historical and cultural claim in that it positions these conceptualizations in a definite historical period and cultural context: it makes the claim that certain ideologies of friendship can only be understood against the backdrop of an economy that is increasingly understood as a disembedded phenomenon. And, as flagged above, the argument revolves in an important sense around authors who attempt to systematize folk theory and practical knowledge into explicit coherent bodies of thought: philosophers such as Xenophon, Plato and Aristotle are analyzed in detail, but the aspiration has been to do so within the context of the system of meaning of folk theory, the knowing-how and the taking-for-granted that repeat and reproduce themselves in everyday thought. And, finally, the analyses offered in this book are informed by the conceptual tools furnished by economic anthropology and sociology: in order to describe and articulate attitudes and folk theory (our EMIC objects of analysis), we need to use descriptive meta-language and models (our ETIC categories and concepts), while, at the same time, remaining aware of the reflexive insight that all theory, every tool, every ETIC notion is in the end itself an object for inquiry in its own right. History of Mentalities is a total game.

But there is more to History of Mentalities than a form of judicious eclecticism. The second point I wish to submit is that this book aspires to make a case for consilience. Or, more precisely, for questioning the degree of commensurability between the conceptual apparatus of different disciplines and subdisciplines. As such, the argument is not built on the application of a single method originating from a single theory, but on using the full array of disciplines that have been devised to study human behavior and attitudes. But, more fundamentally, the argument not only *uses* theories from different disciplines, it also aims to reflect on theory: not merely *using* modern theories to understand and describe ancient conceptualizations but *confronting* modern theories with ancient (folk) theories, modern concepts and categorizations with ancient ones. Analytical distinctions, such as that between objective duties and subjective obligations, or between instrumental relations and elective affinities, are not so much objective tools for descriptive purposes, but rather themselves objects of inquiry.

If therefore this book may appear to speak in too many languages, this is because the story it tries to tell is in part about languages: about the concepts, categories, analogies and oppositions, changes and continuities, unspoken assumptions and crafted theories that enter into the stuff that human attitudes and behaviors are made of. I hope it proves a story worth telling.

CHAPTER 2

Grace under Pressure: The Anatomy of χάρις

Aziz: "If you are right, there is no point in any friendship; it all comes down to give and take, or give and return, which is disgusting."

E.M. FORSTER (1924), 254

•••

Ein Ding als schön empfinden heisst: es nothwendig falsch empfinden.

FRIEDRICH NIETZSCHE (1967–1977), 555

∴

In 5th- and 4th-century Greece, the term that most markedly evokes ideals of reciprocity was probably χάρις: grace, charm, favor and generosity all in one. χάρις is typically associated with the sphere of the long term: it circulates in long-term relations and sustains a long-term order, be it social, political or metaphysical, and that is predominantly positively connoted. χάρις "always invokes the ideals of reciprocity".[1]

The term χάρις operates in all realms of human life. It is inextricably bound up with φιλία,[2] i.e. with all types of long-term reciprocal relations, ranging from the parent-child relationship[3] to political alliances.[4] In religious communication, χάρις characterized the relationship between humans and deities and their exchanges in prayer and sacrifice as a reciprocal endeavor.[5] In an erotic context, χάρις characterized the relationship between lover (ἐραστής) and beloved (ἐρώμενος) as a legitimate and morally unproblematic long-term

1 Goldhill (1998), 115.

2 Blundell (1989), 33.

3 See below in Section 3.1; Cf. Chapter Three.

4 See Section 4.2 below.

5 On the use of χάρις-terminology in dedications, prayers and votive offerings, see Day (2010), 232–280 (esp. 232–245), Bremer (1998), Versnel (1981), 42–62, Van Straten (1981), 65–67, Festugière (1976).

 | DOI:10.1163/9789004416147_003

relationship in which gifts and favors of all sorts are exchanged.[6] Similarly, in political contexts, the χάρις between community and benefactor may be seen as legitimizing differences in wealth and their political repercussions in the context of the Athenian democracy,[7] whereas in a non-egalitarian context political χάρις serves to create, amplify and legitimize asymmetries and imbalances in power.[8]

In all these contexts, the effect of using χάρις-vocabulary is to imply long-term repercussions in long-term relationships and in the long-term order of society or the cosmos at large.[9] In the Greek world of the Archaic and Classical period, the term χάρις, even when referring to the reciprocity between two individuals, always contains potential references to a larger order, representing exchanges as anything but isolated events.

A well-known and suggestive testimony for the civic importance of χάρις is a remark in Aristotle's *Nicomachean Ethics*:

[Text 1]

> ἀλλ' ἐν μὲν ταῖς κοινωνίαις ταῖς ἀλλακτικαῖς συνέχει τὸ τοιοῦτον δίκαιον, τὸ **ἀντιπεπονθὸς κατ' ἀναλογίαν** καὶ μὴ κατ' ἰσότητα. τῷ ἀντιποιεῖν γὰρ ἀνάλογον **συμμένει ἡ πόλις**. ἢ γὰρ τὸ κακῶς ζητοῦσιν· εἰ|$_{1133a}$ δὲ μή, δουλεία δοκεῖ εἶναι [εἰ μὴ ἀντιποιήσει]· ἢ τὸ εὖ· εἰ δὲ μή, μετάδοσις οὐ γίνεται, **τῇ μεταδόσει δὲ συμμένουσιν. διὸ καὶ Χαρίτων ἱερὸν ἐμποδὼν ποιοῦνται, ἵν' ἀνταπόδοσις ᾖ· τοῦτο γὰρ ἴδιον χάριτος; ἀνθυπηρετῆσαι γὰρ δεῖ τῷ χαρισαμένῳ, καὶ πάλιν αὐτὸν ἄρξαι χαριζόμενον.**
>
> In communities based on exchange, however, what binds the parties together is what is just in this way, namely, *reciprocity that is proportionate* and not equal. For it is proportionate reciprocity that *keeps a city together*. For people either seek to return evil for evil (and if they do not, it seems like slavery) or good for good (and if they do not, no giving in exchange takes place), *and it is by giving in exchange that they keep together. That is why cities erect the temple of the Graces in a conspicuous place, in order that there might be a return for what is given. For this is the special characteris-*

6 Davidson (2007), 38–67. See Chapter Six. This representation of the pederastic relationship is by no means uncontested in Classical Athens.

7 Ober (1989), 192–247. On χάρις-terminology and other vocabulary expressive of ideals of reciprocity, see Veligianni (1997) and (1989).

8 On political χάρις, see Chapter Two Section 4.1, 6.1–3, Chapter Three Section 5.

9 E.g. Levine (1985), 190–193 for the importance of χάρις for the polis in Theognis' poetry.

> *tic of gratitude, since we should not only do a service in return for someone who has done us a favor but, on another occasion, start by doing a favor too.*[10]

With an analysis of almost anthropological quality, Aristotle explains the civic function of the prevalence of sanctuaries dedicated to the Grace, the Χάριτες: they serve as a reminder that one ought to return a good turn, thereby securing reciprocation (ἀνταπόδοσις). The defining characteristic (the ἴδιον) of χάρις is that it consists in a double obligation: the obligation to "serve" (ἀνθυπηρετῆσαι) one who has done us a favor (χαρισάμενος) in return and the obligation to take initiatives to extend someone a favor oneself (αὐτὸν ἄρξαι χαριζόμενον).

Aristotle credits χάρις with a cohesive force that has civic implications: it not only keeps people together in bilateral bonds, but, the collectivity of ties of reciprocity "keeps cities together" (συμμένει ἡ πόλις; συμμένουσιν).[11] Cults for the Graces are known from several Greek cities: the oldest known to us are the worship of the Χάριτες as a triad of stones in Orchomenos,[12] the Archaic cult of the Charites on Paros and Thasos,[13] and Kos.[14] In Athens, the Graces had a cult near the Propylaea as well as one near the northwest corner of the Agora.[15] The importance that Aristotle attributes to χάρις must therefore be more than imaginary.

The context of Aristotle's remark is intriguing: it comes right before the famous builder/shoemaker-ratio. With this ratio ("as builder to shoemaker, shoes to a house"), Aristotle lays out the distinct kind of justice that he calls "reciprocal" (τὸ ἀντιπεπονθός) and that describes the exchange that takes place

---

10 Ar. *NE* v.v (1132b31–1133a5); *transl.* Reeve (2014).

11 See Chapter Seven for this Aristotelian conception of civic friendship.

12 Larson (2007), 162; Rocchi (1979), 10–15. Cf. Strabo 9.2.40, who associates the cult of the Charites with the wealth and prosperity of the city.

13 Schwarzenberg (1966), 4–7, Berranger (1992), 195–198, Larson (2001), 170.

14 Pirenne-Delforge (1996).

15 Rozenzweig (2004), 65; *IG* II^2 2798, *Agora* XIV, 160; Harrison (1986). The sanctuary near the Agora probably dates from the second half of the fourth century, but the cult underwent reorganization in the third century and became closely linked to the cult of Demos and, possibly, Aphrodite Pandemos, a newly formed personified deity, as part of a measure to promote and foster cohesion within the community. Wycherley (1957), 59–61 [The Athenian Agora III]; Schwarzenberg (1966), 14–22, 33–42; Mikalson (1998), 172–178. As for the other Athenian cult of the Graces, the one at the Propylaea, ancient reports are even more tantalizing: the relief, depicting the Graces and Hermes, was allegedly produced by Socrates (see Chapter Six Section 5).

between a shoemaker and a builder who are bound together by nothing more than the need that they have for the other's product. Aristotle's analysis is often taken as a rudimentary theory of value, or celebrated as the advent of the "economic" relationship as a distinct concept: the relationship between shoemaker and builder, disembedded from any pre-existing social, political or religious relationship.[16]

This raises a question: *is* there χάρις in the exchange of houses and shoes between shoemaker and builder? The claim made in this chapter is dual: that in the late 5th and 4th century BCE this is a difficult question; and that it is precisely this question that provokes a particular understanding of χάρις, born out of a Hostile Worlds approach.

The Argument

The assumption of this chapter is that proper dealings with χάρις belongs to the core skills of living together with other humans. It is a competence that every Greek is supposed to possess, and it constitutes the very difference between a well-socialized person and a social misfit. Such competencies are typically practical knowledge, i.e. tacit knowledge: everybody knows how to do it, but only a few persons can (or take the trouble to) express this tacit knowledge in a piece of theoretical knowledge, a knowing *that*, in a propositional form.[17] Most of the time there is no need to talk about the norms that we live by, as the very functioning of social norms is premised on their self-evident appeal: what goes without saying need not be said.

So what happens when things *are* said and when the notionally self-evident is made explicit? It will be argued that in our late 5th and 4thcentury sources, we see a perceived need to formulate explicit norms about the proper way of understanding χάρις. We find normative statements about what proper χάρις should be like. We also find contestations of χάρις, claiming that χάρις is merely politeness, a euphemism, hypocrisy, a five-letter word. The norms of χάρις are felt to be less self-evident. As we shall see in this chapter, part of the reason lies in the fact that in all domains χάρις-exchanges have become potentially isomorphous with commercial transactions, i.e. the potentially one-off transactions of equivalent goods that (perhaps ideally) do not necessarily yield a lasting relationship between the people involved.

16 Chapter Seven.

17 On the notion of practical knowledge: Gerrans (2005); Bourdieu (1977), 27.

In Section 1, we shall take a look at three examples of such isomorphism. In all three cases, there are contextual indications that although it is possible to say that isomorphous exchanges are effectively identical, it is not socially acceptable to actually *say* so. To bring such a ban on reductionism into relief we will look at the ways in which the social functioning of χάρις and the use of χάρις-vocabulary involve matters of point of view (focalization) and temporal perspective (Section 2). These perspective requirements of χάρις are at odds with an analytical point of view that understands exchanges as closed events, debts as redeemable, and values as disconnected from the relationships in which they figure.[18] Hence, seeing a situation *as* a χάρις-encounter means also choosing *not* to see other aspects of a situation: to "unsee" an inconvenient truth (Section 3 and 4). This inconvenient truth may come in many forms. It may be an asymmetry in power when one prefers to see equality; or, in the case of 5th- and 4th-century literary texts, it may manifests itself as isomorphism with disembedded exchanges, with the mutuality of the market, the banker's table and the trading port, when one prefers to see graceful and grateful exchange.

1 Three Cases of Isomorphism

Consider the following three cases of isomorphism: the first will deal with the similarity between pederastic encounters and prostitution in erotic exchange, the second of that between religious communication and commerce in religious exchange, and the third of that between friendly aid and credit. In all three cases, a character proclaims the truth about the Emperor's new clothes: that χάρις is an illusion. Whereas every onlooker is aware of this "truth" (as every onlooker knew that the king was naked), it is clear that it is not socially acceptable to say that all these χάρις exchanges are basically the same as market transactions.

1.1 *Case 1: χάρις in Erotics, the Verbal Icing on the Cake of Vice?*

When Chremylus in Aristophanes' *Wealth* is arguing that anything splendid, noble and graceful (τι χαρίεν) happens because of Plutus, the personification

18 The primary and immediate purpose of discrete transactions is to obtain the counterpart value; in contrast, "partial transactions" take place in the context of a larger long-term chain of favors and obligations and contain reference to the relationship between the exchange partners. The terminology of "discrete" and "partial" transactions is taken from Kopytoff (1986), 69.

of wealth, one case in point are the Corinthian courtesans who only show attention to wealthy suitors. According to the slave Carion, something analogous goes for boys, who do "the same thing" (i.e. submit to anal penetration):[19]

[Text 2]

> Κα. καὶ τούς γε παῖδάς φασι ταὐτὸ τοῦτο δρᾶν,
> οὐ τῶν ἐραστῶν, ἀλλὰ τἀργυρίου χάριν.
>
> Carion: And people say that when the young lads do the same thing, *it's not for the sake of their lovers but for the sake of money.*[20]

There is a pun here that revolves around the term χάρις. In one sentence, Carion uses the term χάρις both as a noun (used predicatively "as a grace for", "as a favor") and as a preposition ("for the sake of")—a pun that effectively contrasts the long-term ideals of pederastic encounters and the boys' (real) commercial motivation underlying these ideals.[21] Chremylus objects to this generalization by insisting that "decent boys" do not ask for money as prostitutes do, but for expensive posh gifts instead:[22]

[Text 3]

> 155 Χρ. οὐ τούς γε χρηστούς, ἀλλὰ τοὺς πόρνους· ἐπεὶ
> αἰτοῦσιν οὐκ ἀργύριον οἱ χρηστοί.
> Κα. τί δαί;
> 157 Χρ. ὁ μὲν ἵππον ἀγαθόν, ὁ δὲ κύνας θηρευτικούς.
> Κα. αἰσχυνόμενοι γὰρ ἀργύριον αἰτεῖν ἴσως
> ὀνόματι περιπέττουσι τὴν μοχθηρίαν.
>
> Chremylus: The young *gentlemen* don't do that, it's only the young *professionals*. Decent lads don't ask for *money*. Carion: Oh, what *do* they ask for? Chremylus: One wants a topclass horse, another wants some hunting

---

19 Sommerstein (2001), ad loc.

20 Aristoph. *Plut.* 153–154; *transl.* Sommerstein (2001).

21 Cf. MacLachlan (1993), 161–164 for an argument for semantic continuity between the nominal and prepositional use of χάριν in Archaic and earlyClassical poetry.

22 For the distinction drawn between prostitution and honorable sexual encounters, see Chapter Six.

> dogs ... Carion: *I suppose they're ashamed to ask for money, so they cover up their immorality by a verbal trick.*[23]

To Carion the difference between prostitutes and decent boys comes down to a lexical difference: decent boys simply "put a verbal crust" (ὀνόματι περιπέττουσι) around their immorality (μοχθηρία). The expensive gifts given to decent boys amount to the same as the fees paid to prostitutes and talk about "gifts" is merely giving a different name to the shame of prostitution.[24] Here, in a passage where Chremylus and Carion are reducing all human conduct to behavior motivated by wealth and money, erotic χάρις is reduced to commercial sex with a touch of moral icing.

1.2 *Case 2: χάρις in Religious Communication, a Mere Name for Commerce?*

When Socrates and Euthyphro are examining the nature of the pious (τὸ ὅσιον), Euthyphro comes up with what will turn out to be a last attempt:[25]

[Text 4]

> τόδε μέντοι σοι ἁπλῶς λέγω, ὅτι ἐὰν μὲν κεχαρισμένα τις ἐπίστηται τοῖς θεοῖς λέγειν τε καὶ πράττειν εὐχόμενός τε καὶ θύων, ταῦτ' ἔστι τὰ ὅσια (...).
>
> I'll simply tell you this: If anyone knows how to say and do *what brings χάρις* to the gods through praying and sacrificing, these are the pious things (...).[26]

According to Euthyphro, being pious is simply (ἁπλῶς) knowing how to say and do gratifying things (κεχαρισμένα λέγειν τε καὶ πράττειν) in praying and sacrific-

---

23 Aristoph. *Plut.* 155–159; *transl.* Sommerstein.

24 Although animal gifts are common in depictions of pederastic scenes on vasepaintings, the topclass horses and hunting dogs mentioned here are extremely expensive presents that represent an extreme (and perhaps purely hypothetical) example to imply that extremely decent boys are actually extremely expensive boys. A modern parallel can be found in a comment by hiphopartist 50 Cent on Lindsey Lohan's million-dollar Playboy shoot: "$1 million to pose nude is the same thing strippers do almost every day for way less. If they give you a million dollars, does that change the status of what you've done?" (*Hollyscoop*, December 12, 2011).

25 For the Socratic emphasis on cognition (ἐὰν τις ἐπίστηται ..., "if someone knows ..."), see also Chapter Five Section 2.

26 Pl. *Euth.* 14b2–4.

ing (εὐχόμενός τε καὶ θύων)—i.e. saying and doing things that have and bring χάρις.[27] Socrates paraphrases this working hypothesis of τὸ ὅσιον as "the science of sacrificing and praying,"[28] and rephrases "sacrificing" as giving gifts (δωρεῖσθαι) to gods, and "praying" as making requests (αἰτεῖν) to the gods.[29] Hence, piety turns out to be the science of giving and asking, i.e. asking for what one needs from the gods and giving what the gods need from us.[30] Socrates paraphrases once again:

[Text 5]

> ΣΩ. Ἐμπορικὴ ἄρα τις ἂν εἴη, ὦ Εὐθύφρων, τέχνη ἡ ὁσιότης θεοῖς καὶ ἀνθρώποις παρ' ἀλλήλων.
> ΕΥΘ. Ἐμπορική, εἰ οὕτως ἥδιόν σοι ὀνομάζειν.
> ΣΩ. Ἀλλ' οὐδὲν ἥδιον ἔμοιγε, εἰ μὴ τυγχάνει ἀληθὲς ὄν.
>
> Socrates: So, the craft of piety is a kind of *commercial* skill that men and gods engage in with each other. Euthyphro: A commercial business, if you *prefer calling it that*. Socrates: I don't prefer calling it that unless it is *true*.[31]

The preceding discussion allows for the inference (ἄρα) that piety should be an art of commerce, of traffic, (τις ἐμπορικὴ τέχνη). Euthyphro assents to this reformulation, but only grudgingly so ("Well, fine Socrates, if that is what you prefer to call it"): he acknowledges that it *is* a way to "name" (ὀνομάζειν) the art of piety, but not a pleasant one.[32]

The implications are even more unsettling, as in the exchange that follows Socrates wonders what advantage this traffic possibly yields for the gods. The traffic definition will turn out to be untenable for the absurd implications it yields:[33] not only the paradoxical contention that the gods should need anything at all but also the relapse to an earlier (dismissed) definition of τὸ ὅσιον.[34]

---

27 That the nominalized participle perfect κεχαρισμένα evokes the concept of χάρις seems to be corroborated by 15a9–b2 where the κεχαρισμένα are rephrased as "ὅπερ ἐγὼ ἄρτι ἔλεγον, χάρις". κεχαρισμένα is a regular religious term. Day (2010). E.g. Hom. *Il.* 20.298 (κεχαρισμένα δῶρα θεοῖσι δίδωσι); An. fr. 2,7 (κεχαρισμένης εὐχωλῆς ἐπακούειν).

28 Pl. *Euth.* 14c5–6.

29 Pl. *Euth.* 14c7–9.

30 Pl. *Euth.* 14d8–e5.

31 Pl. *Euth.* 14e6–10.

32 Biernat (2018), 335 n. 30. See also his n. 31 for the theological implications of the adjective ἐμπορικός ("related to traffic", in the sense of foreign trade).

33 Pl. *Euth.* 14e9–15c9.

34 I.e. the definition of τὸ ὅσιον as τὸ τοῖς θεοῖς φίλον (Pl. *Euth.* 7a ff.).

Here, Socrates is capable of reducing piety to commodity trading with gods with χάρις as a middle term: the implication of conceptualizing sacrifice and prayer in terms of gift-giving and making requests is that piety is exchange, and "hence" (ἄρα) traffic and trade. Equally revealing is the way Euthyphro, starting out from conventional premises,[35] is forced to assent to an inference that he resents.[36] What Euthyphro objects to is not so much Socrates' analysis of sacrifice in terms of exchange (to which he subscribes), but to his verbalization. Whereas Socrates is only interested in finding the *true* (ἀληθές) name of piety, naming (ὀνομάζειν) sacrifice "the art of commerce" (ἐμπορικὴ τέχνη) goes against the grain with Euthyphro—as if the name omits something essential, as if the name itself makes the encounter less ἥδιον.[37]

1.3 *Case 3: χάρις in Lending and Borrowing, an "as If"?*

Theophrastus' Compulsive Grumbler (μεμψίμοιρος) is a man who only sees the downside of things and is hence the quintessentially ungrateful man.[38] He reproaches a friend who sends him a present from his table for begrudging him soup and wine (i.e. he reproaches the friend for not inviting him to dinner). He is annoyed with Zeus, not for not raining, but for raining too late. He grumbles at finding a purse on the street for he has never found a treasure. The

35 On this passage, see also Biernat (2018), Mikalson (2010), 14–15, Yunis (1988), 101–, Parker (1998), 118–121. On the function of χάρις-terminology in religious exchange (from a popular morality point of view), see Van Straten (1981), 65–151, Versnel (1981), 1–64, Bremer (1998), 127–138. On the underlying conception of reciprocity in religious prayer and dedication, see Festugière (1976), on the formula "ἀνθ' ὧν", esp. 369 and 413–418, Pulleyn (1997), esp. 16–38 and 39–55. See MacPherran (2002) for an account of Socrates' reformation of popular religion: in rejecting "the age-old model of prayer as barter", Plato's Socrates reinforces the virtue-guiding capacity of religion. Euthyphro's objection against the monetary frame presumably lies in the fact that once long-term relationships with deity are formulated in terms of one-off trades, the long-term asymmetry between god and men disappears from the picture, as if debts to gods are redeemable and relationships of dependence can be dissolved. The underlying notion is not that no human χάρις can be a sufficient return for the good done by the gods (e.g. Xen., *Mem.* IV.iii.15). On the obscuring capacities of χάρις-vocabulary in relationships where permanent asymmetries are covered with the cloak of charity, see Chapter Six.

36 According to Mikalson (2010), 39, neither of the conversation partners subscribes to this view.

37 This seems to be a pun on the affective property of χάρις ("pleasing"). See next section.

38 μεμψιμοιρία is defined as "unsuitable criticism (ἐπιτίμησις παρὰ τὸ προσῆκον) of what you have been given (τῶν δεδομένων)" (Theophr. *Char.* 17.1). There is consensus that the introductory definitions of the *Characters* are later interpolations (added before the time of Philodemus) and must be deleted. Stein (1992).

Grumbler cannot even rejoice at the birth of his son for to him it represents a massive financial setback:

[Text 6]

> καὶ πρὸς τὸν εὐαγγελιζόμενον, ὅτι Υἱός σοι γέγονεν, εἰπεῖν, ὅτι Ἂν προσθῇς· καὶ τῆς οὐσίας τὸ ἥμισυ ἄπεστιν, ἀληθῆ ἐρεῖς.
>
> To the person who brings him the good news 'You have a son' he says 'If you add 'And you have lost half your fortune' you will *not* be *far wrong*.'[39]

The Grumbler is incapable of seeing the birth of a son simply as good news, for he immediately sees the downside: gaining a son is losing half of your property. That is the *whole* truth.

Similarly, the Grumbler cannot react cheerfully (ἱλαρός) to a kindness from his friends:

[Text 7]

> καὶ ἐράνου εἰσενεχθέντος παρὰ τῶν φίλων καὶ φήσαντός τινος· Ἱλαρὸς ἴσθι, Καὶ πῶς; εἰπεῖν, Ὅτε δεῖ τἀργύριον ἀποδοῦναι ἑκάστῳ καὶ χωρὶς τούτων χάριν ὀφείλειν ὡς εὐεργετημένον;
>
> When *his friends* have got together *an ἔρανος loan* and someone says 'Cheer up', he answers 'How do you mean? When I have to *refund* everyone and on top of that *owe χάρις as if* I am done a favor?'[40]

The joke revolves around the phenomenon of *eranos* loans. In his standard work on credit relations in classical Athens, Paul Millett offers a reconstruction of the *eranos* type of credit and the distinct ethos that comes with it.[41] An *eranos* is a "friendly credit group", where friends informally pool credit to help an acquaintance in need. Typically, such contributions are interest-free, rarely contractual, and hence based on personal trust and solidarity. *Eranos*

39 Theophr. *Char.* 17.7; *transl.* Diggle (2004).

40 Theophr. *Char.* 17.9. Steinmetz (1962) II, 211 for an argument for retaining ὅτι (the MSS. reading) instead of Casaubons emendation ὅτε (adopted by Diggle 2004).

41 Millett (1991), 153–159; (2007), 96–98. The word *eranos* could refer to either an individual contribution or the contributors collectively. But see Cohen (1992), 207–215 for the view that *eranos* loans did bear interest.

loans are understood as being distinct from commercial loans, sometimes even in marked contrast.[42] An *eranos* loan is a collective *favor* that is deliberately informal, and that is commonly seen as strengthening the social ties within a community.

To the Grumbler, the contrast with commercial credit is irrelevant as it comes down to the same thing in the end. Hence, the Grumbler fails to rejoice over a χάρις as he fails to recognize a favor as a favor. The only thing he sees is the downside: the obligation to give back the money (ἀργύριον ἀποδοῦναι) to his creditors while owing gratitude (χάριν ὀφείλειν) on top of it, *as if* (ὡς) his creditors have done him a favor.[43] The "as if" (ὡς) qualifies the rationale behind owing someone gratitude (χάρις) as based on a disputable interpretation of events: the Grumbler disagrees that his friends have shown him a kindness, for he will have to pay them back anyway.

1.4 *The Ban on Reductionism*

The three cases of isomorphism above are revealing for several reasons. First of all, they are examples of a **reductionist** response to an isomorphism of χάρις-exchanges and commercial exchanges. They indicate that it is a culturally available option to think of χάρις in erotic encounters as *nothing but* commercial sex (decent boys are just expensive prostitutes), to conceive of religious communication as commerce with the gods, and to regard friendly favors as financial credit. Reductionism involves the claim that one point of view is more fundamentally valid than the other: according to Carion, "gift" is a name that veils an underlying and more valid commercial reality; to Socrates, "the art of commerce" may be a more truthful name for what Euthyphro prefers to name piety; the Grumbler dismisses talk of benefaction as being "as if" talk—a social illusion.[44]

At the same time, they indicate that such reductionism is "not done": it is socially unacceptable. Carion's identification of *erômenoi* with prostitutes is part of a larger reductionist and absurd argument that all human behavior is motivated by money. Euthyphro does consent to Socrates' identification of religious piety with the art of commerce but thinks this somewhat inappropriate. Theophrastus' audience will probably have grasped that the Grumbler does have a point in equating a friendly favor with a bank transaction but will still have dismissed his cynicism as anti-social behavior. Carion, Socrates and

42 Cf. Chapter Two Section 4 and Chapter Three Sections 2 and 3.

43 Cf. Bähre (2007) for the notion of "reluctant solidarity" in neighborly assistance in South Africa.

44 On reductionism see Chapter Four Section 3.

the Grumbler are comical because they say the things that everybody is capable of *thinking*, but that are just not considered as socially acceptable things to *say*.

Improper behavior, as a transgression of "the limits of the thinkable and unthinkable",[45] is informative for popular morality because it marks the boundary between what individuals may "really" think and feel and what may be openly negotiated and commonly thought and "felt".[46] In the Euthyphro case, as has been noted by several commentators,[47] Socrates' analysis of τὸ ὅσιον in terms of commerce amounts to omitting all χάρις-terminology.[48] In the analysis of Carion and the Grumbler too, their interpretation of events eventually removes χάρις from the exchange. As we shall see in the next section, ideally, χάρις-terminology involves a particular point of view and temporal perspective that is at odds with the detached objectifying vision of human behavior maintained by Carion, Socrates and the Grumbler.

2 χάρις and Successful Interaction

The lexeme χάρις is notorious for its semantic complexity. Partly this is because the XAP- word field, comprising verbs such as χαίρειν, χαρίζεσθαι as well as the adjective χαρίεις, seems to bring together domains that we tend to think of as separate: aesthetic appreciation as well as ethical valuation. Beautiful objects and persons are χαρίεις, full of charm, in the sense that they are attractive, but also in that they intend to evoke ethically valued responses: χαρίεις behavior or a χαρίεις gift calls for a response full of χάρις.

Adding to the complex structure of the lexeme is the fact that the noun χάρις challenges the very descriptive **categories** that we use as lexicographical tools when we distinguish between "objective" and "subjective", "active and passive", "concrete" and "internalized":[49]

45 Bourdieu (1990 [1980]), 108.

46 Once implicit individual knowledge is made public and explicit, it has implications for the actions of the conversation partners and their relation.

47 Yunis (1988), 101–102; Day (2010), 240 n. 29.

48 Socrates systematically substitutes Euthyphro's formulation with terminology of advantage (ὠφέλιμον) and need (δέομαι). Mikalson (2010), 39: "The explicit description of 'service to the gods' as a commercial craft is also unique to the *Euthyphro*."

49 E.g. the categories used in LSJ or by Gianotti (1975: 75–76). The prepositional use of accusative χάριν (+ gen.), "for the sake of", is here excluded from analysis. But see n. 16 above.

- **Objective vs. subjective:**[50] χάρις may simultaneously refer to a quality of a beautiful **object** (a person[51] or thing)[52] and to the effect of beauty on the perceiving **subject**[53] who experiences pleasure or delight (χαίρειν);[54]
- **Active vs. passive:**[55] χάρις and χαρίζεσθαι may refer to intentions and dispositions of an **active participant** in an exchange, i.e. the kindness or goodwill of a giver,[56] but may also refer to experiences and dispositions of the **passive participant**, i.e. the gratitude of the recipient (mostly in collocation with the verbs ἔχειν[57] or εἰδέναι).[58]
- **Concrete vs. immaterial**: χάρις sometimes refers to **internalized** intentions, experiences, dispositions and responses in encounters (kindness, delight, goodwill, gratitude), but sometimes also has a **concrete** referent, when it materially denotes a favor done or returned, a gift given, received or returned (frequently in collocation with the verbs φέρειν, τίθεσθαι, διδόναι, and ἀπο- or ἀντι-compounds or ἀμείβεσθαι).[59]

Attempts to reduce these uses to one core meaning differ predominantly over the question of what has semantic priority: χάρις as a **property/quality** ("beauty", "pleasing property") or χάρις as an **effect** ("attraction", "delight"). Primacy of quality is advocated by Otto Löw in his 1908 monograph on χάρις and

50 Categories used in LSJ ad loc. as I and II.

51 E.g. *Od.* 2.12; Hes. *O&D* 65; Aeschyl. *Ag.* 417.

52 E.g. *Il.* 14.183, *Od.* 8.175, 15.320; Hes. *O&D* 720.

53 E.g. E.g. *Od.* 6.232 f., *Il.* 14.183; Hes. *O&D* 73–74, *Theog.* 247; Thgn. 1320; Solon B.13.40; Sappho 368 L&P; Pind.*Ol.*6.76, *Pyth.* 1.33–34, 8.85–86, *Isthm.* 6.50.

54 These uses of χάρις in the aesthetic realm seem to be largely confined to poetic texts, they seem to be a case of metonymia between the adjective χαρίεις ("having χάρις") and the noun χάρις. One of the possible exceptions is the "delight of words" (ἡ τῶν λόγων χάρις) in Dem. 4.38 (and the very similar *Ex.* 1.3.9) contrasted with the truths that are not pleasing to hear (οὐχ ἡδέα ἀκούειν); the χάρις of words is imagined to cause an immediate effect on the perceiving subject who experiences "pleasure". For the overlap between the semantic field of ἡδύς/ἡδονή and χάρις, cf. Eur. *Supp.* 413–414, Isoc. 12.271, Pl. *Leg.* 667b, *Soph.* 222e, *Gorg.* 426c–d; on the near-synonymy between middle voice ἥδομαι and active χαίρω, see Allan (2003), 203.

55 Categories used in LSJ ad loc. as II.1. and II.2. Hewitt (1927), 149: "In many phrases, χάριν as the object of a verb is ambiguous, for it may denote either favor or gratitude." Konstan (2006) attempts to distinguish two senses of χάρις: the emotion of gratitude vs. the favor. See Section 3.2 below.

56 E.g. *Il.* 5.873–874, 9.612–613, 21.458, *Od.* 5.307; Hes. *O&D* 190; Soph. *Aj.* 808; Lys. 14.40.

57 First occurrence probably in Theognis, e.g. Thgn. 1319, 1.957.

58 E.g. *Il.* 14.235; Hdt. 3.21, Lys. 2.23, Isoc. 4.175; Xen. *Cyr.* I.vi.11.

59 Concrete favor done: with φέρειν, e.g. *Il.* 5.211, Eur. *IT* 14, And. 2.24, τίθεσθαι, e.g. Hdt. 9.60.107, Aeschyl. *Pro.* 782, διδόναι, e.g. Soph. *OC* 1489; ἀποδιδόναι, e.g. Lys. 12.60, 28.17, Xen. *Ag.* II.xix, Isoc. 4.56, ἀπαιτεῖν, e.g. Eur. *Hec.* 276; Lys. 18.23; Dem. 20.156, with ἀμείβεσθαι, e.g. Aeschyl. *Ag.* 728 ff.; Soph. *El.* 134; Democr. fr. 92 (Diels) (noun ἀμοιβὰς ἀποδοῦναι for χάριτας); Xen. *Mem.* III.xi.12.

has had consistent supporters ever since.[60] Drawing on the etymological connection of χάρις with χαρά (joy) and χαίρειν (to rejoice), Löw assigned a *factum* or *res laetificans*, a "pleasing property" or "joyful thing" to χάρις; its primary significance would have been a *vis laetificatrix*.[61] From this primary sense emerged a notion of pleasure, grace, favor, and subsequently, the return of a favor.[62] Primacy of effect is argued for by Joachim Latacz.[63] Arguing for the semantic priority of the verb χαίρω over the noun χάρις, Latacz takes the causative sense (*Lustbereitung*, i.e. rousing desire) as logically and semantically prior to the responsive state (*Anziehung, Reiz*, attraction, desire). χάρις in the sense of a quality is secondary.[64]

The question of historical or logical priority set aside, most current approaches of χάρις take the functional unity and the integration of sense as point of departure.[65] The claim set out in this chapter is not a semantic one,

60 Löw is followed by Versnel (1981), 48–49, Philipp (1978) (plural χάριτες as *facta laetificantia*), and MacLachlan (1993) ("charm" as the core meaning of χάρις applicable to physical appearance of persons or things as well as applicable to social behavior). Latacz (1966), 80 criticizes Löw's decription as eclectical and based on an unsystematically diachronical interpretation of passages.

61 On the etymological connection with χαρά, see also Stenzel (1934), 92; for the connection with χαίρω, see Hipp. *Aer*. 22.9 (central to Löw's argumentation).

62 Löw distinguishes between: 1. *factum, quo quis laetitiam parat*, 2. *condicio, qua quis alium laetitia afficit* (*virtus sive animi sive corporis sive utriusque; amabilitas, venustas, Anmut*) 3. *pulchritudinis vis laetificatrix insuper accedens atque consummatrix*.

63 Latacz (1966), 78ff.

64 Latacz (1966), 82: "Indem die χάρις etwas Verschönendes ist, ist sie natürlich zugleich selbst schön." Similarly Burkert (1977), 409, who translates χάρις as "*Gnade*" (mercy, grace) and Moussy (1966), 411–412, who reconstructs the "signification première" of χάρις as "*ce qui provoque de la joie*", "ce qui procure du plaisir". Scott (1983) (who curiously omits any reference to Löw, Latacz and Moussy) takes the sense "source of pleasure" as primary, but adds that in Homeric Greece an articulate distinction between (1) emotion, (2) that which rouses the emotion in experiencers, and (3) the appearance of the experiencers, was not conceptually and lexically available. Verdenius (1979), 14 points out that not only is it questionable to posit a causative sense as the original one, but also that the basis meaning of χαίρω is wider than "to lust".

65 The most fundamental difference between those scholars who postulate a primary sense of χάρις from which all others by logical extension and metonymy derive and those who take the subject-object underdetermination as point of departure seems chiefly methodological in nature and goes at the heart of semantic theory. (As Porzig (1942), 53 already noted). In this subject/object-ambiguity, χάρις also has analogies with some other Greek concepts: e.g. with αἰδώς which may similarly refer to an awe-inspiring source as well as to the feeling of reverence or awe itself. Cf. Cairns (1993). Moreover, Benveniste has pointed out ambiguities in vocabularies of "exchange" in Indo-European languages, where often the same terms signify both the act of receiving and the act of giving. Benveniste (1971).

but a conceptual and functional one: even though the lexeme χάρις challenges our lexicographical categories and distinctions, the **concept** χάρις displays a functional unity. This unity can be grasped along the following principles:[66]

i. χάρις-terminology typically presents a situation (whether current or prospective/hypothetical) as a **successful interaction**, for instance between perceiver and object of perception or between giver and recipient. In this sense, χάρις-vocabulary is **positive** and **evaluative**.

ii. χάρις-terminology tends to describe such successful interaction from the point of view of participants who are involved in the interaction and who experience the interaction as successful: χάρις presupposes **participants' focalization of events**, including the subjective experiences and valuation involved.[67] It does not sit easy with the objectifying perspective of an external observer.

iii. χάρις-terminology tends to approach situations **as an ongoing process** as opposed to discrete events. Presenting situations in terms of χάρις implies seeing the world in terms of long-term structures.

Without committing oneself to semantic essentialism (again, it is not a semantic claim that is being made here), it is possible to expose the anatomy of χάρις by carving the concept closely at its joints. A concept such as χάρις challenges the very categories and distinctions that are used as lexicographical tools: it has an "objective" *and* a "subjective", an "active" *and* a "passive", a "concrete" *and* an "internalized" sense.[68] How does such a concept *work*?

66 I here follow other approaches that focus on functional unity: MacLachlan (1993) and Azoulay (2004a). The principles outlined are my own.

67 For the narratological distinction between focalizers (the vision through which the elements are presented) and narrators (the identity of the voice that is verbalizing this vision), see Bal (1985), 142–161, on embedded focalization Bal & Tavor (1981), 43–53. Focalization is the relationship between the "vision", the agent that sees, and that which is seen. For applications on ancient (especially oral) literature, see De Jong (1987a), (1991), (2001); for the value of the focalization-concept for semantic studies, see De Jong (1987b) on κέρδος in Homer.

68 It is not my aim to make any semantic claim here, but by way of hypothesis, I expect that a semantic description of the lexeme χάρις has a lot to gain from a prototype theory of semantics. See Langacker (1991) and Rosch (1975) for theoretical outlines. For applications on ancient value terminology, see Sluiter-Rosen in Rosen-Sluiter (2003) on ἀνδρεία, Rademaker (2005) on σωφρόσυνη, Peels (2016) on ὅσιος.

2.1 *Successful Interaction between Beauty and Beholder*

When χάρις-vocabulary is used in contexts of aesthetic beauty, it serves to represent beauty and looking at beauty as a reciprocal endeavor. As the noun χάρις is related to the verb χαίρω ("to rejoice"),[69] often the noun not only refers to a quality (beauty) inherent in some object or person, but also to the charming effect on and the delighted response by a subject perceiving the object.[70] Semantically speaking, we could say that this is a case of metonymia (and we may diverge over the question which is more fundamental: quality or effect).[71] In functional terms, we see the following underlying script:

i. **A** perceives **B** who/that "is χαρίεις," "has χάρις" (has pleasing qualities): e.g., a beautiful boy, good wine.
ii. **B**'s χάρις is a quality that affects **A**, i.e. "charm," "attractiveness."
iii. **A** experiences χάρις in perceiving **B** (object of perception): e.g., the pleasure of seeing a beautiful boy, the delight of tasting excellent wine.

Because it is the same χάρις at work in all three steps, χάρις is often conceived of as a force emanating, "breathing" or "radiating" from something or someone beautiful, i.e. something or someone that "has χάρις" or "is χαρίεις",[72] and that,

---

69 The formation of noun (χάρις) in relation to the verb (χαίρω) is contested. Risch (1937) § 60 and Latacz (1966) 78 classify the noun as a *nomen actionis*, deverbative of χαίρω; Porzig (1942) 353 goes as far as supposing that χάρις may originally have been a *nomen agentis* denoting "Ergreifer". Beekes (2009) II.1606 argues for a status independent of the verb on grounds of the antiquity of the substantive.

70 Latacz (1966), 82. Cf. Scott (1983), 4 ff. E.g. Hes. *O&D* 65, *Theog.* 247, 260, 583; Thgn. 1320, Tyrt. 12.5 (Bergk), Solon 13.40 (Bergk). Hence, the noun χάρις displays a distinct articulation of subjectivity and suggests a less clear-cut divide between subject and object. Cf. MacLachlan (1993), 11. This integration of quality, effect and response is distinctive for the noun χάρις and its adjective χαρίεις when compared to the semantic field of κάλλος and καλός: καλός rarely in itself implies an affective or aesthetic response of the perceiver. Cf. Latacz (1966), 99.

71 It has often been noted that the "metonymic use" of vocabulary of perception is a phenomenon typical of early Greek poetry. For instance, in Archaic poetry, ὄψις, "sight", denotes both the object of perception (the thing seen, the appearance, the face) as well as the act of perception (the power of seeing, vision, view): compare English "this is a pretty sight" vs. "coming into one's sight". Lexemes such as ὄψις seem to assimilate action with object. MacLachlan (1993), 11, adduces an instructive English parallel, "good-looking", where "the looking subject has merged with its object." On the object/effect-assimilation in χάρις, see also Verdenius (1979), 14. Cf. Snell (1953), ch. 1. Alternatively, Latacz (1966), 78 ff. takes the causative sense as prior to the responsive state.

72 Hom *Il.* 14.183 (ἀπολάμπομαι "Glittering"), Hom. *Od.* 6.31 (στίλβω, "glittering"), Sapph. fr. 138 (ἀναπετάννυμι "spreading out"), Pind. *fr.* 123.2–3 (μαρμαρύζω, "flashing, sparkling"). Hes. *Theog.* 583 (ἄημι "breathing"; reading χάρις instead of πολλή, cf. West (1966), ad loc.). However, the verb ἄημι is also used in collocation with εἶδος (Hes. *Cat.* fr. 43.74 West & Merkel-

in turn, brings delight (χάρις) to people.[73] It need not surprise us that χάρις is regularly used in collocation with πειθώ, persuasion.[74]

This "glittering" of χάρις, for instance, occurs in "beautification" scenes in the *Odyssey*,[75] e.g., when Odysseus is bathing and oiling himself on the shores of Scheria. Here, Athena helps him to overcome the initial aversion of the Phaeacian girls by making him look taller and mightier and curling his locks like a hyacinth flower[76]—the effect of which is described in terms of χάρις ("poured over" the object):[77]

[Text 8]

ὡς δ' ὅτε τις χρυσὸν περιχεύεται ἀργύρῳ ἀνὴρ
ἴδρις, ὃν Ἥφαιστος δέδαεν καὶ Παλλὰς Ἀθήνη
τέχνην παντοίην, χαρίεντα δὲ ἔργα τελείει,
ὣς ἄρα τῷ κατέχευε χάριν κεφαλῇ τε καὶ ὤμοις.
ἕζετ' ἔπειτ' ἀπάνευθε κιὼν ἐπὶ θῖνα θαλάσσης,
κάλλεϊ καὶ χάρισι στίλβων· θηεῖτο δὲ κούρη.

And as when a man overlays silver with gold, a cunning workman whom Hephaestus and Pallas Athena have taught all manner of craft, and full of χάρις is the work he produces, even so the goddess shed χάρις upon his head and shoulders. Then he went apart and sat down on the shore of the sea, *gleaming with beauty and* χάριτες; and the damsel marveled at him (…).[78]

The χάρις Athena pours (κατέχευε) over Odysseus' head and shoulders is compared to "gold on silver" applied by a skillful craftsman who makes "works full

---

bach) and with κάλλος (*h.H.Dem.* 276–280). Löw (1908), 83–86 on the notion of light in the Indo-European χαρ-root.

73 E.g. the delight, χάρις, of wine (Eur. *Bach.* 535, Aristoph. *Nub.* 311).

74 E.g. Hes. *O&D* 74 (Χάριτες and πότνια Πειθώ), Pind. fr. 123.10–15. See Chapter Six.

75 De Jong (2001), 163 ff. on "beautification" as a typical scene in the *Od.*, consisting of a couple of recurring elements: the presence of a beautifying god (mostly Athena), its function as a prelude to an important performance, the reaction of the onlookers described from embedded focalization (192–193).

76 Hom. *Od.* 6.229–231.

77 Cf. Hes. *O&D* 65–66 (Aphrodite pours χάρις over Pandora's head) and Thgn. 2.1319–1322 (Kypris has given arousing χάρις to the boy). Both passages will be discussed in Chapter Six.

78 Hom. *Od.* 6.231–237; *transl.* Murray (1995). If the text is correct, 6.237 is the only (not personified) instance of plural χάρις in Homer. Latacz (1966) reads χάριτι (following Ap. Lex. 94,26 and codd. K. and H³ (Allen)).

of grace" (χαρίεντα ἔργα). Similarly, Odysseus' beauty (Athena's work of grace) is gilded by divine grace,[79] a glittering beauty and lure that provokes a response in Nausicaa, the focalizer from whose point of view we subsequently see the χάρις: she marvels at him (θηεῖτο).[80]

This χάρις has aesthetic as well as social implications: the grace that perfects his beautification is a gift (a χάρις) from Athena.[81] Moreover, Odysseus' χάρις purports to have a persuasive effect. The same verses reoccur in a similar scene in book 23, when Athena prepares Odysseus for his final confrontation with Penelope—and where his grace purports to have a persuasive effect.[82] Similarly, the beautification on the shore of Scheria aims at persuading the people of Scheria:[83]

[Text 9]

> πολλοὶ δ' ἄρα θηήσαντο ἰδόντες
> υἱὸν Λαέρταο δαΐφρονα. τῷ δ' ἄρ' Ἀθήνη
> θεσπεσίην **κατέχευε χάριν κεφαλῇ τε καὶ ὤμοις**
> καί μιν μακρότερον καὶ πάσσονα θῆκεν **ἰδέσθαι**,
> ὥς κεν Φαιήκεσσι **φίλος** πάντεσσι γένοιτο
> δεινός τ' **αἰδοῖός** τε καὶ ἐκτελέσειεν ἀέθλους
> πολλούς, τοὺς Φαίηκες ἐπειρήσαντ' Ὀδυσῆος.
>
> And many *marveled at the sight* of the wise son of Laertes, for wondrous was *the χάρις that Athena shed upon his head and shoulders*; and she made him taller and sturdier *to behold*, that **he might be welcomed** by all the Phaeacians, and *win awe and reverence*, and might accomplish the many feats wherein the Phaeacians made trial of Odysseus.[84]

---

79 The climactic nature of the description of Odysseus' "makeover" (the first two changes in one single verse (230), next one whole verse on the hair (231), four verses on a comparison) suggests that χάρις is the central feature of the renewed Odysseus, making him golden instead of silver. Latacz (1966), 81–82: "*χάρις bedeutet eine Steigerung über κάλλος hinaus.*" Cf. MacLachlan (1993), 31–32: "*Charis* is more than ordinary beauty; *charis* is gold over silver."

80 Cf. Hom. *Od.* 2.12 (= 17.63), the beautification of Telemachus, for a similar collocation of effective feature (χάρις) and response (θηεῦντο). Latacz (1966), 81–83 on the causal connection between χάρις and θηεῖσθαι. For θηέομαι as gazing at something in wonder, see Mette (1960).

81 On the motif of special abilities as a "gift of the gods" in the *Iliad*, see Van der Mije (1987), 251–254.

82 *Od.* 23.159–162. Cf. Scott (1983), 3.

83 Latacz (1966), 81: "χάρις ist also hier al seine Art Überzug vorgestellt."

84 Hom. *Od.* 8.17–23; *transl.* Murray.

Again, χάρις implies a beholder, as we focalize through the eyes of the admiring Phaeacians:[85] people are looking at Odysseus (ἰδόντες) who is made taller and sturdier "to look at" (ἰδέσθαι), and the spectators are said to marvel (θηήσαντο). Moreover, Odysseus' "makeover" is intended to produce *social* effects: that he may become welcome to and welcomed by (φίλος) the Phaeacians and win awe and reverence (become δεινός τ' αἰδοῖός τε). "The power of *charis* resides in its unerring ability to provoke a response."[86]

In erotic poetry, we frequently find χάρις in the sense of erotic attractiveness,[87] i.e. a quality of an object of perception that has an immediate effect on the onlooking subject. In the example here, χάρις is presented as an utterly subjective experience:

[Text 10]

> Οὐκέτ' ἐρῶ παιδός, χαλεπὰς δ' ἀπελάκτισ' ἀνίας
> μόχθους τ' ἀργαλέους ἄσμενος ἐξέφυγον,
> ἐκλέλυμαι δὲ πόθου πρὸς ἐυστεφάνου Κυθερείης·
> σοὶ δ', ὦ παῖ, χάρις ἔστ' οὐδεμία πρὸς ἐμοῦ.

> I am no longer in love with a boy, I have kicked aside harsh pain, I have gladly escaped from grievous hardships, and the fair-crowned Cytherean has released me from longing. And as for your *χάρις*, boy, it does not exist in my eyes.[88]

χάρις is discussed from a retrospective point of view (*vision par derrière*), from the point of view of *un*successful interaction, of χάρις gone bad. As the thrill is gone and the speaker no longer desires (οὐκέτ' ἐρῶ) the boy (or boys in general), the speaker only sees the downside of his encounters with the boy: pain, hardships, and painful longing. His falling out of love is the result of a process of rejection, escape and release: he has kicked off (ἀπελάκτισα) sorrows,

85 The narrator intrudes upon the embedded focalization by referring to Odysseus as "the wise son of Laertes". De Jong (2001), 192–193.

86 MacLachlan (1993), 37. Löw (1908), 23: "χάρις *hac in re aliquid est quod ad ceteram rei cuiusdam naturam accedens hanc rem laetificantem reddit.*" Along the same lines, the phrase χάριν φέρειν τινί typically refers to a situation in which a person "confers a favor on someone", but may be taken more literally as "brings something to enjoy" or "brings enjoyment to" this person and makes this person rejoice. Verdenius (1979), 14.

87 On the importance of χάρις-vocabulary in the context of erotic seduction, see Chapter Five.

88 Thgn. 2.1337–1340; *transl.* Gerber (1999).

escaped (ἐξέφυγον) from the troubles of courtship and is released (ἐκλέλυμαι) from his longing (πόθος). This process amounts to the result: a change of attitude in the subject and an increase in distance between the subject and the object of desire. The boy's beauty no longer has any effect on him; the boy no longer has charm (χάρις) "from the side of the speaker" (πρὸς ἐμοῦ). Here, χάρις refers to a quality of the boy (his physical beauty) as well as the subjective effect it has on the perceiver (πρὸς ἐμοῦ), for whom the boy has lost his attractiveness. *Both* are required for χάρις: attraction and charm are a reciprocal endeavor.[89] When things go sour, χάρις ceases to be χάρις and turns out, in retrospect, to be troubles and hardship.

In this scenario, χάρις has a direct effect ("attraction") on the onlooking subject, like the earrings "glittering with χάρις" that Hera is wearing when she is about to seduce Zeus.[90] Correspondingly, the subject's *experience* of this effect is also referred to as χάρις:[91] sleep,[92] wine,[93] victory,[94] and ἔρως[95] bring χάρις, the experience of pleasure and delight. Hence, χάρις sometimes occurs in opposition to subjective or emotional responses such as λύπη[96] and πόνος:[97]

---

89 Here we also see how the poet suggests a continuity between the boy's attractiveness and the social dimension of the relationship: the boy will no longer *receive* any χάρις from the speaker.

90 Hom. *Il.* 14.183.

91 This use of χάρις seems to occur predominantly in poetic texts, with the exception of Plato who uses the noun occasionally in juxtaposition with ἡδονή. See n. 50 above.

92 Eur. *Or.* 159.

93 Eur. *Bacch.* 535, Aristoph. *Nub.* 311.

94 Pind. *Ol.*7.5, 10.78.

95 See Chapter Five.

96 E.g. Eur. *Hel.* 654–655: ἐμὰ δὲ χαρμονᾶι δάκρυα· πλέον ἔχει | χάριτος ἢ λύπας. (adopting the causal dative χαρμονᾶι conjectured by Hermann for χαρμονὰ of L.). The speaker disambiguates his/her tears as tears of joy (χαρμονή), containing more delight (χάρις) than sorrow (λύπη). The opposition of χάρις to λύπη indicates that χάρις refers to a subjective, emotional, response, a response moreover caused by χαρμονή, a thing of joy. χαρμονή is probably a metrical alternative for χάρμα. χάρμα is directly derived from the verb χαίρω; the –μα suffix indicates that χάρμα refers to a concrete object of joy (sometimes antonym of πῆμα, "a calamity"), although in *Od.* 19.451 it may be used as a nomen actionis. Latacz (1966), 122. Cf. Porzig (1942), 146, 241–242, 278, F. However, Beekes (2009), II.1606 suggests that χαρμονή is formed after an analogy with ἡδονή.

97 E.g. Soph. *OC* 229–236: X: οὐδενὶ μοιριδία τίσις ἔρχεται ὧν προπάθῃ τὸ τίνειν· ἀπάτα δ' ἀπάταις ἑτέραις ἑτέρα παραβαλλομένα πόνον, οὐ χάριν, ἀντιδίδωσιν ἔχειν.

χάρις is contrasted with distress or pain (πόνος), indicating that a subjective effect or experience may be implied by χάρις (pleasure or delight). This example represents a perverted case of reciprocity: it thematizes vengeance (τίσις), an exchange (cf. ἀντιδίδωσιν) of deceit matching deceit (ἀπάτα ἀπάταις ἑτέραις ἑτέρα), that does involve a return, but not a

[Text 11]

> Η: πρὸς ταῦτα καινέτω τις, εἰ βαρύνεται,
> τῶν ἔνδον ὄντων· ὡς χάρις μέν, ἢν κτάνῃ,
> λύπη δ', ἐὰν ζῶ· τοῦ βίου δ' οὐδεὶς πόθος.
>
> Electra: In face of that let any of those inside kill me, if he resents me; *for if he kills me, it will be a χάρις; to survive will be a pain.* I have no desire for life.[98]

The contrast that Electra draws between χάρις and grief (λύπη) foregrounds the subjective effect or experience of χάρις (pleasure or delight). However, here too χάρις has social or relational implications. The situation is deliberately formulated as a paradox: it does not represent a successful interaction, as Electra's potential killer may not *intend* to do her a favor (he may do so out of resentment (βαρύνεται)), but given the quality of her life, she will *experience* it as a favor (a χάρις) if someone killed her. This is *hypersubjective* χάρις.

In short, χάρις implies successful interaction, between what we would call a subject and an object, between an object and a viewer, between a source of pleasure and an experience of pleasure, between a giver and a recipient. The term χάρις invites us to view a situation from within, from the point of view of the characters.

2.2 *Successful Interaction between Giver and Recipient*

The object/effect-indeterminacy of χάρις that we have seen in the aesthetic realm also manifests itself in the social dimension: acts of χάρις (favors or gifts) arouse χάρις (enjoyment, gratitude) in the receiver.[99] A well-known example of this logic is the adjective χαρίεις in Chryses' prayer, where he reminds Apollo of his past benefactions amongst which the χαρίεις temple that Chryses had roofed for the god:

---

return of favor (χάρις), but of trouble (πόνος)—i.e. a type of reciprocity that does not breed gratitude (χάρις) but pain (πόνος).

98 Soph. *El.* 820–822. For ὡς χάρις μέν, ἢν κτάνῃ, Lloyd-Jones translates "to die will be a pleasure"; Jebb translates "It is a favor if I die." Both translations express different aspects of χάρις (subjective experience vs. favor); however, the fact that both have chosen to convert the third-person κτάνῃ ("if he kills") into a first person correlate ("if I die") also reflects some of the challenges that the "relationality" of the term χάρις poses for our modern lexicon.

99 Nagy (1985), 27: "[*K*]*haris* conveys simultaneously the social aspect of *reciprocity* as well as the personal aspect of *pleasure*."

[Text 12]

> Σμινθεῦ εἴ ποτέ τοι χαρίεντ' ἐπὶ νηὸν ἔρεψα
>
> Sminthian god, if ever I roofed over a temple *to your pleasing* …[100]

Semantically speaking, we could say that χαρίεντα is "proleptic" here (to your pleasing).[101] In functional terms, we see a thicker scenario underlying the prayer, that of a successful interaction. The temple has χάρις in the sense that it is beautiful (quality of the object), but also in the sense that it is a gift with the intention of provoking a response in the recipient, Apollo, who may rejoice (χαίρειν) in the dedication and make this rejoicing manifest in a χάρις, a return of favor.[102] The χάρις refers to both the dedication and its intended response. As such, Chryses' prayer is a corollary of the phrase commonly used in prayer χαρίεσσα ἀμοιβή:[103]

[Text 13]

> Μάντικλός μ' ἀνέθεκε Fεκαβόλοι ἀργυροτόξσοι
> τᾶς {δ} δε|κάτας· τὺ δέ, Φοῖβε, δίδοι χαρίFετταν ἀμοιβ[άν].
>
> Mantiklos set me up for the far-shooting, silver-bowed (god), out of a tithe. As for you, Phoibus, may you grant a *χάρις-filled return*.[104]

The pair of hexameters is incised on the thighs of the famous "Mantiklos statuette", a bronze statuette (probably representing Apollo) from the early seventh century.[105] The "χάρις-filled return" that it calls for implies a prior act of χάρις: Mantiklos' act of dedicating the statuette to Apollo—a dedication filled with χάρις as is effectively visualized by the craftmanship manifest in the artifact. The statuette has χάρις (beauty), embodies a χάρις-event (the act of dedication), embodies a ritual re-enactment of the χάρις-event, invites the passer-by to read

---

100 Hom. *Il.* 1.39.

101 Latacz (2000), ad loc. Cf. Pind. *Pyth.* 8.85–86 (ὤρσεν χάριν).

102 Pulleyn (1997), 16–55.

103 E.g. Hom. *Od.* 3.58–59, *CEG* 359, 360, 326. Cf. Bremer (1998), Versnel (1981), 43 ff., Van Straten (1981), 72 ff., Day (2010), 232 ff.

104 *CEG* 326 (ca. 700–675).

105 For a close reading of the Mantiklos statuette and an analysis of the interactive χάρις implied by dedicatory inscriptions, see Day (1994), (2000), (2010).

the inscription and thereby *re-enact* the χάρις-event,[106] *and* it provokes a χάρις-filled response. The inscription orchestrates a successful interaction.

The Greek expressions for being grateful, χάριν εἰδέναι and χάριν ἔχειν, literally mean "to know the favor" and "to have the favor": to acknowledge a favor and to accept the obligations that go with it—i.e. to respond to a favor properly by reciprocating the favor with a favor.[107] If we take a look at the social script underlying long-term reciprocity, we can distinguish the following events:

(i) A confers a favor on B (χάριν φέρειν/τίθεσθαι/διδόναι), thereby signifying that he (A) recognizes B as a potential partner to cooperate with;

(iia) B receives (δέχεσθαι) or accepts (λάμβανειν) the favor and recognizes A's action as a favor (χάριν εἰδέναι) and, hence, acknowledges A's action as "friendly," as initiating or sustaining a long-term relationship, and acknowledges A as a potential partner to cooperate with, by:

(iib) expressing that he is morally indebted to A (χάριν ἔχειν); recognition of which finds its expression properly in:

(iii) the reciprocation of χάρις, i.e. B "gives back" (ἀποδιδόναι) χάριν in due course.

Characteristically, events (i) and (iii) are concrete manifestations of a long-term relationship, i.e. favors being done and returned, whereas event (ii) is an internalization of the social expectations attached to such long-term relationships. In these cases, rendering χάρις as "gratitude" may serve purposes of translation, but essentially hides from our view that we are still talking about the *same* χάρις as in step (i) of the script: it is the χάρις that A bestowed on B, that B is said to "know" or to "have".[108] "Gratitude" or "kindness" are therefore not distinct "meanings" of χάρις. Rather, the idea of χάρις that is "due" or "needs to be repaid" derives from other contextual indications, such as the noun ἀμοιβή, the verbs ὀφείλειν, τίνειν, or ἀπο-compounds, or the collocation of noun phrases with the preposition ἀντί for manifest behavior and with verbs such as οἶδα or ἔχειν for internalized manifestations of χάρις.[109]

106 Moreover, as an object of dedication, the reading of the inscription re-enacts the act of dedication. Day (2000).

107 On χάριν εἰδέναι see Löw (1908), 6, 10; Scott (1983), 11.

108 This makes the "mechanics" of χάρις comparable to the Maussian phenomenon of *hau*, a quality of an object given, representing a certain spirit of the original giver that sets in motion a drive towards reciprocity. Mauss (1990), 20. The concept itself has been superseded in the anthropological field.

109 Cf. Parker (1998), 108–109; Philipp (1978), 157–159; Versnel (1981), 49; MacLachlan (1993), 4–7, 52; Azoulay (2004a), 28. It should be noted that expressions such as χάριν εἰδέναι, ἔχειν, φέρειν are *descriptive* rather than performative: they are rarely used in Greek con-

χάρις-terminology implies a succesful interaction and succesful interactions imply the script of long-term reciprocity. Within this script of the long run, there is no meaningful difference between givers and receivers, donors and recipients. These are only temporary roles. In a healthy reciprocal relationship, there is no need to separate the χάρις that is bestowed as a favor from the χάρις that is recognized, acknowledged and expierenced by the recipient or the χάρις that is given back (or given *again*) to the original donor.[110]

Hence, the proverbial expression that χάρις begets χάρις:[111]

[Text 14]

Τ. ἀλλ' ἴσχε κἀμοῦ μνῆστιν· ἀνδρί τοι χρεὼν
μνήμην προσεῖναι, τερπνὸν εἴ τί που πάθοι.
Χάρις χάριν γάρ ἐστιν ἡ τίκτουσ' ἀεί·
ὅτου δ' ἀπορρεῖ μνῆστις εὖ πεπονθότος,
οὐκ ἂν γένοιτ' ἔθ' οὗτος εὐγενὴς ἀνήρ.

Tecmessa: *Think of* me also; a man should *remember*, should some pleasure come his way; for it is *always one χάρις that begets another*, and if a man allows the *memory of a kindness* to slip away, he can no longer be accounted noble.[112]

---

versation. Quincey (1966), 133. Cf. Versnel (1981), 49. Neither the expression appropriate for grateful acceptance (αἰνῶ) nor the formulae for grateful refusal (αἰνῶ, ἐπαινῶ, καλῶς, κάλλιστα ἔχει μοι) contain the noun χάρις. Here, it is relevant to distinguish between narrative voice (first person vs. third person) and focalization/point of view (first person vs. third person), as the term χάρις does rarely occur in Greek *expressions* of thanks, i.e. in a first-person *voice* ("I thank you"). See Bal (1985), 142–161 and De Jong (1987a) for the voice/perspective-distinction in narratology. The difference between conferring a favor (χάριν φέρειν) and being grateful (χάριν εἰδέναι or ἔχειν) resembles a distinction made in Classical Latin between *gratiam agere* and *gratiam habere*; however, expressions such as *gratias tibi ago* are used responsively (and in first person reports) in Latin idiom. Cf. Hickson Hahn (2004).

110 Cf. Hewitt (1927), 149: "In many phrases, χάριν as the object of a verb is ambiguous, for it may denote either favor or gratitude." Parker (1998), 108: "*Kharis* words are in fact applied to both sides of the relationship. Mortals seek to bring gifts or sacrifices which are *kharienta* or *kekharismena* to the gods, and request a return which is itself *khariessa* (…)." Cf. Davidson (2007), 38ff.; Kurke (1991), 104; Rocchi (1979), 5–7.

111 Cf. Soph. *OC* 779 (ἡ χάρις χάριν φέροι), Eur. *Hel.* 1234 (χάρις ἀντὶ χάριτος ἐλθέτω), Ar. *Rhet.* 1385a16.

112 Soph. *Aj.* 520–524; *transl.* Lloyd-Jones (1994) *adapt.*

A favor breeds χάρις in the sense that the proper response to receiving a favor (a χάρις), i.e. being treated well (εὖ πάσχειν), is to remember it (cf. μνῆστις twice, μνήμην) and to display gratitude by conferring a favor in turn.[113] The polyptoton χάρις χάριν underscores the fact that within a successful chain of reciprocities, there is no meaningful distinction between favors and counter favors: they are all "acts of grace." In the long run, givers *are* receivers and vice versa. In properly functioning long-term reciprocal relationships, it is barely possible to discern between favors and counterfavors, gifts and countergifts, because the notion of an "original favor" in need of "compensation" has receded in favor of an awareness of a long-term relationship in which each partner is well-disposed towards the other.[114] The reciprocal relationship has logical primacy over the temporary and alternating roles.[115]

The emphatic repetition of the importance of *remembering* (μνῆστις, μνήμη) a favor reflects the fact that the economy of χάρις is premised on a mutual recognition of the history of a relationship. When reciprocity has not yet materialized, a friend needs to know that the other still "knows" the favor:[116]

---

113 The procreative metaphor of τίκτειν, "breeding", not only anticipates the notion of birth and breeding in 524 but may also contain a pun on τόκος in the technical sense of "interest" on loans.

114 Drawing an analogy with the noun ξένος may be illuminating: ξένος may refer to "guest" as well as "host"—displaying a similar active/passive-ambiguity, which may appear paradoxical at first sight; on second thoughts, however, this ambiguity makes perfect sense in light of the institution of ξενία, where there is an expectation of balance in the long run. Conceptually speaking, the reciprocal relationship bears a primacy over the alternating roles of the partners: today's host may be a guest tomorrow. In a similar vein, the noun χάρις embodies the bilateralness of reciprocity in its very meaning. Cf. Bolkestein (1967) for this analogy with ξένος.

115 Benveniste (1971) has observed this phenomenon in vocabulary of gift-giving in other Indo-European languages too.

116 E.g. Hera promises Hypnos (who will do her the favor of inducing sleep in Zeus) that she will keep the χάρις alive in her memory ἤματα πάντα, "for all days" (*Il.* 14.235); for the collocation of χάρις and words expressive of mnemonic activity, *Il.* 23.647–650, Theogn. 503–505 (ἀπεμνήσαντο), Soph. *Aj.* 1267–1269 (ὅτου δ' ἀπορρεῖ μνῆστις εὖ πεπονθότος with its suggestive parallel χάρις διαρρεῖ), Aristoph. *Eq.* 268 (μνημεῖον … ἀνδρείας χάριν (pregnant use of χάριν + gen.)), Soph. fr. 920 (Radt) ((ἀμνήμονος ἀνδρός with χάρις), Lys. 30.27. Similarly, in Pindaric poetry, vulnerable reciprocity (e.g. between descendants and their deceased ancestors) is repeatedly thematized in terms of ancient χάρις that "sleeps" (εὕδει) *Ol.* 8., *Pyth.*9, *Isthm.*4, *Isthm.*7.16–24—until it is awakened by new song. Cf. the theme of "undying grace" (χάριν ἀθάνατον, e.g. Hdt. 7.178), an expression of the importance of keeping the memory of χάρις alive.

[Text 15]

Μηδείς σ' ἀνθρώπων πείσηι κακὸν ἄνδρα φιλῆσαι,
  Κύρνε· τί δ' ἔστ' ὄφελος δειλὸς ἀνὴρ φίλος ὤν;
οὔτ' ἄν σ' ἐκ χαλεποῖο πόνου ῥύσαιτο καὶ ἄτης,
  οὔτε κεν ἐσθλὸν ἔχων τοῦ μεταδοῦν ἐθέλοι.
Δειλοὺς εὖ ἔρδοντι ματαιοτάτη χάρις ἐστίν·
  ἶσον καὶ σπείρειν πόντον ἁλὸς πολιῆς.
οὔτε γὰρ ἂν πόντον σπείρων βαθὺ λήιον ἀμῶις,
  οὔτε κακοὺς εὖ δρῶν εὖ πάλιν ἀντιλάβοις·
ἄπληστον γὰρ ἔχουσι κακοὶ νόον· ἢν δ' ἓν ἁμάρτηις,
  τῶν πρόσθεν πάντων ἐκκέχυται φιλότης·
οἱ δ' ἀγαθοὶ τὸ μέγιστον ἐπαυρίσκουσι παθόντες,
  μνῆμα δ' ἔχουσ' ἀγαθῶν καὶ χάριν ἐξοπίσω.

Let no one persuade you, Cyrnus, to make a base man your friend. Of what use is a base man as a friend? He would not rescue you from hard toil or from ruin nor if he has any success would he be willing to give you a share of this. Doing a good turn to the base is *an utterly useless act of χάρις*; it is the same as sowing the expanse of the white-capped sea. You cannot reap a tall crop by sowing the sea and you cannot get anything good in return by doing good to the base. For the base have an insatiable νοῦς; if you make one mistake, the friendship shown by all former acts is wasted. But the noble enjoy to the highest degree the treatment they have received, they *remember* the good things, and *they have χάρις thereafter*.[117]

The χάρις in line 105 characterizes the conduct of someone who does good (εὖ ἔρδειν). This conduct is utterly "in vain" (ματαιοτάτη) when directed towards *deiloi* or *kakoi* people, i.e.: such acts of χάρις will remain unanswered. *Kakoi* people will not help you in need, nor will they share their successes. While you do good to them (εὖ δρῶν), this will not be returned: *lit.* "you will not receive in return (ἀντιλάβοις) the good given." Moreover, while they fail to reciprocate good treatment, they are resentful too, for they refuse to forgive one single mistake: they only know *tit-for-tat*. Conversely, the *agathoi* are mindful of (i.e. have μνῆμα of) the *agatha* they have received; hence, they "have χάρις" thereafter (ἐξοπίσω).[118] The timeframe implied by ἐξοπίσω indicates that in

117 Thgn. 1.101–112; *transl.* Gerber (1999).

118 The contrast between the *deiloi* and the *agathoi* is even stronger on Ahrens' reading, who

line 111,[119] χάρις characterizes a disposition, or the conduct, of the *recipients* of well-doing: the *agathoi* have χάρις, i.e. they *will* reciprocate χάρις. At the same time, "having χάρις" means that these *agathoi* have "class"—they are chic people who behave with style—as opposed to the δειλοί who "have no χάρις."[120]

To characterize actions and events as χάρις means to recognize them as part of a long-term relationship, to acknowledge the obligations implied by them, to voice the expectations that go with them, to signify that one accepts those obligations and to acknowledge the other as a partner in a χάρις relationship. Within this script, the phrases χάριν ἔχειν[121] and χάριν εἰδέναι represent the introspective, or internalized, moments in these relationships; in situations in which reciprocation has not yet taken place, these phrases refer to the recipient's understanding of the relationship in which he partakes and to his ability to live up to the standards the relationship imposes upon him. The vital point is that the χάρις in the phrases χάριν ἔχειν and χάριν εἰδέναι is, essentially, the same χάρις as the one that is bestowed.[122]

2.3 *The Embodiment of χάρις: Knowing vs. Showing*

In the previous sections we have seen that the noun χάρις cuts across our lexical distinctions of subject/object and active/passive. A third challenge is the distinction between internalized experience (gratitude and favor *felt*) and the concrete gesture that goes with it: the material favor done or returned.[123]

---

conjectures ἀμαυρίσκουσι ("blot out, hide") for ἐπαυρίσκουσι ("enjoy"): the *agathoi* "dim" even the greatest of mistakes but are mindful of the good things and have χάρις thereafter. Cf. Hudson-Williams (1910). For more on vv. 109–102, in See Section 4.1 below.

119 Cf. Hewitt (1927), 149 on ἐξοπίσω in Thgn. 1319. On the recurring theme of friends and enemies and the Theognidea, see Selle (2008), 258–262 (who explains the poems in terms of competition between *hetaireiai*), Donlan (1985), 223–244.

120 For the aristocratic connotations of χάρις-vocabulary, see Section 2.4 below.

121 Hewitt (1927), 149 makes the observation that the expression χάριν ἔχειν "lay dormant for a century after Theognis and blossoms out almost simultaneously in Euripides and Thucydides." A diachronical study of the semantics of χάρις is a desideratum.

122 In approaching the "active" χάρις as essentially the same χάρις as the one experienced and returned by the "passive" receiver, I differ from David Konstan's account of χάρις. Konstan (2006), 157–168. Konstan seeks to draw a fundamental distinction between χάρις in reciprocity (my steps i and iii) on the one hand, and the phrases χάριν ἔχειν or εἰδέναι on the other hand (my step ii); the latter, which he takes to refer to the emotion gratitude, Konstan claims to be fundamentally "distinct from the act of reciprocation", which is "felt, not due as compensation." (167, see T18 below). See Section 3 below. Cf. Chapter Four Section 3.

123 The plural χάριτες presupposes countability and discrete units and hence a more "concrete" contents than an uncountable use of singular χάρις. Analogous to τιμή (referring to

Here too it should be emphasized that χάρις-terminology goes best with internal focalization by participants in a successful interaction: it is a way of seeing objects, a perception of objects and acts *as* gifts and favors. Kindness and gratitude are commonly referred to by their concrete manifestation:[124] kindness is shown only by *doing* someone a favor (offering help, rendering a service, supplying material needs), gratitude is shown by returning such favors in due time. This dispels the necessity to postulate a distinct "concrete" sense of the noun χάρις. Conversely, when concrete services and material objects are referred to as χάρις or χάριτες, the term signals that we should view these services and objects from within a long-term relationship, i.e. as items circulating within a pre-existing or presupposed relationship of long-term reciprocity. For instance, when orators ask jurors for a χάρις in return for antecedent χάριτες, they at once refer to very concrete past services (liturgies) and a very concrete return (a favorable verdict), while at the same time embedding their claims in a (supposedly) pre-existing relationship of mutual favors in which the audience owes the speaker a favor.[125]

Such a pre-existing relationship may even be only a potential one. When faced with the threat of the Persian armies pursuing the Greeks, the Spartan king Pausanias sends for the Athenians with an urgent plea for solidarity:

---

the more abstract notion of "social value") vs. τιμαί (countable concrete manifestations of social value), χάρις may evoke more abstract qualities of pleasant interaction whereas the plural χάριτες refers to concrete boons, i.e. concrete objects or favors that are conferred as favors or tokens of gratitude. However, χάριτες may be less tangible than δῶρα. Mitchell (1997), 20. Löw (1908), 34–35 for χάριτες as *facta laetificanda*; cf. Phillips (1978), 157–159. The plural of χάρις is rare (or non-existent, depending on whether one reads χάριτι or χάρισι in *Il.* 6.237) in Homer, except as personifications, and seems a relatively recent development. Latacz (1996), 81 n. 73.

124 Latacz (1966), 93. Cf. Hewitt (1927) for the argument that in the period until 400 BCE the Greeks did not distinguish between the feeling of gratitude and the result of this feeling, i.e. a concrete act, a gesture of kindness in return. Similarly, MacLachlan (1993, p. 5 n. 2) contends that χάριν εἰδέναι in early Greek literature denotes "an active response as well as a (passive) state of mind. (…) [I]n the early Greek world the expression would take concrete form. The whole experience is a continuum and identified by one word, *charis*."

125 This strategy is by no means uncontested. E.g. in Lyc. 1.139 the χάρις-topos in court is dismissed by Lycurgus who criticizes logographers for claiming χάριτες *for their clients* on grounds of *their own* liturgies; Lycurgus observes that this strategy is a confusion of public and private domains. On the public service theme, see Ober (1989), Liddel (2007). On the (in)transitivity of χάρις, see Christ (1990), 155, Ober (1989), 241–242.

[Text 16]

> Νῦν ὦν δέδοκται τὸ ἐνθεῦτεν τὸ ποιητέον ἡμῖν, ἀμυνομένους γὰρ τῇ δυνάμεθα ἄριστα περιστέλλειν ἀλλήλους. Εἰ μέν νυν ἐς ὑμέας ὅρμησε ἀρχὴν ἡ ἵππος, χρῆν δὴ ἡμέας τε καὶ τοὺς μετ' ἡμέων τὴν Ἑλλάδα οὐ προδιδόντας Τεγεήτας βοηθέειν ὑμῖν· νῦν δέ, ἐς ἡμέας γὰρ ἅπασα κεχώρηκε, δίκαιοί ἐστε ὑμεῖς πρὸς τὴν πιεζομένην μάλιστα τῶν μοιρέων ἀμυνέοντες ἰέναι. Εἰ δ' ἄρα αὐτοὺς ὑμέας καταλελάβηκε ἀδύνατόν τι βοηθέειν, ὑμεῖς δ' ἡμῖν τούς ⟨γε⟩ τοξότας ἀποπέμψαντες χάριν θέσθε.
>
> It is clear what we have to do from now on, then: we must fight back and defend *each other* to the best of our abilities. If the Persian cavalry had started out by attacking you, it would of course have been our duty, along with the Tegeans (who are still with us and have not betrayed Greece), to come and help you. In fact, though, they have come in full force against us, so you should come and support us, since we are the ones who are particularly hard pressed. If for some reason you can't come yourselves, *please do us the* χάρις *of sending us your archers.*[126]

Urging for solidarity (περιστέλλειν ἀλλήλους), Pausanias first elaborates on the hypothetical situation where the Athenian cavalry had been attacked by the Persians first; in which case, the Spartans and the Tegeans would have come to help them. The present situation is that the Spartans are under attack by the Persians; hence, the Athenians are requested "to send their archers and confer a χάρις". The construction, a conjunct participle clause (ἡμῖν τούς τοξότας ἀποπέμψαντες) followed by the main clause χάριν θέσθε, underscores that sending the archers and doing the favor are conceived of as one and the same action: the Athenians are asked to do the favor *of* sending the archers. A translation as "service" or "favor" gives the impression that the request is a call for gratuitous or spontaneous charity in time of need. This downplays the rhetorical force of the use of χάρις in this passage. Pausanias appeals to the solidarity between the Spartans and the Athenians: his speech presents the solidarity asked for as mutual support that might easily have gone the other way round, if the Athenians had been the party in trouble. Here we see how the term χάρις, however concrete the content may be, still *also* serves to evoke ideals of reciprocity. Even in a situation where the reciprocity in question is not yet established (although it is an explicit proposal), the term χάρις can be used persuasively to force the

126 Hdt. 9.60; *transl.* Waterfield (1998) *adapt.*

addressee to adopt the perspective of the speaker and to perceive the situation in terms of mutual solidarity.

In a worldview in which reciprocity of favors needs to be manifest, a "subjective" sense of χάρις can be subsumed under the alleged "concrete" sense. A gift may be said to have χάρις, not only because it concerns a beautifully made object, but also because it embodies the χάρις of its giver towards the receiver and because it, subsequently, provokes χάρις in the receiver. Conversely, in a worldview that revolves around the *perception* of χάρις, the concrete sense *is* subjective: concrete favors and gifts need to be perceived as χάρις, as deriving their meaning from the relationship in which they are embedded.

2.4 *Digression: An Age of Grace?*

How *real* is the "functional unity" that we find in χάρις? That is: to what degree is the "functional unity" of χάρις a product of genre? Many of the examples cited above are poetic and pre-Classical. Could the integration of the aesthetical and the ethical, the subjective and the objective, the active and the passive, the immaterial and the concrete be a result of poetic language, of metonymy and prolepsis—designed to *create* unity and order rather than reflect it?

This is the tenor of Leslie Kurke's work on the ideology of exchange in late-Archaic epinician poetry. Kurke argues that χάρις is "the quality that infuses top-rank occasions":[127] it signifies the "highest virtue of aristocratic style, denoting the perfection of bodily form and movement, the numinous value bestowed on *agalmata*, the radiant circuit of gift exchange, and the pleasures of festivity."[128] The poetic unity of beauty and charm, graceful giving and grateful returning, then, serves to organize "the cosmos within the epinikia in accordance with an aristocratic world view".[129] The articulation and propagation of such a world view takes place against the backdrop of a "system of reciprocity" that is breaking down,[130] or, more aptly formulated: is in the process of being redefined by the emergence of the *polis* as the legitimate representation of long-term order.[131]

Does such reconfiguration mean that the Age of Grace comes to an end in the Classical Period?[132] This depends on how we define it. As many scholars have pointed out, χάρις remains a central term of social and political valuation

127 Kurke (1991), 136; cf. 103–107, 111–112, 116, 120–121, 137–146, 154–159.
128 Kurke (1999), 292.
129 Kurke (1991), 136.
130 Kurke (1991), x.
131 Kurke (1999).
132 The phrase is borrowed from MacLachlan (1993).

well into the Hellenistic era: it is central to the plot of many Attic tragedies,[133] it is the currency of democratic public life,[134] and it belongs to the language of empire.[135] Aristocratic value systems are subsumed into democratic discourse, including the vocabulary of long-term order.[136] At the same time, χάρις-terminology will have acquired a certain archaicizing and elitist ring to it, mobilizing "*certaines résonances archaïques du concept, revoyant à un temps où la notion était encore intimement associée avec le mode de vie des élites sociales et culturelles du monde grec.*"[137] This applies especially to the adjectives χαρίεις/χαρίεντες and χαριέστεροι ("graceful", "elegant"), that in the 4th century came to refer to upperclass persons, "the Graceful".[138]

This suggests a refraction of the χάρις word field and, perhaps, the beginning of a rift between the aesthetic and the ethic, a drive towards disintegration of the functional unity of χάρις. Vincent Azoulay's monograph on Xenophon's ideology of χάρις shows an intriguing dual motion.[139] On a semantic level, Xenophon's use of χάρις-lexemes reveals an increased need to disambiguate active χάρις (for which Xenophon uses the middle verb χαρίζομαι) from passive, performance of χάρις from the personal *quality* of χάρις (for which Xenophon prefers the composits εὔχαρις and ἐπίχαρις).[140] At the same time, Xenophon displays a consistent effort to "re-totalize" the world of χάρις, on his own terms and understanding, and to reintegrate the affective and the ethical aspects of χάρις.[141] χάρις emerges when φίλοι can "rejoice" (χαίρειν) in their exchange, and this rejoicing, in turn, leads to a perception of people and actions in terms of χάρις[142]—etymological play, yes, but also signaling a conscious effort to restore lexical order and to lexicalize the order of things.

As will be argued in the remainder of this chapter, in the case of our 4th-century sources, such efforts to "restore" order are not so much symptomatic of systems of reciprocity breaking down (they are merely being reconfigured).

---

133 Belfiore (2000); Blundell (1989); Wohl (1998), 151–158.
134 Herman (1987), 41–48, 108, 129, 135; Ober (1989), 226–232; Veligianni (1989).
135 Allison (2001).
136 Whitehead (1993).
137 Azoulay (2004a), 29.
138 E.g. Ar. *EN* (1095a18, b22, 1127b31, 1128a31, b1), *Pol.* 1267a1–40, used in contrast with οἱ πολλοί (cf. Pakaluk 1998); Is. *Ep.* IV.2, 9. Cf. Azoulay (2004a), 54.
139 Azoulay (2004a). See also Chapter Six Section 5.
140 Azoulay (2004a), 449–450.
141 Azoulay (2004a), esp. 27–34.
142 For Xenophon's reintegration of affective and ethical, see T29 and T30 below. For Xenophon's distinct redefinition of the ideology of χάρις as emphatically distinct from other modes of exchange, see Chapter Six Section 5 and Chapter Five Sections 2 and 3.

Rather, they are prompted by a potential for confusion, a perceived isomorphism between χάρις-exchanges and other exchanges—an isomorphism that puts an even higher premium on perception, on *seeing as*, the right way of seeing things. Because there is a wrong way too.

3 Perception and *méconnaissance*

3.1 *The Puzzle of Obligation*

One of the odd things about human communication is that nowhere do social norms and guidelines become more articulated and explicit than they do in unsuccessful interactions. This brings a certain asymmetry to value terms such as χάρις. When a friend's failure to reciprocate a good turn, i.e. to participate in a χάρις-relation, leads to a disappearance of χάρις, he is disqualified as ἀχάριστος, "ungrateful," "ingrate." This disqualification is not a judgment about a failure to *experience* a morally appropriate *emotion*. It is a judgment about behavior, about an overt and observable, and hence "objective", breach of a code of conduct: the failure to reciprocate χάρις. ἀχάριστος is not about feeling the right thing; it's about doing the right thing. When the χάρις is gone, there is no longer successful interaction; hence, the situation is no longer focalized from the point of view of the participants in an interaction (for there is none), but from a detached, external observer's point of view.

In the second book of Xenophon's *Memorabilia*, the first of a series of Socratic dialogues on φιλία (II.ii), Socrates reproaches his own son Lamprocles for his lack of χάρις towards his mother.[143] From the outset, the workings of χάρις are discussed from the vantage point of their violation: ἀχαριστία. The dialogue opens with the exchange of uncontroversial observations on ἀχαριστία, failure to reciprocate:

[Text 17]

> ΣΩ. Εἰπέ μοι, ἔφη, ὦ παῖ, οἶσθά τινας ἀνθρώπους ἀχαρίστους καλουμένους;
> ΛΑ. Καὶ μάλα, ἔφη ὁ νεανίσκος.

143 The dialogue sets the standard for subsequent discussions of φιλία-relationships within, as well as beyond, the οἶκος. This "vignette" in the *Memorabilia* can be read as a reaction to the accusation that Socrates taught his companions to treat their parents and other relatives with contempt (I.ii.49–50). Cf. Aristoph. *Nub.* 1312, where Socratic education has led Pheidippides to beat his father and claim that he was right to do so. On the Lamprocles episode, see Chapter Three Section 4.

ΣΩ. Καταμεμάθηκας οὖν τοὺς τί ποιοῦντας τὸ ὄνομα τοῦτο ἀποκαλοῦσιν;
ΛΑ. Ἔγωγ', ἔφη· τοὺς γὰρ εὖ παθόντας, ὅταν δυνάμενοι χάριν ἀποδοῦναι μὴ ἀποδῶσιν, ἀχαρίστους καλοῦσιν.

Look here, my boy, you know that there are some people who are called *ἀχάριστος*?—Yes, of course, said the boy.—Are you clear about what it is that people do to earn this name?—Yes, I am, he said. *People are called ungrateful when they have been well treated and could show χάρις in return, but don't.*[144]

Being a good boy, Lamprocles displays his command of social *etiquette*: ἀχάριστοι is what you call people who fail to return a favor (ὅταν (...) χάριν ἀποδοῦναι μὴ ἀποδῶσιν) after having received good treatment (εὖ παθόντας), despite being capable of doing so (δυνάμενοι ... ἀποδοῦναι).[145] The underlying standard is hardly implicit: one should respond to good treatment by "giving back" χάρις. It is a straightforward definition with nothing problematic about it.

However, let us look back at the three cases of isomorphism set out at the beginning of this chapter. If the norm of χάρις is that one ought to "give back" χάρις, what then was so wrong with the Grumbler who dared to express his displeasure about having to pay back a loan and "owing χάρις on top"? If "giving back χάρις" is precisely what a person needs to do if he is not to be called an ἀχάριστος, the Grumbler seems to be playing by the rules: he shows awareness that he owes his friends χάρις.

There is an awkward tension between the moral imperative of reciprocating χάρις and the idea that χάρις cannot be reduced to a mere returning of a favor—a tension that not only is manifest in our ancient sources, but that also puzzles modern commentators. David Konstan, for instance, argues for semantically separating χάρις in the sense of the emotion "gratitude" (in collocation with εἰδέναι or ἔχειν) and χάρις in the sense of "favor" that needs to be returned:[146]

---

144 Xenophon, *Memorabilia* II.ii.1–2; *transl.* Tredennick & Waterfield (1990) *adapt.*

145 The addition that these people refrain from reciprocating *in spite of* their being δυνάμενος is a necessary condition for a qualification as ἀχάριστος. It is this notion of capacity that allows for a conceptualization of *all* φιλία-relationships in terms of reciprocity including those relationships that may be regarded assymetrical in terms of power and wealth. Elsewhere, Xenophon introduces the notion of reciprocating καδδύναμιν, "according to one's capacity", as a guiding principle in social and religious exchange (*Mem.* I.iii.3). See Chapters Three, Six and Seven for the implications of reciprocating according to desert.

146 Cf. Konstan (2000), 3–4, where a contradiction is assumed between "reciprocity and obligation" on the one hand and on the other hand the Aristotelian requirement that *philia*

[Text 18]

> Whereas Greeks of the classical period demanded and repaid *kharis* (or a *kharis*) in the sense of the good turn deserved by another (…), the terms for asking or paying back are never found in connection with *kharin ekhein* or *eidenai*. The emotion of gratitude is distinct from the act of reciprocation: *it is felt, not due as compensation*. The sentiment of course sustains the social system of reciprocity, but has its own grammar and role. *Gratitude is never owed*.[147]

As we have seen in Section 2.2 above, such separation is unnecessary and not desirable, for it obscures that the χάρις felt ("gratitude") is *the same* as the χάρις due and the χάρις returned. χάρις *is* owed, by gods, by humans, by members of a community, by friends. The solution is not cutting up χάρις into, on the one hand, an isolated emotion of gratitude which supposedly is the foundation of friendship and on the other hand a principle of reciprocation that amounts to sordid business. Rather, we should see the problem for what it is: a problem of isomorphism.

χάρις-reciprocity resembles disembedded exchange, the *tit-for-tat* and *quid-pro-quo* that one finds outside a χάρις-relationship: at the market, at the banker's table, in the harbor. χάρις-reciprocity resembles those exchanges without being completely reducible to them. The crucial difference lies in the nature of obligation. It is in this aspect, the paradoxical nature of obligation, that the concept of χάρις is challenged by the availability of alternative models of mutual obligation such as commercial or contractual exchange. But it is not only challenged: χάρις also finds its articulation in distinction from or in opposition to these alternative models.

3.2 *To See and Not to See:* méconnaissance

In a polemic on the nature of φιλία in Xenophon's *Memorabilia*, David Konstan and Paul Millett appear to choose two opposing positions.[148] Both scholars insist on the importance of reciprocity in φιλία, but operate with different interpretations of the concept:

---

and *kharis* ought to be motivated by a desire to benefit the other. Konstan (1998): "The question of reciprocity exhibits a paradox at the core of the notion of friendship."

147 Konstan (2006), 167.

148 Konstan (1997) devotes a section Friends and finance (78–82) to a reaction to Millett (1991a). Moreover, Millett (1996) also serves as a point of departure for Konstan (1996).

[Text 19]

> But *beneath the surface politeness* was *the calculating attitude* that comes across in the scenes from the *Memorabilia* summarized above. In choosing friends, primary considerations were willingness and ability to repay services in full.[149]

[Text 20]

> (...) the generosity of friends is *imagined as uncoerced and spontaneous*: instead of being motivated by a sense of debt, *philoi* are *presumed to act out of an altruistic desire* to be of benefit to each other.[150]

Millett adduces Xenophon's *Memorabilia* as evidence for his thesis that φιλία is equivalent to an exchange relationship based on balanced or generalized reciprocity. Konstan, on the other hand, attempts to eliminate every element of instrumentality from Xenophontic φιλία-relationships, claiming that friendly acts are primarily motivated by the altruistic desire to benefit the other.[151]

On closer inspection, these quotations represent two interpretations that need not exclude one another. Both approaches assume different levels of analysis and different coexisting perspectives on the nature of friendship and the obligations involved. Millett takes an external point of view and distinguishes between a "surface politeness" of friends and an underlying "calculating attitude"; Konstan's formulation is cautious in that it leaves room for a level of reality beyond *perceived* behavior ("are *presumed* to act out of an altruistic desire") without making any claims about the intentions themselves.[152] The

149 Millett (1991a), 118.

150 Konstan (1997), 81. Cf. Konstan (2018), chapter 3: "The economy of love and gratitude is not that of reciprocity."

151 Konstan (1997), 12: "Friendship is commonly assumed, both today and in antiquity (...), to be an expression of uncoerced love or altruism." p. 82: "Friendship in the classical city was not embedded in relations of economic exchange (however informal in comparison to the modern market) any more than it was entangled in political alliances. It constituted in principle, like modern friendship, a space of personal intimacy and unselfish affection distinct from the norms regulating public and commercial life." Konstan (2000), 3–4 on the Aristotelian definitions of *kharis* and *philia* in terms of benefiting the other: "a description that should give pause to those who interpret *kharis* and indeed *philia* itself as based exclusively on reciprocity and obligation." However, in Konstan (2006), 170–171, Konstan notes that the affective side of friendship in the Greek classical polis remains controversial (in spite of his earlier work).

152 Cf. Konstan (2000), 2, for a more acute formulation: "It is important to recognize that

two approaches diverge over the question of which level or perspective has more reality: Millett is reductionist in dismissing other-regarding behavior as "surface politeness", on the level of presentation, assuming that the "calculating attitude" has more reality;[153] Konstan leaves aside whether friendship may *also* involve calculation and instrumentality, but insists that friends themselves believe in the sincerity of each other's altruistic motivation, lending more reality to the altruistic quality of motivation.[154]

The disagreement boils down to divergent understandings of the nature of reciprocity and reciprocal obligation. Just like Euthyphro who was uncomfortable with the idea of reductionism, modern and ancient authors alike struggle with the nature of reciprocity in friendships and gift-giving. Aristotle's definition of χάρις in the *Rhetoric*, for instance, is careful not to collapse χάρις into a blatant *quid pro quo*-exchange:[155]

[Text 21]

> ἔστω δὴ χάρις, καθ' ἣν ὁ ἔχων λέγεται χάριν ὑπουργεῖν δεομένῳ μὴ ἀντί τινος, μηδ' ἵνα τι αὐτῷ ὑπουργοῦντι, ἀλλ' ἵνα ἐκείνῳ τι·
>
> Let χάρις, in the sense that one is said to "have χάρις," be [defined as] a service to one in need, *not in return for anything nor that* the one rendering the service may get anything but as something for the recipient.[156]

Aristotle emphatically defines χάρις in terms of other-regarding behavior: to qualify as an act of χάρις, a favor should be neither merely a reaction to a preceding favor (ἀντί τινος), nor intended (ἵνα) to obtain a return.[157] Still, as Aristotle is more than ready to recognize elsewhere, there always *is* an expectation of return,

---

altruism is not, in the first instance, a question about behavior but rather about the interpretation of behavior."

153 On reductionism, see Chapter Four.

154 On the egoism/altruism-dilemma, see Chapter Five.

155 See Chapter Four Section 3.

156 Ar. *Rhet.* 1385a17–19; *transl.* Kennedy (1991).

157 Cf. Dem. DK 68b 96: χαριστικὸς οὐχ ὁ βλέπων πρὸς τὴν ἀμοιβήν, ἀλλ' ὁ εὖ δρᾶν προηιρημένος. "The generous person is not he who looks to a return, but rather he who treats another well by choice." βλέπων (χάρις requires perception!), "looking at" or "*aiming* at", defines being χαριστικός in terms of motivation, προηρημένος in terms of choice. Cf. fr. 229. Konstan (2000), 6.

[Text 22]

> ἡ δ' ἠθικὴ οὐκ ἐπὶ ῥητοῖς, ἀλλ' ὡς φίλῳ δωρεῖται ἢ ὁτιδήποτε ἄλλο· κομίζεσθαι δὲ ἀξιοῖ τὸ ἴσον ἢ πλέον, ὡς οὐ δεδωκὼς ἀλλὰ χρήσας·
>
> The type based on character does not operate on stated terms, but presents are given, or whatever else it may be, as to a friend; yet the giver expects to come away with an equal amount, or more, *on the basis that it was not a gift he made but a loan* (…).[158]

—an expectation that effectively turns a gift into a loan.[159] This, in a nutshell, is the Paradox of the Gift:[160]

[Text 23]

> For there to be a gift, there must be no reciprocity, return, exchange, counter gift, debt. If the other *gives* me *back* or *owes* me or has to give me back what I give him or her, there will not have been a gift.[161]

If gifts call for a return, then upon the return the debt is discharged, and the gift will have disappeared. If friendship is all about reciprocity, good turns cancel each other out and the friendship itself becomes inexplicable. Where is the χάρις in this?

The paradox is a paradox of perspective—or rather, of the difficulty of allowing two coexisting perspectives on reciprocity without privileging one as more real than the other. On the one hand there is the perspective of the external observer capable of counting and keeping track: for him, giving and lending are materially identical. On the other hand, there is the analytic perspective of the participants, from within the succesful interaction, who *experience* χάρις, i.e. who experience "uncoerced and spontaneous" behavior, who perceive altruistic motives in the other's behavior.

To see how this works, let us briefly go back to the anthropological textbook definitions of "generalized reciprocity."[162] Generalized reciprocity:

---

158 Ar. *NE* VIII.xiii (1162b31–b33); *transl.* Broadie & Rowe (2002).

159 See for both Aristotelian passages Chapter Four Section 3.

160 See also Chapter Four Section 3.

161 Derrida (1997), 128.

162 See Introduction.

[Text 24]

> (…) includes a system of giving things *without taking account of how much* was given, with the assumption that at some time in *the undefined future something* will be given back.[163]

This definition is an attempt to do the virtually impossible: to capture the experiential insiders' perspective from the analytical outside. To accommodate the experiential perspective, the description contains (at least) four "vague" components: the value of the initial gift or favor is not precisely recorded; the assumption of a return is not formalized into a contractual or otherwise objective obligation; the timespan between prestation and counterprestation is left undefined; and the nature of the counterprestation is undetermined.

What is the function of these indeterminacies? Why is it important to *not* count, *not* record and *not* define? An external observer, e.g. an anthropologist, who only has access to the material manifestations of reciprocity, may observe that within the time span of, say, a couple of years, the favors (help in moving house, drives to the airport, baby-sitting, assistance with filling in tax forms) between a group of adult friends amount to a net result close to neutral: within a stable group of friends, each friend's prestations approximately counterbalance the favors he has received from others. But there is a discrepancy between this analytical perception, from the external viewpoint, and the experience of the participants, the friends, who refuse to see matters this way. They feel that this "reckoning of debts" somehow wipes out the fact that they are doing these things "for free", "for the sake of the other" and "because they are friends"—they may even believe that these acts are "altruistic", because they do not demand immediate returns and leave it to the initiative of the other to decide if and when they are willing to reciprocate their kindness.

However, after a while, these friends become aware of the fact that one of them *never* offers any favors, whereas in the course of years they have all helped him move house, helped him paint his house, stood by him during the painful break-up with his girlfriend and repeatedly invited him to dinner. Now his life seems fairly stabilized and his problems are solved—and he still does not do anything for his friends. His friends feel that he is a sponger, who has "taken advantage of them", and, under these circumstances, finally concede that the external observer does have a point: of course, they do expect *something* in return for their kind favors. The same friends who fiercely objected against the

163 Wilk & Cliggett (2007), 162.

anthropologist's blind spot for their altruistic motives, now all of a sudden feel that their sponger friend has violated an objective Law of Friendship.

Are these friends incoherent? Or did they just *change perspective*? I adopt the latter approach: when the χάρις disappears from the exchange, the friends relapse into an outsider's position and adopt an analytical point of view on their past exchanges. What started out with a light-hearted and cheerful "don't mention it" has now turned into overt counting, keeping track, defining. This would probably also be the verdict of the observing anthropologist, who turns out to be Marshall Sahlins, the architect of the threefold typology of reciprocity that lies behind the textbook definition of T24:[164]

[Text 25]

> "Generalized reciprocity" refers to transactions that are *putatively altruistic*, transactions on the line of assistance given and, if possible and necessary, assistance returned. (…)—the expectation of direct material return is unseemly. *At best it is implicit. The material side of the transaction is repressed by the social: reckoning of debts outstanding cannot be overt and is typically left out of account*. This is not to say that handing over things in such forms, even to "loved ones," generates no counterobligation.[165]

The function of vaguenesses, the indeterminacies of time, quantity and quality, is precisely to sustain the participant's experience of "the social" or of "altruism"—*in defiance of* the material truth accessible to the external observer who is capable of registering the fact that prestations within generalized reciprocity do generate counterobligations. The participant's experience involves an entire system of social meaning that to an external observer can only be accounted for in terms of "vagueness" and "indeterminacy."[166]

It all boils down to the fundamental discrepancy between internal focalization, i.e. the perception of participants, and the perspective of the external observer.[167] In Pierre Bourdieu's terms: there is an irreconcilable discrepancy

164 See Introduction.

165 Sahlins (1972), 193.

166 Note that in Sahlins' definition too, the external perspective is still privileged as a higher reality (e.g. "putatively altruistic"). See also Chapter Four Section 3.

167 Bourdieu (1990 [1980]), 105: "[E]ven if reciprocity is the 'objective' truth of the discrete acts that ordinary experience knows in discrete form and associates with the idea of a gift, *it is perhaps not the whole truth* of a practice that could not exist if its subjective truth coincided perfectly with its 'objective' truth." (my emphasis).

between the perception of agents, or actors, in reciprocal exchanges, who construct reciprocity in time on the one hand, and the omniscient, omnipresent spectator on the other hand who attempts to "objectify" the phenomenon of reciprocity by detemporalizing its mechanics and turning reciprocity into a cycle of reversible practices.[168] Assuming the position of an external observer means excluding the element of time from the workings of reciprocity and to neglect the elements of improvisation and uncertainty that make the "social efficacy" of the little gifts and gestures of ordinary life.[169]

Explanations of social behavior that fail to take improvisation and uncertainty, the effects of time, into account will not be capable of explaining the strategic and interpretative moments in social interaction. Assuming "objective" rules of reciprocity is tantamount to collapsing the difference between a gift, a loan and a swap:

[Text 26]

> In every society it may be observed that, if it is not to constitute an insult, the counter-gift must be deferred and different, because the immediate return of an exactly identical object clearly amounts to a refusal. *Thus gift exchange is opposed to swapping, which, like the theoretical model of the cycle of reciprocity, telescopes gift and counter-gift into the same instant.* It is also opposed to lending, in which the return of the loan, explicitly guaranteed by a legal act, is in a sense already performed at the very moment when a contract is drawn up ensuring the predictability and calculability of the acts it prescribes.[170]

Giving, lending and swapping or paying all amount to the same when the unfolding of time is denied its meaning, when time is "telescoped". It is time that prevents the reduction of the participants' experience to the "objective" truth constructed by the external observer that from a material point of view gift exchange, swapping and lending amount to the same net effect. Interval serves as "an instrument of denial"[171] for agents who must "refuse to know" the objective truth of their exchanges:

---

168 Bourdieu (1990 [1980]), 105. See also Chapter Four Section 3.

169 Bourdieu (1990 [1980]), 99.

170 Bourdieu (1990 [1980]), 105.

171 Bourdieu (1990 [1980]), 107. Davidson (2007), 41 paraphrases *méconnaissance* as "a functional hypocrisy". Both Bourdieu and Davidson are, in the ultimate analysis, reductionistic in privileging the observer's perception as more real than the participants' experience. See Chapter Four Section 3.

[Text 27]

> If the system is to work, the agents *must not be entirely unaware of the truth* of their exchanges, which is made explicit in the anthropologist's model, while at the same time *they must refuse to know it and above all to recognize it.*[172]

It is this element of misrecognition, *méconnaissance*, that enables the partners of a long-term relationship to maintain that a gift is a gift, a favor a favor, and generosity is uncoerced.[173] Therefore, acts of reciprocation, i.e. returning χάρις, are not to be confused with compensation in a commercial sense of obligation. Whereas objectively, i.e. in terms of the material manifestations, "debts" may resemble the obligations incurred by gifts or favors received, from the point of view of the participants in such long-term relationships they are distinct.[174] Debts are burdensome and paying them off a relief. By contrast, within the framework and expectations of a long-term relationship, the same acts are not perceived as inflicting and settling debts, but as a mutual conferring of favors, manifestations of gracefulness and expressions of gratification.

Let us look once again at the χάρις-script and see where perception comes in:

(1) *A brings B a* χάρις, a "favor." A favor should be seen as distinct from a commercial, competitive or hostile allocation, e.g. because it is "uncoerced," "gratuitous," "without expecting a return," "because of B *himself* and not in order to gain something." A "misrecognizes" his expectation of return and, perhaps, of the fact that he felt obliged to do the favor.

(2) *B accepts and recognizes A's action as* χάρις, by ostensibly *not* experiencing χάρις as a debt (misrecognition, e.g. by reacting cheerfully and by postponing mentioning the return), by ostensibly *not* taking account of quantities (misrecognition, e.g. by stressing the unique quality of the χάρις).

(3) *B reciprocates A's* χάρις, not by *compensation* or *retribution*, but by bringing a χάρις himself, a favor that should be seen as distinct from redeeming debts, e.g. because it is "uncoerced", "gratuitous", "without expecting a

---

172 Bourdieu (1977), 6.

173 Bourdieu's analysis applies not only to gift exchange in the sense of exchange of material concrete gifts, but to every transaction that involves a generalization of reciprocity over a longer time span: the generalized exchange of care, help and sustenance work along the same lines.

174 Brandt (1974) draws a similar distinction between two types of obligations.

return", "because of A *himself* and not in order to redeem debts", "because he appreciates A", "because he rejoices in his bond with A". This way, B "misrecognizes" that his χάρις is a reaction to A's antecedent χάρις.

The entire script is premised on perception. χάρις can only circulate when it is, time and again, perceived and acknowledged—at the expense of the perception of other elements that are present in the exchange. Without internal focalization there is no charm, attraction or pleasure in the exchange; focalized from the point of view of successful interaction one misrecognizes the burden of indebtedness. Without internal focalization there are no gifts or favors, only objects and services; from the point of view of successful interaction things cease to have a price. Without internal focalization things are given *back*; from the point of view of successful interaction, χάρις is not given back, but given *again*. To "know" χάρις means to not-know something else.

χάρις-talk is performative language. In order to see χάρις, we must adopt the participants' focalization and be ready to approach things from the vantage point of successful interaction, for χάρις is in the eye of the beholder and everyone involved needs to participate for χάρις to work. Making an effort to see the beautiful may eventually be the same as making an effort *not* to see another truth, the inconvenient truth expressed by Carion, Socrates and the Grumbler who, by adopting a detached external point of view to χάρις-exchanges, made χάρις disappear from the analysis.

4 Conflicts and Cynicism

The phenomena of perception and *méconnaissance* have serious implications for the assessment of our sources of classical conceptualizations of χάρις. Imagine an anthropologist in the remote future who is burdened with the mission impossible of reconstructing 20th-century Western European conceptions of marriage, whereby the only sources available are transcripts of divorce papers. On the basis of the available data, the anthropologist may arrive at the conclusion that 20th-century Western European marriage was little more than a legal transaction between two people who decide to start a joint enterprise. The anthropologist may be shocked by the instrumentalist tenor of his sources: there is little sign of generosity and commitment in these papers, let alone of love, and there are no manifestations of other-regarding behavior.

Clearly, it is the nature of the source that results in love, generosity and commitment being left out of the picture. Divorce papers are drawn up the moment the marriage is effectively over. It basically presents us with a *retrospective* analysis of the efforts and the prestations of the partners during their marriage. This is typically a situation in which vaguenesses and indeterminacies are wiped out and the consensual misrecognition of the material reality that has so long sustained the relationship between the partners has collapsed. Because there are no prospects of continuing their reciprocity *and* because the situation forces them to talk precisely about the material side of the preceding transactions, the ex-spouses switch into a calculating mode as if they were external observers keeping track of the balance sheets.

An ancient analog for divorce drama is the *agôn* of Jason and Medea in Euripides' *Medea*.[175] In a compelling 2001 article, Melissa Mueller offers a reading of the two conflicting worldviews underlying the marital conflict. Jason's use of the language of commerce (his consistent talk about "gain," "profit," "need" and the "better deal")[176] sharply contrasts with Medea who appeals to their pre-existing marriage in terms of χάρις, of doing good turns (including sexual ones) to and fro.[177] However, *both* spouses are painfully explicit in their "precise reckoning of the balance of favors":[178] Medea in her catalog of favors to Jason (saving his life, murdering Pelias, abandoning her family and home),[179] and Jason in recalculating the true extent of Medea's χάρις to him, which he dismisses as "exaggerated" (λίαν πυργοῖς χάριν),[180] because in reality it was Aphrodite who had saved him, not Medea.

[Text 28]

ἀλλ' οὐκ ἀκριβῶς αὐτὸ θήσομαι λίαν·
ὅπηι γὰρ οὖν ὤνησας οὐ κακῶς ἔχει.
μείζω γε μέντοι τῆς ἐμῆς σωτηρίας
εἴληφας ἢ δέδωκας, ὡς ἐγὼ φράσω.
πρῶτον (...)
τοσαῦτα μέν σοι τῶν ἐμῶν πόνων πέρι
ἔλεξ'·

175 On φιλία in marriage: Gill (1996), 166–170, Goldhill (1984), 111–131, (1986) 79–106, Konstan (1997), 53–67.

176 E.g. Medea's exile as "completely a gain" (πᾶν κέρδος, 454), and "not lacking in material resources" (μήτ' ἀχρήμων, 461).

177 Medea about "the benefits received" from her (ταῦθ' ὑφ' ἡμῶν παθών, 498), "favors brought to" Jason (σοὶ χάριν φέρουσα, 508).

178 Mueller (2001), 477.

179 Eur. *Med.* 475–491.

180 Eur. *Med.* 526.

> Jason: No, *I will not make too strict a reckoning on this point*. So far as you did *help* me, *you did well*. But *in return for* saving me *you got more than you gave*, as I shall make clear. *First*, (…) Thus far I have spoken to you *regarding my labors*.[181]

Notwithstanding his disclaimer ("I shall not make too exact an entry of the item," ἀκριβῶς αὐτὸ θήσομαι λίαν, probably accounting terminology),[182] Jason actually does embark on a counter calculation of the marital economy of χάρις. In a very qualified sense (ὅπῃ ὤνησας), Medea has not done too badly (οὐ κακῶς ἔχει, a bit of a stingy litotic complement), but the marital ledger shows that Medea has been more on the receiving end in their marriage (μείζω … εἴληφας ἢ δέδωκας)—something that Jason will demonstrate in systematic and orderly fashion (πρῶτον …), in a catalog of Jason's "labors" (τῶν ἐμῶν πόνων πέρι). (A dubiously smug argument follows, about the gain of living in the civilized Greek world.)[183]

Mueller rightly notes that Jason's "language of profit and gain directly violates the code of silence regarding the balancing of favors between friends,"[184] the "code of silence" being the willful misrecognition (*méconnaissance*) of the marital ledger. But how should one interpret this violation adopted by both marital partners? Central to Mueller's analysis is that both Jason and Medea navigate between two different "incommensurable" concepts of φιλία: kinship φιλία (a φιλία type that allows for hierarchical reciprocity) and aristocratic φιλία (that notionally assumes social equality between φίλοι). On this reading, being "explicit about the content of the *charis* exchanged is problematic" for both Jason and Medea, for their self-presentation as aristocratic φίλοι.

As discussed earlier in this chapter, there is an undeniable social dimension to the use of χάρις-vocabulary: χαρίεις people are people who "know grace", with the style and class that legitimates their position as upper-class persons.[185] Blatantly cataloging good turns is not chic, but the kind of rude behavior that one would expect from the nouveau riche. However, how much of this is social characterization and how much is a (realistic) dramatization of two irreconcilable perspectives on a marriage turned sour and on χάρις that has vanished? Both partners engage in a retrospective interpretation of what was once χάρις by making the terms of their relationship explicit, each according to his/her own

181 Eur. *Med.* 532–546; *transl.* Kovacs (1994).
182 Mastronarde (2002), ad loc.
183 Eur. *Med.* 536–544.
184 Mueller (2001), 476.
185 See Section 2.4 above.

vision and interests. The *agôn* dramatizes the contrast between the point of view of a man who is making up a balance sheet because his marriage is effectively over, and the point of view of a woman who contests the assumption of the possibility that the marriage can be terminated and whose strategy consists in emphasizing the irredeemable nature of her husband's indebtedness.

Therefore, a full understanding of χάρις requires assessing our sources, not only taking into account their referential and rhetorical context, but also accounting for issues of perspective. Important preliminary questions are:

- Who is **focalizing?**
  - **External focalization:** an external observer who analyzes the overt/objective mechanisms of reciprocal exchange. This can be either an "objective" observer or a participant who has switched into analytical mode.
  - **Internal focalization:** character focalization, from the point of view of the participants who have access to non-overt aspects of reciprocal exchange, such as emotions, attitudes and dispositions.
- What is the **temporal perspective?**[186]
  - **A *vision par derrière*:** a temporal point of view that regards χάρις-exchanges as completed events in the past.
  - **A *vision avec*:** a point of view from which χάρις-exchanges are incomplete and χάρις is seen as an ongoing process.

4.1 *Temporal Perspective: Balance Sheets*

If we take these preliminary questions into account, it becomes apparent that it is misguided to understand ancient Greek φιλία as an utterly "objective" or "contractual" relationship,[187] if we do so on the basis of complaints of disappointed friends. Disappointed friends have a *vision par derrière*: they see their friendship, in retrospect, as a balance sheet with unpaid bills.

Take, for instance, the Theognidean lyric subject (T15 above), to whom unreciprocated good turns amount to "χάρις in vain". This does seem to betray a "blatantly pragmatic approach".[188] Yet this does not reflect a utilitarian or dis-

---

186 This has implications for the aspectual difference between χαρίζεσθαι (present aspect) and χαρίσασθαι (aorist aspect). See Chapter Five.

187 Heath (1987), 3–4: "[*Philia*] is not, at root, a subjective bond of affection and emotional warmth, but the entirely objective bond of reciprocal obligation." Donlan (1980), 14. For a reconciliation between the formalist ("instrumentalist") approach of ancient friendship with a position that recognizes affective elements, see Goldhill (1986), 82 who speaks about "complex obligations, duties and claims." Cf. Raccanelli (1998), 20. Both Millett (1991) and Konstan (1997), but esp. (2006), seem to be proponents of a "layered" approach of φιλία (Konstan (1997) uses the term "overdetermination").

188 Scott (1984), 2.

enchanted worldview generalizable to an "ancient Greek mentality", let alone a *Zeitgeist* or a *Volksgeist*. Rather "futile χάρις" expresses an evaluation of a particular case of χάρις, conceived of as closed (and hence concrete) events. Frustrated expectations are made explicit, because the friendship is seen from the *vision par derrière* of a negative experience, voiced, moreover, by a teacher who intends to expose the mechanisms of reciprocity in terms of "objective rules". In unsuccessful interactions, the difference between χάρις and market reciprocity collapses.

At the same time, contrasting *deiloi* friends with an ideal case of friendship, the text hints at the social norms that do demarcate χάρις-exchange from exchanges that are motivated by profit seeking. The better the friendship, the more charitable the interpreter can be and the less concrete χάρις needs to be, up to the point that even if one of the friends is not yet capable of returning the favor, the bond is not seriously at risk. As long as it is clear that he still "knows the favor" (χάριν εἰδέναι), there still is χάρις. Conversely, *deiloi* are immediately resentful after one single failure on the part of the friend because they approach friendship as a one-off interaction, as *tit-for-tat* (like commerce), and thereby reveal their insatiable mind (ἄπληστον νόον).

Another instructive example of the effect of temporal perspective occurs in Socrates' conversation with his friend Aristarchus.[189] In this context, again, the mechanisms of reciprocity that sustain φιλία-relationships are discussed from the vantage point of ἀχαριστία, i.e. from the point of view of a disturbed reciprocity (*vision par derrière*). Due to the upheavals during the Peloponnesian war, an exodus to the Peiraeus has taken place causing a great number of female relatives to seek shelter and sustenance with Aristarchus. As Aristarchus' land has been confiscated by enemies, he has lost his primary source of income, spending his days in utter desperation over his lack of means and the many mouths he has to feed. Socrates' advice is to seek a different source of income in a speech that reveals an implicit "pathology" of a disturbed reciprocal relationship:

[Text 29]

> ἀλλὰ καὶ νῦν μέν, ὡς ἐγῷμαι, οὔτε σὺ ἐκείνας φιλεῖς οὔτ' ἐκεῖναι σέ, σὺ μὲν ἡγούμενος αὐτὰς ἐπιζημίους εἶναι σεαυτῷ, ἐκεῖναι δὲ σὲ ὁρῶσαι ἀχθόμενον ἐφ' ἑαυταῖς· ἐκ δὲ τούτων κίνδυνος μείζω τε ἀπέχθειαν γίγνεσθαι καὶ τὴν προγεγονυῖαν χάριν μειοῦσθαι.

189 Xen. *Mem.* II.vii.

> As things are, I suppose, *there is no* φιλία *lost between you*: you feel that they are *imposing* upon you; *they can see* that you are annoyed with them; and consequently there is a danger that the *ill-feeling* will grow and *the former* χάρις *decline.*[190]

The diagnosis is lucid: in a situation of poverty and lack of viable prospects, the normal mechanisms of reciprocal well-doing are blocked, and the χάρις disappears. This changes the way both parties perceive each other: they no longer *see* the situation *in terms of* (ἡγεῖσθαι) χάρις. Aristarchus is no longer able to express commitment (φιλεῖς) towards his female relatives, who *see* that (ὁρῶσαι); their former χάρις makes way for a sense of irritation (ἀπέχθεια). Socrates predicts that in the face of destitution, where there is no prospect of return of favors, exchanges will be reframed into less favorable terminology: favors (χάρις) and commitment (φιλία) turn into material loss or damage (ἐπιζήμίοι), whereas gratitude turns into a sense of indebtedness that breeds annoyance (ἀπέχθεια).

This reveals an interesting theory of χάρις on Socrates' part—a theory that takes into account the effects of perception, of *seeing-as*, and, perhaps, of *not-seeing*. As long as the turntaking structure remains intact, participants are capable of viewing χάρις as an ongoing process that calls for continuous reinterpretation of mutual exchange acts. As long as exchanges are seen as not-yet-completed (there will always be an act of reciprocation), participants are capable of upholding *méconnaissance*: there is no balance sheet. However, in the absence of viable prospects, the temporal dynamics of exchange are brought to a halt, and the carefully sustained *méconnaissance* collapses. Previous exchanges are viewed as closed events, and the calculating begins. Obligations and expectations that hitherto remained implicit become, retrospectively, objectified—whereas in a healthy relationship, there is no such thing as a *final* bill, and partners silently agree on concealing the balance sheets.

The remedy Socrates has to offer is equally lucid: Aristarchus should force a breakthrough in the situation by creating means of generating income. Aristarchus should borrow capital to make a start with a little wool manufacturing workplace:

190 Xen. *Mem.* II.vii.9; *transl.* Tredennick & Waterfield (1990).

[Text 30]

> ἐὰν δὲ προστατήσῃς ὅπως ἐνεργοὶ ὦσι, σὺ μὲν ἐκείνας φιλήσεις, ὁρῶν ὠφελίμους σεαυτῷ οὔσας, ἐκεῖναι δὲ σὲ ἀγαπήσουσιν, αἰσθόμεναι χαίροντά σε αὐταῖς, τῶν δὲ προγεγονυιῶν εὐεργεσιῶν ἥδιον μεμνημένοι τὴν ἀπ' ἐκείνων χάριν αὐξήσετε, καὶ ἐκ τούτων φιλικώτερόν τε καὶ οἰκειότερον ἀλλήλοις ἕξετε.
>
> But if you encourage them to work, *you will φιλεῖν them, when you see that they are doing something for you*, and they will like you *when they realize that you are pleased with them*; and as you both *remember former acts of kindness with greater pleasure*, you will *increase the χάρις* aroused by these acts with the result that the *relations between you will become cordial and intimate*.[191]

Once everyone is back to work relationships can be restored. *Because* Aristarchus is back in a position in which he can benefit his relatives, and *because* the relatives finally have the opportunity to do something in return, there is an increase of overall χάρις; *because* the women are reciprocating with benefits, Aristarchus is able to φιλεῖν them again. On the whole, commitment and the mutual sense of relatedness will be strengthened (καὶ ἐκ τούτων φιλικώτερόν τε καὶ οἰκειότερον ἀλλήλοις ἕξετε), and sustained by positive emotions (ἀγαπήσουσιν, χαίροντά). The changed situation allows for a more favorable perception—hence the emphatic use of verbs of perception (ὁρῶσι, ὁρῶν, αἰσθόμεναι), as well as words referring to pleasant experiences. When being reminded of one's obligation to the other is a pleasant experience (ἥδιον μεμνημένοι) there is χάρις in the exchange (χαίροντα).

The Aristarchus episode demonstrates not only the vital importance of the mechanism of reciprocal benefit for the continuation of φιλία-relationships; it also demonstrates that framing an exchange in terms of χάρις entails *not* seeing things: concealing balance sheets and suspending the final bill—a feature that demarcates φιλία-reciprocity from seemingly isomorphous ephemeral *quid pro quo*-exchanges in which every single time the accounts need to be balanced.[192]

4.2 *Focalization: Cynicism*

External focalization similarly affects the extent to which χάρις is made concrete and explicit. A well-known example is the phrase "to demand back χάρις"

---

191 Xen. *Mem.* II.vii.9.5; *transl.* Tredennick & Waterfield (1990).

192 On the potentially ironic ending of the dialog, see Chapter Six.

and its variations. As David Konstan has aptly noted,[193] the oratorical record displays a repertory of phrases that explicitly propagate the obligation to make "restitution": one "demands back" χάρις for services performed,[194] "repays"[195] or "owes it",[196] sometimes even in a "payment".[197] Here, χάρις is framed in a Debtor Paradigm of Obligation,[198] where obligations are reduced to debts, givers to creditors, recipients to debtors—formulations that leave little room for vagueness and misrecognition.[199] In third-person perspectives and hindsight analysis, χάρις is said to be "owed" as a debt when it is due. Hence, these texts *are* cynical:[200] they are disenchanting in reducing χάρις entirely to debt, denying the reality of uncoerced generosity, favors and gifts free from expectations.[201]

In these situations, the concept of χάρις itself is subjected to analysis and, hence, is focalized not from within a successful interaction, but from an **external point of view.** External focalization is applied either in didactic contexts where a detached observer (an anthropologist, philosopher, didactic poet) purports to offer an objective analysis of overt behavior, or in contexts of problematic interactions, i.e. disagreements and conflict situations, where participants attempt to maneuver themselves in the position of an external observer and to objectify the situation in terms of concrete observable outstanding debts. The resulting descriptions of reciprocal relationships strike us as cynical.

A notorious example is Pericles' eulogy of Athenian χάρις:

[Text 31]

> καὶ τὰ ἐς ἀρετὴν ἐνηντιώμεθα τοῖς πολλοῖς· οὐ γὰρ πάσχοντες εὖ, ἀλλὰ δρῶντες κτώμεθα τοὺς φίλους. βεβαιότερος δὲ ὁ δράσας τὴν χάριν ὥστε ὀφειλομένην δι' εὐνοίας ᾧ δέδωκε σῴζειν· ὁ δὲ ἀντοφείλων ἀμβλύτερος, εἰδὼς οὐκ ἐς χάριν,

193 Konstan (2006), 166.

194 ἀπαιτεῖν, e.g. Lys. 18.23, 18.27, 21.25.

195 ἀποδιδόναι, e.g. Lys. 18.27.

196 ὀφείλειν, e.g. Soph., *Ant.* 331, Isoc. 18.67, Xen. *Cyr.* 3.2.30, Dem. 4.4.

197 τιμή, e.g. Lys. 25.6; ἀποτίνειν, Aesch. *Ep.* 4.6.7; τίνειν, Lycophron, *Al.* 1092, Hipp. *Ep.* 27.260.

198 For the Debtor Paradigm of Obligation, see Chapter Three and Four.

199 Cf. Blundell (1989), 29: "The language of debt and repayment is pervasive in Greek discussion of both revenge and friendship."

200 Cf. Bourdieu (1998), 95 on the sociologist's task to unveil the material truth of social action: "(…) a truth of their action, a truth which the sociologist unveils, but at the risk of describing as cynical calculation an act which claims to be disinterested and which must be taken as such, in its lived truth, which the theoretical model must also consider and explain."

201 It is no coincidence that the majority of the places that call for a "restitutive" interpretation of χάρις is to be found in the corpus of the orators—i.e. in judicial contexts which are moments where the relationship in question is already problematic.

> ἀλλ' ἐς ὀφείλημα τὴν ἀρετὴν ἀποδώσων. καὶ μόνοι οὐ τοῦ ξυμφέροντος μᾶλλον λογισμῷ ἢ τῆς ἐλευθερίας τῷ πιστῷ ἀδεῶς τινὰ ὠφελοῦμεν.
>
> We are at variance with most others too in our concept of doing good: we make our friends by conferring benefit rather than receiving it. *The benefactor* is the firmer friend, in that by further *kindness* he will maintain gratitude *in the recipient as a current debt*: *the debtor* is less keen, as he knows that any *return* of generosity will be *something owed*, not appreciated as an independent favor. And we are unique in the way we help others—*no calculation of self-interest, but an act of frank confidence in our freedom.*[202]

The cynicism is inherent in the context: what we see here is the Athenian language of imperialism. Pericles not only gives a detached analysis of the mechanisms of χάρις but also a normative rendering of the relationship between Athens and her allies, as part of an effort to legitimate empire. The Athenians acquire φίλοι by conferring favors instead of receiving them; they give (δέδωκε) and confer benefits (ὠφελοῦμεν) out of goodwill (εὔνοια); they do so not out of calculation of interest (τοῦ ξυμφέροντος λογισμός),[203] but out of trust (τὸ πιστόν) in the liberality (ἐλευθερία) of others, i.e. by having confidence that their excellence (ἀρετή) will be reciprocated (ἀποδίδωμι) by the other who is indebted (ἀντοφείλων, ὀφειλομένην). The moral high ground of the virtuous giver results in political superiority: the giver is a βεβαιότερος friend, which not only implies that a giver has proven himself to be the more reliable friend, but also the one in the stronger position.[204] The *hapax legomenon* ἀντοφείλων ("owing in return"), that strictly speaking is semantically rather redundant, makes explicit not only the idea of indebtedness, but also of indebtedness *as a result of* "lagging behind", i.e. of being the reacting party.[205]

Pericles' perspective is a hybrid. Instructing the Athenian citizenry on how to oblige their allies, he speaks from an external perspective, exposing the political mechanics of indebtedness engineering: recipients of χάρις are debtors. At the same time, he appeals to values and perceptions that belong to the internal perspective: the ban on calculation, the imperative of trust, goodwill and

---

202 Thuc. 2.40.4–5; *transl.* Hammond & Rhodes (2009).

203 Hornblower (1991), 307.

204 Hooker (1974), 169. For the adjective βέβαιος ("steady") qualifying φίλος, cf. Aeschyl. *Prom.* 299. Cf. Thuc. 1.32.1 where the Corcyreans insist that the χάρις of a city seeking alliance must remain βέβαιος.

205 Allison (2001), 63; Hornblower (1991), 307.

liberality—Bourdieu's "instruments of denial". The analytical perspective of *Realpolitik* breaks this "code of silence" as it makes explicit what in the internal perspective ought to remain unsaid. But what exactly is it that ought to remain unsaid, what is being misrecognized? Here we see how χάρις-terminology not only has the potential to misrecognize the **balance** in exchanges, but also the **imbalance** in asymmetrical relations. What once started out as the League's common effort and contribution has been transformed into a reciprocal relationship between Athens and her allies where Athens claims the upper hand.[206] The vocabulary of χάρις serves to render Athens' imperialistic politics as morally legitimate:[207] it transmutes "overt domination" into misrecognized, "socially recognized domination", in other words, *legitimate authority*.[208]

5 Concluding Remarks

Χάρις is grace under pressure. The case of χάρις is illustrative for the mechanisms and norms that are operative in long-term reciprocal relations such as φιλία. Early poetic uses of χάρις-lexemes shape a notion of order that transcends the individual, suggesting a worldview where the reciprocal relationship has logical primacy over the temporary and alternating roles of the participants, and where the ethical and aesthetical coincide. The case of χάρις also shows us how such order has to be won against competing systems of order and valuation: the emphasis on perception and aesthetic quality stipulates a way of perceiving interactions, of *seeing* them *as* full of grace—as opposed to interactions with a mechanics that may resemble χάρις exchange, but that lack those distinct qualities.

The case of χάρις also confronts us with the distorting effects of language: we have seen how the linguistic representation of the "grammar" of exchange and social interaction is distorted in essential respects depending on factors of focalization and temporal perspective. Detached analysis (external focalization) and spiteful retrospection (*vision par derrière*) imply a particular mode of perception, a way of seeing exchanges as discrete and completed events, that

206 This change is described in Thuc. 1.99. See Kallet-Marx (1993), 65–66.

207 Cf. Mitchell (1997), 28–44.

208 See Chapter Six Section 5. Bourdieu (1977), 191–192. This ideal of "Active Partnership", i.e. a moral privileging of the (first) donor, the initiator of χάρις, recurs later in Pericles' speech, when Pericles incites the Athenian citizens to become ἐρασταί of the city and to give away "the finest contribution", κάλλιστον ἔρανον, to it. Thuc. 2.43.1–2. See Sara Monoson (1994).

can be looked upon in an objectifying and quantifying manner and that can be made explicit. This mode of perception is at odds with the workings of χάρις in a fully functional relation, where χάρις is approached as an ongoing process (from a *vision avec*) and interpreted charitably by internally focalizing participants.

From an internal point of view, Carion and the Grumbler, who reduce honorable sex and friendly aid to prostitution and credit, *see* things the wrong way; from the socially detached point of view of Carion and the Grumbler, people give concealing *names* ("euphemisms") to the inconvenient truth that it all comes down to the same thing. Euthyphro, hesitant to concede that "traffic" is the more truthful name for "piety", in any case, thinks it an "ugly" name—but is pulled towards an external perspective by Socrates to analyze the "true" grammar of religious relations. χάρις-talk is performative language, inviting the onlooker, listener or reader to adopt participants' focalization, to make an effort to see and know the χάρις and to make an effort to *not* see another, inconvenient, truth.

This inconvenient truth may come in many guises. Although Bourdieu seems to think that the opposition of gift exchange to swapping and loaning is something universal ("in every society ..."),[209] I do not believe in the universal validity of such claims. Having meaning implies choice. Distinctions and oppositions are only meaningful in specific cultural circumstances: there can only be a ban on establishing value through counting, for instance, when value is countable; "pricelessness" can only be appreciated if there is a price to be transcended in the first place. Similarly, gift exchange can only be meaningfully opposed to lending when formal credit with legal backing is a culturally available option and can only be meaningfully opposed to swapping when the immediate transaction of equivalent values is a current practice. Neither can be taken for granted.[210]

But my argument for the world of the Classical Greek polis is that much of the χάρις-talk that goes on in this period is better understood if we see that here the inconvenient truth, the "objective truth" that needs to be misrecognized

209 T27.

210 This is not to say that before monetization, there was no *méconnaissance* involved in gift exchange, but only that *méconnaissance* had a somewhat different meaning as there were other truths to be misrecognized before the development of market economy. On the "Myth of Barter", i.e. the misunderstanding that barter was a precursor of monetary exchange, see Introduction and Chapter Four. Instantaneous exchange between neutral strangers only became a current and everyday model of exchange with the monetization of the Mediterranean world and the rise of markets.

in order to preserve the χάρις in the exchange, is the truth of disembedded exchanges: the truth of the market, the banker's table, the harbor—a powerful truth to think with, proclaiming that it all comes down to traffic, trade and credit. This is not a universally inconvenient truth, nor a scientifically established "objective" truth behind exchange according to our own modern standards. It simply means that 5th- and 4th-century literary texts, from a diversity of genres and contexts, could reflect, express and appeal to the experience that χάρις-exchanges sometimes resemble disembedded exchanges, to the *awkwardness* of such isomorphism and to a desire to eliminate such isomorphism and to make χάρις-exchanges conceptually "immune" against the market model that seems to force itself upon the situation because it is easy to think with.[211] In other words: these literary texts seem to reflect an articulation of a Hostile Worlds Thesis.[212]

The ultimate historical cause behind such a Hostile Worlds thesis is a complex interplay of political, judicial and economic factors.[213] But from a synchronic point of view, there seems to have been a widespread association, or clustering, of a diversity of phenomena such as credit transactions, paid labor, trade and traffic. With all due qualifications, these phenomena seem to have represented a realm of disembedded exchange in a short-term transactional order, that was in principle morally underdetermined (not good or bad *per se*),[214] but that in situations of isomorphism formed a threat to the conceptualization of the values and bonds of the long-term order. Money occupies an ambiguous position in this conceptual clustering. As we have seen in Chap-

211 The term *méconnaissance* is potentially misleading in sounding deliberate and intentional, smacking of hypocrisy and insincerity, because it seems to presuppose that agents know the truth they are suppressing. This depends on the conception of "knowledge". The knowledge possessed by agents in social interaction is "practical knowledge", i.e. social know-how (analogous to linguistic competence), as opposed to a knowing-that that can be propositionally formulated (analogous to grammatical knowledge). *Méconnaissance* requires a less intentionalist approach of both knowing and not-knowing: an agent that "intentionally" and theoretically "knows" is capable of representing means and ends of the contents of his knowledge; misrecognition is a matter of practical knowledge and agents who "choose" to misrecognize an aspect of a situation without having full access to the reason why they are doing so except from "knowing" that they do the socially appropriate thing. Cf. Gerrans (2005). *Méconnaissance* is deliberate in the sense that it requires effort by the agents: the suppressed material reality is perfectly accessible to the agents of exchange, and it takes effort to suppress it (to remove the price tag from a gift, to *not* compare the value of Christmas gifts etc.).

212 See Introduction.

213 See Chapter One.

214 See Chapter One.

ter One, there is no intrinsic or historical connection between money and the short-term order: money can be given as a gift or a token of honor and hence participate in a long-term order.[215] However, money can, in specific contexts, also become a symbol or a shorthand for the short-term order and become the quintessentially disembedded and promiscuous object.[216]

The literary sources of the Classical period offer us several examples of such a tension between the notion of χάρις and the powerful conceptual model of disembedded obligations. It is in situations where there is a risk of isomorphism, i.e. in contexts where both χάρις and the notions of market exchange are activated, that tacit know-how, implicit social competence, is articulated into social grammar rules. Implicitly, most Athenians "know" that Carion, Socrates and the Grumbler are socially incompetent: the extreme position that χάρις can be entirely reduced to debt is a taboo. However, within the bounds of the socially acceptable, there is room for negotiating the grammar rules and we find our sources explore several strategies of demarcating χάρις and the paradigm of finance and banking.

It is not only on the lexical level that we find a Hostile Worlds attitude. In the next chapters we shall see the Hostile Worlds thesis recur on different levels of analysis: in the conception of a particular relationship, the parent-child bond, where thicker conceptions of obligation are articulated against the push of a Debtor Paradigm of Obligation (Chapter Three); but also in the conception of the Debtor Paradigm itself (Chapter Four), of the utility of friends (Chapter Five), the value of Active Partnership (Chapter Six) and the value of value itself (Chapter Seven).

We started this chapter with Aristotle's testimony of the civic function of χάρις: sanctuaries dedicated to the Χάριτες serve to remind people of the dual imperative to reciprocate a good turn and to take initiatives in extending favors. We have wondered about the immediate juxtaposition of this socio-religious etiology with Aristotle's famous monetary theory in *NE* v.v: is there a difference between χάρις-reciprocity and the exchange of goods for money? As we will see in the chapters to come, there is no unequivocal answer to this question, not even for Aristotle. But if we rephrase the question as "is there a way to *create* a distinction between χάρις-reciprocity and disembedded exchanges", Aristotle gives a possible answer: we could *see* χάρις-exchanges *as* reciprocity beyond requital. Requital is passive, χάρις implies taking initiatives and being the first to extend a favor. We will see in the next chapter how in the 5th and

215 See also Chapter Five.

216 See also Chapter Six.

4th century, this notion of χάρις starts to serve as the ideological underpinning of filial duty: the idea that honoring one's parents is never-ending, precisely because they began first.

CHAPTER 3

The Most Ancient of Obligations: The Nature of Filial Duty

> Of all crimes that human creatures are capable of committing, the most horrid and unnatural is ingratitude, especially when it is committed against parents, and appears in the more flagrant instances of wounds and death.
>
> DAVID HUME (1969 [1739]), 16

∴

What do we owe our parents and why? This is the question raised by the opening anecdote in Margaret Atwood's *Payback*:

[Text 1]

> Canadian nature writer Ernest Thompson Seton had an odd bill presented to him on his twenty-first birthday. It was a record kept by his father of all the expenses connected with young Ernest's childhood and youth, including the fee charged by the doctor for delivering him. Even more oddly, Ernest is said to have paid it. I used to think that Mr. Seton Senior was a jerk, but now I'm wondering. What if he was—in principle—right? Are we in debt to anyone or anything for the bare fact of our existence? If so, what do we owe, and to whom or to what? And how should we pay?[1]

If this anecdote makes us feel uncomfortable, well, this is exactly what it is designed to do.[2] There is something truly upsetting about fathers demanding compensation for living expenses from their sons, and something equally disquieting about the idea of sons discharging the debt of rearing. If not a jerk, at

1 Atwood (2008), 1.

2 Cf. the use of the anecdote in Graeber (2011: 92–93) that ultimately aims to dismantle the notion that moral obligations can be conflated with debts. See for this argument Chapter Four Section 1.

 | DOI:10.1163/9789004416147_004

least we can say that Mr. Seton Senior is somewhat *antisocial.* (From the point of view of anecdotal potential, it almost seems too good to be true that Mr. Seton Senior was an accountant by trade.) Perhaps this is because we feel that the desire to square accounts with someone is at odds with having an ongoing relationship with them: presenting a bill to someone means wanting to get rid of them. In the case of Seton this is what happened. Allegedly Seton never spoke to his father again.[3]

1 The Parent-Child Bond: A Paradigm Case

1.1 *The Obligation to Nurture One's Parents*

While owing parents a check sounds preposterous, the notion that children have *some* sort of obligation towards their parents is found in many cultures, ancient and modern—think of the fifth of the Ten Commandments in the Hebrew Bible ("Honor thy father and mother!") or of the ideals of filial piety in Confucian ethics. In 5th- and 4th-century Athens too, the idea that children owe their parents specific duties was prevalent in Athenian legal and popular discourse and was made an object of analysis in several philosophical texts.[4] The topic of filial duty was commonly referred to with terminology of "feeding"—τρέφειν or βόσκειν, to provide τὰ τροφεῖα (support), γηροτροφία (support of the aged) or γηροβοσκία (nurture of the aged)—but typically covered more than material nurture alone, including norms of reverent behavior towards parents and the obligation to take care of their burial, their tomb and their post-mortem memory.

Filial obligation was enshrined in Attic law: Solonic legislation codified that, unless a father had failed to teach his son a trade, a son should maintain his parents after they became old.[5] This duty to provide parental support[6] was

3 Graeber (2011), 93.

4 Garland (1990), 261–262, Lacey (1968), 116–117.

5 On Solon's legislation, see Plut. *Sol.* 22.1.4 (νόμον ἔγραψεν υἱῷ τρέφειν τὸν πατέρα μὴ διδαξάμενον τέχνην ἐπάναγκες μὴ εἶναι.); Aesch. 1.28 (ἐάν τις λέγῃ ἐν τῷ δήμῳ τὸν πατέρα τύπτων ἢ τὴν μητέρα, ἢ μὴ τρέφων, ἢ μὴ παρέχων οἴκησιν). See also Scafuro (2006); Pomeroy (1997), 141. 5th- and 4th-century Athenians attributed the institution of public suits to Solon (whether or not this was historically correct). Cf. Hunter (1994), 125; Scafuro (2006); Rhodes (2006).

6 Our sources for Solonian law suggest a distinction between "passive" offences (failure to provide support (μὴ τρέφειν), housing (μὴ παρέχειν οἴκησιν) or burial (τοὺς τάφους μὴ κοσμεῖν)) and "active" offences (striking (τύπτειν) a parent). See Scafuro (2006), 187–188 for an inventarisation and analysis of the sources. Cf. the parody of Solonian law in Aristoph. *Av.* 1356–1357, where the birds in Cloudcuckooville are under the obligation to "feed in turn" (πάλιν τρέφειν)

enforced by a public suit for "maltreatment of parents (γονέων κάκωσις)"[7] and by a provision in the δοκιμασία τῶν ῥητόρων, a procedure of preliminary scrutiny by which a public speaker could pre-emptively be barred from exercising the right to address the Council, Assembly, and law courts.[8] Similarly, one of the criteria in the examination of candidates for the archonship was the question of whether they treated their parents well.[9]

More than a matter of legislation or "law enforcement",[10] treatment of parents was typically subject to informal social control.[11] Filial obligation was an issue with rhetorical potential: maltreatment of parents was regarded the worst type of immoral behavior only paralleled by treason or entering the *agora* with polluted hands.[12] Boasts of good treatment of one's parents were part of a standard strategy to construct one's civic ethos, moral standing or patriotism; accusing one's opponents of bad treatment of his parents was oratorical stock-in-trade in forensic character assassination.[13] And it was a matter

---

their fathers if they have fed them (τρέφων); with Lacey (1968), 290 n. 115 (on *Birds* 1349–1369) and Dunbar (1995), ad loc. For the legal obligation to support one's parents (τοὺς γονέας τρέφειν), see also Dem. 24.107 and Aristoph. *Vesp*. 341, 729–759, 1004–1006. Rubinstein (1993), 64–68 on the duty to look after one's parents in 4th-century Athens.

7 [Ar.], *Ath. Pol.* 56.6; cf. Din. 2.17–19. Violation was punished with complete *atimia*. And. 1.74; Dem. 24.60, 103, 107. The public suit belonged to a group of *graphai*, the *graphê kakôseôs*, that were designed to protect individuals not in a legal position to take legal action for themselves (e.g. orphans and aged parents). Hunter (1995), 125. Isaeus I.39 and VIII.32 suggest that grandchildren may have been under the same legal obligation to support their grandparents. Cf. Rubinstein (1993), 64 n. 3.

8 [Ar.], *Ath. Pol.* 42.2, 49.1–2, 4, 55.3–4. Notorious instances are the case against Timarchus (Aesch. 1.28–30, with Fisher (2001), 137) and the case against Philon (Lys. 31 with Hunter (1994), 107–108); cf. Dem. 57.66–67. Cf. Harris (2014), 55; Adeleye (1983); Rhodes (1981), 619.

9 *Ath. Pol.* 55.3 (with Rhodes ad loc.). Candidates who neglected their duty towards their parents were to be disqualified for office. E.g. Timarchus suffered *atimia* for breaking this law. cf. Dem. 19.257, 284; Harris (2014), 55. The process of *dokimasia* primarily served to monitor a candidate's legal and moral qualifications and thereby reinforce the social norms of the community; Liddel (2007), 117; Robertson (2000), 163. MacDowell (1978), 168 points out that failure to pass *dokimasia* for office was not necessarily followed up with punishment.

10 "Law enforcement" is an anachronistic notion: classical Athens knew no professional police force to investigate crime or arrest offenders. Hunter (1994), Todd (1993).

11 Hunter (1994), 107. Cf. Lanni (2009) for an argument that although Athenian courts did not reliably enforce *laws*, they did enforce *norms*—generally norms of social behavior that were not subject to explicit legal regulation.

12 Dem. 24.60, Hyp. *Eux*. 6. Cf. Liddel (2007), 215.

13 E.g. in Din. 2.17–18 the unknown speaker in the trial against Aristogeiton (implicated in the Harpalus scandal of 323 BCE) holds the accused to the standards of a *dokimasia*-procedure (εἰ γονέας εὖ ποιεῖ)—a rhetorically effective pretext for gossip and moral censure; for the historical background, see Worthington (1992). Cf. And. 1.59, Din. 2.8; Cf. Dem. *Ep*. 4.11. Cf.

with moral implications: the substance of debates in comic and tragic theater, and a topic for analytical exploration in philosophical dialogues and treatises.

While it was uncontroversial that children have obligations towards their aging parents, the nature of this obligation and its underlying moral foundation did raise questions. Consider the following statements:

[Text 2]

> Lawgiver to settlers of a newly found colony: Children ought to take care of their parents because they *owe* it to them to discharge the debt of rearing.[14]

[Text 3]

> Deceased child speaking from an epitaph to its grieving mother: In vain did my mother's breasts provide me with milk for which I was not able to fulfill my filial duties as an act of *gratitude*.[15]

[Text 4]

> Angry son to father who refuses to die for him: I have always been a good son. And now this is the repayment you and my mother have made to me![16]

All three statements picture the relation between parents and children as a form of exchange over a long period of time, but they do so differently. T2 uses an analogy between parental care and credit—much like Seton's father, probably evoking a similar sense of unease in the modern reader. T3 approaches filial duties as acts of gratitude, which may seem more appropriate to a parent-child relation than debt, but the idea that nurturing a baby is futile if care cannot be reciprocated (because the child has died before his time) has an insensitive and utilitarian feel to it. T4 also understands the bond between parents

Liddel (2007), 215. MacDowell (1978), 168; Adeleye (1983), 296. On forensic oratory, and *dokimasia*-cases in particular, as a "repository of innuendo, rumor, hearsay, and gossip", see Hunter (1994), 104–108.

14 Paraphrase of Pl. *Leg.* 717b4–c6; see Section 2.1, T5.

15 Paraphrase of 3rd-century epitaph found in Karanis, Egypt; see section 3.2, T22.

16 Paraphrase of Eur. *Alc.* 658–668; see section 7.2, T41.

and children as a mutual exchange, but here it is the son who feels entitled to a repayment on the grounds of previously rendered services—suggesting that the son, at this point, feels he has discharged any obligation arising from the care he had received earlier in life and, even more so, feels entitled to a service in return. Are these three statements all part of the same social script? And do they imply the same understanding of filial obligation? Is it possible to discharge one's obligations towards one's parents, to *pay them off completely*, and will that dissolve the relationship?

This is the question at the core of this chapter: what does it mean to *owe* something to one's parents?

1.2 *Generalized Reciprocity and Filial Duty*

Why are we expected to care for our parents? Why *ought* we treat them with respect? Why are we *obliged* to honor our father and mother? And why do we *owe* them our love and attention?

In the anthropological model of reciprocity introduced by Marshal Sahlins, the bond between parents and children is the paradigm case of "generalized reciprocity", a mode of reciprocity characterized by acts of "giving things without taking account of how much was given, with the assumption that at some time in the undefined future something will be given back."[17] The determinant factor in the degree of "solidarity" is, according to Sahlins, kinship distance.[18] At the unsociable extreme there is "negative reciprocity", where parties aim to gain as much as possible from an encounter at the expense of the other, e.g. by means of exploitation or theft. Generalized reciprocity is the solidarity extreme, involving an overwhelming but unspecified and often implicit obligation to reciprocate; identification of individual transfers is experienced as impossible or inappropriate. Somewhere midway between these poles there is the phenomenon of "balanced reciprocity", exchange operations which assume an equal or equivalent return within a finite, often specified, period of time.

The parent-child bond is often adduced as an obvious and unproblematic example of such generalized reciprocity: "parents provide for children over years and years, giving food, clothing, birthday parties, and paying for school. Parents usually expect nothing tangible at the time; they may hope for love,

17 Sahlins (1972: 193–194). Cf. Wilk & Cliggett (2007), 162. For a convincing and influential application of this model to ancient Greek economy, see esp. Millett (1991), 110; for a salutary reminder of the perils of imposing such a model wholesale onto classical Greek social and economic configurations, see Mitchell (1997), 1.

18 Sahlins (1972), 196. See also Chapter Four Section 3.2.

affection, and care later in life, but that's something unmeasured and certainly a long time away."[19]

The parent-child example is particularly appealing because of its presumed universal validity: mothers who suckle their babe, without any security as to a return (a return that may be expected, at best, only after a maximum span of time), seem to constitute an example of the "nearly-perfect gift" (a gift given without *any* expectation of return!) transcending boundaries of culture or history; it is only *self-evident* that such an overwhelming gesture deserves unquestionable reciprocation—it is simply a matter of *gratitude*. Anyone who fails to do so, not only shows himself an *ingrate*, an ungrateful child, but a defective human being with questionable morals! Ingratitude towards parents is, after all, "the most horrid and unnatural" of all crimes.

But is it? Are parent-child bonds universally understood as reciprocal relations? And is such reciprocal solidarity necessarily premised on kinship distance (and how is kinship in turn constructed?) or are there other determinant factors (such as the organization of the household)?[20] And if so, how universal, natural or self-evident is the ideological motivation underlying such an understanding of the relationship and the ensuing obligations on the part of the child? Even universally shared norms can be motivated in ways that are culturally variable and subject to discursive negotiation and construction.[21]

To start with the first question: cross-culturally, there is a range of distinct interpretations of filial obligation; reciprocity, i.e. a prolonged give-and-take, is only one of them. In a recent anthropological study on Dutch welfare policy, it has been observed that the retreat of the welfare state in the Netherlands has been premised, in the ultimate analysis, on the assumption that family ties would "take over" from the state and ensure the care of the elderly. In reality, however, Dutch family life is not structured in this way: due to all sorts of culturally and demographically specific causes, neither parents nor children have a strong understanding of being in a reciprocal relationship. Once their children reach adulthood and move out of the parental house, Dutch parents feel they are supposed to grant them absolute "freedom" and "autonomy". Parents are

19 Cf. Wilk & Cliggett (2007), 162. On the perception of life as a series of exchanges, see Schieffelin (1980), Strathern (1990), 1–31, Davis (1992).

20 Cf. Foxhall (1998), 52 on affective economies in the Athenian household: "Household, not kinship, constituted the most important "limit of trust", hence affection changes qualitatively beyond this boundary." See Section 3.1 below.

21 Cf. the starting point of the general introduction in Rosen & Sluiter (2010: 2), here on notions of "fairness" and "trust": "Although there is an evolutionary rationale for such norms, their expression in *specific* value terms and concepts is culturally embedded".

not keen on asking children for assistance: they "do not want to be nuisance", or infringe on their children's (notionally absolute) freedom.[22]

Remarkably, in Germany, concerns with intergenerational independence are believed to produce a *stronger* connection between the norm of reciprocity and the obligation to support parents. Here, the crucial factor is a concern with independence on the part of the children (adult daughters, in this particular case):[23] the intention to support parents is affected by a perceived imbalance in exchanges of support. Due to the relatively high pensions awarded to the German elderly, more financial support flows from old parents to their daughters than the other way round. Because daughters feel they receive more than they give back, there is an increased willingness among them to tolerate their burden and to support their parents—a willingness in part based on the value of independence and the desire to be not overmuch indebted to others. It is an open question if this line of thought presumes that it is possible, ultimately, to fully *pay off* filial debt.

On a different note, it has been observed that anxiety about "overbenefiting" from reciprocity may motivate elderly parents in the United States to "strategically interpret" support by their children as reciprocation for the support and care that they as parents provided years earlier.[24] Here we see the order of explanation reversed: instead of being the motivating ground of filial obligation, reciprocity becomes a "strategical interpretation" that enables the recipient of care to accept support without perceiving himself as overbenefiting; "reciprocity" becomes a discursive strategy. Note that as an analytical category, "strategical interpretation" is not neutral: it implies an element of make-believe or disingeniousness[25]—it implies that reciprocity not only is a category that human actors use to understand their behavior, relations and obligations, but also a discursive strategy that helps people to position themselves and to manipulate the ground rules of the relations in which they find themselves.

Notions of "reciprocity" may be invoked as part of explicit government policy. In China, for instance, centuries of Confucianism have nurtured conceptions of mutual generational interdependence and filial piety:[26] there is a strong ideological stimulus to provide daily care to elderly parents and to co-

22 Risseeuw (2005).

23 Schwarz, Trommsdorff, Zheng & Shi (2010), 238; 248–251.

24 Uehara (1995), 494; Antonucci (1985).

25 Cf. the criticism on Bourdieu's notion of "strategy"; see Chapter Four Section 3.6.

26 Hwang (1999).

reside with them.[27] However, Confucian ideas were rejected by the Communist Chinese government until the 1980s.[28] Although they are partly rehabilitated,[29] active government reinforcement to ensure care of parents was deemed necessary: the government of Beijing enacted a law in July 2013 that allows parents to sue their children for failing to take care of them.[30] In an analogous case, the government of Shanghai enacted a similar law in 2016 with the remarkable stipulation that children who fail to visit their parents on a regular basis will have their credit scores lowered.[31] Failure to reciprocate care to parents is explicitly constructed as indicative of one's ability to observe obligations in general. Conversely, state regulation of care may lead to a decline of perceived filial obligation, as was reportedly the case in Japan after the nationwide long-term care insurance in 2000 as a universal right for older adults.[32]

This all goes to show that there is a range of possible interpretations of filial duties towards parents that all assign different weight and meaning to reciprocity. Considerations of reciprocity may be absent *because* of a strong valuation of children's autonomy (as in the Dutch case, where filial obligations are also less normative); they may be present and *motivated* by a strong desire to restore one's independence (as in the case of the German daughters)—a line of thought that possibly implies that one can redeem filial debt; or they may be interpretative strategies constructed out of a desire to perceive oneself as not overly indebted (as in the case of the American elderly parents). Mechanisms of reciprocity may be (mistakenly) taken for granted by government policy, as in the Netherlands, or explicitly made an object of policy as in Beijing or Shanghai.

1.3 *Reciprocity vs.* Emic *Conceptions*

What, then, is the analytical value of a notion such as "reciprocity"? As David Graeber argues in his radical reconceptualization of debt, "almost everyone" (i.e. social scientists and "natives" alike) overestimates the importance of reciprocity as a social principle, which leads to the assumption that all human interactions somehow take the form of exchange (which, in turn, leads to the perception that morality can be reduced to dealing with debt).[33]

---

27 Zhang (2014).

28 Schwarz, Trommsdorff, Zheng & Shi (2010), 237.

29 Zheng et al. (2005).

30 Wong, "A Chinese virtue is now the law," *New York Times* July 2, 2013.

31 Ruiyao, "Shanghai says people who fail to visit parents will have credit status lowered," *Caixin Online* April 11, 2016.

32 Tsutsui, Muramatsu, and Higashino 2014.

33 Graeber (2011), 91. For other objections against the explanatory value of "reciprocity", see MacCormack (1976), 10, Parry (1986), 466.

Graeber's objections go to the heart of the concept of "generalized reciprocity", the idea of sharing and contributing to a common pool without keeping account. For this is the paradox of generalized reciprocity: it is only experienced as reciprocity at the moment when everyday sharing loses its taken-for-grantedness. In other words: it only becomes reciprocity when it has ceased to be reciprocity. For this reason, Graeber, abolishes the concept of reciprocity entirely,[34] offering a tripartite reorganization of "modalities of morality" instead, i.e. the broad moral principles on which economic behavior and relationships rest:

- **baseline communism**, the moral relation in which no accounts are taken, in which there is no quantification nor reciprocity;[35]
- **hierarchy**, the moral relation in which relationships of rank between people are recognized in repeated acts of deference made over and over again; here too, there is no quantification, reciprocity or debt in these relations;[36]
- **exchange**, all relations that strive towards equivalence (of people, things, words, deeds), therefore quantifying debts, expecting reciprocity and giving rise to debts;[37]

The interesting point about this distinction is that it enables Graeber to analyze human interactions without reducing everything to exchange, by allowing for everyday and effortless shifts between modalities of morality: when debt goes unpaid, the moral regime of "hierarchy" rules—i.e. there is a shift from "exchange" (the modality from which debt arises) to "hierarchy" (the modality in which people are understood to be unequal).[38] Similarly, one might argue that the default in the everyday dealings within the οἶκος, between parents and children, is "baseline communism"; only in times of crisis or disruption is there a modal shift to "exchange", i.e. the language of reciprocity. In such an analysis, "reciprocity" is more a discursive strategy that helps participants to articulate the idea that someone is, or is not, "overbenefiting"—as we saw in the case of the elderly parents in the US who "strategically interpret" filial support as an act of reciprocation.

Graeber's classification is elegant and analytically compelling. His motivation for denying specific status for "generalized reciprocity" is justified to the

---

34 Graeber (2011). Graeber dismisses concepts such as "generalized reciprocity" and "alternating reciprocity" that ultimately demonstrate "that if one has already decided that all relations are based on reciprocity, one can always define the term so broadly as to make it true." (405 n. 21).

35 Graeber (2011), 99.

36 Graeber (2011), 111.

37 Graeber (2011), 103.

38 Graeber (2011), 121.

extent that it acknowledges the paradoxical nature of this somewhat hybrid category. For the purposes of analysis of our ancient Greek sources, however, it remains justifiable to use the term "reciprocity" as distinct from the broader "exchange", because it provides us with the granularity that enables us to do justice to emic conceptions of family solidarity and kinship obligation that do seem to distinguish between different types of exchange and to attach different moral modalities to them. As we will see in this chapter and the next, the transactional logic of the market and of commercial debt (with the vocabulary of "buying", "paying" and "discharging") and that of φιλία-reciprocity (with the vocabulary of "giving" and "returning") are experienced and discussed as distinct in our 5th- and 4th-century sources. This becomes particularly relevant in the case of conceptions of filial duty: 5th- and 4th-century sources all seem to presuppose a form of parent-child "exchange", but sometimes disagree on the nature of the exchange and its implications. What we should take away from Graeber, however, is the awareness that reciprocity not only serves as an analytical instrument *for us*, but also for the sources and characters that we study: they too may revert to the language of reciprocity (or, as Graeber has it, the "rhetoric of reciprocity") *in moments of analysis* or *as a discursive strategy*.

1.4 *The Argument*

This chapter will focus on the conception of filial duty in 5th- and 4th-century Greece. It will lay bare the conceptual configurations that shape ideas about obligations towards parents. When talking about one's duties to one's parents, to what extent do notions of reciprocity have an explanatory force, and in what way exactly? And how is "reciprocal duty" itself conceptualized? Is being indebted the same as having a debt, is reciprocating the same as returning a debt?

It will be argued that, down to the 4th-century BCE, the dominant conception of filial duty was an implicit Gratitude Theory (Section 3): the duty to nurture one's parents and to take care of them was understood as a reciprocal obligation, arising as a response to being treated well by them earlier in life. This theory is akin to, but not identical with, the Debtor Paradigm, Seton Senior's model of obligation, according to which filial duty comes down to the obligation to repay a debt (Section 2). The Debtor Paradigm has a certain analytical rigor that is compelling, but at the same time gives rise to conceptual and moral problems. The Gratitude Theory has less analytical force (at its strongest moments it coincides with the Debtor Paradigm) but offers a morally thicker account of obligation by integrating affects, emotions and intentions (Sections 3 and 4). In its pure form, the Debtor Paradigm in 5th- and 4th-century discourse about filial duty is rare.[39] However, I will argue that, as early as Euripides, the Debtor Paradigm functions as a foil in situations in which the script of filial obligation is subject to negotiation (Section 5).

Let us now turn to the Debtor Paradigm of Obligation, the worldview of Seton Senior—the petty accountant who had Plato on his side.

2 The Debtor Paradigm of Obligation

Filial duty is a topic addressed by present-day philosophers as well. One of the prevalent accounts of filial duty is the so-called Debt Theory or Debtor Paradigm:[40] we have specific duties towards our parents because they have done so much for us, i.e. we are *indebted* to them and have the duty to *repay*—pretty much the way financial debts work.

The Debtor Paradigm of filial duty has obvious precedents in classical reflection on the nature of obligations.[41] The debt theory exploits the isomorphism between "commercial" transactions and φιλία-exchanges for purposes of analysis: prescriptive statements about the economy of χάρις are cast in a vocabulary of monetary exchange where obligations can be quantified and objectified. Especially in didactic contexts, the seemingly unambiguous terminology of banking and commerce may help to articulate and objectify the far more implicit and "vague" obligations within long-term φιλία-relationships such as parent-child bonds.[42]

2.1 *Primordial Debt*

This is what we see in Plato's *Laws*. The context is an imaginary address by the unnamed Athenian Visitor to the future settlers of Magnesia. The speech revolves around the power of god over human affairs and that prescribes that each man ought to try to become "dear to god" (θεῷ φίλος).[43] As a direct consequence (τούτοις ἑπόμενον)[44] of this general prescription, the Athenian discusses the worship of gods (θεραπείᾳ θεῶν), described in terms of gift-giving to the

39 For the theoretical discussion on the Debtor Paradigm, see Chapter Four.

40 Blustein (1982); English (1979) and Keller (2006) for the shortcomings of this model of filial duty.

41 Keller (2006), 256: "Throughout much of the history of philosophy, in the West and in the East, the debt theory has been regarded as unproblematic and transparently true."

42 As will be argued in Chapter Four, commercial and financial concepts such as "debt" are themselves shifting and subject to discursive processes.

43 716d2.

44 716d3.

gods (δῶρα, δέχεσθαι):[45] priority goes to the gods of the underworld and the Olympian gods; next the spirits (δαίμονες) and the heroes. Last in line are the obligations towards the ancestral gods and living parents:

[Text 5]

> ἐπακολουθοῖ δ' αὐτοῖς ἱδρύματα ἴδια πατρῴων θεῶν κατὰ νόμον ὀργιαζόμενα, γονέων δὲ μετὰ ταῦτα τιμαὶ ζώντων· ὡς θέμις ὀφείλοντα ἀποτίνειν τὰ πρῶτά τε καὶ μέγιστα ὀφειλήματα, χρεῶν πάντων πρεσβύτατα, νομίζειν δέ, ἃ κέκτηται καὶ ἔχει, πάντα εἶναι τῶν γεννησάντων καὶ θρεψαμένων πρὸς τὸ παρέχειν αὐτὰ εἰς ὑπηρεσίαν ἐκείνοις κατὰ δύναμιν πᾶσαν, ἀρχόμενον ἀπὸ τῆς οὐσίας, δεύτερα τὰ τοῦ σώματος, τρίτα τὰ τῆς ψυχῆς, ἀποτίνοντα δανείσματα ἐπιμελείας τε καὶ ὑπερπονούντων ὠδῖνας παλαιὰς ἐπὶ νέοις δανεισθείσας, ἀποδιδόντα δὲ παλαιοῖς ἐν τῷ γήρᾳ σφόδρα κεχρημένοις.
>
> Next in priority will be rites celebrated according to law at private shrines dedicated to ancestral gods. Last come the honors paid to living parents. It is meet and right that *a debtor* should *discharge* his first and greatest *obligation* and pay the *debt* which comes before all others; he must consider that all he has and holds belongs to those who bore and bred him, and he is meant to use it in their service to the limit of his powers. He must serve them first with his property, then with hand and brain, and so give to the old people what they desperately need in view of their age: *repayment* of all that anxious care and attention they *lavished* on him, the long-standing *"loan" they made* him as a child.[46]

The duty to respects one's parents is motivated according to the debt theory of filial obligation, a subcategory of the so-called Debtor Paradigm of Obligation.[47] The child-parent bond is understood as a debtor-creditor relationship, in which parental care is reduced to a loan (a δάνεισμα),[48] while the filial obli-

---

45 716e3–717a1.

46 Plato, *Leg.* IV 717b4–c6; *transl.* Saunders (2005).

47 This terminology is coined and explored by Card (1988).

48 In 4th-century Attic Greek δανείζειν is the most common verb for "to lend". Modern lexica, including LSJ and Chantraine (1968–1980, s.v. δάνος), identify δανείζειν and cognate terminology as having the specific sense of lending at interest—as opposed to lending on a "friendly" basis, which is commonly denoted by κίχραναι. Korver. 79–84; Bogaert (1986), 22 n. 22. Cf. Millett (1991), 28–29 for the qualification that the verb δανείζειν, and its associated nouns δάνειον and δάνος, possibly originally denotes giving and gifts; however the basis for this reconstruction (supported by Chantraine who links δάνος with the root of

gation to care for one's parents is formulated in terms of a debt (a χρέος) and of "repaying" (ἀποτίνειν) "what is owed" (ὀφειλήματα).[49] The moral connection between the "care and pain" (ἐπιμελείας τε καὶ … ὠδίνας) spent by the parents on the children and the obligation of these children towards their parents is highlighted by the intentional repetition παλαιάς … παλαιοῖς: the debts are old, and by the time they are to be repaid the creditors are old as well.[50] The most binding of all family obligations is "expressed as a loan transaction, complete with security and repayment."[51]

Within the Debtor Paradigm, fulfilling obligations is a matter of settling accounts and ethics comes down to bookkeeping.[52] The paradigm provides a powerful tool to objectify moral concepts such as obligation, duty and guilt, because it is capable of encapsulating a larger timeframe.[53] It is especially in cases where the timespan between original favor and the favor done in return is extremely long, as in the case of parents and children, that the Debtor Paradigm provides a transparent and formalized analogy that makes a moral and causal connection between the two events objectifiable: one has the duty to take care of one's parents *because* one has received care earlier in life from one's parents.

The Athenian Visitor continues to lay out the obligations towards parents: the "repayment" of the debt of parental care consists of three elements: financial aid (ἀπὸ τῆς οὐσίας), physical help (τὰ τοῦ σώματος) and help for the soul (τὰ τῆς ψυχῆς). The obligations towards parents acquire a religious dimension:[54] throughout his life, in addressing his parents, the son ought (χρή)[55] to observe reverent speech (πρὸς αὑτοῦ γονέας εὐφημίαν διαφερόντως) as his parents' rights are protected by Retribution (Νέμεσις), messenger of Justice (Δίκη) who oversees everything;[56] he is to submit (ὑπείκειν) to his parents when they get angry

---

δίδωμι) consists in relatively late sources (*Etymologicum Magnum*, the third-century poet Euphorion (fr. 90) and a first century B.C. grammarian Tryphon).

49 Similar analyses of the parent-child relationship can be found elsewhere in Plato (*Rep.* 538b–c; *Leg.* 869a–c, 930–931a; *Symp.* 207a–209e).

50 England (1976), 454, also for parallels for the use of the poetical παλαιός for "aged" persons.

51 Millett (1991), 133.

52 Card (1988), 115. An extreme example is deontological ethics where being in debt is "the paradigm ethical relationship." Card (1988), 115. In Germanic languages the lexeme for moral guilt, *Schuld*, incorporates the debtor's paradigm. Cf. Nietzsche (1968), 498–501. See Chapter Four for a full exploration of this paradigm.

53 Card (1998). Cf. Card (1988) for a distinction between a "debtor's paradigm" and a "trustee's paradigm" of duty and obligation.

54 Morrow (1960), 467. In 931a parents are said to be the "living images" of the divine.

55 717c7.

56 717c6–d3. cf. 931d.

and to forgive them (συγγιγνώσκοντα) if they act out their anger upon him,[57] because (ὡς) it is only natural (εἰκότως) for a father to be angry if he is convinced that he is being wronged by his own son.[58] When the parents die, there will have to be a most modest burial (ταφὴ ἡ σωφρονεστάτη) and the ceremonies should be fitting: not more elaborate than custom demands, not less than stipulated by ancestral tradition. Even the way of commemorating is prescribed: every year, the son is to bestow "acts of care that bring honor" (τάς ... ἐπιμελείας τὰς κόσμον φερούσας ἀποδιδόναι), never failing to provide a perpetual memorial, spending a due share (τὸ μέτριον) on the deceased with the means that he has available (δαπάνη).[59] (Note that rites of commemoration are explicitly constructed as the reciprocation of care received earlier in life: τάς ἐπιμελείας ... ἀποδιδόναι, "to bestow *duly*", or "to give *back*"). "If we manage this and thus observe these rules of life," the Athenian Visitor says, "we will all receive due reward from the gods (τὴν ἀξίαν ἂν παρὰ θεῶν (...) κομιζοίμεθα) and live in the enjoyment of hopes of happiness."[60]

Not surprisingly, the filial duties prescribed by Plato's Athenian Visitor are in line with general conceptions in 5th- and 4th-century Athens: filial duty goes beyond the mere performance of direct and material duties to help one's parents materially and financially—i.e. beyond "nurturing" (τρέφειν) in a literal sense. Filial duty includes the obligation to respect one's parents, with deference in speech and behavior, a forgiving attitude in cases of conflict and the duty to take care of burial, tomb and commemorative practices after the parents' demise. The average Athenian would have found these prescriptions self-evident. How about the *motivation behind* these duties?

The Debtor Paradigm of Obligation is compelling. It has a ring of self-evident and unproblematic truth to it:[61] there is barely anything as transparent and self-evident as the obligation to repay a debt.[62] But on closer inspection the paradigm raises questions.

In the case of filial duty, the Debtor Paradigm raises the question of whether the debt towards parents can ever completely be repaid. The prescription of annual ἐπιμελεία after their death suggests that it cannot. Moreover, in T5, the prefix ὑπερ- in the formulation "care and attention that they *lavished* (ὑπερπονούντων) on him" gives the impression of an excessive gift that cannot be

57 717d3–5.
58 717d5–6.
59 717d7–718a3.
60 718a4–6.
61 Blustein (1982).
62 However, we will see this view problematized in Chapter Four Section 2.

balanced—an idea reinforced by the formulation that a child is "to serve parents to the limit of his powers (κατὰ δύναμιν πᾶσαν)". Reciprocity between parents and children is not only long-lasting, but also unequal: a child can never do or give enough to balance out his parents' favor; but he can reciprocate to the best of his ability. In other words, we have a case here of **primordial debt**, a debt we are born into, just by the grace of being born, a debt that cannot be redeemed.

Moreover, some of the norms of behavior prescribed by the Athenian Visitor are easily understood as "paying back" a "debt" of care, e.g. the financial and physical aid while the parents are alive, as well as the ἐπιμελεία of the deceased parents. Other norms of behavior towards parents, for instance being polite, respecting them, yielding to their anger, describe treatment that is plausibly "due" to the parents, but here the transparency of the debt metaphor starts to wear thin: what exactly is the connection between the pain endured by parents and the patience that is to be endured by children?

As we will see in Chapter Four, to Plato, even the seemingly exact paradigm of debt is not self-evident: knowing what we owe presupposes knowledge of what we *ought* to do—not the other way round. More specifically, the phenomenon of credit with legal backup will turn out to be problematic (or qualified) in the broader context of the *Laws*.[63] Another indication that the Debtor Paradigm alone fails to carry sufficient normative force both in the address to the settlers here and, as we will see, in Cephalus' version of the paradigm in *Republic* I,[64] is the dominant and emphatic presence of the idea of divine retribution: just as "real" debts function with legal back-up, the idea of divine retribution (both negative or retaliatory, Νέμεσις, and positive in the sense of rewards in the afterlife) serves as the ultimate safeguard for adherence to the moral law of reciprocity.

Nevertheless, in the present context, the Debtor Paradigm seems to fulfill its didactic purpose.

---

63 For the Platonic laws on credit, see Chapter Four Section 1.2. We have to bear in mind that the account of filial duty precedes the discussion of the laws on credit in books V (742c3–6) and XI (915d6–e9). It is part of a "prelude" to the entire law code and it immediately precedes a discussion about legislation as a form of πείθειν, civic instruction, that, like a good doctor, not only "treats" but also gives the rationale for the treatment in view (718a6–723b). See Buccioni (2007) and Bartels (2014), 175–208.

64 Chapter Four Section 2.

2.2 *The Isomorphism between Debt and Filial Duty*

The Debtor Paradigm of Obligation recurs in the Aristotelian account of φιλία in the *Nicomachean Ethics*. Discussing the hierarchy of claims attached to various types of φιλία, Aristotle supposes that when it comes to support (τροφή), parents have priority, because children are "in a position of debt" (ὡς ὀφείλοντας):

[Text 6]

> Δόξειε δ' ἂν τροφῆς μὲν γονεῦσι δεῖν μάλιστ' ἐπαρκεῖν, ὡς ὀφείλοντας, καὶ τοῖς αἰτίοις τοῦ εἶναι κάλλιον ὂν ἢ ἑαυτοῖς εἰς ταῦτ' ἐπαρκεῖν·
>
> But it would seem that one should give priority to parents when it comes to giving support, *on the basis that a debt is owed to them*, and that it is a *finer* thing to give support in this way to those who caused one's existence than to oneself.[65]

The analogy between children and debtors is qualified: ὡς with participle indicates internal focalization, suggesting that here the Debtor Paradigm is *a* way of looking at the state of affairs.

Note furthermore that in T6 the decisive criterion for prioritizing parents is what is "finer" (κάλλιον), i.e. the obligation to reciprocate support to one's parents is a *moral* obligation. This sheds light on Aristotle's conception of parent-child φιλία. At the basis of Aristotle's understanding of reciprocity lies his famous tripartite classification of kinds (εἴδη) of friendships according to their proper objects (φιλητά)[66]—utility (διὰ τὸ χρήσιμον),[67] pleasure (δι' ἡδονήν)[68]

---

65 Ar. *EN* IX.ii (1165a22–24); *all translations of Aristotle's Nicomachean Ethics are by* Broadie & Rowe (2011).

66 Also: φιλούμενον, φιλητέον, φίλον. For more on this terminology, see Dirlmeier (1962), 376, (1958), 254–256. The distinction in three types of friendship on the basis of their φιλητά corresponds to the three standard categories of value, the beneficial or useful, the pleasant, and the fine (*NE* II.iii (1155b17–19)), and hence involve distinct interactional structures: *exchanging* utilities, *sharing in* pleasure, *sharing* in the activity of virtue. In *Rhet.* II.iv (1381b33 ff.) Aristotle makes a categorization into εἴδη of φιλία that is presumably more in touch with common usage: εἴδη δὲ φιλίας ἑταιρεία οἰκειότης συγγένεια καὶ ὅσα τοιαῦτα. More on this distinction in Chapters Four and Seven.

67 Also ὠφέλιμον, συμφέρον.

68 Or διὰ τὸ ἡδύ. Cf. *EE* VII.ii (1236a12–14), *MM* II.xi (1209b2–4, 17–19, 1210a30 ff.). Moreover, Aristotle uses τὸ χρήσιμον interchangeably with ὠφέλιμον, συμφέρον. *NE* VIII.ii (1155b17–19), VIII.iii (1156a7 ff.); Cf. *EE* VII.ii (1236a15 ff.), VII.iii (1238b15); *MM* II.xi (1209a19–21, 28 ff.; 1210a6–24).

and the development of virtue (κατ' ἀρετήν; δι' ἀγαθόν).[69] However, nowhere is it made unambiguously explicit how parent-child φιλία fits into this typology.[70] Parent-child ties seem to revolve around a blend of the three objects:

[Text 7]

> ἔστι δ' ἡ μὲν πρὸς γονεῖς φιλία τέκνοις, καὶ ἀνθρώποις πρὸς θεούς, ὡς πρὸς ἀγαθὸν καὶ ὑπερέχον· εὖ γὰρ πεποιήκασι τὰ μέγιστα· τοῦ γὰρ εἶναι καὶ τραφῆναι αἴτιοι, καὶ γενομένοις τοῦ παιδευθῆναι· ἔχει δὲ καὶ τὸ ἡδὺ καὶ τὸ χρήσιμον ἡ τοιαύτη φιλία μᾶλλον τῶν ὀθνείων, ὅσῳ καὶ κοινότερος ὁ βίος αὐτοῖς ἐστίν.
>
> Now children's friendship for parents, and human beings' for gods, is *as for something good and superior, since it is they who have bestowed the greatest benefits on them*, being responsible for their *existence* and their *upbringing*, and their *education* once they have come into existence; though such friendship also has more of *the pleasant and the useful* about it than friendship between those not related by family, in so far as they have more of a shared life.[71]

The three categories of value are mentioned here, the good (ἀγαθόν), the pleasant (τὸ ἡδύ) and the useful (τὸ χρήσιμον), although it does not become entirely clear if the child's commitment towards his parents is *directed towards* the good (or only motivated by their being good). What becomes evident is that to Aristotle the quality and intensity of children's φιλία towards their parents is contingent on the fact that they have been given existence (εἶναι), nurture (τραφῆναι) and education (παιδευθῆναι): the child's φιλία is, somehow, understood as a response to this good treatment (εὖ πεποιήκασι). Moreover, child-parent φιλία is fundamentally unequal in nature,[72] similar to that of men towards

---

69 There is some discussion over the precise interpretation of the διά-phrases: prospectively expressing final cause (coming close to ἕνεκα with genitive), i.e. what the potential friend hopes to achieve by his friend's prosperity (Irwin 1999), or retrospectively expressing efficient cause, i.e. a causal condition in recognition of which a friend wishes his friend well (Cooper 1977, Alpern 193), or covering both goal and ground (Price 1989, 151, referring to *Phys.* II.vii 198a14–21). The distinction between retrospective διά and prospective ἕνεκα is dealt with in Plato's *Lysis* (217–219, 220c–d). Cf. Whiting (2006), 285, Glidden (1981), 39–59.

70 Nagle (2006), 196.

71 Ar. *EN* VIII.xii (1162a4–9).

72 Cf. *EN* VIII.xi (1161a14–21): the bond between parent and child is analogous to that between king and subjects, i.e. based on superiority in beneficence (ἐν ὑπεροχῇ εὐεργεσίας); the superior party receives esteem (τιμῶνται). On unequal friendships (as opposed to dissim-

gods, because of an element of moral superiority (ὑπερέχον) on the part of the parents—a moral superiority grounded in the fact that parents have rendered to their children the *greatest* good (τὰ μέγιστα). Note that at this point the *type* of response (reciprocation? reciprocation *with what*? *useful* things? material benefits? deference? recognition?) remains unspecified.

Inasmuch as utility is concerned, unequal relations require that one aims at what is equitable (ἐπιεικής), not at the numerically equal:[73]

[Text 8]

> ὅταν δὲ γονεῦσι μὲν τέκνα **ἀπονέμῃ ἃ δεῖ** τοῖς γεννήσασι, γονεῖς δὲ [υἱέσιν] **ἃ δεῖ** τοῖς τέκνοις, **μόνιμος** ἡ τῶν τοιούτων καὶ **ἐπιεικὴς** ἔσται φιλία.
>
> [W]hen children *render* to parents *what should be rendered to those who gave one birth*, and parents render *what should be rendered to children*, such parties' friendships are *lasting* and *good of their kind*.[74]

Obligations to and fro are expressed in the language of exchange ("portioning out" (ἀπονέμειν)), with an objectifying "ought" (δεῖ).[75] The idea that functioning reciprocity safeguards the longevity of parent-child φιλία (its being μόνιμος) is striking: it cuts across any distinction between "ascribed" and "achieved" relations. One *is born* into a parent-child φιλία and one can *choose* to keep the relation sound and functional by securing its reciprocal structure.

Combined with the notion that parent-child φιλία is fundamentally asymmetrical, the Debtor Paradigm of Obligation yields a conception of filial duty as a debt that can never be repaid in full:

[Text 9]

> τὸ δυνατὸν γὰρ ἡ φιλία ἐπιζητεῖ, οὐ τὸ κατ' ἀξίαν· οὐδὲ γὰρ ἔστιν ἐν πᾶσι, καθάπερ ἐν ταῖς πρὸς τοὺς θεοὺς τιμαῖς καὶ τοὺς γονεῖς· οὐδεὶς γὰρ τὴν ἀξίαν ποτ' ἂν **ἀποδοίη**, εἰς δύναμιν δὲ ὁ θεραπεύων **ἐπιεικὴς** εἶναι δοκεῖ. διὸ κἂν δόξειεν οὐκ ἐξεῖναι υἱῷ πατέρα ἀπείπασθαι, πατρὶ δ' υἱόν· **ὀφείλοντα** γὰρ **ἀποδοτέον**, οὐδὲν

ilar or heterogeneous friendships) and on the function of τιμή in such friendships, see Chapter Seven.

73 Aristotle elaborates on the notion of equity in *NE* v.xiv.

74 Ar. *EN* VIII.vii (1158b21–23).

75 See Redard (1953), 56, Benardete (1965), Liddel (2007), 159 and Barrett (1964) for the semantic difference between objective and external δεῖ and internalized χρή.

> δὲ ποιήσας ἄξιον τῶν ὑπηργμένων δέδρακεν, ὥστ' ἀεὶ ὀφείλει. οἷς δ' ὀφείλεται, ἐξουσία ἀφεῖναι· καὶ τῷ πατρὶ δή.
>
> For friendship looks also for what is possible, not what accords with merit, for such a thing is not even possible in all cases, e.g. where it is a matter of honoring the gods or one's parents; for no one could ever *render* them the honor they deserve, and the person who serves them to the best of his ability is thought to be behaving *decently*. This is why it might well not be thought permissible for son to disavow father, while father may disavow son; for the son *must return the debt he owes*, and since there is nothing he can do that is worthy of the benefits he has already received, he is always a *debtor*. On the other hand, a *creditor* can remit a debt; so too, then, can a father.[76]

In the case of parents and gods, it is impossible to honor them according to merit (κατ' ἀξίαν), because adequate compensation cannot possibly be rendered.[77] This fundamental asymmetry is explained with the aid of the Debtor Paradigm: the debts (ὀφείλοντα) owed (ἀποδοτέον) by a son to his father can never be redeemed. Whereas creditors (οἷς ὀφείλεται) are free to discharge their debtors, debtors cannot remit their creditors.

In the lines that follow, Aristotle admits that it is highly improbable that a father will ever disavow his son:

[Text 10]

> ἅμα δ' ἴσως οὐδείς ποτ' ἂν ἀποστῆναι δοκεῖ μὴ ὑπερβάλλοντος μοχθηρίᾳ· χωρὶς γὰρ τῆς φυσικῆς φιλίας τὴν ἐπικουρίαν ἀνθρωπικὸν μὴ διωθεῖσθαι. τῷ δὲ φευκτὸν ἢ οὐ σπουδαστὸν τὸ ἐπαρκεῖν, μοχθηρῷ ὄντι· εὖ πάσχειν γὰρ οἱ πολλοὶ βούλονται, τὸ δὲ ποιεῖν φεύγουσιν ὡς ἀλυσιτελές.
>
> At the same time presumably no one would dissociate himself from a son unless he was an exceedingly bad character; for apart from the natural

76 Ar. *EN* VIII.xiv (1163b15–22); *transl. adapted.*

77 Cf. *EN* IX.i (1164b6): towards parents and gods, only reciprocation according to ability (τὸ ἐνδεχόμενον) is possible. According to Pakaluk (1998), 148 this emphatically exceptional quality of the relationship with parents and gods may be taken to imply that in other relationships deference (τιμή) may serve to discharge debts. This is partly right: Aristotle does acknowledge τιμή as a form of symbolic capital that accrues to the superior party in unequal utility friendships but does not accept the implication that debts in unequal friendships can ever be balanced. See Chapter Seven Section 3.5 on τιμή.

> friendship of father for son, it is human not to reject a source of assistance. But if the son is a bad character, then for him assisting his father is something to be avoided, or something not to take trouble about; for most people wish to receive benefits, but conferring them they avoid as *unprofitable.*[78]

Not only is the parent-child bond "natural" (φυσική), it is also all too human to not reject the future assistance (ἐπικουρία) the son is able to offer—whereas a bad son seeks to avoid (φεύγειν) his impending duty.[79] The digression closes with a somewhat cynical remark: most people (οἱ πολλοί) prefer to *receive* good (εὖ πάσχειν), but avoid *doing* good (εὖ ποιεῖν), as if that were unprofitable (ὡς ἀλυσιτελές)—with ὡς pointing out that this, again, is a subjective take on things. It is the *wrong* take, for it presupposes an accounting model based on the utility of the benefits instead of the goodness of the act of benefaction.

It is not only in cases of filial obligation that Aristotle applies the Debtor Paradigm. In a more generic discussion of φιλία, Aristotle claims that in cases of conflicting claims, it is as a general rule better to fulfill outstanding obligations towards benefactors before doing any favor to friends. Here too the Debtor Paradigm is applied:

[Text 11]

> Καὶ τὰς μὲν εὐεργεσίας ἀνταποδοτέον ὡς ἐπὶ τὸ πολὺ μᾶλλον ἢ χαριστέον ἑταίροις, ὥσπερ καὶ δάνειον ᾧ ὀφείλει ἀποδοτέον μᾶλλον ἢ ἑταίρῳ δοτέον.
>
> [A]nd one should for the most part sooner pay someone back for benefits received than give to a comrade, *just as one should also sooner repay a loan to a creditor* than give favors to comrades.[80]

Discharging outstanding obligations (ἀνταποδοτέον) to a benefactor has precedence over making investments in long-term reciprocities (to oblige, χαρίζεσθαι,

78 Ar. *EN* VIII.xiv (1163b22–27).

79 Smith-Pangle (2003: 131) is somewhat disillusioned to see "the unqualified love of parents" thrown "into a new shadow". As will be argued in Chapters Four and Seven, reading "unqualified love" or "selflessness" into Aristotle's concepts of φιλία presupposes a clean-cut egoism-altruism dichotomy that was alien to Aristotle. For the study of ancient conceptions of φιλία, the dichotomy has little analytical value—although it certainly is an interesting *object* of analysis.

80 Ar. *EN* IX.ii (1164b31–32).

one's ἑταῖροι—paraphrased as gift-giving (ἡ δόσις) a few lines later):[81] giving *back* (ἀποδιδόναι, or ἀνταποδιδόναι) before giving (διδόναι)! Here, the priority of obligations of a beneficiary towards his benefactor is constructed as analogous (ὥσπερ) to an outstanding debt (δάνειον).[82] The realm of long-term reciprocity (benefits, giving, giving what is due, χάρις) is conflated with, or reduced to, debtor-creditor relationships—with only ὥσπερ to indicate that it is merely an *analogy* that we are dealing with.

Aristotle exploits the isomorphism between the formal credit and phenomena of long-term reciprocity for didactic purposes. When reciprocal obligations require explanation, the analogy with debt serves to articulate the precise debt relation: who owes what to whom and on what grounds? In Chapter Four, we will see that Aristotle also takes care to make plain that despite all the similarities, the Debtor Paradigm is still only an analogy, *a way of seeing things*. Filial duty is not *really* about repaying debts. The imperfect nature of the analogy is already hinted at in T9: Aristotle, like Plato, sees filial obligation as an *irredeemable* debt. In Graeber's terminology, this would be hierarchy—not exchange.

Nevertheless, as the Athenian Visitor did, Aristotle uses the terminology of debt and repayment as an **analytical model**. The Debtor Paradigm may not be the last word on the nature of obligation, but it may provide a model good enough for didactic purposes. Or does it?

2.3 *Children as Credit Instruments?*

Like the anecdote about Ernest Thompson Seton, the type of analysis of filial duty in terms of debt strikes modern readers by its "remarkable lack of any mention of love", as it "reads painfully like a balance sheet".[83] This reaction is not the prerogative of a modern audience; similar objections recur in Plutarch,

81 A few lines later (*EN* IX.ii (1165a2–5)) the "general rule" (καθόλου) is repeated, that one must first pay back the debt (τὸ ὀφείλημα ἀποδοτέον), unless the balance of nobility or urgency (τῷ καλῷ ἢ τῷ ἀναγκαίῳ) is on the side of the gift (ἡ δόσις).

82 Possibly the contrast between asymmetrical (benefaction involves a superior and an inferior party with respect to access to utilities) and symmetrical (*hetairoi* are equally useful for one another) is also relevant. Note furthermore that Aristotle here emphatically discusses rules of thumb: the priority of redeeming debt with a benefactor over gratifying a friend applies "in most situations" (ἐπὶ τὸ πολύ); it is not, as the next lines (*EN* IX.ii (1164b34–35)) make plain, a universal law (ἴσως δ' οὐδὲ τοῦτ' ἀεί); on a more general note, Aristotle repeats his famous reservation that discussion about affections and actions have the same degree of determinacy as their subject matter (*EN* IX.ii (1165a12–13), referring back to I.iii (1094b11–14), I.vii (1098a26–33), II.ii (1104a1–7); cf. *Met.* 995a15–16).

83 Stevenson (1992), 428. See also English (1991); Keller (2006), 256–257.

who in his work *On Affection for Offspring* ridicules the idea of having children as a sort of credit instrument. It is in this context that we see Plato's Debtor Paradigm recur.

It is important to appreciate that there is a different perspective here. Rather than inquiring after the grounds of the obligation that children have towards their parents, Plutarch is involved in a polemic about the nature of **parental affection** (φιλοστοργία), concentrating on the internalized aspects of the relation (rather than on overt behavior alone), from the point of view of the parent. The prime target of the discussion is Epicurus who claims that although parents do love their children, this commitment (στέργειν) is not natural, but motivated by the expectation of some benefit to be derived from these children.[84] According to Epicurus (i.e. in Plutarch's polemical representation) human parents are incapable of loving their children without prospect of gain (φιλεῖν ἄνευ χρείας).[85] "It is for pay (μισθοῦ)," says Epicurus, "that fathers love sons, mothers love children and children love their parents."[86] Here the Debtor Paradigm is taken to deny the possibility of genuine other-regarding dispositions or emotions: the prospect of gain changes the depth and the nature of the experience of φιλία.

This is absurd, according to Plutarch, for animals love their offspring not for pay (οὐ ... ἐπὶ μισθῷ ... φιλοῦσιν),[87] but "gratuitously and naturally" (προῖκα καὶ φυσικῶς). Given that animals bear the burden of childbirth and nurture as a matter of nature (φυσίν) and as an act of χάρις, it would be a moral digrace (αἰσχρόν) if humans were only capable of caring for their children as loans (δάνεια), for wages (μισθούς) and security money (ἀρραβῶνας) on the condition of a return (ἐπὶ χρείαις).[88] In the hands of Plutarch, the same Debtor Paradigm that to the Athenian Visitor served as an explanatory model for the inculcation of virtue in Magnesia turns into an object of moral reprehension: it is a pathetic conception of the parent-child relation, one that is mean and less evolved than plainly observable animal behavior.

Next Plutarch embarks on a thought experiment about the condition of primitive mankind:

84 See Roskam (2011), 186–187 on the Epicurean background of this statement.

85 Plut. *De Amor. Prol.* 495a4.

86 495a5, citing a comic fragment μισθοῦ γὰρ ἄνθρωπον τίς ἀνθρώπων φιλεῖ (Kock III, 450, adesp. 218).

87 495a11–12.

88 495b5.

[Text 12]

> Ἐπὶ τοὺς παλαιοὺς ἀνάγαγε τὸν λόγον, ὧν ταῖς μὲν τεκεῖν πρώταις, τοῖς δ' ἰδεῖν συνέβη τικτόμενον βρέφος· οὔτε νόμος ἦν ἐκείνοις τεκνοτροφεῖν προστάττων οὔτε προσδοκία χάριτος ἢ τροφείων 'ἐπὶ νέοις δανειζομένων'.
>
> Carry the discussion back to primitive mankind, to those whose women were the first to bear, and whose men were the first to see a child born; they had neither any law which bade them rear their children, *nor any expectation of gratitude or of receiving the wages of maintenance 'lent to their children when they were young.'*[89]

The first parents were not guided by any law for the rearing of their children nor by any expectation of χάρις or "reward for nursing" (τροφεία) for the "loan they made their children" (ἐπὶ νέοις δανειζομένων)—a literal citation of the passage from Plato's *Laws*. Under such circumstances, it would be reasonable to expect that women would be harsh and malicious (χαλεπὰς ... καὶ μνησικάκους) to their children because of the great dangers and travail that comes to them from childbirth. But even then, nature instills φιλοστοργία in mothers, who instantly care for their infants "reaping nothing sweet or profitable in return (μηδὲν ἡδὺ καρπουμένη μηδὲ χρήσιμον)",[90] but enduring pain and discomfort instead.

Plutarch's analysis of parental affection shows that in Hellenistic and Imperial philosophical discourse, a tension was felt between the format of a balance sheet with its objectifiable and quantifiable obligations on the one hand, and the subjective first-person experience of commitment on the other hand. His main objections are directed against the notion that a relationship as fundamental as that between parent and child would be based, in the ultimate analysis, on ulterior motives and on self-interest.[91] To Plutarch, this is what the Debtor Paradigm boils down to: an Epicurean worldview in which every relationship is based on a calculus of what is useful.[92]

---

89 496c5–8; *transl.* Helmbold (1939).

90 496d9–e1.

91 This raises the topic of the egoism-altruism dichotomy. On the emergence of the distinction and its limited analytical value, see Chapter Five.

92 Roskam (2011), 186.

2.4 *The Problem with the Debtor Paradigm*

We have seen that although the Debtor Paradigm of Obligation can be a compelling analogy, problems arise when this model is applied to the parent-child bond too strictly. Even in the context of Plato's *Laws* we see that the metaphor of debt can only be applied loosely to the parent-child situation: concrete direct duties (to nurture or to provide care for parents) are more easily explained with the debt metaphor than deferential behavior or post-mortem care.[93] Moreover, the one obvious problem with the debt analogy is that debts can be discharged whereas filial duty is not a definite list of specific acts of care, nurture or respect that can be ticked off.[94]

The conceptual solution to this apparent mismatch between the Debtor Paradigm and the nature of filial obligation is to regard the debt as a debt so large that it cannot be redeemed. The perpetuity of the debt makes the relation between debtor and creditor unequal—which in turn is in line with the fact that children *owe* their parents deferential behavior and language. We will see how this idea of unequal reciprocity and obligations beyond redemptions recurs in Xenophon's conceptualization of parent-child relations (Section 4).

Plutarch's problems with the Debtor Paradigm are not analytical or conceptual in nature but moral: to Plutarch, the analogy with credit relations affects the qualitative aspects of the parent-child bond. Following Epicurus' reductionist approach, Plutarch takes the analogy as a statement about the parents' motivations and intentions, and by implication their emotions, somewhat along the following lines: the filial obligation to return nurture implies an *expectation* on the part of the parents that their efforts will be returned; this in turn says something about the parents' *motivation* to beget and take care of children in the first place; this means that parents have *ulterior reasons* to care of their children, which means that they cannot really care *about* their children, because ulterior reasons are at odds with affective qualities and emotional aspects that are commonly associated with parental commitment. (Strictly speaking, none of these steps is self-evident or purely deductive). In Chapter Four we will see that a similar tension is felt by Aristotle, who concedes that the Debtor Paradigm is "a way of looking" at a reciprocal interaction, but in the end he judges the analogy to be defective as it fails to grasp the moral moment in parent-child exchanges.

To Plato, the analogy between formal credit in the form of a δάνεισμα and long-term reciprocity between parents and children serves as a didactic instru-

93 Cf. Keller (2006), 256: "The trouble with the debt theory is that it leads to implausible claims about what filial duties we actually have."

94 English (1979), 354–356.

ment. To Plutarch, the same analogy is symptomatic of a misguided view on interpersonal relationships. In 5th- and 4th-century popular discourse, the analogy was, as we shall see, anomalous.

3 The Gratitude Theory

3.1 *The Language and Logic of Generalized Reciprocity*

Is there an alternative theory of filial duty? An obvious candidate would be the Gratitude Theory.[95] In 5th- and 4th-century popular discourse, filial obligations were routinely formulated in terms that expressed their reciprocal nature: children are expected to support parents "in their turn" (πάλιν)[96] and to "make a return" (ἀποδίδοναι)[97] for their rearing (θρεπτήρια, τροφεῖα); even seemingly one-sided phrases such as "treating well" (εὖ ποιεῖν) or "to be a benefactor to" (εὐεργετεῖν) may be presumed to evoke the ideal of "reciprocating a good turn" and of reciprocal χάρις.[98]

Like the Debtor Paradigm of Obligation, the reciprocity-model of filial duty establishes a moral connection between the care bestowed by parents upon their children and the children's obligation to support their parents in their old age. The *locus classicus* of filial obligation occurs in a pre-classical text: Hesiod's well-known doom prophecy of the Iron Race, the generation that will witness the breakdown of reciprocal ties, between fathers and children, guests and hosts, comrades and brothers (180–185), and between children and their aging parents:

[Text 13]

> αἶψα δὲ γηράσκοντας ἀτιμήσουσι τοκῆας·
> μέμψονται δ' ἄρα τοὺς χαλεποῖς βάζοντες ἔπεσσι,
> σχέτλιοι, οὐδὲ θεῶν ὄπιν εἰδότες· οὐδέ κεν οἵ γε
> γηράντεσσι τοκεῦσιν ἀπὸ θρεπτήρια δοῖεν·

---

95 For modern analyses of the Gratitude Theory of filial duty, see: Keller (2006), Berger (1975).

96 Aristoph. *Birds* 1356–1357 (see n. 5 above); [Ar.] *Oec.* I.iii.3.

97 Eur. *IA* 1228–1230; Men. *Xen.* fr. 354 (T23), Men. *Sam.* 18 (T24), Alexis fr. 280 (T30), Lyc. 1.53, Xen. *Mem.* II.ii.2 (T34), Xen. *Mem.* II.ii.13 (T37), Ar. *EN* 1163b22–27 (T10); outside the strict context of 5th- and 4th-century Athens: Hes., *O&D* 188 (T5; cf. Hom. *Il.* 4.447), IG IX-1² 313.7 (T20).

98 τὸν εὖ παθόντα ἀντευποιεῖν: e.g. Aristoph. *Plutus* 1029; εὖ ἔρδων εὖ πάσχε: e.g. Thgn. 573–574; εὖ δρᾶν εὖ παθών: e.g. Soph. *Phil.* 672. For reciprocal χάρις, see Chapter Two. Cf. Fragoulaki (2013); Blundell (1989), 26–59; Millett (1991), 109–116.

> Men will dishonor their parents as they grow quickly old, and will carp at them, chiding them with bitter words, hard-hearted are they, not knowing the fear of the gods. They will not repay their aged parents the cost of their nurture.[99]

The children will withhold from their parents the treatment that is due to them (ἀτιμήσουσι) and will treat them disrespectfully and withhold from them the return (ἀπὸ … δοῖεν) for the effort of rearing (θρεπτήρια). What is presupposed in this prophecy of doom is, of course, its reverse, i.e. an understanding of, and an adherence to, the norm of filial duty: it is part of the treatment that is due (τιμή) to parents to return the favor of nurture. This formulation of filial duty too reads like a balance sheet and the similarities with the Debtor Paradigm of Obligation are obvious: children are obliged to take care of their aging parents *because* they have received nurture from them in the past. Care is due (note the ἀπο-prefix) because it is *owed*.

In fact, in many of our sources it is difficult to see a difference between the Debtor Paradigm and the Gratitude Theory: both models picture the bond between parents and children as a form of exchange over a long period of time. While perfectly transparent and persuasive, our Hesiod passage above (T13) is illustrative for the skewed nature of our source material about conceptions of filial duty: social norms function by the grace of their implicitness and are only explicated when they are perceived to be problematic,[100] not self-evident[101] or in need of theorization.[102] The Hesiod passage is an example of the *breakdown* of parent-child reciprocity. It is in such contexts where relations are problematic, negated or subject to negotiation that norms are made explicit; it is in such contexts too that the difference between the Debtor Paradigm and the Gratitude Theory collapses.

As we have seen in Chapter Two, there is something about analytic discourse, i.e. the act of formulating and formalizing social rules, that is alien, or even hostile, to the workings of χάρις. To get a better grasp of this phenomenon, let us once again revert to Sahlins' description of the phenomenon of "generalized reciprocity":

---

99 Hes. *O&D* 185–188.

100 As for instance in cases of their violation; see Sections 3.2, 3.4, 6 and 7.

101 As for instance in cases of adoption; see Sections 3.2 and 3.3.

102 As for instance in analytical discourse: Xenophon (see Section 4) and Aristotle (see Section 2.2 above).

[Text 14]

> "Generalized reciprocity" refers to transactions that are putatively altruistic, transactions on the line of assistance given and, if possible and necessary, assistance returned. (…)—*the expectation of direct material return is unseemly. At best it is implicit. The material side of the transaction is repressed by the social: reckoning of debts outstanding cannot be overt and is typically left out of account.* This is not to say that handing over things in such forms, even to "loved ones," generates no counter-obligation.[103]

As we have seen, generalized reciprocity is the type of extreme solidarity that occurs between people with minimal social distance. In such close and intimate bonds, there is a generalized sense of solidarity in which individual transfers cannot, or *must not*, be identified: there is no counting of meals or diapers. Returns may be expected, but not made explicit, for that would be "unseemly" and inappropriate—i.e. it violates the sense of solidarity associated with this notional form of "sharing".

Whereas Sahlins took kinship distance to be the determinant factor of solidarity, for the 5th- and 4th-century Greek world, Lyn Foxhall has argued that the οἶκος, the household, is the fundamental unit:[104] within the household information and resources[105] are shared, i.e. "held in common"—"baseline communism", in Graeber's model. A passage often quoted in this context is Xenophon's *Oeconomicus* where Ischomachus explains to his young new wife the principles of the household:

[Text 15]

> τέκνα μὲν οὖν ἂν θεός ποτε διδῷ ἡμῖν γενέσθαι, τότε βουλευσόμεθα περὶ αὐτῶν ὅπως ὅτι βέλτιστα παιδεύσομεν αὐτά· κοινὸν γὰρ ἡμῖν καὶ τοῦτο ἀγαθόν, συμμάχων|13 καὶ γηροβοσκῶν ὅτι βελτίστων τυγχάνειν· νῦν δὲ δὴ οἶκος ἡμῖν ὅδε κοινός ἐστιν. ἐγώ τε γὰρ ὅσα μοι ἔστιν ἅπαντα εἰς τὸ κοινὸν ἀποφαίνω, σύ τε ὅσα ἠνέγκω πάντα εἰς τὸ κοινὸν κατέθηκας. καὶ οὐ τοῦτο δεῖ λογίζεσθαι, πότερος ἄρα ἀριθμῷ πλείω συμβέβληται ἡμῶν, ἀλλ' ἐκεῖνο εὖ εἰδέναι, ὅτι ὁπότερος ἂν ἡμῶν βελτίων κοινωνὸς ᾖ,|14 οὗτος τὰ πλείονος ἄξια συμβάλλεται.

103 Sahlins (1972), 193; my emphasis.

104 The household cuts across boundaries between kin and non-kin. Foxhall (1998), 52.

105 Foxhall (2007), 51–52.

> Now, as far as children are concerned, we will wait to see if God grants us any before thinking about how best to bring them up: *one of the advantages we will share with each other* is having them to support us and look after us as well as they can when we grow old. *But what we share now is this household of ours*, and we share it because I make *all* my income available *for both of us*, and you have deposited *all* that you brought with you *in the same common pool. There's no need to tot up* which of us has made the greater contribution *quantitatively*, but we must appreciate that whichever of us is the better partner contributes more *qualitatively*.[106]

The household is envisaged as a common pool (a κοινόν) to which both husband and wife contribute, without keeping track in a quantitative sense (οὐ τοῦτο δεῖ λογίζεσθαι; ἀριθμῷ).[107] Although the passage focuses on the generalized solidarity between husband and wife, it is interesting to note that the prospective support by future children too is understood as something that husband and wife will share (will have κοινόν). As we will see, children too are imagined as being participators in the common pool of the household, where resources are shared with the implicit understanding that at some point everybody will have to contribute according to his or her capacity.

Whereas this generalized mode of sharing may be seen as the default practice within the οἶκος, the sources that thematize filial obligation, by their very perspective, analytically break down the mechanics of generalized solidarity, or baseline communism, into a form of reciprocal exchange—reciprocity that may not involve precise and numerical quantification, but that does presuppose awareness of "more", "less", "great (favor)", "small (favor in return)". This "analysis" typically occurs in situations of disruption and crisis when the everyday taken-for-grantedness of reciprocity is suspended: when one of the partners is unable, unwilling or unlikely to reciprocate or when the conditions of a relation are, for some reason, being questioned or renegotiated.

We will see that in 5th- and 4th-century popular discourse, this "analysis" of filial duty in terms of reciprocal gratitude will generally adhere to one of two related but distinct templates: the general model of χάρις or the related, but more specific, model of *eranos* credit. Both models are distinct from the Debtor Paradigm of Obligation.

---

106 Xen. *Oec.* VII.12–14; *transl.* Tredennick & Waterfield (1990) *adapted*.

107 Ischomachus takes care to stress that the generalized sharing of resources does not imply that husband and wife are *equal*: qualitative differences in their contributions legitimate inequality between husband and wife.

3.2 *Futile χάρις*

Occasionally, the Debtor Paradigm and Gratitude Theory seem dangerously close to each other. As we have seen, once made explicit, the norm of reciprocity may exude a sense of utilitarianism that "reads painfully like a balance sheet". An extreme example that tramples on modern sensitivities can be found in literary and epigraphical representations of parents who are grieving for their deceased children—a situation in which one of the partners is, simply, *unable* to reciprocate. In Euripides' *Suppliant Women*, for instance, the chorus consisting of Argive mothers responds to Adrastus' Funeral Oration for the fallen Argive warriors with a song of lament:[108]

[Text 16]

> Χο. ἰὼ τέκνον, δυστυχῆ
> σ' ἔτρεφον ἔφερον ὑφ' ἥπατος
> πόνους ἐνεγκοῦσ' ἐν ὠδῖσι· καὶ
> νῦν τὸν ἐμὸν Ἀίδας
> ἔχει μόχθον ἀθλίας,
> ἐγὼ δὲ γηροβοσκὸν οὐκ ἔχω, τεκοῦσ'
> ἁ τάλαινα παῖδα.

> Alas, my son, it was for misery | that *I carried you* next to my heart and *nourished you*, | bearing the *pain* of childbirth! And now Hades has taken | *the fruits of my labor*, wretch that I am, | and *I have no one to tend my old age*, though I, | unhappy one, *have borne* a child![109]

The lament is typically shaped as a complaint: the lament starts off with a single comment on the dead (proleptic δυστυχῆ, "to your misery") and then moves on to the mothers' grief—a grief that is circumscribed in almost objectifying terms of distress. Nurture (ἔτρεφον), gestation (ἔφερον) and the pain of childbirth (πόνους ... ἐν ὠδῖσι) were all in vain, for the mothers are not able to reap the fruit of their labor (μόχθον), that is: to have someone to tend them in their old age (to act as a γηροβοσκός). The postposed participle τεκοῦσα adds a concessive flavor:[110] *despite* the fact that the mothers have given birth to children, they are bereft of a caretaker in their old age.

---

108 On the political aspects of the mothers' lament, especially in contrast to Adrastus' Funeral Oration, Loraux (2006 [1981]), with the critical discussion in Pelling (1997), 230–235.

109 Eur. *Suppl.* 918–924; *transl.* Kovacs (1998).

110 Collard (1975), ad loc.

The bereaved mothers resume their complaint in 1133–1137 in a series of rhetorical questions:

[Text 17]

> Χο. ἰὼ ἰώ·
> ποῦ δὲ πόνος ἐμῶν τέκνων,
> ποῦ λοχευμάτων χάρις
> τροφαί τε ματρὸς ἄυπνά τ' ὀμμάτων τέλη·
> καὶ φίλιαι προσβολαὶ προσώπων;
>
> Ah me! | Where is the *labor* I spent on my sons? | Where is the *thanks for the pains of childbirth*? | Where is a mother's tendance, the sleepless devotion of her eyes, | the sweet touch of her face?[111]

In this "triple expansion of motherhood's πόνος and χάρις",[112] the interrogative ποῦ underscores the idea that the toil (πόνος) of rearing has been in vain, because there is no reciprocation (χάρις) for the act of childbirth (λοχευμάτων).[113] The "triple expansion of motherhood's πόνος and χάρις"[114] that follows, though syntactically on the same level as λοχευμάτων χάρις, seems to presuppose the idea of χάρις: maternal nurture (τροφαί), devotion and affection (ἄυπνά … προσώπων) all seems "lost" now because all expectation of reciprocation is thwarted with the demise of the children. Note that we see a seamless juxtaposition of the typically tender and affectionate details of motherhood (1136–1137) with the almost utilitarian idea that all of this has been "in vain" now that reciprocity has been made impossible.

These notions of "fruit of labor" and "affection lost" give rise to the idea of the "unprofitable" child. Hecuba, for example, referring to her murdered son Polydorus, qualifies giving birth to him as "in vain" (or "unprofitable", ἀνόνητά):[115]

---

111 Eur. *Suppl.* 1133–1137.

112 Collard (1975), ad loc.

113 λοχευμάτων is a conjecture by Musgrave. Manuscript L reads πολυχευμάτων (which is nonsensical); Tr offers a supralinear correction ου νῦ, which results in the reading ποῦ νυχευμάτων χάρις ("where is the thanks for nightly watches", i.e. "where is the thanks for the wakeful nights"), which makes no less sense in the context and, in addition, anticipates the ἄυπνα τ'ὀμμάτων τέλη. For the idea of maternal lucubration, see also Xen. *Mem.* II.ii.6.

114 Collard (1975), ad loc.

115 The adverbially used ἀνόνητα qualifies an understood ἔτεκον.

[Text 18]

Αγ. ἦ γάρ τιν' ἄλλον ἔτεκες ἢ κείνους, γύναι;
Εκ. ἀνόνητά γ', ὡς ἔοικε, τόνδ' ὃν εἰσορᾷς.

Agamemnon: But did you bear *another* son besides those, lady?
Hecuba: Yes, *but to no purpose*, it seems: the man you see before you.[116]

—the underlying script being that Polydorus' death before his time has deprived Hecuba of the fruit of parent-child reciprocity. To modern sensitivities, particularly this notion of "bearing children unprofitably" is revolting because it seems to violate the cultural construct of the "priceless" child; as Viviana Zelizer has argued for American culture, the nineteenth century has witnessed a transformation in the social valuation of the child, from economically "useful" (the child being expected to make a valuable contribution to the family economy) to economically "useless" but emotionally "priceless", i.e. to an "exclusively emotional and affective asset".[117] For our ancient lamentations we should note that seemingly utilitarian complaints over the "economic" implications of the loss of a child need not imply an absence of an affectionate and emotional dimension: complaints are part of the expression form of ancient lament and talk of thwarted reciprocity is a natural way of thematizing the tragedy of premature death that does not diminish or eliminate the affectionate nature of the mother-child bond.[118]

A similar script recurs in funerary epigrams of deceased youths—albeit with a different, somewhat twisted, perspective: the epitaphs are conventionally cast in first-person perspective, formally giving voice to the deceased youth and suggesting internal focalization, but in effect voicing the parents' grief and sense of loss. The tragedy of premature death is foregrounded by the idea of natural order reversed: parents are burying their child instead of the child adhering to the norms of γηροτροφία (which include providing a proper burial to one's deceased parents):[119]

116 Eur. *Hec.* 766–767; *transl.* Kovacs (1995).

117 Zelizer (1985) documents this transformation by analyzing sources on child labor, adoption, insurance and legal cases concerning wrongful deaths and accidents. She argues that although demographic and market economic factors have been relevant to the social development she describes, ultimately the key is a process of "sacralization" of the child.

118 For complaints as a standard element of laments, see Alexiou (1974), 182–184.

119 The tragedy of a parent receiving his child's remains instead of τροφεῖα is poignantly brought out in IG XII-1 140 (Rhodes, late 3rd century BCE; Peek (1955), no. 920): Ἀνδρόμαχος με(τ)ὰ πένθος | Ἀριστάνακτος ἀδελφοῦ | [κ]άλπιν ἐπ' ἄστυ Πάφου πάτριον ἵξει ἄγων. |

[Text 19]

πένθους καὶ στοναχῆς ἐτράφην χάριν, οὐχὶ βοηθός
μητρὶ φίλῃ γήρως εἰς τέλος ἐρχομένῃ·
ἐννεετεῖς γὰρ ἰδὼν κυκλίους ὥρας ἐνιαυτῶν
θνήισκω δυσξυνετῶι δαίμονι χρησάμενος.

For the sake of grief and groaning *did I grow up*, not to become a *helper* | for my dear mother who is progressing towards the end of her old age | For after having seen for nine years the cycling seasons of the years | I die, having met a senseless Daimon.[120]

In this late-4th-century epitaph from Peiraeus, the voice of a nine-year-old laments his premature death in terms of his inability to return the χάρις of rearing (ἐτράφην) by becoming his mother's helper (βοηθός). Although syntactically speaking, the noun χάριν functions as a postpositive ("for the sake of", with the genitives πένθους and στοναχῆς), its juxtaposition with ἐτράφην evokes the idea that τροφή of children should be reciprocated with τροφεῖα for parents in their old age—the cycle of χάρις made impossible by the child's premature death:

[Text 20]

οὔ με πατήρ, ὦ ξεῖνοι, ὁ δύσμορος οὐδέ με μάτηρ
νυμφιδίων θαλάμων ἔδρακον ἁπτόμενον,
ἀλλὰ πάρος διὰ νύκτα κατὰ πτόλιν Ἄρεϊ λυγρῶι
φωτὸς ὑπὸ στυγερᾶς οὐλόμενον παλάμας·
εἰκοσιπενταέτης δὲ γόνος πινυτοῖο Ξένωνος
Νίκαρχος μύσταις ἄμμιγα ναιετάω
οὐδὲ γονεῦσιν ἑοῖς ἀποδοὺς χάριν· ὦ μέγας Ἅιδα,
τόν με κατακτείναντ' αἶψα καταστορέσαις.

πρέσβυ, σὺ δ' οὐχὶ τροφεῖα, | τὰ δ' ὀστέα παιδὸς ἐπόψει, | Μεννέα, ἐν ξείνῃ γῇ Ῥοδίων φθιμένου. ("With grief will come Andromachos | bringing of his brother Aristanax | the urn to his hometown Paphos. | And you, old man, will not behold *care* | but the bones of your child, | who has died on Rhodian soil abroad, Menneas.")

120 IG II² 13102. The inscription which is dated in the last quarter of the 4th century is currently located in the Peiraeus Museum. For the epigraphic details, see Peek (1936), 4–6; see also Peek (1955), no. 1118, Verilhac (1982), no. 169.

> Not did my hapless father, dear strangers, nor my mother | have the sight of me reaching the bridal bedroom. | Instead, aforetime, towards night, in town through baneful fight | by the loathed hands of man I was killed. | Aged twenty five, a child of prudent Xenon, | I, Nikarchos, dwell with the initiated, | *without having reciprocated* kharis *to my parents*. Mighty Hades, | may you soon cover my killer with dust.[121]

The voice of the young man mourns his untimely death by bringing out the lamentable fact that he dies an unmarried man (v.2), without having reciprocated (ἀποδούς) grace to his parents—the two most harrowing loose ends of premature death. Similarly, an epitaph from Phocis (3rd century BCE) for a youth named Damotimos closes with a description of his mother's grief:

[Text 21]

> πολλάκι δ' ἀμφὶ τεὸν μάτηρ τάφον οἰκτρὸν ἄϋσεν
> Δεξώ, στενάζουσα ὀρφανὰν τέκνου χάριν.

> Often has your mother been heard wailing around your grave | Dexo, *bemoaning her child's orphaned grace*.[122]

With delicate metonymia, the aborted cycle of mother-child reciprocity is called "orphaned grace" (ὀρφανὰν χάριν) or "grace bereft of a child" (ὀρφανὰν τέκνου χάριν). At once mirroring the childless state of the mother and evoking the proverbial expression that "grace begets grace" (χάρις χάριν ἐστιν ἡ τίκτουσ' ἀεί),[123] the image closely ties together the reproductive order of mother and child and the moral order of *kharis*.

Occasionally, the theme of an inverted order of nature prompts the use of a vocabulary that seems blatantly at odds with the deeply affectionate bond that we would expect between parents and children:

[Text 22]

> τί πλέον ἐστ' εἰς τέκνα πονεῖν, ἢ πρὸς τί προτιμᾶν,
> εἰ μὴ Ζῆνα κριτὴν ἕξομεν, ἀλλ' Ἀΐδην;

121 IG IX-1² 313 = GV 1822; Akarnania, 2nd century BCE.

122 IG IX-1 163.7–8 = Geffcken 155; GV 1502; Elateia, Phokis; 3rd century BCE.

123 Soph. *Aj.* 520–524; cf. Soph. *OC* 779 (ἡ χάρις χάριν φέροι), Eur. *Hel.* 1234 (χάρις ἀντὶ χάριτος ἐλθέτω), Ar. *Rhet.* 1385a16. See Chapter Two, Section 2.2.

> δὶς δέκα γάρ μ' ἐκόμησε πατὴρ ἔτη, οὐδ' ἐτέλεσσα
> νυμφιδίων θαλάμων εἰς ὑμέναια λέχη,
> (…).
> μαστοὶ μητρὸς ἐμῆς κ̣ε̣νεὸν γάλα τοί με ἐκόμησαν,
> οἷς χάριν οὐ δυνάμην γηροτρόφον τελέσαι.

> What good is it to *suffer toil* for children, why trouble oneself about them | when we will not have Zeus as judge, but Hades? | For twice ten years my father *took care of me*, but *not did I reach* | my bridal chamber's wedding bed. (…) In vain did my mother's breasts *provide* me with milk | for which *I was not able to fulfill my filial duties as* kharis.[124]

Again, the drama of premature death is made palpable with the theme of the doubly unfulfilled (οὐδ' ἐτέλεσσα, τελέσαι) life: not getting married and not being able to provide γηροτρόφος χάρις, the grace of taking care for the elderly. The parallelism is brought out by the repetition of the verb κομέω, "to take care of" (3: ἐκόμησε, 9: ἐκόμησαν),—a care remaining unrequited in both cases (note the repetition οὐδ' ἐτέλεσσα … τελέσαι). The toil (1: πονεῖν) of child-rearing is "in vain" (9: κενεὸν γάλα; cf. the rhetorical questions in 1: τί πλέον ἐστ' … πρὸς τί …), like the ματαιοτάτη χάρις, the "useless grace" of Theognis, like sowing the expanse of the white-capped sea.[125]

Between parents and their deceased child, the lament of futile χάρις may strike us as awkward and somewhat alienating, as though the child's voice is channeling a deeply utilitarian attitude on the part of the parents. However, this "utilitarian" theme of aborted χάρις need not imply a lack of affection:[126] the *vision par derrière*, the temporal point of view that regards χάρις-exchanges as completed events in the past, is inherent in the situation of a child's premature death; but the concern with the disruption of reciprocity itself is rarely voiced from the perspective of the parents (T13, 14 and 16 are focalized by the indebted child; T15 from the point of view of an empathic outsider). On the level of the child, these epitaphs express awareness of *kharis* not redeemed: it is part of the tragedy of untimely death that these children shall never be able to do what full-grown persons do, i.e. reciprocating care to their greatest benefactors—but their inability to reciprocate does not make them ingrates,

124 *GV* 1680 1–4, 9–10 = *Annales du Service des Antiquités de l'Égypte* 21 (1921), 165 ff. = Bernand, E., *Inscriptions métriques de l'Égypte grécoromaine* 83; Karanis, Egypt; 3rd/2nd century BCE; Bernand: 2/1 BCE.

125 Thgn. 1.105–106; see Chapter Two Section 2.2.

126 Cf. Strubbe (1998), 47.

for they do "know" the *kharis*, and even attempt to *show* it, albeit by means of the verbal substitute of a 1st-person epitaph. On the level of the parents, it is striking for us to see how even emotions as profound as grief for a deceased child are mediated and structured by the norms and expectations of reciprocity.

3.3 *Reciprocity and Affection*

In everyday reality, the norm of reciprocity remains implicit—only to be explicated in situations where the norm is threatened, violated or subject to detached analysis. For instance, in a fragment from Menander's *Xenologos*, we find a young man enlisting as a mercenary in order to save his father from poverty:[127]

[Text 23]

> ἀνδρὸς πένητος υἱός, ἐκτεθραμμένος
> οὐκ ἐξ ὑπαρχόντων, ὁρῶν ᾐσχύνετο
> τὸν πατέρα μίκρ' ἔχοντα· παιδευθεὶς γὰρ εὖ
> τὸν καρπὸν εὐθὺς ἀπεδίδου χάριτος καλόν.

> The son of a poor man, *who had been brought up* | beyond his father's means, saw that his father | had only a little and *was ashamed. Being properly raised* | *he at once set on returning the fair fruit of gratitude.*[128]

There is a clear moral link between the young man's upbringing (ἐκτεθραμμένος) and its reciprocation (τὸν καρπὸν ἀπεδίδου χάριτος καλόν), the long-term time frame encapsulated in the metaphor of καρπός ("fruit", "yield"): an investment in something that takes time to materialize.[129] This moral norm is internalized (παιδευθεὶς εὖ: the product of proper socialisation) and mediated by moral emotions (ᾐσχύνετο: the young man is ashamed about his poor father's predicament).[130]

---

127 For father-son relationships in Greco-Roman comedy, see Sherberg (1985).

128 Men. *Xen.* Kock fr. 354.

129 Cf. Eur. *Ion* 475 where children are καρποφόροι, "fruit bearing".

130 The adverb εὐθύς potentially suggests that the son manages to discharge altogether ("at once") his moral indebtedness to his father—something that seems to run counter to the logic of χάρις-terminology that tends to approach situations as ongoing processes instead of discrete definitive events. However, the imperfectual aspect of the verb ἀπεδίδου may support a processual and dynamic interpretation of the act of reciprocation.

A child's ability to experience χάρις (i.e. to "know the χάρις", to be grateful) is considered a sign of proper upbringing and good socialization. In the prologue of another play by Menander, the *Samia*, it is the young man Moschion who displays his ability to "know χάρις" by setting out the comfortable lifestyle he had enjoyed through the generosity of Demeas, his adoptive father:

[Text 24]

> [......]ο τοῦτο ἐσόμενον λογίζομαι,
> μᾶλλον] δὲ τοῦτ' ἂν εὐλόγως ὑμῖν ποεῖν
> [......] τὸν ἐκείνου διεξελθὼν τρόπον.
> οἷς μὲ]ν ἐτρύφησα τῶι τότ' εὐθέως χρόνωι
> ὢν παι]δίον, μεμνημένος σαφῶς ἐῶ·
> εὐεργέ]τει γὰρ ταῦτά μ' οὐ φρονοῦντά πω.
> [......]εγράφην οὐδὲν διαφέρων οὐδενός,
> τὸ λεγόμενον δὴ τοῦτο "τῶν πολλῶν τις ὤν",
> [......]α μέντοι, νὴ Δί', ἀθλιώτερος·
> [......] γάρ ἐσμεν. τῶι χορηγεῖν διέφερον
> καὶ τῆι] φιλοτιμίαι· κύνας παρέτρεφέ μοι,
> ἵππο]υς· ἐφυλάρχησα λαμπρῶς· τῶν φίλων
> τοῖς δεομένοις τὰ μέτρι' ἐπαρκεῖν ἐδυνάμην.
> δι' ἐκεῖνον ἦν ἄνθρωπος. ἀστείαν δ' ὅμως
> τούτων χάριν τιν' ἀπεδίδουν· ἦν κόσμιος.
>
> I reckon it will be (?) [| But sensibly [I'd like] to make this [clear] | To you by spelling out the kind of man he is. | I well *remember* [how], just after that, | [In child]hood I was spoiled—but let that pass. | *This* [*served*] *me* [*well*], before I learned to think. | [Next], I was registered—an average chap, | [That's how the] phrase goes, just like any other. | And I've [become] in fact more wretched—all | Because we're [loaded]! I shone with my payments | For choruses [and] public service. He kept hounds | For me, and [horses]. I starred as a colonel of | Hussars! I could give modest help to needy | Friends. He made me grow up. *I paid my debt* | *For that, though, nobly; I behaved myself.*[131]

The benefits that Moschion has enjoyed from his father are divided into two categories. First there are the luxurious circumstances (ἐτρύφησα)[132] of his

131 Men. *Sam.* 4–18; *transl.* Arnott (2000).

132 As Sommerstein (2013) ad loc. points out, the verb τρυφᾶν often suggests *excessive* luxury

early childhood. These Moschion remembers clearly (μεμνημένος σαφῶς, the perfective aspect contributes to Moschion's self-characterization as a considerate son); but which he will not catalog in the present context (ἐῶ, by way of *praeteritio*) given that (γάρ) it benefited (εὐεργέτει)[133] him at a point when he was not yet able to fully grasp the moral implications (οὐ φρονοῦντά πω).[134] Then, there is the treatment he received once he was registered (… εγράφην),[135] when he, being an average young man, was in the exceptional position of distinguishing himself by fulfilling choregies and phylarchies and keeping horses and hounds—signs of extraordinary luxury.[136] The entire catalog is framed as a demonstration by Moschion of the character (6: τρόπον) of his adoptive father Demeas. After the general remark "he made me a person" (δι' ἐκείνων ἦν ἄνθρωπος), Moschion breaks off his catalog (ὅμως) insisting that he has responded to Demeas' generosities by being a good and appreciative son: he has reciprocated with "some refined grace for that" (ἀστείαν τούτων χάριν τιν(α)),[137] i.e. he has been well-behaved (κόσμιος).[138]

(in a negative way), but not so much when it is used to describe good treatment by another person from which one has benefited.

133 If this restoration is correct.

134 Cf. Ar. *EN* 1155b33–1156a5 on one of the moral requirements for φιλία that φίλοι be aware of each other's εὔνοια. Sommerstein (2013) interprets οὐ φρονοῦντα as "not having a matured intelligence"; cf. Aesch. 1.39. Grant (1986: 177) infers from this passage that Moshion does not speak "in terms of the father-son relationship, in which a son's debt of gratitude to his father has nothing to do with his awareness of the benefits at the time he enjoyed them, but in terms of a relationship between friends." As has been argued in Chapter One, this is a false opposition.

135 Gomme & Sandbach (1973), 545, supply εἶτ' ἐν …, reading εἶτ' ἐνεγράφην, "subsequently I was enrolled in my deme". If this is right, Moschion is implying that as a citizen he was of equal status as the rest, although financially his position was of a different order (Gomme & Sandbach 1973) and he was "privileged and pampered" in his home (Sommerstein 2013).

136 Weissenberger (1991), 419 n. 17.

137 The effect of the indeterminate pronoun τινα is not straightforward. It seems to indicate awareness on Moschion's part that his χάρις is only "partial" reciprocation, not a full redemption. Alternatively, τινα may "quantify" χάριν by making it concrete (*an act of* grace); the resulting vagueness ("some act of grace") seems uncalled for in this context.

138 On the moral connotations of κόσμιος, see Mette (1969), Weissenberger (1991), 419–420 ("die Summe derjenigen Verhaltensweisen (…) die Vater bei ihren heranwachsenden Söhnen gern sehen"); Lape (2004), 146 n. 25 suggests a link with Moschion's status as a (quasi) ephebe: eukosmia (orderliness and discipline) was a quality expected from ephebes. For the filial duty to be obedient, polite and well-behaved, see also Xen. *Mem.* II.ii. Cf. Blustein (1982), 167–172, for obedience as the typical duty that young children owe their parents.

As has been pointed out,[139] the sense of gratitude professed by Moschion is rather exceptional in Greek comedy where ideals of filial behavior seem to be defined by their perversion or absence. But is he merely representing "the behavior of an ideal son in the eyes of Greek society",[140] unproblematically restating a general social norm—the kind of norm that owes its efficacy to its implicit or tacit nature? *What stake* does Moschion have in making explicit the reciprocal nature of the bond with his father?

Gomme and Sandbach[141] suggest that part of the reason may be Moschion's status as an adopted son: "[A]n adopted son has not the same claim on his father's affections as a son by birth. Demeas' indulgent treatment of Moschion, described in 7–17, and his attempt to preserve his reputation (352) are therefore the more creditable, and he has the greater reason for reproaching him for ingratitude (698–710)."

However, the element of adoption is not exploited by Demeas in 698–710. It is obliquely mentioned in the phrase "ε[.......]αλαβών σε παιδίον" (698: "I took you in when you were a child"), but serves mainly to underscore the fact that Demeas *is* Moschion's father (698: εἰμὶ γὰρ πατήρ, "for I am your father"). The drift of Demeas' argument is that he is nothing *less* than a biological father; not that he is *more*.

Rather, as Lape has pointed out, Moschion's defensive tone serves as a prelude to the conflict that is about to unfold between father and son: it is a preemptive invalidation of any potential reproach that he may show himself to be an ungrateful son. There is something apologetic, and perhaps even forensic, in the pose assumed by Moschion, a pose reinforced by his casual mentioning of the liturgies taken on by him at such a young age[142]—a trope commonly used by wealthy ligitants in court "seeking special consideration from a jury"[143] when they mention their liturgical merits in order to elicit χάρις from the jury.[144] In other words, the father-son reciprocity is highlighted and thematized to set the stage for the play that centers around a model father-son relation that is nonetheless under pressure due to the familiar misunderstandings that make up a comic plot.

139 Grant (1986), 177, Wehrli (1936), 70.

140 Grant (1986), 177.

141 Gomme & Sandbach (1973), 544.

142 On the exceptional (and perhaps irreal) nature of such grand liturgies at this age, see Weissenberger (1991), 419 n. 18, Lape (2004), 143–144.

143 Lape (2004), 143–144.

144 Cf. Ober (1989), 228.

Still, the line of reasoning taken on by Gomme and Sandbach is interesting for what it presupposes: Moschion's overly explicit father-son bookkeeping is somehow at odds with the affective nature of the parent-child bond and requires explanation and may be explained by the fact that their parent-child bond is, in a sense, "manufactured". It is true that explicit discourse abounds in the extant legal cases about adoption: adoption cases prove to be an arena for "kinship engineering" in the course of which norms and expectations tend to be made explicit.[145] There is an obvious contextual reason for this: inheritance cases require obligations between parties to be spelled out and negotiated and hence give rise to explicit normative discourse about interpersonal relations that may have an instrumental or reductionist feel to it:

[Text 25]

> Μετὰ δὲ ταῦτα χρόνου διαγενομένου ἐσκόπει ὁ Μενεκλῆς ὅπως μὴ ἔσοιτο ἄπαις, ἀλλ' ἔσοιτο αὐτῷ ὅστις ζῶντά τε γηροτροφήσοι καὶ τελευτήσαντα θάψοι αὐτὸν καὶ εἰς τὸν ἔπειτα χρόνον τὰ νομιζόμενα αὐτῷ ποιήσοι.
>
> Some time after this, Menecles began to consider how not to remain childless but instead to have someone to look after him in his old age, bury him when he died, and afterwards perform the customary rites for him.[146]

The speaker, adopted by his uncle Menecles twenty-three years prior to his demise, narrates the events leading up to his adoption. Menecles' considerations are presented as dryly pragmatic: remaining childless (ἄπαις) is not an option; instead he opts for adopting a son to support him in his old age (γηροτροφήσοι) and look after his funeral and tomb-cult after his death—the filial duties that we have seen in the legislation in Plato's *Laws* and in Athenian law as well.

---

145 In her anthropological study about the social construction of kinship, Janet Carsten (2004) rightly objects against the term "fictive kinship", because it essentializes biological notions of kinship. In 4th-century Athenian parlance, however, it was common to refer to adoptive kin in terms of "created children" (παῖδες ποιητοί) in opposition to "children by nature" (φύσει παῖδες) (e.g. Is. 2.11.6, 6.28.4, 7.16.2, Isocr. 19.46, [Dem.] 40.47); for references to epigraphical parallels, see Wyse (1904), 248. Cf. Rubinstein (1993), 63–66. Nonetheless, it is important to keep in mind that it is in judicial speeches that kinship and household are negotiated and shaped. Cf. Wohl (2010), 244: "Like the crime, the family does not pre-exist the speech but is its rhetorical product."

146 Is., 2.10; *transl.* Edwards (2007).

According to the adopted son, expected reciprocity played an explicit role in Menecles' considerations,[147] and the ensuing relation is explicitly described as a faithful imitation of a biological father-son relation:

[Text 26]

> Κἀκεῖνός τε τὴν πρόνοιαν εἶχεν ἥνπερ εἰκός ἐστι πατέρα περὶ ὑέος ἔχειν, καὶ ἐγὼ τὸν αὐτὸν τρόπον ὥσπερ γόνῳ ὄντα πατέρα ἐμαυτοῦ ἐθεράπευόν τε καὶ ᾐσχυνόμην, καὶ ἐγὼ καὶ ἡ γυνὴ ἡ ἐμή, ὥστ' ἐκεῖνον πρὸς τοὺς δημότας ἐπαινεῖν ἅπαντας.
>
> Menecles *was concerned* for me *as is reasonable for a father to be for his son*, and I and my wife together *took care of him and respected him in the same way as if he were my natural father*; and so he praised us to all his demesmen.[148]

Menecles' behavior and disposition towards the speaker was "as was reasonable (εἰκός) for a father for his son"; his adopted son reciprocated with care and respect (ἐθεράπευον, ᾐσχυνόμην) "as if he were my biological father" (ὥσπερ γόνῳ ὄντα πατέρα ἐμαυτοῦ). The imitation of the father-child bond goes beyond the mere replication of its reciprocal structure—there is an affective dimension to it as well (πρόνοιαν εἶχεν; also implicit in the praise (ἐπαινεῖν) towards the demesmen)[149]—an affective dimension that is understood as part of (and symptomatic of) a reciprocity bond that functions well.

Beyond this remark, the emotional dimension is never emphasized or foregrounded throughout the speech: the presence of affections and emotions are not part of a *proof* that the speaker's relation with Menecles resembles a "real" father-child relation. Nonetheless, it is noteworthy that even in a context that requires a reduction of interpersonal relations down to the bare bones of instrumental obligations and expectations, the subjective or affective dimension is never entirely absent. Unlike Plutarch, who argued that instrumental

147 This is not surprising given the fact that an old, childless person has very few economic possibilities—especially as he lacks the means to maintain balanced *quid pro quo* exchanges with his relatives at an age at which he is unable to reciprocate. Rubinstein (1993), 66.

148 Is. 2.18.

149 This emotional dimension is less likely to have occurred in cases of posthumous adoption (although the legal implications would effectively be the same). Rubinstein (1993), 66. The analogy in Lyc. *Leocr.* 47 between one's attitude towards foster parents and towards a country that is not one's own reveals a reality somewhat remote from the ideal.

reciprocity denies the possibility of affection between parent and child, here we see an adopted son who does not experience a contradiction between the explicitly instrumental motivations and the logic of reciprocity behind his adoption and the full-fledged parent-child bond within which he has grown up.

This suggests that affective emotions do not occur *in spite of* reciprocity; rather, they are part and parcel of the economy of the family, being mediated and produced by the mechanisms of reciprocal exchange. In Sections 4 and 5 we will see examples of analytical discourse in Xenophon and Aristotle that attempt to account for the affective economy of the household.

3.4 *ἔρανος: Pooling Resources*

A very specific metaphor from the vocabulary of reciprocity is the terminology associated with ἔρανος-credit.[150] This is the vocabulary to which the Compulsive Grumbler (the μεμψίμοιρος), whom we have met in Chapter Two, is tone-deaf:

[Text 27]

> **καὶ ἐράνου εἰσενεχθέντος παρὰ τῶν φίλων καὶ φήσαντός τινος· Ἱλαρὸς ἴσθι, Καὶ πῶς; εἰπεῖν, Ὅτε δεῖ τἀργύριον ἀποδοῦναι ἑκάστῳ καὶ χωρὶς τούτων χάριν ὀφείλειν ὡς εὐεργετημένον;**
>
> "When *his friends* have got together *an* ἔρανος *loan* and someone says 'Cheer up', he answers 'How do you mean? When I have to *refund* everyone and on top of that *owe* χάρις *as if* I am done a favor?'"[151]

By violating the social norms, Theophrastus' Grumbler offers us a glimpse of the socially presupposed scenario. An ἔρανος-loan is (1) gathered (εἰσενεχθέντος), (2) by friends (παρὰ τῶν φίλων), (3) that creates an obligation to "give back to each" (τἀργύριον ἀποδοῦναι ἑκάστῳ) at some point, (4) that makes the recipient "owe gratitude" (χάριν ὀφείλειν), because (5) the loan is to be experienced as a benefaction (ὡς εὐεργετημένον), (6) and is to be reacted upon appropriately by, at least, being cheerful (ἱλαρός).[152] "ἔρανος" belongs to the semantic field of

---

150 On the stability of the terminology associated with *eranos* credit, see Millett (1991), 153; Vondeling (1961).

151 Theophr., *Char.* 17.9.

152 The *eranos* loan recurs in other character descriptions: 1.5, 15.7, 22.9, 23.6. Cf. Millett (1991), 154–156.

φιλία, χάρις, beneficence, giving and giving back.[153] The *faux pas* of the Grumbler is that he applies the Debtor Paradigm to a scenario that is supposed to work on different principles: although an *eranos*-loan *is* a form of credit, it does not function according to the Debtor Paradigm.

Eranos-credit refers to loans made by an *eranos*, a "friendship group", or a "rotating savings and credit association":[154] it is an informal system of pooled credit in which a multiplicity of friends contribute a sum of money to help an acquaintance in times of need.[155] Lenders contributed according to their means, and although economic returns were clearly expected,[156] the loans were typically interest free[157] and returns were not expected directly or immediately:[158] *eranos* loans were conceptualized as collective *favors* and as such were perceived to strengthen social ties within a community (this social function is obviously undermined by the Compulsive Grumbler who refuses to "know the favor", i.e. to recognize and acknowledge the χάρις involved in the exchange!). Contributors were usually among the debtor's φίλοι,[159] who had the best access

---

153 Millett (1991), 27–36.

154 Bresson (2016), 279.

155 Millett (1991), esp. Ch. 1, 2, and 6. In contexts of credit transactions, the word *eranos* could refer to either an individual contribution (e.g. Dem. 53.8), to the total collected funds (Antiph. *Tetr.* 1.2.9; [Dem.] 59.31, Theophr. 15.7) or to the collectivity of the contributors (IG II^2 1291.7, 1369.24–27; see e.g. Arnaoutoglou (1998), 68 on religious ἔρανος associations). In its earliest, Homeric, use, ἔρανος referred to a shared meal (a "picnic", as LSJ have it) to which a group of participants contributed a share (e.g. Hom. *Od.* 1.226). Vondeling (1961), 4–15; Hewitt (1927), 160. By the end of the fifth century, "the term had evolved to include a credit system" (Millett 1991: 155); in the Hellenistic period, "*eranos* was regularly a loan of cash, stripped of its civic ethos, but still typical of friends" (Von Reden (2010), 96). We have no surviving source that gives a detailed and systematic account of the precise mechanisms of *eranos* credit, but references in forensic oratory and in *horos*-inscriptions allow for a global reconstruction of the mechanisms. It should however be stressed that we do not have sufficient evidence to assess whether *eranos* credit was a phenomenon functioning outside the social circles of the wealthy and well-to-do Athenians. Foxhall (2007), 50–51.

156 *Eranos* loans too were secured by property. Millett (1991), 153–154; Foxhall (2007), 46–47. Foxhall argues that this underscores the notion of "limits of trust": trust in reciprocity changes qualitatively beyond the boundaries of the household; mechanisms of generalized reciprocity rarely transcend the boundaries of the household (for long) and tend to lapse into more balanced kinds of reciprocity. Cf. Foxhall (1998), 55.

157 Millett (1991), 153–159; (2007), 96–98; Maier (1969), 120–125; Rauh (1993), 260–261. However, Cohen (1992: 207–215) insists that the sources are silent on the matter of interest on *eranos* loans.

158 Millett (1991), 153–159; Foxhall (2007), 46.

159 Dem. 53.4. Millett (1991), 156–159.

to information regarding the debtor's reliability;[160] conversely, extending *eranos* credit was perceived as an act that strengthened the existing bonds of φιλία: as the speaker in Lysias' *For Polystratus* exclaims, ἐν τοῖς τοιούτοις μάλιστα δηλοῦσιν οἳ ἂν φίλοι ὦσιν, "it is in such situations that it becomes most manifest who a man's friends are!"[161] Moreover, the loans often served purposes associated with the long-term social order, such as the performance of liturgies or the collection of dowries.[162]

To the 5th- and 4th-century Athenian, *eranos* credit is part of the repertory of embedded economic exchanges, i.e. of long-term reciprocity. Consequently, the vocabulary of *eranos* credit is the vocabulary of χάρις, of giving, receiving, acknowledging, remembering and returning grace. However, *eranos* credit presupposes a more specifically *collective* scenario, involving collectives and acts of pooling: the regular verbs for making contributions are εἰσφέρειν ("bring in, contribute")[163] and συλλέγειν ("bring together");[164] the lenders were identified as ἐρανισταί ("members of an ἔρανος") or πληρῶται (literally "completers", hence "joint lenders").[165] The vocabulary stands out in marked distinction with the terminology of commercial credit.[166]

In several contexts, we find a metaphorical use of ἔρανος-terminology to prescribe norms of filial duty. In a fragment of an otherwise unknown tragedy, the fourth-century tragedian Dicaeogenes of Athens has a character say:

[Text 28]

> αὐτὸς τραφεὶς δὲ τῶν φυτευσάντων ὕπο
> καλῶς, τὸν αὐτὸν ἔρανον αὐτοῖσιν νέμεις.

160 Bresson (2016), 279.

161 Lys. 20.12: ἐν τοῖς τοιούτοις ("in such situations") refers back to the fact that the speaker's father refused to contribute (οὐκ εἰσήνεγκεν) to a fund that served to enable Phrynichus to pay a fine to the Treasury.

162 Foxhall (2007), 46–47, who (to my mind pertinently) prefers the notions of long-term and short-term transactional orders (Parry & Bloch 1989) over the distinction "productive" vs. "non-productive"-credit used by Millett (1991: 71–72, 229–232). Foxhall emphasizes that for rich households, lending money on *eranos* terms was a rational way of "storing" wealth (2007: 47). But note that *eranos* credit also seems to have been associated with poor credit history (Aristoph. *Ach.* 614–617, Dem. 27.25) and acute short-term financial difficulties (Antiph. 1.2.9).

163 εἰσφέρειν is also the standard verb used for women who are "bringing in" a dowry to the household of their husbands. E.g. Dem. 40.19; Foxhall (1989), 32.

164 Millett (1991), 151.

165 Millett (1991), 151; Vondeling (1961), 229–231.

166 Millett (1991), 27–36; Korver (1934), Bogaert (1986).

> Having been reared well yourself by your parents
> *grant them the same contribution.*[167]

The ideal of τροφεῖα, reward for rearing, is clearly expressed: "the same contribution" (τὸν αὐτὸν ἔρανον) refers back to the idea of nurture (αὐτὸς τραφείς καλῶς) (and perhaps, obliquely, to the favor of being "begotten" (φυτευσάντων))—the symmetry delicately brought out by the repetition of the determinative pronoun (αὐτὸς … τὸν αὐτὸν … αὐτοῖσιν).[168]

The image concurs with the ideology of reciprocal χάρις that we have seen in the previous sections—*eranos* imagery indeed belong to the same semantic field of long-term order and balance. It should however be noted that here the image is more **distributive** in nature: contributions and portions are distributed or measured out (νέμεις).

In other metaphorical uses of *eranos* imagery, the interactions seem to be structured not so much as exchanges of **direct** (or **restricted**) **reciprocity**, i.e. forms of exchange in which two actors exchange resources *with each other*, but as **indirect reciprocity**:[169] the recipient of benefit does not return benefit directly to the giver, but to another actor in the social circle. In **net-** or **group-generalized** exchanges, each participant contributes to the resources of a group and, in return, receives goods from the group.[170]

This structural characteristic of *eranos* credit is activated in its metaphorical use in some gnomic statements:

---

167 Dicaeogenes 52F4 (Snell).

168 A similar image, but with a more self-serving (and hence reductionistic) purport can be found in Antiphanes' fr. 260 (*CAF* II.121): Υἱῷ γὰρ ἀγαπητῷ τι πράττων πρὸς χάριν | ἔρανον ἐμαυτῷ τοῦτον οἴομαι φέρειν. "For in doing my beloved son a favor to his pleasure I think I'm doing this as a favor to myself." χάρις ("pleasure") evokes the idea of reciprocal favors—made explicit in the next verse where "favor to son" and "favor to myself" are conflated.

169 For the distinction between direct and indirect reciprocity, see Molm, Colett & Schaefer (2007), 206–208. A similar distinction is made by Ekeh (1974), but with different terminology: restricted (= direct) and generalized (= indirect).

170 Ekeh (1974) distinguishes net-generalized exchange from chain-generalized forms of exchange, in which A benefits B, B benefits C, and C benefits A; a classic example of chain-generalized exchanges is the Kula ring (Malinowski 1922). Cf. Yamagashi & Cook (1993) on "network-generalized" exchanges. Ekeh further distinguishes two forms of group-generalized exchange: group-focused (the pooled benefits are shared by all the participants) and individual-focused (the pooled resources benefit one participant at the time). *eranos* credit is an example of individual-focused group-generalized reciprocity. The theoretical status of "group-generalized exchanges" has been questioned (e.g. Bearman (1997)) on the grounds that such exchanges can be reduced to direct dyadic exchange between a group member and the group as a whole.

[Text 29]

οὓς ἂν ἐράνους εἰσενέγκῃς, φησί, τοῖς γονεῦσιν, τοὺς αὐτοὺς προσδέχου καὶ παρὰ τῶν τέκνων.

He says, "*The very same favors that you conferred on* you parents, expect them from your children too."[171]

The Thales-fragment expresses the identity of the "contributions" (τοὺς αὐτοὺς ἐράνους) that one has "brought in" (εἰσενέγκῃς) for one's parents and the contributions that one may expect to receive from one's own children. Note that the orientation is different here from the earlier discussions of filial duty that we have seen: the obligation to care for parents is not grounded in antecedent favors done by them but motivated by future favors to be expected from the next generation.

A fragment by the fourth-century comic poet Alexis is more overtly normative and argumentative in tone:

[Text 30]

ὦ παῖ, μέγιστος ἔρανος ἐστί μοι τὸ σὲ
θρέψαι κατὰ τρόπον· ὃν γὰρ αὐτὸς ἀπέλαβον
παρὰ τοῦ πατρός, δεῖ τοῦτον ἀποδοῦναί με σοί.

The *greatest eranos* I can give you is *to bring you up* properly. That is what I *received* from my father, and I must *return* to you.[172]

The greatest "contribution" (ἔρανος) that the father-character has to offer to his son is to nurture him properly (θρέψαι), *for* (γάρ) that what he has received (ἀπέλαβον) from *his* father he must (δεῖ) "give back" (ἀποδοῦναι). Note that the ἀπό-prefix does not imply direct or dyadic reciprocity; rather, the idea of "giving back" presupposes a long-term and supra-individual order (e.g. the continuity of the οἶκος) that transcends the timeframe of direct reciprocity between two individuals. What is striking is that what is motivated here is not filial obligation, but the obligation (δεῖ) of the parent to take care of his child, an obligation grounded in the antecedent favor granted by the previous generation—a perfect corollary to the Thales-fragment.

171 Thales 1.64.5 DK 11A1.144 = DL 1.37.185–187.
172 Alexis, *CAF* fr. 280 = *FAC* II p. 510 fr. 280.

A synthesis of these two lines of intergenerational group-generalized reciprocity may be found in an early instance of the *eranos* image occurring in Euripides' *Suppliant Women* (423 BC). At the end of his *rhêsis*, in which he complies with Aethra his mother's urgent request to take pity on the Argive mothers and help them retrieve the bodies of their sons, Theseus clasps hands with his mother and turns to the Chorus of Argive mothers, ending his speech with a gnomic statement:

[Text 31]

> ἀλλ', ὦ γεραιαί, σέμν' ἀφαιρεῖτε στέφη
> μητρός, πρὸς οἴκους ὥς νιν Αἰγέως ἄγω,
> φίλην προσάψας χεῖρα· τοῖς τεκοῦσι γὰρ
> δύστηνος ὅστις μὴ **ἀντιδουλεύει** τέκνων,
> **κάλλιστον ἔρανον· δοὺς** γὰρ **ἀντιλάζυται**
> παίδων παρ' αὑτοῦ τοιάδ' ἂν τοκεῦσι **δῷ**
>
> So, aged women, remove your suppliant boughs | from my mother so that I may bring her to Aegeus' house, | taking her dear hand in mine. | A poor wretch is he who does not *serve* his parents *in return*,| *the noblest contribution*. For when he *has made it, he receives back*| from his own children services like those he *gave* his parents.[173]

The idea of filial duty is first expressed in terms of direct reciprocity: a good son is expected to "serve his parents *in return*" (τοῖς τεκοῦσι … ἀντιδουλεύει)[174]—the reactive and reciprocal nature of the obligation being unequivocally expressed in the ἀντι-prefix. In apposition to the phrase τοῖς τεκοῦσι … ἀντιδουλεύει follows the accusative κάλλιστον ἔρανον,[175] shifting the image from the idea of direct reciprocity to a more group-generalized form of reciprocity—a shift made explicit in 363–364, where the ἀντι-prefix is repeated, but worked out in a different way: when a child makes "his gift" (δούς, i.e. the "gift" of "serving his parents in turn") he "receives in turn" (ἀντιλάζυται) in kind what he gave to his parents (τοιάδ' ἂν τοκεῦσι δῷ).[176] Anticipating the Argive mothers' lament over

---

173 Eur. *Suppl.* 359–364; *transl. is my own.*

174 The verbal form ἀντιδουλεύει is a *hapax*, but the noun ἀντίδουλος occurs at Aeschyl. *Choeph.* 135.

175 κάλλιστον ἔρανον is not (merely) to be read as an internal accusative to ἀντιδουλεύει. Cf. Collard (1975), 201.

176 Although Theseus here appears as "a model of filial piety", in the rest of the play his role as

their unreciprocated care for their children (T 16 and 17), here we are offered a foil that emphasizes parent-child reciprocity that is still going strong.[177]

The *eranos* metaphor expresses the idea of a favor or service for which there will be a later return to the giver, but not necessarily from the recipient of the original favor. Originating in contexts of group-generalized reciprocity, *eranos* imagery is capable of telescoping intergenerational solidarity (grandparents—parents—children) into one pool of resources to which generations are expected to contribute in turns and from which they receive favors and resources in due course.

This ties in with an observation made by Lin Foxhall about the "timescales" in which *eranos* credit operated: "*Eranos* loans, stored commodities and raw materials, and agricultural produce are oddly comparable. All bear returns only in the medium- to long-term. Timescale was vital to the use of resources for ancient households. (…) Households were intended to continue into the future, if not indefinitely, and at least for more than a single generation."[178] *Eranos* credit was associated with the transgenerational and supra-individual long-term order of the οἶκος; conversely, as a metaphor, *eranos* vocabulary served to articulate the very idea of the long-term order of the household.

3.5 *The Gratitude Theory*

At first sight, the Gratitude Theory of filial obligation resembles the Debtor Paradigm: both models picture the bond between parents and children as a form of exchange over a long period of time. In situations of conflicts or premature death of the child, the cycle of χάρις is disrupted and Gratitude Theory comes to coincide with the Debtor Paradigm: it is against the very nature of generalized reciprocity that acts of χάρις come to be identified as individual discrete transfers and expectations of return become explicit—like loan transactions and repayments are. In such situations, the rearing of a child can be called "unprofitable", "in vain". Similarly, when "officialized" in legal contexts or in proverbs and maxims (the currency of social norms), the obligation to reciprocate is expressed in a way that resembles the Debtor Paradigm.

---

a son and his identity as an intemperate youth his problematized. See Strauss (1993: 113–115, 143–148) for an argument that father-son conflicts in late-5th-century drama were not so much symptomatic for some sort of epidemic filial rebellion but rather symbolic for tensions between "the old" and "the new" in education (the sophists), the military (Pericles' revolutionary defensive strategy) and politics (the lacuna after the demise of Pericles, Athens' "father-figure"); Danes (2011: 22–24) argues that the *Supp.* destabilize the old-young opposition and the standard association of youth with intemperateness and ὕβρις.

177 Cf. Storey (2008).

178 Foxhall (2007), 51. Cf. Foxhall (1989), 28–29, n. 32; (1994), 139; cf. Plato, *Resp.* 330b.

However, the ancient Greek Gratitude Theory of filial obligation draws on concepts associated with the long-term transactional order: it is a model of understanding obligations from the perspective of the household that transcends and survives the lives of the individual members, and, by analogy, of the city-state. An example is the analogy with *eranos*-credit, a model according to which parent and child both contribute to a common stock, the *oikos*, from which they both at a particular point in life draw resources, just like their ancestors did and their offspring will. Sometimes it is the parent who is pictured as the contributor, sometimes the child, but the point is that the system is bigger than both of them and the moral obligation arises from the simple fact of being a member of a collective. Nobody *ought* to be a free rider.

When fully functional, the Gratitude Theory offers a more fleshed out account of the parent-child bond in which the reciprocal exchange of good treatment is intertwined with moral emotions, affects and dispositions. There is an important qualitative side to both parental care and filial acts of reciprocation. Hence our sources often focus on the appropriateness of the affective responses involved. The ability to experience shame when failing to reciprocate, the ability to exhibit personal moral concern towards an adopted son, to grasp the moral implications of excessive good treatment by an adoptive father and to be cheerful in response to benefactions—these are the abilities that distinguish the well-socialized properly brought up Athenian from the cynics, the social misfits and the boors. To get a better grasp of the role and the production of emotions and affects in parent-child reciprocity, let us now turn to the analytical discourse of Xenophon's Socrates.

4 The Gratitude Theory Analyzed

4.1 *Gratitude and Filial Duty as Divine Law*

To Plato's Athenian Visitor, filial duty was "the first and greatest obligation", part of the common ground on the basis of which the city of Magnesia could start its process of legislation—a primordial ground rule. In Xenophon's *Memorabilia*, the norm to reciprocate parental care recurs as a Divine Law. The obligation to reciprocate a good turn is not only *just*, but also *legal* and prescribed by law. Here "legal" is not necessarily to be understood in terms of "positive law" (the law written down by citizens in agreement about what to do and what not to do),[179] but of "natural law", the kind of law that is universally accepted and

179 IV.iv.13.

observed, endorsed by the gods and that does not need to be written down.[180] What does this particular concept of law imply for the nature of reciprocal obligations?

The context is *Memorabilia* IV.iv, a conversation between Socrates and Hippias, the sophist who famously expressed cynicism over the conventional nature of existing laws and who therefore favored φύσις over νόμος.[181] In the dialogue, Socrates and Hippias, discussing the relation between the just (τὸ δίκαιον) and the lawful (τὸ νόμιμον), apparently progress towards the position that the just and the lawful are to be identified: the lawful is just, the lawful and the just are the same thing.[182]

A crucial concept in this identification is that of Unwritten Laws: laws that are universally recognized, adopted by all men regardless of community or culture.[183] As such unwritten laws cannot possibly have been enacted by any human lawgiver they must therefore be divine.[184] Among these universally accepted unwritten laws are the duty to honor one's parents and to reciprocate a good turn.[185]

There are some serious interpretative and philosophical problems with this dialogue, most importantly the curious fact that in this dialogue Socrates seems

---

180 IV.iv.19.

181 Pl. *Prot.* 337c–d. *Mem.* IV.iv interrupts Xenophon's account of Socrates' education of Euthydemus. Strauss (1939) suggests that Hippias is chosen as an interlocutor in this conversation because of his well-known cynicism about the law. See Classen (1984) for the argument that in this dialogue Xenophon represents Hippias as a conversation partner of a serious intellectual caliber—as Xenophon tends to represent the sophists in general as intellectuals to be taken seriously.

182 IV.iv.12–13.

183 This dialogue reflects a late fifth- and fourth-century debate on the status of law (*locus classicus* Soph. *Ant.* 450–457)—a debate that was prominent in Socratic circles (see e.g. DL 6.11; ps-Pl. *Minos*, Pl. *Hippias Major* 284d–285b) and that found due resonance in Xenophon's works (*Mem.* I.ii.40–46, *Cyr.* I.iii.16–17). The invocation of unwritten laws in Athens has often been misunderstood as reflecting a conflict between written law and higher moral principles. As several scholars have convincingly pointed out, the Athenians did not see a fundamental conflict between written and unwritten law, but regarded written and unwritten law as complementary and compatible rather than as competing. Carey (1994), Allen (2005), Thomas (2005). Although originally all laws are unwritten, in the post-403 constitution νόμος came to refer by definition to "written law" in Athens: the Athenians had adopted a resolution that banned the use of "unwritten laws" to ensure that magistrates could only enforce laws that had been inscribed. By this time, the notion of "unwritten divine law" had probably become suspect due to anti-democratic parties who attempted to invoke the notion in order to overrule the written, democratic law of Athens. Thomas (2005), 53, Allen, (2005), 390 n. 350.

184 IV.iv.19.

185 IV.iv.20–24.

to both adhere to a positivist theory of law, according to which there is a perfect identification between law and justice (which, strictly speaking, implies that there can be no unjust law), *and* to a (rudimentary) theory of natural law that conceives of the rules of morality as a kind of legal system—but one that has not been enacted by any legislature that is only capable of expressing conventional laws liable to change.[186] However, it is striking that in *Mem.* IV.iv Xenophon's Socrates nowhere acknowledges a tension between a position that accords supreme validity to the legislation of the polis and a position that presupposes the existence of laws of a higher legislative status: nowhere in the dialogue do the conversation partners address the potential for conflict between the positive law of the city and the unwritten laws.[187] Socrates simply seems to be in favor of both.

In the course of this discussion both partners agree on the existence of unwritten divine laws. In contrast to the written laws of the city, divine laws are universally recognized. The first universal law is the requirement that one worships the gods (θεοὺς σέβειν);[188] the second is to honor one's parents—Plato's "first and greatest obligation":

---

186 For this definition, see Striker (1989), 79. In modern scholarship, there have been several attempts to account for this tension. Some readings understand Socratic divine law as just another instance of positive law (albeit on a higher level than the laws of the city). E.g. Morrison (1995: 340), arguing that in *Mem.* IV.iv it is the gods who enact divine law; the authority of these laws depends on this fact of enactment; but see Johnson (2003: 264), for the objection that according to the logic of *Mem.* IV.iv, unwritten laws are identified by their universal presence, not by their divine mandate. Other readings point out that Socrates avoids strict identification of law and justice. E.g. Danzig (2009) argues that the position that Socrates defends is that "it is always just to obey the law" (IV.iv.13–18), which merely implies that justice is a *characteristic* of the lawful. This characterization of the lawful as just is grounded in a distinct criterion: obeying the law is just because it is beneficial. Other interpretations accept the tension between the two positions as real and that explain the tension from Xenophon's apologetic agenda. Johnson (2003) argues that the tension between the two positions in *Mem.* IV.iv (somewhat similar to the tensions concerning the status of law between Plato's *Crito* and *Ap.* 29b–d and 37e–38a) results from Xenophon's effort to both show that Socrates did value and obey the laws of the city *and* to prevent his Socrates from making the naïve and exaggerated claim that the lawful and just are to be identified. In IV.iv the tension is left implicit, according to Johnson, because the belief that divine law may overrule the positive law of the city was a politically controversial position that harmed Xenophon's apologetic intentions. Cf. Johnson (2012), 144, Dorion (2010), 296–301.

187 Johnson (2003) makes a compelling case that, although in *Mem.* IV.iv Socrates seems to ignore the possibility that positive law and natural law could come into conflict, Xenophon was aware of such potential conflicts.

188 IV.iv.19: θεοὺς σέβειν.

[Text 32]

> Οὐκοῦν καὶ γονέας τιμᾶν πανταχοῦ νομίζεται;
>
> "Isn't it a custom everywhere to *honor* parents?"[189]

In its immediate context, there is no further explanation that explicates what it means to τιμᾶν, to "honor" one's parents, i.e. to give them the treatment that is due.[190] It is characteristic of this discussion that the substance of the unwritten laws remains underspecified, stipulating only fundamental and general precepts that are universally recognized—no detailed code of law covering all eventualities.[191]

At this point in the discussion, the defining characteristic of the unwritten laws is that they are universally respected. The two divine laws that follow, however, seem to be defined on different grounds. Hippias remarks that the third "law", the ban on parent-child incest,[192] is harder to construe as a divine law, as this is a law that is occasionally transgressed. Here, Socrates introduces a new criterion: divine laws need not be universally respected (they may be transgressed), but in contrast with laws instituted by human legislators, in the case of divine laws transgressors cannot escape penalty. The gods see to it that transgressors pay a penalty (δίκην διδόασιν), as the crime entails its own punishment: transgressors of the ban on incest will be punished by dysgenic offspring.[193]

A similar self-entailing punishment can be observed in the workings of the last law: one should benefit those from whom one has benefited:[194]

[Text 33]

> Τί δέ; τοὺς εὖ ποιοῦντας ἀντευεργετεῖν οὐ πανταχοῦ νόμιμόν ἐστι;
> Νόμιμον, ἔφη· παραβαίνεται δὲ καὶ τοῦτο.

---

189 Xen. *Mem.* IV.iv.20; *all* Memorabilia *translations are by* Tredennick & Waterfield (1990).

190 On τιμή as expressive of what is due *on relational grounds*, see Cairns (1993), Blok (2017), chapter 4, Van Wees (1992), chapter 3.

191 Johnson (2003), 268, argues that this general nature of the unwritten laws limits the scope of these laws, leaving ample room for written legislation without necessarily entailing conflict between the two realms of law.

192 IV.iv.20: οὐκοῦν καὶ μέτε γονέας παισὶ μίγνυσθαι μήτε παῖδας εἶναι.

193 This notion of self-enforcing laws that involve no direct divine intervention resembles Antiphon's dictates of nature. DK 87A44a.

194 Cf. Hobbes' Fourth Law of Nature, the imperative of gratitude in *Leviathan* I.15.

> Οὐκοῦν καὶ οἱ τοῦτο παραβαίνοντες δίκην διδόασι, φίλων μὲν ἀγαθῶν ἔρημοι γιγνόμενοι, τοὺς δὲ μισοῦντας ἑαυτοὺς ἀναγκαζόμενοι διώκειν; ἢ οὐχ οἱ μὲν εὖ ποιοῦντες τοὺς χρωμένους ἑαυτοῖς ἀγαθοὶ φίλοι εἰσίν, οἱ δὲ μὴ ἀντευεργετοῦντες τοὺς τοιούτους διὰ μὲν τὴν ἀχαριστίαν μισοῦνται ὑπ' αὐτῶν, διὰ δὲ τὸ μάλιστα λυσιτελεῖν τοῖς τοιούτοις χρῆσθαι τούτους μάλιστα διώκουσι;
>
> Νὴ τὸν Δί', ὦ Σώκρατες, ἔφη, θεοῖς ταῦτα πάντα ἔοικε· τὸ γὰρ τοὺς νόμους αὐτοὺς τοῖς παραβαίνουσι τὰς τιμωρίας ἔχειν βελτίονος ἢ κατ' ἄνθρωπον νομοθέτου δοκεῖ μοι εἶναι.
>
> "Well now, isn't it customary everywhere *to repay benefits*?"
>
> "Yes, it is, but this is transgressed too."
>
> "Don't those who transgress it pay a penalty as well, by being deprived of good friends and being compelled to pursue the company of people who dislike them? Isn't it a fact that *those who do good to their associates* are good friends, whereas those *who don't repay their debts* are disliked *for their ingratitude*, but still try with all their might to form such associations because of the profit to be gained from them?"
>
> "Certainly, Socrates," he said, "all this looks like the work of the gods. That the laws themselves should entail penalties for their transgressors seems to me to imply a lawgiver of more than human excellence."[195]

This example of unwritten divine law contains a clear description of the morphology of friendship. Good friends (ἀγαθοὶ φίλοι) are defined as people who treat well (εὖ ποιοῦντες) those who deal with them (τοὺς χρωμένους ἑαυτοῖς) and who should be treated well in return (ἀντευεργετεῖν). In accordance with the self-enforcing quality characteristic of divine law, failure to reciprocate will eventually lead to the termination of a friendship. No one wants to deal with people who fail to reciprocate (μὴ ἀντευεργετοῦντες), whereas to associate with good friends is profitable (τὸ μάλιστα λυσιτελεῖν).

It should be noted how smoothly the rule of reciprocity is identified as the mechanism that keeps φιλία going. Although Socrates does not explicitly state that "reciprocating good treatment" is co-extensive with "being a good friend", he does suggest that mutual benefaction is a defining feature of friendship, whereas friendship, if not co-extensive, must at least be a good example of relationships based on reciprocating good treatment. Moreover, ἀχαριστία, failure to meet the standard of reciprocity, will eventually lead to the loss of φίλοι—a punishment for breaking the divine law of reciprocity. In accordance with

195 Xen. *Mem.* IV.iv.24.1.

the new definition of divine law, this punishment is entailed within the law itself: it does not require punitory institutions and legal enforceability, because the punishment is grounded in the very nature of φιλία. Just as transgressors of the ban on parent-child incest will beget weaker offspring, by virtue of the simple law of nature that at least one of the parents will not be in full physical vigour,[196] the punishment imposed by the law of reciprocity on its transgressors is entailed in the logic of φιλία. Sound reciprocity, premissed on gratitude, defines φιλία. Whoever fails to play the game is simply no longer a participant: if you do not meet the basic requirements of friendship, you fail to *be* a friend, and, consequently, you will not *have* friends.

Hence, in the conversation between Socrates and Hippias, the obligation to reciprocate good treatment is constructed not only as an unwritten law with universal validity, but also as a self-enforcing law that entails punishment for transgression by a natural process of cause and effect. How does this reflect on the nature of filial obligation? As we have seen, the first two laws that were declared to be divine were not explicitly defined in terms of their punitory potential. Does the criterion of self-entailing punishment retrospectively apply to the first two laws, to the obligation to honor gods and parents? According to Leo Strauss,[197] it is conceivable that Socrates' omission of the criterion for the first two cases is meaningful: Socrates may have thought that in these cases punishment may not automatically follow the transgression but requires active agency of men or gods.

In response, David Johnson suggests that the fourth law, the law against ingratitude, is the most fundamental principle in *Mem.* IV.iv,[198] containing the earlier laws because parents and gods are benefactors as well.[199] Along this line of reasoning, the absence of an explicit argument that the violation of the law to respect one's parents entails its own punishment may be less of a hint and more of a reflection on the logic of conversation.[200] In addition, this approach also makes filial duty, the obligation to "honor one's parents", more substantive: honoring one's parents is to reciprocate their beneficence.

Still, for our purposes it remains somewhat unsatisfactory that nowhere in the conversation can we find an explicit statement as to the nature of

196 IV.iv.22–23.

197 Strauss (1972), 112.

198 Johnson (2003), 269; Johnson (2012), 151 points out that according to Xenophon this law featured prominently in the Persian educational system (*Cyr.* I.ii.7). Cf. Dorion (2010), 309.

199 Gods as our benefactors: *Mem.* I.iv, IV.iii; parents as our greatest benefactors: *Mem.* II.ii. See Section 4.2 below.

200 Cf. Danzig (2009), 283, who also attempts to explain the ban on parent-child incest in terms of a law of reciprocity.

our obligation towards the gods and our parents. In addition, it is less clear what the punishment for transgressing the law of filial duty would look like. How can a failure to honor one's parents entail its own punishment? Gabriel Danzig reconstructs a plausible punishment for parental neglect in terms of "the loss of allies who despite physical infirmity may be a source of valuable wisdom".[201] But there may be a different explanation. For this we need to turn to book II of the *Memorabilia* where we meet with a concrete example of a transgressor of the Second Unwritten Law: Socrates' own son Lamprocles.

4.2 *χάρις and the Genesis of Moral Obligation*

In book II of the *Memorabilia* a series of Socratic dialogues on the topic of φιλία starts off with Socrates reproaching his son Lamprocles for his lack of χάρις towards the boy's mother.[202] In the arrangement of *Mem.* II, the discussion about filial obligation is placed to set the standard for the subsequent discussions of φιλία-relationships within the οἶκος and beyond.[203]

From the outset the workings of χάρις are discussed from the vantage point of its violation: ἀχαριστία. The dialogue opens with the exchange of observations based on popular morality on this phenomenon of ἀχαριστία, failure to reciprocate:

[Text 34]

> Εἰπέ μοι, ἔφη, ὦ παῖ, οἶσθά τινας ἀνθρώπους ἀχαρίστους καλουμένους;
> Καὶ μάλα, ἔφη ὁ νεανίσκος.
> Καταμεμάθηκας οὖν τοὺς τί ποιοῦντας τὸ ὄνομα τοῦτο ἀποκαλοῦσιν;
> Ἔγωγ', ἔφη· τοὺς γὰρ εὖ παθόντας, ὅταν δυνάμενοι χάριν ἀποδοῦναι μὴ ἀποδῶσιν, ἀχαρίστου καλοῦσιν.
>
> [H]e said, "Look here, my boy, you know that there are some people who are called **ungrateful**?"
> "Yes, of course," said the boy.
> "Are you clear about what it is that people do to earn this name?"

201 Danzig (2009), 283.

202 *Mem.* II.ii.

203 Within the larger framework of the *Memorabilia* this 'vignette' may be read as a reaction to the accusation that Socrates taught his companions to treat their parents and other relatives with contempt (I.ii.49–50). One can think of Aristoph. *Nub.* 1312, where Socratic education has led Pheidippides to beat his father and claim that he was right to do so.

> "Yes, I am," he said, "People are called ungrateful **when they have been well treated and could show gratitude in return, but don't.**"[204]

The didactic method is typically Socratic: Socrates draws out Lamprocles' latent moral knowledge, as he is made to agree that ἀχάριστος is what we call people who fail to return a favor (ὅταν (…) χάριν ἀποδοῦναι μὴ ἀποδῶσιν) after having received benefits (εὖ παθόντας) while capable of doing so (δυνάμενοι).[205] Socrates goes on to claim that being ἀχάριστος is tantamount to being ἄδικος, without further qualification: benefits should be reciprocated, to friends and enemies (πολεμίοι) alike.[206] Then, making a transition to the parent-child case, Socrates suggests that failure to reciprocate a favor (ἀποδιδῷ χάριν) is an offense, the more heinous in proportion to the benefits received:[207] as our parents are our greatest benefactors, it is to them that we owe the greatest obligation imaginable. Hence, in the course of the conversation, the mother-child relationship acquires a paradigmatic status: a mother is a super-φίλος, one's φίλος *par excellence*[208] and the ultimate test for a person's capability to maintain healthy reciprocal relationships.

Thus far Socrates' account of filial χάρις is very close to the Debtor Paradigm: the child is framed as the indebted party for he is born into a web of obligations. However, the approaches differ over the nature of the indebtedness. Whereas the Athenian Visitor takes recourse in the formalized discourse of banking, Socrates frames the child's obligations consistently in terms of χάρις: the didactic goal is that Lamprocles recognizes the χάρις bestowed on him, i.e. that he "knows the favor" (χάριν εἰδέναι). In part, this difference may be a difference in perspective: Plato's analysis of filial obligation takes the external perspective of the lawgiver, Xenophon's Socrates gives his son instructions from an internal point of view of a relation that can still be fixed. But the differences run deeper.

---

204 *Mem.* II.ii.1–2.

205 The addition that these people refrain from reciprocating *in spite of* their being δυνάμενος is a necessary condition for a qualification as ἀχάριστος. It is this notion of capacity that allows for a conceptualization of *all* φιλία-relationships in terms of reciprocity, ranging from bonds between parent-children to brothers, from brothers in arms to drinking buddies, from contacts in the neighbourhood to political affiliations—i.e. including those relationships that may be regarded assymetrical in terms of power and wealth. Elsewhere, Xenophon introduces the notion of reciprocating καδδύναμιν, "according to one's capacity", as a guiding principle in social and religious exchange (*Mem.* I.iii.3).

206 *Mem.* II.ii.2.

207 *Mem.* II.ii.3.

208 *Mem.* II.ii.13: τὴν δὲ μητέρα τὴν πάντων μάλιστά σε φιλοῦσαν οὐκ οἴει δεῖν θεραπεύειν. See Chapter Six Section 5 for some of the ideological consequences of the paradigmatic status of the asymmetrical parent-child bond (and gods).

4.3 *The Moral Quality of the Act*

In what respect exactly does Socrates think a mother is the paradigm case for φιλία? What makes her supremely entitled to χάρις? What makes her a benefactor? Socrates substantiates the notion with a vivid description of the hardship and pain endured by parents, especially by the mother, in bringing up a child:[209] parents give the greatest gift (the gift of life, the one we never give up voluntarily), with great carefulness (men select women who are likely to produce the best offspring). The moment selection has taken place, a chain of care and sustenance is put into operation: men sustain their wives and provide their future children with things that will benefit them later in life; women carry the burden of pregnancy, go through labor, risk their lives, share food; both parents share with their children all knowledge they have and spend money to send them off to good teachers.

This type of χάρις may be understood within the framework of the Debtor Paradigm: the moral need to reciprocate a favor seems to be proportionate with the size of the original beneficence, just as, within the Debtor Paradigm, the size of the repayment is proportionate to the size of the original debt. However, taking a closer look at Socrates' representation of the mother as the φίλος *par excellence*, we see how χάρις calls for alternative accounting principles. It is not only the size of the gift that matters, but also the moral quality of the *act* of giving:

[Text 35]

> ἡ δὲ γυνὴ ὑποδεξαμένη τε φέρει τὸ φορτίον τοῦτο, βαρυνομένη τε καὶ κινδυνεύουσα περὶ τοῦ βίου καὶ μεταδιδοῦσα τῆς τροφῆς, ᾗ καὶ αὐτὴ τρέφεται, καὶ σὺν πολλῷ πόνῳ διενεγκοῦσα καὶ τεκοῦσα τρέφει τε καὶ ἐπιμελεῖται, οὔτε προπεπονθυῖα οὐδὲν ἀγαθὸν οὔτε γιγνῶσκον τὸ βρέφος ὑφ' ὅτου εὖ πάσχει, οὐδὲ σημαίνειν δυνάμενον ὅτου δεῖται, ἀλλ' αὐτὴ στοχαζομένη τά τε συμφέροντα καὶ τὰ κεχαρισμένα πειρᾶται ἐκπληροῦν, καὶ τρέφει πολὺν χρόνον καὶ ἡμέρας καὶ νυκτὸς ὑπομένουσα πονεῖν, οὐκ εἰδυῖα εἴ τινα τούτων χάριν ἀπολήψεται.
>
> The wife conceives and carries this burden, bearing the weight of it, risking her life and giving up a share of her own nourishment; and after all her trouble in carrying it for the full time and bringing it to birth, she feed and cares for it, *although the child has never done her any good and does not know who his benefactor is.* He cannot even communicate what

---

209 *Mem.* II.ii.5.

> he wants; his mother's attempts to supply what will be good for him and give him pleasure depend upon her powers of guessing. And she goes on rearing him for a long time, putting up with drudgery day and night, *without knowing whether she will receive any gratitude.*[210]

A mother's care for her child is a shot in the dark, an investment in an insecure future: she starts taking care of the child long before the child is capable of recognizing his benefactor and acknowledging the χάρις involved, let alone reciprocating χάρις—long before she can have any indication *if* there will ever be a return of χάρις. As we shall see in Chapter Six, to Xenophon's Socrates, this notion of "paying it forward" is of central importance to good friendship: being a good friend requires "active partnership", i.e. not only avoiding being ἀχάριστος, but also taking initiatives and investing in the relationship, thinking along with the other and guessing his needs—the same way a mother tries to guess her infant child's needs. Mothers are exemplary φίλοι not only because of the magnitude of their "gifts", but also because they take initiative, because their generosity is not a mere reaction to a preceding gift or favor, because she has few to no expectations of return in the short run and because the future of the relationship as a whole is insecure.[211] Mothers display risky exchange behavior.

4.4 *The Principle of Active Partnership*

Having made the case that mothers are exemplary φίλοι, Socrates points out that for Lamprocles the stakes are higher than merely preserving the reciprocal relationship with his mother:

[Text 36]

> Οὐκοῦν, ἔφη ὁ Σωκράτης, καὶ τῷ γείτονι βούλῃ σὺ ἀρέσκειν, ἵνα σοι καὶ πῦρ ἐναύῃ, ὅταν τούτου δέῃ, καὶ ἀγαθοῦ τέ σοι γίγνηται συλλήπτωρ καί, ἄν τι σφαλλόμενος τύχῃς, εὐνοϊκῶς ἐγγύθεν βοηθῇ σοι;
>
> Ἔγωγε, ἔφη.
>
> Τί δέ; συνοδοιπόρον ἢ σύμπλουν, ἢ εἴ τῳ ἄλλῳ ἐντυγχάνοις, οὐδὲν ἄν σοι διαφέροι φίλον ἢ ἐχθρὸν γενέσθαι, ἢ καὶ τῆς παρὰ τούτων εὐνοίας οἴει δεῖν ἐπιμελεῖσθαι;
>
> Ἔγωγε, ἔφη.

---

210 *Mem.* II.ii.5–6.

211 Cf. Gigon (1956), 93.

"Well then," said Socrates, "do you want to be pleasant to your neighbor, so that he may give you a light for your fire when you need it, and both contribute to your success and give you prompt and *friendly* help if you meet with any misfortune?"

"Yes, I do."

"Take the case of a fellow traveler or fellow voyager, or anyone else you might meet: would it make no difference to you whether he became your friend or your enemy? Do you think that you ought to concern yourself with the *goodwill* of people like these?"

"I do think so."[212]

The subsidiary point that Socrates here establishes is that it is in Lamprocles' own interest to be concerned with the εὔνοια, the goodwill, of others. The examples chosen are significant, as similar cases recur in *Mem.* II.iii when Socrates advises Chaerecrates to make amends with his brother Chaerephon by taking the initiative to restore their relationship that had turned sour. Again, the didactic moment consists in making Chaerecrates aware of his own latent moral knowledge:

[Text 37]

Λέγε δή μοι, ἔφη, εἴ τινα τῶν γνωρίμων βούλοιο κατεργάσασθαι, ὁπότε θύοι, καλεῖν σε ἐπὶ δεῖπνον, τί ἂν ποιοίης;

Δῆλον ὅτι **κατάρχοιμ'** ἂν τοῦ αὐτός, ὅτε θύοιμι, καλεῖν ἐκεῖνον.

Εἰ δὲ βούλοιο τῶν φίλων τινὰ προτρέψασθαι, ὁπότε ἀποδημοίης, ἐπιμελεῖσθαι τῶν σῶν, τί ἂν ποιοίης;

Δῆλον ὅτι **πρότερος** ἂν ἐγχειροίην ἐπιμελεῖσθαι τῶν ἐκείνου, ὁπότε ἀποδημοίη.

Εἰ δὲ βούλοιο ξένον ποιῆσαι ὑποδέχεσθαι σεαυτόν, ὁπότε ἔλθοις εἰς τὴν ἐκείνου, τί ἂν ποιοίης;

Δῆλον ὅτι καὶ τοῦτον **πρότερος** ὑποδεχοίμην ἄν, ὁπότε ἔλθοι Ἀθήναζε· καὶ εἴ γε βουλοίμην αὐτὸν προθυμεῖσθαι διαπράττειν μοι ἐφ' ἃ ἥκοιμι, δῆλον ὅτι καὶ τοῦτο δέοι ἂν **πρότερον** αὐτὸν ἐκείνῳ ποιεῖν.[213]

"Tell me, then," said Socrates, "if you wanted to prevail upon one of your acquaintances to invite you to dinner whenever he was holding a celebration, what would you do?"

---

212 *Mem.* II.ii.12.

213 *Mem.* II.iii.11–13.

> "Obviously I should **begin** by inviting him when I was celebrating."
> "And if you wanted to induce one of your friends to take care of your property when you were away from home, what would you do?"
> "Obviously I should **first** try to take care of his when he was away."
> "And if you wanted to make a foreigner give you hospitality when you visited his country, what would you do?"
> "Obviously I should **first** give him hospitality when he came to Athens. And if I wanted him to be eager to achieve the object of my visit for me, obviously I should have **first** to do the same for him."

The principle of χάρις, whether with neighbours, ξένοι or other φίλοι is shockingly simple: make the first move (πρότερος εὖ ποιεῖν). If you want to be invited to dinner by an acquaintance, you should invite him first. If you want your friends to look after your property when you're out of town, attend to theirs first. If you want a ξένος to receive you when you're abroad, receive him first when he comes around. Taking initiatives is imperative in all kinds of reciprocal relationships.[214]

Let us look back at Sahlins' definition of generalized reciprocity: generalized reciprocity manifests itself in transactions that are "putatively altruistic".[215] The Socratic imperative to take initiatives, to think along with the other and to guess his needs, may be seen as a way of defining the social competences that serve to sustain *méconnaissance*, to construct a consensual interpretation of events in which it is for the sake of the other person for whom we are acting;[216] or formulated alternatively, to preserve the χάρις, the grace, pleasure and gratitude, in the exchange. "Risky exchange behavior", i.e. making investments in an insecure future, signals goodwill and trust—all the more so when other types of exchange behavior are culturally available that are more reactive or restitutive in character: transactions in the context of commercial or contractual relationships. In effect, we may say that the idealization of "risky exchange behavior" is part of an ideology that aims to demarcate Socratic φιλία from transactions,

214 See Chapters Five and Six. This appears to be a motive under the Minor Socratics. E.g. DL mentions a conflict between Aristippus of Cyrene and his friend Aeschines of Sphettus. Aristippus makes the first move towards reconciliation; (frg. 112 B Mannebach) Cf. 112 A (= Plut. *Cohib. ira* 14,462d–e), 112 C (= Stob. 4,27,19). A similar story is attributed to Euclides of Megara who attempts to assuage a conflict with his brother. Stob. 4,27,15. The sentiment is akin to Seneca's "*si vis amari, ama*" (*Ep.* IX.4).

215 See Section 1. Cf. Chapter Two Section 3.2; Chapter Four Section 3.2.

216 Cf. Davidson (2007), 41: "Altruistic *charis* is simply a more extreme version of the reciprocal *charis*, the most charitable, the furthest from necessity, the freest kind of giving."

obligations and expectations that are premised on legal backing, framed in a Debtor's Paradigm of Obligation.[217]

The language of χάρις provides an accounting model that is fundamentally distinct from the Debtor Paradigm of Obligation. Both models serve to articulate and explain long-term obligations, but involve different perspectives on the exchange between parents and children. Xenophon's Socrates, carefully avoids legal discourse and financial terminology in favor of a discourse of goodwill, generosity and gratitude—the language of χάρις.[218] Once participants are *in* a relationship that can be characterized as φιλία, the relationship is sustained by χάρις, a mutual conferring of benefits, favors and gifts in response to antecedent expressions of generosity. χάρις serves as the moral memory of a relationship, incorporating the past in the construction of reciprocal friendship. As such, χάρις-reciprocity is more than requital. The consequence of seeing filial obligation in terms of χάρις is that one has to acknowledge that nothing can ever be enough to compensate for the biggest χάρις of all, a mother's χάρις. Debts are redeemable. χάρις creates lasting bonds of indebtedness.

Within this understanding of obligation, the figure of the mother, as we have seen, serves as the personification of the principle of active partnership. Filial duty is a special case of a more general normative economics of χάρις—the obligation to reciprocate a good turn. We have also seen that the economy of χάρις, as Socrates envisages here, is a moral economy that not only prescribes that good turns are to be reciprocated, but that also prominently privileges the active partner, the giver, the instigator.[219] Here, and in the conversations that follow in *Mem.* II,[220] Socrates' theory of χάρις is morally thicker than most of our non-analytical sources allow:[221] although the conversation with Lamprocles started out from the vantage point of ἀχαριστία, the failure to reciprocate,

217 This explains why Socrates characterizes Lamprocles' mother as εὔνους, a qualification that, as Gigon notices, seems a *Fremdkörper* in the portrayal of Xanthippe. Gigon (1956), 115.

218 That Xenophon is deliberately avoiding financial terminology is plausible given the abundant use of commercial analogies and metaphors in the rest of *Mem.* II and the *Oec.* See Chapter Four.

219 As we will see in Chapter Six, the economics of χάρις allows "receivers" to become "givers" themselves and to "win back" initiative by "giving back" in a way that transcends mere requital. Good reciprocity is about good turns alternating each other (good turns that can each be seen as acts of χάρις), instead of turns cancelling each other out and annulling the relationship.

220 E.g. II.iii; see Chapter Six.

221 The discussion of the fourth unwritten law (that one must reciprocate good treatment) in *Mem.* IV.iv also amounts to a "thin" conception of χάρις that stays close to the Debtor Paradigm. See Chapter Four.

it moved on to hint at an understanding of χάρις that includes more than the mere return of favors. It provided the first starting point of the notion of Active Partnership, a notion that Socrates develops in several conversations in *Mem.* II and III.

In T36 too we see a hint at the principle of active partnership, the logic being that if you want your neighbor to help you in times of need, it is meet and expedient to display good intent (εὔνοια) and offer help (εὐνοϊκῶς βοηθεῖν) to him first; if you attach value to the goodwill (εὔνοια) of your travel companions and shipmates, it makes sense to be attentive (ἐπιμελεῖσθαι) to them. The common denominator is the notion of active partnership: if you want a good neighbor, *be* a good neighbor; if you want a friend, *be* a friend. Note how εὔνοια here is constructed as proactive behavior: taking the lead breeds εὔνοια, precisely because it *signifies* εὔνοια itself.

However, in the direct context of *Mem.* II.ii, the principle of active partnership serves a didactically more mundane function: it offers Socrates the opportunity to convince Lamprocles that, in the ultimate analysis, being moral is in his own best interest:

[Text 38]

> Εἶτα τούτων μὲν ἐπιμελεῖσθαι παρεσκεύασαι, τὴν δὲ μητέρα τὴν πάντων μάλιστά σε φιλοῦσαν οὐκ οἴει δεῖν θεραπεύειν; οὐκ οἶσθ' ὅτι καὶ ἡ πόλις ἄλλης μὲν ἀχαριστίας οὐδεμιᾶς ἐπιμελεῖται οὐδὲ δικάζει, ἀλλὰ περιορᾷ τοὺς εὖ πεπονθότας χάριν οὐκ ἀποδόντας, ἐὰν δέ τις γονέας μὴ θεραπεύῃ, τούτῳ δίκην τε ἐπιτίθησι καὶ ἀποδοκιμάζουσα οὐκ ἐᾷ ἄρχειν τοῦτον, ὡς οὔτε ἂν τὰ ἱερὰ εὐσεβῶς θυόμενα ὑπὲρ τῆς πόλεως τούτου θύοντος οὔτε ἄλλο καλῶς καὶ δικαίως οὐδὲν ἂν τούτου πράξαντος; καὶ νὴ Δία ἐάν τις τῶν γονέων τελευτησάντων τοὺς τάφους μὴ κοσμῇ, καὶ τοῦτο ἐξετάζει ἡ πόλις ἐν ταῖς τῶν ἀρχόντων δοκιμασίαις. σὺ οὖν, ὦ παῖ, ἐὰν σωφρονῇς, τοὺς μὲν θεοὺς παραιτήσῃ συγγνώμονάς σοι εἶναι, εἴ τι παρημέληκας τῆς μητρός, μή σε καὶ οὗτοι νομίσαντες ἀχάριστον εἶναι οὐκ ἐθελήσωσιν εὖ ποιεῖν, τοὺς δὲ ἀνθρώπους φυλάξῃ μή σε αἰσθόμενοι τῶν γονέων ἀμελοῦντα πάντες ἀτιμάσωσιν, εἶτα ἐν ἐρημίᾳ φίλων ἀναφανῇς. εἰ γάρ σε ὑπολάβοιεν πρὸς τοὺς γονέας ἀχάριστον εἶναι, οὐδεὶς ἂν νομίσειεν εὖ σε ποιήσας χάριν ἀπολήψεσθαι.

> "So you are prepared to concern yourself with these people, and you see no need to show consideration for your mother, who is committed to you more than anyone else does? Don't you know that the *polis* cares nothing for any other kind of ingratitude, and prescribes no penalty for it, but turns a blind eye when beneficiaries fail to repay a favor; but if anyone

> shows no consideration for his parents, the *polis* imposes a penalty upon him and disqualifies him from holding public office, on the presumption that the sacrifices could not be performed on behalf of the *polis* with the proper piety if he performed them, nor any other act be well and duly carried out if he were the agent? And what is more, if anyone fails to tend the graves of his dead parents, even this becomes the subject of a State inquiry when candidates for office are having their conduct scrutinized. So if you are sensible, my boy, you will beseech the gods to pardon any disregard that you have shown towards your mother in case they count you as ungrateful and refuse to do you good; and at the same time you will take care that your fellow men don't observe you neglecting your parents and all lose respect for you so that you stand revealed as destitute of friends; for if they once got the notion that you were ungrateful to your parents, none would expect gratitude in return for doing you a kindness."[222]

Socrates points out that although the polis does not apply legal sanctions against other forms of ingratitude (ἄλλης ἀχαριστίας),[223] ingratitude towards parents is a transgression formally recognized by the city's legislation: a person found guilty of ἀχαριστία towards parents is deemed unfit to perform sacrifices on behalf of the *polis*;[224] a person who neglects his parents' grave will be investigated by the polis in case he runs for office and has to undergo δοκιμασία.[225] If you show yourself incapable of recognizing and expressing χάρις to the φίλος that matters most, you are publicly recognized as an unfit citizen—somewhat along the same line of argument that lies behind the 2016 Shanghai regulation that makes children who fail to reciprocate care to their elderly parents less likely candidates for consumer's credit.[226]

---

222 *Mem.* II.ii.13–14.

223 *Mem.* II.ii.13.

224 *Mem.* II.ii.13. A central term in the description of morally legitimate and religiously sanctioned behavior is ὁσίη/ὅσιος. See Peels (2016).

225 *Mem.* II.ii.14.

226 A similar correlation between private behavior towards parents and public virtues is used by Aeschines against Timarchus: ἐάν τις λέγῃ ἐν τῷ δήμῳ τὸν πατέρα τύπτων ἢ τὴν μητέρα, ἢ μὴ τρέφων, ἢ μὴ παρέχων οἴκησιν· τοῦτον οὐκ ἐᾷ λέγειν. Νὴ Δία καλῶς γε, ὡς ἔγωγέ φημι. Διὰ τί; ὅτι εἴ τις, οὓς ἐξ ἴσου δεῖ τιμᾶν τοῖς θεοῖς, εἰς τούτους ἐστὶ φαῦλος, τί ποτε, φησίν, ὑπ' αὐτοῦ πείσονται οἱ ἀλλότριοι καὶ ἡ πόλις ὅλη; ("If any one addresses the people who beats his father or his mother, or fails to support them, or fails to provide a home for them," such a man he does not allow to speak. And quite rightly, by Zeus, I say. Why? Because if a man is mean towards those whom he ought to honour on an equal level with the gods, how on earth are other people going to be treated by him, how will the city as a whole be treated?) (1.28; *transl.* Fisher).

But perhaps the even stronger deterrent is the mechanism of cause and effect inherent in the logic of χάρις: someone incapable of expressing χάρις towards his mother will become an unlikely object of investment to others. He will lose εὔνοια, people will not be inclined to give him the benefit of the doubt and to pay it forward to him, and he will end up without friends (ἐν ἐρημίᾳ φίλων), because no one expects any χάρις from him anymore.[227]

There *is* an automatic sanction that punishes transgressors of the Divine Law of filial duty: because filial duty is understood as being a form of gratitude, and as a *supreme* form at that, it is subject to the same causal logic of reciprocity.[228] This is the "ought" in the obligation to obey the divine law of honoring one's parents.

4.5 *The Economy of χάρις and the Debtor Paradigm*

In the *Memorabilia*, Xenophon's Socrates articulates a Gratitude Theory of filial obligation that makes χάρις, the obligation to reciprocate morally thicker than the duty to repay a debt in the Debtor Paradigm. χάρις is consistently understood as reciprocity that is more than requital. Whereas the Debtor Paradigm stresses the performance of duties, the Gratitude Theory insists on acting from the right internal dispositions: recognizing (or "knowing") χάρις and remembering it is key to the correct performance of obligations.

Moreover, in the case of mother-child χάρις, it is crucial that the child recognizes that nothing can ever be enough to compensate for the biggest χάρις of all. The moral origins of the mother's superior position lie in her Active Partnership: her willingness and ability to take the risky initiative of exhibiting generosity and goodwill towards a recipient whom she does not yet know. The Debtor Paradigm is **reactive** in nature: it stresses the obligation to repay a debt and places an emphasis on restoration. The Gratitude Theory is **proactive**: it emphasizes the moral moment of taking the leap of faith and initiating χάρις.

This has implications for the meaning and functioning of emotions, affects and internal dispositions. Interestingly, the idea of the parent not expecting a return, or not knowing if she will get a return, recurs in Plutarch's argument (Section 2.3): while the hypothetical "first parents" could not have been guided by an expectation of gratitude or a reward for nursing they still instantly took the trouble to take care of their infants. To Plutarch, this observable behavior leads to the conclusion that parents *must feel something*, i.e. experience parental affection (φιλοστοργία). Xenophon's Socrates departs from the related

227 *Mem.* II.ii.14.

228 This is in line with the interpretation of Johnson (2003) and (2012), who unfortunately misses the parallel of *Mem.* II.ii.13–14 that may have strengthened his case.

observation that mothers in general can never be sure that their care will be reciprocated. But to him, this is not so much evidence of the presence of affective emotions, but rather indicative of the moral quality of the act of giving.

This does not mean that the Gratitude Theory yields an understanding of the parent-child bond destitute of emotions. Quite to the contrary. But whereas Plutarch saw a contradiction between the mechanism of reciprocity and the presence of affection, Xenophon's Socrates understands emotions such as goodwill (εὔνοια) and gratitude (knowing χάρις) as part of reciprocity: goodwill is manifested in proactive behavior, just like knowing χάρις is manifested in performing χάρις.

5 Tensions in the Script: The Possibility of χάρις

One could say, of course, that both the Debtor's Paradigm and the Gratitude Theory are *theories*—or, on a slightly less charitable reading: *only* theories. Such an assessment is fair in the sense that, yes, Plato, Aristotle and Xenophon are theoreticians of social behavior and ethical norms. However, it is important to bear in mind that philosophical discourse is not the only place where we can find theory. Social actors, "real humans", act on social scripts (condensed theories), modelling their behavior in accordance with implicit theories and making those theories explicit when they feel such is needed: especially in situations of conflict. It is in such situations when the taken-for-grantedness of the script vanishes that actors turn into theoreticians and cracks appear in the scripts that people live by. Often these are conflict situations.

In this section I will argue that Euripides' *Alcestis* can be read as an artistic dramatization of this mechanism: of the ways in which a conflict situation (in this case on the extreme premise of a human life at stake) prompts people to resort to theorizing, to "strategical interpreting", to framing and formulating arguments—until the χάρις disappears from every exchange.

5.1 *Alcestis: Excessive χάρις*

These tensions and contradictions are brought out acutely in Euripides' satyr play *Alcestis* (c. 438 BCE). The dramatic action is set in motion by a divine act of χάρις: prior to the play, Apollo had rewarded the mortal Admetus for the good treatment that the god had received during the period when he was Admetus' servant. Apollo grants Admetus the chance to avoid a premature death if he can find someone to take his place. However, everyone, even Admetus' parents, refuses Admetus' request to die on his behalf—except for Admetus' wife Alcestis. The play proper opens, significantly, with a failed exchange: Apollo attempts to convince Death not to take Alcestis, Death refuses him this χάρις, for such χάρις is not in his nature (60–61) and making an exception for Alcestis would amount to privileging the wealthy (57). Death is perfectly egalitarian and a phenomenon of necessity[229] (and as Empedocles has it, χάρις "abhors intolerable necessity").[230] Apollo's response sets the tone for the contradictions that run throughout the play: he prophesies that Death will perform the favor anyway (71: δράσεις θ' ὁμοίως ταῦτ'), referring to Alcestis' eventual rescue from the underworld, but without receiving χάρις from Apollo (70) and in a spirit of resentment (71: ἀπεχθήσῃ)—the χάρις disappears from the exchange.

Hence, the plays kicks off with a divine act of χάρις that violates the life/death boundary,[231] the supreme act of χάρις of Alcestis who is willing to die on behalf of her husband and an act of non-χάρις of Death.[232] These basic premises set in motion a chain of events that unsettles every φιλία-relation in a play that reads as an inquiry into the possibility of χάρις.[233] Alcestis' ultimate gift, the gift of her life for that of her husband's, establishes an "economy of excess",[234] that proves to be an *impossible* economy, as no grace, favor or gift can be a sufficient response to the gift of life:[235]

229 Cf. the chorus in the *kommos* (962–975).

230 Empedocles fr. 116: Χάριτος στυγέει δύστλητον Ἀνάγκην. On the role of the voluntariness of χάρις in the construction of erotic seduction (πείθειν) (as opposed to βία, forcing oneself on one's object of desire), see Chapter Six.

231 This violation of the life/death boundary is a theme prepared in the events preceding the play and recounted in the prologue. Apollo's son Asclepius had dared to bring mortals back to life, inflicting on himself the punishment of Zeus who kills him with the thunderbolt and thereby reestablishes the boundary between mortal and immortal (112–131, 122–129, 455–459, 962–990, 988–999). Apollo retaliates by killing the Cyclopes (the manufacturers of the thunderbolt) and eventually has to pay for his insubordination by having to serve Admetus as a shepherd.

232 MacLachlan (1993), 153.

233 Cf. Scodel (1979), who reads the play as "a study in φιλία, benefaction and response (…)" (54). Cf. Schein (1988), who points out how Euripides brings out "contradictions among these relationships (i.e. of φιλία), thus making them and their ethical value problematic" (190–191) and Conacher (1988), who shows how "[t]he virtue of hospitality, and the closely related idea of *charis* (…), may be said to provide the ethical theme of the play" (37).

234 Wohl (1998), 152–153.

235 See Wohl (1998), 153ff. and Padilla (2000) for an analysis of the play as structured by a series of excessive gifts: Apollo's offer to Admetus (transgression of the life/death-boundary), Alcestis's gift to Admetus (excessive for it cannot reciprocated), Admetus' hospitality to Heracles (excessive in times of mourning), Heracles' gift to Admetus (transgression of the life/death-boundary). Cf. Pearson (1962), 148–149 for an interpretation of Admetus' excessive hospitality towards Heracles ("that is no real favour at all") as an attempt to match or duplicate the excessive gift of Alcestis.

[Text 39]

Αλ: εἶέν· σύ νύν μοι τῶνδ' ἀπόμνησαι χάριν·
αἰτήσομαι γάρ σ' ἀξίαν μὲν οὔποτε
(ψυχῆς γὰρ οὐδέν ἐστι τιμιώτερον),
δίκαια δ', ὡς φήσεις σύ·

Well, then. *Remember to show your gratitude for this*. I shall not ask you for the return my act *deserves* (for *nothing is more precious* than a life), but for what is right, as you will agree.[236]

The dying Alcestis asks her husband Admetus to "remember the χάρις"—a request that becomes all the more urgent in the prospect of death, as Alcestis will not be able to remind Admetus of her χάρις. Alcestis makes explicit the problem of the situation: she cannot ever ask Admetus for an equivalent return (ἀξία), simply because for a mortal there is nothing more valuable (τιμιώτερον) than life. This radical incommensurability of value disrupts the equilibrium between all the characters in the play and eventually disintegrates the social bonds between the characters.[237]

As Victoria Wohl observes, the chorus and Admetus[238] repeatedly thematize that Alcestis is unique and irreplaceable;[239] moreover, Alcestis actually makes her own irreplaceability a condition for her own death:[240] Admetus may never remarry.[241] Alcestis carefully constructs her χάρις as an absolutely singular object: the unique and irreplaceable gift of her life, a debt that can never be repaid.[242]

No stranger to hyperbole and rhetorical pathos,[243] Admetus assures his dying wife that he will mourn her forever, worship her statue and never remarry (343–346), but in the end he betrays his promise. Heracles, wishing to reciprocate the hospitality that he had enjoyed from Admetus, offers his host the χάρις of an Alcestis revived from the dead (1024). But there is a catch to this tale of "virtue rewarded": Alcestis is in disguise, hence effectively "another woman",

236 Eur. *Alc.* 299–302; *all* Alcestis *translations are by* Kovacs (2001).
237 Padilla (2000).
238 Wohl (1998), 329–333.
239 Wohl (1998), 153.
240 305–316.
241 A promise which Admetus violates by taking in the veiled "gift" brought by Heracles.
242 Wohl (1998), 152–153 compares Alcestis' extraordinary gift with the *potlatch*.
243 Padilla (2002) understands Admetus' hyperbolic commitment in words as a form of rhetorical χάρις that can never match Alcestis' heroic χάρις (192).

constituting a direct threat to Admetus' promise to Alcestis.[244] Admetus, reluctantly, accepts the woman—an exchange that, although in appearance an act of χάρις by Heracles, seals the transformation of Alcestis from a heroic donor of irredeemable χάρις into the object of exchange between two men.[245] She ceases to be absolutely unique; she has replaced herself.

5.2 *Admetus: Perverted χάρις*

It is against this backdrop of the impossible economy instigated by Alcestis' excessive χάρις, that we have to read the debate scene between Admetus and his father Pheres,[246] that unsettles and problematizes the obligations and rights between father and son. As we have seen, father-son conflicts are stock-in-trade in Athenian drama;[247] however, the conflict between Pheres and Admetus escalates beyond resolution into a disconcerting perversion of standard rhetorical repertory.

Alcestis' willingness to die at such a young age for the sake of her children[248] casts an unfavorable light on Admetus' parents who refuse to do so in their old age.[249] Consequently, when his father Pheres comes to pay respect to Alcestis, Admetus refuses to accept his burial gifts (631) and embarks on a harsh and humiliating speech that, by exposing his father's cowardice, inadvertently draws attention to his own hypocrisy.

Admetus preemptively subverts the ethics of primordial indebtedness: refusing to accept the burial gifts brought by Pheres (631–632) and brushing aside

244 Goldfarb (1992) accordingly reads the play as an enactment of the tensions between φιλία and ξενία, with Admetus betraying his φιλία towards Alcestis because of the obligations engendered by his ξενία with Heracles. Such a contradiction is contrived: ξενία falls under the broader heading of φιλία (see Introduction). It is more productive to read the conflicts in the play as arising from tensions within the very notion of φιλία and its concomitant script. Cf. Schein (1988), Scodel (1979).

245 Cf. Wohl (1998), 175. Cf. MacLachlan (1993), 15.

246 On the *agon* between Pheres and Admetus (606–746) see Collard (1975), Conacher (1972) and (1981), esp. 5–9; Thury (1988), Lloyd (1992), Iakov (1999), (2012), 281–304 & 305–318; Dubischar (2001), Halleran (2005), 175–177.

247 See Section 3.3.

248 Schein (1988: 194–195) rightly warns us that we must be careful to attribute a particular motivation to Alcestis as her decision to die for Admetus takes places prior to the beginning of the play—which means that Euripides has left out Alcestis' motivation from the dramatic action; it can however be observed as Schein points out, that Alcestis nowhere speaks of her affection for Admetus, but solely concentrates on her concern for their children. Dyson (1988), 16, suggests that Alcestis, saying that she dies "ὅτε ζῆν χρῆν μ'", acknowledges her obligations to her children.

249 Schein (1988), 195–196.

his father's sympathy, he treats parent-child φιλία (typically an "ascribed" relation)[250] as a relation based on achievement and desert:

[Text 40]

> **οὐκ ἦσθ' ἄρ' ὀρθῶς τοῦδε σώματος πατήρ,**
> **οὐδ' ἡ τεκεῖν φάσκουσα καὶ κεκλημένη**
> **μήτηρ μ' ἔτικτε,** δουλίου δ' ἀφ' αἵματος
> μαστῶι γυναικὸς σῆς ὑπεβλήθην λάθραι.
> ἔδειξας εἰς ἔλεγχον ἐξελθὼν ὃς εἶ,
> καί μ' οὐ νομίζω παῖδα σὸν πεφυκέναι.
>
> *You were not, as it now seems clear, truly my father, nor did she who claims to have borne me and is called my mother really give me birth*, but I was born of some slave and secretly put to your wife's breast. When you were put to the test you showed your true nature, and I do not count myself as your son.[251]

Put to the test (εἰς ἔλεγχον ἐξελθών), Pheres turns out to be a counterfeit φίλος, not a true father to Admetus after all; nor is the woman who bears the name of "mother" truly the one who bore him. Both were merely parents in name,[252] not in reality: Admetus no longer recognizes them as his φίλοι (630: οὔτ' ἐν φίλοισι σὴν παρουσίαν λέγω) and he refuses to consider himself as being their natural child (παῖδα σὸν πεφυκέναι).

Admetus does what Aristotle, more than a century later, thought impossible and against the logic of parent-child φιλία: he disowns his parents, as he does even more explicitly later in 737–738 when he virtually renounces his paternal hearth by proclamation (ἀπειπεῖν ... κηρύκων ὕπο | τὴν σὴν πατρῴαν ἑστίαν)—a reference to, and wry reversal of, the formal legal proceeding of ἀποκήρυξις, the public disinheriting of a son by his father.[253] Instead, Admetus claims with grotesque absurdity, *Alcestis* (an outsider)[254] is his true mother and father (646–647).

---

250 Konstan (1997), 6; cf. Chapter One Section 2.

251 Eur. *Alc*. 636–641.

252 Cf. Admetus, speaking to Alcestis, about his parents in vv. 338–339: στυγῶν μὲν ἥ μ' ἔτικτεν, ἐχθαίρων δ' ἐμὸν | πατέρα· λόγῳ γὰρ ἦσαν οὐκ ἔργῳ φίλοι. "hating her who bore me and loathing my father. For their love was in word, not deed."

253 Thury (1988), 200–201.

254 On the irony of Admetus using the term ὀθνεία for Alcestis, see Schein (1988), 195–196.

There is no ambiguity about Admetus' sense of entitlement: his father should have "shared his trouble" (633: ξυναλγεῖν χρῆν σε) when Admetus was dying instead of "allowing a young person to die" (634–635: παρεὶς ἄλλωι θανεῖν | νέωι), for Pheres, being so old, had little life left to lose (643: ὅς τηλικόσδ' ὢν κἀπὶ τέρμ' ἥκων βίου). And the calculus goes on: Pheres could have gained the prestige of dying for his son (648–649: καλόν γ' ἂν τόνδ' ἀγῶν' ἠγωνίσω | τοῦ σοῦ πρὸ παιδὸς κατθανών) for the low price of the short span of life he had left (649–650: βραχὺς δέ σοι | πάντως ὁ λοιπὸς ἦν βιώσιμος χρόνος) that was, besides, qualitatively already complete, as Pheres had already enjoyed the privilege of spending the prime of his life as a king and of having yours truly, Admetus, as his secure successor, and of not dying childless (654–657).

To Admetus, this calculus adds up to an almost mercantile valuation of one life against another—effectuating a reversal of conventional ethics that must have horrified the audience and that certainly discomfited the chorus (673–674). Failing to meet these standards and refusing to adhere to the calculus of life, Pheres has disqualified himself as Admetus' father. According to the conventional ethics of primordial debt, every son is born into a web of irredeemable obligations towards his parents, spending a lifetime trying to (however defectively) deserve them. To Admetus, Pheres has to deserve being his father and moreover fails to do so—because Pheres has failed to reciprocate Admetus' good treatment:

[Text 41]

{Αδμ.} οὐ μὴν ἐρεῖς γέ μ' ὡς ἀτιμάζοντα σὸν
γῆρας θανεῖν προύδωκας, ὅστις αἰδόφρων
πρὸς σ' ἦ μάλιστα· κἀντὶ τῶνδέ μοι χάριν
τοιάνδε καὶ σὺ χἠ τεκοῦσ' ἠλλαξάτην.
τοιγὰρ φυτεύων παῖδας οὐκέτ' ἂν φθάνοις,
οἳ γηροβοσκήσουσι καὶ θανόντα σε
περιστελοῦσι καὶ προθήσονται νεκρόν.
οὐ γάρ σ' ἔγωγε τῆιδ' ἐμῆι θάψω χερί·
τέθνηκα γὰρ δὴ τοὐπὶ σ'. εἰ δ' ἄλλου τυχὼν
σωτῆρος αὐγὰς εἰσορῶ, κείνου λέγω
καὶ παῖδά μ' εἶναι καὶ φίλον γηροτρόφον.

{Admetus} *Surely you cannot say that you abandoned me to death because I dishonored you in your old age,* for I have always shown you every respect. *And now this is the repayment you and my mother have made to me.* You had better hurry, therefore, and beget other children *to take care*

> *of you in old age* and, when you have died, to dress you and lay you out for burial. |665 I for my part shall never bury you myself. For as far as in you lay I am dead. And if I have found another savior and still look upon the sun, I am that savior's child and fond *support in old age*.[255]

The reversal is complete. Anticipating the defense that Pheres was right to have handed him over to death (θανεῖν προύδωκας) *because* Admetus failed to give him the treatment that was due to him in his old age (ὡς ἀτιμάζοντα σὸν γῆρας),[256] Admetus now claims that he has been perfectly respectful (αἰδόφρων ... μάλιστα) towards his father and that it is *Pheres* who has failed to reciprocate: in exchange for all Admetus has done for his parents (ἀντὶ τῶνδε, i.e. his being respectful), they have given him "such a favor in return" (χάριν | τοιάνδε ... ἠλλαξάτην, i.e. they have withheld him the favor of dying for him). Admetus turns his father's refusal to die for him into an issue of χάρις—using a rhetoric well-known in father-son conflicts, but with the not so subtle difference that now it is Pheres who is pushed into the debtor's position: whereas in conventional ethics, sons owe their parents respect (αἰδώς) and deference (τιμή) in return for being treated well by them, Admetus thinks that his respectful behavior towards his parents has placed them under obligation to him.

What is more, Admetus' claim that he respects his father is immediately undermined by his threat that he will not bury him (662–665)—a radical rejection of the most binding of all family obligations. Pheres will have to produce other children to tend him in his old age (γηροβοσκήσουσι), as Admetus (picking up the absurd trope of 646–647) will only be a caretaker (γηροτρόφον) for his newly adopted mother Alcestis whose child he chooses to be (παῖδά μ'εἶναι).

5.3 *Pheres: Disenchanted χάρις*

Apollo's initial χάρις to Admetus has destabilized the most sacred and fundamental of human relations: parents can be disinherited or chosen, children can be substituted, there are no pre-existing obligations. This "disenchanted monetarism"[257] is aggravated in Pheres' reply, who, rightly, exposes his son's hypocrisy and selfishness[258] but nonetheless fails to restore χάρις himself:

---

255 Eur. *Alc.* 658–668.

256 On τιμή in relation to one's parents, see Section 2.2 and 4.1 above.

257 Wohl (1988), 155.

258 Padilla (2002), 197; Goldfarb (1992), 115: "Pheres' unwillingness to die does of course reflect Admetus' own reluctance."

[Text 42]

{Φερ.} ἐγὼ δέ σ' οἴκων δεσπότην ἐγεινάμην
κἄθρεψ', ὀφείλω δ' οὐχ ὑπερθνήισκειν σέθεν·

I *begot* you and *raised* you to be the master of this house, but *I am not obliged* to die for you.[259]

Pheres ticks all the boxes of 5th-century parenthood: he has engendered (ἐγεινάμην) his son, maintained him (ἔθρεψ') and taught him a trade (i.e. made him οἴκων δεσπότην).[260] He does not *owe* it to his son (ὀφείλω) to die on his behalf. If anything, Admetus should be the one owing his father: using the verb τρέφειν, Pheres brings up the issue of filial duty and "clarifies the question of rights and duties between father and son",[261] thus reestablishing the conventional norm. His legalistic take on paternity is reinforced in the verses that follow, where he insists that there is no tradition (683: πατρῷιον νόμον) or Greek custom that requires a father to die for his son (683–684).[262]

Pheres continues his defensive catalogue of fulfilled duties:

[Text 43]

(…) ἃ δ' ἡμῶν χρῆν σε τυγχάνειν ἔχεις.
πολλῶν μὲν ἄρχεις, πολυπλέθρους δέ σοι γύας
λείψω· πατρὸς γὰρ ταὔτ' ἐδεξάμην πάρα.
τί δῆτά σ' ἠδίκηκα; τοῦ σ' ἀποστερῶ;

What you should in justice have received from me you have: you rule over many subjects, and I shall leave to you many acres of land, for I received the same from *my* father. What *injustice have I done* you? Of what am I *robbing* you?[263]

---

259 Eur. *Alc.* 681–682.

260 Thury (1988), 199–200.

261 Parker (2007), 189.

262 It is conceivable that Euripides makes Pheres refer to laws and customs to bring to mind to the audience that such norms *do* exist for the other side of the coin, the obligations of sons to fathers. It should be noted that Pheres' arguments are predominantly apologetic and defensive in tone: the focus is on the fact that *he* has fulfilled all obligations, *not* on Admetus' shortcomings as a son. Nor is the issue of disinheritance directly addressed by Pheres.

263 Eur. *Alc.* 686–689.

Within his narrowly legalistic framework, Pheres has done everything that can be demanded of a father. He has created the right material and dynastic conditions for his son, he has properly preserved family property and will transfer it accordingly. He has done his son no injustice (ἠδίκηκα) nor is he robbing him of anything (ἀποστερῶ). It is striking how Pheres' arguments are based on a "narrow and rigid interpretation of the legal obligations binding him,"[264] an approach that boils down to the defense that he has committed no offense, that he has not committed any act of negative reciprocity. Be that as it may, denial of negative reciprocity does not amount to sound and sustainable relations. The χάρις has irrevocably disappeared from Pheres' worldview. Pheres may be right; but he is not noble.[265]

Once χάρις disappears, human relations dissolve into ephemeral exchanges between atomistic individuals who may or may not manage to strike a deal. But when human life is at stake, there *is* no plausible deal. In the end fortune strikes us as individuals (685 σαυτῶι γὰρ εἴτε δυστυχὴς εἴτ' εὐτυχὴς | ἔφυς) and we all equally value our own lives:

[Text 44]

> μὴ θνῆισχ' ὑπὲρ τοῦδ' ἀνδρός, οὐδ' ἐγὼ πρὸ σοῦ. |690
> χαίρεις ὁρῶν φῶς· πατέρα δ' οὐ χαίρειν δοκεῖς;
> ἦ μὴν πολύν γε τὸν κάτω λογίζομαι
> χρόνον, τὸ δὲ ζῆν σμικρὸν ἀλλ' ὅμως γλυκύ.
>
> Do not die on my behalf, and I shall not die on yours. |690 You *enjoy* looking on the light. Do you think your father does not? Truly I *regard* the time below as long and life as short but sweet for all that.[266]

The only χάρις that yields a valid premise is the simple fact that we rejoice (χαίρεις ... χαίρειν) in our own lives—the wordplay with the XAP-root effectively underscoring the contrast between Alcestis' χάρις, saturate with virtue and value, and the simple pleasure that Pheres takes in living another day.[267]

---

264 Golden (1970), 119. This line of defense seems to be the last resort of a man who *is* slightly uncomfortable with his refusal to die for his son. Luschnig & Roisman (2003), 134.

265 Schein's (1988: 196) remark "as often in Euripides, each (i.e. both Admetus and Pheres), while telling the truth, lacks any real moral authority in the eyes either of the antagonist or of the audience or reader" applies more to Pheres than to Admetus.

266 Eur. *Alc*. 690–693.

267 Cf. Wohl (1998), 155: "Both philosophies (*i.e. both Alcestis' and Pheres'*) start from the same

Admetus compared the value of his father's life against that of his wife; Pheres points out that love of life is universal and that this point of departure takes away any possibility of privileging one life over another.[268] Admetus calculated the price of his father's life against the prospect of prestige to be won by Pheres for the noble act of dying for his son; Pheres' countercalculation (λογίζομαι) departs from the premise that nothing is more valuable than life, however short it may be,[269] which cancels out all considerations of honor and virtue.[270] Admetus challenged his father to substitute him with other sons to take care of him in old age; Pheres retorts the argument of substitutability against Admetus and insinuates that he may infinitely postpone death by successively persuading one wife after another to die on his behalf (699–700; cf. 720).

With hindsight, we see that even Pheres' initial gesture of bringing adornments to Alcestis' burial had been narrowly instrumental:[271] he had praised her noble sacrifice because it had prevented him from becoming childless (and hence bereft of filial care) in old age (621–622)—the fate of aborted χάρις that is lamented in the epitaphs of prematurely deceased children. His praise does not acknowledge virtue or nobility, merely personal advantage, and his valuation of marriage is plainly mercantile:[272] it is profitable (λύειν) for a man to marry a woman like Alcestis; otherwise a marriage is "not worthwhile" (οὐκ ἄξιον; 627–628).

In the ensuing stichomythia we see how Pheres' premise of the ultimate and irreducible value of life narrows his moral universe and eclipses considerations

premise: "Nothing is more valuable than a life" (301, cf. 691–693, 703–704, 712, 722). But starting from this point, Alcestis' economy denies the possibility of an equivalent to life or of equating values at all; Pheres, on the other hand, takes this premise as the foundation for an economy in which everything is equitable."

268 Cf. 704–705: νόμιζε δ', εἰ σὺ τὴν σαυτοῦ φιλεῖς | ψυχήν, φιλεῖν ἅπαντας ("Consider that if you love life, so do all men.") On Pheres' "democratization" of life, that follows Death's apolitical egalitarianism against Apollo's aristocratic stance at the beginning of the play (55–59), see Padilla (2002), 206; Luschnig & Roisman (2003), 134. On the possible sophistic origins of Pheres' argumentations, see Thury (1988), 206–207.

269 This seems to be a variation on Soph. *Ant.* 74–76 where Antigone makes a similar calculation regarding the length of time spent among the living compared to the time spent in Hades. Whereas the same calculation motivates Antigone to display loyalties to her dead relatives, it makes Pheres want to live. Luschnig & Roisman (2003), 135.

270 Golden (1970), 120.

271 Wohl (1988), 155, argues that the ornaments (613: κόσμον) brought by Pheres are "an attempt to compensatie Alcestis for her sacrifice and Admetus for his suffering (…): the τιμή they represent is honor, but also recompense". This may explain why Admetus rejects them right away: there is no proper compensation for the loss of life.

272 On Pheres' monetary vocabulary, see also Golden (1970).

of honor, virtue and obligation. Whereas at the beginning of the scene, Pheres seemed to adhere to social conventions and to admire Alcestis' sacrifice (619–627),[273] he now reveals his true evaluation of her act: she may not have been shameless (728: ἀναιδής), but senseless she was (ἄφρονα). Disparaging Alcestis' heroism Pheres catagorically denies the value of a good death.[274] Apart from the stipulations of law, there remains only one obligation: the only thing that we are truly "bound to" (or that we truly "owe"; 712: ὀφείλομεν) is that we only live once.

5.4 *What We Owe*

Admetus' take on the obligations that bind father and son to and fro is perverted. He does the morally impossible, disowning his father, and reveals himself to not "know the χάρις". Pheres, being the second speaker in a Euripidean debate, wins the discussion, but it appears that while Pheres' arguments exposes Admetus' hypocrisy they simultaneously lay bare his own worldview that knows no χάρις and is destitute of meaning.[275] His rejoicing (χαίρειν) in mere living is a reduced form of χάρις—reduced to the point where we may wonder if there is any grace left.

What started as a debate about the question of who owes whom and on what grounds now leaves us with a reduced and narrow notion of what constitutes obligation. Making the value of life absolute Pheres ultimately eliminates the things that give life meaning. Virtue and honor cease to be recognized, the χάρις disappears from social interactions and even the most sacred φιλία-bond, that between parent and child, dissolves into ephemeral deals between atomistic individuals who each take pleasure in mere survival.

Within the dramatic plot, the central *agon* is mainly instrumental to Admetus' "tragic education": it is through his confrontation with Pheres that Admetus morally and socially hits rock bottom. Having disinherited his own father and being virtually "stripped of any significant relationship to another human being",[276] Admetus recognizes that his life, prolonged at the expense of Alces-

---

273 619–627.

274 Luschnig & Roisman (2003), 134.

275 Thury (1988) argues that the Athenian audience would have sympathized with Admetus rather than with Pheres. Although it can be argued that Athenian law and civil institutions "placed fathers and sons … on a level of political equality" (Reinhold 1979: 353) and that Athenian custom stipulates that old men retire from managing the family estate and transfer power to their sons (Lacey 1968: 106–107; Thury 1988: 200), this has no bearing on the moral quality of Admetus' arguments.

276 Schein (1988), 204. The exception is of course, as Schein points out, the "quasi-divine" Heracles, before whom Admetus tries to regain a sense of social meaning by fulfilling his

tis, may not be the greatest gain after all.[277] Beyond the logic of the play we see how a conflict situation—especially on the extreme premise of a human life at stake—prompts people to resort to a Debtor Paradigm of Obligation, yielding an overly legalistic interpretation of what they owe to one another that fails to do justice to the relations involved. It leads fathers and sons into thinking of themselves as atomistic individuals engaged in discrete exchange events, in a mutual ticking off of obligations that seems to dissolve relations rather than keeping them together.

6 Concluding Remarks

We have seen how, much to the disgust of later thinkers such as Plutarch, in the Classical period, models of filial duty always involve **mutuality**—in the sense that the parent-child bond is invariably imagined as a *kind of exchange*. The notions typical of modern Dutch family life (filial freedom and autonomy) play no role whatsoever in the Athenian discussion. There *is* a form of to-and-fro: we *ought* to take care of our parents, because we *owe* it to them. But what is the nature of this "owing"?

Among the two available models in Classical Athens, the Debtor's Paradigm is analytically the most compelling and the easiest to explain: we owe our parents respect and care because we are *indebted* to them. However, we have also seen that this model is never fully endorsed. If it is used, it is only as a didactic analogy (Plato, Aristotle) with locally circumscribed validity, or as a "strategic interpretation" in the heat of a conflict situation (Admetus and Pheres). This is because in the ultimate analysis the model is seriously flawed:

- A Debtor Paradigm assumes that a debt can be **redeemed**, and an obligation can be, therefore, discharged. This goes against the very nature of the parent-child relationship: we can never cease to *be* our parents' child.
- A Debtor Paradigm is **too reductionistic**: in exposing the bare bones of our interpersonal obligations we lose the very "flesh" of the parent-child relationship: the emotions, the affective and subjective aspects of the relation.

Both Plato and Aristotle address the first objection by grouping the parent-child bond with relations between humans and the gods. They are beyond the

obligation of hospitality (albeit in a hyperbolic, and therefore not entirely appropriate, way).

277 Conacher (1988), 37: "Even, indeed *especially*, before the happy ending, Admetus finds reason to believe that Alcestis, by her death, has gained more than he has by his avoidance of death."

sociable extreme of Sahlins' "kinship distance"-model: the debts are of such a magnitude that they are, by definition, irredeemable. They are **primordial** debts, debts that can never by discharged, and that define the relation as perpetually unequal or hierarchical. The second point is Plutarch's objection to the Epicurean take on human relations, and one of the reasons why Aristotle insists on the fact that the Debtor Paradigm is an analogy, and *only* an analogy. We shall elaborate on this in Chapter Four.

The Gratitude Theory offers a more fleshed out account of the parent-child bond and a thicker notion of what it means to *owe* care to one's parents. Social actors who model their relations on an implicit Gratitude Theory insist on the fact that there is more to their relationship than mere mechanics. There is an important qualitative side to the give-and-give-again in a parent-child bond:

(i) Whereas the Debtor Paradigm is **reactive** in orientation, the Gratitude Theory is **proactive.** Being a parent, the initial donor of χάρις, requires a primordial goodwill towards the child, i.e. absolute trust.

(ii) Whereas the Debtor Paradigm insists only on **performance**, the Gratitude Theory **prescribes moral emotions** on the part of child, the recipient of primordial χάρις: he must first and foremost *know* the χάρις, i.e. experience gratitude.

(iii) Whereas the analytical strength of the Debtor Paradigm is its **objectifying potential**, the Gratitude Theory insists on the **subjective** aspects of the relationship: being in a reciprocal relationship means experiencing positive emotions and affects.

(iv) Whereas the Debtor Paradigm imagines debt relations as **isolated** and discrete, the Gratitude Theory is **holistic:** one's ability to do the right thing in a parent-child relation is indicative of one's social performance and ethical standing.

The parent's initial shot in the dark (i) makes the χάρις of the parent outrank the χάρις of any possible act of reciprocation. The primordial χάρις accounts for the unequal relation between parent and child, in which the child *owes* perpetual gratitude, obedience, respect and care to the parent. The child's first task is to recognize this (ii), and many a didactic effort goes into *showing* the χάρις where a child fails to know it—as we have seen Socrates try to do with his son Lamprocles.

Contrary to what Plutarch seems to presuppose, in classical Athens there is no contradiction perceived between the reciprocal nature of filial obligation and the presence of emotions (iii). Emotions and subjective dispositions such as goodwill, gratitude, affection and appreciation are part of the mechanism of reciprocity. People who fail to reciprocate χάρις experience shame; conversely, people who are capable of reciprocating experience a sense of social pride and ethical conformity. This also means that the epitaphical theme of the "futile χάρις" of parents of prematurely deceased children is not symptomatic for an absence of emotions. On the contrary: it is a way of *voicing*, channeling or articulating grief.

Filial obligation is not an isolated duty (iv) and one's ability to observe such obligation is a sign of character, not of sufficient funds. Being in a reciprocal relationship means exercising social virtues and ethical dispositions. People who fail to *know* or reciprocate χάρις are seen as social misfits. In the Gratitude Theory, filial duty has repercussions beyond the immediate bounds of the parent-child relationship.

One final remark about the list of characteristics of the Gratitude Theory: they are all defined **in contrast to** the Debtor Paradigm. This is no coincidence. It is hard to give an account of the Gratitude Theory without resorting to such a contrast—not only for us, but, as I will argue in the next chapter, also in the conceptual world of Classical Greece. Both the Debtor Paradigm and the Gratitude Model find their full articulation because of each other. The models develop in tandem, in a dynamic process of mutual contrastive definition.

CHAPTER 4

A Debtor Paradigm of Obligation: Principles of Moral Accounting

> "But when," asked Pantagruel, "will you be free of debt?" (…) Panurge responded: "God help me from ever being free of debt. I'd never again find anyone to lend me a penny. (…) [A]ll my life, I've imagined debt to be like a bond between Heaven and earth, the sole sustenance of humanity—without which, I say, all humans would die—, perhaps to be the universe's great soul, which the philosophers claim gives life to all things."
>
> FRANÇOIS RABELAIS, *Tiers Livre* (1546)

•••

> The more precise the measurement of position, the more imprecise the measurement of momentum, and vice versa.
>
> WERNER HEISENBERG (1927)

∴

Our feeling of guilt, or personal obligation, has its origin in "the oldest and most primitive personal relationship there is, in the relationship of buyer and seller, creditor and debtor."[1] Thus spoke Friedrich Nietzsche in the Second Essay of his *On the Genealogy of Morality*.[2] These relationships are the most fundamental of human interactions, according to Nietzsche, for it is within this relationship that "person met person for the first time, and measured himself person against person."[3] To Nietzsche, this is not only a statement with genealogical pretensions but also a proposition about man's true and essential nature:

---

1 Parts of this chapter are published in Risseeuw & Van Raalte (2017).

2 "Das Gefühl der Schuld, der persönlichen Verpflichtung, um den Gang unsrer Untersuchung wieder aufzunehmen, hat, wie wir sahen, seinen Ursprung in dem ältesten und ursprünglichsten Personen-Verhältnis, das es gibt, gehabt, in dem Verhältnis zwischen Käufer und Verkäufer, Gläubiger und Schuldner." *English translation by* Diethe (1997).

3 "[H]ier trat zuerst Person gegen Person, hier *maß sich* zuerst Person an Person."

 | DOI:10.1163/9789004416147_005

[Text 1]

> Fixing prices, setting values, working out equivalents, exchanging—this preoccupied man's first thoughts to such a degree that in a certain sense *it constitutes thought*: the most primitive kind of cunning was bred here, as was also, presumably, the first appearance of human pride, man's sense of superiority over other animals. Perhaps our word 'man' (manas) expresses something of this first sensation of self-confidence: *man designated himself as the being who measures values, who values and measures, as the 'calculating animal as such'*. Buying and selling, with their psychological trappings, are older even than the beginnings of any social form of organization or association: it is much more the case that the germinating sensation of barter, contract, debt, right, duty, compensation was simply transferred from the most rudimentary form of the legal rights of persons to the most crude and elementary social units (in their relations with similar units), together with the habit of comparing power with power, of measuring, of calculating.[4]

This is Homo Economicus dressed up to the nines: a calculating animal, defined by a conceptual apparatus that is geared towards establishing equivalences and setting values. This portrait forms part of an argument that, in a deliberately provocative vain,[5] tries to establish that even reciprocal contractual relations did not emerge from moral sentiments but rather find their origins in violence: in primordial times, the debt relation used to be an intimate rela-

4 Nietzsche (1887), II.8; *transl.* Diethe (1997). "Preise machen, Werte abmessen, Äquivalente ausdenken, tauschen—das hat in einem solchen Maße das allererste Denken des Menschen präokkupiert, daß es in einem gewissen Sinne *das* Denken ist: hier ist die älteste Art Scharfsinn herangezüchtet worden, hier möchte ebenfalls der erste Ansatz des menschlichen Stolzes, seines Vorrangs-Gefühls in Hinsicht auf anderes Getier zu vermuten sein. Vielleicht drückt noch unser Wort »Mensch« (*manas*) gerade etwas von *diesem* Selbstgefühl aus: der Mensch bezeichnete sich als das Wesen, welches Werte mißt, wertet und mißt als das »abschätzende Tier an sich«. Kauf und Verkauf, samt ihrem psychologischen Zubehör, sind älter als selbst die Anfänge irgendwelcher gesellschaftlichen Organisationsformen und Verbände: aus der rudimentärsten Form des Personen-Rechts hat sich vielmehr das keimende Gefühl von Tausch, Vertrag, Schuld, Recht, Verpflichtung, Ausgleich erst auf die gröbsten und anfänglichsten Gemeinschafts-Komplexe (in deren Verhältnis zu ähnlichen Komplexen) *übertragen*, zugleich mit der Gewohnheit, Macht an Macht zu vergleichen, zu messen, zu berechnen."

5 The context is Nietzsche's polemics against the utilitarians (the "English psychologists"), where he explains the delight that they take in "moral genealogies" in terms of a perverse need "to debase any little piety or sympathy left". Mirowski (2001), 432.

tionship, because the creditor was entitled to the bodyparts of a defaulting debtor.[6] Exploiting the polysemy of Germanic *Schuld* ("guilt" and "debt"), Nietzsche argues that even religions are rooted in this "oldest and most primitive" relation between debtor and creditor. Morality follows a logic of compensation.

The line of reasoning in this genealogy is not unlike Adam Smith's account of the evolution of a complex society driven by a basic and universal human constant, the "propensity to truck, barter, and exchange one thing for another".[7] Although discredited in the anthropological record, this Myth of Barter, as it is called by its detractors, still dominates the popular understanding, and economic textbooks' accounts, of how our economies and societies have come about.[8] This is probably due to the very compelling protagonist of this myth: the Homo Economicus, driven by the universal propensity to seek their own advantage. Even language and communication can be understood as "trucking":

[Text 2]

> "(...) If we should enquire into the principle in the human mind on which this disposition of trucking is founded, it is clearly the naturall inclination every one has to persuade. The offering of a shilling, which to us appears to have so plain and simple a meaning, is in reality offering an argument to persuade on to do so and so as it is for his interest."[9]

Genealogies and *Kulturentstehungslehre* tend to be more about a particular anthropology than about history. The historical claim that humans have always "trucked, bartered and exchanged" is in essence a retrojected conjecture about human nature: as creatures that, by their very nature, always seek their own advantage.[10]

Historical discourse enables us to undress mankind, strip off the fancy garments of socialization, and to expose the bare human looming underneath its oversized moral clothing. The darker, the more reductionistic, the truer. Nietzsche was well aware of this pseudo-scientific use of origin stories, and,

---

6 Cf. Shakespeare's Shylock "pound of flesh" in Act 4 of the *Merchant of Venice*.

7 Adam Smith, *Wealth of Nations*, 1.2.1–2.

8 The Myth of Barter is one of the two main targets of criticism in Graeber (2011), 21–42.

9 Smith (1978 [1763]), 56.

10 On this Flintstones Effect, see Chapter One Section 3.3.

with almost sardonic iconoclasm, employs the discourse of backward-looking morality to lay out his God-less understanding of the world and its implications.[11]

Historical discourse may also be a vehicle for nostalgia, for a discourse of decline and moral corruption.[12] The common denominator of such accounts is a postulated Golden Age, a romanticized notion of the archaic societies as more socially integrated and less individualistic and morally degenerate than the present age—think of Marcel Mauss's account of an evolution of complex societies from a pure gift economy.[13] In their introduction to the volume *Gift Giving and the Embedded Economy*, Filippo Carlà and Maja Gori also point to an ancient equivalent of such a romantic valorization of the past.[14] The context is the banquet hosted by Seuthes II, king of the Odrysian kingdom of Thrace, that turns into an occasion of lavish gift-giving to the king.[15] In a lineup of people giving horses, slaveboys, and clothes for the wife,[16] the Athenian Gnesippus stands up, celebrating old times:

[Text 3]

> Γνήσιππος δέ τις Ἀθηναῖος ἀναστὰς εἶπεν ὅτι ἀρχαῖος εἴη νόμος κάλλιστος τοὺς μὲν ἔχοντας διδόναι τῷ βασιλεῖ τιμῆς ἕνεκα, τοῖς δὲ μὴ ἔχουσι διδόναι τὸν βασιλέα, ἵνα καὶ ἐγώ, ἔφη, ἔχω σοι δωρεῖσθαι καὶ τιμᾶν.
>
> [A]n Athenian called Gnesippus stood up and praised the ancient tradition that those who had possessions should show their regard for the king by giving, while the king should do the giving to those who had nothing, "so that," he said "I too will have something to give you to show my regard for you."[17]

11 Graeber (2011: 78–79) does not fully do justice to Nietzsche's contrarian use of genealogical discourse: "It's a worthy game and no one has played it better, (…) but it's a game played entirely within the boundaries of bourgeois thought. It has nothing to say to anything that lies beyond that."

12 Well-known examples are the theories by George Simmel (1907: 661–676), Karl Marx (1890: 70–82), Emile Durkheim (1902: 133–138) about the socially corrosive effects of money and capitalistic production. Cf. Carlà & Gori (2014), 18.

13 Mauss (1990 [1954]).

14 Carlà & Gori (2014), 18.

15 On the complex exchange relation and the dynamics of meaning-making between Seuthes and Xenophon in this episode, see Azoulay (2004b).

16 Xen. *An.* VII.iii.26–27.

17 Xen. *An.* VII.iii.28.

As Carlà and Gori note, this passage (that struck Mauss as "enigmatic")[18] not only confirms "the strength, already in classical times, of this historical construction opposing an 'ancient' and a 'modern' gift", but also how "such a construction represents a discursive device whose main aspect resides in its moral undertones."[19] In this particular case, as Evelyne Scheid-Tissinier has convincingly argued, the Gnesippus is projecting the Athenian democratic logic of redistribution, of liturgies and *eisphorai*, on Odrysian practice.[20] Golden Age narratives always tell a story about the here and now and how we got where we are.

Much more could be said about the different traditions of evolutionist thinking lumped together here. However, the point I would like to make is, of a different order. It is about genealogical discourse in general, about how grand narratives are essentially reductionistic programs: they either tell the story of how a pre-existing quality unfolds itself in the course of human history, or how some extraneous phenomenon penetrates and contaminates human society over time.

This chapter is about the story of debt. Did morality follow the logic of debt, of compensation, as Nietzsche had it? Did the monetization of credit inform conceptions of justice and morality? What was the place and nature of morality in a world shaped by monetary exchange, commercial relations and financial concepts?

1 Moral Bookkeeping

1.1 *The Root of All Morality?*

Nietzsche and Smith share a fundamental assumption: that life revolves around exchange. As George Lakoff's work on conceptual metaphors has demonstrated, this is an assumption that has trickled down all through our day-to-day thinking deep into our moral language, manifesting itself in the pervasive metaphor of "moral bookkeeping": MORALITY IS A FORM OF ACCOUNTING. Behind this cluster of metaphors lies the implicit assumption of moral self-interest, "based on a folk version of Adam Smith's economics",[21] i.e. "if each person tries to maximize his own wealth, then by an invisible hand, the wealth of all will be maximized."[22]

---

18 Mauss (1921), 393 n. 19.
19 Carlà & Gori (2014), 18.
20 Scheid-Tissinier (1994), 287.
21 Lakoff (1995), 190.
22 Lakoff (1995), 190.

Similarly, one of the centerpieces of David Graeber's monograph on the history of debt is the argument that Adam Smith's Myth of Barter has resulted in a worldview where:

[Text 4]

> [a]lmost everyone continues to assume that in its fundamental nature, social life is based on the principle of reciprocity, and therefore that all human interaction can best be understood as a kind of exchange. If so, then debt really is at the root of all morality, because debt is what happens when some balance has not yet been restored.[23]

This requires some clarification of Graeber's use of the phrase "principle of reciprocity": in the reductionist program of Graeber (as we have seen in the previous chapter),[24] all forms of exchange ultimately aim towards equivalence, hence "reciprocity" here is a synonym for "exchange" or "mutuality". Terminological issues aside, Graeber's monumental monograph is a sustained attempt to prove the historical and factual inadequacy of this fundamental assumption and at the same time to demonstrate the implications of this fallacy: what does it mean when we reduce moral obligations to debt? In the case of classical Athens, Graeber points out how the logic of debt and finance informed moral discourse:

[Text 5]

> In Athens, the result was extreme moral confusion. The language of money, debt, and finance provided powerful—and ultimately irresistible—ways to think about moral problems. (...) people started talking about life as a debt to the gods, of obligations as debts, about literal debts of honor, of debt as sin and of vengeance as debt collection.[25]

This is in line with some of the sources in the previous chapter, where we saw how the logic of debt provides an explanatory (or at least a rhetorical) model to articulate certain moral and social obligations. However, we also saw resistance against this logic, in the idea that what makes an obligation and its observance "social" or "moral" escapes analysis in terms of a Debtor Paradigm. This in itself

23 Graeber (2011), 91.
24 Chapter Three Section 1.2.
25 Graeber (2011), 195.

implies a particular understanding of debt and the obligation to repay it: i.e. as an obligation that is *not* social or moral (or has certain *a-social* or *a-moral* aspects to it). It suggests that debt itself is a relatively fluid notion in 5th- and 4th-century discourse, requiring disambiguation from other types of obligation.

Whereas Graeber is certainly right in pointing out that Classical Greek moral discourse was informed by the phenomenon of monetary debt, his understanding of this "moral confusion" assumes only unilateral influence. It all comes down to the idea that people start to assimilate everything to monetary phenomena and reduce all obligations to debt. There is a blind spot in this analysis: the simple fact that the cultural participants, i.e. the ancient Greeks, *themselves* seem invested in the idea that *not* all obligations work according to the Debtor Paradigm and that some relations, although involving exchange, are notionally free from "economic" expectations. This blind spot is due to the "lumping" nature of Graeber's analysis: because he chooses to lump together as forms of "exchange" all interactions that involve a two-sided allocation of goods between notional equals (ranging from barter, commercial credit and the buyer-seller relation to informal varieties of reciprocity) he fails to see the differences that are relevant from an *emic* point of view.[26]

The relevance of such an *emic* perspective is elegantly brought out in Allan Silver's work on emerging conceptions of obligation in the Scottish Enlightenment. As Silver argues, the development of "commercial societies" has produced an ideological distinction between relations based on formal obligations on the one hand and personal relations that are supposed to inhere in the "subjective definition of the situation" on the other:

[Text 6]

> Smith, Hume, and other contemporaries argue that "commercial society" introduces a historically unprecedented distinction between self-interested relations and personal bonds that are normatively free of instrumental and calculative orientations. On this view, market society has constitutive significance for the emergence of a new sphere of the private characterized by new forms of personal relations, the ethos of which is quite distinct from that of market exchange. This newly "private" world

26 See Chapter Three Section 1.

> of personal relationships is not residual, fragile, fugitive, or interstitial, but is rather made possible by the new "public" world of commerce, contract, and impersonal administration.[27]

Rather than the logic of commerce and debt *subsuming* private ethics, we see here how an increasingly articulated discourse of commerce enables the articulation of a realm of private interactions that is notionally free from utilitarian considerations. The social is emancipated from the economic—*and the other way around.*

The problem with Graeber's argument is that he, in the final analysis, seems to assume that debt is a monolithic non-changing notion, that somehow pervades and influences moral discourse. However, as we see in our ancient Greek evidence, debt itself is a fleeting notion: terminology such as δάνειον and δάνεισμα may be "etymologically rooted in notions of gift-giving",[28] but in 4th-century discourse, they are often defined in distinction from or opposition to gift-giving or other forms of long-term reciprocity—while gift-giving itself also acquires new social functions and meanings.[29] This is the conceptual problem in a nutshell: while it may be true that the very idea of "moral bookkeeping" is in the boils down to a conceptual metaphor from the source domain of finance (i.e. the notion of moral accounting is a way of understanding moral/social obligations *as if they were* financial), the financial concepts themselves, in turn, may historically have emerged from pre-existing moral notions, in a dialectic of interdefining and reciprocal molding.

1.2 *Two Vignettes*

To illustrate this conceptual point, let us turn to two examples that we already touched upon in the previous chapter. Exploring the landscape of 5th- and 4th-century conceptualizations of filial duty, one recurring model was the Debtor Paradigm of Obligation of Plato's *Laws*, where parental care was reduced to a loan (δάνεισμα) and the filial obligation to care for parents was formulated in terms of a debt (χρέος), that is owed (ὀφείλειν) and needs to be repaid (ἀποτίνειν).[30] Although this model has the force of the self-evident, in the broader context of Plato's *Laws*, however, "debt" itself, i.e. the phenomenon of credit with legal backup, turns out to be a fluid and problematic notion. The very type

27 Silver (1997), 45.

28 Von Reden (2010), 96; Millet (1991), 28f.

29 Carlà & Gori (2014).

30 See Chapter Three, Section 2.1.

of credit (δάνεισμα) that the Athenian Visitor uses as a model for filial obligations is explicitly excluded from the domain of legislation in the blueprints of Magnesia:

[Text 7]

> μηδὲ νόμισμα παρακατατίθεσθαι ὅτῳ μή τις πιστεύει, μηδὲ δανείζειν ἐπὶ τόκῳ, ὡς ἐξὸν μὴ ἀποδιδόναι τὸ παράπαν τῷ δανεισαμένῳ μήτε τόκον μήτε κεφάλαιον·
>
> Money must not be *deposited with anybody whom one does not trust.* There must be no *lending at interest*, because *it will be perfectly possible* for the borrower *to refuse* absolutely *to return* both interest and principal.[31]

Credit mechanisms are denied any form of legal backup: deposits (νόμισμα παρακατατίθεσθαι) should only be based on trust (πιστεύει), since in the case of lending at interest (δανείζειν ἐπὶ τόκῳ) there is no possibility of redress in court (or other ways to reclaim payment). It is important to appreciate the fact that there is no *ban* or prohibition on these kinds of transactions; they are merely not backed up by the force of law and the authority of the city.[32] The reason is explained somewhat later by the Athenian Visitor: the whole point of legislation is to enable citizens to live their lives as happily as possible and in the greatest possible friendship (ὅτι μάλιστα ἀλλήλοις φίλοι);[33] the latter goal is impossible if citizens inflict injuries and lawsuits on each other.[34]

As we shall see in Section 3 below, this seems in line with a remark by Aristotle, in what probably is a reaction to this passage, that legal backing is precisely what renders the element of trust, the stuff that friendships are made of, obsolete.[35] Does Platonic legislation recognize a similar relation between trust and friendship in matters of credit? This is suggested by the discussion of laws of sale and exchange:

---

31 Pl. *Leg.* V 742c3–6; *all translations of Plato's Laws are by* Saunders (2005). *Here adapted.*

32 Skultety (2006), 193.

33 743c5–6.

34 743c7–d2. Schöpsau (2003), 323–324.

35 Ar. *EN* VIII.xiii (1162b22–b31). A more explicit reference to Plato's abolition of δίκαι περὶ συμβολαίων occurs in Ar. *Pol.* 1263b21. See Section 3 below.

[Text 8]

> ὅσα δὲ διά τινος ὠνῆς ἢ καὶ πράσεως ἀλλάττηταί τις ἕτερος ἄλλῳ, διδόντα ἐν χώρᾳ τῇ τεταγμένῃ ἑκάστοις κατ' ἀγορὰν καὶ δεχόμενον ἐν τῷ παραχρῆμα τιμήν, οὕτως ἀλλάττεσθαι, ἄλλοθι δὲ μηδαμοῦ, μηδ' ἐπὶ ἀναβολῇ πρᾶσιν μηδὲ ὠνὴν ποιεῖσθαι μηδενός· ἐὰν δὲ ἄλλως ἢ ἐν ἄλλοις τόποις ὁτιοῦν ἀνθ' ὁτουοῦν διαμείβηται ἕτερος ἄλλῳ, πιστεύων πρὸς ὃν ἂν ἀλλάττηται, ποιείτω ταῦτα ὡς οὐκ οὐσῶν δικῶν κατὰ νόμον περὶ τῶν μὴ πραθέντων κατὰ τὰ νῦν λεγόμενα. ἐράνων δὲ πέρι, τὸν βουλόμενον ἐρανίζειν φίλον παρὰ φίλοις· ἐὰν δέ τις διαφορὰ γίγνηται περὶ τῆς ἐρανίσεως, οὕτω πράττειν ὡς δικῶν μηδενὶ περὶ τούτων μηδαμῶς ἐσομένων.
>
> When one person makes an exchange with another by buying or selling, the transfer must be made by handing over the article in the appointed part of the market-place (and nowhere else), and by receiving the price on the nail; no payment *for delivery later* or sale on credit is to be allowed. If a man exchanges with another man any thing for any other thing in any other place or under any other arrangement, *trusting* to the honesty of the other party to the exchange, he must do so on the understanding that when sales are made other than under the rules now stated the law does not permit him to sue. Anyone may *collect contributions to clubs on a friendly basis*, but if some disagreement arises over the collection, he must do so on the understanding that in this business no one under any circumstance will be allowed to go to law.[36]

There is to be no purchase on credit and no backup for deferred payment—a prohibition in line with a general tendency in Plato's *Law* to reduce all exchanges to cash or barter.[37] Extending ἔρανος-credit (ἐρανίζειν), a system of pooling credit,[38] is allowed, but it is insisted that such credit is extended informally, "as a friend among friends" (φίλον παρὰ φίλοις); in case of disagreements, again, they are not recoverable. As Paul Millett comments on this passage, here the point seems to be not so much to discourage citizens of Magnesia to help each other out with ἔρανος-loans; rather, the point is to convey that the very phenomenon of legal sanctions is at odds with the spirit of friendship.[39] Instantaneous cash- or barter-transactions are conducted on the market

36 Plato, *Leg*. XI 915d6–e9.

37 Morrow (1960), 138–139.

38 See Chapter Three Section 3.4.

39 Millett (1991), 187.

between non-φίλοι between whom trust cannot be taken for granted (it is presented as *exceptional* if someone allows deferred payment, and it can only be based on trust, πίστις); ἔρανος-loans function in the context of friendship, and friendships presuppose and engender trust, and may even strengthen citizen-solidarity.[40] By contrast, the reason to exclude the more formal type of credit, the δάνεισμα (T7), from legislation is of a different order: it is permissible (ἐξόν) for a debtor to refuse to return both interest and principal, for there can be no violation of trust if the exchange was never premised on trust in the first place.

The Platonic discussions of moral duties and more disembedded types of obligations that function without personal trust may indeed vouch for the "extreme moral confusion" that Graeber sees in the classical period, they certainly do not demonstrate a wholesale assimilation of the moral domain to monetary phenomena. Rather, they testify to a lively conceptual debate about the nature of debt and obligation—a debate that took place not only in the realm of detached ethical analysis to which a large part of this chapter is devoted, but also in the everyday world of conflicts that make up the bulk of the examples that Plato and Aristotle draw on, and in the petty realities of judicial court.

This last category of sources, court speeches by litigants and defendants in conflict situations, form the basis of Paul Millett's standard work on credit relations in classical Athens.[41] Evidence in the Attic orators shows how Athenian social life works with two distinct sets of credit relations, "that could be presented as either complementary or contradictory, according to the circumstances":[42] professional moneylending, on an impersonal basis and with the charging of interest, and non-professional loans, in the spirit of reciprocal help among φίλοι and therefore interest-free. Working with Sahlins' "social-distance model",[43] Millett shows how, although both credit types are forms of "monetary debt", money derives its meaning from the social relations in which it finds itself embedded.

The social mechanisms of interest-free credit imply a distinct ethos of personal, or informal, credit: obligations are understood in a broader and thicker

40 Millett (1991), 42.

41 Millett (1991). But see Shipton (1997) and Harris (1993), who point out that Millett downplays the importance of private banks (as opposed to informal "friendly" credit) in 4th-century Athens too much. Private banks were an important factor in connecting the economics of citizen-owned land and the world of money, where metics and other "outsider" play a prominent part.

42 Millett (1991), 37.

43 See Chapter Three, Section 1.2, and Chapter Four, Section 3.2 below.

way than the mere obligation to repay a debt. It is inherent in the social nature of informal debt that friendly loans impose certain "feeling rules", prescribing good will and trust on the part of the donor and gratitude on the part of the recipient. Hence, when things go pear-shaped and conflicts get to court, litigants not only charge their defaulting debtors with non-payment but also reproach them with not displaying the gratitude due to them:

[Text 9]

> (…) τότε ἡγήσεσθε τὸν μὲν πατέρα τὸν ἐμὸν βέλτιστον γενέσθαι περὶ Τιμόθεον, τοῦτον δὲ **οὐ μόνον ἀχάριστον εἶναι,** $|_2$ **ἀλλὰ καὶ ἀδικώτατον** πάντων ἀνθρώπων, ὅς γε τυχὼν παρὰ τοῦ πατρὸς τοῦ ἐμοῦ ὅσων ἐδεήθη καὶ **λαβὼν ἀργύριον ἀπὸ τῆς τραπέζης**, ἐν πολλῇ ἀπορίᾳ ὢν κἀν κινδύνοις τοῖς μεγίστοις καθεστηκὼς περὶ τῆς ψυχῆς, **οὐ μόνον οὐκ ἀπέδωκε χάριν, ἀλλὰ καὶ τὸ δοθὲν ἀποστερεῖ με.** καίτοι σφαλέντος μὲν τούτου ἀπώλλυτο καὶ τῷ πατρὶ τῷ ἐμῷ **τὸ συμβόλαιον· οὔτε γὰρ ἐπ' ἐνεχύρῳ οὔτε μετὰ μαρτύρων ἔδωκεν·** σωθέντος δὲ ἐπὶ τούτῳ ἐγίγνετο, ὁπότε βούλοιτο εὐπορήσας ἡμῖν ἀποδοῦναι.

> (…) then you'll understand that my father was as kind as could be to Timotheus, while the latter *not only is ungrateful but also is the most unjust of all men.* $|_2$ Indeed, although he got from my father all that he had asked for and *received the money from the bank* at a time when he was without resources and in the greatest peril for his life, *not only did he not show any thanks, but he's even trying to rob me of the money he received.* And yet, if the defendant had suffered loss, *the loan,* too, was lost for my father, *for he gave it neither on security nor in the presence of witnesses*; but if the defendant survived, he could pay us back at his own discretion when his resources should be secure.[44]

[Text 10]

> ἀλλ' **οὔτε ὁ χαλκὸς ὑπετέθη**, ὦ ἄνδρες δικασταί, οὔτε ὁ Βοιώτιος ναύαρχος ἐδανείσατο τὰς χιλίας δραχμὰς παρὰ τοῦ πατρὸς τοῦ ἐμοῦ, ἀλλὰ Τιμόθεος οὑτοσὶ ἐν ἀπορίᾳ ὢν πολλῇ: τήνδε χρείαν, εἰς ἣν **κατεχρήσατο** τῷ ἀργυρίῳ, εἴρηκα ὑμῖν. **ἀντὶ δὲ τοῦ χάριν ἀποδοῦναι ὧν ἐπιστεύθη** καὶ ἔλαβεν παρὰ τοῦ πατρὸς τοῦ ἐμοῦ, οἴεται δεῖν καὶ **τὰ ἀρχαῖα, ἂν δύνηται, ἀποστερῆσαι.**

44 [Dem.] 49.1–2; *transl.* Scafuro (2011).

> But in fact *neither was the copper given as security*, judges, nor did the Boeotian admiral borrow the thousand drachmas from my father, but Timotheus here did so because he was in dire straits. I've told you what he *used* the money for. But instead of repaying the favor of being trusted by my father and receiving loans from him, he even thinks it right to defraud us of the capital, if he can.[45]

The speaker Apollodorus (the banker Pasion's son) blames Timotheus for failing to display the proper reaction to his creditor from whom he had borrowed (T9 λαβὼν ἀργύριον ἀπὸ τῆς τραπέζης; T10 κατεχρήσατο) a considerable sum of money. Instead of showing gratitude (T9 οὐκ ἀπέδωκε χάριν; T10 χάριν ἀποδοῦναι) for the trust that Pasion had put in him (T9 ἐπιστεύθη), he thought fit to rob Pasion and his son of the principal (T10 τὰ ἀρχαῖα, T9 τὸ δοθέν).[46]

The element of trust (ἐπιστεύθη) refers to the fact that the loan was granted without security and witnesses (T9 οὔτε ἐπ' ἐνεχύρῳ (*lit.* "not on security") οὔτε μετὰ μαρτύρων): "copper was not put down as a pledge" (T10 οὔτε ὁ χαλκὸς ὑπετέθη).[47] Lending money without security requires a leap of faith, trust, because return of loan is insecure and the creditor runs a serious risk of ending up with empty hands (T9 ἀπώλλυτο … τὸ συμβόλαιον). As Apollodorus presents the case, the proper reaction of a debtor to a creditor's trust would be gratitude (χάρις).

There is some discussion over the question whether Pasion charged interest for his loan to Timotheus:[48] κατεχρήσατο suggests an informal interest-free loan,[49] as also does the emphatic mentioning of gratitude (χάριν ἀποδοῦναι)—not only in the passage quoted above, but throughout the entire speech there are lavish references to χάρις and to the personal nature of the relationship

45 [Dem.] 49.54.

46 ἀποστέρειν is a common term for failing to repay a loan. Aside from the places quoted above, it occurs seven times in Dem. 49 (12, 16, 21, 41, 45, 61, 68). Cf. Dem. 21.44, 32.5 (contrasted with ἀποδοῦναι τὰ χρήματα), 33.24, 34.27, 56.4 (contrasted with τὰ χρήματα ἀποδίδωσιν). See Cohen (1983), 18–22. For the details of the case: MacDowell (2009), 103, Millett (1991), 125–126.

47 Aside from land as security for a loan, pledges sometimes consisted of high-value items, such as jewellery or mass of copper. Millett (1991), 77.

48 Millett (1991), 286 n. 27 for an overview of the diverging positions: "The problem could be resolved by assuming that although interest *was* charged, Apollodorus wanted to mislead the jury into thinking that the loans were interest-free. But it is probably impossible to penetrate Apollodorus' rhetorical posturing, and the question of an interest charge must remain open." See Millett (1991) on the nature of χάρις in formal and informal credit-transactions.

49 κατεχρήσατο is probably put in opposition with ἐδανείσατο that is a technical term in the 4th-century for interest-bearing formal loans.

between Pasion and Timotheus,[50] a relationship that suggests informal interest-free loans rather than commercial "professional" loans.[51] On the other hand, throughout the speech it is clear that the loan, unlike personal non-professional loans, was contractual (T9 τὸ συμβόλαιον).[52]

Moreover, the division within the debt of Timotheus between the χάρις owed and the principal to be returned essentially leaves open the option of interest: the idea is either that Timotheus' behavior towards Pasion (e.g. his refusal to pay back his loans) falls short of displaying gratitude to a friendly creditor ready to accommodate a loan without security, *or* that Timotheus was expected to display χάρις in a material sense on top of the return of the loan. In the last case, the χάρις in play would materially amount to interest on the loan, and Apollodorus would apparently have had reason to frame the history of loan transactions of Pasion to Timotheus in terms of friendship and χάρις.

Either way, it is significant that the failure to evince χάρις (being ἀχάριστος) is a flaw of a different kind from the failure to repay a debt (which amounts to being ἀδικώτατος, most unjust). In both quotations there is a build-up in the charge from the moral flaw of failing to display gratitude (T9 οὐ μόνον ἀχάριστον εἶναι, T10 ἀντὶ δε τοῦ χάριν ἀποδοῦναι) to the legally more objectifiable offense of non-payment of debt (T9 ἀλλὰ καὶ τὸ δοθὲν ἀποστερεῖ με; T10 οἴεται δεῖν καὶ τὰ ἀρχαῖα ἀποστερῆσαι). The formal charge is focused around the "hard" obligation of repayment (failing to do so equals theft);[53] the rhetoric also makes an appeal to the "softer" and more "voluntary" obligation to display χάρις (be it material or not) as a reaction to the creditor's voluntary gesture of displaying trust in a debtor.

This goes to show that here in a court context, χάρις is a moral obligation "owed over and above the formal repayment of the money borrowed",[54] that is: as an obligation understood as complementary to the financial obligation—not identical. Sometimes to owe χάρις is distinct from owing a debt.

1.3 *The Argument*

In this chapter it will be argued that, quite in line with Graeber's general analysis and Nietzsche's provocative pronouncements, classical Greek think-

50 Millett (1991), 125–126, 213–215.

51 Millett (1991), chapters VI, VII and VIII explore and analyze the distinction between different types of loans in 4th-century Athens.

52 Millett (1991), chapter VI.

53 Cohen (1983), 18 on Dem. 32.5: "Here, as is commonly the case, *aposterein* is used in connection with *apodounai*, and describes a failure or refusal to repay what one is legally obliged to repay, the obligation arising out of the contract of which the loan was a part."

54 Millett (1991), 125.

ing about moral obligations is informed by the phenomenon of monetary debt (Section 2): one of the foundational and most influential philosophical works in the Western tradition, Plato's *Republic*, indeed starts off from the hypothesis that doing right consists in repaying one's debts, i.e. that justice follows the logic of compensation and that debt is at the root of morality. However, we will also see that this account of morality is contested and that it is far from evident *why* one should repay one's debts. What is the nature of this obligation? It will turn out, indeed, that rather than providing an explanatory framework for justice and morality, the notion of debt is an *explanandum* in itself: to know what we *owe*, we must first understand how we *ought* to act.

In Classical Athens, money and monetary debt become an instrument to think with. An analysis of the famous passage in Aristotle's *Nicomachean Ethics*, VIII.xiii, that shows some similarities with Sahlins' "social-distance model", shows how "the language of money, debt, and finance" indeed does provide powerful ways to think about moral problems, but not always in a straightforward way (Section 3). Moral obligations can be modelled on financial debt in a Debtor Paradigm of Obligation, that can both provide an **analogy** (a moral obligation or a gift *is like* a loan) or a more **reductionist(ic) explanation** (a moral obligation *fundamentally is* a loan). However, moral obligations can also be articulated in contrast to financial debt: *genuinely* moral acts, such as benefaction, are irreducibly distinct from financial credit (a *real* gift must not be seen as a loan) and call for qualitatively different responses or no responses at all (the perfect gift must not be reciprocal).

Both case studies will show how grand narratives of the impact of monetization and the development of commercial credit on morality tend to assume too easily that conceptual impact and influence work like a percolator, as if ready-made concepts from one domain trickle down to other domains to permeate, and, as the case may be, contaminate them. But this is not the way cultural concepts are brewed. They take shape in processes of active meaning-making, of actors experimenting with analogies, simplifications, operations of lumping and splitting, having been invested with the possibility of virtue or taking delight in debunking contemporary moral myths. In this process, it is not only "the moral" that is shaped by or through "the financial", the gift being defined by the loan; conversely, it is through the gift that credit is better understood, through the moral that the financial takes shape.

2 Morality as Paying Debts

It is generally recognized that money plays a central role in book I of Plato's *Republic*,[55] and may even be said to constitute one of the "architectonic principles" of the whole work.[56] Historical-materialist interpretations of the *Republic* have attempted to demonstrate that underneath the abstractions of Platonic philosophy and its "duplication" of the world lies the "real abstraction" of the money form as an embodiment of abstract social labor.[57] In her 2013 monograph on Plato's criticism on money and wealth, Anna Schriefl has argued that the famous property arrangements introduced at the end of book III find their philosophical underpinning in specific psychology of money according to which appetite for money is "by nature insatiable";[58] the abolition of private property can therefore be directly understood as a measure to promote justice, a proper constitution of the soul. This conception of justice replaces a more externalistic and rule-based one, introduced in book I, where justice is understood as the opposite of πλεονεξία, greed, i.e. the quite conventional notion that justice consists in a proper dealing with wealth: refraining from theft and deceit—*and paying back one's debts*. Scholars of the history of debt, such as Graeber and Douglas, are eager to point out that one of the foundational texts at the core of the Western tradition of moral and political theory starts off with two deceptively simple questions: what does it mean to pay our debts, and can we understand justice as the obligation to repay a debt?[59]

While it probably goes too far to claim that *Republic* I "revolves" around the morality of debt, we will see how the *Republic's* introductory discussion is preoccupied with what we may term the "transactional logic" of justice. In a series of thought experiments that involve a variety of transactional orders, ranging from poetics and religion to finance and the continuity of the *oikos*, the quest for justice itself becomes part of a rich texture of debts and dues.

2.1 *Of Debts, Dues and Duties: Children, Poems and Money*

As is to be expected in a Platonic dialogue, the setting of the conversation matters: the dialogue partners meet up in the Peiraeus, in the house of Cephalus—a

55 Schriefl (2013), Rudebush (2007), Miller (2017).

56 E.g. Shell (1978).

57 E.g. Noutsopoulos (2015). For "real abstraction", see Sohn-Rethel (1973), Castoriadis (1978); Seaford (2012) for the argument that the articulation of the Western subject in early Greek philosophy is an instance of real abstraction.

58 Pl. *Rep*. IV 442a; Schriefl (2013), chapter IV, Schriefl (2018). Cf. Schofield (2006), chapter 6.

59 Graeber (2011), 195–196; Douglas (1016), 5.

respected and successful businessman, and a long-time friend of Socrates'. As has been pointed out by several commentators,[60] the famous opening lines κατέβην χθὲς εἰς Πειραιᾶ, "I went down yesterday to the Peiraeus", foreshadows a range of salient "descents" in the *Republic*: into the first cave, where Gyges will find his golden ring,[61] into the allegorical cave where mankind is held captive by its inability to see sensory reality for what it is,[62] and finally the descent to Hades in the eschatological myth of Er.[63] Moreover, by setting the dialogue spatially in the economic center of Attica[64] and temporally in the course of a large-scale religious festival,[65] Plato lets the conversation start off right in the comfort zone of the first interlocutor: Cephalus, the wealthy and pious weapon manufacturer.

The conversation starts off rather casually with a discussion of Cephalus' old age and his lifestyle. Socrates, impressed by Cephalus' praise of moderation in the enjoyment of sex and wine,[66] is interested in the perspective on life of a man "on the threshold of death". According to Cephalus it is character (τρόπος) that matters in relations, both sexual and familial, and it is character that makes old age tolerable or not.[67] Socrates is sympathetic to this idea, but adds that most people would think that it is not character but wealth that makes old age bearable.[68]

This provides the starting point for an inquiry into the value system of Cephalus, the self-proclaimed money-maker (χρηματιστής).[69] Is it "character or rather wealth that is the condition for easily bearing old age?" asks Socrates.[70] Cephalus concedes that excellence of character excellence is not sufficient for a happy old age; wealth is a necessary condition too. Substantially, this statement will be refuted by the end of the first book;[71] however, Cephalus' claim also sets up a wider frame of reference that allows Plato to explore the nature of debt, obligation and responsibility in contexts of credit deposits and of φιλία, of inheritance, of poetical exegesis and philosophy.

60 Noutsopoulos (2015).
61 359d–e. Cf. Shell (1978) on the ring's power to make its bearer invisible as a symbol for money's power to make relations invisible.
62 514a–520a.
63 614–621.
64 Noutsopoulos (2015).
65 Miller (2017).
66 329a–d.
67 329d2–6.
68 329e1–2.
69 E.g. 330b1.
70 329e.
71 353e. Cephalus himself leaves the conversation at 331d to attend to a ritual.

The thematic nexus of credit, inheritance and philosophy is immediately flagged at the outset of the discussion. Socrates, noticing that Cephalus is not overly fond of money (οὐ σφόδρα ἀγαπᾶν τὰ χρήματα),[72] guesses that he must have inherited (παραλαμβάνειν) his possessions rather than acquired them himself (ἐπικτᾶσθαι);[73] Cephalus calls himself a money-maker, χρηματιστής, somewhere halfway between his grandfather, who inherited great wealth and multiplied it many times, and his father, who reduced the family fortune to less than the present amount. (Note that the measure of their money-making ability is the way they have dealt with their inheritance: one has multiplied it, the other reduced it.) Cephalus proudly claims a middle position: he will be content if he leaves to his children (καταλίπω) slightly more than he had inherited himself (βραχεῖ τινι πλείω ἢ παρέλαβον).[74] This background explains Cephalus' attitude towards money. As Socrates explains, people who have made their own money have "a double reason" to appreciate it (ἀσπάζονται). Not only do they value money for its use (χρεία), as any other person would do; in addition, self-made rich people are attached to (ἀγαπῶσιν) money the way poets like their poems or father are attached to their children: they take it seriously as their own produce (ὡς ἔργον ἑαυτῶν).[75]

It is instructive to see how this comparison turns money into an object of *production* instead of merely a (neutral) object of exchange. On a more thematic level, it may be noted that by evoking the term τόκος, connoting "offspring" as well as "interest", the parallel between natural procreation and money-making prepares the image that Socrates uses in book VI, where he poses as a banker-philosopher, dispensing the τόκος, 'interest', of the principal that is the Good.[76] Moreover, the link between creative production, procreation and money-making is suggestive of the types of obligations that will be at stake in the immediately following discussion, which will revolve around the correct

72 330c1.

73 330a7. Aristotle also makes the observation that *nouveaux riches* tend to be more attached to their riches than people wealthy by inheritance. *EN* 1125b1–b26, *Rhet.* 1371b18–25, 1391a14–19.

74 330b6–7. Reeve (2006) notes that tragic touch given by the dramatic date: the historical Cephalus will lose his fortune and his son soon after this dialogue—an eary reminder of the transcience of Cephalus' kind of happiness.

75 330c2–8. See Section 3.1 below for an Aristotelian analogue of this idea.

76 Pl. *Rep.* VI 506c–507a with Shell (1978), 46–48. cf. VIII 555e and X.612c where Socrates claims back the philosophical surplus value of what the interlocutors have borrowed from him in the argument (ἃ ἐδανείσασθε ἐν τῷ λόγῳ). For puns on τόκος, see also Aristoph. *Nub.* 1156 (cf. 34), *Thesm.* 845, Arist. *Pol.* I 1258b6. Golden (1990), 211. Cf. Baracchi (2001), n. 14. For the metaphysical resonances of τόκος (as reduplication of reality), see Noutsopoulos (2015), Shell (1978), Sohn-Rethel (1973).

interpretation of a quotation from a poet, about a son who has the obligation to act as the heir to his father's definition of justice and about the obligation to pay a debt.

2.2 *The Deposit Paradigm: Returning a Debt*

Cephalus explains what to him constitutes the value of wealth: old people are more sensitive to the stories of old, telling people that in Hades "someone who does/has done wrong here must pay the penalty there" (τὸν ἐνθάδε ἀδικήσαντα δεῖ ἐκεῖ διδόναι δίκην).[77] An old man, closer to the end and having a clearer view, starts to reckon up (ἀναλογίζεται) and consider whether he has ever wronged anyone[78]—he will check the ledger of his life. Rights and wrongs are now objects of reckoning (ἀναλογίζεσθαι)—a conceptual move that sets the tone for the ensuing conceptions of morality in terms of debts.

It is in light of this final reckoning that Cephalus affirms that the possession of wealth is the greatest value (τὴν τῶν χρημάτων κτῆσιν πλείστου ἀξίαν εἶναι):[79] it enables a person not to cheat someone even unintentionally or play him false (τὸ γὰρ μηδὲ ἄκοντά τινα ἐξαπατῆσαι ἢ ψεύσασθαι) and to not remain in debt to a god for some sacrifice, or to a man for money (μηδ' αὖ ὀφείλοντα ἢ θεῷ θυσίας τινὰς ἢ ἀνθρώπῳ χρήματα). Although there are many other uses (ἄλλας χρείας πολλάς), this, to Cephalus, is the prime use of wealth (πλοῦτον χρησιμώτατον).[80] Wealth allows us to be honest and to pay our debts—it allows us to go to the Underworld in righteousness.

Socrates is quick to draw out the implication that Cephalus may just have offered a definition of morality (δικαιοσύνη):[81]

[Text 11]

> Παγκάλως, ἦν δ' ἐγώ, λέγεις, ὦ Κέφαλε. τοῦτο δ' αὐτό, τὴν δικαιοσύνην, πότερα τὴν ἀλήθειαν αὐτὸ φήσομεν εἶναι ἁπλῶς οὕτως καὶ τὸ ἀποδιδόναι ἄν τίς τι παρά του λάβῃ, ἢ καὶ αὐτὰ ταῦτα ἔστιν ἐνίοτε μὲν δικαίως, ἐνίοτε δὲ ἀδίκως ποιεῖν; οἷον τοιόνδε λέγω· πᾶς ἄν που εἴποι, εἴ τις λάβοι παρὰ φίλου ἀνδρὸς σωφρονοῦν-

---

77 330d8. Shell (1978), 21–22 for an analysis of the terminology of "seeing", "visibility" and "invisibility" (e.g. the pun on Ἅιδης) in Book I of the *Republic* and the analogy of Gyges' Ring with money's invisible power.

78 330e5.

79 331a9.

80 331b5–7.

81 In the following analysis I will follow Waterfield (1993) in using "morality" as a translation of the noun δικαιοσύνη; however, I will also, interchangeably, use "justice" and "doing right". The same applies *mutatis mutandis* to the adjective δικαιός.

τος ὅπλα, εἰ μανεὶς ἀπαιτοῖ, ὅτι οὔτε χρὴ τὰ τοιαῦτα ἀποδιδόναι, οὔτε δίκαιος ἂν εἴη ὁ ἀποδιδούς, οὐδ' αὖ πρὸς τὸν οὕτως ἔχοντα πάντα ἐθέλων τἀληθῆ λέγειν.

Ὀρθῶς, ἔφη, λέγεις.

Οὐκ ἄρα οὗτος ὅρος ἐστὶν δικαιοσύνης, ἀληθῆ τε λέγειν καὶ ἃ ἂν λάβῃ τις ἀποδιδόναι.

Πάνυ μὲν οὖν, ἔφη, ὦ Σώκρατες, ὑπολαβὼν ὁ Πολέμαρχος, εἴπερ γέ τι χρὴ Σιμωνίδῃ πείθεσθαι.

Καὶ μέντοι, ἔφη ὁ Κέφαλος, καὶ παραδίδωμι ὑμῖν τὸν λόγον· δεῖ γάρ με ἤδη τῶν ἱερῶν ἐπιμεληθῆναι.

Οὐκοῦν, ἔφη, ἐγώ, ὁ Πολέμαρχος, τῶν γε σῶν κληρονόμος;

Πάνυ γε, ἦ δ' ὃς γελάσας, καὶ ἅμα ᾔει πρὸς τὰ ἱερά.

"A thoroughly commendable sentiment, Cephalus," I said. "*But what about this thing you mentioned, doing right? Shall we say that it is, without any qualification, truthfulness and giving back anything one has borrowed from someone*? Or might the performance of precisely these actions sometimes be right, but sometimes wrong? This is the kind of thing I mean. I'm sure everyone would agree that if you'd borrowed weapons from a friend who was perfectly sane, but he went insane and then asked for the weapons back, *you shouldn't give them back, and if you were to give them back you wouldn't be doing right*, and neither would someone who was ready to tell the whole truth to a person like that."

"You're right," he agreed.

"It follows that this isn't the definition of morality, to tell the truth and to give back whatever one has borrowed."

"Yes, it is, Socrates," Polemarchus interjected. "At least, it is if we're to believe Simonides."

"Well now," said Cephalus, "*I shall pass the discussion on to you two*, since it's time for me to *attend* to the ceremony."

"*You don't mean I am to be the legatee of what is yours*?" asked Polemarchus.

"Of course," he said with a chuckle, and promptly left for the ceremony.[82]

Doing right consists in truth-telling and the act of "giving back if one has received something from someone" (τὸ ἀποδιδόναι ἄν τίς τι παρά του λάβῃ)—

82 Pl. *Rep.* I 133c1–d10; *all translations from Plato's* Republic *are by* Waterfield (1994). *Here adapted.*

a typical and seemingly undisputable case of doing what is due. It is notable how Socrates, in reformulating Cephalus' description of what he thinks are preconditions to enter the afterlife in righteousness, rephrases the crucial word ὀφείλοντα: to not be indebted to god or man means to give back if one has received something. In the example that follows, Socrates distorts Cephalus' formulation even more by exploiting the ambiguity of the ἀπό-prefix in ἀποδιδόναι that can both express the idea of giving *back* and giving *what is due*: he moves from "giving back *whenever* (ἄν) someone has received something from someone" to "giving back *whatever* (ἃ ἄν) someone has received". Socrates' example centers around the case of literal and physical return of an object (e.g. a weapon, a significant example given that Cephalus is a salesman of weapons—does this problematize the fact that commerce only cares for instrumental reasoning?) to a friend who in the meanwhile has lost his mind. It is evident that this is a bad idea. What is more, to Socrates it is evident that in this case one *ought not* (οὔτε χρή) return the object, nor would giving it back be *just*.

In reformulating Cephalus' traditional ideas about justice, Socrates seems to simplify Cephalus' value system and exaggerate its externalist character: on this reformulation, Cephalus' idea of justice is simply "the performance of those debt-repaying actions prescribed by the lex talionis."[83] Morality is reduced to a set of actions: life is a ledger and if we manage to be in the black when we die, the good afterlife is ensured; the kind of person that we are does not matter—as long as our obligations are fulfilled.

The ensuing *elenchus* is so shockingly easy (Cephalus immediately gives in and leaves the scene politely and smiling) that we may pause to wonder what the significance of this scene might be. Is Cephalus a gentle caricature of an un-philosophical conception of virtuous living?[84] Or does Plato dramatize here an uncomfortable tension between virtue and knowledge in the person of Cephalus, who is manifestly un-philosophical, but who nonetheless remains an embodiment of virtue, living his life in moderation and happy to leave the philosophical conversation to attend to his religious duties?[85]

---

83 McPherran (2006), 86 (who seems to miss the distorting role of Socrates). A similar understanding of divine justice is held by Euthyphro (*Euth.* 14c–15c; Yunis 1998).

84 E.g. Annas (1981), 20.

85 E.g. Reeve (2006), 6: Cephalus "may not know what justice is, but his experience of life has given him a kind of wisdom that Plato by no means despises." According to Reeve, the person of Cephalus, being "to some degree moderate, just, pious, and wise without having studied philosophy or knowing what the virtues are" challenges the notion, articulated later in the dialogue, that one needs philosophy in order to be just and virtuous.

For one thing, the easy *elenchus* of Cephalus is crucial for the thematics of debt and dues about to be unfold. It triggers Polemarchus to do his duty as a good son and intervene to help his father, whereupon Cephalus decides to "make over his argument" (παραδίδωμι τὸν λόγον) to his son, making him the heir (κληρονόμος) to his argument—father and son thus exemplifying the harmonious order of parent-child reciprocity and succession.

Moreover, as easy as the *elenchus* may be, Socrates' distortion of Cephalus' theory of justice does help to bring out the nature of debts, dues and duties: the far-fetched example of the friend turned mad makes it clear that knowledge of what we *owe*, what we have borrowed, is not sufficient to understand what we *ought* to do. To know what we *owe*, we must first understand how we *ought* to act. "Debt is understood via duty rather than the other way around."[86]

2.3 *Helping Friends and Harming Enemies: To Give Everyone Their Due*

Polemarchus, having inherited the obligation to explain Cephalus' account of justice (ὁ τοῦ λόγου κληρονόμος),[87] is asked to clarify his intervention: what does he think the poet Simonides has to add to the discussion about morality?

[Text 12]

> Ὅτι, ἦ δ' ὅς, τὸ τὰ ὀφειλόμενα ἑκάστῳ ἀποδιδόναι δίκαιόν ἐστι· τοῦτο λέγων δοκεῖ ἔμοιγε καλῶς λέγειν.
>
> "That it is right *to give anyone back what you owe them,*" he said. "In my opinion, this is a fine remark/this account is the correct one."[88]

Citing Simonides, Polemarchus is close to bringing back Cephalus' original wording (μηδ' αὖ ὀφείλοντα ἢ θεῷ θυσίας τινὰς ἢ ἀνθρώπῳ χρήματα) into the discussion: justice is to render to each (ἑκάστῳ ἀποδιδόναι) what is due or owed (τὰ ὀφειλόμενα). Although there is nothing resembling this quotation in the extant fragments of Simonides, the saying is consistent with the image attached to the poet, already in antiquity, according to which Simonides was the first poet to receive payment for his poetry, introducing "meticulous calculation

86 Douglas (2016), 5.
87 331e1.
88 Pl. *Rep.* I 331e3–4.

into songmaking"[89]—resulting in the unfavorable image of Simonides the miser and the moneylover.[90]

In the manner characteristic of his treatment of fragments in other dialogues, Socrates and Polemarchus devote themselves to exegesis of Simonides' statement: the crucial question now turns out to be what is meant by "due" or "owed" (τὰ ὀφειλόμενα). How is this definition different an improvement of the discussion about the case of the manic friend?

[Text 13]

> **δῆλον γὰρ ὅτι οὐ τοῦτο λέγει, ὅπερ ἄρτι ἐλέγομεν, τό τινος παρακαταθεμένου τι ὁτῳοῦν μὴ σωφρόνως ἀπαιτοῦντι ἀποδιδόναι.|$_{332a}$ καίτοι γε ὀφειλόμενόν πού ἐστιν τοῦτο ὃ παρακατέθετο·**
>
> I mean, he obviously doesn't mean what we were talking about a moment ago, *the returning of something one has been deposited with one to someone insane who's asking for it back. And yet something lent is owed, wouldn't you say?*[91]

The case of the manic friend is now reformulated in the more abstract and general terms of "safe keeping" (παρακαταθεμένου, παρακατέθετο): Simonides does evidently not mean giving back something to "someone asking it back when he is not in his right mind" (ὁτῳοῦν μὴ σωφρόνως ἀπαιτοῦντι), although the deposit may "in a sense" (που) be due/owed (ὀφειλόμενον) to the person in view. Polemarchus offers an alternative interpretation of "what is owed" (τὰ ὀφειλόμενα):

[Text 14]

> **Ἄλλο μέντοι νὴ Δί', ἔφη· τοῖς γὰρ φίλοις οἴεται ὀφείλειν τοὺς φίλους ἀγαθὸν μέν τι δρᾶν, κακὸν δὲ μηδέν.**

---

89 Schol. Aristoph. *Pax* 697b (pp. 107–108 Holwerda): ἐκ τοῦ Σοφοκλέους· ὁ Σιμωνίδης δοκεῖ πρῶτος σμικρολογίαν εἰσενεγκεῖν εἰς τὰ ᾄσματα καὶ γράψαι ᾆσμα μισθοῦ. ("From Sophocles: Simonides seems to have been the first to introduce stinginess into song and to have put a song in writing for pay.") Cf. Suidas s.v. Simonides.

90 Aristotle sees Simonides as the stock example of ἀνελευθερία, miserliness (*EN* 1121a6–7; *Rhet.* 1391a8 ff.). One of the characters in Aristophanes' *Peace* characterizes Simonides as someone who "put out to sea on a bathmat for profit" (695). Cf. Carson (1999); Noutsopoulos (2015), 143.

91 Pl. *Rep.* I 331e8–332a2; *transl. adapted.*

> Μανθάνω, ἦν δ' ἐγώ—ὅτι οὐ τὰ ὀφειλόμενα ἀποδίδωσιν ὃς ἄν τῳ χρυσίον ἀποδῷ παρακαταθεμένῳ, ἐάνπερ ἡ ἀπόδοσις|b καὶ ἡ λῆψις βλαβερὰ γίγνηται, φίλοι δὲ ὦσιν ὅ τε ἀπολαμβάνων καὶ ὁ ἀποδιδούς—οὐχ οὕτω λέγειν φῂς τὸν Σιμωνίδην;
>
> "Yes, of course it was something else," he said. *"His view is that friends owe friends to do them good, not bad ones."*
>
> "I see," I said. "So if someone gives money back to someone who lent it to him, and his repayment and returning turns out to be harmful, and both the giver and the receiver are friends, then this is not a case of giving back what is owed: is this Simonides' meaning, according to you?"[92]

What is "owed" is good to friends and harm to enemies—a definition that easily avoids the difficulties of the Manic Friend scenario: returning a knife to a friend who has turned mad is not doing this friend good, hence "not owed" or "due" in any sense. (Note that the example has shifted in the course of the discussion, from the deposit of a weapon, to a not specified deposit, to a deposit of gold.) In other words, justice is now relationally defined as the virtue to do good to friends and to harm enemies:

[Text 15]

> Ἠινίξατο ἄρα, ἦν δ' ἐγώ, ὡς ἔοικεν, ὁ Σιμωνίδης ποιητικῶς τὸ δίκαιον ὃ εἴη. διενοεῖτο μὲν γάρ, ὡς φαίνεται, ὅτι τοῦτ' εἴη δίκαιον, **τὸ προσῆκον ἑκάστῳ ἀποδιδόναι, τοῦτο δὲ ὠνόμασεν ὀφειλόμενον.**
>
> "There was apparently a certain obscurity, then, in Simonides' definition of morality," I remarked. "How typical of a poet! Although, as it turns out, he meant that it is right *to give back to people what is appropriate for them, he called it what is owed to them.*"[93]

Socrates concludes (ἄρα) that what Simonides, in a poetic fashion (ποιητικῶς), expressed in a kind of riddle (ᾐνίξατο) by the somewhat ambiguous name (ὠνόμασεν) of "owed" (ὀφειλόμενον) is the virtue "to render to each what befits him" (τὸ προσῆκον ἑκάστῳ ἀποδιδόναι).[94]

---

92 Pl. *Rep.* I 332a9–b3; *transl. adapted.*

93 Pl. *Rep.* I 332b9–c3.

94 The verb αἰνίσσομαι ("to riddle") is used in the *Theaetetus* to characterize Protagoras' Man Measure Statement (152c9–10; cf. 194b), a statement that has become an ὀρφα-

2.4 *The Art of Giving Each His Due*

Overthrowing this last definition is a bit more work. Socrates offers four counter-arguments[95]—not all of them equally compelling.[96] Three of the four arguments depend heavily on an analogy between morality and (other) skills (τέχναι)[97]—to the extent that some commentators argue that Plato here deliberately presents a Socrates with serious argumentative deficiencies.[98] However, if we approach Socrates' counter-arguments as an experimental garden for ideas about debts, dues and duties, we may see how the τέχνη-analogy amplifies and distorts characteristics that are central in conceptualizations of reciprocal obligation.

The first counterargument (332c–333e) tries to pin down the precise object of the art of justice or morality. Different τέχναι "render" (ἀποδιδοῦσα) different kinds of "dues" (ὀφειλόμενα);[99] the art of medicine, for instance, gives to bodies drugs, foods, and drinks. To what particular area of human activity does the art or skill of justice apply? Polemarchus thinks that justice is the skill that gives benefits to friends and harms to enemies (ἀποδιδοῦσα ἡ τοῖς φίλοις τε καὶ ἐχθροῖς ὠφελίας τε καὶ βλάβας), i.e. to treat friends well and enemies ill (τὸ τοὺς φίλους ἄρα εὖ ποιεῖν καὶ τοὺς ἐχθροὺς κακῶς).

Socrates still has doubts: each τέχνη enables its experts to help friends and harm enemies—*with respect to something*; physicians are good at helping friends and harming enemies with respect to health. What is the "with respect to which" that an expert in justice is good at? In extreme situations such as wars, it is not hard to imagine how there is a place for an expert in benefiting friends and harming enemies; but what about peacetime? Is the just man useless (ἄχρηστος) in such a situation? Polemarchus retreats

---

νόν without its author to help him and without further context; hence, the Man Measure Statement is in need of a guardian (ἐπίτροπος, Pl. *Theaet.* 165a1). This ties in with the statement earlier in *Rep.* 330c2–8 where the attachment of self-made people to their money is compared to the love of fathers for their children and poets for their poems.

95 Sheppard (2009), 29–33.

96 Ferrari (2010), 25–27 argues that Socrates, in his refutation of Polemarchus' definition, exemplifies what Aristotle recommends to the "dialectical inquisitor": Socrates uses dialectical tricks (smuggling into the discussion the assumption that justice is a τέχνη for instance) to ensure that Polemarchus loses (so that he can be enlightened).

97 Only the third counterargument (334c1–335a10) does not rely on the τέχνη-analogy, but rather on the possibility of being mistaken who one's friends and enemies are.

98 Reeve (2006), 8 argues that Plato deliberately draws attention to the deficiencies in Socrates' argumentation.

99 Rosen (2005), 40: "There is something very odd about these examples. An art is not obligated to do anything." 40–41: objections against these examples.

to the position that in peacetime, the just man is useful (χρήσιμος) in dealings with money (εἰς ἀργυρίου).[100] The τέχνη-analogy turns out to be a Trojan horse harboring the assumption that justice is in itself neutral, merely a means to achieve an ulterior end. Justice and money-making have been conflated.

Moreover, as Socrates goes on, even on this minimalistic interpretation, justice as a skill is redundant. In moneymaking, the business of using money (τὸ χρῆσθαι ἀργυρίῳ) too, you need specialists concerning the objects of purchase or sale: when buying or selling a horse, the expert is a hippic specialist.[101] Moneymaking does not have a distinct proper object.[102] Justice, it turns out, is only useful when one wishes to keep one's money safe (ὅταν παρακαταθέσθαι), i.e. when there *is* no object of purchase or sale, because money is "there is no need to put the money to use, it is enough just to let it rest" (ὅταν μηδὲν δέῃ αὐτῷ χρῆσθαι ἀλλὰ κεῖσθαι).[103] It is when money is without use (ἄχρηστον) that justice in relation to it is useful (χρήσιμος ἐπ' αὐτῷ ἡ δικαιοσύνη).[104] In the use of each thing (ἐν χρήσει), justice is useless (ἄχρηστος); in its uselessness (ἐν ἀχρηστίᾳ) it is useful (χρήσιμος). Is this merely a clever sophism building on the etymological connection between χρήματα, money, and χρῆσις, use? And is this devaluation of justice premised on a logic of safekeeping—the same hoarder's logic that separates money from objects with use value?[105]

Or is it an effective way to demonstrate the emptiness of a chrematistic value system that conflates justice and moneymaking?

The second counterargument (333e–334b) builds on the purported neutrality of justice as a skill: if doctors are able to cure people and to make them ill, then, along the same lines, the best guard will also be the most accomplished thief.[106] Therefore, the just man is clever at looking after money (δεινὸς φυλάττειν) *and* at stealing it (κλέπτειν δεινός).[107] Hence, the just man is "some kind of a thief" (κλέπτης τις) and justice turns into some art of stealing (κλεπτική τις)

100 Here κτῆσιν or an alternative *nomen actionis* must be understood, analogous to εἰς πεττῶν θέσιν in 333b1.

101 333b11–13.

102 This resistance to seeing money as an end (and a phenomenon) in itself resembles the argumentation of Socrates in Xenophon's *Memorabilia*. See Chapter Five.

103 333c9.

104 333c11–d1.

105 Noutsopoulos (2015), 143–146 contrasts Polemarchus' "logic of hoarding" with Thrasymachus "logic of usury", a logic of limitless exploitation and violation of the notion of self-sufficiency.

106 334a1–5.

107 334a7–8.

"but with a view to helping friends and harming enemies" (ἐπ' ὠφελίᾳ μέντοι τῶν φίλων καὶ ἐπὶ βλάβῃ τῶν ἐχθρῶν).[108]

The third counter-argument (334c–335b) is the only argument that does not rely on the τέχνη-analogy, but revolves around the distinction between reality and reputation: are "friends" people that one "believes to be good" or those "who really are good, even if one does not realize it" (and likewise with enemies). Polemarchus, wishing to keep open the possibility of being mistaken, opts for "those who one believes to be good" and quickly runs into difficulties: if mistakes are possible and if you mistakenly think a person is bad while in fact he is good, then it would follow that it is moral to "harm those who do no wrong".[109] "Helping friends and harming enemies" may sound like a simple, and mechanistically applicable, principle of morality, but once again it turns out that we need morality in order to find out who one's friends and enemies are, or ought to be, rather than the other way round.

Polemarchus adjusts his position and defines a friend as someone "who seems to be good *and* is" (and vice versa for enemies).[110] This adjusted definition becomes the target of Socrates' final objection: is it really moral to treat enemies, or *anyone*, in the world badly?[111] For to cause anything harm is to make it worse; in the case of justice, this would result in making an enemy more immoral, i.e. to corrupt him: justice produces injustice.[112] Here, the τέχνη-analogy is invoked again: just as it is impossible to use music to make people unmusical, similarly it is impossible that a moral person would make others immoral by the practice of morality or justice.[113] It is never moral to harm others. In fact, people who claim that it is are very likely to be people like Periander, Perdiccas, Xerxes or Ismenias, or "someone else like that—a rich man who fancied himself to be highly powerful" (τινος ἄλλου μέγα οἰομένου δύνασθαι πλουσίου ἀνδρός); the morality of a plutocrat.[114]

It is evident that Socrates' argumentation depends for a large part on the introduction of the τέχνη-analogy—in its insistence of a clearly defined

108 Reeve (2006), 8 articulates the flaws in Socrates' application of the τέχνη-analogy in his second counterargument.

109 334d.

110 335a.

111 335b.

112 It is commonly noted that the argument here trades on an ambiguity of βλάπτειν: whereas Polemarchus means "to hurt" enemies in the sense of damaging their interests, Socrates takes the verb to mean "to harm" in the sense of making them worse men. See Cross & Woosley (1964), 20–22; Annas (1981), 33.

113 335d.

114 336a.

domain or object of application for morality, in the assumption that morality is a neutral skill that can be put to use for good and for bad ends and in the (contrary) assumption that morality, as a skill, cannot produce its opposite. In all three cases, the argumentation seems contrived at best. In all three cases, dealings with money and wealth play an important role in characterizing the putatively moral or just person as someone of questionable standing: a moneymaker with inactive property, a thief, a plutocrat. Not exactly a debt-paying truth-telling model of reliability.

On a more charitable view, we could say that the τέχνη-analogy helps Socrates raise questions about the seemingly self-evident nature of debts and dues: Polemarchus' "giving to each what is due" may seem a step forward in sophistication compared to Cephalus' (or actually: Socrates') "giving back what you borrowed", but it is still deceptive in its simplicity. It suggests that justice is mechanistic and rule-based, as a kind of skill, but skills are means towards "achieving an antecedently determined end"[115]—an approach that leads us to conceive of justice as either useless or as the art of both safekeeping and theft.

Moreover, in his arguments Socrates pushes Polemarchus towards the most "monetized" version of the "helping friends and harming enemies"-rule: justice is reduced to the art of moneymaking or the art of safekeeping and theft. On one level, this simplification may be seen as the ultimate consequence of Cephalus' value system that may be characterized as "externalistic" in that it puts too great an emphasis on externalities, such as money, and that locates morality in the performance of actions that adhere to rules; it may be a gentle caricature or a *reductio ad absurdum*. But it also poses a challenge to the idea that monetary debts are transparent and easy to grasp: that it is self-evident and self-explanatory that we need to repay our debts and that we can model our entire moral system on the paradigm case of monetary debts. Although of dubious philosophical quality, Socrates' counterarguments at least demonstrate how reducing morality to bookkeeping is not only a dead-end street, but also reversing the order of explanation. The "obligation to repay a debt" is not something that can help us understand justice and moral obligations in general, because in order to know what we owe we need first to know what justice is.

2.5 *The ἔρανος Paradigm*

But then Thrasymachus bursts onto the scene, and the antagonism between money and morality takes the form of open rivalry. Socrates begs Thrasy-

115 Annas (1981), 26–28.

machus to be patient with him and the painstaking process of dialectics, for if they would have been looking for gold they wouldn't have given in one little bit to each other (οὐκ ἄν ὑποκατακλίνεσθαι ἀλλήλοις)[116] in their search; now their quest is for morality (δικαιοσύνην ζητοῦντας), "a matter more valuable than loads of golden coins" (πρᾶγμα πολλῶν χρυσίων τιμιώτερον), so it would be silly to give in to each other (ὑπείκειν ἀλλήλοις) and not do their every best to discover it.[117]

Socrates assures Thrasymachus that it is lack of competence, not bad faith, that causes him to relentlessly ask questions rather than offering a definition of morality himself. Thrasymachus does not buy the irony Socrates is famous for,[118] and after somewhat crude banter to and fro Thrasymachus ends up confirmed in his suspicion that Socrates is not willing to provide a definition of morality himself: Thrasymachus will elaborate on his own account of morality, his famous theory that "justice is simply what is good for the stronger",[119] a program of cynical Realpolitik, holding that in the ultimate analysis, nobody owes anything to anyone—everything else is naïve idealism. But first, the terms of the debate need to be clearly articulated: "Suppose that I can demonstrate that there is an alternative answer you can give about morality," asks Thrasymachus, "what penalty would you expect (τί ἀξιοῖς παθεῖν)"—inviting Socrates to propose his own penalty as was customary in some legal cases:[120]

[Text 16]

> Τί ἄλλο, ἦν δ' ἐγώ, ἢ ὅπερ προσήκει πάσχειν τῷ μὴ εἰδότι; προσήκει δέ που μαθεῖν παρὰ τοῦ εἰδότος· καὶ ἐγὼ οὖν τοῦτο ἀξιῶ παθεῖν.
> Ἡδὺς γὰρ εἶ, ἔφη· ἀλλὰ πρὸς τῷ μαθεῖν καὶ ἀπότεισον ἀργύριον.
> Οὐκοῦν ἐπειδάν μοι γένηται, εἶπον.
> Ἀλλ' ἔστιν, ἔφη ὁ Γλαύκων. ἀλλ' ἕνεκα ἀργυρίου, ὦ Θρασύμαχε, λέγε· πάντες γὰρ ἡμεῖς Σωκράτει εἰσοίσομεν.
>
> "The penalty which is appropriate for ignorance, of course," I said, "which is learning from an expert. That's the penalty I expect."

116 Note how in monetary matters competition becomes a norm.
117 336e4–9.
118 337a.
119 338c.
120 Most notoriously in Pl. *Ap.* 36b where Socrates gets to formulate a counterproposal as to his punishment. Socrates, seeing his "crime" more as a service to the community, proposes treatment similar to that of a victorious athlete: to dine at the city hall. In his conversation with Thrasymachus too, Socrates (albeit in jest) unsettles the very notion of crime by refusing to conform to what other people may see as a reasonable punishment.

> "Don't be naïve," he said. "You can't just learn: *you must pay for it too.*"
> "If I ever have the money, I will," I said.
> "He has it," said Glaucon. "We'll all *help* Socrates out financially, *so as far as the money is concerned*, Thrasymachus, go ahead and speak."[121]

The "penalty" (πάσχειν) Socrates proposes fits (προσήκει) the fault of ignorance: learning from an expert. Thrasymachus reacts along the same lines as the Athenian jury in the *Apology*: this doesn't count as a full act of compensation (ἀποτίνειν), Socrates will have to pay as well—i.e. Socrates will have to *actively contribute* something to the conversation as well, instead of merely asking questions. He *owes* the others an answer.

Although the theory of justice that Thrasymachus will expound is in appearance a far cry from Polemarchus' Debtor's Paradigm, here, in the opening advances of the discussion with Thrasymachus, the topic of debts and the question what is due are playfully dramatized.[122] This becomes even more explicit in Socrates' reply: he will pay, when he has the "money", i.e. an answer, but for now he can only buy on tick. Here Glaucon comes to the rescue, reassuring Thrasymachus that he and his companions will "contribute" (εἰσοίσομεν) for Socrates—using the metaphor of a banquet (ἔρανος) where each contributes (εἰσφέρειν) his share, or the vocabulary of ἔρανος-loans, a system of crowdfunding or pooled credit where each contributor lends a sum of money to help an acquaintance in need.[123] What is being played out under the veil of banter are different models of obligation and valuation: what does a person caught in ignorance "owe" to others? Is he under an obligation to pay back an answer or is it his duty to learn? Are dialectical conversations shaped in a way analogous to exchanges? Can we learn on credit? What *kind* of credit would that be: a commercial banker's credit, or on a model of collective contributions?

Although more than eager to speak about his ideas,[124] Thrasymachus pretends to object against the ease by which Socrates is let off the hook: this way, Socrates will never be encouraged to give answers instead of merely questioning—he will forever be a dialectical freeloader, never repaying his debt of knowledge. Socrates sticks to his guns: he cannot answer his questions

121 Pl. *Rep.* I 337d3–337d10.

122 On the sophistic nature of Thrasymachus' intervention and the underlying issues of commercialized education, see Chapters Five and Six.

123 Cf. Pl. *Symp.* 177c. On *eranos*-credit, see Chapter Three Section 3.4. A famous example of friends pooling resources to help someone out is the case of Socrates' friends bailing him out of jail (or at least, attempting to do so).

124 339a4–6.

because he does not *know* any answers,[125] whereas Thrasymachus obviously does. "Don't be obstinate," Socrates says, "do me the favor (χαρίζου) of giving an answer (ἀποκρινόμενος) and don't refuse (or: don't begrudge, μὴ φθονήσῃς) to teach Glaucon and the rest of us about it".

It is this reproach of "being stingy" (φθονέω) and the pressure to be "gracious" and "generous", or to be a good sport (to χαρίζεσθαι), that eventually provokes Thrasymachus:

[Text 17]

> τελευτῶν δὲ συνεχώρησεν, κἄπειτα, Αὕτη δή, ἔφη, ἡ Σωκράτους σοφία· αὐτὸν μὲν μὴ ἐθέλειν διδάσκειν, παρὰ δὲ τῶν ἄλλων περιιόντα μανθάνειν καὶ τούτων μηδὲ χάριν ἀποδιδόναι.
>
> Ὅτι μέν, ἦν δ' ἐγώ, μανθάνω παρὰ τῶν ἄλλων, ἀληθῆ εἶπες, ὦ Θρασύμαχε, ὅτι δὲ οὔ με φῂς χάριν ἐκτίνειν, ψεύδῃ· ἐκτίνω γὰρ ὅσην δύναμαι. δύναμαι δὲ ἐπαινεῖν μόνον· χρήματα γὰρ οὐκ ἔχω. ὡς δὲ προθύμως τοῦτο δρῶ, ἐάν τίς μοι δοκῇ εὖ λέγειν, εὖ εἴσῃ αὐτίκα δὴ μάλα, ἐπειδὰν ἀποκρίνῃ· οἶμαι γάρ σε εὖ ἐρεῖν.
>
> Eventually, however, he gave in, and then added, "Now you can see what Socrates is deft at—he refuses to do any teaching himself, but he goes around learning from other people and *doesn't even give them thanks in return.*"
>
> "You're quite right to say that I learn from other people, Thrasymachus," I said, "but quite wrong to say that I don't *repay them with gratitude. I pay what I can*—and compliments are all I can give, since I don't have money. If I think someone has a good idea, I'm quick to applaud it—as you'll find out very soon when you tell us your opinion, since I'm sure it will be a good one."[126]

It is Socrates who lacks grace: he is almost a reverse sophist, going around *learning* from others, but refusing to pay thanks in return (τούτων μηδὲ χάριν ἀποδιδόναι). Socrates insists that he does reciprocate the χάρις, albeit not in monetary form: he pays gratitude according to his means, and being ignorant, this comes down to paying thanks in the alternative "coin" of praise, i.e. he gives praise to those who he thinks are speaking well—a more proper form of reciprocating in reaction to λόγος.

---

125 337e.

126 Pl. *Rep.* I 338a8–b9; *transl. adapted.*

Two distinct models of reciprocal obligation are at play. The kind of obligation that Thrasymachus has in mind is one of direct compensation (ἀποτίνειν), of singing for your supper and paying penalties (πάσχειν)—the language of negative reciprocity. Socrates and Glaucon operate in a distinct paradigm: of voluntary contributions (εἰσφέρειν), of generosity (χαρίζομαι) and gratitude (χάρις). In response to this, Thrasymachus ostensibly presents himself as a participant in this χάρις-economy; however, from his mouth, the language of χάρις is merely a thin disguise for the mercenary model of obligation.

The issue running in the background here is sophistic self-presentation. Plato comments on the way some sophists tend to present their business in terms of civic service[127] or cloak the mercenary nature of their practice by adopting χάρις-terminology[128] that suggests that a professional teacher is more than a businessman, a mercenary or a prostitute[129]—until Plato's Socrates exposes this χάρις-talk as a mere euphemism for money.[130]

In the argument that follows, the monetary paradigm prevails: Thrasymachus stresses "the financial advantages of immorality",[131] pointing out that the immoral man makes more money in business deals (ἐν τοῖς πρὸς ἀλλήλους ξυμβολαίοις),[132] pays less property taxes (εἰσφοραί),[133] makes lots of profit (πολλὰ κερδαίνει),[134] avoids monetary damages (ζημία)[135] and makes money in public office;[136] "being immoral profits oneself" (τὸ ἄδικον ἑαυτῷ λυσιτελοῦν τε καὶ ξυμφέρον).[137] It is not hard for Socrates to make it felt that Thrasymachus' account of rulers amounts to the claim that they are moneymakers (χρηματισταί)[138] versed in wage-earning (μισθωτική, μισθαρνητική);[139] it is somewhat more of a challenge to get Thrasymachus to admit, by the end of Book I, that in fact morality is more "profitable" than immorality.[140] By then, the discussion has moved from exploring the nature of morality to the question whether morality

127 See Chapters Five and Six.
128 See Chapter Six.
129 On the ideological battle about the nature of education, see Chapter Five.
130 Or, as Fredal (2008), calls it: "mystification". See Chapter Six.
131 Rudebusch (2007), 82 n. 14.
132 343d4.
133 343d8.
134 343e1.
135 343e3.
136 343e1–7.
137 344c8–9. This claim is rephrased by Socrates as ἀδικίαν δικαιοσύνης κερδαλεώτερον εἶναι (345a3).
138 345d1.
139 345a–c.
140 354a.

is "profitable". When Thrasymachus admits defeat at the end of Book I, Socrates finds this hardly a reason to celebrate. They have allowed themselves to be distracted from the question for a definition of morality to discuss questions about attributes of morality.

2.6 *Money and the Debtor's Paradigm*

We have seen how Socrates, in typically Socratic fashion, strips the very norms that his companions (and audience) live by of their self-evident appeal. After scratching their surface, the obvious, basic norms, such as the obligation to repay a debt or the ethical injunction that one ought to benefit one's friends and harm one's enemies, turn out to be question-begging. Although Socrates and his conversation partners do not rule out that there may be a connection between morality or justice and repaying debts,[141] knowing what we owe presupposes knowledge of what we *ought*; "helping friends and harming enemies" is not a principle that helps us understand morality, but *requires* an understanding of morality: in the course of the opening conversation, the idea of "debt" itself shifts from the return of a numerically identical object (the deposit model) to the reciprocation of equivalent or equitable objects. More fundamentally, in his arguments against Polemarchus' view (however flawed or fallacious), Socrates manages to give the audience a first intuition as to why mere formalistic or mechanistic standards of *actions* fall short of adding up to a theory of justice. We will see how the action- or performance-oriented approach targeted here by Plato's Socrates will recur as an account of moral obligation that falls short of being ethical to/by Aristotelian standards (Section 3).

We have also seen how Plato embeds Socrates' explicit inquiry after the nature of morality and obligations in a context that dramatizes several orders of exchange, raising questions about their comparability: ranging from poetics, religion and the intergenerational transmission of the οἶκος to the conversational trading of question and answer and the alternative philosophical model of a dialectics of collective contributions.

Money plays a crucial part in thinking through the implications of the various perspectives: it generalizes Cephalus' paradigm case of the deposit into a more abstract statement of a businessman's view of morality; and it shows the ultimate consequences of Polemarchus' understanding of morality as thoroughly externalistic and instrumental. In both discussions, money proves to be

141 In book IV, the δίκαιος is described as someone to whom one can entrust a deposit of money (παρακαταθήκην χρυσίου ἢ ἀργυρίου) (442e–443a).

an analytical instrument that helps the conversation partners to articulate the nature of obligation and morality and as such, it helps to bring to light that money can never be part of a *substantive* answer to moral questions (it is never what justice is really *about*) and that as a *formal* model or analytical instrument it is only question-begging (even if we understand morality as giving to each what is due, we need first to understand what is due).

But the abstracting force of money may be even more fundamental. Throughout the series of conversations in Book I we have seen how the dialogue partners experiment with the idea of the comparability of exchanges and relations: the attitude of moneymakers towards their money is compared with the appreciation shown by parents towards their children or by poets towards their poetic production; the moral quality of a life is compared with a credit balance on a ledger (rights and wrongs are objects of reckoning, ἀναλογίζεσθαι); taking over someone's position in a discussion is compared to coming into a family fortune; ignorance is compared to a failing that requires punishment, acquiring knowledge, or alternatively answering questions, is compared with punishment; to "owe" an answer is compared to deferred payment of a debt; making conversation is compared to collectively pooling resources, a conversational "debt" to informal pooled credit, dialectics to a χάρις-economy; and, in turn, χάρις is compared to debt, or exposed as a mere euphemism for debt.

These comparisons give us a vivid impression of intellectual banter that will soon develop into a full-fledged philosophical discussion with high stakes. But the comparisons seem to do more. They experiment with reductionism and problematize the very idea of comparability, by consistently raising questions: is every kind of obligation an instance of debt? And if so, are all debts the same? Does one and the same model, the Debtor's Paradigm of Obligation, apply to every kind of obligation in life, and in a life hereafter?

It is the analytical force of money as an object *and* a means for abstraction that gives rise to the idea of isomorphism.[142] Book I of Plato's *Republic* simultaneously explores the analytical value of this isomorphism and stages resistance against the kind of reductionism that people apply too easily when analyzing moral obligations.

---

142 See Graeber (2011), 196 for a comparable observation: "It's only the existence of money, Socrates suggests, that allows us to imagine that words like "power" and "interest" refer to universal realities that can be pursued in their own right, let alone that all pursuits are really ultimately the pursuit of power, advantage, or self-interest." See Shell (1978).

3 Debts, Gifts and Morality

With Aristotle, the question of isomorphism narrows down to the question of the relation between two prototypical exchange objects that are often believed to stand for larger systems: the gift and the loan. *Is* there a difference between a loan and a gift? If a gift elicits the obligation to reciprocate,[143] how is this different from the obligation to repay a debt? It is a socially appropriate intuition to feel that there *must* be a difference. It is also a rationalistic virtue to appreciate the type of analysis that *denies* the reality of such a difference. In this section we shall see that Aristotle displays both propensities, i.e. both a commitment to a form of analytical reductionism *and* a need to disambiguate things that are similar but not identical. We shall see how Aristotle's analysis of the gift is shaped by the use of analogy (gifts *are like* loans), reductionism (gifts *really are* loans), rational debunking and unmasking (most donors *only pose* as donors, their gifts are *not real*)—culminating in the firm normative pronouncement, that sets the bar nearly too high, that the donor's intentions are defining for a real gift (*a real* gift must …).

As we saw in Chapter Three, Aristotle recognizes and exploits the similarities between the credit relationship and the parent-child bond:

[Text 18]

> τὸ δυνατὸν γὰρ ἡ φιλία ἐπιζητεῖ, οὐ τὸ κατ' ἀξίαν· οὐδὲ γὰρ ἔστιν ἐν πᾶσι, καθάπερ ἐν ταῖς πρὸς τοὺς θεοὺς τιμαῖς καὶ τοὺς γονεῖς· οὐδεὶς γὰρ τὴν ἀξίαν ποτ' ἂν ἀποδοίη, εἰς δύναμιν δὲ ὁ θεραπεύων ἐπιεικὴς εἶναι δοκεῖ. διὸ κἂν δόξειεν οὐκ ἐξεῖναι υἱῷ πατέρα ἀπείπασθαι, πατρὶ δ' υἱόν· ὀφείλοντα γὰρ ἀποδοτέον, οὐδὲν δὲ ποιήσας ἄξιον τῶν ὑπηργμένων δέδρακεν, ὥστ' ἀεὶ ὀφείλει. οἷς δ' ὀφείλεται, ἐξουσία ἀφεῖναι· καὶ τῷ πατρὶ δή.
>
> For friendship looks for what is possible, not what accords with desert, for the latter is not even possible in all cases, e.g. where it is a matter of honoring the gods or one's parents; for no one could ever render them what they deserve, but the person who serves them to the best of his ability is thought to be behaving decently. This is why one might well think it is not permissible for son to disavow father, though it is for a father to disavow his son; for the son *must return the debt he owes*, and since there is noth-

143 See Chapter One.

> ing he can do that is worthy of the benefits he has already received, he is always a *debtor*. On the other hand, a *creditor* can remit a debt; so too, then, can a father.[144]

A father can disown a son, just as a creditor can let a debtor off the hook by remitting his debt; a son cannot disown a father, just as it would be absurd for a debtor to remit a creditor.[145] Here, the Debtor Paradigm serves the didactic purpose of illustrating the reciprocal obligation and the asymmetry underlying the parent-child bond: despite everything a son may think or feel, he is *like a* debtor. There may also be a different way to read this passage. Does Aristotle imply that the son, in the final analysis, *actually* and *really is* a debtor? In other words: does Aristotle use the credit relation as an *analogy* for filial obligation or does he regard filial obligation as a *species* of it and ultimately *reduce* filial obligation to debt?

3.1 *Analogy: Gifts, Favors and Benefactions* are like *Loans*

To say that gifts, favors and benefactions *are like* loans is to say that on a particular way of seeing things, the relation between donor and recipient can be understood as a relation between creditor and debtor. There is a certain degree of isomorphism and this isomorphism sometimes helps us to articulate outstanding obligations as well as people's ultimate motivations.

Nonetheless, we are still talking *analogy, a way of seeing things*. Aristotle takes care to point out the shortcomings of the Debtor Paradigm. Inquiring into (ἐπιζητεῖται) why benefactors appear to be more committed to the people they benefit than vice versa, Aristotle first expounds the popular explanation, the Debtor Paradigm:

[Text 19]

> Οἱ δ' εὐεργέται τοὺς εὐεργετηθέντας δοκοῦσι μᾶλλον φιλεῖν ἢ οἱ εὖ παθόντες τοὺς δράσαντας, καὶ ὡς παρὰ λόγον γινόμενον ἐπιζητεῖται. τοῖς μὲν οὖν πλείστοις φαίνεται ὅτι οἳ μὲν ὀφείλουσι τοῖς δὲ ὀφείλεται· καθάπερ οὖν ἐπὶ τῶν δανείων οἱ μὲν ὀφείλοντες βούλονται μὴ εἶναι οἷς ὀφείλουσιν, οἱ δὲ δανείσαντες καὶ ἐπιμελοῦνται τῆς τῶν ὀφειλόντων σωτηρίας, οὕτω καὶ τοὺς εὐεργετήσαντας βούλεσθαι εἶναι τοὺς παθόντας ὡς κομιουμένους τὰς χάριτας, τοῖς δ' οὐκ εἶναι ἐπιμελὲς τὸ ἀνταποδοῦναι.

---

144 Ar. *EN* VIII.xiv (1163b15–22); *all translations of EN are by* Broadie & Rowe (2002). *Adapted.*
145 See also Chapter Three, Section 5.

> Benefactors seem *to be commited to* beneficiaries *more* than receivers are to bestowers of benefits; and this is made a problem for investigation, as if it were an unreasonable thing to happen. Now to most people it appears that one party are *debtors*, the other *creditors*; as *in the case of a loan*, then, where *debtors* wish *creditors* not to exist, while those who made the loan even take care to ensure *the safety of their debtors*, so the view is that benefactors too wish the recipients to exist so that they can recoup the favours they have bestowed, while recipients do not take the same care to repaying them.[146]

The fact that we are talking analogy here is flagged by comparison markers (καθάπερ ... οὕτω). According to popular perception (τοῖς πλείστοις φαίνεται), benefaction is *like a* loan (a δάνειον), receivers are *like* debtors (οἱ ὀφείλοντες, "those who owe"), and benefactors *like* creditors (οἷς ὀφείλουσιν, "those to whom they owe"). Within relationships on such terms, there is an asymmetry of care (ἐπιμελέομαι) that can be explained by pointing out the conflict of interests underlying the relation: it is in the interest of the creditors that the debtors are preserved, whereas debtors may not be very keen on the existence of their creditors.

The Debtor Paradigm allows for an analytically convenient form of reductionism: it takes away the fluff of relationships and reduces everything to bare interest—or, in Aristotle's terminology: utility. There is a certain analytical appeal to such deconstruction. Benefactions are *unmasked*, revealed and exposed for what they *really* are: loans, and nothing more elevated than that. The more reductionistic, the darker, the truer.

Interestingly, Aristotle refrains from committing to such reductionism. The Debtor Paradigm is *only* an analogy, a way of seeing things—and a dark and cynical one at that:

[Text 20]

> Ἐπίχαρμος μὲν οὖν τάχ' ἂν φαίη ταῦτα λέγειν αὐτοὺς ἐκ πονηροῦ θεωμένους, ἔοικε δ' ἀνθρωπικῷ· ἀμνήμονες γὰρ οἱ πολλοί, καὶ μᾶλλον εὖ πάσχειν ἢ ποιεῖν ἐφίενται. δόξειε δ' ἂν φυσικώτερον εἶναι τὸ αἴτιον, καὶ οὐδ' ὅμοιον τὸ περὶ τοὺς δανείσαντας· οὐ γάρ ἐστι φίλησις περὶ ἐκείνους, ἀλλὰ τοῦ σῴζεσθαι βούλησις τῆς κομιδῆς ἕνεκα· οἱ δ' εὖ πεποιηκότες φιλοῦσι καὶ ἀγαπῶσι τοὺς πεπονθότας κἂν μηδὲν ὦσι χρήσιμοι μηδ' εἰς ὕστερον γένοιντ' ἄν.

146 Ar. *EN* IX.vii (1167b17–24); *transl. adapted.*

> Now Epicharmus might perhaps claim that those who say this say it because they are "*observing* from the bad side", but it seems human enough; for most people are forgetful, and aim more at receiving benefits than at bestowing them. But it would seem that the explanation lies, rather, in nature, and that the case of *the lender does not even resemble this one*; for with the lender there is *no commitment* involved, only wishing for the other's preservation for the sake of what is to be got back from him; by contrast those who have bestowed benefits *are committed and appreciative towards* he recipients *even if the latter are of no use* and will not become useful in the future either.[147]

The precise meaning of Epicharmus' saying is, as Michael Pakaluk remarks, not so easy to establish.[148] However, the expression seems to suggest that the Debtor Paradigm is one way of *seeing* (θεωμένους) things—the way most people see it (πλείστοις φαίνεται, T19)—but that somehow fails to capture the truth or the whole truth about the logic of benefits: it is an *incomplete*, and vulgar, take on things. To Aristotle, the analogy between a debt-relationship and benefaction falls short (οὐδ' ὅμοιον), because the former does not involve commitment (φίλησις) to a *person*,[149] but only a concern with the debtor's well-being *for the sake of* repayment, whereas the benefactor does feel committed (φιλοῦσι) to the beneficiary irrespective of ulterior utility (κἂν μηδὲν ὦσι χρήσιμοι). The Debtor Paradigm ultimately assumes that people interact with each other on the basis of utility—only one of the possible forms of cooperative interactions according to Aristotle—and leaves the elements of commitment (φίλησις, φιλεῖν) and

---

147 Ar. *EN* IX.vii (1167b24–32); *transl. adapted.*

148 Pakaluk (1998a), 184. The main problem is that without the original context, it is impossible to establish the meaning of ἐκ πονηροῦ. The interpretations suggested by Pakaluk are: (1) "from a bad point of view", i.e. like a bad seat at the theatre that prevents seeing what is actually going on; (2) "at the bad side of thing", i.e. with neglect of the good in what is to see. Pakaluk thinks (1) is most likely the correct reading. I would suspect the expression is closer to (2), the counterpart to Brian's looking at the bright side of things; or, more precisely, "on the basis of", "or on the assumption of" badness or vulgarity.

149 Aristotle defines φιλία as a bond of mutual φιλεῖν of two partners who are aware of each other's φίλησις. (*EN* XIII.ii (1155b28–1156a5)). τὸ φιλεῖν, the verb, and its corresponding *nomen actionis* ἡ φίλησις, are defined as goodwill (εὔνοια), which consists in "wishing the other good things" (βούλεσθαι ἀγαθά) for his own sake (ἐκείνου ἕνεκα)—good things, i.e. either useful, pleasant or intrinsically good things. Hence, φιλεῖν and φίλησις are a πάθος (*EN* XIII.v (1157b28); *Rhet.* 1380b34–1382a37), characterized by introspective qualities. φιλία, on the other hand, is not only a relational term that denotes a bond, but is also a disposition, a ἕξις (*EN* VIII.v (1157b28–30)), that involves deliberate choice (προαίρεσις, *EN* VIII.v 1157b31).

appreciation (ἀγαπᾶν)[150] out of the analysis.[151] Benefit circulates in relationships that are based on fundamentally different dispositions and motivations. There is a deep difference within the dispositions and motivations underlying the exchange relation.

In the passage that follows, Aristotle proposes an alternative model to analyze the benefactor-beneficiary-relationship, based on an analogy with the craftsman-product-relationship: the benefactor and the craftsman are actualizing their potential by the acts of giving and creation.[152] As Aristotle notes, for the benefactor there is an element of moral excellence (καλόν) in the act of benefaction; whereas the beneficiary is merely a passive recipient (ὁ παθών) of something useful (τὸ χρήσιμον).[153] This may remind us of the observation that children have φιλία towards their parents "as towards something good and superior" (ὡς πρὸς ἀγαθὸν καὶ ὑπερέχον):[154] a benefaction-relationship, like a

150 Whereas φιλεῖν is a verb of interaction that signifies the level of commitment the subject feels towards a φίλος, ἀγαπᾶν is rather an evaluative verb indicating a subject's positive response ("appreciation") of a person, thing or situation, ranging from "to value", "to appreciate" to "to be pleased with". Cf. Schmidt (1879 [1969]), 485: "In dem ganzen Gebrauche also erweist sich ἀγαπᾶν als der schwächste Ausdruck, der ebenso sehr unserm *schätzen* als unserm *lieben* entspricht." Cope & Sandys (1877), 296: "ἀγαπᾶν (…) gives the intellectual aspect of love in the shape of esteem; no longer a mere emotion, but an affection acquired and conceived after an exercise of judgement, consisting in a valuation or estimate formed of the worth of the object of preference." See Introduction.

151 Note that at this point, Aristotle only mentions φίλησις and φιλεῖν from the point of view of the benefactor/giver. Another objection frequently formulated against the Debtor's Paradigm is that it fails to explain and take into account positive dispositions and emotions from the side of the receiver, such as gratitude. Cf. Card (1988), 118: "Aristotle also had views about the dischargeability of obligations to a benefactor. But they leave no more room than Kant's for gratitude. According to Aristotle, a noble person 'is apt to confer greater benefits in return; for thus the original benefactor besides being paid will incur a debt to him, and will be the gainer by the transaction. (…) Noble people, said Aristotle, are ashamed of receiving benefits. Instead of gratitude, we have a game of One-Up."

152 *EN* IX.vii (1167b34–68a10). It seems significant that Aristotle's famous formulation that the φίλος is "another self" first occurs in the context of parental commitment to children (1161b28–29): parents are committed to children "as their own" or even "as themselves" (1161b18, b28) because they "spring from them". Cf. Smith-Pangle (2003: 86) on the almost "perfectly selfless" love of parents for their children (although the term "self-less" is infelicitous in this context and implies an egoism/altruism-dichotomy that has little analytical value for an understanding of Aristotelian notions of φιλία).

153 *EN* IX.vii (1168a10–19). On the primacy of active φιλεῖν over passive φιλεῖσθαι see *EN* VIII.viii (1159a27 ff.).

154 See Chapter Three Section 2.1. Children too have the possibility to exercise virtue in their relation towards their parents as is implied in the remark that prioritizing obligations towards one's parents is "the finer thing" (κάλλιον, T6).

parent-child bond, is not an undiluted case of Utility Friendship, but a Heterogeneous Friendship:[155] the benefactor may be χρήσιμος to the beneficiary (i.e. he offers him access to utilities), but the beneficiary offers the benefactor the opportunity to exercise virtue.[156] One of them is in it for the money, the other for the virtue. This means that there is no genuine isomorphism with full utility friendships such as credit-relations. Therefore, the Debtor Paradigm is merely an analogy and, treating the dissimilar as similar, a defective one at that. It assumes that all friendships are Utility Friendships, it assumes that there is only one fundamental category of value: the useful.[157]

3.2 *Reductionism: Gifts, Favors and Benefactions* Really are *Loans*

But there are some tell-tale signs of reductionism in Aristotle's ethics, i.e. the claim that in the final analysis gifts are *really*, or *nothing but*, loans. Aristotle's reorganization of forms of friendship in terms of their objects (utility, pleasure and the good) does, indeed, come down to a form of reductionism: all utility friendships share the structural feature of being reciprocal; if, in addition, reciprocation is deferred, this amounts to a credit relation. This is the gist of an intriguing passage where Aristotle classifies utility friendships by degrees of formality, i.e. in degrees to which the obligation to reciprocate is made explicit between utility friends:

[Text 21]

> ἔοικε δέ, καθάπερ τὸ δίκαιόν ἐστι διττόν, τὸ μὲν ἄγραφον τὸ δὲ κατὰ νόμον, καὶ τῆς κατὰ τὸ χρήσιμον φιλίας ἡ μὲν ἠθικὴ ἡ δὲ νομικὴ εἶναι. (…) ἔστι δ' ἡ νομικὴ μὲν ἡ ἐπὶ ῥητοῖς, ἡ μὲν πάμπαν ἀγοραία ἐκ χειρὸς εἰς χεῖρα, ἡ δὲ ἐλευθεριωτέρα εἰς χρόνον, καθ' ὁμολογίαν δὲ τί ἀντὶ τίνος. δῆλον δ' ἐν ταύτῃ τὸ ὀφείλημα κοὐκ ἀμφίλογον, φιλικὸν δὲ τὴν ἀναβολὴν ἔχει· διόπερ ἐνίοις οὐκ εἰσὶ τούτων δίκαι, ἀλλ' οἴονται δεῖν στέργειν τοὺς κατὰ πίστιν συναλλάξαντας. ἡ δ' ἠθικὴ οὐκ ἐπὶ ῥητοῖς, ἀλλ' ὡς φίλῳ δωρεῖται ἢ ὁτιδήποτε ἄλλο· κομίζεσθαι δὲ ἀξιοῖ τὸ ἴσον ἢ πλέον, ὡς οὐ δεδωκὼς ἀλλὰ χρήσας·

---

155 On this category of φιλία, see Chapters Four and Seven.

156 Aristotle is here preparing the claim he will make in the next chapter that the benefactor actually gets the greater good (*EN* IX.viii (1169a18–b1)). Cf. Pakaluk (1998a), 183.

157 Modern analyses of the Debtor Paradigm of Obligation similarly point out that something gets lost in the paradigm, working "best for relatively formal obligations. It presents problems for informal and personal relationships." (Card (1988), 116). For our purposes, this is begging the question: *why* would a paradigm be problematic for informal and personal relationships and what defines these relationships as informal and personal?

> Now it seems that, just as what is just is twofold, part of it being unwritten and part what accords with written law, so too friendship in terms of the useful falls into a type based on character and a type based on legal requirements. (…). The legal type is *the one that operates on stated terms, the wholly commercial sort* from hand to hand, the more cultivated sort over time, *but still by agreement* as to the question "What against what?" With this type what is due is clear and not open to dispute, *but if it is based on friendship it will allow for postponement*; hence the fact that in some places lawsuits to recover such debts are not allowed, the thought being that those who have made an exchange *on the basis of trust* should be contented. The type based on character does not operate on stated terms, *but presents are given as to a friend*, or whatever else it may be; yet the giver expects to come away with an equal amount, or more, *on the understanding that it was not a gift he made but a loan* (…).[158]

The first distinction is between those utility friendships that find their basis in law (νομική) and those that are based on character and good manners (ἠθική).[159] Within the law-based utility friendship, the epitome of explicitness is the utterly commercial (πάμπαν ἀγοραία) one-off cash transaction: the legally backed, contractual (καθ' ὁμολογίαν) and immediate (ἐκ χειρὸς εἰς χεῖρα) transaction on fixed and explicit terms (ἐπὶ ῥητοῖς). This sounds an awful lot like a buyer-seller deal and it may very well be just that: for Aristotle, even a blatantly contractual and instrumental interaction, destitute of any form of personal involvement, still deserves the name of what we call friendship, for it still requires a modicum of cooperation, of mutual goodwill, to come about.[160]

Compared to this schematic extreme, there is a more "liberal" (ἐλευθεριωτέρα) variety of the law-based type of utility friendship: it is more liberal "in time" (εἰς χρόνον), for it allows for a deferral of payment (ἀναβολή), which is "an element of friendship" (φιλικόν), because it presupposes trust (πίστις). Here loans are distinguished from swaps: although deferral of payment still leaves the debt unambiguous and explicit (καθ' ὁμολογίαν τί ἀντὶ τίνος and οὐκ ἀμφίλο-

158 Ar. *EN* VIII.xiii (1162b22–b33); *transl. adapted.*

159 The distinction is set up after an analogy with the distinction between written and unwritten law that Aristotle elaborates on in *EN* V.vii.

160 Such an instrumental friendship is premised on "the individual's lack of self-sufficiency" (τὸ μὴ αὐταρκεῖν, *EE* VII. (1242a7–9)), since it is a matter of mutually supplying in each other's needs, complementing each other in what we lack. It does meet some minimum demands as to what we would be willing to regard as a "friendly" relation: both partners are consenting and co-operating in a mutual endeavor. Stern-Gillet (1995), 150; Cooper (1976–1977), 14. See also Chapter Seven.

γον), yet it requires a leap of faith to forego on a guarantee for immediate compensation. This is why some city-states refuse to formalize debt-relationships by legal backing: for that would destroy precisely this element of trust that signifies commitment (cf. στέργειν) by rendering it obsolete.[161]

Next, gifts are distinguished from swaps and loans. The less explicit and fixed, ἐπὶ ῥητοῖς, obligations are, the more important good manners and character, ἦθος, become: exchanges acquire different names, they come to be labeled as "gifts" (δωρεῖται, δεδωκώς), and the obligation becomes less explicit, both in timing and in value.

Note that this passage gives an *analytical* account of the differences and similarities between distinct types of utility friendship. There is a tendency in scholarship to read the passage as a genealogy of friendship types. Kenneth Alpern, for instance, rephrases the passage in such genealogical terms, speaking of "the next variety or stage in the development of utility-friendship", "this stage (…) developing naturally out of the first one", "the moral stage", "still" and "eventually".[162] It should be noted that Aristotle's language shows no signs of genealogical development; if anything, in the passage immediately following T21, there is talk of an almost inevitable "relapse" from the high-minded ideals of character-based utility friendships to the more base and simple realities of law-based friendships. Aristotle's is a language of timeless and analytical classification, not of anthropological development. The passage serves not to explain the historical emergence of prosocial virtues, but the causes of complaints and recriminations (τὰ ἐγκλήματα καὶ αἱ μέμψεις) that utility friendship is prone to.[163]

More illuminating, therefore, is the analysis of Paul Millett, who has noted the similarities between the Aristotelian classification of exchange relations and Marshal Sahlins' model of reciprocity in terms of degrees of solidarity. Sahlins model works with gradations of solidarity, ranging from the solidarity extreme of "generalized reciprocity" (giving without taking account), via "balanced reciprocity" (exchanging under the assumption of an equivalent return within a specified period of time) to "negative reciprocity" (taking without giv-

161 Cf. *EN* IX.i (1164b13ff.) for a further analysis of the reason why some city-states prohibit lawsuits for voluntary contracts: transactions voluntarily entered in should be ended in the same manner in which one entered into it. Historically we know that the colony Locri in Italy did not regulate credit in law. See Zenobius *Prov.* V.4 with Millett (1991), 42. See Section 3 above on Plato's argument for the irrecoverability of friendly loans on the same grounds (trust presupposes risk). Cf. *Rep.* 556a10–b4.

162 Alpern (1983), 312.

163 *EN* VIII.xiii (1162b5–7). Pangle (2003), 125–126.

ing, gaining as much as one can from an encounter).[164] Leaving aside "negative reciprocity" (for obvious reasons not relevant for Aristotle's utility friendship), both Sahlins and Aristotle recognize a correlation between solidarity (or: things being φιλικόν) and a degree of flexibility in exchange, particularly in the *timing* (how deferred?) and *nature* (how explicit?) of reciprocation—an almost mechanical explanation of sociality.

This is reductionism. Aristotle shows commitment to an objectivist external viewpoint and all but dismisses the difference between a swap and a loan on the one hand and a gift on the other as merely nominal. It is only its *not*-explicit nature (οὐκ ἐπὶ ῥητοῖς) that turns the encounter into one of gift-giving (δωρεῖται), and from Aristotle's analytical viewpoint, there is an element of *as-if* to this sort of friendship: we "give" *as to a friend* (ὡς φίλῳ), or, if we take ὡς to qualify the verb as well, we exchange *as if gifts are given to a friend* (ὡς φίλῳ δωρεῖται). Does this mean that in the final analysis gift-giving, or friendly reciprocity, is a sort of *as if*? Is a gift *really* a loan, a deferred swap? Is there something not entirely "real" about the ἠθική variety of utility friendships—are these not friendships after all?

3.3 *Two Truths and a Qualitative Leap in Between*

The importance of time flagged by Aristotle in T18 above also reminds us of Pierre Bourdieu's analysis of the crucial irreversibility of time in gift exchange.[165] It is this irreversibility, the workings of time, that accounts for the fundamental discrepancy between the perspective of an external observer and the perception of participants: where friends see gifts, generosity and gratitude, the omniscient spectator sees a loan and, simultaneously, the return of the loan that was "in a sense already performed at the very moment when a contract is drawn up ensuring the predictability and calculability of the act it prescribes".[166] The difference between the two perspectives is the qualitative leap between the absolute certainty that a loan is recoverable and the pretty-sure-expectation that good turns will be reciprocated, between expectation-as-legal-certainty and expectation-as-trust: the difference, the fundamental uncertainty that only exists when participants construct reciprocity in time, is what accounts for the rhythm and the irreversibility of the participants' experience, what makes the dialectics of reciprocity more than a mechanics of allocations.[167] The more time is allowed to run its course, the less explicit reciprocal

164 Sahlins (1972), 196; Millett (1991). See Chapter Three Section 1.
165 See Chapter Two Section 3.2.
166 Bourdieu (1990), 105.
167 Bourdieu (1990), 99.

obligation becomes (the less νομική, Aristotle would say) and the easier it gets for participants to uphold their "subjective illusion"[168] and to misrecognize the "objectivist" truth, the truth of the external observer: that the gift is nothing but a swap.[169] (We catch a glimpse here of the paradox in Bourdieu's description of the logic of practice: an insistence on the irreducibility of the subjective experience to an objectivist account, combined with a systematic privileging of the objectivist account as "more real" than the subjective "illusion"—we shall get back to this tension in Section 3.6 below).

We may see something of the co-existence of the "two truths" of reciprocal exchange in Aristotle's typology of utility friendships. What from the point of view of an external observer may appear as "vagueness"—vagueness surrounding the assumption of a return of favor, the vagueness of the time-span—may be experienced differently on the inside: as a measure of solidarity, as a matter of moral quality and character.[170] For instance, the idea that deferred repayment (ἀναβολή) is "friendly" because of the trust (πίστις) it presupposes is expressive of a perspective shift from third person description ("postponement") to first-person experience ("friendly", "trust"). The attribution ἐλευθεριωτέρα, "more liberal" (than the "wholly commercial" swap), for the "loan" variety of law-based utility friendship is also telling: more than an objective description of the type of exchange that allows for a certain flexibility, it also expresses an evaluation. As an adjective, ἐλευθέριος refers to "behavior and qualities appropriate to a free person",[171] such as being generous—a virtue in Aristotelian ethics;[172] conversely, being ἀνελεύθερος, i.e. exhibiting the behavior of an unfree or servile person, amounts to being acquisitive and mean.[173] One has to be able to afford flexibility and vagueness, engagements beyond the immediate swap; and one will be *credited* with virtue for being able to exhibit such behavior and accrue symbolic capital.

However, in contrast to Bourdieu, Aristotle arguably remains committed to what we might call a "realist" viewpoint. As we shall see in the next sections, for Aristotle, the "inside", i.e. the realm of intentions and expectations, may be a hidden world, sometimes in opposition to manifested behavior (people may lie, pretend and make false suggestions), but it remains, in the end, a knowable world: a world that allows for an objective and stable description,

168 Cf. Bourdieu [1980] (1990) 107.

169 On time as "an instrument of denial", see Chapter Two Section 3; Bourdieu (1990), 105.

170 Alpern (1983), 312–313.

171 Webb (1996), 163.

172 Cf. Ar. *EN* IV.1 (1119b22 ff.) on ἐλευθεριότης, "generosity". See also Chapter Seven Section 3.3.

173 E.g. Ar. *EN* 1107b10, 1108b22, 1119b27, 1121a11, 1121b13.

answering to the same principles as the outside world. There is no articulated and explicit conception of an independent domain of the subjective that can only be described in phenomenological terms, a first-person domain that is irreducible to third person description.

3.4 *Fake Gifts*

In not acknowledging a fundamental disparity between 1st- and 3rd person perspective, Aristotle is more reductionist than Bourdieu—i.e. in privileging one perspective over the other, assigning more reality to one account over the other. We saw a hint of this in Aristotle's use of "reality markers", such as the ὡς in the phrase ὡς φίλῳ δωρεῖται that may indicate false appearance (we all pretend to be *giving* gifts) belied by the reality of *true* intentions underlying the exchange. Let us take a second look at this description of ἠθική-exchanges:

> [Text 22; cf. Text 21] ἡ δ' ἠθικὴ οὐκ ἐπὶ ῥητοῖς, ἀλλ' ὡς φίλῳ δωρεῖται ἢ ὁτιδήποτε ἄλλο· κομίζεσθαι δὲ ἀξιοῖ τὸ ἴσον ἢ πλέον, ὡς οὐ δεδωκὼς ἀλλὰ χρήσας·
>
> The type based on character does not operate on stated terms, *but presents are given as to a friend*, or whatever else it may be; yet the giver expects to come away with an equal amount, or more, *on the understanding that it was not a gift he made but a loan* (…).[174]

The *second* ὡς points us to something different, not a quasi-truth, an as if, but to a reality underlying exchanges: intentions and orientations. A donor in an ἠθική utility friendship expects an equal return "on the grounds that it was not a gift he made but a loan" (ὡς οὐ δεδωκὼς ἀλλὰ χρήσας). This ὡς qualifies the participles δεδωκώς and χρήσας as giving a *subjective* motivation,[175] and thereby forging a subjective connection between expecting a return and not giving a gift: the expectation of a return is, according to Aristotle's voice, a denial of the gift.

In this line of reasoning, the difference between a gift and a loan lies not only in the flexibility and explicitness of the exchange, but also in the presence or absence of an expectation of a return. Character-based utility friendships are ambiguous: it looks like one gives to a friend, but the expectation of an equal or greater return effectively reduces the gift to a loan. Aristotle is being normative here. A *real* gift "ought" to be free of the expectation of a return and the intention to elicit one, a sentiment crisply verbalized in the pseudo-Aristotelian *Problemata*:

---

174 Ar. *EN* VIII.xiii (1162b31–33).

175 I take this ὡς as a rudimentary conjunction (ὡς ἂν δεδωκὼς εἴη).

[Text 23]

οὗ δὲ τὸ χρέος, οὐ φίλος· οὐ γὰρ δανείζει, ἐὰν ᾖ φίλος, ἀλλὰ δίδωσιν.

[W]here there is a *debt*, there is *no friend*; for if a man is a friend, he does not *lend* but *gives*.[176]

There is a mutual incompatibility between friendship and credit. Note that this not only runs counter to real everyday practice in Athens,[177] but also to the Aristotelian understanding of Utility Friendship set out in T18 where debt constitutes one of the interaction forms within the law-based variety of utility friendships. Here, as in the "ὡς φίλῳ"-phrase in T19 ("as to a friend"), we see a dismissal of Utility Friendship as an inferior kind of friendship—as *less genuine*.

The Logic of the Gift is the same as the Logic of χάρις:[178] to qualify as an act of χάρις, a favor should be neither merely a reaction to a preceding favor (ἀντί τινος), nor *intended* (ἵνα) to obtain a return:[179]

[Text 24]

ἔστω δὴ χάρις, καθ' ἣν ὁ ἔχων λέγεται χάριν ἔχειν, ὑπουργεῖν δεομένῳ μὴ ἀντί τινος, μηδ' ἵνα τι αὐτῷ ὑπουργοῦντι, ἀλλ' ἵνα ἐκείνῳ τι·

Let χάρις, in the sense that one is said to "have χάρις," be [defined as] a service to one in need, *not in return for anything* nor *in order that* the one rendering the service *may* get anything but that the *recipient* may get something.[180]

176 Ar. *Probl.* 950a40.

177 See Section 1.2 above.

178 Although chapter 3 in Konstan (2018) analyzes the same paradox of gratitude and liberality as the present analysis, Konstan insists on a qualitative difference between gratitude (which he sees as an emotion; see also Chapter Two Section 3) and the mechanism of reciprocity (which he considers a "semi-contractual relation", the "territory of commercial exchange"). As I have argued in Chapter Two, χάρις is the matter (material, cognitive and emotional) that long-term reciprocity is made of. Aristotle's "quarantaine" of material reciprocity from perfect friendship is and his insistence on intentions and emotions is, as I argue in this chapter, a *reaction* to the paradox of gratitude.

179 Cf. Dem. DK 68b 96: χαριστικὸς οὐχ ὁ βλέπων πρὸς τὴν ἀμοιβήν, ἀλλ' ὁ εὖ δρᾶν προῃρημένος. "The generous person is not he who looks to a return, but rather he who treats another well by choice." βλέπων, "looking at" or "*aiming* at", defines being χαριστικός in terms of motivation, προῃρημένος in terms of choice. Cf. fr. 229. Konstan (2000), 6.

180 Ar. *Rhet.* II.vii (1385a16–18); *transl.* Kennedy (2007 [1991]) *adapted.*

Gratitude is a response to the gratuitous: mere return of prior benefaction (ἀντί τινος) would be to discharge an obligation.[181] Moreover, the expectation of return would effectively cancel out an act of χάρις:[182] the ἵνα-phrases sharply contrast services (acts of ὑπουργεῖν) that serve the donor (αὐτῷ)—which do not qualify as acts of χάρις—with those that serve the recipient (ἐκείνῳ).[183]

181 Cf. Emmons (2004), 5: "At the cornerstone of gratitude is *the notion of undeserved merit*. The grateful person recognizes that he or she did nothing to deserve the gift or benefit, it was *freely bestowed*." However, a crucial difference with Aristotle's concept of χάρις is that modern "gratitude" is understood as an emotion (Emmons: "Gratitude is an emotion, the core of which is pleasant feelings about the benefit received."). On some differences between modern conceptualizations of emotions and the Greek conception of πάθη, see Nussbaum (2001) and Konstan (2007), 3–40. On Aristotle's conception of emotions see, e.g., Fortenbaugh (1975) and Leighton, Cooper, Frede and Striker in Oksenberg Rorty (1996). What to my view and knowledge is lacking in cross-cultural accounts of emotion is a sensitivity not so much for the cultural variability of emotions but for the way emotions themselves become part of theories of the world. A full-fledged theory of the socially constructed nature of emotions would, to my view, need to account for the way in which emotions, in post-Renaissance discourse, are embedded in notions of authenticity, sincerity and subjectivity—notions that have no exact analogue in classical antiquity (Gill (1994)). There is no ancient equivalent to the modern notion of the "private self", which lies behind the bearer of roles and participant in communal action that is the social self (Gill (1994), Stern-Gillet (1995), 11–30). See e.g. Baily (1983) for a promising approach to modern discourse of emotion that approaches the *term* "emotion" as a social strategy, a discursive practice used for identity maintenance, and Van Alphen & Bal (2009) on the economy of "sincerity".

182 Elsewhere in *EN* IX.i (1164a33–b6), when discussing potential conflicts over the valuation of services, Aristotle makes clear that within Virtue Friendship the value of the return is to be determined with reference "to the donor's intention" (κατὰ τὴν προαίρεσιν, in accordance with his deliberate decision to exercise virtue). In other cases, Aristotle continues (1164b6–14), exchanges are by implication conditional (ἐπί τινι), as "in the case of buying and selling" (ἐν τοῖς ὠνίοις).

183 Similarly, εὔνοια (cf. Section 1.1), φιλία (cf. Section 1.1 and 1.2) and ἔλεος (pity/compassion) are defined by Aristotle as phenomena that explicitly have the welfare of others as ends in themselves. Konstan (2000); Konstan (2018). A valid act of χάρις that meets the requirements is productive of φιλία: Aristotle, *Rhetoric* II.iv (1381b34–36): ποιητικὰ δὲ φιλίας χάρις καὶ τὸ μὴ δεηθέντος ποιῆσαι καὶ τὸ ποιήσαντα μὴ δηλῶσαι· αὐτοῦ γὰρ οὕτως ἕνεκα φαίνεται καὶ οὐ διά τι ἕτερον. (Friendship is produced by a favor and by conferring it in an unsolicited way and by not disclosing the deed; under these circumstances it *is perceived* as having been done *for the sake of the friend* and *not on a different ground*. [own translation]) For an act of χάρις to be productive of solidarity it needs to be recognized as gratuitous and supererogatory: by being unsolicited and not public it may appear as other-regarding behavior, free of expectations of return and ulterior motivations. Aristotle presumably has virtue friendship in mind here—although it also remains the case that here, in accordance to the aims of rhetoric (*arousing* gratitude and solidarity in one's audience), Aristotle is

On this passage George Kennedy notes that Aristotle is "[t]hus excluding *kharis* in the sense of gratitude".[184] This is missing the point. μὴ ἀντί τινος serves as a qualification on the level of *intention*, not on the level of objectively observable sequentiality.[185] Even when temporally speaking an act of χάρις is a reaction to an antecedent grace, it is not *intended* as the mere redemption of a debt. Even if from the outside acts of χάρις may be seen as sequential, from the inside, from the point of view of participants' intentions, each act of χάρις is a new gratuitous act.[186] χάρις is not given *back*, but given *again*.[187] We are grateful (we "have χάρις") in response to a gratuitous act (an act of χάρις), one that is given "not motivated by the expectation of a return (the future) (…) or by a prior obligation (the past)."[188]

What is a conditional gift? It is instructive to reflect on the nature of "the subjective", the intentionality that is made the defining mark of the true gift. Here again, we see an instructive contrast between the analyses of the gift given by Bourdieu and by Aristotle. To Bourdieu, making a gift conditional is to remove the flexibility and the temporal fluidity of gift exchange out of the dynamics: the space for future improvisation and continuous reinterpretation of past "prestations" collapses. The person expressing the condition (making the friendship ἐπὶ ῥητοῖς) controls the meaning of the exchange and forces his perspective on it, closing off the open-endedness of the gift; the implicit has become explicit. For Bourdieu, it is the difference between implicit open-ended exchanges and explicit transactions that accounts for the "excess of meaning" of the gift *vis-à-vis* the defined and exhaustively defined nature of the object of contract.[189]

---

discussing *appearance*: if you want to forge a tie of solidarity with someone, it helps if you refrain from bragging about your favors and good deeds.

184 Kennedy (2007), 137 n. 53.

185 Cope (1877), ad loc., reads χάρις in this passage "exclusively in its subjective sense (…), to denote one of the instinctive feelings" as distinct from "the actual requital of the benefit conferred". My reading differs in that I believe that χάρις refers not so much to an emotion itself, nor to a material object of requital, but to a qualitative aspect of an exchange that precludes emotions nor reciprocation. See also Chapter Two.

186 More in general, Aristotle construes πάθη as reactions to the merits and intentions of others. Kennedy's interpretation of χάρις as "kindliness" makes it hard to understand why Aristotle treats χάρις as one of the πάθη: "This short chapter differs from others on the emotions in that it focuses on what *kharis* is, neglecting the state of mind of those of exhibit it (…)." (137). For similar objections against Kennedy's interpretation, see Konstan (2006), 156–158. On χάρις in late-Archaic and Classical Greek see Chapters Two and Three.

187 Cf. Godelier (1996), 44, on the implicit logic of gifts.

188 So Webb (1996), 47 on the theological notion of gratitude. Webb also includes "the requirements of the situation (the present)"; this does not seem to apply to Aristotle's notion of χάρις, that explicitly includes reference to the recipient's need (δεομένῳ).

189 Cf. Hénaff (2014), 80.

To Aristotle, the qualitative leap between gift and loan is not an epiphenomenon of the interval between prestation and counterprestation or the vagueness of the conditions. These phenomena merely account for the *appearance* of a difference, for the *as if*, for the good manners of the free man who can afford to keep up appearances and not act in a vulgar manner. At the end of the day, gifts-with-expectations are loans and loans are swaps: they are all motivated by, and aimed at, utility. The *real* qualitative leap between a gift and a loan lies in the intention of the donor, i.e. his orientation to the good (the noble and fine, as distinct from the useful). The point of Aristotle's analysis is that it reveals how, in the end, implicit and explicit utility friendships come down to the same thing: they revolve around conditional exchanges, in which the obligation to reciprocate is understood—at the very least by the donor. Explicit "legal" reciprocity is not qualitatively different from implicit "moral" reciprocity, there is only the appearance of a difference. "To make a gift conditional" is, to Aristotle, nothing more than stating one's true intentions: that it wasn't a gift to begin with.

A *true* gift is not motivated by the expectation of a return; it is determined by the donor's orientation towards the good.[190] Aristotle's classification of friendship in terms of their object (virtue, pleasure and utility) forges a dividing line between those friendships that revolve around virtuous intentions and those friendships that reveal utilitarian expectations of return. The category of character-based utility friendship seems an awkward hybrid at first sight—a tension that is flagged elsewhere in the Aristotelian corpus:[191]

[Text 25]

> ὅταν μὲν οὖν καθ' ὁμολογίαν ᾖ, πολιτικὴ αὕτη φιλία, καὶ νομική·[192] ὅταν δ' ἐπιτρέπωσιν αὐτοῖς, ἠθικὴ βούλεται εἶναι φιλία καὶ ἑταιρική. διὸ μάλιστα ἔγκλημα

---

190 Cf. the analysis of gratitude and liberality in Konstan (2018), chapter 3. Konstan, however, notes a "radical distinction between a favor spontaneously bestowed upon a person for that person's sake, without expectation of return and with solely the other's interests at heart, and an act of liberality which is a manifestation of one's own virtue and undertaken for the sake of the *kalon*."

191 Yack (1993), 116–118. Schofield (1998), 49 makes the observation that compared to *EE* VII. (1242a–b), the *NE*-passages (VIII.xiii (1162b16, 1163a6)) lack "both the cynical tone struck in these quotations and their suggestion that ethical friendship is generally doomed to collapse into political." On the relation of the *Eudemian Ethics* to the *Nicomachean Ethics*, See discussion in Chapter Seven Section 2.3.

192 Reading ᾖ (not ἥ) and retaining καί. Spengel's deletion of καί is based on his conjecture ἥ for ᾖ. Cf. Solomon (1915), Dirlmeier (1979).

> ἐν ταύτῃ τῇ φιλίᾳ· αἴτιον δ' ὅτι παρὰ φύσιν. ἕτεραι γὰρ φιλίαι ἡ κατὰ τὸ χρήσιμον καὶ ἡ κατὰ τὴν ἀρετήν· οἱ δ' ἀμφότερα βούλονται ἅμα ἔχειν, καὶ ὁμιλοῦσι μὲν τοῦ χρησίμου ἕνεκα, ἠθικὴν δὲ ποιοῦσιν ὡς ἐπιεικεῖς, διὸ ὡς πιστεύοντες οὐ νομικὴν ποιοῦσιν.
>
> When, then, friendship proceeds by contract, it is of the civic and strictly legal kind; but when they trust each other for repayment, it aspires to be a moral friendship, that of comrades. Hence this is the kind of friendship in which recriminations most occur, the reason being that it is *contrary to nature*; for friendship based on utility and friendship based on goodness are different, but these people wish to have it both ways—they bond together for the sake of utility but make it out to be a moral friendship *as between good men*, and so represent it as not merely legal, *pretending that it is a matter of trust.*[193]

Character-based utility friendships (here also dubbed ἑταιρική, "of comrades") are unnatural (παρὰ φύσιν), for they are a hybrid of utility friendship (ἡ κατὰ τὸ χρήσιμον) and virtue friendship (ἡ κατὰ τὴν ἀρετήν): they attempt to be both, with friends who hang out together for the sake of utility (τοῦ χρησίμου ἕνεκα), but who make it a character-based encounter *as* decent people do (ὡς ἐπιεικεῖς), *as* they would do if they would trust one another (ὡς πιστεύοντες) without legal backing (οὐ νομικήν).[194] These are merely weak attempts to be noble, only outward manifestations, not anchored in internal dispositions, intentions and a true orientation towards the good. Aristotle's categorization allows for no compromises: utility friendships are utility friendships, even when they sometimes purport to be more than that.[195]

This is the analytical power of Aristotle's discussion of character-based utility friendships. It is a debunking, or unmasking, move: while doing justice to social reality (people find character-based utility friendships nobler, more liberal, civilized and friendly), Aristotle drives home the point that in the ultimate analysis "moral-like" is still a far cry from the true virtue that forms the basis of Virtue Friendship. As such, it provides the conceptual tools to understand conflict:

---

193 Ar. *EE* VII.x (1242b35–43a2); *transl.* Rackham (1971), *adapted.*

194 Cf. *EN* VIII.xiii (1162b34–63a1): Character-based utility friends wish to do what is morally fine (τὸ βούλεσθαι τὰ καλά), but in the end choose to do what is beneficial (προαιρεῖσθαι τὰ ὠφέλιμα). Pangle (2003), 126; Alpern (1983), 31.

195 On "political friendship" (πολιτικὴ φιλία), see Chapter Seven.

[Text 26]

> δυναμένῳ δὴ ἀνταποδοτέον τὴν ἀξίαν ὧν ἔπαθεν καὶ ἑκόντι[196] (ἄκοντα γὰρ φίλον οὐ ποιητέον· ὡς δὴ διαμαρτόντα ἐν τῇ ἀρχῇ καὶ εὖ παθόντα ὑφ' οὗ οὐκ ἔδει—οὐ γὰρ ὑπὸ φίλου, οὐδὲ δι' αὐτὸ τοῦτο δρῶντος—καθάπερ οὖν ἐπὶ ῥητοῖς εὐεργετηθέντα διαλυτέον.)
>
> A person should, then, if he can, pay back the value of what he has been treated to, and voluntarily, *for he must not make a man his friend against his will*; he should pay it back, then, on the basis that he made a mistake at the beginning, and received benefits from someone he shouldn't have had them from—because they weren't from a friend, or from someone doing it just for its own sake—and so he should dissolve the friendship as if the benefits had been bestowed on stated terms.[197]

In a world where the intentions of a donor determine the meaning of an exchange, it is the recipient who bears the burden of misunderstanding and misinterpretation. A recipient may be mistaken: he may mistake the civilized ἠθική behavior of a donor for real virtue, may mistake a utility friendship for a virtue friendship (or "a real friendship", as Aristotle says here!),[198] and hence mistake a loan for a gift. In such a situation, Aristotle explains, there is nothing more one can do than to follow the true intentions of the donor: if the donor, in hindsight, turns out to have been motivated by utility, there is no point in insisting on a friendship being virtuous—that would be treating the friend as an involuntary friend (one cannot *force* anyone into a virtue friendship). The recipient should, therefore, return the favor (ἀνταποδοτεόν), as he would do if (καθάπερ) the exchange were on stated terms (ἐπὶ ῥητοῖς). If obligations are thus met, the bond is dissolved.

3.5 *The Great Rift*

Recipients who mistake loans for gifts mistake business relations for "real friendships"; after a while, it turns out that the donor never was a real friend (T23: οὐ γὰρ ὑπὸ φίλου).[199] This dismissal of utility friendship as not being *real*

---

196 καὶ ἑκόντι is omitted in Laurentianus LXXXI as well as in Aspasius' commentary. There is no reason to accept this omission. *Pace* Burnet (1900).

197 Ar. *EN* VIII.xiii (1163a1–6); *transl. adapted.* I follow Pakaluk (1998), 140, Pangle (2003), 126–127, and Stern-Gillet (1995), 65.

198 Cf. Price (1989), 154–156.

199 Cf. Price (1989), 154–156.

friendship is not simply an incidental slip of the pen, but part of an effort on Aristotle's part to debunk *quasi*-ethical exchanges as in the end self-serving and utilitarian exchanges.[200]

The other side of the coin is a gift given with the sole intention of benefiting the recipient and without any hint of expectations of a return on the part of the donor:

[Text 27]

> ὁ μὲν γὰρ εὐεργετηθεὶς ἀνθ' ὧν πέπονθεν ἀπονέμει τὴν εὔνοιαν, τὰ δίκαια δρῶν· ὁ δὲ βουλόμενός τιν' εὐπραγεῖν, **ἐλπίδα ἔχων εὐπορίας δι' ἐκείνου**, οὐκ ἔοικ' εὔνους ἐκείνῳ εἶναι, ἀλλὰ μᾶλλον ἑαυτῷ, **καθάπερ οὐδὲ φίλος, εἰ θεραπεύει αὐτὸν διά τινα χρῆσιν**. ὅλως δ' εὔνοια δι' ἀρετὴν καὶ ἐπιείκειάν τινα γίνεται, ὅταν τῳ φανῇ καλός τις ἢ ἀνδρεῖος ἤ τι τοιοῦτον, καθάπερ καὶ ἐπὶ τῶν ἀγωνιστῶν εἴπομεν.
>
> For a person who has been benefited metes out good will in return for what he has been treated to, and justly so; but one who wishes someone else to do well in the *hope of doing well through him* does not seem to manifest good will towards the other person as towards himself, *just as he won't be a friend, either, if he cultivates the other because of some use he wants to get out of him*. And generally good will occurs on account of excellence, or some kind of decency, where one person appears to another as noble or courageous, or something like that, as we said happens when we support contestants.[201]

Just as any expectation of a return (ἐλπίδα ἔχων εὐπορίας δι' ἐκείνου) cancels out εὔνοια, similarly the presence of an ulterior motivation (διά τινα χρῆσιν) cancels out friendship (οὐδὲ φίλος).[202] The decisive criterion for true friendship, a real gift, genuine goodwill and real benefaction is the absence of calculation, interest and the expectation of a return—a gift that ceases to be reciprocal at all.

---

200 The dismissal of utility friendship as not friendship in the proper sense of the word is more characteristic of the treatment of the varieties of friendship in *EN* (where the inferior types of friendship are only similar to *real* friendship) than in *EE* (where the author seems far less dismissive of the inferior types). (See discussion in n. 191). See discussion in Chapter Seven Section 2.3.

201 Ar. *EN* IX.vi (1167a14–21); *transl. adapted.*

202 Cf. the discussion of utility in 1156a9–14: to φιλεῖν someone because of utility is not to φιλεῖν someone for the person that he is himself (δι' αὐτούς), but for accidental reaons.

Aristotle's revision of reciprocity in friendship is therefore twofold. There is a reductionist movement where he debunks ἠθική-friendships as ultimately motivated by utility. And there is an insistence on irreducible difference where he defines the *true* gift as an act of benefaction and hence as an exercise of virtue that does not seek reciprocation.[203] By making virtuous choice (προαίρεσις), an intentional category, the defining criterion for the true gift, Aristotle may have given a major boost to the "frenzy of disinterest" in the Western tradition of thinking about the gift.[204] After Aristotle, the analytically hard to grasp topics of gratitude and the nature of social obligation continued to be a popular subject matter in the philosophical schools.[205] Among the Stoic treatises on the subject that have survived are Cicero's *De Officiis*[206] and Seneca's *De Beneficiis*.[207]

Seneca's *De Beneficiis* provides a *lex vitae* with instructions "how to give, receive, and return benefits correctly and willingly".[208] The high-minded moral code of beneficence is, as has often been noted, aimed primarily at the obligations of the givers of benefits and favors.[209] Analogously with Aristotle, Seneca too makes the moral quality of benefaction dependent on intentions and character as opposed to performance: benefits are composed of a material part (*re*) as well as an intentional part (*animoque*), and it is the recipient's obligation to remember the favor, for the donor is expected to be indifferent to material returns and to forget about his gift (*nihil inputare*);[210] a donor's expectation of a return for a benefit extended cancels its moral quality;[211] comparable to Aristotle's προαίρεσις, the intentional category of *voluntas* is the central consid-

203 Cf. Konstan (2018), chapter 3.

204 The phrase is coined by Mirowski (2001), 447–448.

205 Starting in the Peripatos, where both Theophrastus and Demetrius of Phaleron wrote treatises titled περὶ χάριτος (DL 5.48, 5.81), the topic was adopted by Epicurus' περὶ δώρων καὶ χάριτος (DL 10.28) and the early Stoicists Cleanthes' περὶ χάριτος (DL 7.175) and Chrysippus' περὶ χαρίτων and περὶ κατορθωμάτων (SVF 3.674, 2.1081) as well as Dionysius of Heraclea's περὶ πλούτου καὶ χάριτος καὶ τιμωρίας (DL 7.167). Unfortunately, none of these treatises has survived.

206 Cicero seems to have followed Panaetius in treating beneficence as a duty. Griffin (2003).

207 Cf. Konstan (2018), chapter 3, for an analysis of the "split between intention and deed" in Seneca's *De Beneficiis*.

208 Seneca, *De Beneficiis* 1.4.2: *docendi sunt libenter dare, libenter accipere, libenter reddere.*

209 See Inwood (2005) on the position of *De Beneficiis* in the Stoic context; Griffin (2003) for a contextualization in Roman society.

210 Seneca, *De Beneficiis* 1.4.3. Cf. Dem. 18.268–269.

211 2.31.2–3.

eration in assessing the moral quality of a benefit;[212] sellers and investors may have expectations of a return,[213] may receive returns that are not necessarily voluntarily conferred,[214] may keep records and fix time-spans,[215] but a benefactor aims for gratitude and the recipient's mere intention to reciprocate.[216] The Debtor Paradigm of Obligation does not apply to benefaction:

[Text 28]

> *Mira in quibusdam rebus verborum proprietas est et consuetudo sermonis antiqui quaedam efficacissimis et officia docentibus notis signat. Sic certe solemus loqui: 'ille illi gratiam rettulit'. Referre est ultro, quod debeas, adferre. Non dicimus 'gratiam reddidit', reddunt enim et* ***qui reposcuntur et qui inviti et qui ubilibet et qui per alium;*** *non dicimus 'reposuit beneficium' aut 'solvit nullum nobis placuit',* ***quod aeri alieno convenit,*** *verbum. Referre est ad eum, a quo acceperis, rem ferre. Haec vox significat voluntariam relationem: qui rettulit, ipse se appellavit.*
>
> Here is a marvellously accurate phraseology applied to certain subjects, a long-established terminology which indicates certain acts by means of symbols that are most efficient and that serve to outline men's duties. We are, as you know, wont to speak thus: "A. has made a return for the favour bestowed by B." Making a return means handing over of your own accord that which you owe. We do not say, "He has paid back the favour"; for "pay back" is used of a man upon whom a demand for payment is made, of those who pay against their will. Of those who pay under any circumstances whatsoever, and of those who pay through a third party. We do not say, "He has 'remitted' the benefit," or 'settled' it; we have never been satisfied with a word which applies properly to a debt of money. Making a return means offering something to him from whom you have received something. The phrase implies a voluntary return; he who has made such a return has called himself to account.[217]

---

212 1.1.8, 6.10.2, 1.5.2, 1.5.5, 2.1.2, 2.2.1, 2.25.2, 3.29.2, 4.21.6, 5.2.2, 5.3.2, 5.4.1, 5.25.6, 6.9.2, 6.11.3, 6.21.4, 6.23.1, 7.15.4. Inwood (2005), 93.

213 4.13.3, 1.1.9, 3.15.4, 4.3.3.

214 1.1.3, 3.15.1.

215 1.2.3, 3.15.2–3, 7.14.5. Seneca too is aware of the potential isomorphism between lending/borrowing/ buying/selling/renting/leasing and benefaction. See Griffin (2003), 99–100.

216 7.14.4–5, 1.1.3, for the transaction "is in the minds" (2.34.1).

217 Sen. *Ep.* 81.9; *transl.* Gummere (1917), *adapted.*

The traditional idiom for returning a favor, *referre gratiam*, is to be preferred over expressions that include *reddere, reponere*, or *solvere*, for it expresses a *voluntaria relatio*—it preserves the voluntary nature of the act (*ultro adferre*), that is free from external demand (*reposcuntur*), reluctance (*inviti*), arbitrariness (*ubilibet*) or (inter)acting at a distance (*per alium*). The benefaction relationship is fundamentally removed from the world of credit (*quod aeri alieno convenit*), where debts can be resolved.[218]

The passage reveals not only that to Seneca "the language of commercial and monetary obligation is not appropriate to the sphere of good deeds";[219] it also displays awareness of the importance of verbal framing which is the logical counterpart of the internalization of benefit: if the moral quality and assessment of *beneficium* and *gratia* become a matter of intention and character, they become less visible and more subjective (they are "in our minds" 2.34.1) and verbal demarcation becomes all the more crucial.[220] Moral accounting obeys principles different from commercial bookkeeping:

[Text 29]

> *Beneficiorum simplex ratio est: tantum erogatur; si reddet aliquid, lucrum est, si non reddet, damnum non est. Ego illud dedi, ut darem. Nemo beneficia in calendario scribit nec avarus exactor ad horam et diem appellat. Numquam illa vir bonus cogitat nisi admonitus a reddente; alioqui in formam crediti transeunt. Turpis feneratio est beneficium expensum ferre.*
>
> In benefits the book-keeping is simple—so much is paid out; if the beneficiary gives anything back, there is a gain, if he doesn't, this is not a loss. I made the gift for the sake of giving. No one enters his benefactions in his account-book, or like a greedy collector calls for payment upon a set day and time. The good man never thinks of them unless he is reminded of them by having them returned; otherwise, they transform themselves into a loan. To regard a benefit as an amount advanced is putting it out as a shameful investment.[221]

---

218 cf. Cic. *Off.* 2.69: *pecuniam qui habeat, non reddidisse, qui reddiderit, non habere, gratiam autem et qui rettulerit habere et qui habeat rettulisse.* ("A man has not repaid money, if he still has it; if he has repaid it, he has ceased to have it. But a man still has the sense of favour, if he has returned the favour; and if he has the sense of the favour, he has repaid it." (*transl.* Miller)) cf. Cic. *Amic.* 31: *neque enim beneficium faeneramur.*

219 Inwood (2005), 79.

220 As Griffin (2003), 99 points out, Seneca too does discuss the exchange of benefits in credit terminology (*Ben.* 1.1.1, 1.4.6, 3.2.2, 5.16.5). Cf. Moussy (1966), 253, 267–269.

221 Sen. *De Ben.* 1.2.3; *transl.* Basore (1928), *adapted.*

The metaphorical account (*ratio*) is simple. One gives a gift for the sake of giving (*ut darem*), being indifferent towards the return, for there is no losing in conferring a benefit: one either receives a return (which is gain), or does not, which is not a loss from a moral point of view. If a donor keeps a record of his *beneficia* done (*in calendario scribit*) and thinks about the return, he turns into a tax collector (*exactor*) while the favor he has done turns into credit (*in formam crediti*) for shameful interest (*turpis feneratio*).[222] Within this moral economy, liberality is backed up by *fides*, not the legal enforcement that protects credit[223] and commerce.[224] Moreover the spirit of the return manifests itself in timing: a recipient who repays too soon turns into a debtor who wants to be clear of debt.[225]

It can be argued that Aristotle's normative language of genuine friendship and real "pure" gifts not only anticipates the ideal of the "perfect gift" in Christian thought, but also instigates a "hermeneutic of suspicion", a hermeneutic of unmasking, demystification and reduction of illusions:[226] something may seem like a gift but turn out to be a conditional bribe; someone may appear like a friend but turn out to be a self-interested business partner with ulterior motives. Real friendship is a realm free of calculable interests; the pure gift is an act of self-negation.[227] All other gifts can be unmasked as self-seeking investments.

It may also be argued that Aristotle's distinction between reciprocal utility and non-reciprocal gifts born out of virtue is the germ of a Great Rift. Modern legislation defines gifts as one-sided allocations.[228] Any service ren-

---

222 Cf. 3.15.1–3. *Faeneratio* refers to money lending at interest, usury. Cf. Cic. *Ver.* 3.168, *Fin.* 2.117.

223 3.7.1. In 3.6–17 Seneca, in a discussion whether ingratitude should be made punishable by law, comes up with (practical and) moral objections: benefit and return of gratitude will lose moral standing. See Griffin (2003), 101.

224 3.51.1.

225 4.40.5, 6.35.3–4, 6.40.

226 For the phrase, see Ricoeur (1970), 9. Cf. Graeber (2001), 30, on the hermeneutics of false consciousness in Marxism: "When Marxism, semiotics and the rust burst on the academic scene in the 1960s and '70s, they were seen above all as ways to probe beneath the surface of reality. The idea was always to unmask the hidden structures of power, dominance, and exploitation that lay below even the most mundane and ordinary aspects of daily life."

227 Cf. Bourdieu (1997), 233–234: "If one adopts the standpoint of a philosophy of mind, *by asking about the intentional meaning of the gift*, and … wondering whether the gift, conceived as the free decision of an isolated individual is a real gift, is really a gift … then this is indeed sufficient to raise insuperable antinomies (a gift is really a gift only if neither the giver nor the receiver sees it as such) that force one to conclude that a gratuitous gift is impossible."

228 E.g. the German Civil Code of 1900 defines the gift as an unpaid transfer of assets (that

dered with the intention of acquiring something of equal value is not considered as a gift, but as a purchase or exchange. This is the ultimate implication of the "frenzy of disinterest", of conflating intentionality with calculation and making intentionality the defining mark of the gift.[229] The gift may be not so much an illusion, as Bourdieu has it, but impossible and unknowable:

[Text 30]

> Pour qu'il y ait don, il faut qu'il n'y ait pas de réciprocité, de retour, d'échange, de contre-don ni de dette. Si l'autre me rend ou me doit, ou doit me rendre ce que je lui donne, il n'y aura pas eu don (…) C'est que ces conditions de possibilité du don (que quelqu'un «donne» quelque « chose » à quelqu'un «d'autre ») désignent simultanément les conditions de l'impossibilité du don.
>
> For there to be a gift, there must be no reciprocity, return, exchange, countergift, debt. If the other *gives* me *back* or *owes* me or has to give me back what I give him or her, there will not have been a gift. (…) [The] conditions of possibility of the gift … designate simultaneously the conditions of the impossibility of the gift.[230]

Derrida takes Aristotle's ban on reciprocal expectations a stap further: selfless intentions on the part of the donor do not suffice to guarantee the possibility of the gift; the mere act of the *recipient* "giving back", of showing gratitude, is to destroy the comedy of innocence—enough to annul the gift.[231] Paradoxically, the *real* gift, the gift wrapped in profuse avowals of disinterest, is an anti-social gesture:[232]

---

is *unentgeltlich*) and a one-sided allocation (it is *einseitig verpflichtend*). Paragraph 516 of the Civil Code ("Begriff der Schenkung"); cf. the Dutch Civil Code 7:175. This code was perceived as a drastic innovation of previous legislation that acknowledged the category of "mutual gifting" (e.g. the Prussian *Allgemeines Landrecht* of 1794, paragraph 1169) and instigated conceptual and ethical discussions about the possibility of a "free gift" and the possibility to subject a "social" phenomenon such as the gift to legislation. Cf. Von Gierke (1917), II.432. For an overview of the legal discussion, see Wagner-Hasel (2003), esp. 150ff.

229 Mirowski (2001), 447–448.

230 Derrida (1997), 128.

231 See Webb (1996), 69, for an illuminating explanation of this much-quoted passage.

232 Mirowski (2001), 447–448.

[Text 31]

> Refusing requital puts the act of giving outside any mutual ties.[233]

This is a far cry from the ancient commonplace that reciprocity breeds relationality—as we see for instance in a Pseudo-Aristotelian letter:

[Text 32]

> χάριτος ἀμοιβὴ καὶ δόσις συνέχει τοὺς τῶν ἀνθρώπων βίους, τῶν μὲν διδόντων, τῶν δὲ λαμβανόντων τῶν δ' αὖ πάλιν ἀνταποδιδόντων.
>
> The giving and interchange of favors holds together the lives of men—of the ones who give, those who receive and again who return.[234]

Having seen the ultimate consequence of Aristotle's analysis of the gift, it is hard to see how it can hold anything together.[235]

3.6 *Reductionism and Beyond*

In this section we have seen how Aristotle's method results in both a new "lumping" as well as a "splitting" against the anatomy of existing social concepts. We have noted both reductionism and an insistence on irreducible difference:

(i) Reductionism *within* the category of utility friendships: character-based friendships *look* moral, liberal and civilized because of the deferral of repayment they allow for and because obligations remain implicit; but in the final analysis (and after some debunking) these friendships turn out to be based on mere utility. Here gifts *are really* loans, and loans *are really* swaps.

(ii) Irreducible differentiation *between* utility friendships and virtue friendships: sometimes they may be isomorphous, because both friendship types use the language of gifts, favors and benefaction. However, within utility friendships these terms are misnomers, because what they are *really* referring to are loans, exchanges based on utility. Within virtue friendships undue focus on the "objects" of exchange (the gift, favor or benefit) distracts from what truly defines the gift: the quality of the *act* of

233 Douglas (1990), ix.
234 [Ar.], *Letter to Phillipus* (fr. 3 Plezia), 2–5.
235 See Chapter Seven.

giving, a quality that inheres in the donor's intention and his orientation towards the good—a category fundamentally and irreducibly different from utility.

Aristotle's reductionism (i) may appear less subtle than a modern phenomenological analysis like Bourdieu's. As we have seen, Aristotle's ethical or psychological worldview does not allow for an "elusive, ultimate subject of experience," an "'I' that cannot be reduced to an object",[236] one that commands an internal subjective perspective that stands in contrast to an external objective one. To Bourdieu, the gift receives its meaning from the "response it triggers off",[237] a meaning that therefore may have a certain open-endedness, flexibility and excess to it. To Aristotle, the meaning of an allocation is a given, predetermined by the intention of the donor. Misunderstandings between exchange partners do not occur due to an excess of meaning, or to a phenomenological process of constant redefinition of an exchange object, but purely due to the recipient not getting right the donor's fixed intentions—because the donor was being too implicit about the terms of the exchange, or simply deceptive and insincere.

On the other hand, as we shall see in Chapter Seven, Aristotle's insistence on the fundamentally different nature of the genuine gift, the virtuous *act* of giving (ii), opens up possibilities to conceive of a kind of incommensurable capital—a genuine surplus value that cannot be reduced to utility, interest or calculations. Although Bourdieu professes to pursue the "full truth" of the gift, by bringing together Mauss's phenomenological, subjectivist, truth with Lévi-Strauss's structural, objectivist, truth, his vocabulary tells a different story. Critics of Bourdieu, accusing him of "sociologizing" morality out of existence,[238] have pointed out that the vocabulary of "as if", "game", "strategy", "capital", "misrecognition" (*méconnaissance*), "illusion" and "self-deception" reveals a commitment to the idea that in the end all individuals are driven by self-interest, by narrow economic calculation and by power.[239] If gift exchange is a "fake circulation of fake coin",[240] if the external material side of the exchange is dubbed the "objective truth" and the first-person internalized intentional aspects are merely "subjective illusions", then, in the end, Bourdieu may have established

236 Formulations from the description of the "psycho-metaphysicians"' modern conceptions of the subject by Oksenberg Rorty (1990), 33. Cf. Nagel (1986), 34; Engberg-Pederson (1990), 121, on possible Stoic precursors for the articulation of such an irreducible subjective viewpoint.

237 Bourdieu (1987), 5.

238 Sayer (1999), 413.

239 Alexander (1995); Graeber (2002), 28–29; Evens (1999), 22–23.

240 Bourdieu (1977), 6.

"*the perception* of the possibility of a gift", not the possibility itself.[241] Aristotle's account of the genuine gift provides an alternative axiology by fundamentally resisting such reductionism: it places the true gift, the true act of benefaction, in a distinct realm of value where value is an attribute of acts rather than things, measured by the deliberate intention to do the right thing.

4 Concluding Remarks: The Ledger under Taboo

In this chapter we have seen some extended accounts and examples of the ways in which "the language of money, debt, and finance provided powerful—and ultimate irresistible—ways to think about moral problems".[242]

In the changing world of Classical Athens, money and monetary debt could indeed be part of a conceptual cluster of disembedded relations, contractual clarity, rigorous and precise accounting, and unambiguous indisputable obligations. However, as Paul Millett's account of credit forms in Classical Athens has established, monetary debt could equally be embedded in friendly reciprocal relations, where the charging of interest and overly assiduous keeping track were considered taboo. Debt itself turned out to be a fleeting and fluid notion under construction—and its articulation was in an important sense formed by moral questions: what does it mean to trust someone? And what does it mean to owe a debt? Even though the notion of debt lays the groundwork for Plato's *Republic*, one of the indisputably foundational philosophical works in the Western tradition, the Debtor Paradigm of Obligation has turned out to raise more questions than it answers. Moreover, Aristotle's analysis of the difference between loans and gifts, while at first verging towards an assimilation of gifts and loans (and hence of moral obligations with financial ones), in the end established an irreducible distinction between moral gifts and financial credit—to the extent that gifts on this view had ceased to be reciprocal at all.

Rather than a wholesale assimilation of moral obligation to financial ones, of gifts to loans, we have seen the reverse: gifts, benefactions and other social interactions to which there is a moral moment, come to be defined *in opposition to* the financial and the commercial—an opposition that would open a

---

241 Evens (1999), 22. Carlà & Gori (2014), 13: "Bourdieu himself, defining these perspectives "objective" (the external one) and "subjective" (the internal one) ended up falling again in the structuralist trap, by representing as "objectivity" the reality of the economicistic interpretation of the gift [n. 30: see Graeber (2001), 26–30] as it can be seen by a not involved spectator, but he opened the way to further important reflections."

242 Graeber (2011), 195 (= T5 above).

long tradition in Western thinking that, directly or indirectly, has culminated in the grand narratives of Adam Smith, Friedrich Nietzsche, Marcel Mauss, Georg Simmel and David Graeber. It may be salutary to remind ourselves that:

[Text 33]

> one should not confuse the synchronic quarantine of money from gifts with some diachronic precedence of gifts over money. Gifts are an attempt to transcend the system of value; but that system transcendence already presupposes some form of monetary structure.[243]

Evolutionary accounts tend to work more readily with unidirectional influences from one concept to another than with the concerted twin emergence of a polar distinction. But this may be just what we have witnessed in our 4th-century sources: "the very idea of a pure and unencumbered gift can only be formed as a mirror image of an equally pure and marketable commodity. Both ideas are theoretical fictions,"[244] i.e. constructs that make up the conceptual architecture, ideas to think with and to think against.

The late Allan Silver noted with reference to friendship in modern culture, how:

[Text 34]

> [t]he essence of the "personal" is understood to inhere, *not in formal roles and obligations, but in subjective definitions of the situation.* Not normatively constituted by public roles and obligations—indeed, often constituted in distinction from them—friendship is, in principle, the "purest" and most widely available instance of personal relations in this sense. Spouses, lovers, kin, and colleagues are "friends" to the extent that *they treat the objective conditions of their bond as collateral or inessential.* Friendship as *a continuous creation of personal will and choice,* is ungoverned by the structural definitions that bear on family and kinship and, unlike erotic relations, may ignore gender. It is an ideal arena for that *individualized conception of personal agency* central to modern notions of *personal freedom.*[245]

243 Mirowski (2001), 453.
244 Morris (1993), 344.
245 Silver (1997), 46.

As we have seen, neither Plato nor Aristotle catered for anything like "a subjective definition of a situation". However, we have seen how Aristotle has made the intention of the donor the decisive criterion for the meaning of a gift, thereby awarding the subjective *aspects* of a situation (the internalized dispositions, intentions and expectations) a central place in the process of meaning-making.

It may be noted that in the course of this analysis I have attempted to avoid the use of the ready-made distinctions that populate our modern conceptual landscape: between instrumental relationships and elective affinities; between ascribed and achieved relationships; between objective obligations and subjective favors; between coerced or enforceable duties and the supererogatory; between self-interest and other-regarding behavior; between "formal" relationships and informal "personal" ones.

Although these oppositions may sometimes facilitate analysis, they not only tend to obscure our understanding of relationships in various cultures; moreover, because they are held to be self-evident, it often escapes notice that these oppositions themselves may turn out to be the product of certain cultural preoccupations, and should therefore be handled with caution when describing and analyzing phenomena in a culture different from ours.

CHAPTER 5

Pricing the Invaluable: Socrates and the Proper Use of Friends

> Money is baaaaaaaaad.
>
> BILL MAURER (2006), 19

•••

> Nowadays people know the price of everything and the value of nothing.
>
> OSCAR WILDE (1890), Chapter IV

∴

In the Netherlands,[1] every student in Dutch higher education is invited to participate in an annual national survey (The National Student Survey) that rates students' satisfaction with their program. The ratings are informative and hence useful for departments to improve their course programs; moreover, they help prospective students choose a degree program. The value of the survey, of course, depends on the response rate, and every year universities, departments, and student associations are involved in elaborate campaigns that stimulate students to take the questionnaire without raising the suspicion that the students are put under pressure to give their program a favorable rating—walking the fine line between incentives and bribes. Among the more standard examples of incentives conjured up by departments are prizes put up for raffle among the respondents, such as travel checks or gift vouchers. Of a somewhat different order are examples such as this:

[Text 1]

> The faculty donates €25 for every % of the response rate to UAF: foundation for Refugee Students.[2]

1 Parts of this chapter are published in Rosen & Sluiter (2010) and Danzig & Johnson (2018).

2 Leiden University Humanities, NSE media campaign.

 | DOI:10.1163/9789004416147_006

The rationale behind this particular type of incentive may be manifold. There may be a calculating or manipulative motive: for instance, the idea may be that, being primed with such an "altruistic" incentive and hence being *appealed to* in their capacity as other-regarding humans, the students participants are pre-emptively put in a mindset that looks beyond immediate short-term interests and impulses (such as the ulterior motive to exerting influence over the value of one's own degree, or motives of retaliation towards teaching staff), to fill out the questionnaire accordingly. There may also be the intention to manufacture a common goal: department and students "team up" in helping out the less fortunate, the subliminal message being that "we're in this together" (sc. in the endeavor to make our program as good as possible). However the most fundamental reason is, arguably, symbolic in nature: the department converts one "currency" (the number of student respondents) into another (euros to be spent on a good cause), thereby allowing for a diversion of interests and resources from a sphere of competition and conflict of interests into a sphere of cooperation, other-regarding motives and restoration. This incentive is not a bribe; it is sublimated beyond doubt.

Or perhaps *cooked* beyond doubt. The Malay men of the fishing villages on the island of Langkawi are known in the anthropological record to be averse towards money: while they do *make* money, handling and spending money is the exclusive domain of their wives. In her ethnographic study of gender relations in the Malay fishing community, anthropologist Janet Carsten exposes the mechanism underlying this puzzling situation.[3] Central to her analysis is the kitchen, the *dapur*, which represents the physical and notional center of the house. The *dapur*, like the Greek οἶκος, is a space where individual ownership of property is downplayed and where expenses (*belanja dapur*) are explicitly left uncalculated.[4] It is also the locus of transformation: where raw fish, caught and exchanged by the Malay men in highly competitive fishing crews, is cooked by women and eaten by the household;[5] and where money, earned by men in competitive and divisive contexts, is "cooked" in a sphere of unity and indivision, i.e. symbolically transformed and socialized, being endowed "with the values of kinship morality":[6]

---

3 Carsten (1989).

4 Carsten (1989), 131, 136–138. Cf. Foxhall (1989). See also Chapter Three Section 3.

5 Carsten (1989), 137.

6 Carsten (1989), 137.

[Text 2]

> Women's close association with money is founded on consumption. In spending money for the house women reproduce the household.[7]

While to most readers the second example may seem more exotic than the first, both cases can be seen as manifestations of the same tension between two distinct *orders* or *spheres* of exchange. This tension is well described by the model of transactional orders or cycles as proposed by Maurice Bloch and Jonathan Parry.[8] According to this model, many societies distinguish two different spheres of exchange: a short-term order of "transactions concerned with the arena of individual competition"[9] and a long-term cycle in which transactions between people "are concerned with the reproduction of the long-term social or cosmic order,"[10] this order being the household, the polity or any other stable order. The short-term order of individual acquisition is morally neutral or underdetermined; the long-term cycle is "positively associated with the central precepts of morality",[11] representing an understanding of individual transactions as "part of the reproduction of social and ideological systems concerned with a time-scale far longer than the individual human life".[12] Short-term gain is condoned or even considered morally legitimate provided that it does not jeopardize the stability of an "enduring social and cosmic order"[13] by interfering with the long-term cycle. Moral problems typically arise when these two basic transactional orders get confused when resources of the long-term order are diverted for short-term individual acquisition.

Bloch & Parry's model was first introduced in the context of a series of anthropological case studies on the meaning of money[14] that sought to accommodate both for universal factors as well as for the fact that the meaning of money "is not only situationally defined but also constantly re-negotiated".[15]

---

7 Carsten (1989), 137.
8 Bloch & Parry (1989), 1–32.
9 Bloch & Parry (1989), 24.
10 Bloch & Parry (1989), 24.
11 Bloch & Parry (1989), 26.
12 Bloch & Parry (1989), 1.
13 Bloch & Parry (1989), 28.
14 Parry & Bloch (1989).
15 Bloch & Parry (1989), 22–23. Cf. "[T]he meanings with which money is invested are quite as much a product of the cultural matrix into which it is incorporated as of the economic functions it performs as a means of exchange, unit of account, store of value, and so on. It is therefore impossible to predict its symbolic meanings from these functions alone."

Instead of attributing transformative forces to money, ("money is baaaaa-aaaaad"), investing it with an intrinsic power to change cultural, social or cognitive structures, this model explains how a phenomenon such as money derives its meanings from the cultural context in which it circulates.[16] Although money is commonly associated with the short-term cycle and invested with the capacity to divert resources from the long-term cycle to the short-term cycle, it may equally itself be converted into goods belonging to the long-term cycle: think of companies making large donations to international relief organisations, or rituals attested in the anthropological records such as the "drinking" of cash in Fiji,[17] the "digesting" of pilgrim gifts by the Brahmans of Benares,[18] or gift-giving rituals in Northern-American celebrations of Christmas[19]—or the εἰσφορά and liturgies in the classical Athenian polis that ritually convert privately acquired riches into communal valuables.[20] Money gained in the competitive and acquisitive realm of commerce is physically or symbolically transformed into public goods or temples treasures.

Bloch & Parry's model has become commonplace in economic anthropology as well as in historical and cultural studies on the ancient economy. Sitta von Reden, Leslie Kurke and Richard Seaford, amongst others, have applied the model to their respective analyses of exchange practices,[21] ideological representations of early Greek coinage,[22] and pre-Socratic projections of money into cosmological abstractions.[23] All three approaches are rooted in a substantivist perspective on the ancient economy, holding that the ancient Greek economy was fundamentally embedded in social, political and religious structures. The precise application of the Bloch & Parry-model differs among these studies.

Seaford uses the model of transactional order in his overarching argument that seeks to explain the *genesis* and *essence* of money: in his reconstruction

---

16 Bloch & Parry (1989), 19: "[A]n existing world view gives rise to particular ways of representing money." A complex example is the value of salt in Baruya society described by Godelier (1977): within the community, salt is exchanged as a gift in ritual exchanges, acquiring emotional value, while at the same time also being an all-purpose means of exchange; in exchanges with other communities salt functions as a measure of value and as currency (the Baruya do not export anything else). In both contexts, it can be said, salt functions as money—but with different meaning in each.

17 Toren (1989).

18 Parry (1989).

19 Carrier (1995: 203–204) for an analysis of Christmas as a celebration and re-creation of the family as the foundation of social order.

20 Von Reden (2003) [1995], 96–97.

21 Von Reden (1995), 3, 96, 172.

22 Kurke (1999), 14–15, 126–127, 168–170.

23 Seaford (2004), 13–15, 95.

of the genesis of coinage as based on the dual models of sacrificial distribution and gift exchange, early Greek coinage derives its effectiveness from a "revolutionary fusion of transactional orders".[24] Emphasizing the metaphysical qualities of money, its functional potential from a user's point of view is no essential part of Seaford's analysis.[25]

Von Reden and Kurke's analyses are concerned with the discursive implications of the model: both examine the ways in which economic exchanges are integrated into larger cultural and political systems and both offer impressive analyses of the role of different actors in creating, sustaining and solving tensions between different spheres of exchange. However, Kurke distinctly focuses on *what counts as* the long-term order.[26] The emergence of coinage is related to the establishing of the city as an embodiment and symbol of the long-term order. In this context, voices that dismiss coinage as belonging to the sphere of short-term transactions are part of an aristocratic reactionary discourse that sought to contest the shift of political power to the *polis*. Von Reden by contrast, less committed to a one-to-one correspondence between symbolic categories and concrete political actors, displays more interest in the negotiability of the transactional spheres and in the rich variety of tensions and dichotomies that the tensions between the transactional orders produce in different contexts.[27]

Differences set aside, both Von Reden and Kurke have greatly enriched our understanding of Archaic and Classical Greek economies *as systems* and have contributed to the study of these systems as a totality of transactions that form general patterns that adhere to the transactional logic of Bloch & Parry's long- and short-term orders of exchange. In the world of 6th- to 4th-century BCE Greece, we see a constant dialectics between the long-term cycle of exchange of χάρις in the context of φιλία and ξενία and a sphere of short-term transactions that typically revolve around utility and profit (κέρδος), mediated through wages (μισθός).[28]

24 Seaford (2004), 14ff.

25 As Aarts (2005: 16) points out, Seaford comes close to "fetishizing" money—precisely the approach that Bloch & Parry sought to avoid and reject with the model of transactional orders.

26 According to Kurke (2004: 15–17), Von Reden fails to integrate the "oppositional voice" (i.e. the voices contesting the *polis* as embodiment of the long-term order) because of a focus on predominantly Athenian sources.

27 For example, Von Reden draws attention to the ways in which the elite, far from rejecting coinage as belonging to the short-term sphere of trade, attempted to appropriate it as a symbol of value in civic exchange. (176–216).

28 Gottesman (2010), 290.

The Argument

This chapter and the next will deal with such "total patterns", i.e. with the understanding of individual transactions as part of a totality of transactions belonging to different spheres of exchange. The specific focus will be **the role of philosophical discourse** in marking off distinct transactional spheres and protecting such demarcation lines, and in facilitating the philosophical conversion from one sphere to another. It will be argued that whereas Plato oeuvre exhibits an altogether dismissive attitude towards coinage, money and monetary compensation ("money is baaaaaaaaaad"), Xenophon's moral philosophy reveals a subtler analysis of the tensions between the distinct orders of exchange and the potential for moral confusion. Xenophontic philosophical discourse is invested in establishing, or re-establishing, a particular long-term order and in reproducing what it sees as the *status quo*, and in regulating possible conversions from one sphere to another.

Two specific transactions will be at the center of our discussion:

(i) the exchange of wisdom for money—as discussed by Socrates with his "colleague" Antiphon in *Memorabilia* I.vi (Sections 1 and 4);

(ii) the purchase of a Hermogenes as a friend when his price is still low—as discussed by Socrates with his friend Diodorus in *Memorabilia* II.x (Sections 2 and 3).

At stake in the Antiphon-episode is the **demarcation** between the sphere of short-term acquisitive self-indulgence, gratification and individualistic pleasures, and the long-term order of philosophy, friendship, and virtue. The Diodorus-episode revolves around **conversion**: what is the proper relation between money, the currency of utilitarian and individualistic acquisition, and the long-term value of friendship and the reproduction of the household? Crucial both in preserving the demarcation between the spheres and in making possible a conversion from one sphere into another are the concepts of ἐγκράτεια, self-mastery and self-restraint, and of ὀρθὴ χρῆσις, the "proper use" of both things and people.

1 Framing Socratic Conversation

We start with Xenophon's report of one of a series of encounters between Socrates and the sophist Antiphon.[29] Addressing the controversial topic of

29 The identity of Antiphon is surrounded by controversy. For the debate around the ques-

commercial education Xenophon carefully stages a clash between two conflicting interpretations of one exchange event, thereby dramatizing two conflicting moral worldviews.

1.1 *Antiphon's Challenge*

Antiphon opens the conversation by disqualifying Socrates' refusal of fees as irrational behavior:

[Text 3]

> Πάλιν δέ ποτε ὁ Ἀντιφῶν διαλεγόμενος τῷ Σωκράτει εἶπεν· Ὦ Σώκρατες, ἐγώ τοί σε δίκαιον μὲν νομίζω, σοφὸν δὲ οὐδ᾽ ὁπωστιοῦν· δοκεῖς δέ μοι καὶ αὐτὸς τοῦτο γιγνώσκειν· οὐδένα γοῦν τῆς συνουσίας ἀργύριον πράττῃ. καίτοι τό γε ἱμάτιον ἢ τὴν οἰκίαν ἢ ἄλλο τι ὧν κέκτησαι νομίζων ἀργυρίου ἄξιον εἶναι οὐδενὶ ἂν μὴ ὅτι προῖκα δοίης, ἀλλ᾽ οὐδ᾽ ἔλαττον τῆς ἀξίας λαβών. δῆλον δὴ ὅτι εἰ καὶ τὴν συνουσίαν ᾤου τινὸς ἀξίαν εἶναι, καὶ ταύτης ἂν οὐκ ἔλαττον τῆς ἀξίας ἀργύριον ἐπράττου. δίκαιος μὲν οὖν ἂν εἴης, ὅτι οὐκ ἐξαπατᾷς ἐπὶ πλεονεξίᾳ, σοφὸς δὲ οὐκ ἄν, μηδενός γε ἄξια ἐπιστάμενος.

> On another occasion when Antiphon was talking to Socrates, he said, 'You know, Socrates, I think that you are an honest man, but not at all a *wise* one. And it seems to me that you realize this yourself; at any rate, *you don't charge anyone for your company*. But if you thought that your cloak or your house or *any other item of your property* was *worth money*, so far from *giving it away*, you wouldn't even accept a price lower than its value. So obviously, if you thought that your company was *worth anything*, you would charge a fee for it *no less than its value*. Therefore, honest you may be, since you don't deceive *with a view to your own advantage*; but *wise* you cannot be, if your knowledge *is worthless*.'[30]

---

tion whether "Antiphon the sophist" and "Antiphon from Rhamnous" are the same person, see Pendrick (2002) and Gagarin (2002). Antiphon is introduced in *Mem.* I.vi.1 as "the sophist" (τὸν σοφιστήν). This has been understood as a disambiguating device. However, in the fourth century BCE the term "sophist" was applied more broadly than we would expect from overmuch reliance on Plato, so that orators engaging in forensic argument were also designated as sophists: see Apollodorus ([Dem.]) 59.21 about Lysias, and Aeschines 1.173 about Socrates. On the active role of Plato and Xenophon in attributing a group identity to the sophists, see n. 31 below.

30 Xen. *Mem.* I.vi.11–12; *all translation of the* Memorabilia *are by* Tredennick & Waterfield (1990).

The issue at hand is education on a commercial basis, a problem well-known in the Classical Period: the fact that the sophists, self-proclaimed teachers of wisdom, citizenship, and rhetoric, made a living out of teaching.[31] One generation after the famous great sophists had burst onto the scene of Athenian public life they started to be defined by the very fact that they charged fees for their teachings[32]—a definition largely due to sources hostile to the sophists, such as Plato, Aristotle and, to a certain extent, Xenophon,[33] all having a vested interest in representing the activities of the sophists as an occupational group as fundamentally distinct from whatever it was that Socrates the Athenian was doing.

It is invariably through this hostile lens that we find Socratic reflections on the sophists' habit of teaching for pay. A variety of reasons to disapprove of this practice are attributed to Socrates.[34] Some of these reasons are only

---

31 It should be kept in mind that in the time of the famous sophists (Protagoras, Gorgias, Prodicus, Hippias) themselves, the sophists were by no means a well-defined homogenous group. It is to a large extent due to the polemical efforts of Plato, Xenophon and Aristotle that the sophists retrospectively started to appear as an intellectually homogenous group. See Schiappa (2003), Nightingale (1995) and Tell (2011), for the role that Plato, Xenophon and Aristotle have played in establishing the "otherness" of the sophists as an intellectual movement; Classen (1984) argues that Xenophon does not conceive of the sophists as a homogenous group or movement and has less of a vested interest in polemicizing against them than Plato does; on the *status aparte* of Antiphon, Gagarin (2002), 5; Bett (1989) for an argument that relativism, as a philosophical position, can only be attributed (with great caution) to Protagoras.

32 It is around this period that the term σοφιστής, previously used broadly to refer to persons skilled in a wide range of trades, started to refer to a well-defined class of intellectuals. Cf. Kerferd (1981), 24–41, Guthrie (2005), 27–54.

33 The prototypical definition is the one offered by Aristotle (*Soph. El.* 165a): (…) ἔστι γὰρ ἡ σοφιστικὴ φαινομένη σοφία οὖσα δ' οὔ, καὶ ὁ σοφιστὴς χρηματιστὴς ἀπὸ φαινομένης σοφίας ἀλλ' οὐ οὔσης (…). ("for the sophistic art consists in apparent and not real wisdom, and the sophist is one who makes money from apparent and not real wisdom.") (*transl.* Forster). For similar definitions, see: Pl. *Apol.* 19e–20a, *Prot.* 311e, 313c, 357e, *Gorg.* 519c–d.; Blank (2014), 379 n. 4, Blank (1985).

34 See Blank (1985) for an overview of sources; Corey (2002) for an evaluation for the various objections raised by the Socratic authors against teaching for pay; Tell (2009 and 2011) for an assessment about the historical reality and ideology behind the Socratics' hostile representation of sophistic practice (the Platonic representation is largely slander); Fredal (2008) for a hypothesis about the sophists' motivation to charge fees (to demystify the economics of gift-giving in which wisdom and rhetoric used to circulate among aristocrats); Schriefl (2013), chapter 3, for an interpretation of Plato's objection against the sophistic practice to charge fees in terms of a conflict between the sophists' conception of ἀρετή (financial dexterity is an important component of ἀρετή) and Socrates' (financial skills are not a part of ἀρετή); Blank (2014), 383, for an objection against the common interpretation of the theme of sophistic fee-charging as part of an invective representation

conditional: the sophists' practice of charging fees for lessons in virtue raises questions about the nature of virtue (e.g. no one seems to know what virtue actually *is*) or the teachability of virtue (does charging money for lessons in virtue imply that it can, in fact, be taught?).[35]

The objections against teaching for a fee that Xenophon attributes to Socrates are of a different order: they go to the heart of what it means to be teaching, or rather, to be sharing knowledge.[36] The objections against fee-taking imply particular preconceptions and ideas about the effects that the *structure* and the *nature* of a transaction have on teaching practices.[37]

The Antiphon passage is a compelling example. The encounter centers around two co-existing interpretations of a single event: Socrates not receiving fees.[38] According to Antiphon, there is only one interpretation conceivable for the fact that Socrates refuses to accept fees: not accepting pay means giving away commodities for free (προῖκα δοίης)—a clear indication of the seller's low valuation of his own goods (μηδενός γε ἄξια).[39] Not charging a fee is tantamount to pricing the goods on offer (e.g. Socratic conversation) as worthless.

---

that serves to dissociate the sophists from the Sages and philosophers such as Socrates and Plato. According to Blank, such interpretations (in particular Tell 2011) run the risk of overestimating the rhetorical invective component of the sources while underestimating the historical basis for such an invective (e.g. the idea that fee-charging was a sophistic innovation).

35 Corey (2002), 191–195.

36 An argument I have made in Van Berkel (2018) requires qualification. I have argued that the criticism against sophistic fee-taking expressed by Plato's Socrates is less programmatic and integrated in grander ethical and economical ideas than is the case with his Xenophontic counterpart. But see Schriefl (2013), chapter 3, for an argument that in Plato's rejection of the practice a conflict between two competing conceptions of ἀρετή is played out.

37 For instance, Socrates argues that money changes the economics of education in a fundamental way: fees make teachers select their students on grounds that are not relevant for education in virtue, i.e. fees make teachers *not* available *enough* (only available to the rich): e.g. Pl. *Soph.* 231d3: sophists (only) hunt young rich people; Xen. *Cyn.* XIII.8. Cf. Corey (2002: 196–203.) or *too* available (instead of only to those susceptible for the inculcation of virtue): e.g. Pl. *Euthyd.* 304c1–5; Corey (2002), 196–203).

38 In the introduction to a previous conversation between Antiphon and Socrates, reported in *Mem.* I.vi.1–10, Xenophon makes plain that Antiphon's motive behind instigating the discussion is professional rivalry: Antiphon came to Socrates "with the intention of drawing his companions away from him" (βουλόμενος τοὺς συνουσιαστὰς αὐτοῦ παρελέσθαι) and hence deliberately stages the conversation in the presence of the companions (παρόντων αὐτῶν).

39 *Soph.* 234a may be read as Plato's answer to a similar sophistic challenge. Socrates points out to Theaetetus that the sophists are selling great things (knowledge of everything) for comparatively low fees. Xenophon and Plato effectively apply the same strategy in disqualifying the sophistic practice of charging fees for lessons in wisdom: they both attempt

This line of reasoning surely has a self-evident ring to it. But the logic is premised on the framing: Antiphon is applying a commercial paradigm to Socratic practice. This paradigm, evoked by the use of the language of finance, rests on three pillars:

(i) **value monism:**[40] in Antiphon's world view, there is only one single standard of value to which everything can be reduced; the value of Socratic conversation can and should be expressed in terms of monetary currency. See for instance his unreflective assimilation of τινὸς ἀξίαν ("to be worth something") with ἀργυρίου ἄξιον ("to be worth money", i.e. to have its worth measured by money), or, conversely, the equation of not charging monetary fees (προῖκα δίδοναι) with deeming one's goods worthless (μηδενός ἄξια). The ultimate consequence of value monism is the "fetishization" of the single standard to which all value is related: to Antiphon money has become an end in itself.[41]

(ii) **commodification:**[42] Socrates' company is characterized as a possession, something one acquires (κτάομαι), comparable to a cloak or a house; moreover, the very saleability of wisdom and virtue presupposed by Antiphon, serves as an indicator of commodity status;[43]

(iii) **business rationality**: in plainly assuming that *not* charging a fee is tantamount to giving away services for free[44] Antiphon resembles Syloson

---

to immunize virtue and wisdom against commodification, either by showing the moral consequences (Xenophon) or by revealing the logical absurdities inherent in the commodification of wisdom (Plato).

40 I use the term "value-monism" to refer to ethical systems which recognize only one thing as having value in itself and which, consequently, contend that the good is fundamentally unitary. Other entities only have value by reference to this single measure of value. E.g. utilitarianism only recognizes happiness as intrinsically valuable; other "goods" in our lives are only good in as far as they contribute to happiness. Cf. Craig (1998), Anderson (1993), 117 ff.

41 In a previous conversation with Socrates, reported in the passage immediately preceding this one (I.vi.1–11), Antiphon does seem to imply that money (τὰ χρήματα) is an end in itself: the mere acquiring of money is a delight (ἃ καὶ κτωμένους εὐφραίνει); in addition, money, according to Antiphon, enables one to live more independently and pleasantly (κεκτημένους ἐλευθεριώτερόν τε καὶ ἥδιον ποιεῖ ζῆν).

42 Commodities are commonly defined as entities that have use value and that can be exchanged in a discrete transaction for a counterpart that has, in the immediate context, an equivalent value. Cf. Kopytoff (1986), 68.

43 Cf. Kopytoff (1986), 69: "(…) in the West, as a matter of cultural shorthand, we usually take saleability to be the unmistakable indicator of commodity status, while non-saleability imparts to a thing a special aura of apartness from the mundane and the common."

44 Cf. anecdotes about Protagoras who allowed pupils less than the standard fee if they were prepared to state on oath that they did not think his teaching worth so much. E.g. Pl. *Prot.*

who, at first, thought of his gift as a loss (ἀπολωλέναι).[45] It is from this commercial point of view that Socrates is said to lack in σοφία—which yields a very particular understanding of σοφία as a form of mercantile cleverness.[46] In other words: σοφία is drawn into a short-term sphere of individual acquisition, made morally neutral and hence liable for self-serving abuse.[47]

Transactional models have implications beyond the immediate transaction. They shape the ways in which transactional "objects", such as wisdom and knowledge, are understood. The commodification of both education and sexuality raises critical ethical questions: *what* exactly is being sold?[48] Can it be detached from the person selling it, or is it embodied?[49] In this particular case, Antiphon's worldview implies a conception of wisdom and knowledge as discrete objects, as separated from the knower.[50] Disembedded transactions imply "disembedded" σοφία.

328b–c. Cf. Ar. *EN* 1164a24–26, DL 9.56. Cf. Demont (1993), 41–44, who relates this anecdote to the χρήματα in Protagoras' Man/Measure-fragment. I agree that the anecdotal tradition reflects a particular interpretation of the Man/Measure fragment (χρήματα in its narrow and specific sense as "money"), but am inclined to think that this *ad hominem* interpretation is a product of negative spin and hostile reception by post-platonic authors. Cf. Van Berkel (2013).

45 On the ideology of "business" that propagates norms to seek "value for money" and ridicule the "sucker" who pays over or undercharges, see Davis (1992), 7–8, 56–58. Cf. Polanyi (1968), 69, Van Wees (1998), 19–20. Cf. Zelizer (2005), 125, about attitudes among prostitutes about "freely giving away sexual favors".

46 On σοφία in the *Memorabilia*, see Chernyakhovskaya (2014), Dorion (2008b), and Morrison (2010).

47 Cf. Schriefl (2013), chapter 3, for a comparable discursive battle on the value of ἀρετή in Plato: Plato's sophists understand *oikonomia* and financial skills as an important part of ἀρετή, whereas to Plato's Socrates money and wealth are irrelevant to the human pursuit of ἀρετή.

48 The etymology of πόρνος/πόρνη, prostitute, from πέρνημι, to sell, is suggestive. The verb πέρνημι originally did not so much refer to a commercial transaction but to the act of transferring or export, and may originally have been restricted to the transfer of prisoners and captives (as opposed to commodities for purchase and sale), just as the verb ὠνέομαι ("to buy") that applies only to persons in Homer. Benveniste (1973), 112. In the Classical Period the nouns πόρνος and πόρνη seem to refer predominantly to unfree brothel workers. Cohen (2002). Cf. Citti (1997) who points out that in Classical Greek the terms πόρνη and δούλη form *una coppia nominale* ("a verbal coupling") (92). Female brothel workers were often represented as depersonalized and reified, bearing cash names such as Dicrachmon or Obole. Davidson (1997), 188–189.

49 The political discourse about δωροδοκία, bribery (literally "accepting gifts") cashes in on this slippage. E.g. Dem. 18.46–47 where bribed politicians are described as *thinking* that they are selling (πωλεῖν) everything except themselves, but turning out to have sold themselves (ἑαυτοὺς πεπρακόσιν).

50 This episode is the middle one in a series of three encounters between Socrates and

1.2 *Socrates' Analogy*

Back to Antiphon and Socrates and their object of valuation and contention: Socratic "company" or "being together" (συνουσία). The term συνουσία and its cognates (forms of the verbs σύνειμι, συγγίγνεσθαι), refers to male bonding by intellectual encounters—encounters that are characterized by "an educational purpose, repeated contacts, and a relationship between pupil and a mentor".[51] Although the term seems specifically associated with sophists,[52] in Xenophon's *Memorabilia*, συνουσία and cognates are frequently used to characterize *Socrates* and his associates.[53] The noun συνουσία, "intercourse", was also a common euphemism for sexual intercourse—a connotation exploited by Socrates in his reaction to Antiphon:[54]

[Text 4 = Text 33]

> ὁ δὲ Σωκράτης πρὸς ταῦτα εἶπεν· Ὦ Ἀντιφῶν, παρ' ἡμῖν νομίζεται τὴν ὥραν καὶ τὴν σοφίαν ὁμοίως μὲν καλόν, ὁμοίως δὲ αἰσχρὸν διατίθεσθαι εἶναι. τήν τε γὰρ ὥραν ἐὰν μέν τις ἀργυρίου πωλῇ τῷ βουλομένῳ, πόρνον αὐτὸν ἀποκαλοῦσιν, ἐὰν δέ τις, ὃν ἂν γνῷ καλόν τε κἀγαθὸν[55] ἐραστὴν ὄντα, τοῦτον φίλον ἑαυτῷ ποιῆται, σώφρονα νομίζομεν· καὶ τὴν σοφίαν ὡσαύτως τοὺς μὲν ἀργυρίου τῷ βουλομένῳ

Antiphon in *Mem.* I.vi. The encounters (interpreted by Gray (1998) as extended *chreiai*) serve to showcase the Socratic principles of ἐγκράτεια and καρτερία: his self-mastery or control over his needs and desires, and his capacity to endure physical pain and discomfort. In this light, it is intriguing to see the Suda attributing to Antiphon the view that he (perhaps: god?) "lacks nothing and receives nothing from anyone, but is unlimited and unlacking." (DK 87 B 10 (= Suda A.435) ἀδέητος· ὁ μηδενὸς δεόμενος καὶ πάντα ἔχων. Ἀντιφῶν ἐν α' Ἀληθείας· «διὰ τοῦτο οὐδενὸς δεῖται, οὐδὲ προσδέχεται οὐδενός τι, ἀλλ' ἄπειρος καὶ ἀδέητος.») It is not easy to see if this statement propagates limitation of needs or (more probably) unlimited acquisition.

51 Tarrant (2005), 133.

52 Tarrant (2005). Robb (1994) argues that συνουσία also refers to traditional pre-sophistic mentoring, but, as Tarrant (2005) points out, this is hard to establish on the sources that have been influenced by late fifth-century educational trends. The term seems to be associated in particular with Protagoras.

53 The noun συνουσία occurs frequently in the *Memorabilia* (e.g. I.ii.14, I.ii.38, I.ii.60); οἱ συνόντες is the standard term for Socrates's young companions (e.g. I.i.4, I.i.5, I.ii.5, I.ii.8, I.ii.9, I.ii.17, I.ii.49, I.ii.56, I.ii.64), as is also (the more technical) συνουσιασταί (I.vi.1). Cf. Tarrant (2005), 138 n. 28.

54 See Tarrant (2005); in Plato's authentic dialogues the terminology, although referring to Socratic conversation, is non-technical and under-specific, mostly used for its sexual overtones.

55 Tamiolaki (2014), n. 51: For the aristocratic connotations of *kalokagathia* see Bourriot (1995). Cf. Bevilacqua (2010), 187–196, 448 n. 42, 454 n. 66.

> πωλοῦντας σοφιστὰς ἀποκαλοῦσιν, ὅστις δὲ ὃν ἂν γνῷ εὐφυᾶ ὄντα διδάσκων ὅ τι ἂν ἔχῃ ἀγαθὸν φίλον ποιεῖται, τοῦτον νομίζομεν, ἃ τῷ καλῷ κἀγαθῷ πολίτῃ προσήκει, ταῦτα ποιεῖν.
>
> To this Socrates replied, 'In our society, Antiphon, the same rules with regard to what is creditable and what is not are thought to apply equally to the disposal of physical attractions and of wisdom. A man who *sells his favours for a price to anyone who wants them* is called a prostitute; but if anyone forms a love-attachment with someone whom he knows to be truly good, we regard him as perfectly respectable. In just the same way, *those who sell wisdom at a price to anyone who wants it* are called sophists; but if anyone, by imparting any edifying knowledge that he possesses, makes a friend of one whom he knows to be naturally gifted, we consider that he is behaving as a truly good citizen should behave.'[56]

Socrates retorts by replacing Antiphon's commercial paradigm with an alternative way of framing Socratic συνουσία—a frame that implies a conception of σοφία different from Antiphon's mercantile cleverness, that undoes the separation of knowledge and knower and that operates on a different transactional logic.

Let us state the obvious first: here we see an example of the principle, well-known in economic anthropology, that the distinction between "gifts" and "commodities" has less to do with the identity of the objects of transaction and more with the mode of exchange, i.e. with the relation between the transactors and the way this relationship is understood.[57] The same exchange object can be a commodity in one context and a friendly loan, gift, donation or deposit in another; in all these "identities", the object has particular social potential.[58] The object may shift between these identities by processes of "singularization" (the object is made unique, unexchangeable and withdrawn from the market into a more restricted sphere of exchange) and the reverse process "commodification" (the object is made exchangeable for other items). Each of the identities that

---

56 *Mem.* I.vi.13; *transl. adapted.*

57 The *locus classicus* is the programmatic Kopytoff (1986), 68 and Appadurai (1986). For an important and fundamental critique on the approach taken by both Appadurai and Kopytoff, see Graeber (2001), esp. 33.: "Both Appadurai's essay and Kopytoff's emphasize the possibility of writing the "social biography of a thing"; but both also define their terms in such a way that it becomes impossible to consider that an object's biography could *itself* contribute to its value."

58 Appadurai (1986), 6.

are culturally available for the object implies a particular transactional logic, i.e. a scenario or social code comprising the expectations of the exchange partners, the way they read the exchange and understand the value of the object in view.[59]

Socrates is obviously objecting against Antiphon's reading of the scenario of συνουσία, and he, therefore, proposes an alternative reading. Key to this attempt to reframe Socratic συνουσία is the analogy between wisdom and youthful physical beauty (ὥρα). Both wisdom and beauty allow for two distinct uses or ways to "spend" them (διατίθεσθαι):[60]

- The shameful way (αἰσχρόν), meaning "the commercial way", i.e. selling it irrespectively to anybody (τῷ βουλομένῳ),[61] thereby rendering oneself a prostitute (πόρνος) in case of beauty and a sophist in case of wisdom.[62]
- The noble way (καλόν),[63] meaning, in case of beauty: acquiring a reputation for self-restraint (for being σώφρων) by bestowing this beauty on a gentleman-lover (καλόν τε κἀγαθὸν ἐραστήν) and making him one's friend (φίλον ἑαυτῷ ποιῆται); in case of wisdom: befriending (φίλον ποιεῖται) someone selected on basis of his moral qualities (ὃν ἂν γνῷ εὐφυᾶ ὄντα) by teaching him all the good one can (διδάσκων ὅ τι ἂν ἔχῃ ἀγαθόν), thereby acquiring the reputation of a gentleman-citizen (τῷ καλῷ κἀγαθῷ πολίτῃ).

Socrates uses the analogy with the opposition between the ἐραστής—ἐρώμενος-relationship and prostitution[64] to construct an opposition between Socratic συνουσία, modeled as φιλία, and sophistic practices. He defies Antiphon's commodification of συνουσία by presenting him with an alternative scenario according to which συνουσία needs to be conducted. So what is this scenario?

---

59 E.g. whereas the value of commodities is measured by how much one would give up to possess it, the value of an extremely singularized object such as an heirloom is measured by how little one would wish to give up on it. Cf. Weiner (1992).

60 διατίθεσθαι (middle voice) with direct object in accusative case denotes "to dispose of" property (e.g. τὴν οὐσίαν) or merchandise (e.g. φόρτον). LSJ διατίθημι B2 and 3.

61 Blank (1985), 11 n. 45, points out that ὁ βουλόμενος is also a legal term "indicating that anyone has the right to bring a particular action." The dative case, τῷ βουλομένῳ, is reminiscent of the Athenian bureaucratical formula τῷ βουλεμένῳ σκοπεῖν. Hedrick (1990).

62 Xenophon is obviously drawing on the etymological derivation of πόρνος/πόρνη from πέρνημι, to sell. Cf. Chantraine (1977). See n. 48 above.

63 Which is possibly also the "correct" (ὀρθός) use. See Section 2 below.

64 Cf. Pausanias' two Erotes (Pl. *Symp.* 180c1–185c3); Aesch. 1; Lys. III. Dover (1978); Halperin (1997); Winkler (1990); Fisher (2001), 36–52, Davidson (2007), 38 ff.

1.3 *Socrates' "Conversion" of Commercial Language*

The beauty/wisdom analogy effectively opposes erotic and didactic transactions on a commercial basis to the type of erotic and didactic exchange embedded in a morally elevated long-term relationship.[65] What does such συνουσία look like?

[Text 5]

> ἐγὼ δ' οὖν καὶ αὐτός, ὦ Ἀντιφῶν, ὥσπερ ἄλλος τις ἢ ἵππῳ ἀγαθῷ ἢ κυνὶ ἢ ὄρνιθι ἥδεται, οὕτω καὶ ἔτι μᾶλλον ἥδομαι φίλοις ἀγαθοῖς, καὶ ἐάν τι ἔχω ἀγαθόν, διδάσκω, καὶ ἄλλοις συνίστημι παρ' ὧν ἂν ἡγῶμαι ὠφελήσεσθαί τι αὐτοὺς εἰς ἀρετήν· καὶ τοὺς θησαυροὺς τῶν πάλαι σοφῶν ἀνδρῶν, οὓς ἐκεῖνοι κατέλιπον ἐν βιβλίοις γράψαντες, ἀνελίττων κοινῇ σὺν τοῖς φίλοις διέρχομαι, καὶ ἄν τι ὁρῶμεν ἀγαθὸν ἐκλεγόμεθα· καὶ μέγα νομίζομεν κέρδος, ἐὰν ἀλλήλοις φίλοι γιγνώμεθα.
>
> 'As for myself, Antiphon, I *take as much pleasure* in good friends as other people take in a good horse or dog or bird—in fact, I take more; and if I have anything good to teach them, I teach it, and I introduce them to any others from *whom I think they will get help* in the quest for goodness. And *in company with my friends*, I open and read from beginning to end the books in which the wise men of past times have written down and bequeathed to us their *treasures*; and when we see anything good, we take it for ourselves; and we regard our mutual friendship as great gain.'[66]

Extending the Beauty/Wisdom analogy, Socrates elaborates on the nature of the exchange: whereas a beautiful ἐρώμενος might enjoy (ἥδεται) the gift of a horse, dog or bird (gifts commonly bestowed by aristocratic ἐρασταί to their ἐρώμενοι),[67] Socrates takes even more pleasure (καὶ ἔτι μᾶλλον ἥδομαι) in excellent friends (φίλοις ἀγαθοῖς). Here the analogy breaks down: noble dealings with wisdom seem even superior to noble dealings with beauty, because in the case of wisdom, the excellent friend, the object of Socrates' pleasure, seems to be the reward itself.

---

65 The opposition between φιλία and prostitution recurs in Xen. *Symp.* VIII.21 where Socrates asks the rhetorical question how there can be any more commitment (στέργειν) between a prostitute and customer than between a buyer and a seller (ὁ ἐν ἀγορᾷ πωλῶν καὶ ἀποδιδόμενος).

66 *Mem.* I.vi.14.

67 Cf. Pl. *Lys.* 211d and the horses that are exorbitantly expensive gifts to the Corinthian boys in Aristoph. *Pl.* 157 (see Chapter Two Section 1).

The transactional logic of wisdom exchange is characterized by sharing and holding things in common (κοινῇ) in a generalized way.[68] Whenever Socrates has something good to teach a friend, he does so without begrudging him anything. The sharing even applies to the friends themselves: whenever Socrates expects a friend to benefit (ὠφελήσεσθαι) from others in their quest for virtue (εἰς ἀρετήν), he introduces the friend to them too.[69] Socratic "teaching" turns out to be: reading collectively (κοινῇ), exploring the treasures (τοὺς θησαυρούς) of the wise men of old, and extracting the valuables out of them. Didactic συνουσία is not shaped as a bilateral *quid-pro-quo*-exchange but as a collective endeavor of a community of friends mining a common pool of written treasures from the past.

Reshaping the transactional structure of συνουσία requires at least one out of two options: using new vocabulary or using existing vocabulary in a novel way. Socrates' reaction, characteristically, consists in reforming existing language, in particular, the terms θησαυρός ("treasure") and κέρδος ("gain"). Although the use of θησαυρός for treasuries of metaphorical, non-material, "wealth" such as wisdom and learning is quite common in Attic literature,[70] in this context the term also underscores Socrates' attempt to redefine wealth, making wisdom, not money, the *real* treasure. Further on in the *Memorabilia*, this line of thought is made explicit:

[Text 6]

> Νὴ τὴν Ἥραν, ἔφη ὁ Σωκράτης, ἄγαμαί γέ σου, διότι οὐκ ἀργυρίου καὶ χρυσίου προείλου θησαυροὺς κεκτῆσθαι μᾶλλον ἢ σοφίας· δῆλον γὰρ ὅτι νομίζεις ἀργύριον καὶ χρυσίον οὐδὲν βελτίους ποεῖν τοὺς ἀνθρώπους, τὰς δὲ τῶν σοφῶν ἀνδρῶν γνώμας ἀρετῇ πλουτίζειν τοὺς κεκτημένους.
>
> 'I really do admire you for preferring to stockpile wisdom rather than silver and gold,' said Socrates. 'Evidently you think that silver and gold make people no better, whereas the maxims of the wise enrich their possessors with moral goodness.'[71]

68 On κοινόν and the transactional logics of generalized sharing, see also Chapter Three.

69 For Socrates directing his companions to people with expert knowledge, cf. *Mem.* IV.vii.1 (ὅ τι μὲν αὐτὸς εἰδείη, πάντων προθυμότατα ἐδίδασκεν. ὅτου δὲ αὐτὸς ἀπειρότερος εἴη, πρὸς τοὺς ἐπισταμένους ἦγεν αὐτούς). Cf. Is. 1.51–52. On the "eclectic" encyclopedic (and non-competitive) character of wisdom literature, see Gray (1998). For the image of Socrates as matchmaker, see Xen. *Symp.* IV.56–64; cf. Chapter Six. Cf. Epictetus, *Discourses* 4.8.22–23.

70 E.g. Soph. *Ant.* 30, Pl. *Phlb.* 15e.

71 *Mem.* IV.ii.9.

Comparing two types of treasures (θησαυρούς with genitives ἀργυρίου καὶ χρυσίου vs. ἡ σοφίας), Socrates discusses the relative value of gold and silver and wisdom, suggesting that his conversation partner Euthydemus might prefer wisdom because of its capacity to "enrich" (πλουτίζειν) with virtue (ἀρετή). Comparisons between material wealth and riches of the soul are commonplace in Socratic literature. However whereas Plato's Socrates takes care not to contaminate the realm of the soul with the language of the body and the material world, Xenophon's Socrates tends to *appropriate* material and commercial terminology and to endow them with normative value: whereas gold and silver are treasures, the real treasure in human existence is wisdom; whereas both prostitutes and beloved boys use their beauty, only beloved boys "spend" it in a noble way; whereas both beloved boys and philosophers enjoy rewards for their "noble" use of their beauty and wisdom, the philosopher's reward is more enjoyable.

When applied metaphorically to knowledge and wisdom, the term θησαυρός has the capacity to reify the goods of the soul—in part a consequence of the technology of writing, which is often associated with facilitating a separation of knowledge and knower and hence with a commodification of knowledge or wisdom. In *Mem.* IV.2, Socrates' conversation partner Euthydemus seems to fall prey to such reification: he *collects* (συλλέγειν) writings[72] and confuses possession of books (γράμματα) with the possession of expertise.

In contrast, in Socrates' retort to Antiphon, reading is emphatically depicted as a *social* activity (**κοινῇ σὺν τοῖς φίλοις**) and as a *critical* activity (**καὶ ἄν τι ὁρῶμεν ἀγαθὸν ἐκλεγόμεθα**). The treasure stores, θησαυροί, are not to be identified with the books themselves, but the things written *in* the books (οὓς … ἐν βιβλίοις γράψαντες); this implies that recovering the treasures requires critical examination and discussion of texts.[73] Whereas in the Euthydemus episode, the metaphor θησαυρός may have been chosen to underscore Euthydemus' misguided understanding of books as unproblematic containers of knowledge and wisdom, here θησαυρός may suggest an element of "unlocking" a treasure that does not yield just like that to any random treasure hunter.

Moreover, treasures typically take part in restricted circuits of circulation: they belong to the realm of "inalienable possessions", valuables that are kept

---

72 Xen. *Mem.* IV.ii.1: (…) Εὐθύδημον τὸν καλὸν γράμματα πολλὰ συνειλεγμένον ποιητῶν τε καὶ σοφιστῶν τῶν εὐδοκιμωτάτων (…).

73 For reading as a social activity, cf. Pl. *Parm.* 127c–d, *Phdr.* 230e–235e (the reading of Lysias' speech), *Theaet.* 143a–c (Euclides asks slave to rade to him and Terpsion a dialogue that he has taken note of), [Pl.] *Epist.* VI 323c. Learning from written texts is in itself suboptimal compared to live discussion, but social reading is a superior practice to solitary reading, because the group context allows for examination of text, reader and reading. See Cambron-Goulet (2012).

from exchange as much as possible, being exchanged only under exceptional circumstances.[74] This phenomenon may tie in with Socrates' insistence on *choosing* worthy "wisdom partners" instead of selling to all comers. Socrates' portrayal here is benign: he is a generous friend sharing his wisdom ungrudgingly (even Antiphon concedes that Socrates is a just man because of his lack of greediness, πλεονεξία) and he is by no means the typical hoarder who conceals his riches by burying his treasures; but he is also elitist, carefully selecting his φίλοι, the companions whom he deems worthy of the enterprise of sharing and exploring treasures with. Insisting that particular goods are priceless is tantamount to keeping them out of circulation or to restricting their circulation.[75]

In contrast to the term θησαυρός that is associated with the long term transactional cycle in which goods circulate at a slow rate within a restricted circuit, the term κέρδος is typically associated with the fast lane of short term exchanges. Socrates' application of the term in the last sentence of T5 is deliberately paradoxical: κέρδος comes to refer to a process of joint realization, yielding benefit to all parties.[76] It is an instance of Xenophon's Socrates appropriating and twisting commercial terminology: to someone like Antiphon, receiving high fees may seem profitable, but *real* profit resides in becoming mutual friends (ἐὰν ἀλλήλοις φίλοι γιγνώμεθα).[77]

1.4 *Socrates' Economics of Wisdom*

In short, we see Socrates reconfiguring Antiphon's commercial framework by insisting on the idea that wisdom and beauty may be exchanged according to an alternative logic and logistics:

(i) In Antiphon's **monistic** universe, valuing something implies reducing it to a mere means, setting a price on it so as to sell it and to part from it. To Socrates beauty, wisdom, and virtue, as well as good friends, have an

74 Weiner (1992), 150. Cf. Gottesman (2010), 307–308, on κειμήλια. Aarts (2005), 13.

75 See also Chapter Six Section 6.

76 κέρδος ("gain") should not be mistaken for the morally neutral modern notion of gain or profit; the term κέρδος implies that the exchange at hand is not committed to a long-term relationship, but is a satisfaction of immediate needs. Morris (2002); Gottesman (2010); Cozzo (1998). On κέρδος in political thought, Balot (2001). On the use of the root *κερδ-, see Roisman (1987), 66; on the association between the adjective κέρδιον and trickery in the *Iliad*, see Roisman (1990). De Jong (1987b) on the difference between κέρδος (advantage for oneself) and ὄφελος (advantage for some else). κέρδος is suitable for derogatory use when a person's behavior is characterized as anti-social: "profit *at the expense* of the other"—evoking a seesaw, or zero-sum, conception of wealth. On this notion of wealth, see: Millett (1984).

77 Cf. I.ii.7: μέγιστον κέρδος ἕξειν φίλον ἀγαθόν κτησάμενον.

intrinsic value: they are ends in themselves and, once obtained, are not for sale. But their value structure does promote sharing without diminishing: the economy of intrinsic valuables is not a zero-sum game.[78]

(ii) Whereas Antiphon's **commodification** of wisdom forges a separation of knowledge and knower (also implying a reified notion of wisdom), Socrates firmly (re)embeds wisdom in relationships between φίλοι. Wisdom and beauty become **relational goods.** Selling wisdom means delivering to anyone; by contrast, in the friendship-model one **elects** the receiver on the basis of his moral qualities.[79] Selling takes places according to the logic of short-lived interactions to be immediately dissolved after the transaction has taken place; sharing wisdom leads to the establishment and strengthening of a **relationship.**

(iii) Whereas according to Antiphon's **business rationality** not charging a fee plainly means loss and σοφία comes down to mercantile cleverness, Socrates implies that being a prostitute or a sophist is at odds with practicing self-restraint (being σώφρων).[80] That is: not charging a fee is motivated by considerations, norms or values that lie outside Antiphon's business rationality.[81]

In this dialogue, the same exchange event, Socratic company, συνουσία, is framed in two radically opposed ways, presenting us with a neat confrontation of two different world-views. To Antiphon, Socrates is doing the same thing as he and many other contemporaries did: teaching for pay with a price-range including zero. Within his commercial framework, which only allows for short-

78 In classical game theory, a "zero-sum game", or a "strictly competitive game", describes a situation in which a participant's gain or loss is exactly balanced by the losses or gains of the other participant(s). At first sight, the zero-sum concept may appear to be the basic metaphor underlying modern market economy and politics, as was initially assumed by the founding fathers of game theory Neumann and Morgenstern. (Neumann (1928) and Neumann & Morgenstern (1944)). In reality, zero-sum situations are rarely encountered in economic and political applications. Much more common are situations in which the participants' interests are only in partial conflict. See Bicchieri (1998).

79 Interestingly, Xenophon elsewhere (1.ii.60–61) apparently feels the urge to exonerate Socrates from the charge of being too 'elitist'. In reply to the complaint that Socrates was elitist, Xenophon claims that Socrates was φιλάνθρωπος, someone committed to (φιλεῖν) everyone—as opposed to those teachers of virtue who demand pay and therefore do not cater to the less wealthy.

80 The example of prostitution is obviously also chosen for its moral charge. For philosophers' dismissive attitudes and proposed constraints on sex, see e.g. Pl. *Rep.* 458d–461b, *Leg.* 840d–841e, Ar. *Pol.* 1334b29–35b37, 1335b38–36a2. See Cohen (2006) and (2000) on the unrepresentative nature of these sources for Athenian attitudes towards prostitution.

81 For the relation between prostitution, sophistry and self-restraint see Section 3 below.

lived discrete transactions, goods are valued irrespective of the relationship in which they figure: sophistic education is a commodity. By contrast, Socrates' notion of value is dynamic, always referring to relationships: wisdom and virtue are not commodities for sale, but goods that arise out of a process of friends sharing virtues and sharing friends becoming virtuous.

The salient point is that behind the staging of these two alternative worldviews stands a Xenophon who is orchestrating this clash, being manifestly *aware* of the ambiguities surrounding exchanges. Although we may see in this dialogue a corroboration of the idea that "Athenian morality (…) focused on the structure of work relationships, and not on the actual nature of the labor undertaken",[82] more fundamentally we see how in late 5th- and 4th-century Athenian upper-class morality the "actual nature" of labor, or any other exchange "object", is a derivative of the way we construct the exchange relationship in question. It is liable to discursive negotiation—a negotiation that the socio-cultural circumstances in Classical Athens provided conceptual space for.[83]

Within every society, there are more and less conventional manners in which things (objects, acts) can be exchanged or commodified, certain socially regulated "paths" that one needs to know to be a well-socialized participant.[84] However, existing paths can be renegotiated and diverted: for instance, new objects can be made a "commodity for sale in an open market economy" as opposed to a gift "given and reciprocated within a restricted (elite) gift economy".[85]

What is at stake in the Antiphon-episode is the position of wisdom (σοφία) in the transactional system. By exchanging wisdom (σοφία) for direct short-term compensation (μισθός), the sophists threaten to draw wisdom and its reproduction into the short-term order—ready to subvert the long-term order and to undermine the cultivation of traditional virtues. Wisdom becomes mercantile cleverness in the short-term realm, which means: morally neutral or underdetermined, and hence liable for abuse to the wrong ends.

82 Cohen (2006), 101.

83 The ambiguous or paradoxical character of Socrates' relations with his pupils/friends was probably evident to many Athenians, as it is played on in Aristophanes' *Clouds*, where Socrates confuses Strepsiades by not showing interest in his offer of a fee (244–245). Note moreover that Strepsiades' unspecified gift (1146–1147), that is not contracted and sarcastically offered as a sign of admiration or gratitude, appears to be disregarded by Socrates. *See* VanderWaerdt (1994), 59 and Dover (1968) ad loc. on these passages.

84 Fredal (2008) for an application of the notion of "path" to the sophist's practice; Fredal argues that the sophists were economic innovators who demystified the exchange of wisdom along the same lines as they demystified religion and (other) social conventions. The notion of "path" is first explored by Gouldner (1960), 226–259. Cf. Appadurai (1986), 15.

85 Fredal (2008), 158.

Socrates' reaction is conservative: by decommodifying wisdom and virtue, he attempts to take it off the open market and to control its distribution—thereby marginalizing the sophists. As we will see in Chapter Seven, Aristotle similarly attempts to immunize philosophy from commodification: to Aristotle, philosophy is not an exchange object, but something one can "share in" (κοινωνέω). Xenophon's Socrates too engages in a struggle to control the distribution of virtue and wisdom. Whereas Aristotle's strategy is to insist on the embodied state of wisdom and virtue (they are activities, not κτήματα that can be exchanged and alienated),[86] his precursor Socrates emphasizes the distinct nature of the economies of wisdom and virtue: they are to be shared, for it is in the sharing that virtue can be developed.

2 False Friends, Part One: Utility, Ancient and Modern

Does this all imply a wholesale renunciation of money and monetary exchange on Xenophon's part? Is money baaaaaaaaaad? Such a bland repudiation would sit uneasily with the ubiquitousness of commercial terminology in the second book of the *Memorabilia* where Socrates discusses the topic of φιλία, long-term reciprocal relationships. In this series of Socratic conversations, friends are conceived of as commodities,[87] possessions,[88] having a precise cash equivalent,[89] and being objects of purchase.[90]

2.1 *Valuing Friends*

A particularly baffling example is *Memorabilia* II.x, where we see Socrates, urging his friend Diodorus to take steps to befriend the impoverished Hermogenes, draw a comparison with the trouble good estate managers invest in their treatment of their servants:

[Text 7; cf. Text 23]

> Εἰ δέ τίς σοι τῶν γνωρίμων, ἔφη, πολὺ τῶν οἰκετῶν χρησιμώτερος ὢν κινδυνεύει δι' ἔνδειαν ἀπολέσθαι, οὐκ οἴει σοι ἄξιον εἶναι ἐπιμεληθῆναι ὅπως διασωθῇ; καὶ μὴν οἶσθά γε ὅτι οὐκ ἀγνώμων ἐστὶν Ἑρμογένης, αἰσχύνοιτο δ' ἄν, εἰ ὠφελού-

86 See Chapter Seven Section 2.1.
87 *Mem.* II.iii (φίλοι as χρήματα).
88 *Mem.* II.iv (φίλοι as κτήματα).
89 *Mem.* II.v.
90 *Mem.* II.x.

μενος ὑπὸ σοῦ μὴ ἀντωφελοίη σε· καίτοι τὸ ὑπηρέτην ἑκόντα τε καὶ εὔνουν καὶ παραμόνιμον καὶ τὸ κελευόμενον ἱκανὸν ποιεῖν ἔχειν, καὶ μὴ μόνον τὸ κελευόμενον ἱκανὸν ὄντα ποιεῖν, ἀλλὰ δυνάμενον καὶ ἀφ' ἑαυτοῦ χρήσιμον εἶναι καὶ προνοεῖν καὶ προβουλεύεσθαι πολλῶν οἰκετῶν οἶμαι ἀντάξιον εἶναι. οἱ μέντοι ἀγαθοὶ οἰκονόμοι, ὅταν τὸ πολλοῦ ἄξιον μικροῦ ἐξῇ πρίασθαι, τότε φασὶ δεῖν ὠνεῖσθαι· νῦν δὲ διὰ τὰ πράγματα εὐωνοτάτους ἔστι φίλους ἀγαθοὺς κτήσασθαι.

'And if one of your acquaintances who is *much more useful* to you than your house-slaves is in danger of dying of want, don't you think that you should see to it that he is saved? You must surely know that Hermogenes is not insensitive, and that he would feel ashamed *if he didn't return your kindness*. Also, to have an assistant who is willing, loyal, reliable and able to carry out instructions—and not only that, but capable of independent action, foresight and planning—this is surely worth a good many house-slaves. Now, good estate-managers say that when you can *purchase something valuable at a low price*, you ought to *buy* it; and at the present time, owing to circumstances, it is possible to acquire good friends *very reasonably*.'[91]

The same Socrates who dismissed Antiphon's educational practice as mere wisdom prostitution does not come across as particularly coy or contrite about framing friendship in commercial discourse. Here we see talk of the "acquisition" (κτήσασθαι) of Hermogenes, a friend who is said to be "useful" (χρήσιμος), even "more useful (χρησιμώτερος) than servants". The process of "befriending" him is described through the practical accounting metaphor of buying a commodity when it is cheap, implying a notion of a discrepancy between the friend's real value (πολλοῦ ἄξιον) and his market price at the moment (him being εὐωνότατος).[92]

---

91 Xen. *Mem.* II.x.2–5.

92 The analysis by Mitchell (2009: 11) that "the language of *philia* and quality in exchange is being used to describe another kind of relationship, a patronage relationship based on an unequal distribution of power" only works on the assymption that φιλία notionally implies exchange between equals. While this is disputable in general, this is definitely not true for Xenophon's *Memorabilia* II, where the series of conversation about φιλία is started off with the model case of mother-child φιλία, which sets the standards for the conversations to come. Moreover, in this particular case, Xenophon does not so much show "a certain amount of contempt for those of reduced circumstances who are forced into subservient positions" (Mitchell 2009: 11); rather, the position of superiority is legitimized. Cf. Azoulay (2004) on the "*glissement*" of χάρις is Xenophon's oeuvre.

Here we find Socrates exploiting the isomorphism between friendship and market transactions: he uses a commercial metaphor to make the point that a good friend reciprocates benefits (summarized in the negative in the phrase εἰ ὠφελούμενος ὑπὸ σοῦ μὴ ἀντωφελοίη σε).[93] Socrates motivates his conversation partner to strike up φιλία with Hermogenes, by holding out the prospect of return of benefit: Hermogenes is the kind of person who is very likely to reciprocate in a valuable manner; moreover, he is in need, which makes it easy to benefit him—in this sense, he is cheap while rewarding: a good bargain. Socrates' didactic strategy thus consists in presenting this friendship as a rationally justified investment, imposing a "debtor's paradigm of obligation" on gratitude, making generosity an investment out of enlightened self-interest, and reducing the good of friendship to the fruit of rational investment.

In another conversation (II.v) with Antisthenes (later to become the founder of the Cynics' school), Socrates even raises the question of a friend's cash value He interrogates his conversation partner whether one can set a price on friends along the same lines as one does with house servants (εἰσί τινες ἀξίαι φίλων ὥσπερ οἰκετῶν),[94] who are sometimes worth two minae, sometimes a half, five, ten, sometimes even a talent.[95] Antisthenes gives the question a thought:

[Text 8]

> Ναὶ μὰ Δί', ἔφη ὁ Ἀντισθένης· ἐγὼ γοῦν βουλοίμην ἂν τὸν μέν τινα φίλον μοι εἶναι μᾶλλον ἢ δύο μνᾶς, τὸν δ' οὐδ' ἂν ἡμιμναίου προτιμησαίμην, τὸν δὲ καὶ πρὸ δέκα μνῶν ἑλοίμην ἄν, τὸν δὲ πρὸ πάντων χρημάτων καὶ πόνων πριαίμην ἂν φίλον μοι εἶναι.
>
> "'Yes, indeed,' replied Antisthenes. 'At any rate, I would rather have A as my friend than two minae, while I wouldn't rate B higher than half a mina; and I would choose C in preference to ten minae, and I would spend any amount of money and effort to obtain the friendship of D.'"[96]

---

93 E.g. *Mem.* II.ii.1–2; IV.iv.24 ff. Cf. Chapter One.

94 Gigon (1953), 122: "Das Ziel des Gesprachs wird angegeven, wobei ἄξιος das Stichwort ist, das den ganzen kurzen Dialog beherrscht, und ἐξετάζειν ἑαυτον an Platon Apol. 23c, 9e, 33c, besonders aber die gleichlautenden Stellen Apol. 28e und 38a (wozu Laches 187e–188b) erinnert."

95 *Mem.* II.v.2–3.

96 *Mem.* II.v.3.

Just like it is common practice to set a price on slaves, particular friends are given a cash equivalent. Desirable friends are worth all the wealth and labor in the world (πρὸ πάντων χρημάτων) to purchase them (πριαίμην); others run the risk of being sold (II.v.4.5–5: τοῦ δ' ὅτι μνᾶν ἀνθ' ἑαυτοῦ μᾶλλον εἵλετο ἀνήρ). Friends are commodities, fungible for money.

It is passages such as these that have provoked an understanding of Xenophon's Socrates as thoroughly instrumentalist, as an adherent to a type of utilitarianism *avant la lettre* that frames friendship in rational economic cost-benefit analysis.[97] This instrumental attitude towards friendship tends to rub us the wrong way. *We* may prefer to understand friendship as something that resists means/ends-reasoning. In contemporary Western thought, there is a conceptual polarity of individualized persons and commoditized things,[98] and we prefer to adhere to an axiomatic distinction between the use of natural resources and the use of other people.[99] Friends are not supposed to be chosen on the grounds of selfish motives alone nor to be interchangeable.

Moreover, this episode poses an additional problem for the interpretation of Xenophon: is Socrates' account of φιλία intrinsically coherent? There appears to be a severe tension between Socrates' dismissal of Antiphon's commercial paradigm as unfit to characterize Socratic conversations with friends and Socrates' own rational economic model of friendship. Why should Socrates take the trouble to disambiguate the friendship model of sharing intrinsic goods from the commercial model in which everything has a monetary price when at the same time he urges his companions to buy friends when they are cheap?

2.2 *Utility and Use and the Kantian Kingdom of Ends*

To alleviate this tension, we should take a closer look at Socrates' use of commercial terminology. To start with Socrates' characterization of Hermogenes as a useful (χρήσιμος) friend: we need to be aware that our understanding of the terminology of "use", "utility" and "usefulness" is essentially informed by modern market economic conceptualizations. Within such a framework, "useful" applies to something that is a means to our independently defined end[100] (the

97 According to Danzig (2018), Socrates is revolutionary in "disembedding" φιλία-ties and economizing them. For the utilitarian perspective, see also Chernyakhovskaya (2014), 154–166.

98 It is remarkable how easily any suggestion that persons (or, e.g., their organs) can be incorporated in a commodified universe elicits charges of "slavery" in public debate—which is apparently "the readiest metaphor when commoditization threatens to invade the human sphere". Kopytoff (1986), 84.

99 Von Reden (1995a), 218. Cf. Weber (1972) [1922], p. 32.

100 Anderson (1993), 144–145.

realm of value)[101] as opposed to an "end in itself" (the realm of values). Hence, in post-Enlightenment thinking, there is a strong moral impediment against framing friendship in terminology of use. Our fellow-humans are inhabitants of the Kantian Kingdom of Ends: they ought to be valued as ends in themselves as opposed to means to our own ulterior ends.[102]

The egoism/altruism dilemma, at least in its philosophically challenging form, generally presupposes a zero-sum notion of the good. Since Hobbes,[103] modern philosophical discourse has a tendency to privilege one special type of the human situation as paradigmatic for the whole of moral life, i.e. "the situation in which I and someone else have incompatible aims and my aims are connected only with my own well-being".[104] Hence, in modern philosophical discourse that is moreover influenced by rudimentary notions of Darwinism,[105] the burden of proof lies with the proponents of altruism. Universal egoism is taken for granted.[106] Therefore, the possibility of altruism can only be proven persuasively when we find an action that not only is performed for the sake of the other, but that also meets the condition that it is *at the expense of ourselves*—for these are the only cases when altruism appears

101 Graeber (2005).

102 Kant (1797), 4.429, with Kaulbach (1988). E.g. Anderson (1993), 144 regarding use a "lower, impersonal, and exclusive mode of valuation" that sees things as fungible and capable of being "traded with equanimity for any other commodity at some price." Cf. Badhwar (1993): "(…) Many philosophers still seek to accommodate friendship within the framework of Kantian or consequentialist theories." Or, conversely: Helm (2005): "Often, the appeal to friendship is intended to bypass traditional disputes among major types of moral theories (consequentialism, deontology, and virtue ethics) (…)."

103 Hobbes (1650). Since Hobbes (1650), most of the philosophical definitions of altruism require an element of self-negation, to the extent that "the interests of another person can be a reason for acting, without any reference to one's own interests." E.g. Monroe (2001), Annas (1977). Combined with the Hobbesian doctrine that most instances of altruism are a disguise of a substitute for self-seeking, altruistic behavior has come to be an unexplained, and possibly unexplainable, property in human nature. (MacIntyre (1972)). But see Butler (1726) for an early and influential rejection of the view that altruism is rooted in self-negation.

104 MacIntyre (1972), 466.

105 Recent developments in social darwinism persuasively demonstrate that the egoism/altruism-dilemma is only relevant on the level of conscious individual motivation. The social processes studied by social darwinism move on a different level of analysis, to which the dilemma is not applicable at all. E.g. Sober & Wilson (1998).

106 Conceptually speaking, the origins of this "universal egoism" is to be found in what MacIntyre (1972) labels the "genetic fallacy", i.e. the confusion of the question what motives there are in some original state (of human kind according to Hobbes or in early childhood according to Freud) with the question of what the fundamental character is of motives for action in our present/adult state.

to be salient enough to justify belief in it (and not to regard it as a mere disguise or substitute for self-seeking behavior).

This intellectual "game of gotcha",[107] of course, presupposes a zero-sum notion of happiness (or survival) and of distribution of the good. Socratic philosophy beforehand undercuts this conception of happiness and the good from the outset. It propagates an ethical individualism[108] that is directed towards a univocal notion and ideal of the good grounded in reality—a model that allows for no happiness and virtue that goes at the expense of the other.

Such a dichotomy between "useful as a means to an end" and "valuable as an end in itself" may not be the best key for understanding classical applications of use-terminology to the realm of friendship (although it may be equally hard to do altogether without this distinction). For one thing, it often prematurely steers the discussion in the direction of the *cul-de-sac* of the egoism/altruism discussion, raising the tediously overrated question of the possibility of altruism.[109] The opposition between self-serving utility and altruism is an inadequate tool for understanding Socrates' account of friendship, as modern conceptions of "use" and "utility" do not seamlessly correspond with Greek notions. They are false friends.

As has often been noted, the verb χρῆσθαι displays a semantic pluriformity,[110] denoting states of affairs ranging from "being in want of", to "having", "using", "experiencing" and "dealing with" something; applied to persons the verb may denote "to treat X as", "to be intimate" or "to have intercourse with" X;[111] in addi-

107 Mirowski (2001), 436: "It is easy to learn as any proleptic two-step: posit an ontology of 'individuals' (selfish genes, isolated consciousness, strategic organisms, anomic atoms), and then run the numbers in a 'disguised self-interest' narrative."

108 In this context it is highly confusing that the philosophical eudaemonism of Greek philosophy is often labeled "ethical egoism" in scholarship. E.g. Hughes (2001). Cf. Chapters Six and Seven.

109 E.g. Nagel (1970). This goes at the heart of the terminological confusion around "altruism": a thick conception of altruism demands self-negation (the interests of another person are a reason for acting, without any reference one's own interests; e.g. Monroe 2001, Annas 1977, MacIntyre 1972); the "thinner" conception requires merely a regard for the well-being of others for its own sake or as a general disposition to regard the interests of others as making some claim on one (e.g. Blum 1992, Williams 1977, 250). I concur with Gill that overmuch emphasis on altruism "understates the range and complexity of human thinking about the motives and ideals that lead people to benefit others" in Greek ethical thought (303). Cf. Annas (2007).

110 In his seminal semantic study Rédard (1953) lists twenty-three *sens*, "meanings", of χρῆσθαι, making the observation that the verb does not seem to have a "proper meaning" but to acquire its meaning from its complements.

111 Rédard (1953); Cohen 1992, 65–66 on χρῆσθαι in the context of credit operations: "Clients are said to "use" (χρῆσθαι) bankers ... But "use" implied not only a business relationship

tion, the term may be applied to external circumstances (νιφετῷ, χειμῶνι: to be caught in a snowstorm or bad weather; συμφορᾷ), perceptions and sensations (ὀργῇ: to be angry), characteristics such as "good birth" (εὐγενείᾳ, to be of noble stock), or language (λογῷ: to speak), truth (ἀληθεῖ λογῷ: to tell the truth), sexual pleasures (ἀφροδισιῶν: to enjoy sexual pleasures; ἐπιθυμίαις: to give way to one's passions),[112] opinions (ταῖς δόξαις: by conjecture), and knowledge (τῇ ἐπιστήμῃ: actualizing the contents of one's knowledge).

This range suggests a sense of "usage" that is broader than the purely pragmatic and instrumental sense "to make use of" or "to utilize". The semantic field implies a closeness or interdependence of subject and object,[113] possibly an adaptation or accommodation of *both* subject and object to the requirements of a given context. Or, strictly speaking, not a subject/object relationship at all (χρῆσθαι is, after all, not a purely transitive verb going with an object in the accusative case, but a middle verb going with a dative, or genitive, case),[114]

but also a social intimacy". See *LSJ*, s.v. "χράομαι": "The Greek term does not carry the negative connotation sometimes present in colloquial English "use" of someone". For the broader, not exclusively exploitative meaning of "use", cf. German *Nutz* ("usefulness") and *genießen* ("to enjoy", also in the sense of receiving X or having the advantage of X, as in "to enjoy benefits") that are formed from the same root. See Mourelatos (1970), 652 and Schein (1998), 295 for the notion that XPH-terminology refer to "subjective, internally based needs, requirements, and constraints" as opposed to δεῖ and cognates that tend to refer to external, objective constraint or causal necessity; Robbiano (2006), 74–79 (following Jonkers (1981 unpublished)) for the notion that control is a central semantic feature of XPH-terminology. Bundy (1962), 57–59 for the notion that in Archaic poetry χρέος typically does not designate contractual obligation and occurs in contexts where references to payment are suppressed. Cf. Kurke (1991), 85–107. For the semantic connection between χρεία (need) and χρῆσις (use), see Rédard (1953), 80–82, 93–98; a striking analogy can be found in the German verbs *brauchen* (to need) and *gebrauchen* (to use) that are formed from the same root. See also Chapter Three Section 1.2 and 3.1 (esp. n. 84).

112 This phrase is central to Michel Foucault's famous discussion of the χρῆσις of pleasures in the second volume of his History of Sexuality as the manner in which "an individual managed his sexual activity" (1986: 53) and gives sexual acts a meaning in his life (1986: 53–56).

113 Rédard (1953), 41; Agamben (2015), 27: "It is probable that precisely the subject/object relationship—so marked in the modern conception of the utilization of something on the part of someone—emerges as inadequate to grasp the meaning of the Greek verb."

114 Rédard (1953), 41–43, following Benveniste (1950), attaches great importance to the fact that χρῆσθαι is a *medium tantum*, indicating "a process that takes place in the subject" (Benveniste p. 172/148) as opposed to processes that "start from the subject and beyond him" (what we might term: "causative"). Agamben is particularly interested in the ancient Greek semantic field of XPH-vocabulary because in the verb χρῆσθαι he finds a relationality between subject and world that is differently structured than the subject-object relationship that is analytically so prevalent since Kant (to whose "split ontology" Agamben

but rather a "relationship with something", the nature of which is "so indeterminate that it seems impossible to define a unitary sense of the term."[115] In any case, it is safe to establish that XPH-terminology is underdetermined in comparison with modern conceptions of utility and allows for discursive negotiation unknown to our concept of use. Moreover, this Protean quality of XPH-terminology did not escape the attention of 4th-century native speakers themselves—most notably Aristotle and the Socratics.

2.3 *Aristotle's Useful Friends*

The most obvious example of Aristotelian reflection on XPH-terminology is his distinction in *Politics* I between the proper use "οἰκεία χρῆσις" of a commodity and its use "for the sake of exchange" (ἀλλαγῆς ἕνεκεν).[116] Another Aristotelian distinction that springs to mind is his discussion of the use (χρῆσις) or property: property can be used as means to the acquisition of revenues (χρήσιμα) or for the sake of the *activity* of using, i.e. as an intrinsically valuable activity.[117]

For present purposes, the more relevant case is Aristotle's Utility Friendship (φιλία διὰ τὸ χρήσιμον).[118] It is easy to misconstrue Utility Friendships as ultimately self-seeking and utilitarian relations motivated by selfish concerns, in which one basically "uses" the friend, not valuing him as an end in itself but as a mere instrument for attaining an ulterior end, and, as such, opposed to Virtue Friendships that are defined by other-regarding sentiments.[119] And here we find ourselves facing the Egoism/Altruism conundrum again.

On closer analysis, however, it appears that Aristotle's tripartite analysis of friendship follows fault lines that do not fully coincide with the dichotomies

attributes the philosophical "crisis of modernity"). χρῆσις, according to Agamben, points towards an original unity, an interdependent relation between the act and that on which it relies.

115 Agamben (2015), 25. It is indeed this indeterminateness that has necessitated Rédard (1953) to offer the quite tautological definition of χρῆσθαι as "*rechercher l'utilisation de quelque chose*", a definition he later nuances to reflect that χρῆσθαι expresses expresses an attempt at accommodation and appropriation on the part of the subject ("*appropriation occasionelle …*", "*Le Procès exprimé est restraint a la sphere du sujet qui fait un recours occasionnel à l'object.*" Rédard (1953), 44).

116 Ar. *Pol.* I.ix (1257a6–13). Cf. Chapter Seven Section Four.

117 Ar. *EN* IV.i (1120a4–9); cf. *Rhet.* 1361a11–24 Cf. Chapter Seven Section 2.

118 See also Chapter Seven.

119 It is, however, equally problematic to assimilate Aristotle's virtue friendship with modern ideals of altruism. To many commentators, Aristotle appears to reduce apparent altruism in virtue friendship to egoism. E.g. Allan (1970), 138. But Stern-Gillet (1995), 85 for a clear statement of the point that self-love is inaccessible for those who are not virtuous.

that we are conditioned to use. As we carve the Aristotelian concept of the Utility Friend closer to its joints, a different anatomy emerges.

2.3.1 Utility Friendships *are* Other-Directed

Aristotle explicitly acknowledges that the three types of friendship do share the general (and absolutely fundamental) characteristic that there is a basic other-directed concern:[120]

[Text 9]

> δεῖ ἄρα εὐνοεῖν ἀλλήλοις καὶ βούλεσθαι τἀγαθὰ μὴ λανθάνοντας δι' ἕν τι τῶν εἰρημένων.
>
> [T]he parties must *have goodwill towards each other*, i.e. wish good things for each other, and be aware of the other's doing so, the feeling being brought about by one of the three things mentioned.[121]

Among the basic criteria of φιλία, Aristotle stipulates: (i) that a friendship be mutual (ἀλλήλοις, there needs to be ἀντιφίλησις, hence friendship cannot involve inanimate objects like wine),[122] (ii) that this mutual goodwill be explicitly shared knowledge (μὴ λανθάνοντας) and (iii) that it involve being well-disposed towards the other (εὐνοεῖν, εὔνοια). Being well-disposed towards the others means that one wishes the other good things (βούλεσθαι τἀγαθά) on account of one of the three qualities mentioned in the immediately preceding passage: Virtue Friends wish each other well on account of virtue, Pleasure Friends on account of the pleasant, Utility Friends on account on the useful.[123]

Aristotle finds it essential to remark that in popular conception, well-wishing is, by definition, *about the other*:

---

120 Smith-Pangle (2003), 39: "Here, then, is the paradox of friendship as Aristotle presents it: In seeking and choosing friends, we seek the god for ourselves, and apparently we only love another if and so long as he seems good for us; yet we are persuaded that we are not real friends unless we wish one another good apart from what is good for ourselves."

121 Ar. *EN* VIII.2 (1156a4–6); *all translations of NE are by* Broadie & Rowe (2002).

122 *EN* VIII.ii (1155b28).

123 Note that to Aristotle, goodwill is a necessary, but not sufficient condition for φιλία: εὔνοια alone lacks a sense of responsibility for treating friends well (1166b32–1167a3); goodwill is "idle friendship" (ἀργὴν φιλίαν, 1167a8–12), verbal declarations of intention without actual support.

[Text 10]

τῷ δὲ φίλῳ φασὶ δεῖν βούλεσθαι τἀγαθὰ ἐκείνου ἕνεκα.

[A]nd people say friendship demands that one wish a friend good things *for his sake.*[124]

It is in the very nature of well-wishing (βούλεσθαι τἀγαθά) that it involves a concern for the other (ἐκείνου ἕνεκα). This other-directed quality applies *to all three kinds of friendships*. Even the inferior types of friendships do involve an active concern for the wellbeing of the other, however defective this may be.

Therefore, Utility Friendships are by no means egoistic or motivated by "purely selfish" concerns. This is not to say that Utility Friendship (or the other two friendship types for that matter) are altruistic in a thick sense of the word, i.e. in the sense that the interests of the other person are the *only* reason for acting without any reference to one's own interests.[125] It simply means that the interests of the other are *a* reason for acting in a certain way.

2.3.2 Utility Friendships are Accidental, but Not Necessarily Exploitative

What, then, makes Utility Friendship and Pleasure Friendship inferior types of friendships according to Aristotle? If they are all about well-wishing, what more do we want from our friends?

---

124 Ar. *EN* VIII.ii (1155b31–32).

125 Gill (1998), 319 for the point that the qualification ἐκείνου ἕνεκα does not necessarily remove any reference to self-interest. So too Cooper (1977), 621 n. 7. To Cooper the fact that the needs of another person can form a sufficient (though possibly not the only or strongest) reason for acting for his sake justifies the attribution of altruistic elements to Aristotle's account of friendship. However, Aristotle's definition of φιλία in the *Rhet.* (2.4 1381a5–6) adds the provision to act "for no other reason than the other's sake." Cf. Konstan (2000), 6. On the terminological confusion around the notion of altruism, see n. 110 above. As for antiquity: Blum (1992), 36 for the contention that Plato and Aristotle "entirely lack a concept of altruism"; MacIntyre (1972), 462 that Plato and Aristotle do not conceive of altruistic benevolence as a distinct cardinal virtue; Annas (1993) for the preference to avoid terminology of "egoism" and "altruism"; Ross (1923) and Prichard (1968) for the idea that Greek ethical thought principally presupposes the priority of self-interest; Irwin (1977) and (1995), Kahn (1981) and Kraut (1989) for the view that Aristotle's account of Virtue Friendship leaves room for substantial altruism; Gill (1998), 317 for the argument that although Aristotle's account does offer "linguistic and conceptual equivalents for the "self-other"-contrast", the possibility of altruism is not a central concern for Aristotle. As Konstan (2000) points out, in his rhetorical works, Aristotle does insist on altruistic motivations (in the strong and thick sense) as crucial features of some other-

As becomes clear in VIII.3, the inferior types of friendship are concerned with the other κατὰ συμβεβηκός, in an "accidental way", i.e. not for what the other essentially is,[126] but "in his quality as useful or pleasant" (ᾗ χρήσιμος ἢ ἡδύς)—the fact remains that these friends *are* concerned with each other.[127] As a virtue friend you are concerned with your friend for the virtuous person he is, and you wish him good things and virtue; along the same lines, as a utility friend you wish your friend useful things and you cooperate with him on the basis of utility. Your concern is confined to concern for the friend in his quality as a utility friend.

Utility presupposes need and needs are fleeting—they change or they are met—and therefore fail to offer a solid base for a long-term relationship:[128] Utility Friendships tend to be unstable and dissolve quickly,[129] as the rationale

---

benefiting sentiments; Aristotle remarkably does so not in order to make a contribution to ethics, but to an analysis of emotion.

126 The contention that virtue friends are committed to each other κατ' αὐτούς, "for what they really are", of course implies a close connection between moral excellence and what human being essentially is. Cooper (1977), 634; Price (1989), 105. Smith-Pangle (2003), 39–40.

127 See Cooper (1977) for the argument that the oppositions (i) loving a person for what he essentially is vs. loving a person for his incidental qualities and (ii) loving a person for the sake of himself vs. loving a person for the sake of oneself, are distinct. Cf. Alpern (1983). See Vlastos (1973) for the view that neither Plato's nor Aristotle's accounts of friendship accommodates for personal love for whole persons as opposed to "love for place-holders of the predicates "useful" and "beautiful"" (26); Penner & Rowe (2005), 280–290 for a response to Vlastos that calls for a broad construction of utility: e.g. parental love is not conditioned by a child's usefulness in producing income, but rather by the role it plays in the parent's happiness.

128 The idea that "utility" is the *raison d'être* of friendship also figures prominently among the Cyrenaics, which seems to support the idea that this conceptualization may have been originally associated with Socrates (Fürst (1996), 57–59). E.g. Aristippus (DL 2.91 = frg. 232 Mannebach): τὸν φίλον τῆς χρείας ἕνεκα. Protest against this conceptualization is found among the followers of Anniceris of Cyrene: Friendships should not be based on utility alone (μὴ διὰ τὰς χρείας μόνον), for that makes them short-lived, but also on stable goodwill (τὴν γεγονυῖαν εὔνοιαν) that makes one willing to endure hardships. (frg. 234 Mannebach). On utility and need as basis of φιλία in Plato and Aristotle, see Chapter Seven Section 2.1.

129 *EN* VIII.iii (1156a19–23, 34–b4), VIII.v (1157a3f., 14–16, 24–26), VIII.viii (1158b4f., 9f.), VIII.x (1159b10–12); *MM* II.xi (1209b21–23, 29–10a2). Utility friendships and Pleasure friendships are not μόνιμος, quickly turn into (μεταπίπτειν) their opposites, are quickly formed (ταχέως γίνεσθαι) and similarly quickly ended (ταχέως παύεσθαι), are hence ἀβέβαιος and εὐδιάλυτος (a neologism of Aristotle and a hapax legomenon in his work (*EN* VIII.iii 1156a19); cf. Dirlmeier (1979), 514). Virtue Friendship is stable and lasting: *EN* VIII.iv (1156b11f., 17f.), VIII.v (1156b33f.), VIII.viii (1158b9), VIII.x (1159b4f.); *EE* VII.ii (1236a33–b19, 37b9–12, 38a11); *MM* II.xi (1209b11–17). The duration of friendships is explicitly thematized in IX.iii (1165a36–b36; also IX.i 1164a8–13). Cf. Fürst (1996), 86–101, for an argument that duration

of their existence is cancelled as soon as the partners' needs are fulfilled.[130] More fundamentally, the very basis of Utility Friendships is goal-relative: as a category of value, the useful (τὸ χρήσιμον) represents a goal-relative value, a "good-*for*" some further end (i.e. the pleasant or the good).[131] When a friendship is based on utility, the basis is not an end in itself—as opposed to Virtue Friendships where the end is virtue-in-friendship.

2.3.3 Although Both Can Be "Used", Friends are Not Tools

But this would take us back to the idea that Utility Friendships are self-serving utilitarian relations. If Utility Friends are said to connect to one another not for what the other is (οὐ καθ' αὐτοὺς φιλοῦσιν), but to be committed to the other because of what is good for themselves (διὰ τὸ αὐτοῖς ἀγαθόν στέργουσι),[132] then a useful friend is a friend who offers access to the utilities that the other needs.[133] This suggests that Utility Friends *are* a means towards the acquisition of utilities. In other words: Utility Friendships are useful because the *friend* is being "used"—a far cry from the earlier idea that a Utility Friend is someone for whom one wishes useful things. Although not incompatible with it, it does change the tone of the story: talking about "using friends", we find ourselves on the other side of the Kantian fence.

---

is a more central criterion for Aristotelian φιλία than is commonly assumed. The idea that the duration/viability of friendship is correlated to utility is also Cyrenaic. E.g. frg. 234 Mannebach. Cf. *Mem.* I.ii.53.

130 Therefore, both Utility Friendships and Pleasure Friendships are dismissed as "friendships" only in the analogical sense (καθ' ὁμοιότητα); *EN* VIII.v (1157a25–30); *EN* VIII.iii (1156a16–17). Cf. Smith-Pangle (2003), pp. 39–40. On the nature of the similarity and differences between the three εἴδη, see Chapter Seven Section 2.1. The dismissal of utility friendship as not friendship in the proper sense of the word is more characteristic of the treatment of the varieties of friendship in *EN* (where the inferior types of friendship are only similar to *real* friendship) than in *EE* (where the author seems far less dismissive of the inferior types). On the problem of the relation between these two Aristotelian ethical works, see Chapter Seven Section 2.3.

131 *EN* VIII.ii (1155b19–21). Cf. *EE* VII. (1235b31–37).

132 Ar. *EN* VIII.iii (1156a10–15). στέργω is often used as a "marked" term in relation to φιλέω, as "unreserved commitment" in relation to "connection". Cf. Soph. *El.* 1102 where Clytaemnestra complains that Electra "πέφυκας πατέρα σὸν στέργειν ἀεί", i.e. "structurally *chooses* your father's side."

133 Aristotle suggests that utility friends are more fungible than virtue friends because the friendship is based on characteristics that are accidental (κατὰ συμβεβηκός) and not intrinsic (καθ' αὐτούς) to the friends; but this still does not necessarily preclude even a utility friend wishes a friend well for the sake of the other; even in a utility friendship, a friend cannot be reduced to a mere means to one's own ulterior ends.

An important proviso is required here. In the *EN*, Aristotle seems to avoid the adjective χρήσιμος as a direct attribute of φίλος and to prefer formulations such as φίλοι διὰ τὸ χρήσιμον or κατὰ τὸ χρήσιμον.[134] Moreover, in the *Eudemian Ethics*,[135] Aristotle takes the trouble to disambiguate two ways of "use" in order to preserve the fact that even in a utility friendship, a friend cannot be reduced to a mere means to one's ulterior ends:[136]

[Text 11]

> ἄλλον γὰρ τρόπον συνῆλθον πρίων καὶ τέχνη, οὐχ ἕνεκα κοινοῦ τινος (οἷον γὰρ ὄργανον καὶ ψυχή) ἀλλὰ τοῦ χρωμένου ἕνεκεν. συμβαίνει δὲ καὶ τοῦτο ὄργανον ἐπιμελείας τυγχάνειν, ἧς δίκαιον πρὸς τὸ ἔργον· ἐκείνου γὰρ ἕνεκεν ἐστίν. καὶ τὸ τρυπάνῳ[137] εἶναι διττόν, ὧν τὸ κυριώτερον ἡ ἐνέργεια, ἡ τρύπησις. καὶ ἐν τούτῳ τῷ εἴδει σῶμα καὶ δοῦλος, ὥσπερ εἴρηται πρότερον. τὸ δὴ ζητεῖν πῶς δεῖ τῷ φίλῳ ὁμιλεῖν, τὸ ζητεῖν δίκαιόν τι ἐστίν.
>
> The coming together of a saw with the craft that uses it is on different lines—it is not for the sake of some common object, for saw and craft are like instrument and spirit, but for the sake of the man who employs them. It does indeed come about that even the tool itself receives attention which it deserves with a view to its work, since it exists for the sake of its work, and the essential nature of a gimlet is twofold, the more important half being its activity, boring. And the body and the slave are in the class of tool, as has been said before. Therefore to seek the proper way of associating with a friend is to seek for a particular kind of justice.[138]

---

134 Occasionally, Aristotle does apply the attribute χρήσιμος directly to the noun φίλος: e.g. *EN* VIII.iii (1156a16), VIII.vi (1158a29, 33) VIII.xiii (1159b), IX.ix (1169b23); *EE* VII. 1243b25, 1244a15, 1244a21, 1236a13, 1238a22, 1238a8, 1238b2, 1244a18, a33, 1243b26. This may also be a case of focal predication: "the person with whom I have a utility friendship", or "utility friend" instead of "useful friend". The collocation χρήσιμος φιλία only occurs in *EE* 1242b31. Cf. Dirlmeier (1969), 445 ad loc.: "Zu χρήσιμος φιλία kenne ich keine Parallele. ἡδεῖα φιλία gibt es nicht. Aber an χρησίμων darf man wegen 43a2.6 nicht denken."

As Engen (2010: 213–216) points out, the word χρήσιμος is sporadically used to refer to persons in the epigraphic record after the mid-fourth century: in honorary decrees, the term may have been used to avoid the antidemocratical connotations of χρηστός.

135 On the relation between these two Aristotelian ethical works, see Chapter Seven Section 2.3.

136 φίλος as direct object of χρῆσθαι: e.g. *EE* VII. (1237a41–b1) ("Treating" (χρῆσθαι) an object of φιλεῖν (φιλόμενον)).

137 Conceivably a response to the example of the "use" of a knife in the Platonic *Alcibiades*.

138 Ar. *EE* VII.10 (1242a14–19); all translations of *EE* are by Rackham (1981).

Saw and craft "come together" (συνῆλθον) without having a common purpose (οὐχ ἕνεκα κοινοῦ τινος),[139] but for the sake of the person using them (τοῦ χρωμένου ἕνεκεν). Similarly, the person using the tools (a τεχνίτης) does not have an association (κοινωνία) with his tool (ὄργανον):[140]

[Text 12]

> ἐπεὶ δ' ὁμοίως ἔχει ψυχὴ πρὸς σῶμα καὶ τεχνίτης πρὸς ὄργανον καὶ δεσπότης πρὸς δοῦλον, τούτων μὲν οὐκ ἔστι κοινωνία. οὐ γὰρ δύ' ἐστίν, ἀλλὰ τὸ μὲν ἕν, τὸ δὲ τοῦ ἑνός [οὐδέν].[141] οὐδὲ διαιρετὸν τὸ ἀγαθὸν ἑκατέρῳ, ἀλλὰ τὸ ἀμφοτέρων τοῦ ἑνὸς οὗ ἕνεκα ἐστίν. τό τε γὰρ σῶμά ἐστιν ὄργανον σύμφυτον, καὶ τοῦ δεσπότου ὁ δοῦλος ὥσπερ μόριον καὶ ὄργανον ἀφαιρετόν, τὸ δ' ὄργανον ὥσπερ δοῦλος ἄψυχος.
>
> But since the relations of soul and body, craftsman and tool, and master and slave are similar, between the two terms of each of these pairs there is no partnership; for they are not two, but the former is one and the latter a part of that one; nor is the good divisible between them, but that of both belongs to the one for whose sake they exist. For the body is the soul's tool born with it, a slave is as it were a member or tool of his master, a tool is a sort of inanimate slave.[142]

Craftsman and tool are not two independent agents with a common purpose (a κοινόν) consisting of a good that can be shared or divided (οὐδε διαιρετόν); the tool is simply an extension or part (μόριον) of the craftsman; only one of them is a "one" (τὸ μὲν ἕν), the other is "of one" (τὸ δὲ τοῦ ἑνός).[143] The crucial difference is that Utility Friends have "something in common", i.e. they pursue a common goal that harmonizes the needs and ends of both friends, e.g. an exchange of

---

139 Cf. *EN* 1161a30–35.

140 Cf. *EN* 1160b32–1161a3.

141 οὐδέν is deleted by Fritzsche (1849). Rackham (1935), Apelt (1894) and Jackson (1900) read οὐδ' ἕν. Dirlmeier (1979), who suspects οὐδέν to be a proleptic dittography of the subsequent οὐδὲ, and Walzer & Minger (1991) follow Fritzsches deletion.

142 Ar. *EE* VII.9 (1241b17–24); *transl. adapted.*

143 A tool exists for the sake of its work (τὸ ἔργον), i.e. its activity (ἐνέργεια)—also "use" (χρῆσις) in the case of tools: *De Part. An.* 645b14–18. This forms a marked contrast with what Aristotle in *Pol.* II.1 (1262b7–23) takes to be Plato's conception of φιλία in the *Symposium*: as the merging of two lovers into a single unity (συμφῦναι καὶ γενέσθαι ἐκ δύο ὄντων ἀμφοτέρους ἕνα). Aristotle conceives of this merging as a destruction (ἐφθάρθαι) of both individuals, or at least one. Cf. Hutter (1978), 110–111.

five pairs of shoes for a bed, that meets the needs of both.[144] In such a situation, the good is "divisible", in the sense that the person who needed a bed gets one and the person who needed five pairs of shoes gets what he wants too. Using a tool means making it realize your goals; "using" a friend, i.e. dealing with a friend, means making an arrangement in which both of you can realize your goals—not using him as a tool for your ulterior ends. "Using" friends is distinct from "using" tools.

By distinguishing two kinds of "use", Aristotle attempts to harmonize his analysis that Utility Friendships are ultimately grounded in need and lack with his contention that friends in *all* types of friendship meet the basic requirement that they wish one another well. Utility friendships are grounded in mutual benefit, not mutual exploitation.

2.4 *Use and Usability According to Xenophon*

One thing that emerges from Aristotle's analysis of XPH-terminology is his awareness of a degree of lexical polysemy in the verb χρῆσθαι. It is this lexical flexibility that is being exploited by Xenophon in his *Oeconomicus*, the Socratic dialogue on estate management (οἰκονομία or οἰκονομικὴ τέχνη). Socrates and his conversation partner Critoboulus, attempting to define possessions (κτήματα),[145] the realm of οἰκονομία,[146] establish a criterion of value:[147] wealth, χρήματα, is defined in terms of usefulness.[148] Using the example of a flute, Socrates redefines χρήματα so as to cover anything beneficial (τὰ ὠφελοῦντα),[149] provided that the user in view knows how to use it (χρῆσθαι):[150] a flute is wealth in the hands of a skilled user (τῷ ἐπισταμένῳ ἀξίως λόγου αὐλεῖν), but "useless

144 For Aristotle, κοινωνία is a generic term for any community of interest, any social group emerging out of social interaction. See also Chapter Seven Section 3.2. For the difference between having a common interests and having *identical* interests, see *EN* IX.v–vi (1167a20–b2), *EE* VII. (1241a27–29).

145 *Oec.* I.5: wealth is defined as "everything that a man possesses" (πάντα τοῦ οἴκου εἶναι, ὅσα τις κέκτηται). Gernet (1981) for the argument that the term κτῆμα, in contrast to the noun χρῆμα, always contains reference to the object's mode of acquisition. Cf. Gottesman (2010).

146 Critoboulus' first definition of *oikos* is that it encompasses "everything a man possesses". *Oec.* I.5: πάντα τοῦ οἴκου εἶναι, ὅσα τις κέκτηται.

147 *Oec.* I.6–7: Possession (κτήματα) may encompass wealth (χρήματα) as well as liabilities.

148 As Schaps (2003: 142) notes, Critoboulus here makes a shift from Socrates' κτήματα, that contains both wealth, χρήματα, as well as liabilities, ζημίαι, such as enemies, towards χρήματα. Socrates leaves the shift unjustified, but takes the conceptual space to explore the etymology of χρήματα.

149 *Oec.* I.9.

150 *Oec.* I.10–11.

stones" (ἄχρηστοι λίθοι) to someone who isn't (τῷ μὴ ἐπισταμένῳ).[151] Here Critoboulus appears to make an important proviso:

[Text 13]

> εἰ μὴ ἀποδιδοῖτό γε αὐτούς.
> τοῦτ' ἄρα φαίνεται ἡμῖν, ἀποδιδομένοις μὲν οἱ αὐλοὶ χρήματα, μὴ ἀποδιδομένοις δὲ ἀλλὰ κεκτημένοις οὔ, τοῖς μὴ ἐπισταμένοις αὐτοῖς χρῆσθαι.
> Καὶ ὁμολογουμένως γε, ὦ Σώκρατες, ὁ λόγος ἡμῖν χωρεῖ, ἐπείπερ εἴρηται τὰ ὠφελοῦντα χρήματα εἶναι. μὴ πωλούμενοι μὲν γὰρ οὐ χρήματά εἰσιν οἱ αὐλοί· οὐδὲν γὰρ χρήσιμοί εἰσι· πωλούμενοι δὲ χρήματα.
>
> "Unless he *sells* them."
> "So our impression is that, for those who don't know how to make use of them, pipes are assets if they sell them, but are not assets if they don't sell them but hang on to them."
> "Yes, Socrates, and the stages of our argument are perfectly consistent, based on the premise that beneficial things are assets. Unsold pipes are not assets, because they are useless; sold pipes are assets."[152]

This almost looks like a rudimentary distinction between an object's "value in use" (which is dependent upon the subject's ability to use it) and its "value in exchange" (one can sell an object for money if one is not capable of using it oneself).[153] However, this distinction between the purely individual subjective notion of value in use and a more objective concept of wealth is only apparent, as even exchangeability for money does not secure value in anything:

[Text 14]

> πρὸς ταῦτα δ' ὁ Σωκράτης εἶπεν· Ἂν ἐπίστηταί γε πωλεῖν. εἰ δὲ πωλοίη αὖ πρὸς τοῦτο ᾧ μὴ ἐπίσταιτο χρῆσθαι, οὐδὲ πωλούμενοί εἰσι χρήματα κατά γε τὸν σὸν λόγον.
>
> Socrates' response was as follows: "Yes, *if* the seller knows how to sell. But if he sells the pipes for something else which he doesn't know how

151 *Oec.* I.10.
152 *Oec.* I.10–11; *all translations of* Oeconomicus *are by* Tredennick & Waterfield (1990).
153 Sedlacek (2011), 101, Lowry (1987), 77.

to make use of, then it follows from your argument that pipes are not assets even if they're sold."[154]

The seller needs to know how to sell, i.e. how to exchange an object for something that he does know how to use.[155] This leads to the paradoxical observation that even money (ἀργύριον) is not wealth (χρήματα) to one who does not know to use (χρῆσθαι) it—obviously drawing on the polyvalence of χρήματα (also used for money):

[Text 15]

Λέγειν ἔοικας, ὦ Σώκρατες, ὅτι οὐδὲ τὸ ἀργύριόν ἐστι χρήματα, εἰ μή τις ἐπίσταιτο χρῆσθαι αὐτῷ.

'You seem to be implying, Socrates, that not even *money* is an asset, unless one knows how *to make use* of it.'[156]

Utility becomes a quality of an object that refers not primarily to its potential utility but rather to the ability of the owner to use it rightly. Knowledge is a crucial component of wealth because it "transforms otherwise useless objects into tools which serve a good purpose".[157] In other words: whereas modern discourse tends to associate "utility" and "use" with the short-term transactional order of individual competition and acquisition, to Socrates the notions of *real* utility and *proper* use always and by definition bear reference to the long-term order of things.

---

154 *Oec.* I.12.

155 Note that in this analysis of exchange value the value to the *buyer* is left out of account.

156 *Oec.* I.12.

157 Danzig (2003 rev. 2010), 59–60. Cf. Von Reden (2003 [1995]), p. 174: "In classical Athens the term *chrêmata* could still be used for a variety of things; these included money, but also other valuables for exchange. (…) *Chrêma* (…) was not the term for any specific valuable, nor did it have precise moral connotations. Its meaning shifted according to the context in which it was used and the ends to which it was applied." Tamiolaki (2014), n. 26, in response to Van Berkel (2010), insists on maintaining a distinction between χρήματα and ὠφέλεια and on crediting ὠφέλεια with ethical priority. I am inclined to think that the difference is more one of perspective and normativity: while ὠφέλεια is by definition beneficial, the noun χρήματα may be applied to valuables on false grounds and always requires the question whether the χρήματα in view are *true* χρήματα.

2.5 *Socratic Proper Use*

The notion of proper use (ὀρθὴ χρῆσις) of wealth and money is not unique to Xenophon's Socrates. In Plato's *Euthydemus* too, it is argued that wealth is premised on proper use:[158]

[Text 16]

> {—} Δεῖ ἄρα, ἔφην, ὡς ἔοικεν, μὴ μόνον κεκτῆσθαι τὰ τοιαῦτα ἀγαθὰ τὸν μέλλοντα εὐδαίμονα ἔσεσθαι, ἀλλὰ καὶ χρῆσθαι αὐτοῖς· ἢ οὐδὲν ὄφελος τῆς κτήσεως γίγνεται.
> {—} Ἀληθῆ λέγεις.
> {—} Ἆρ' οὖν, ὦ Κλεινία, ἤδη τοῦτο ἱκανὸν πρὸς τὸ εὐδαίμονα ποιῆσαί τινα, τό τε κεκτῆσθαι τἀγαθὰ καὶ τὸ χρῆσθαι αὐτοῖς;
> {—} Ἔμοιγε δοκεῖ.
> {—} Πότερον, ἦν δ' ἐγώ, ἐὰν ὀρθῶς χρῆταί τις ἢ καὶ ἐὰν μή;
> {—} Ἐὰν ὀρθῶς.
>
> Socrates: So it seems one must *not merely have acquired* such goods if one is to be happy, *but use them too*; else there is no benefit gained from their possession.
> Cleinias: True.
> Soc.: Then have we here enough means, Cleinias, for making a man happy—in the possession of these goods and using them?
> Cl.: I think so.
> Soc.: Shall we say, I asked, *if he uses them rightly*, or just as much if he does not?
> Cl.: If rightly.[159]

To be happy, one must not only have acquired (κεκτῆσθαι) goods (ἀγαθά) but use (χρῆσθαι) them too; moreover, one must use them *correctly* (ὀρθῶς). And it is knowledge (ἐπιστήμη) that makes right use (τὸ ὀρθῶς χρῆσθαι) possible:[160]

---

158 *Euthyd.* 280b–e, 281b, 281d, 288e–289a. Similarly, in Plato's *Republic* it is the soul that makes goods such as riches (πλοῦτος) good and beneficial (ἀγαθά, ὠφέλιμα) or harmful (βλαβερά; *Meno* 88d–e). Here too, value is subjective, in the sense that it is defined with reference to the owner: the possession of wealth (τὴν τῶν χρημάτων κτῆσιν) is of most value (πλείστου ἀξίαν) to the good man (ἐπιεικεῖ; *Rep.* 1.331a–b).

159 Pl. *Euthyd.* 280d–e; *transl. by* Lamb (1924).

160 *Euthyd.* 281b.

[Text 17]

> ἆρ' οὖν, ἦν δ' ἐγώ, καὶ περὶ τὴν χρείαν ὧν ἐλέγομεν τὸ πρῶτον τῶν ἀγαθῶν, πλούτου τε καὶ ὑγιείας καὶ κάλλους, τὸ ὀρθῶς πᾶσι τοῖς τοιούτοις χρῆσθαι ἐπιστήμη|ᵦ ἦν ἡγουμένη καὶ κατορθοῦσα τὴν πρᾶξιν, ἢ ἄλλο τι;
> ἐπιστήμη, ἦ δ' ὅς.
> οὐ μόνον ἄρα εὐτυχίαν ἀλλὰ καὶ εὐπραγίαν, ὡς ἔοικεν, ἡ ἐπιστήμη παρέχει τοῖς ἀνθρώποις ἐν πάσῃ κτήσει τε καὶ πράξει.
> ὡμολόγει.
> ἆρ' οὖν ὦ πρὸς Διός, ἦν δ' ἐγώ, ὄφελός τι τῶν ἄλλων κτημάτων ἄνευ φρονήσεως καὶ σοφίας;
>
> Then similarly, I went on, in the use of the goods we mentioned at first—wealth and health and beauty—was it *knowledge* that showed *the way to the right use of all those advantages* and rectified their conduct, or was it something else?
> Knowledge, he replied.
> So that knowledge, it would seem, supplies mankind not only with good luck, but with *welfare, in all that he either possesses or conducts.*
> He agreed.
> Then can we, in Heaven's name, get any benefit from all the other possessions without understanding and wisdom?[161]

Goods are not good or evil by themselves. It is right use, made possible by knowledge of the owner, that makes them good.[162]

Similarly, in the platonic dialogue *Eryxias*, the sophist Prodicus' stance on wealth is remarkably reminiscent of the *Oeconomicus*:

[Text 18]

> Ἠρώτα γὰρ αὐτὸν τὸ μειράκιον πῶς οἴεται κακὸν εἶναι τὸ πλουτεῖν, καὶ ὅπως ἀγαθόν. ὁ δ' ὑπολαβών, ὥσπερ καὶ σὺ νυνδή, ἔφη, Τοῖς μὲν καλοῖς κἀγαθοῖς τῶν ἀνθρώπων ἀγαθόν, καὶ τοῖς ἐπισταμένοις ὅπου δεῖ χρῆσθαι τοῖς χρήμασι, τούτοις μὲν ἀγαθόν, τοῖς δὲ μοχθηροῖς καὶ ἀνεπιστήμοσιν κακόν. ἔχει δ', ἔφη, καὶ τἆλλα πράγματα οὕτω πάντα· ὁποῖοι γὰρ ἄν τινες ὦσιν οἱ χρώμενοι, τοιαῦτα καὶ τὰ πράγματα αὐτοῖς ἀνάγκη εἶναι.

---

161 *Euthyd.* 281a–b.

162 Goods (ἀγαθά) do not have any value (οὐδενὸς ἄξια εἶναι) without guidance by understanding and wisdom (φρόνησίς τε καὶ σοφία); *Euth.* 281d.

> The young man asked him in what respect he thought wealth was bad and in what respect good. Prodicus responded as you did just now: 'It's good for gentlemen, *the people who know in what situations they should use their property*; but it's bad for those who are wicked and ignorant. The situation is the same with everything else as well: the nature of the things people deal in inevitably reflects the people themselves.'[163]

Being wealthy (τὸ πλουτεῖν) is good for καλοὶ κἀγαθοί and those who know how to use wealth (ἐπισταμένοις ὅπου δεῖ χρῆσθαι τοῖς χρήμασι) but bad for the μοχθηροί and the ignorant. Later on in the dialogue, Socrates professes to have the same opinion on wealth as everyone else: being wealthy (τὸ πλουτεῖν) means possessing a lot of χρήματα. This equivocation begs the question what χρήματα are, as some property (e.g. pieces of leather) are considered riches (πλοῦτος) among some people (the Carthaginians), but not among others (the Greeks).[164] Similarly, whereas houses are χρήματα among the Greeks, they are not χρήματα for the Scythians, because they have no use for houses:

[Text 19]

> Ἐπεὶ καὶ ἐν τοῖς Σκύθαις τούτου ἕνεκα αὐτοῖς οἰκίαι οὐ χρήματά ἐστιν, ὅτι οὐδεμία αὐτοῖς οἰκίας ἐστίν· οὐδ' ἂν προτιμήσειεν Σκύθης ἀνὴρ οἰκίαν αὐτῷ τὴν καλλίστην εἶναι μᾶλλον ἤπερ σίσυραν δερματίνην, ὅτι τὸ μὲν χρήσιμον, τὸ δ' ἀχρεῖον αὐτῷ ἐστιν. αὖθις αὖ ἡμῖν τὸ Καρχηδόνιον νόμισμα οὐκ οἰόμεθα χρήματα εἶναι· οὐ γάρ ἔστιν ὅτι ἂν αὐτοῦ κομισαίμεθα ὅσων δεόμεθα, ὥσπερ τῷ ἀργυρίῳ, ὥστ' ἀχρεῖον ἂν ἡμῖν εἴη.
>
> {—} Εἰκός γε.
>
> {—} Ὅσα μὲν ἄρα τυγχάνει χρήσιμα ὄντα ἡμῖν, ταῦτα χρήματα· καὶ ὅσα δ' ἀχρεῖα, ταῦτα δ' οὐ χρήματα.

> "And that's also why among the Scythians houses are not property, because the Scythians have no use for a house; nor would a Scythian prefer the finest house over a heavy leather coat, since the one thing is useful to him while the other isn't. Again, we don't think that the Carthaginian coinage is property, since we couldn't possibly obtain from it what we need, as we do with silver; therefore it would be useless to us."
>
> "Fair enough."

163 [Pl.], *Eryx.* 397e; *transl. by* Joyal, in Cooper (1997).

164 *Eryx.* 400a–b.

"It follows *that everything that turns out to be useful to us* is property, while everything useless is not."[165]

Wealth (χρήματα) is what is useful (χρήσιμος) for its owner. Carthaginian coinage (νόμισμα) is not χρήματα among Greeks because it is useless (ἀχρεῖον) for them. In the (pseudo-)Platonic texts as well as in Xenophon's *Oeconomicus*, we see a common strategy in bringing out the subjective nature of wealth by analyzing XPH-terminology in terms of a subject who "uses" (χρῆσθαι) possessions that are "useful" (χρησιμός) to *him*.[166] Utility is subjective, i.e. dependent on the subject of use, and knowledge is a crucial component of wealth.

2.6 *Xenophon on Using Friends*

Whereas the doctrine of proper use suggests considerable common ground between various Socratic authors, there are differences as well. Xenophon's *Memorabilia* is an outlier when it comes to conceptual architecture. Central to (ps.-)Plato's discussion of money and the proper use of wealth and money[167] is the body-soul dichotomy. "Money" and "wealth" are relegated to the realm of the body[168] and subordinated to other goods;[169] they are, in short, baaaaaaaaaad. Riches (πλοῦτος) pervert the soul[170] and gold, silver and coin money cause degeneration in state and individual.[171]

165 *Eryx*. 400e.

166 Nestle (1936) suggests Prodicus as a common source of the idea of proper usage in both the *Oeconomicus* and the 3rd century *Eryxias*. See also the dialogue *Callias* by Aeschines Socraticus (fr. 17) for a paradoxical twist to the idea of ὀρθὴ χρῆσις of wealth: the correct use of poverty is even more admirable (because it is harder) than the correct use of wealth.

167 Plato never seems to systematically distinguish between wealth and money. Cf. Schaps (2003: 154).

168 Money is related to the lowest part of the soul (*Rep*. 9.581a); the concern for money ranks lowest, after concern for the body (*Leg*. 5.743e). Cf. the ps.-Platonic *Eryxias* 401a–e where wealth (χρήματα) is predominantly described with reference to the body. See Plato, *Phd*. 64d–67a for Plato's little regard for the body. Cf. Sedlacek (2011: 109 ff.).

169 Material wealth is inferior to other goods; e.g. *Leg*. 3.697bl; Cf. *Rep*. 9.581 ff.: love for gain and money is the lowest of the different types of pleasure. *Leg*. 9.870a2–c1: bodily goods should serve the body and the body should serve the soul. Cf. *Leg*. 3.679a10–c3, 5.727c7–728a5, 5.743e1–8, 11.913b3–c1.

170 *Leg*. 11.919c. However, in Pl. *Men*. 88d–e "wealth and the like" (πλοῦτός τε καὶ τὰ τοιαῦτα) are characterized as being "sometimes good and sometimes harmful" (τοτὲ μὲν ἀγαθὰ τοτὲ δὲ βλαβερά); it is the soul that, through right use and guidance (ὀρθῶς χρωμένη καὶ ἡγουμένη), makes wealth beneficial (ὠφέλιμα).

171 In the *Republic* the guardians of the state are not allowed to possess money. In the constitution of the *Laws*, Magnesia, money is reduced to token-money that is useless beyond

Whereas Plato embeds his criticism of material wealth in a hierarchy of goods,[172] Xenophon's discussion of money and wealth is shaped by an opposition between short-term and long-term goods, expanding the notion of the "proper use" of wealth to include interpersonal relationships. Hence, it is in the context of Socrates leading Critoboulus to the baffling conclusion that even money is not χρήματα for one who lacks the knowledge of its proper use (εἰ μή τις ἐπίσταιτο χρῆσθαι αὐτῷ),[173] that we find Socrates' infamous statement that friends are wealth, as the same notion is applicable to friends:

[Text 20]

> Τὸ μὲν δὴ ἀργύριον, εἰ μή τις **ἐπίσταιτο** αὐτῷ **χρῆσθαι**, οὕτω πόρρω ἀπωθείσθω, ὦ Κριτόβουλε, ὥστε μηδὲ χρήματα εἶναι. οἱ δὲ φίλοι, ἄν τις **ἐπίστηται** αὐτοῖς **χρῆσθαι** ὥστε **ὠφελεῖσθαι ἀπ' αὐτῶν**, τί φήσομεν αὐτοὺς εἶναι;
>
> —Χρήματα νὴ Δί', ἔφη ὁ Κριτόβουλος, καὶ πολύ γε μᾶλλον ἢ τοὺς βοῦς, ἂν ὠφελιμώτεροί γε ὦσι τῶν βοῶν.
>
> 'So if one doesn't *know how to make use of it*, Critobulus, then money must be kept at such a distance that it isn't even included among one's assets. Now, what about friends: if one knows how *to make use of them*, so as *to derive benefit from them*, then how should they be described?'
>
> 'Most emphatically as assets,' said Critobulus, 'They deserve the description far more than cattle, provided they are more beneficial than cattle.'[174]

If one knows how to deal with (χρῆσθαι) friends so as to benefit from them, friends may be called wealth (χρήματα) too. Although the notion of benefit (ὠφελεῖσθαι) does much to alleviate it, the idea that the value of friends may be assessed in terms of the benefit they provide may still have a utilitarian ring to it. But this, of course, depends on what can properly be seen as "benefit".

---

the boundaries of the state (5.742a), the citizens are restricted in the amount they may accumulate, and contact with gold and silver (and hence with shipowning, trading, retail trading, innkeeping, mining, lending, interest etc.) is restricted to non-citizens (8.842d). *Leg.* 5.743d, 5.742a–b, 7.801b. Superabundance of gold and silver coins (νομίσματος ἀργυροῦ καὶ χρυσοῦ) is most fatal to the state (*Leg.* 4.705e).

172 Whereas in the *Republic*, Plato only issues the warning that in a society where wealth and the wealthy are honored, virtue and the virtuous tend to be neglected (8.551a), in the *Leges* he plainly states that a very rich person cannot be a good one (5.742e–743c).

173 *Oec.* 1.12–13.

174 *Oec.* 1.14.

In the second book of the *Memorabilia*, Socrates appeals to Chaerecrates to make his brother Chaerephon an asset instead of a liability. Socrates opens his conversation with the rhetorical question that surely Chaerecrates does not consider wealth (χρήματα) to be more useful (χρησιμώτερον) than brothers:

[Text 21]

> Εἰπέ μοι, ἔφη, ὦ Χαιρέκρατες, οὐ δήπου καὶ σὺ εἶ τῶν τοιούτων ἀνθρώπων, **οἳ χρησιμώτερον νομίζουσι χρήματα ἢ ἀδελφούς**; καὶ ταῦτα τῶν μὲν ἀφρόνων ὄντων, τοῦ δὲ φρονίμου, καὶ τῶν μὲν βοηθείας δεομένων, τοῦ δὲ βοηθεῖν δυναμένου, καὶ πρὸς τούτοις τῶν μὲν πλειόνων ὑπαρχόντων, τοῦ δὲ ἑνός. θαυμαστὸν δὲ καὶ τοῦτο, εἴ τις τοὺς μὲν ἀδελφοὺς ζημίαν ἡγεῖται, ὅτι οὐ καὶ τὰ τῶν ἀδελφῶν **κέκτηται**, τοὺς δὲ πολίτας οὐχ ἡγεῖται ζημίαν, ὅτι οὐ καὶ τὰ τῶν πολιτῶν ἔχει, ἀλλ᾽ ἐνταῦθα μὲν δύνανται **λογίζεσθαι** ὅτι κρεῖττον σὺν πολλοῖς οἰκοῦντα **ἀσφαλῶς τἀρκοῦντα**[175] ἔχειν ἢ μόνον διαιτώμενον τὰ τῶν πολιτῶν **ἐπικινδύνως πάντα κεκτῆσθαι**, ἐπὶ δὲ τῶν ἀδελφῶν τὸ αὐτὸ τοῦτο ἀγνοοῦσι·[176]
>
> 'Tell me, Chaerecrates, surely you aren't one of those who think *that possessions are more useful than a brother*, although they are not endowed with sense and he is, and they need protection whereas he can give it, and, what is more, they are many while he is only one? It is extraordinary, too, that anyone should regard brothers as a *liability* because he doesn't *possess* their property as well as his own, and not regard his fellow citizens as a liability on the same ground. Since in the one case people can *reason* that it is better to have *a secure sufficiency* and live in a group than *to have precarious possession* of all their fellow citizens' *property* and live alone, it is curious that they fail to realize the same fact in the case of their brothers.'[177]

Socrates sums up the reasons why he thinks that valuing χρήματα over brothers is misguided: a brother has sense (is φρόνιμος), is capable of offering help and protection (βοηθεία) and is unique—whereas χρήματα lack these qualities. But not only do some people think that χρήματα have higher utility (χρησιμώτερον) than brothers, brothers are even regarded as a liability, a ζημία. The underlying argument is a zero-sum approach to family property: a brother is a liability

175 Cf. *Oec.* II.1–11.

176 On "use" as the most important relationship to property in Athenian attitudes towards ownership, see Ar. *Rhet.* 1361a; Foxhall (1989), 26; cf. Kränzlein (1963), 31–33, 61.

177 *Mem.* II.iii.1–3.

because anything possessed by the brother goes at the expense of one's own property.[178] This is a shortsighted and inconsistent line of argument, according to Socrates. We do not apply the same zero-sum model to our relations with fellow-citizens, because then we are capable of making the rational calculation (λογίζεσθαι) that there is an added value to living together: it is better to have a sufficient part of the pie with security (ἀσφαλῶς), than to have the whole pie without (ἐπικινδύνως).

In the course of the conversation, Socrates urges Chaerecrates to turn his brother, a liability (ζημία) at present, into an asset, someone he can benefit from. To this end, he introduces the notion of "knowing how to deal with someone":

[Text 22]

> Ἆρ' οὖν, ἔφη ὁ Σωκράτης, ὥσπερ ἵππος τῷ ἀνεπιστήμονι μέν, ἐγχειροῦντι δὲ χρῆσθαι ζημία ἐστίν, οὕτω καὶ ἀδελφός, ὅταν τις αὐτῷ μὴ ἐπιστάμενος ἐγχειρῇ χρῆσθαι, ζημία ἐστί;
>
> 'Well,' said Socrates, 'a horse is a liability to a person who tries to manage it *without having enough knowledge*. Perhaps in the same way a brother is a liability when one tries to manage him *without knowledge*.'[179]

This passage emphatically underscores the indispensability of knowledge in valuing the other; if one does not know how to deal with X, X is a liability, no matter how useful X may be in other situations. Socrates explains to Chaerecrates that knowing how to deal with a brother may at times require that one take the lead in treating the other well. The conversation closes with an analogy between the synergy of limbs and the relationship between brothers: they are designed for mutual benefit (ἐπ' ὠφελείᾳ ἀλλήλοιν).[180]

Hence, just as one has to know how to use something (χρῆσθαι) in order to turn it into wealth (χρήματα), one has to know how to deal (χρῆσθαι) with some person in order to make him more useful (χρησιμώτερος). Being useful is, in turn, paraphrased in terms of being mutually beneficial, an interpretation that logically excludes the possibility of "using the other as a means to your own ends at his expense". If your dealing with the other is grounded in

178 Greek property law puts a strain on relations between brothers. See Cox (1998), chapter 4.

179 *Mem.* II.iii.7.

180 *Mem.* II.iii.18.

genuine knowledge there is no such thing as conflicting interests, because genuine knowledge will point out that happiness and the good are not distributed according to the logic of a zero-sum model.

To wrap up, Socrates' rehabilitation of XPH-terminology occurs in three distinct steps. First of all, Socrates articulates what he regards as the commonly acknowledged "real" meaning of χρῆσθαι and χρήματα: he makes his conversation partners accept as self-evident the observation that the correct use of XPH-terminology should take into account that we are talking about *genuinely useful* things and *real utility*. Although it can be questioned to what extent the etymological connection between χρήματα and χρῆσθαι is really active in the mind of the Athenian language user, it is uncontroversial that the etymological connection *can* be activated and recognized by native speakers of Greek such as Socrates' conversation partners: they are supposed to be susceptible to Socrates' semantic essentialism.

The second step is distinctly Socratic: in redefining "usefulness" and "correct use" Socrates emphasizes the indispensability of knowledge. Use, that is: *correct* use, implies knowledge, the know-how of using X. The third step applies exclusively to cases in which X is a *person*: the only correct way of "using" a person is treating him well and being beneficial to him. In the case of persons, "correct use" becomes a bilateral engagement. This reshaping of the notion of utility and use makes Socratic friendship incompatible with a zero-sum conception of the good. Socrates' use of XPH-terminology does not reflect an "empty" valuation of persons or assets as merely means to independently defined ends; he carefully redefines XPH-terms to invest them with intrinsic meaning and direct them towards what is genuinely good.

Although not made explicit in the use of terminology, Socrates' reaction to Antiphon in T4 appeals to the idea of "proper use" in two ways. First of all, there seems to be a proper use to both physical beauty and wisdom: they can be wealth to their owner if he knows how to use them; but they are worthless for the prostitute and the sophist, who are incapable of proper use. Moreover, bearing in mind the *Oeconomicus*' distinction between use value and exchange value (see Section 1 above), the implicit suggestion may be that just as the flute is only sold for money if one does not know how to use it oneself, one only sells wisdom if one does not know how to use it oneself.

Both the insight that money is not always the same as wealth and that friends can be wealth too are clearly premised on Socrates' redefinition of χρήματα. Therefore, the conceptualization of friends as χρήματα should not be understood as incorporating the phenomenon of friendship in a commercial discourse, or of diverting and abusing the goods of the long-term order (friendship) for short-term individual gain. Rather, both friends and material wealth are redefined and framed in Socrates' ideal of estate management based on knowledge—an ideal grounded in a long-term conception of benefit and virtue.[181]

3 False Friends, Part Two: Economics, Ancient and Modern

On a small scale, this manipulation of terminology demonstrates Socrates' reform of a commercial paradigm towards a positive model for understanding interpersonal relationships: the central component of this model is genuine and thorough knowledge of how to deal with the other—the other being a person as opposed to a mere instrument.

Working with ancient normative discourse always involves this conceptual two-step: (1) we need to start from a pervasive awareness of the false friends that cover up the divergences between ancient and modern worldviews and (2) we need to account for the fact that authors such as Xenophon and Aristotle are themselves actively invested with re-defining and reforming contemporary discourse. This goes for XPH-terminology, with its deceptive congeniality with modern notions of utility, need and use. Moreover, it goes for the very term οἰκονομικός—a distant ancestor, and a false friend, of "economist".

3.1 *Banking on φίλοι: Estate Management*

Let us look back to the final sentence of the Diodorus episode:

[Text 23 = Text 7]

> οἱ μέντοι ἀγαθοὶ οἰκονόμοι, ὅταν τὸ πολλοῦ ἄξιον μικροῦ ἐξῇ πρίασθαι, τότε φασὶ δεῖν ὠνεῖσθαι· νῦν δὲ διὰ τὰ πράγματα εὐωνοτάτους ἔστι φίλους ἀγαθοὺς κτήσασθαι.
>
> Now, *good estate-managers* say that when you can purchase something valuable at a low price, you ought to buy it; and at the present time, owing to circumstances, it is possible to acquire good friends very reasonably.[182]

---

181 The distinction between short- and long-term goods does not stipulate anything as to the precise identity or substance of this good and the vexed question whether to Xenophon virtue and the good are in the end instrumental in nature. For this discussion, see Danzig (2018).

182 *Mem.* II.x.4.

Does this piece of Socratic wisdom, that strikes us as calculating, indeed imply a commercial framing of the acquisition of Hermogenes as a friend? Remarkably, this line of reasoning in the Hermogenes episode is the exact opposite of the so-called Banker's Paradox according to which people who need money most desperately are the least likely to receive a loan, because they are the poorest credit risks:

[Text 24]

> Bankers have a limited amount of money, and must choose who to invest it in. Each choice is a gamble: taken together, they must ultimately yield a net profit, or the banker will go out of business. This set of incentives leads to a common complaint about the banking system: that bankers will only loan money to individuals who do not need it. The harsh irony of the Banker's Paradox is this: just when individuals need money most desperately, they are also the poorest credit risks and, therefore, the least likely to be selected to receive a loan.[183]

Here is where Socratic and modern conceptions of economics most manifestly diverge: where the prototypical banker sees a credit risk, the Socratic οἰκόνομος looks upon a deprived acquaintance as a good investment. The Socratic estate manager is not a banker. So who is this οἰκόνομος and what does his economics look like?

As one would expect in a Socratic context, the οἰκόνομος is defined by his expert skill (τέχνη) and by the function (ἔργον) of his field of expertise.[184] Critoboulus' first attempt at a definition is somewhat tautological: a good οἰκόνομος "manages his own estate well" (εὖ οἰκεῖν τὸν ἑαυτοῦ οἶκον).[185] When Socrates asks if estate-management is a skill that can be performed for pay on someone else's estate (or conversely: if estate-management can be outsourced), Critoboulus comes up with a more substantial description of οἰκονομία:

[Text 25]

> Νὴ Δία καὶ πολύν γε μισθόν, ἔφη ὁ Κριτόβουλος, φέροιτ' ἄν, εἰ δύναιτο οἶκον παραλαβὼν τελεῖν τε ὅσα δεῖ καὶ περιουσίαν ποιῶν αὔξειν τὸν οἶκον.

183 Tooby & Cosmides (1996), 131.
184 *Oec.* 1.2–3.
185 *Oec.* 1.3.

> "Yes, indeed," said Critobulus. "He could earn a great deal of money, if he were able to take over an estate, *pay all necessary expenses and increase the estate by providing a surplus*."[186]

A good estate-manager (or at least: an estate-management who is appreciated by his patron and rewarded with a generous μισθός) is one who manages to pay the bills and to create a surplus (περιουσία), the necessary condition for increase of the estate. This is the most fundamental premise that defines Critoboulus' attitude towards the occupation that he will soon take up: the end of οἰκονομία is growth (αὔξειν)—and as such, this premise has led commentators to infer that "the thrust of much of the *Oeconomicus* is to apply purposive, opportunizing behavior to increase the *oikos*"[187] and that "[a]ccording to the *Oeconomicus*, profit is the chief goal of estate management".[188]

It is true that Socrates refrains from directly challenging Critoboulus' presupposition. However, the conversation on the subjective nature of χρήματα (value always bears reference to the abilities of the owner)[189] prepares for a second Socratic hobbyhorse: the relativity of wealth. When Critoboulus tries to direct the conversation to the topic of increasing his estate in Xenophon's *Oeconomicus*, he jokingly asks Socrates whether he believes that they are rich enough already (ἱκανῶς πλουτεῖν):

[Text 26]

> Ὁ οὖν Κριτόβουλος ἐκ τούτων ὧδέ πως εἶπεν· Ἀλλὰ περὶ μὲν τῶν τοιούτων ἀρκούντως πάνυ μοι δοκῶ τὰ λεγόμενα ὑπὸ σοῦ ἀκηκοέναι· αὐτὸς δ' ἐμαυτὸν ἐξετάζων δοκῶ μοι εὑρίσκειν ἐπιεικῶς τῶν τοιούτων ἐγκρατῆ ὄντα, ὥστ' εἴ μοι συμβουλεύοις ὅ τι ἂν ποιῶν αὔξοιμι τὸν οἶκον, οὐκ ἄν μοι δοκῶ ὑπό γε τούτων ὧν σὺ δεσποινῶν καλεῖς κωλύεσθαι· ἀλλὰ θαρρῶν συμβούλευε ὅ τι ἔχεις ἀγαθόν· ἢ κατέγνωκας ἡμῶν, ὦ Σώκρατες, ἱκανῶς πλουτεῖν καὶ οὐδὲν δοκοῦμέν σοι προσδεῖσθαι χρημάτων;
>
> Next, Critobulus spoke somewhat as follows: "I don't think you need to tell me any more about them: when I examine myself, I think I find that my control over them is adequate. So if you were to advise me *how to increase my estate*, I don't think it could be these mistresses, as you call them, who

186 *Oec.* 1.4.
187 Figueira (2012), 677.
188 Pomeroy (1994), 52.
189 Sections 2.4 and 2.6 above.

> would prevent me from doing it. So don't hesitate to give me all the good advice you have. *Or have you decided, Socrates, that we are rich enough and don't need further assets*?"[190]

Critoboulus' impatience reveals his failure to grasp the gist of Socrates' warning sermon immediately prior to this passage: a good estate-management needs to be wary of the "mistresses" that enslave the soul by alluring her in the guise of pleasure (ἡδονή) and that force the estate-manager to squander the fruits of his labor by instilling insatiable desires in him.[191] The message is hard to miss: the estate manager's success depends not only on his capacity to increase production, but all the more so on his ability to limit, or at least control, consumption—a point lightheartedly brushed aside by Critoboulus who presses Socrates to come up with advice more relevant to his endeavors. Hence his rhetorical question: does Socrates think that they are rich enough (ἱκανῶς πλουτεῖν) and that they do not have an additional need (προσδεῖσθαι) for assets (χρήματα)?

Socrates takes the question at face value and provocatively takes up the notion of "need" (προδεῖσθαι) brought up by Critoboulus:

[Text 27]

> Οὔκουν ἔγωγε, ἔφη ὁ Σωκράτης, εἰ καὶ περὶ ἐμοῦ λέγεις, οὐδέν μοι δοκῶ προσδεῖσθαι χρημάτων, ἀλλ' ἱκανῶς πλουτεῖν· σὺ μέντοι, ὦ Κριτόβουλε, πάνυ μοι δοκεῖς πένεσθαι, καὶ ναὶ μὰ Δί' ἔστιν ὅτε καὶ πάνυ οἰκτίρω σε ἐγώ.
>
> "If you're including me," said Socrates, "No, I *don't think I need any further assets*: I'm *rich enough*. But I think that *you are very hard up*, Critobulus, and indeed there are times when I feel very sorry for you."[192]

Socrates, with his humble possessions, claims to be wealthier than Critoboulus with his vast fortune, for he has no further need (προσδεῖσθαι) and thinks he is rich enough (ἱκανῶς πλουτεῖν). This is an outright provocation to Critoboulus who challenges Socrates to calculate the monetary worth of his property (i.e. to establish how much it will yield after a sale, πωλούμενα),[193] momentarily forgetting the limited value of money as a standard for wealth. Not so long ago,

---

190 *Oec.* II.1.

191 *Oec.* I.19–23.

192 *Oec.* II.2.

193 *Oec.* II.3.

Critoboulus had agreed to Socrates' subjective definition of value that stipulated not only that money is only an asset for one who knows how to use it correctly, but also that selling something indicates that the owner lacks knowledge of its proper use.[194]

Critoboulus' thought experiment points out that in terms of monetary worth, Critoboulus' owns property one hundred times more valuable than Socrates'.[195] Still, to Socrates, Critoboulus' lifestyle renders him poor (πένεσθαι) whereas he himself is wealthy: a rich aristocrat's life comes with expensive habits and expectations—with many needs in short—whereas Socrates' needs and desires are limited. Wealth is relative to need. And if wealth is the total of things that are useful for satisfying one's needs, it is by implication finite. This finite notion of wealth and need presupposes a conceptual distinction between the objective requirements of a good life ("needs" in modern terminology), which are finite in quantity, and desires that are psychologically defined ("wants", i.e. "things that I want")[196] and infinitely expandable.

The definition of πλοῦτος and πενία as relative to what one needs ([προσ]δεῖσθαι) is a theme that recurs in other texts from the Socratic circle as well. In Plato's oeuvre too we see poverty psychologically defined in terms of an insatiability wants,[197] that is rooted in the lowest part of the soul, that is "most insatiate by nature of wealth".[198] In the context of Xenophon's *Oeconomicus*, we see how Socrates' finite conception of wealth flies in the face of Critoboulus' axiomatic notion of growth (increasing the estate is an objective of estate-management). The objective of growth, so fundamental to Critoboulus' belief

194 *Oec.* 1.10–12. Section 2.4 above.

195 5 minae makes Socrates a member of the property class of thetes. Pomeroy (1994), ad loc.

196 Skidelsky (2012: 25–26). προσδεῖσθαι (and in general cognates of δεῖ) tends to refer to external objective constraints or causal necessity as opposed to XPH-terminology that refers to "subjective, internally based needs, requirements, and constraints." Mourelatos (1970: 652).

197 Pl. *Leg.* 5.736e. Furthermore, Plato's notion that unlimited acquisition should be prevented (*Leg.* 5.736e, 5.741e) presupposes a conception of wealth that is limited, and hence also an implicit distinction between needs and wants.

198 Cf. the notion of happiness as absence of wants: according to Socrates, those who want nothing (οἱ μηδενὸς δεόμενοι) are happy (Pl. *Gorg.* 492e)—a position that Callicles, overtly attaching a positive value to appetitive needs, reacts to with disgust. Socrates attempts to make Callicles choose a life that is contented with what it happens to have (493c: τὸν κοσμίως καὶ τοῖς παροῦσιν ἱκανῶς καὶ ἐξαρκούντως ἔχοντα βίον) over one of insatiate licentiousness (493c: ἀντὶ τοῦ ἀπλήστως καὶ ἀκολάστως ἔχοντος), and compares the soul to a leaking jar (493b–d, 493e–494a)—clearly locating insatiability, and hence poverty, in the soul. See also Xen. *Mem.* 1.vi; cf. Chernyakhovskaya (2018).

system, is never wholeheartedly endorsed by Socrates in the *Oeconomicus*.[199] Worse still: it is fundamentally compromised by Socrates' take on wealth as subjective and relative—but the point is lost on Critoboulus who refuses to see its implications and perseveres in his quest of knowledge that can help him increase his estate.[200]

Meanwhile, Socrates points out an additional difference between Critoboulus' lifestyle and his own:

[Text 28]

> καὶ ἐμοὶ μέν, εἴ τι καὶ προσδεηθείην, οἶδ' ὅτι καὶ σὺ γιγνώσκεις ὡς εἰσὶν οἳ καὶ ἐπαρκέσειαν ἂν ὥστε πάνυ μικρὰ πορίσαντες κατακλύσειαν ἂν ἀφθονίᾳ τὴν ἐμὴν δίαιταν· οἱ δὲ σοὶ φίλοι πολὺ ἀρκοῦντα σοῦ μᾶλλον ἔχοντες τῇ ἑαυτῶν κατασκευῇ ἢ σὺ τῇ σῇ ὅμως ὡς παρὰ σοῦ ὠφελησόμενοι ἀποβλέπουσι.
>
> Now, if *I* needed something, you know as well as I do that there are people who would help me out and whose contributions would not have to be at all large to overwhelm me with more than I need to live. Your friends however, although they have enough for their own situations and are therefore far better off than you, since you do not have enough, still look to you for your help![201]

The difference is in the moral quality of their friends (φίλοι): Critoboulus' friends only cost him money, whereas Socrates can be confident that should he be in dire need, he will not have a lack of friends to help him out.[202]

---

199 It has been pointed out (e.g. Perrotta 2004) that Socrates' idea that wealth is a finite concept contradicts Xenophon's famous statement in *De Vectigalibus* IV.7 about the insatiable desire for silver. The tension is only apparent, as Xenophon merely makes an observation about the psychological effects of money without evaluating these; the tenet seems in line with Aristotle's claim that there is no natural limit to the amount of money or silver that people wish to acquire (Ar. *Pol.* 1). See also Figueira (2012, 681).

200 I follow Danzig (2003; rev. 2010) in attempting to read the *Oeconomicus* not so much as either a simple book of prescriptions or an "ironic" negation of these prescriptions, but rather as a polyphonous dialogue that aims to *problematize* (as opposed to prescribe). On the topic of irony, cf. Strauss (1972); see also Stevens (1994) for an interesting ironic reading of the *Oeconomicus*. See also Dorion (2008a) on the vexed problem of the relation between Socrates' philosophy and Ischomachus' ideas.

201 *Oec.* II.8.

202 Cf. *Hiero* IV.6–10; *Mem.* IV.ii.37, I.vi.1–10. Cf. the wealth contest between Cyrus and Croesus in *Cyr.* VIII.2.16–19 (Von Reden (1995: 87): "an experiment which proved the effect of gift-giving") in the context of their conversation about the good life (*Cyr.* VIII.ii). The idea is

This take on the quality of friends casts a different light on the Diodorus-episode (T7 & 23), where Socrates urged his friend to reach out to Hermogenes by holding out the prospect of the return of benefit: a good estate-manager knows that one should invest when the price is low. Was Socrates really committing the social crime of reductionism, of conflating two categorically distinct forms of interaction (friendship and market transactions)? I propose to integrate the episode into Socrates' reform of the idiom of estate management as we know it from Xenophon's *Oeconomicus*. Although the οἰκόνομος engages in monetary transactions, he does so on different grounds and in a different manner than our stereotypical modern banker does, with a different objective and with a different state of mind and soul. Using money to help a friend is an outstanding example of proper use—both of money and of friends.

3.2 *Bad Friends, or: The Importance of Being ἐγκρατής*

Modern economics attempts to describe relations between persons and things, with individuals only as allocating forces. Socratic economics pertains to relationships between *persons*. In such economics, the risk of an investment is not measured in terms of a person's material wealth, but in terms of the person's moral quality. We have seen that the point that Socrates makes in the Diodorus episode is that one should not dismiss potential friends for their short-term "value", but rather should attempt to envision long-term interests.[203] The metaphor that illustrates this point does not evoke a "commercial discourse", but rather, more specifically, the paradigm of estate management. But what exactly does it mean to be "*like* a good estate manager" in friendship?

Let us first look at how *not* to be a φίλος, according to Socrates. In his conversation with young Critoboulus in *Mem.* II.vi, a dialogue on the selection and acquisition of φίλοι,[204] Socrates sketches a pathology of bad friends. The best way of testing (δοκιμάζειν)[205] whether a potential φίλος is worth acquiring (ἄξιος

---

that μισθός, typically belonging to the short-term conception of resources and wealth that Croesus embodies, does not guarantee loyalty in guardians.

203 Gigon (1953), 122.

204 As commentators like to point out, in *Mem.* II.vi the theme of φιλία appears as a euphemism for more overtly erotic vocabulary. As I argue in Chapter Six, the terminology of φιλία indeed serves as a euphemism *for Critoboulus*; by contrast, Socrates is interested in universal and general rules of conduct that apply to all kinds of φιλία-relationships, including those with an erotic interst without being confined to them. For the discussion here, the erotic innuendos are irrelevant.

205 For the metaphor/idea that friends can best be tested by their behavior, cf. Chapter One n. 257. On δοκιμάζειν as monetary metaphor, see Hangard (1963).

κτᾶσθαι) is to look at his past behavior towards his φίλοι.[206] Some character types can be immediately dismissed as inherently unfit:[207]

(i) someone overpowered by his appetites, for not being able to do what he should either for himself or for a friend;[208]

(ii) the spendthrift who is not self-sufficient, because he will always be in need, getting favors from others without ever being *capable* of returning them, whereas getting resentful of the one who does not give;[209]

(iii) the businessman (who does have wealth), whose desire for money makes him drive a hard bargain and causes him to be *unwilling* to return favors;[210]

(iv) the fanatical businessman who only has leisure for the pursuit of gain;[211]

(v) the quarrelsome person who brings a host of enemies along for his friends;[212]

(vi) someone who receives good treatment while *not considering* return.[213]

By picturing types of *defective* reciprocity, three of these six caricatures (ii, iii, vi) evoke, by implication, the rule of reciprocating favors received (λαμβάνων ἀποδιδόναι): the bad friend being unwilling, incapable or unthoughtful of returning a favor. Nos. (i) and (iv) too can be understood as addressing the issue of discharging reciprocal obligations. In case of the first character type, the underlying idea seems to be that someone dominated by his appetites will not be able to meet obligation (τὰ δέοντα πράττειν) because a sense of obligation requires the ability to suspend the immediate fulfillment of appetites and to overrule one's desires. This presupposes an understanding of these obligations as going beyond immediate fulfillment of appetites, which is at least coherent with imperatives of benefiting someone and returning benefits received.

---

206 *Mem.* II.vi.1.

207 Cf. *Mem.* II.vi.19 for a recapitulation of the inventory of vices in φιλία: πῶς γὰρ ἂν ἢ ἀχάριστοι ἢ ἀμελεῖς ἢ πλεονέκται ἢ ἄπιστοι ἢ ἀκρατεῖς ἄνθρωποι δύναιντο φίλοι γενέσθαι;

208 *Mem.* II.vi.1: ἆρα πρῶτον μὲν ζητητέον, ὅστις ἄρχει γαστρός τε καὶ φιλοποσίας καὶ λαγνείας καὶ ὕπνου καὶ ἀργίας; ὁ γὰρ ὑπὸ τούτων κρατούμενος οὔτ' αὐτὸς ἑαυτῷ δύναιτ' ἂν οὔτε φίλῳ τὰ δέοντα πράττειν.

209 *Mem.* II.vi.2: ὅστις δαπανηρὸς ὢν μὴ αὐτάρκης ἐστίν, ἀλλ' ἀεὶ τῶν πλησίον δεῖται, καὶ λαμβάνων μὲν μὴ δύναται ἀποδιδόναι, μὴ λαμβάνων δὲ τὸν μὴ διδόντα μισεῖ, οὐ δοκεῖ σοι καὶ οὗτος χαλεπὸς φίλος εἶναι;

210 *Mem.* II.vi.3: ὅστις χρηματίζεσθαι μὲν δύναται, πολλῶν δὲ χρημάτων ἐπιθυμεῖ, καὶ διὰ τοῦτο δυσσύμβολός ἐστι, καὶ λαμβάνων μὲν ἥδεται, ἀποδιδόναι δὲ μὴ βούλεται;

211 *Mem.* II.vi.4: ὅστις διὰ τὸν ἔρωτα τοῦ χρηματίζεσθαι μηδὲ πρὸς ἓν ἄλλο σχολὴν ποιεῖται ἢ ὁπόθεν αὐτός τι κερδανεῖ;

212 *Mem.* II.vi.4: ὅστις στασιώδης τέ ἐστι καὶ θέλων πολλοὺς τοῖς φίλοις ἐχθροὺς παρέχειν;

213 *Mem.* II.vi.4–5: Εἰ δέ τις τούτων μὲν τῶν κακῶν μηδὲν ἔχοι, εὖ δὲ πάσχων ἀνέχεται, μηδὲν φροντίζων τοῦ ἀντευεργετεῖν;

Similarly, the fanatical businessman of (iv), whose priorities are only with the pursuit of gain (κερδανεῖ), is not likely to be concerned about returning goods received. The crucial point seems to be that friendship is too time-consuming and costly to seem rewarding to someone ruled by the short-sightedness of short-term gain.

Types (i) and (ii) are reminiscent of Socrates' discussion of Slavery of the Soul,[214] where two types of "mistresses" (δέσποιναι) are distinguished: those appetites and vices that keep the enslaved οἰκόνομος from doing what he should (cf. type (i) bad friend),[215] and those appetites and vices that perpetuate the estate manager's neediness by driving him to squander the fruits of his labor (cf. type (ii) bad friend).[216] More in general, we could say that bad friends are typically inhabitants of a world ruled by short-term transactions. These character types are incapable of envisioning the long-term perspective needed to be able or willing to perform the reciprocal exchanges that constitute friendship. In a world ruled by appetites directed at short-term "goods", only immediate gain can be conceived as a good. Gratitude, generosity, favors, and gifts cannot exist in such a world, because of the time span they presuppose. In contrast, the good friend is characterized by virtues that somehow pertain to the suspension of immediate gratification of short-term needs: a good friend is continent (ἐγκρατής).[217]

Both φιλία and the art of estate-management revolve around the realization of long-term goods. Key to the dialectics of the long-term is ἐγκράτεια, self-mastery, controlling the impulses of appetites that demand satisfaction in the short run, but that pose a threat to the pursuit of these long-term goods.[218] Together with the concepts of καρτερία (physical endurance) and αὐτάρκεια (self-sufficiency), ἐγκράτεια forms the core of Socratic ethics in the *Memorabilia*.[219] It constitutes the precondition for the development of virtue in an individual,[220] as virtue is the result of practice (ἄσκησις)[221] and requires a complete mastery of body and soul.[222]

---

214 *Oec.* I.17–23.

215 *Oec.* I.19–20.

216 *Oec.* I.22.

217 *Mem.* II.vi.5.

218 *Mem.* I.ii.14, I.iii.5–14, I.v.1, I.v.6, I.vi.8, II.i, III.xiv, IV.v.9, IV.viii.11.

219 Dorion (2006). See however the Edmunds (2018) for an argument that there is no such "triad": ἐγκράτεια is primary; καρτερία overlaps somewhat in meaning with ἐγκράτεια whereas αὐτάρκεια if of a different order.

220 *Mem.* I.v.4–5.

221 *Mem.* I.ii.19–23, II.i.20, II.i.28, II.vi.39, III.iii.6, III.v.14, III.ix.1–3.

222 *See* Dorion (2006) for an overview of the functions of ἐγκράτεια in Socrates' moral philosophy in the *Memorabilia*.

As such, ἐγκράτεια is the prerequisite for anyone who aspires to become successful, virtuous and beneficent in life: in productive life as an estate manager, in politics as a citizen qualified to rule for the common good and capable of serving public interest, in personal life as a member of an οἶκος—and as a friend. ἐγκράτεια is the first precondition to initiating and cultivating relationships that are genuinely beneficial to both partners—long-term relationships that are impossible in a world that revolves around short-term needs and appetites.[223]

The practice of estate management provides both the *arena* in which virtues and other long-term goods can be realized (including the proper treatment of friends) and a *model* for behavior that successfully integrates an understanding of the long term good. The proper care of an estate always takes into account the long-term perspective, the paradigm-case being land cultivation, i.e. tilling soil and taking care of crops and trees that will eventually yield fruit:

[Text 29]

> ἀλλ' ὅμως ἔνιοι δένδρα μὲν πειρῶνται θεραπεύειν τοῦ καρποῦ ἕνεκεν, τοῦ δὲ παμφορωτάτου κτήματος, ὃ καλεῖται φίλος, ἀργῶς καὶ ἀνειμένως οἱ πλεῖστοι ἐπιμέλονται.
>
> Nevertheless, while some strive to cultivate a tree for its fruit, most bestow but an idle and listless care on their most fruitful possession, the name of which is 'friend.'[224]

Here Socrates explicitly compares the cultivation (θεραπεύειν, the *care*) that people, motivated by the prospect of its yield (τοῦ καρποῦ ἕνεκεν), tend to invest in trees with the paradoxically indolent and slack care (ἀργῶς καὶ ἀνειμένως ἐπιμέλονται) they exhibit towards a friend, their "all-productive possession *pur sang*" (τοῦ παμφορωτάτου κτήματος).[225] The tenor of the comparison is apparent: both fruit cultivation and friendship require looking beyond short-term effects and aim at the realization of long-term goods. The same goes for farmland that allows for different uses:

---

223 The intricate connection between ἐγκράτεια and φιλία is most evident in *Mem.* II.vi.1–6. Cf. Pl. *Gorgias* where φιλία is a natural limit to πλεονεξία: friendship contains in itself a tendency to limit appetite. Cf. Duncan (1974).

224 *Mem.* II.iv.7.

225 The adjective πάμφορος ("all-bearing", "all-productive") is typically used for land (χώρη, e.g. Hdt. 7.8.α; γαῖα: Aeschyl. *Pers.* 618).

[Text 30]

> καὶ γὰρ δὴ δοκεῖ μοι ὁ μὲν τῷ εἴδει τὸν νοῦν προσέχων μεμισθωμένῳ χῶρον ἐοικέναι. οὐ γὰρ ὅπως πλείονος ἄξιος γένηται ἐπιμελεῖται, ἀλλ' ὅπως αὐτὸς ὅτι πλεῖστα ὡραῖα καρπώσεται. ὁ δὲ τῆς φιλίας ἐφιέμενος μᾶλλον ἔοικε τῷ τὸν οἰκεῖον ἀγρὸν κεκτημένῳ· πάντοθεν γοῦν φέρων ὅ τι ἂν δύνηται πλείονος ἄξιον ποιεῖ τὸν ἐρώμενον.
>
> I think that the man who pays attention to looks is like a tenant farmer: he's not concerned to make the land worth more, but just to get himself as handsome a profit from it as he can. The man seeking friendship is by contrast like the farmer who owns his land: he brings his beloved whatever he can from every source, and so improves his quality.[226]

Farmland and lovers can be used for short-term exploitation (ὅπως αὐτὸς ὅτι πλεῖστα ὡραῖα καρπώσεται), as land on lease and rent boys, only to be left to lie fallow, waste and out of crop afterwards, barren of any value.[227] Or they can be used properly, i.e. treated with respect, as a proper farm of friend, so that their value increases (πλείονος ἄξιον ποιεῖ).[228]

Similarly, the programmatic choice between Virtue and Vice in Prodicus'[229] myth of Heracles, revolves around the toil and effort that long-term goods require as opposed to the lures of short-term gratification. Against Vice's promise of a life without toil,[230] stands the truth of Virtue that the gods give nothing without toil and effort:[231]

---

226 *Symp.* VIII.25; *transl.* Bowen (1998).

227 ὡραῖα (ripe fruits) is also a pun on ὡραῖος ("in youthful bloom"). Cf. Huss (1999).

228 On the apparent body and soul contrast in this passage, see Chapter Six. Cf. Hindley (2010) [1999], 90–91 on *Mem.* II.vi.22: "The point is, once again, self-restraint, not abstinence." Cf. Pentasugglio (2018).

229 Xenophon characterization of Prodicus, and of his relation with Socrates, stands out as remarkably sympathetic: Prodicus' moral theory is congenial to Socrates' views and is quoted by Socrates as authoratitative. Plato's representation of Prodicus is more hostile: for instance, his portrayal of Prodicus lying on a bed in the house of Callias, covered with soft blankets and surrounded by attractive boys, (Pl. *Prot.* 317d10–e2), seems to allude to the Life of Vice, denounced in Prodicus' own myth. For the unique status of Prodicus among the sophists in the Socratic authors, see Corey (2015), 69–95. Cf. Mayhew (2011).

230 *Mem.* II.i.25.

231 Virtue lives up to Socrates' prescriptions of φιλία, as she emphatically tells Heracles that she has been observing his qualities for a long time. Where Vice prostitutes herself, Virtue carefully embeds her promises to Heracles in a long-term relationship: she knows his parents and his qualities. *Mem.* II.i.27.

[Text 31]

> τῶν γὰρ ὄντων ἀγαθῶν καὶ καλῶν οὐδὲν ἄνευ πόνου καὶ ἐπιμελείας θεοὶ διδόασιν ἀνθρώποις, ἀλλ᾽ εἴτε τοὺς θεοὺς ἵλεως εἶναί σοι βούλει, θεραπευτέον τοὺς θεούς, εἴτε ὑπὸ φίλων ἐθέλεις ἀγαπᾶσθαι, τοὺς φίλους εὐεργετητέον, εἴτε ὑπό τινος πόλεως ἐπιθυμεῖς τιμᾶσθαι, τὴν πόλιν ὠφελητέον, εἴτε ὑπὸ τῆς Ἑλλάδος πάσης ἀξιοῖς ἐπ᾽ ἀρετῇ θαυμάζεσθαι, τὴν Ἑλλάδα πειρατέον εὖ ποιεῖν, εἴτε γῆν βούλει σοι καρποὺς ἀφθόνους φέρειν, τὴν γῆν θεραπευτέον, εἴτε ἀπὸ βοσκημάτων οἴει δεῖν πλουτίζεσθαι, τῶν βοσκημάτων ἐπιμελητέον, εἴτε διὰ πολέμου ὁρμᾷς αὔξεσθαι καὶ βούλει δύνασθαι τούς τε φίλους ἐλευθεροῦν καὶ τοὺς ἐχθροὺς χειροῦσθαι, τὰς πολεμικὰς τέχνας αὐτάς τε παρὰ τῶν ἐπισταμένων μαθητέον καὶ ὅπως αὐταῖς δεῖ χρῆσθαι ἀσκητέον· εἰ δὲ καὶ τῷ σώματι βούλει δυνατὸς εἶναι, τῇ γνώμῃ ὑπηρετεῖν ἐθιστέον τὸ σῶμα καὶ γυμναστέον σὺν πόνοις καὶ ἱδρῶτι.
>
> 'Nothing that is really good and admirable is granted by the gods to men without some effort and application. If you want the gods to be gracious to you, you must worship the gods; *if you wish to be appreciated by your friends, you must be kind to your friends*; if you desire to be honored by a State, you must help that State; if you expect to be admired for you fine qualities by the whole of Greece, you must try to benefit Greece; *if you want your land to produce abundant crops, you must look after your land*; if you expect to gain wealth from your livestock, you must take care of your livestock; if you have an impulse to extend your influence by war, and want to be able to free your friends and subdue your enemies, you must both learn the actual arts of war from those who understand them, and practice the proper way of applying them; and if you want to be physically efficient, you must train your body to be subject to your reason, and develop it with hard work and sweat.'[232]

Real happiness and self-fulfillment consist in αὐτάρκεια that results from self-restraint (ἐγκράτεια) and endurance (καρτερία),[233] the foundational principles of all virtues. Instead of making appealing promises of short-term gratification,

---

232 *Mem.* II.i.28; *transl. adapt.*

233 Cf. O'Connor (1994), 159–163. Socrates' re-telling of Prodicus' myth is aimed at a distorted understanding of Socratic self-sufficiency on Aristippus' part: Aristippus professes to be a hedonist, who refrains from taking part in public life and being part of a community, i.e. investing in interpersonal relationships. See O'Connor (1994) for Socratic self-sufficiency and its distorted versions of Socrates' followers.

Virtue tells Heracles the truth that the gods give nothing without toil (πόνος) and effort (ἐπιμελεία). If you want to be appreciated by your friends, you need to benefit them; if you want your land to yield a bounty of fruit, you should cultivate it.

Virtue's "rhetoric of πόνος"[234] is part of Socrates' moral-philosophical ideology that runs through the whole of the *Memorabilia.* It is an ideology of voluntary endurance of deprivations and self-imposed toil—an ideology that defines genuine benefit as grounded in an understanding of and an investment in long-term goods and a cultivation of the self, and that opposes the appeals of short-term self-indulging gratification that in the long run corrupts body, soul and one's interpersonal relationships.

To Xenophon's Socrates, the salient opposition is therefore not so much between disembedded monetary exchanges and a sharing economy embedded in ties of φιλία, nor between the instrumental pursuit of self-interest and other-regarding behavior. Rather, to Socrates, the more fundamental opposition is between two outlooks on life: between a life driven by a short-term cycle of instant gratification and short-lived interactions on the one hand and a life oriented to the long-term good, to one's genuine interests. Although money and monetary exchanges are easily subsumed into the short-term cycle and hence lend themselves to use for the wrong ends, they are not pernicious in and by themselves: money *can* be used for good ends.

The estate manager, the οἰκόνομος, is the model inhabitant of Xenophon's moral order, displaying a deep understanding of this order and a keen eye on the long-term perspective. At the other end of the scale we find the prostitute, the sophist, and the businessman: the flashy drives on the fast lane who display opportunistic and exploitative behavior, because, having condemned themselves to a life driven by the impulses of the moment, they are incapable of taking in the long-term perspective. Our easygoing Antiphon

---

234 Johnstone (1994). Cf. a fragment scribed attributed to the followers of Anniceris (fr. 234 Mannebach = DL 2.97): τόν τε φίλον μὴ διὰ τὰς χρείας μόνον ἀποδέχεσθαι ὧν ὑπολειπουσῶν μὴ ἐπιστρέφεσθαι, ἀλλὰ καὶ παρὰ τὴν γεγονυῖαν εὔνοιαν, ἧς ἕνεκα καὶ πόνους ὑπομενεῖν. καίτοι τιθέμενον ἡδονὴν τέλος καὶ ἀχθόμενον ἐπὶ τῷ στέρεσθαι αὐτῆς ὅμως ἑκουσίως ὑπομενεῖν διὰ τὴν πρὸς τὸν φίλον στοργήν.

"A friend should be cherished not merely for his utility—for, if that fails, we should then no longer associate with him—but for the good feeling for the sake of which we shall even endure hardships. Nay, though we make pleasure the end and are annoyed when deprived of it, we shall nevertheless cheerfully endure this because of our love to our friend." (*transl.* Hicks).

On the political dimension of the valorization of πόνος, see Tamiolaki (2014), 4§16.

(T3) is characterized as an inhabitant of this world, guided by the short-sightedness of blind appetites and short-term needs, with no clear view of long-term interests, because his understanding of value is not grounded in knowledge.[235]

4 Education and the Logic of Wage-Earning

The sophist who teaches for pay operates on a misguided understanding of the teacher-student relationship. However, the central concept of ἐγκράτεια suggests that there is more at stake in Socrates' refusal to accept pay than this formal objection alone: a more substantive objection that charging fee is incompatible with the very subject matter of teaching virtue.

4.1 *Xenophon's Dual Economics*

Throughout Xenophon's oeuvre runs the idea that interacting with others with the mediation of pay (μισθός) yields a distinct type of relationship with a dynamics of its own:

- There is a tension between the logic of wage-earning and trust: paying guardians μισθός does not optimally guarantee loyalty in them; giving gifts[236] to friends is more effective because it renders them more reliable (πιστοτέροι) and prone to reciprocate.[237]
- Offering compensation by sale or wage discharges all parties from further obligations to one another; χάρις-exchanges and benefactions incite positive emotions in the recipients and make them be of service permanently.[238] χάρις-exchanges are a more effective model for forging, maintaining, and legitimating a position of superiority.[239]

235 In *Mem.* I.vi.3 Antiphon proclaims that the mere possession of money is a pleasure in itself. This of course contrasts with Socrates' approach that it all depends on how we use money.

236 E.g. Xen. *Cyr.* VIII.ii.17: δῶρα.

237 For the Croesus episode as a literary reaction on Herodotus' representation of the encounter between Croesus and Cyrus, see: Lefèvre (1971); Gray (2011: 151, 170 ff.).

238 E.g. Xen. *Ag.* IV.iv.1: doing free favors is preferable over taking payment for services, because gratuitous (προῖκα) favors presuppose trust (προεπιστεύθησαν) and hence breeds structural (ἀεί) gratitude (it is a παρακαταθήκη χάριτος, a deposit of χάρις) that the recipient is happy to reciprocate (ἡδέως ὑπηρετοῦσι).

239 On this mechanism, see also Azoulay (2004), a thorough study about the role of χάρις in

- Accepting μισθός implies acting out of compulsion; actions performed out of compulsions cannot be qualified as acts of χάρις and do not deserve to be reciprocated with χάρις.[240]

χάρις and εὐεργεσία, phenomena premised on an understanding of a long-term moral order, are systematically contrasted with μισθός, a transaction mode that belong to a short-term system of immediate compensation and gratification. Not only are χάρις and εὐεργεσία morally superior—as methods of governance they are also far more successful than coercion.

The opposition recurs in Xenophon's Socratic work where we find continuity between the characterization of the ideal leader and the portrayal of Socrates, who is prone to maintain "his position at the head of the benefaction chain".[241] In Xenophon's *Apology*, for instance, Socrates defends his refusal to accept money for teaching, emphasizing that he is indebted to nobody (χάριτας ὀφείλειν).[242] Moreover, we find that the incompatibility of μισθός with long-term relations shaped by χάρις and πίστις is made philosophically productive. Long-term moral economics not only constitutes a precondition for the transmission of wisdom and virtue; it **constitutes** its very substance.

Socrates typically associates this moral short-sightedness with the phenomenon of "money"; a telling example can be found in a passage that bears many similarities to the Antiphon episode:

Xenophon as a political tool that establishes moral relationships of indebtedness. See also Tamiolaki (2018).

240 E.g. Xen. *Cyr.* IV.ii.12: Cyrus' followers join their leader not out of compulsion (οὐκ ἀνάγκῃ), but willing (ἐθελούσιοι) and "for χάρις". Here χάρις is ambiguous between prospective ("for the sake of future gratitude from Cyrus", i.e. "in order to obtain gratitude from Cyrus") and retrospective ("because of gratitude towards Cyrus", i.e. "because they have received gratitude from Cyrus"). Cyrus' reaction is in keeping with their χάρις: he prays that he may be able to return the favor (χάριν ἀποδοῦναι) of their readiness (προθυμία). There is an effective contrast between ready and willing behavior that yields χάρις and the idea of compulsion, a disjunction between moral obligations and enforceable obligations. Actions performed out of compulsion cannot be qualified as acts of χάρις and do not deserve to be reciprocated with χάρις. Cf. the opposition between compelling followers by means of coercion (ἀνάγκη) and "persuasion of the willing" (τὸ ἑκόντας πείθεσθαι) (Xen. *Cyr.* I.ii.21); and the opposition between serving out of compulsion (ἀνάγκῃ) vs. out of goodwill and friendship (εὐνοίᾳ καὶ φιλίᾳ) (Xen. *Cyr.* III.i.28). Cf. Empedocles fr. 116: Charis "στυγέει δύστλητον Ἀνάγκην".

241 O'Connor (1994: 57).

242 Xen. *Ap.* XVII.

[Text 32]

> οὐ μὴν οὐδ' ἐρασιχρημάτους[243] γε τοὺς συνόντας ἐποίει. τῶν μὲν γὰρ ἄλλων ἐπιθυμιῶν ἔπαυε, τοὺς δ' ἑαυτοῦ ἐπιθυμοῦντας οὐκ ἐπράττετο χρήματα. τούτου δ' ἀπεχόμενος ἐνόμιζεν ἐλευθερίας ἐπιμελεῖσθαι· τοὺς δὲ λαμβάνοντας τῆς ὁμιλίας μισθὸν ἀνδραποδιστὰς ἑαυτῶν ἀπεκάλει διὰ τὸ ἀναγκαῖον αὐτοῖς εἶναι διαλέγεσθαι παρ' ὧν ἂν[244] λάβοιεν τὸν μισθόν. ἐθαύμαζε δ'εἴ τις ἀρετὴν ἐπαγγελλόμενος ἀργύριον πράττοιτο καὶ μὴ νομίζοι τὸ μέγιστον κέρδος ἕξειν φίλον ἀγαθὸν κτησάμενος, ἀλλὰ φοβοῖτο μὴ ὁ γενόμενος καλὸς κἀγαθὸς τῷ τὰ μέγιστα εὐεργετήσαντι μὴ τὴν μεγίστην χάριν ἕξοι. Σωκράτης δὲ ἐπηγγείλατο μὲν οὐδενὶ πώποτε τοιοῦτον οὐδέν, ἐπίστευε δὲ τῶν συνόντων ἑαυτῷ τοὺς ἀποδεξαμένους ἅπερ αὐτὸς ἐδοκίμαζεν εἰς τὸν πάντα βίον ἑαυτῷ τε καὶ ἀλλήλοις φίλους ἀγαθοὺς ἔσεσθαι.
>
> Nor again did he make his associates *money*-lovers: he rid them of all other desires except for his company, and for that he charged no fee. In eschewing fees, he considered that he was protecting his own independence; those who accepted a fee in return for their services he nicknamed '*self-enslavers*', *because they were obliged to converse with all from whom they could take a fee*. He expressed surprise that a man who offered to teach goodness should demand to be paid for it and, instead of anticipating the greatest possible gain through obtaining a good friend, should be afraid that the person who has become truly good will feel less than the deepest gratitude to his supreme benefactor. Socrates never made any such offer to anyone, but he believed that those of his associates who accepted the principles which he himself approved would be good friends all their life long to himself and to one another.[245]

Fee-taking is voluntary self-enslavement (being an ἀνδραποδιστής ἑαυτῶν). The image itself is leading: it evokes the same morally biased universe as the πόρνος from the Antiphon episode. The difference is in the underlying argumentation: the trouble with taking fees is not so much the impossibility to discriminate and select one's conversation partner on the basis of his moral quality;[246] rather, the

243 This adjective is a neologism of Xenophon, coined by analogy with φιλαργυρία, probably intended to highlight the compulsory aspects of money-driven behavior.

244 'ἄν' is deleted by Dindorf (1910). See n. 82.

245 *Mem.* I.ii.5–7; *transl. adapted.*

246 *Pace* Corey (2002), 196–197: "Taking pay places constraints upon the free discretion that any conscientious teacher will want to exercise."

problem is that fee-taking yields a dynamics of its own. Accepting payment not only puts one under the legal obligation to deliver;[247] it is even suggested that the very mediation of money makes one cultivate the wrong ἐπιθυμίαι and hence causes compulsory behavior: one is under compulsion to διαλέγεσθαι with whomever one *can* get money from.[248]

Socratic economics strikingly stands out from this sophistic discourse ruled by compulsion and fear (φοβοῖτο): for Socrates, the greatest gain is making friends and making one's friends morally excellent; in light of this objective fear turns into trust (ἐπίστευε), and obsession with gain (κέρδος) is replaced by a belief in χάρις, of generosity and gratitude. This switch of discourse enables Socrates to recognize the paradox of sophistic teaching and formulate what may be seen as a clever inversion of Antiphon's paradox. The practice of fee-raising flies into the face of the sophist's claim of teaching virtue, for fee-raising is a symptom of distrusting one's pupil—of which there is no need if one has succeeded in making the pupil virtuous![249] The bottom line is that χάρις, virtue, and trust presuppose a time-frame that surpasses the short-term world of the businessman, sophist, and prostitute.

This may eliminate one final potential misreading of the Antiphon episode:

[Text 33 = Text 4]

> ὁ δὲ Σωκράτης πρὸς ταῦτα εἶπεν· Ὦ Ἀντιφῶν, παρ' ἡμῖν νομίζεται τὴν ὥραν καὶ τὴν σοφίαν ὁμοίως μὲν καλόν, ὁμοίως δὲ αἰσχρὸν διατίθεσθαι εἶναι. τήν τε γὰρ

247 Blank (1985). This is an objection expressed by Socrates in *Mem.* I.vi.5: once you take money, you are under an obligation (ἀναγκαῖον) to carry out the task whereas when you refrain from it you can talk to whomever you like (οὐκ ἀνάγκη διαλέγεσθαι ᾧ ἂν μὴ βούλωμαι). Alternatively, in *Mem.* I.v.6 the image of slavery recurs: whomever takes money makes himself a δοῦλος of a δεσπότης.

248 This reading diverges from current interpretations of this passage. The disagreement hinges upon the interpretation of the optative ἂν λάβοιεν. The standard translation "because they were obliged to converse with those from whom they took pay" presupposes that ὧν ἂν λάβοιεν is an optative of secondary sequence replacing a subjunctive construction: ὧν ἂν λάβωσιν, λάβωσιν being a distributive-iterative subjunctive. However, it is extremely uncommon that "ἄν" is retained in indirect discourse after a past tense when the verb has been changed to the optative. Among the few alleged "exceptions" of this rule mention is made of precisely this particular case (Xen. *Mem.* I.ii.6). See Goodwin (1897), section 702. Kühner-Gerth (1890) do not postulate such exceptions to the rule. I do not see a necessity to do so either. The optative ἂν λάβοιεν should be read as a potential optative. Cf. Kühner (1882) who paraphrases this sentence as: *quia necessitas iis imposita esset cum iis colloquendi, a quibus mercedem accipere possent.*

249 This paradox recurs on several occasions in Socratic literature and other manifestations of criticism against the sophists. E.g. Pl. *Gorg.* 519c, 460e; Is. *Soph.* 5–6.

> ὥραν ἐὰν μέν τις ἀργυρίου πωλῇ τῷ βουλομένῳ, πόρνον αὐτὸν ἀποκαλοῦσιν, ἐὰν δέ τις, ὃν ἂν γνῷ καλόν τε κἀγαθὸν ἐραστὴν ὄντα, τοῦτον φίλον ἑαυτῷ ποιῆται, σώφρονα νομίζομεν· καὶ τὴν σοφίαν ὡσαύτως τοὺς μὲν ἀργυρίου τῷ βουλομένῳ πωλοῦντας σοφιστὰς ἀποκαλοῦσιν, ὅστις δὲ ὃν ἂν γνῷ εὐφυᾶ ὄντα διδάσκων ὅ τι ἂν ἔχῃ ἀγαθὸν φίλον ποιεῖται, τοῦτον νομίζομεν, ἃ τῷ καλῷ κἀγαθῷ πολίτῃ προσήκει, ταῦτα ποιεῖν.

> To this Socrates replied, 'In our society, Antiphon, the same rules with regard to what is creditable and what is not are thought to apply equally to the disposal of physical attractions and of wisdom. A man who sells his favours for a price to anyone who wants them is called a prostitute; but if anyone forms a love-attachment with someone whom he knows to be truly good, we regard him as perfectly respectable. In just the same way, those who sell wisdom at a price to anyone who wants it are called sophists; but if anyone, by imparting any edifying knowledge that he possesses, makes a friend of one whom he knows to be naturally gifted, we consider that he is behaving as a truly good citizen should behave.'[250]

In accord with the general outlines of Xenophon's moral economics, prostitution and sophistry, and monetary compensation at large, are constructed as incompatible with self-restraint (σώφρονα);[251] by contrast, friendship is conceptualized in terms of self-restraint, i.e. the suspension of short-term needs of gratification in favor of long-term goods. In this particular passage, however, it is tempting to make too much of the body-soul dichotomy that is implicitly present in this episode—and here it is instructive to point out a fundamental difference between Plato and Xenophon.

To Plato, the body-soul dichotomy functions as an architectonic principle in his ontology: wealth and money are dismissed by being relegated to the realm of the body, and they are subordinated to other goods.[252] The body-soul dichotomy functions differently in Xenophon's Socratic thought: it does not construct an opposition between the economy of the body and a distinct economy of the soul. Rather, *both* body and soul are potentially involved in two different types of economies: a shameful one, oriented towards immediate grati-

---

250 *Mem.* I.vi.13.

251 E.g. Socrates' first conversation with Antiphon (I.vi.1–10) shows Socrates redefining notions of poverty, happiness and the ends of wisdom.

252 See Section 2.6 above.

fication of short-term needs, as opposed to an honorable one, informed by moral concerns.[253] This accords with the overall tenor of Xenophon's Socratic work, where a soul-body distinction is acknowledged,[254] but rarely to the extent that the realm of the body and the physical is dismissed as secondary, subservient or hostile to that of the soul.[255] Xenophon's Socrates insists just as much on caring for the body as for the soul.[256]

In a nutshell, we may say that Socrates' problem with demanding and accepting payment for his conversations is twofold. The formal objection is that accepting pay presupposes a wrong interpretation of the teacher-student relationship, confusing friendly reciprocity premised on trust, generosity, and gratitude with a commercial notion of exchange. The substantial problem is that demanding pay is in itself incompatible with the contents of Socratic moral-philosophical teaching that takes as its point of departure the principle of ἐγκράτεια.

4.2 *Plato: Collapsing the Distinction*

To Xenophon's Socrates, charging fees for lessons in virtue turned out to be a self-contradictory endeavor (T32). Plato's *Gorgias* features a very similar trope when Plato's Socrates constructs an alternative version of the paradox of charging fees:

[Text 34]

> καὶ γὰρ οἱ σοφισταί, τἆλλα σοφοὶ ὄντες, τοῦτο ἄτοπον ἐργάζονται πρᾶγμα· φάσκοντες γὰρ ἀρετῆς διδάσκαλοι εἶναι πολλάκις κατηγοροῦσιν τῶν μαθητῶν ὡς ἀδικοῦσι σφᾶς [αὐτούς], τούς τε μισθοὺς ἀποστεροῦντες καὶ ἄλλην χάριν οὐκ ἀποδιδόντες, εὖ παθόντες ὑπ' αὐτῶν. καὶ τούτου τοῦ λόγου τί ἂν ἀλογώτερον εἴη πρᾶγμα, ἀνθρώπους ἀγαθοὺς καὶ δικαίους γενομένους, ἐξαιρεθέντας μὲν ἀδικίαν ὑπὸ τοῦ διδασκάλου, σχόντας δὲ δικαιοσύνην, ἀδικεῖν τούτῳ ᾧ οὐκ ἔχουσιν; οὐ δοκεῖ σοι τοῦτο ἄτοπον εἶναι, ὦ ἑταῖρε;

---

253 Here I disagree with (the otherwise admirable and spot-on) analysis of Tell (2009), who reads in this episode "a thematic sequence consisting of wisdom, money, and prostitution, in which the interference of the intermediary phase—money—runs the danger of corrupting and even *conflating the things of the mind with the sphere of the body*" (16, my emphasis).

254 E.g. *Mem.* IV.i.2.

255 With the possible exception of Socrates' notorious speech in *Symp.* VIII.6–41. On this speech, see Pentassuglio (2018). See also Chapter Six.

256 *Mem.* I.ii.4, III.xii; Cf. Dorion (2006), 96, (2011), 16.

> For all their cleverness in other respects, there's an anomaly in the sophists' affairs: they claim to be teachers of virtue, but they often accuse their pupils of wronging them, their benefactors, by withholding their gratitude in some form, and especially by not paying fees.|d But can you think of anything more absurd than this argument? It claims that people who have had injustice removed by their teacher, and have had it replaced with injustice—who have become, then, good and moral people—are acting with injustice, which is something they don't have. Doesn't that strike you as as implausible, Callicles my friend?[257]

Good teachers succeed in instilling their students with virtue. Virtuous students cannot fail to reciprocate (χάριν ἀποδιδόντες) when treated well (εὖ παθόντες). Hence, teachers of virtue who accuse their students of non-payment and ingratitude are being absurd: either they haven't done their job well enough (in which case they do not deserve to be paid), or they have (in which case, the student's education being successful, they will be paid).

Although this paradox resembles the one in Xen. *Mem.* I.ii.5–7 (T32), the difference is instructive as well.[258] Here in the *Gorgias*-passage, the paradox is in complaining and accusing students of non-payment *after* the lessons have taken place—in which case, the very accusation proves to be an unwitting diagnosis of the teacher's failure. In the *Memorabilia*-passage, the point is that the very act of asking a fee *beforehand* is a gesture of mistrust on the part of the teacher that is incompatible with the ethics of χάρις that is all about taking the leap of faith and paying it forward. The teacher's complaints in the *Gorgias*-passage are not inherent to the workings of money; the analysis in the *Memorabilia*-passage concern the very logic of exchange.

5 Concluding Remarks: The Givenness of the Good

One of the cornerstones of modern economic theory is the "givenness of wants": consumption is a matter of satisfying wants, wants are psychological facts, and there is no point in disputing what constitutes the *summum bonum*, "whether the best relish [is] to be found in apples, plums, or nuts."[259] Consumption is the only area in the economic cycle in which people are not supposed to

---

257 Pl. *Gorg.* 519c3–d7; *transl.* Waterfield (1994).
258 On this passage see also Chapter Six Section 6.
259 Locke (1894), 351.

be acting rationally;[260] it is the arena where individual freedom is exercised—the ultimate consequence being that "there is no intrinsically desirable life, only a range of desired lifestyles."[261]

In this chapter we have seen how Socrates' understanding of οἰκονομία makes consumption the arena of virtue:[262] it is through consumption, or "proper use", that the resources of the short-term sphere are converted into long-term goods; and it is through ἐγκράτεια, self-restraint, and self-mastery, that the long-term order of the οἶκος, the estate, is protected, sustained and reproduced. In the wake of this articulation of a long-term order, Xenophon "converts" the potentially sordid terminology of wealth, money, value and utility, terms that originate in the short-term order of the sophist, the prostitute and the money-maker, into ethical notions that sustain and legitimate the long-term order of the philosopher, the friend and the estate-manager.

As such, Xenophon's *Memorabilia* provide us with an instructive alternative to post-Enlightenment notions of utility, use, and the good. At first sight, the Antiphon episode seemed to suggest an opposition between commercialized transactions mediated by money and the "sharing economy" among φίλοι. On second thought, however, the genuine opposition turned out to be between the short- and the long-term sphere—a dialectics that is most explicitly articulated in Xenophon's interpretation of the Socratic doctrine of "correct use" (ὀρθὴ χρῆσις), a way of interacting with one's surroundings in a sustainable way that accords with the long-term good. While the notion of "correct use" features in other Socratic authors too, it is Xenophon who turns it into one of the pillars of his understanding of οἰκονομία by applying the doctrine not only to the use of material and natural resources but to persons as well. The correct treatment of φίλοι becomes an integral part of οἰκονομία—as Socrates attempts to point out to Diodorus.

In both domains, in friendship as well as in estate-management, it is imperative to look beyond the appeal of short-term gratification and to envision the long-term perspective. Without such a perspective it is impossible to understand long-term bonds such as φιλία—bonds that transcend the opposition between egoism and altruism in favor of a notion of mutual benefit, as he

260 Graeber (2005).

261 Skidelsky & Skidelsky (2012), who locate the roots of economics in "the empiricist revolt against Aristotle."

262 A similar ethical attempt to make demand or consumption a rationally controllable element we find in the Parable of the Leaky Jars (Pl. *Gorg.* 493c), where the concept of unlimited demand is exploited: the rational individual can minimize losses through leakage by desiring less rather than more. Lowry (1987), 113 and (1998), 22.

points out to Chaerecrates. The ideal of the long-term care of the self automatically entails the care of one's φίλοι. After all, they are part of one's χρήματα, wealth. Socratic economics, therefore, is never a zero-sum game: there is no such thing as a conflict of interests between two genuine φίλοι, two people who treat each other well, because their dealings are grounded in genuine knowledge and virtue.

CHAPTER 6

Active Partnership: Socrates and the Art of Seduction

> Tomas did not realize at the time that metaphors are dangerous. Metaphors are not to be trifled with. A single metaphor can give birth to love.
>
> MILAN KUNDERA (1984)

•••

> Cressida (…) My lord, *come* you into my chamber: you smile and mock at me as if I meant naughtily.
>
> Troilus. Ha, ha!
>
> Cressida. *Come*, you are deceived, I think of no such thing.
>
> WILLIAM SHAKESPEARE, *Troilus and Cressida* IV.ii. 36–99

•••

> Analyzing humor is like dissecting a frog. Few people are interested and the frog dies of it.
>
> E.B. WHITE[1]

What exactly is wrong with taking money for bodily services? Isn't it something that we all do, to a certain extent? Such is Martha Nussbaum's opening statement in her analysis of the moral arguments advanced against sexual commodification and the legalisation of prostitution. To elicit the implicit values that underlie the stigmatization of sex work, Nussbaum starts her analysis with

1 A range of multiforms of E.B. White's statement is in circulation. The quote printed in *A Subtreasury of American Humor* (1941) runs as follows: "Humor can be dissected, as a frog can, but the thing dies in the process and the innards are discouraging to any but the pure scientific mind".

 | DOI:10.1163/9789004416147_007

a systematic comparison of prostitutes with other women "who take money for bodily services", such as the factory worker in the Perdue chicken factory, the domestic servant in a prosperous upper-middle class house, the nightclub singer in middle-range clubs who sings request songs, the skilled masseuse employed by a health club, the "colonoscopy artist", and, somewhat hidden in this inventory, the professor of philosophy:[2]

[Text 1]

> The Prostitute and the Professor of Philosophy. The two figures have a very interesting similarity: both provide bodily services in areas that are generally thought to be especially intimate and definitive of selfhood. Just as the prostitute take money for sex, which is commonly thought to be an area of intimate self-expression, so the professor takes money for thinking and writing about what she thinks—about morality, emotion, the nature of knowledge, whatever—all parts of a human being's intimate search for understanding of the world and self-understanding. (…) The fact that we do not think that the professor (even one who regularly holds out for the highest salary offered) thereby alienates her mind or turns her thoughts into commodities—even when she writes a paper for a specific conference or volume—should put us on our guard about making similar conclusions in the case of the prostitute.[3]

The analogy is, of course, an old one. In his retort to the market-proud wise guy Antiphon, Xenophon's Socrates uses the same analogy (SOPHIST : GENTLEMAN CITIZEN = PROSTITUTE : VIRTUOUS BOY-LOVER) to make a simple point, though one that is diametrically opposite to the inference reported by Nussbaum: according to Socrates, prostitution is dishonorable, *therefore* taking pay for teaching is too. Nonetheless, the underlying cluster of ideas seems very similar: taking pay for something "intimate", something very close to us, an area of "intimate self-expression", results in a form of alienation—the most grotesque form of alienation, according to Georg Simmel in his classic *Philosophy of Money*:

2 Nussbaum (1998), 700–707.
3 Nussbaum (1998), 704.

[Text 2]

> Of all human relationships, prostitution is perhaps the most striking instance of mutual degradation to a mere means, and this may be the strongest and most fundamental factor that places prostitution in such a close historical relationship to the money economy, the economy of means in the strictest sense.[4]

There is something unsettling about trading something bound up so closely with the irreplaceable uniqueness of the individual for something so interchangeable and exchangeable as money. It is as if some of the characteristics of money rub off on the person taking it. This is the "ominous analogy" that Simmel sees between the use of money and prostitution: both are premised on an indifference in use, a lack of attachment to any individual, the exclusion of relatedness and emotions.[5]

Whereas Simmel treats the alienating effect of taking money for bodily services as a given, sociologist Arlie Hochschild reverses the question to see when and how people providing bodily services detach themselves from the work they do: by what kind of "feeling rules" is their emotional involvement (or disinvolvement) regulated? When do they feel they *should* feel in a certain way?[6] A central notion in her study is Milton Friedman's notion of a forward moving Market Frontier, a notional frontier between the "unpaid activities of family, friends, and neighbors" on the one hand, and "the goods and services for rent or sale" on the other.[7] The movement of this Market Frontier necessitates a continuous crafting of new strategies to shield off intimate life from commodification and alienation: commercial surrogate mothers in India carrying babies for infertile couples living in Canada try to think of their womb as a mere carrier and of their baby as a jewel on loan ("if you put a jewel in my hand, I don't covet it. I give it to its owner"),[8] suburban upper-middle class American parents who hire birthday planners and party animators for their children's birthday party reconcile themselves with their imminent feelings of failure by telling themselves that "the experts do it better".[9] Both groups are engaged in "emo-

4 Simmel (1978 [1900]), 379.

5 Simmel (1978 [1900]), 378: "Only money, which does not imply any commitment, and which in principle is always at hand and welcomed, is the appropriate equivalent to the fleetingly intensified and just as fleetingly extinguished sexual appetite that is served by prostitution."

6 Hochschild (2011).

7 Hochschild (2011), 2.

8 Hochschild (2011), 5.

9 Hochschild (2011), 9.

tion work", in making up feeling rules to come to terms with their changing positions *vis-à-vis* the Market Frontier.

While Hochschild's examples seem as heterogeneous as the list of "body workers" explored by Nussbaum, what they have in common is the implicit idea that there are separate spheres of life that are regulated by distinct transaction rules. The distinctions that we make between sexual intimacy among married couples, paid prostitutes and casual hookups (each comes with its own interaction pattern, its own expectations and obligations) require what Viviane Zelizer calls "relational work":[10] we set boundaries to make meaningful distinctions between types of social relations, marking off sets of practices and transactions that we find appropriate, or not, stipulating what methods or media of reckoning and interacting are appropriate, or not. We feel that such boundaries may not be stable (we may feel the forward movement of the Market Frontier) and that they are worth fighting for. Boundaries are high maintenance, they require constant creation, enforcement and renegotiation.

Moral philosophical discourse is invested with such boundaries, both with renegotiating and restoring them. One of the more bizarre achievements in Socrates' philosophical career is his successful seduction of the most beautiful woman of Athens: the hetaera Theodote. When hearing from his companions that Theodote's beauty is "beyond words", Socrates proposes that they go see this lady for themselves, for evidently mere hearsay does not suffice to fully know such beauty. In the course of this visit, Socrates smoothly seduces the courtesan into a genuine Socratic conversation on the topic of how to hunt for friends and how to incite desires in others. At the end of the encounter, Theodote desires Socrates to stay with her and to come back to her as often as he can. But Socrates declines for he is a busy man with lots of "girlfriends". *She* come and visit *him*. She will, she says, but he should welcome her. Socrates closes the conversation with the enigmatic words: "I will, unless there is some dearer girl with me".

This encounter, reported in Xenophon's *Memorabilia* (III.xi), has provoked a variety of reactions from scholars, ranging from outright disgust[11] to delight for showing us an "unbuttoned"[12] and roguish Socrates and (finally) a Xenophon capable of complexity and irony. By and large the episode appears to challenge

10 Zelizer (2005), 35–36.

11 Kierkegaard (1841), XIII.120. Kierkegaard (1989), 24: "We are even more disgusted, because we cannot perceive the possibility of Socrates ever having been capable of it!" Cf. Delatte (1933), 151: "One is above all astonished that Xenophon would have presented Socrates in this light in the book consecrated to defending his memory!"

12 Pangle (2018), 174.

common preconceptions of Xenophon's Socratic work as pedestrian and prone to apologetic overkill, as its paradoxical nature does not straightforwardly fit in with the overall didactic strategy of the *Memorabilia* and reminds us more of the delicate irony of Plato's Socrates than its Xenophontic counterpart.

There is certainly something funny about this episode, but what exactly is the joke? At the risk of dissecting a frog (but like in most dissecting project: this frog is already dead!), there is surely something provocative and "roguish" about the juxtaposition of a courtesan seductive beauty and the rather prosaic and obnoxious Socrates, for juxtapositions invite comparison and comparisons imply comparability. So *in what* are Socrates and Theodote compared? In their distinct kinds of beauty? In their seduction techniques? In the profit they gain from their interactions with their "friends"? Are they on the same side of the Market Frontier?

A range of interpretations have been proposed.[13] One class of interpretations focuses on what may be understood as a "role reversal" between Socrates and Theodote. What does this "reversal" consist in? The most influential interpretation, by Simon Goldhill, reads the episode as dramatizing a reversal in the "economy of looking": it dramatizes how Socrates gains control over Theodote by claiming the position of the object of the gaze, and concomitantly, of desire.[14] This reading can be understood within a wider framework of "erotic irony", the idea that Socrates, by pretending to be in love, provokes his object of his amorous attentions to fall in love him.[15] Such erotic irony is understood as an extension of Socrates' dialectic irony, his disavowal of knowledge that provokes his interlocutor to answer his questions. For Xenophon's Socratic works, such an ironic reading is controversial for a range of reasons.[16] Most importantly in this context is that because Xenophon's Socrates openly professes to be a teacher and never avows ignorance the way his Platonic counterpart does, dialectical irony does not seem to be as prominent a technique in Xenophon's Socratic works.[17]

A second class of interpretations read the Theodote episode as a demonstration of the principle of self-restraint (ἐγκράτεια), highlight Socrates' capability to resist the courtesan's physical beauty and his own physical desire,[18]

13 Azoulay (2004a), Delatte (1933), Dorion (2003), Goldhill (1998), Hindley (2004), Kierkegaard (1841), Narcy (2004), O'Connor (1994), Thomsen (2002), Tilg (2004).

14 Goldhill (1998).

15 Hadot (1995), Dorion (2006).

16 For a comprehensive critique on Straussian ironic readings, see Gray (2011), 56–69.

17 Dorion 2006, Kierkegaard 1841, Vlastos 1991, Nehamas 1998, 45.

18 Narcy (2004); Dorion (2003).

sometimes in contrast to Pericles who was not capable of such control when confronted with Aspasia.[19] There are some complications and controversies to these interpretations as well: is ἐγκράτεια to be understood as a principle of celibacy and does it presuppose a body/soul dichotomy (love for the soul is good, love for the body is baaaaaaaaaad)?[20] As Xenophon's Socrates gives much weight to the proper care of the body and actually shows relatively little interest in the soul as an independent entity, scholars are still divided over the question if and to what extent Socrates actually propagates absolute celibacy.[21]

What all interpretations share is the assumption that the dialogue is essentially an *erotic* conversation, overlooking a very elementary fact: the Theodote episode is a dialogue on φιλία and χάρις, on friendship and long-term reciprocity—instead of, say, ἔρως,[22] desire, that in Classical Athens is clearly conceptualized as an asymmetrical bond, between an active and a passive partner, and hence allows more readily for a reading in terms of role reversal.[23] If Socrates' concerns in this episode lie overtly in the interpersonal realm, what exactly is the significance of a role *reversal*? What is the point in reversing the roles in a reciprocal engagement?

---

19 Tilg (2004).

20 Xenophon's Socrates does acknowledge a soul/body opposition of some sorts (e.g. *Mem.* IV.i.2), but he rarely does so to the extent that the realm of the body and the physical is dismissed as secondary, subservient or hostile to that of the soul—with the exception of his notorious speech in *Symp.* VIII.6–41. (*See* Hindley (2004) and Thomsen (2002) for a discussion of this speech.)

21 See e.g. Thomsen (2002) and Hindley (2004) for subtle and balanced accounts of Socrates' erotic doctrine in Xenophon's works. See Buffière (1980), 404 ff. and Thornton (1997), 103 for more anti-hedonistic interpretations of the Socratic sexual attitude (at least as far as same sex contacts are concerned), and Vlastos (1991) and Dover (1978) for the sublimation doctrine. The key-passages are the mentioned speech in *Symp.* VIII where Socrates declares the superiority of "love of soul" over love of body and the programmatic passage in *Mem.* I.iii.8 where Socrates is said to avoid sexual relations (ἀφροδίσια) with beautiful people for fear his self-control may get compromised. Cf. Pangle (2018), 66.

22 In contrast to Plato's treatment of the paradoxical relation of Socrates with erotics (beauty, desire, seduction, love), in Xenophon's *Memorabilia* ἔρως hardly seems to be a significant concept. In the few isolated discussions of erotic desire and sexual contacts in the *Memorabilia* the term used is ἀφροδίσια, the context invariably being ἐγκράτεια. (I.ii.1, I.ii.2, I.iii.8, I.iii.15, I.iv.12, I.v.1, II.1.3, II.1.4, II.1.5, II.ii.4, IV.v.9). See also Ludwig (2002).

23 Dover (1978) and Foucault (1984), followed by Halperin (1997) and Winkler (1990) remain foundational works. A recent reappraisal is offered by Davidson (2007) who criticizes Dover, Foucault and Halperin as overly "phallocentric" in their undue emphasis on penetration as an intrinsically unidirectional act.

The Argument

In the previous chapter we have seen how in Xenophon's representation, the demarcation between commercial sophistics and Socratic φιλία is organized along the opposition **between the short and the long term**, between the immediate gratification impersonated by the businessman and sophist on the one hand and the ideology of ἐγκράτεια practiced by the estate manager, the philosopher and anyone who grounds his conduct in an understanding of the long-term good on the other hand.

In this chapter we shall elaborate on a related opposition central to Xenophon's moral thought: the active/passive-dichotomy. To Xenophon, for interaction to qualify as moral exchange it not only needs to be embedded in a long-term order of things; moral exchange requires **active participation** by both exchange partners. This ideal of Active Partnership is contrasted with forms of exchange that reduce both partners to passive consumers: business transactions, sophistic demonstrations of knowledge and prostitution—as opposed to estate management, philosophical dialectics and Socratic φιλία.

This reading suggests an interesting contrast with Plato's erotic doctrine. In Plato's oeuvre, it is "the fine" or "the noble" (τὸ καλόν) and erotic desire (ἔρως) that are invested with protreptic potential and hence made philosophically productive: the fine, if well-understood, has the potential to inspire an active philosophical disposition in us and to stimulate the ascent of the soul to the realm of the Forms. In Xenophon's philosophy, we see a different pair of concepts at work: not beauty (one-sided) but charm, χάρις (two-sided), not desire (unidirectional), but friendship, φιλία (reciprocal). These concepts, χάρις and φιλία, turn out to shape the **preconditions** for, the **setting** of and the very **substance** of philosophical ethics.

A reading of the Theodote episode along these lines takes its overt subject matter, φιλία, seriously while simultaneously integrating its thematics within the larger framework of the moral philosophy in Xenophons' *Memorabilia* and of the larger issues at stake. As we shall see this episode not only dramatizes the "relation work" done by Theodote and Socrates at the Market Frontier of fifth- and fourth century Athens, but also the language games that go with it. This is as much a dialogue about reciprocity and philosophy as it is about the power and proper use of language: the proper application of terms, the use of euphemisms, the power of metaphors and the function and value of dialogue.

1 Amazing Grace: Looking as a Reciprocal Endeavor

1.1 *The Look of Love: χάρις and Display*

Let's see what happens if we take the terms of the dialogue at face-value and read the encounter between Socrates and Theodote as a dialogue on the Art of Friendship. From the outset, the idea of active reciprocity is hinted at. For instance, by Socrates' use of χάρις-terminology. In tandem with the hunting metaphor later exploited in the dialogue, the use and analysis of the term χάρις become Socrates' most important vehicle to destabilize conventional role divisions and to shape a notion of reciprocity as a mutually active endeavor.

The apparent "role reversal" between Socrates and Theodote is most strongly suggested by the shifting application of the verb πείθειν. The narrator's framing of the dialogue is crucial:

[Text 3]

> Γυναικὸς δέ ποτε οὔσης ἐν τῇ πόλει καλῆς, ᾗ ὄνομα ἦν Θεοδότη, καὶ οἵας συνεῖναι τῷ πείθοντι (...).
>
> At one time there was in the city a beautiful woman called Theodote, who was the sort *to consort with anyone persuasive* (...).[24]

Right at the outset, the narrator calls attention to the role of euphemistic language (and perhaps to the role of language in general, given the emphatic introduction of Theodote's ὄνομα, *name*): Theodote is introduced generically as "the sort of woman" (οἵας) who is ready to "keep anyone company" (συνεῖναι) who "persuades" (πείθειν) her. Both verbs συνεῖναι and πείθειν are verbs commonly applied in the sexual realm, denoting "having intercourse"[25] and "seducing".[26] The verb πείθειν, persuading and seducing, reflects the fundamentally unidirectional character of the situation. Theodote is emphatically characterized as the *object* of "persuasion", a position that yields certain expectations: visitors may expect that Theodote will respond to overtures without initiating them and Theodote herself expects her visitor, Socrates, to seduce her. Nobody in Xenophon's original audience will have missed the point: the terms

---

24 Xen. *Mem.* III.xi.1; *all translations of the* Memorabilia *are by* Tredennick & Waterfield (1990).

25 Henderson (1991), 159: "συνεῖναι, which often has the high tone "live with," was also a standard euphemism for intercourse itself." See also Chapter Five Section 1.2.

26 Buxton (1982). Cf. Goldhill (1998), 113.

do not encode a secret message; rather, they are lexicalized euphemisms[27] that leave little doubt as to the category of women ("the sort of woman") to which Theodote belongs.

Fast forward to the end of the dialogue, where Theodote invites Socrates to become her "co-hunter of friends". Socrates' reply is in character:

[Text 4]

> Ἐάν γε νὴ Δί', ἔφη, πείθῃς με σύ.
>
> 'I will, believe me,' said Socrates, 'if you persuade me.'[28]

Here it is Socrates who has turned into the object of "persuasion", seduction, or rather: who claims the position of the object of seduction. The role reversal is underscored by Theodote's taking on the role of pursuer, willing and eager to visit Socrates, instead of the other way around, and Socrates' playing the part of the hard to get object of seduction.

As commentators have pointed out, this is not only a matter of playful role reversal between the allegedly most beautiful woman of Athens and the notoriously ugly Socrates who manages to outbid her; it is also a destabilization of prevailing morality: an adult male citizen is not supposed to indulge in coquetry, nor is a respectable female expected to be an active pursuer or spectator. Simon Goldhill, for instance, offers a reading of the episode as a Socratic challenge to the conventional role of vision in the construction of citizenship, and aptly identifies the problem: "Socrates confuses the modes of exchange—words, teaching, gratitude, desire, vision—by which a citizen is placed".[29]

So how do these "modes of exchange (…) by which a citizen is placed" precisely work? The destabilization of traditional role-divisions is foreshadowed in Socrates' opening question:

27 Lexicalized euphemisms are euphemisms "in which the figurative meaning is regarded as the normal or literal meaning", as opposed to semi-lexicalized euphemisms ("the substitute is associated with the taboo because of its inclusion in a conceptual domain traditionally tied to the forbidden concepts") and creative euphemisms ("the result[s] of a novel association with the taboo, only accessible in its phraseological context"). Crespo Fernández (2008), 98.

28 *Mem.* III.xi.15.

29 Goldhill (1998), 123. A problematizing reading of the gaze in Xenophon's *Symposium* is offered by Gilhuly (2009), 98–139.

[Text 5]

> παυσαμένου δὲ τοῦ ζωγράφου, Ὦ ἄνδρες, ἔφη ὁ Σωκράτης, πότερον ἡμᾶς δεῖ **μᾶλλον Θεοδότῃ χάριν ἔχειν**, ὅτι ἡμῖν τὸ κάλλος ἑαυτῆς **ἐπέδειξεν**, ἢ ταύτην ἡμῖν, ὅτι **ἐθεασάμεθα**; ἆρ' εἰ μὲν ταύτῃ **ὠφελιμωτέρα** ἐστὶν ἡ **ἐπίδειξις**, ταύτην ἡμῖν **χάριν ἑκτέον**, εἰ δὲ ἡμῖν ἡ **θέα**, ἡμᾶς ταύτῃ; εἰπόντος δέ τινος ὅτι δίκαια λέγοι, Οὐκοῦν, ἔφη, αὕτη μὲν ἤδη τε παρ' ἡμῶν ἔπαινον **κερδαίνει** καί, ἐπειδὰν εἰς πλείους διαγγείλωμεν, πλείω **ὠφελήσεται**· ἡμεῖς δὲ ἤδη τε ὧν **ἐθεασάμεθα** ἐπιθυμοῦμεν ἅψασθαι καὶ ἄπιμεν ὑποκνιζόμενοι καὶ ἀπελθόντες ποθήσομεν. ἐκ δὲ τούτων εἰκὸς ἡμᾶς μὲν **θεραπεύειν**, ταύτην δὲ **θεραπεύεσθαι**. καὶ ἡ Θεοδότη, Νὴ Δί', ἔφη, εἰ τοίνυν ταῦθ' οὕτως ἔχει, ἐμὲ ἂν δέοι ὑμῖν **τῆς θέας χάριν ἔχειν**.
>
> When the painter had finished, Socrates said: 'Gentlemen, ought we to *be more grateful to* **Theodote** for *letting us see* her beauty, or she to us for *looking* at her? I suggest that, if the *display has been more to her advantage*, she *ought to be grateful* to us, and if the *sight* has been more to ours, we ought to be grateful to her.' Someone said, 'That's right.' 'Well then,' he went on, 'she is already *enjoying the tribute* of our admiration, and when we have spread our report, she *will benefit* still further. On the other hand, we are now desirous of touching *what we have seen*; we shall go away with our emotions titillated; and when we have gone, we shall feel an unsatisfied longing. The natural inference from this is that *we are performing the service* and she is receiving it.' 'I *must say,' said Theodote, 'if that's how it is, I should have to* be grateful to you for looking at me.'[30]

This brief but very dense exchange reads as a witticism or paradox, though one not easily unraveled. Socrates evidently demystifies something that is essential to Theodote's practice and self-definition, for it is only with some reluctance that Theodote draws an inference that she herself finds somewhat surprising.

The exchange revolves around χάρις and the way the acts of displaying and looking should be mapped onto the logic of χάρις: who is doing a favor to whom? Is the spectacle, the beauty on display, conferring on favor on the spectators?[31] Or is it the other way around, are the spectators being benevolent

30 *Mem.* III.xi.2–3.

31 Note also the use of the verb θεραπεύειν, "to benefit", "to confer a service", a term frequently used in erotic contexts for the "care" and "attention" the lover offers his beloved, and hence is the counterpart of χαρίζεσθαι. Both evoke the long-term order (θεραπεύειν is al used in contexts of the care for one's parents, gods and land) and both have a capacity towards euphemization. Cf. Goldhill (1998), 116.

towards the spectacle? Socrates' question is, of course, prompted by the dialogue's setting, featuring not only the Socratic visitors but also painters attending the spectacle, situated in a position where they quench themselves at the sight of Athens' most beautiful woman. And she, as the narrator significantly adds, displays "as much of herself as decency allows" (ἐπιδεικνύειν ἑαυτῆς ὅσα καλῶς ἔχοι)[32]—a phrase that immediately brings the thematic issues of visibility and vision to the fore.

James Davidson's reading of the passage beautifully exposes the "economy of looking" beneath the surface of the dialogue. Building on Luce Irigaray's notion of the "dominant scopic economy",[33] Davidson describes "the whole business of hiding women only to discover them later" in Classical Athens: as the visibility of women in Classical Athens is subject to careful negotiation (women are supposed to live secluded from sight, at least from the company of men outside the family),[34] the sight of a woman becomes erotically charged by virtue of its sheer scarcity.[35] Within the limits imposed by status and propriety, women are endowed with the power to manage their desirability: to manipulate their visibility, to carefully regulate exposure and invisibility.[36] Theodote is staged in command of the situation: it is up to her to decide how much she is willing to display, and to walk the fine line between "the extreme exposure of the brothel prostitute and the complete invisibility of the decent lady".[37] Her display becomes a *favor* to which the spectator can respond with gratitude for what he is allowed to see.

The magic of seduction is immediately gone when Socrates spells out the rules of engagement, making explicit the terms of the economy of looking

32 *Mem.* III.xi.1. Goldhill (1998), 114: "[F]or Xenophon to describe Theodote as showing ὅσα καλῶς ἔχοι, is to mark the fine line of propriety."

33 Irigaray (1977), 26.

34 Cf. the extreme shame experienced by the nieces and sisters of the anonymous defendant in Lys. 3.6.

35 Davidson (1997), 127 ff.; Goldhill (1998), 114. This forms a marked contrast with male nudity. As Goldhill remarks, a man's body is displayed openly in gymnasium and assembly: "[H]is status is formed in the gaze of the citizens. (...) Within the idealized (male) discourse of propriety, a woman who is properly controlled—in all senses—is not open to the gaze of men, except under carefully regulated circumstances."

36 Ultimately, this unilateralness of the gaze of course reinforces the object-status of women and boys. Steiner (1998): "[W]ithin the realm of visual representation, depicting a body in a manner that emphasizes its 'to-be-looked-at-ness,' which codes its appearance for strong visual and erotic impact, turns that body from subject into spectacle, and constructs it as the passive and powerless object of the unseen viewer's gaze."

37 Davidson (1997), 127.

and lusting:[38] having seen them, the spectators long to touch her (ἐπιθυμοῦμεν ἅψασθαι), they feel "a bit titillated" (ὑποκνιζόμενοι) and they end up with an unsatisfied longing (ποθήσομεν). This blunt recalculation of the scopic economy leads to the deduction that Theodote is not doing her spectators a favor at all as she arouses ἐπιθυμία and πόθος in them, states of mind that are generally negatively qualified in Classical Greek ethos for the implied loss of control and agency;[39] moreover, Theodote *does* benefit from them spreading the news of her beauty.[40]

Socrates' spell breaking recalculation of what is *really* beneficial, ὠφέλιμος, is well in line with Socrates' general didactic strategy in the *Memorabilia* in which he teaches his companions to look beyond the appeal of short-term gratification and to envisage their real long-term interests and goals.[41] But in this situation, there is more at stake: the proper use of χάρις-vocabulary in the economy of seduction.

1.2 *Erotic χάρις: Misrecognition and Euphemism*

As we have seen in Chapter Two, the noun χάρις typically figures in an order sustained by long-term reciprocities where, in the long run, givers of favors (χάρις) are receivers of gratitude (i.e. favors reciprocated, also χάρις). Moreover, we have seen that within this order, beauty is experienced as a mutual delight: a boy's or a woman's physical attractiveness (χάρις) afflicts the perceiver with attraction (χάρις) to the object of his attraction and causes an experience of delight (χάρις) in the perceiver: χάρις is grace, attraction, and pleasure at once. As such, χάρις is a quality that cannot exist without it, being seen; χάρις-exchanges depend upon perception, on seeing the grace of things; typical use of χάρις-vocabulary presupposes internal focalization, the point of view of participants in a successful interaction.

χάρις plays a central role in the way seduction is understood. To pass for an act of seduction, of πείθειν, it is of vital importance that the seduced party has the choice to consent or decline:[42] satisfaction of lust without the consent of

38 Davidson (1997), 128.

39 Davidson (2007), 23 ff.; Faraone (1999), 29 and 29 n. 121.

40 Azoulay (2004a), 405. See Goldhill (1998), 116 for the observation that the word spreading the news of Theodote's beauty goes against the Periclean adage that a good citizen woman is someone not spoken about. Theodote's fame emphatically marks her as a non-citizen woman, the category not addressed by Pericles.

41 See Chapter Five. On the concept of ὠφέλεια in Xenophon, see Tamiolaki (2014), Dorion (2013), Bevilacqua (2010), 157–171.

42 Cf. the incompatibility of χάρις and ἀνάγκη in Chapter Three Section 5.

the object of seduction is simply brutal force, βία.[43] If the object of desire is not given choice and the autonomy to decline, then there is no seduction but coercion or prostitution.[44] If the object of desire is courted with flattery, gifts and marks of attention and (s)he is free to decide whether or not to reciprocate this kindness, (s)he is being seduced[45] and (s)he has the choice to respond to the lover's gifts and marks of attention by yielding to the lover—literally "gratifying", χαρίζεσθαι, a central term in the Greek erotic lexicon. χαρίζεσθαι, a denominative verb derived from χάρις,[46] denotes the act of bestowing χάρις on someone.[47]

43 Hence in some situations seduction is *worse* than force Xen. *Symp.* VIII.20; cf. Lys. 1.

44 To us, the connection between prostitution and coercion is not self-evident. Contrary to modern conceptions, in Classical Athens money and the delivery of services for pay is commonly framed in terms of slavery and coercion. Selling services, for instance, is seen as degrading (self-enslaving: ἀνδραποδιστὰς ἑαυτῶν), because fee-taking places one under coercion (ἀνάγκη). E.g. *Mem.* I.vi.5. Whereas we may feel that there is an element of autonomy or choice in accepting pay, in Classical Athens fees often represent asymmetrical and exploitative labor relations. See Chapter Five Section 1; Cf. Cohen (2006), Von Reden (1995).

45 The commonplace of the thankless boy in Greek elegy reflects precisely the fact that an object of seduction is supposed to be free to decline and that the boy has a possibility of *not* returning the favors of his seducer at the price of having a reputation of thanklessness. See Davidson (2007), 38ff.

46 The active form χαρίζω is rare in Greek sources before Philo and the Christian authors.

47 Latacz (1966), 105–107. See Schmoll (1955), 121 for the claim that χαρίζεσθαι is not an action verb but a static verb, analogous to other verbs on -(ί)ζω, denoting a state of the subject (that has the quality of χάρις); this seems to be correct in Christian literature, but, as Latacz observes, not for Homeric Greek, nor for Classical Greek. See Davidson (2007), 46–50 for the difference in aspectual stem between χαρίζεσθαι (present aspect) and χαρίσασθαι (aorist aspect): as the aorist aspect tends to characterize a situation as a bounded event, χαρίσασθαι tends to be more concrete and specific than the underdetermined present χαρίζεσθαι. This has implications for the *méconnaissance* inherent in χάρις: the present aspect of χαρίζεσθαι is more tolerant towards the "vagueness" of the transaction, whereas χαρίσασθαι refers to more concrete favors (often specific sexual acts). Moreover, as the aorist *tense* (i.e. in the indicative) is obviously suited to describe a past event, it implies a hindsight perspective on χάρις of specific and concrete past favors or a person's failure to deliver such a concrete favor. Hesychius, in providing two distinct entries (χαρίζεσθαι and χαρίσασθαι), suggests that a meaningful distinction between aorist and present aspect was also perceived in late antiquity: χαρίζεσθαι· τὸ δρᾶν τὰ κεχαρισμένα. ("to do pleasing things.") χαρίσασθαι· παρασχεῖν. λέγονται γὰρ χώρας γυναῖκες χαρίζεσθαι πρὸς συνουσίαν αὐτοῖς ἐκδιδοῦσαι. ("To supply. Women are said to gratify as a profession in relation to intercourse when they hire out.") The two definitions seem to be conflated in Hupperts (2000), 39. Suidas gives Χαρίζεσθαι: κοινῶς μὲν ὡς οἱ πολλοί, ἰδίως δὲ ἐπὶ ἀφροδισίων, ἢ ὑπὸ τοῦ ἐν λόγῳ ὑποκατακλίνεσθαι. ("In common usage as the majority [uses it], but specifically [it is used] in reference to sexual acts, or for submitting to someone in word.")

Hence, the terms χάρις and χαρίζεσθαι serve to define the situation in terms of seduction, consenting and responding to favors—as opposed to sexual contacts that lack this freedom of response and the theoretical possibility to say no, such as prostitution and other forms of coerced sex.[48] Moreover, the term suggests that we are not talking about isolated sexual acts, but about erotic encounters within the context of a long-term relationship, participating in a long-term transactional order, in which generosity, gratitude, and grace prevail.[49]

At the same time, the term χάρις has euphemistic potential in two ways. First of all, in an erotic context, the use of χάρις-vocabulary may be felt, even by participants in the situation (who focalize internally), to be a mere verbal veil. Whereas in non-erotic contexts the instrument of gratification is made explicit with a noun in the accusative case (e.g. χαρίζεσθαι τινι δῶρα, "to gratify someone with a gift"), in erotic contexts "to grant a favor" (χαρίζεσθαι) is predominantly used absolutely, with an implied object: specific acts of sexual gratification. In such situations, χάρις-vocabulary still serves to prescribe an internal focalization of events and people may still perceive requests and acts in terms of long-term relations, but there is less *méconnaissance*, the veil is thinner, as the concrete dimension of the exchange is never completely misrecognized but always present and unambiguously implied:[50] it is a *double entendre*. The social function of χάρις-vocabulary diminishes to politeness and a face-saving device. A lover asking a boy for "gratification" comes close to the modern-day equivalent of walking a girl home and inviting oneself for a "cup of coffee": you both know that you are not talking about a cup of coffee, but you both have the escape clause that sometimes a cup of coffee is just a cup of coffee.

Secondly, operative on a more systemic level, there is a form of active misrecognition, *méconnaissance*:[51] in erotic contexts, χάρις-terminology is euphemistic in its emphatic propagation of reciprocity in a situation where there is a clear asymmetry and a rigid division of roles. To be sure, reciprocity by

---

48 Cf. Hindley (2004), 134: "It is the opposite of forcing oneself upon an unwilling boy (…)".

49 Davidson (2007), 47: "Sexual *charis* stand for a particular construction of sex as part of a gracious exchange (…)."

50 Henderson (1991), 160. It is, however, important to keep in mind that "[s]exual charis (…) is never merely a euphemism for buggery or frottage, though sometimes, of course, that is exactly what charity meant in practice." (Davidson 2007: 47), although χάρις tends to have a concrete obscene reference in comedy, where, depending on contextual cues, the term can stand for "penis" (e.g. *Ecl.* 1047, *Frogs* 202) or "vagina" (e.g. *Av.* 1100). See Henderson (1991), 160.

51 For *méconnaissance*, see Chapter Two.

no means implies equality or perfect symmetry;[52] what is more, the language of reciprocity tends to be silent on power-relations. However, it is precisely *because* of this silence that an emphasis on the reciprocal quality of an encounter can serve to obfuscate imbalances in power and conceal the fact that, whereas the object of desire does have the power to lend or withhold consent to his or her suitor, he or she never has the power to control the terms of the exchange and actively become a subject of desire and pursuit. It is no coincidence that in homo-erotic contexts, χαρίζεσθαι refers predominantly to the *eromenos* "gratifying" the *erastes*—not the other way around.[53] In an erotic context, the term χαρίζεσθαι facilitates misrecognition of the power balance by suggesting an equal distribution of agency.

This is why, in erotic contexts, we encounter a very ambivalent attitude towards χάρις. On the one hand, χάρις embodies the grace that the lover "gracefully" begs for:

[Text 6]

> Ὦ παῖ, ἐπεί τοι **δῶκε** θεὰ **χάριν ἱμερόεσσαν**
> Κύπρις, σὸν δ' εἶδος πᾶσι νέοισι μέλει,
> τῶνδ' ἐπάκουσον ἐπῶν καὶ **ἐμὴν χάριν** ἔνθεο θυμῶι,
> γνοὺς ἔρος ὡς χαλεπὸν γίνεται ἀνδρὶ φέρειν.
>
> Boy, since the Cyprian goddess *gave* you *a beauty that arouses desire* and all the young men are obsessed with your looks, listen to these words of mine and take them to heart *as a favor to me*, knowing that love is hard for a man to bear.[54]

Here we see the recurring idea that charm or physical attractiveness (χάρις) is a gift (δῶκε) from Aphrodite: the goddess has done the boy the favor (χάρις) of desire-rousing charm (χάρις), a force that makes many young men be affected by the boy's looks (σὸν εἶδος πᾶσι νέοισι μέλει). The pun on χάρις is repeated and amplified in the second half, where the speaker urges the boy to listen to his words and take them to heart "as my χάρις". The possessive pronoun makes the χάρις ambiguous between a favor from the speaker to the boy ("listen to my

52 Azoulay (2004), 281–326 for an analysis of the role of χάρις-vocabulary in masking relationships of dependence; cf. Tamiolaki (2014). For a critique on Azoulay's approach, Gray (2011), 291–329.

53 Thomsen (2002), 155ff.

54 Thgn. 2.1319–1322; *transl.* Gerber (1999).

words and put my χάρις, i.e. my wise words, in your heart") or a favor from the boy to the speaker ("listen to me and do me a favor"). Moreover, the speaker suggests a reasonable connection (ἐπεί) between the gift of the Cyprian goddess and his appeal to the boy: since the Cyprian goddess has given you the favor of beauty, you must do me a favor *in turn*, for desire is hard to bear: "you are beautiful, give me pleasure", or rather: "pass on the χάρις."[55] χάρις is here represented as a quality circulating in a divine order of things; hence the boy is urged to "participate" in this long-term order of things and do the speaker a favor: the boy is to comply with his wishes and to gratify (χαρίζεσθαι) him. χάρις-vocabulary is used to strengthen the case of the lover, but at the same time functions as a thin verbal veil that serves to give a sexual request a refined and cultivated (and witty) outlook.

There is a counter-discourse. Within this discourse of victimization, male lovers emphatically represent themselves as victims of desire (and definitely not coercing lovers), fallen prey to the deceitful force of χάρις.[56] There is a long and persistent tradition of representing χάρις as a coercive force capable of persuading men to do things they maybe should not, i.e. a force capable of seducing (πείθειν) men.[57] In Hesiod's *Works and Days*, we see a close link between the aesthetic (and here fatal) χάρις of the object of desire and the divine economy of χάρις where beauty circulates as a gift from the gods. The gift is ambivalent from the start, as it is designed by Zeus as a punishment for Prometheus. The vocabulary of gift-giving conceals the underlying mechanism of revenge, of negative reciprocity, where a beautiful gift is always a *don fatal*. Zeus orders the gods to make an evil gift to men as price for the fire (ἀντὶ πυρὸς δώσω κακόν)—"a gift in which all be glad of heart while embracing their own destruction":[58] woman. To this gift of Zeus the gods, in turn, each attach a gift (δῶρον ἐδώρησαν)—hence her name Pandora,[59] and each gift contributes to Pandora's nature as an evil embraced by men, a destructive force that men

55 MacLachlan (1993), 68: "The repetition of the word in the same position in both hexameters underscores the fact that the pleasure requested (*charin* 1321) is in fact the possession of the boy's desirable body (*charin* 1319)."

56 See Section 2.3.

57 The archetype is perhaps Hera who, while seducing Zeus, wears earrings "glittering with χάρις" (Hom. *Il.* 14.183), to make him fall asleep—a favor (χάρις) of Hypnos to Hera who promises him to "always remember" the favor (χάρις).

58 Hes. *O&D* 57–58.

59 Hes. *O&D* 81–82. Vernant (1974), 179–186 for an analysis of both Hesiodic versions (*Theog.* 507–616 and *O&D* 42–105) of the Pandora myth as a series of deceitful gifts given, refused, withheld and stolen. Cf. Zeitlin (1996).

willingly yield to: a shameless mind, and deceitful nature, the likeness to a modest girl, a beautiful outfit and jewellery, lies and crafty words.[60] Amongst these gifts, is the gift from Aphrodite:

[Text 7]

> καὶ χάριν ἀμφιχέαι κεφαλῇ χρυσέην Ἀφροδίτην
> καὶ πόθον ἀργαλέον καὶ γυιοβόρους μελεδῶνας·
>
> and golden Aphrodite to shed *grace* upon her head and *cruel longing* and cares that weary the limbs.[61]

Aphrodite's contribution is attractiveness (χάριν) and cruel longing and limb-loosening sorrows (πόθον ἀργαλέον καὶ γυιοβόρους μελεδῶνας) poured over (ἀμφιχέαι) Pandora's head.[62] Aphrodite's gift is more than physical beauty alone: it is characterized in terms of the *effects* that Pandora's beauty will have on men—an invasive conception of emotions and affects, where longing and desire enter a person from without, emanating from the object of longing.[63] Pandora will *attract* her victims, rouse painful longing in them and bring them worries. A couple of lines further on, the necklaces of gold hung around Pandora's neck are described as gifts from the divine Graces (οἱ Χάριτες) and Persuasion (πότνια Πειθώ)—[64] clearly hinting at the intended effect of Pandora's adornment. "The power of *charis* resides in its unerring ability to provoke a response."[65] Here we see how the discourse of victimization is built on a χάρις that connects beauty and attraction with divine vengeance, erotic reciprocity with negative reciprocity: the "gift" Pandora is given by Zeus as an act of vengeance in return for an act of theft by Prometheus, and Pandora's χάρις is a gift attached to her by Aphrodite designed to amplify the efficacy of Zeus' revenge. And ultimately, the efficacy of the revenge is dependent upon the effect Pandora has on the men who gaze at her beauty.

---

60 Hes. *O&D* 60–79.

61 Hes. *O&D* 65–66; *transl.* Evelyn-White (1914).

62 For a conceptualization of χάρις as a kind of substance, cf. Hom. *Od.* 6.232–235.

63 Verdenius (1985), 52; West (1978), 159 ad loc.

64 For the collocation of πειθώ and χάρις, cf. Pind. fr. 123.14.

65 MacLachlan (1993), 37. Löw (1908), 23.

1.3 *Hetaeras and Prostitutes*

How does this reflect on Theodote? How exactly is she positioned in the χάρις-landscape? It should be noted that nowhere in the dialogue is Theodote's profession explicitly defined or named. This is not to say that Xenophon's representation does not provide the ancient Greek reader with clear clues as to the status of the lady: the fact that unlike most women she is mentioned by name,[66] her economic autonomy,[67] the fact that her encounters with men are not regulated by male relatives, all leave little doubt as to her professional occupation.[68] In fact, her emphatic presentation as an object of seduction already serves as a marker of her status, for to be an object of seduction presupposes a freedom of response that is the privilege of Greek boys and those exceptional women who do exercise some autonomy (however compromised) in the erotic sphere: courtesans. Theodote is one of those few women who *do* have χάρις, for she only "keeps company" with those men who "persuade" her.[69]

Theodote is one of the few women to participate in the system of erotic exchange that *allows* for a framing in terms of χάρις. Moreover, to Theodote's self-definition as a hetaera, this framing is *essential*. As several commentators, amongst whom most groundbreakingly Leslie Kurke and James Davidson have argued,[70] to the hetaera, the language of reciprocity is an indispensable discursive tool for representing her art as distinct from the occupation of the πόρνη (who takes her name from the verb πέρνημι, to sell), the unfree brothel worker who inhabits the world of commercialized sex and commodified bodies, a world that is naturally hostile to seduction and consensual gratification.[71] The hetaera emphatically participates in a long-term order, an

---

66 On naming women, see Schaps (1979), Faraone (1999), 156, Davidson (2007), 45, Fantham (1975).

67 Cohen (2006); see also below in n. 73 and n. 75; Cartledge (2002), 160.

68 Athenaeus XII 5535c (cf. 5743) lists Theodote explicitly as "the Athenian courtesan" (τὴν ἀττικὴν ἑταίραν).

69 As the elegists notice, the terminology of χάρις and πίστις simply does not apply to regular women, the faithful wives of Athenian citizens, for they lack the autonomy that makes such behavior meaningful: Παιδός τοι χάρις ἐστί· γυναικὶ δὲ πιστὸς ἑταῖρος | οὐδείς, ἀλλ' αἰεὶ τὸν παρεόντα φιλεῖ. (Thgn. 1367–1368). This of course reflects masculine discourse on ideal wives rather than reality.

70 Kurke (1997), Davidson (1997). Cf. Peschel (1987), 19–20; Harvey (1988), 249; Calame (1989), 103–104; Dover (1989), 20–21.

71 Traditionally, the distinction between the hetaera and the prostitute is explained away in terms of differences in "status". This is begging the question of how differences in status are constructed in the first place.

economy of grace, gifts and friendship, "which maintains, rather than severs, the connection between individuals".[72] She cultivates relations with people rather than establishing exchanges between commodities,[73] always operating in the realm of plausible deniability and the possibility of refusing her favors.

As both Kurke and Davidson insist, in terms of concrete *acts* it may not always be easy to distinguish between the prostitute's occupation and the hetaera's way of life (in some cases, the same woman is referred to as both *hetaera* and *pornê*),[74] and the distinction is best not overly reified.[75] However, the hetaera's insistence on the vocabulary of long-term reciprocity suggests that one of the markers of the distinction was the extent to which concrete acts could be understood as engagements embedded in a φιλία-relationship. Here too, χάρις-vocabulary serves to uphold *méconnaissance*—easily slipping towards the extreme of euphemism.

In this connection, the name hetaera is also relevant. Davidson suggests that the term, the female form of "companion" or "friend", is "ambiguous,

72 McClure (2003).

73 Davidson (1997), 109–110. Davidson rightly insists that "the distinction between these two kinds of relationship is not simply the difference between an exchange of objects and a payment of money, although thanks to its interchangeability, money naturally tends to establish more impersonal relationships," (111–112), pointing out that the reification of the *pornê* is exemplified by nicknames such Didrachmon and Obole, terms for Attic currency (118–119).

74 McClure (2003), 9–24. Cf. Cohen (2006), 98–99. But see also Davidson (1997), 124–125, who points out that more is involved in the hetaera's (and customers') misrecognition of the transaction, as public prostitutes who worked in brothels were charged with *pornikon telos* (the "whore-tax") and subjected to income limits and other legislation. Cf. Aesch. 1.119; Poll. 7.202.

75 Cf. Cohen (2006), who places the *hetaera-pornê*-contrast against the backbone of a broader Hellenic tendency to understand phenomena in terms of inclusive antitheses. Cohen argues that the ideological distinction between *hetaera* and *pornê* is best explained in terms of labor conditions as a contrast between free and unfree (slave) labor. In contexts where this distinction is relevant, the name "hetaera" may serve to flag the woman's free status. In the case of Theodote, for instance, her freedom of selection is emphasized, which indicates that her relations with "friends" have been "elevated from the master/servant or customer/commodity variety to one in which she possesses the independence inherent in personalized reciprocity" (113). It is instructive to make a comparison with modern conceptions of "prostitution", where the conceptual metaphor A PROSTITUTE IS A WORKER functions as a *euphemism* that allows for a conceptualization of prostitution as "a job like any other", as a socially acceptable option. See Crespo Fernández (2008), 104. In the classical Greek conception, something being a "job" hardly makes it socially acceptable—it has little euphemistic potential.

a euphemism".[76] Kurke, in contrast, makes the crucial observation that the term "hetaera" is never used but in contexts of ridicule (and, hence, of external focalization); it is, therefore, a term of derision, "applied by those outside the aristocratic symposium to mock the sympotic equality of prostitute and elite participant (*hetairos*)."[77] This fits into Kurke's larger argument about a late-archaic symbolical conflict between aristocratic and democratic discourses with the elite symposium featuring as an "anti-city":[78] whereas the ἑταῖρα/πόρνη-*distinction* is an invention of the elitist discourse of the aristocratic symposium that shields itself from the public egalitarian sphere that applauds the universal availability of *pornai* as a democratization of sex, the *term* ἑταῖρα originates in a democratic discourse hostile to the exclusionist symposium and its restricted circulation of valuables. In other words, according to Kurke, the term ἑταῖρα is not a euphemism (as Davidson argued), but typically a dysphemism: instead of veiling and covering up an obscene and debasing reality, the term ἑταῖρα, being a parody of such revealing language, unveils and exposes the true nature of the companionship.

The linguistic nature of the courtesan/prostitute-distinction is well illustrated by two comic fragments by Anaxilas, featuring the types of "the good hetaera" and "the bad hetaera (i.e. the whore")":[79]

[Text 8]

> {A} ἐὰν δέ τις μέτρια † καὶ λέγουσα ...
> τοῖς δεομένοις τινῶν ὑπουργῇ πρὸς χάριν,
> ἐκ τῆς ἑταιρίας ἑταίρα τοὔνομα
> προσηγορεύθη· καὶ σὺ νῦν οὐχ ὡς λέγεις
> πόρνης, ἑταίρας δ' εἰς ἔρωτα τυγχάνεις (5)
> ἐληλυθώς. {B} ἆρ' ὡς ἀληθῶς· {A} ἔστι γοῦν
> ἁπλῆ τις; {B} ἀστεία μὲν οὖν, νὴ τὸν Δία.

And if someone [even when saying *moderate things*?] *does service to those in need of something as a favor, from her companionship she has been called*

76 Davidson (1997), 118–119.

77 Kurke (1997), 113. For the democratic framing of prostitution ("the somatics of Athenian democratic ideology") see Halperin (1990), 88–104.

78 Kurke (1997). This is also the context in which the symbolical opposition between metals and freeling circulating interchangeable money originates. Cf. Kurke (1999).

79 Fr. 22 originates from Anaxilas' comedy Νεοττίς ("The Chick"); fr. 21 possibly too. Cf. Auhagen (2009), 49.

> *a hetaera*—and you now happen to have come to desire, not a *pornê* (*as you say*), but a *hetaera*. (b) *Really*? (a) She is someone honest then? (b.) Yes, by Zeus, and refined.[80]

Here speaker A tackles the difference between a πόρνη and a hetaera in terms of the proper "name" for each (τὸ ὄνομα). Speaker B seems to be referring to a lady as a πόρνη (ὡς λέγεις), but according to speaker A, person B *in reality* (ὡς ἀληθῶς)[81] turns out to have come to desire a hetaera. The lady in question should be addressed with the name "hetaera" (ἑταίρα τοὔνομα προσηγορεύθη), if she meets the condition that she is moderate or speaks moderate things (μέτρια)[82] and that she serves (ὑπουργῇ) those who are "in need of some things" (τοῖς δεομένοις τινῶν) as a favor (πρὸς χάριν).[83] When these conditions are met, a lady is not a prostitute for pay, but someone whose company (ἑταιρία) one can enjoy. Isomorphism is clearly acknowledged as the speakers discuss whether a particular lady is to be called a hetaera or a prostitute. At the same time, the company of a hetaera is constructed as distinct from a prostitute's: the sexual acts, euphemistically referred to in terms of serving (ὑπουργέω) and needs (δέομαι), are conferred as a favor (χάρις) in the context of company (ἑταιρία) of a lady who is moderate (μέτρια, perhaps as opposed to promiscuous; or speaks moderate things), straightforward (ἁπλῆ) and refined (ἀστεία).[84]

However, this demarcation line is fragile and liable to contextual negotiation, as another fragment by Anaxilas, the famous fragment 22, demonstrates.[85] There, in the middle of an invective of greedy and treacherous hetaeras (ἑταίραν in line 1), the speaker suddenly refers to the hetaeras as whores (τὰς πόρνας), who may just as well be called Theban Sphynx:

80 Anaxilas fr. 21 (K-A).

81 I follow the punctuation of Schweighauser (1801).

82 There is a textual problem here: ms A reads μέτρια λέγουσι; CE reads μέτρια λέγουσα καὶ ∪ ∪. The conjectures by Blaydes (1905), 146 μετρίως ἔχουσα ⟨χρημάτων⟩ and Meineke (1970), 267 καὶ μέτρι' ἔχουσα ⟨χρήματα⟩ are interesting.

83 For the phrase πρὸς χάριν as "as a favor", cf. Eur. *Med.* 538.

84 On the meaning of ἁπλῆ and ἀστεία in this context, see also Auhagen (2009), 49.

85 In *Oec.* I.xiii, discussing bad uses of wealth, Socrates adduces the example of someone "buying a *hetaera* who makes him worse off in body and soul and estate", with ἑταίραν as direct object with πριάμενος. This corroborates Kurke's point that the term "hetaera" is predominantly used in a derogatory way. Kurke (1997).

[Text 9]

> Σφίγγα Θηβαίαν δὲ πάσας ἔστι τὰς πόρνας καλεῖν,
> αἳ λαλοῦσ' ἁπλῶς μὲν οὐδέν, ἀλλ' ἐν αἰνιγμοῖς τισιν,
> ὡς ἐρῶσι καὶ φιλοῦσι καὶ σύνεισιν ἡδέως.
>
> It is not too much to call all these *whores* Theban Sphinxes, as they *speak nothing plain*, but *only riddles, how* they '*desire*', and '*care for*' and '*enjoy company*'.[86]

The distinction between prostitutes and hetaeras is crushed and reduced to verbal chitchat: a hetaera is simply a whore and may be called "Theban Sphinx" because of her mystifying chatter about "desiring" (ἐρῶσι), "being committed" (φιλοῦσι) and "keeping pleasant company" (σύνεισιν ἡδέως).[87] Talk about ἔρως, φιλία, and συνουσία is demystified as mere euphemisms, as babbling (λαλοῦσ') farfetched things (ἁπλῶς οὐδέν, perhaps even duplicitous or insincere—note the opposition with ἁπλῇ in T8!), talking in riddles (ἐν αἰνιγμοῖς), *as if*-talk (ὡς).[88] The bottom line is: behind the refined verbal veil a hetaera is simply a

86 Anaxilas fr. 22.22–24 (K-A).

87 The fragment goes on elaborating the analogy between *hetaera* and Sphinx, as the hetaera gives an obscene version of the famous Oedipus-riddle (vv. 25–27).

88 The *as if*-talk is akin to the notion of "bounded authenticity", coined by Elizabeth Bernstein (2001) in her ethnographic study among male clients of commercial sex-workers: in her interviews with these clients, the notion frequently emerged that it was the experience of "a mutually desired, special, or even romantic sexual encounter (…), the semblance of genuine erotic connection (…) the fantasy of sensuous reciprocity" (401–404) that clients thought they were purchasing—as opposed to a purely mechanical sex act. In these cases, the sexual marketplace is imagined as the great social equalizer, "where consumer capitalism democratizes access to goods and service that in an earlier era would have been the exclusive province of a restricted elite" (400–401). Note that in such a scenario, euphemization, or "bounded authenticity", serves the desire of the *clients*, not those of the prostitute. An analogous mechanism may account for the phenomenon (recorded by, amongst others, Hoigard & Finstad (1992)) that many sex-workers prefer street prostitution (an unambiguous sale of the body) to hotel prostitution that mimics free encounters and that, hence, requires more time and effort: hotel encounters appear to be more respectful towards the person, but require more effort of euphemization, as prostitutes need to talk to their customers and pretend to be interested in them as persons. Euphemisms are *costly* for the person performing them. Along a different dividing line, it may be felt that euphemisms fool women into charity: in a historical survey between 1900 and 1918 among prostitutes, mapping out different kinds of prostitution, Ruth Rosen (quoted in Zelizer (2005), 125) reports how low-paid prostitutes pride themselves on their professionalism, expressing contempt for the "charity girls" who gave away sexual favors for free. (In other words: euphemisms fool women into charity).

whore—just as man-devouring and treacherous, i.e. greedy and promiscuous. Whereas the speaker of T8 takes much trouble to make a linguistic distinction and to decide which of the two "names", hetaera or prostitute, the lady deserves, the speaker of T9 dismisses the distinction between hetaera and prostitute as merely verbal.

Socrates has his own characteristic ways of dealing with mystifying chatter: pretending to be literal-minded. When Socrates notices the sumptuous wealth in Theodote's household, he (in a faux-naïve vain) cannot help but wonder about her source of income:[89]

[Text 10]

> Εἰπέ μοι, ἔφη, ὦ Θεοδότη, ἔστι σοι ἀγρός;
> —Οὐκ ἔμοιγ', ἔφη.
> —Ἀλλ' ἄρα οἰκία προσόδους ἔχουσα;
> —Οὐδὲ οἰκία, ἔφη.
> —Ἀλλὰ μὴ χειροτέχναι τινές; Οὐδὲ χειροτέχναι, ἔφη.
> —Πόθεν οὖν, ἔφη, τὰ ἐπιτήδεια ἔχεις;
> —Ἐάν τις, ἔφη, φίλος μοι γενόμενος εὖ ποιεῖν ἐθέλῃ, οὗτός μοι βίος ἐστί.
>
> So he now said, 'Tell me, Theodote, have you got a farm?' 'Not I,' she said. 'Well then, a house that brings in money?' 'Nor a house.' 'Perhaps you have some slaves who work at a craft?' 'No, none.' 'Then how do you support yourself?' 'If anyone *gets friendly with me* and wants *to be generous*, that's how I get my living.'[90]

Theodote carefully describes relationships with her visitors in terms of φιλία: her source of income consists in her φίλοι who "treat her well" (εὖ ποιεῖν).[91] From a reductionist approach, Theodote's talk of friendship is euphemistic ("being just good friends"), a "verbal veil".[92] To Theodote, the function of her χάρις-talk

89 As Cartledge (2002), 160 points out, this passage is revealing about what the normal and openly recognized sources of a rich Athenian's wealth were: a large farm, a tenement house, and skilled slave craftsmen.

90 *Mem.* III.xi.4–5.

91 Narcy (2004), 228 n. 2 notes that εὖ ποιεῖν is normally construed with a participle or a complement (e.g. a personal pronoun in the accusative case). The absence of both may be taken as an indication that the phrase is used euphemistically. However, it may be argued that the complement is already implied in (be it in dative case) φίλος μοι γενόμενος as well as in οὗτος μοι βίος ἐστί.

92 Goldhill (1998), 117. See Konstan (2013) for an analysis of the *hetaera* in New Comedy and

is to demarcate her profession from the seemingly isomorphous profession of the brothel-worker: she does not "sell" "sex" or "her body" to a "client" but she is an autonomous subject who "gratifies" "friends" who do her "favors".[93] Even Theodote's name, "God's gift", has a programmatic ring to it: from the outset, the courtesan's business is located within an economy of long-term gift exchange between φίλοι.[94]

The Anaxilas-examples above betray an awareness of isomorphism of χάρις-exchanges and commercial transactions and, more than that, an acute awareness of the linguistic frailty of the demarcations.[95] This leaves scope for Socrates to renegotiate Theodote's status. Oh yes, Theodote does have grace and charm, χάρις; after all she *is* the most wanted woman of Athens and artists are eager to have her posing. But in asking which party ought to "have more χάρις", i.e. to "be more grateful" (μᾶλλον χάριν ἔχειν) in this ἐπίδειξις, Socrates restores the reciprocal set-up of the spectacle: the act of displaying and the act of looking are parts of a reciprocal engagement.[96] This not only breaks the spell of the seductive magic of showing and concealing; it also puts Theodote's identity as

---

Roman Comedy as a contested figure through whom the logic of the gift is both played out and demystified.

93 Davidson (1997), 120: "References to clients and prices and payments and sex are carefully avoided. The talk is all of friendship and favours."; Kurke (1997), 112: "(…) the impulse to mystify economic relations for sex generates the category of the *hetaira* within the framework of gift exchange. (…) the *hetaira* gratified her patron πρὸς χάριν, "as a favor.""

94 According to Azoulay (2004a) the name Theodote evokes the myth of Pandora; his glossing of "Pandora" as "*don de tous* [*les dieux*]" (404) seems a problematic interpretation of a πᾶν-composite. The gloss "All-Gifts" for Pandora is unique for *O&D* 81–82; in other occurrences of the name (e.g. as epithet for the goddess Gaia), the meaning is active "Giver of All". Vernant (1974), 74; Zeitlin (1996), 60.

95 Cf. Chapters Two and Three. Attic Comedy and Oratory testify how reductionism and demystification were available options, especially in the case of χάρις in erotic contexts: one of the issues at stake in the trial against Timarchus was to establish that Timarchus was prostituting himself instead of being engaged in a long-term relationship (Fisher 2001, 36–52); moreover several jokes in Attic Comedy are based on the fragile ("merely lexical") demarcation of honorable sexual encounters and commercial sex. E.g. the Socratic authors represent Aspasia as a hetaera, a respected lady and the mother of some of Pericles' children; Eupolis fr. 98 represents one of these sons (Pericles the younger) as "the whore's son" (τὸ τῆς πόρνης κακόν). Cf. Chapter Two Section 1. Moreover, the appropriation of the long-term order by the institution of pederasty and the transactions with hetaeras could be problematized when compared to the civic institution of marriage. Apollodorus' *Against Neaera* is concerned with the demarcation between transactions with courtesans and the institution of marriage linked to the reproduction of the city (the long-term order). Cf. Gilhuly (2009), 29–57.

96 Goldhill (1998), 115: "The gaze, for Xenophon's Socrates, even—especially—when directed by a man at a beautiful woman, is not a unilinear process of objectification."

a courtesan on the line. If we are *really* talking about χάρις, instead of payment-in-disguise, there is no reason to suppose why the spectator alone should "owe gratitude".

2 The Hunter Hunted: Role Reversals and the Paradox of the Hetaera

2.1 *Goodwill Hunting*

Meanwhile, Socrates has succeeded in luring the very topic of his conversation with his companions, Theodote, into the discussion: from object of conversation she turns into a subject, and from xi.4 onwards, Socrates addresses Theodote directly. The dialogue turns to a discussion of φιλία, friendship:

[Text 11]

> Ἐάν τις, ἔφη, φίλος μοι γενόμενος εὖ ποιεῖν ἐθέλῃ, οὗτός μοι βίος ἐστί.
> Νὴ τὴν Ἥραν, ἔφη, ὦ Θεοδότη, καλόν γε τὸ κτῆμα καὶ πολλῷ κρεῖττον ⟨ἢ⟩ οἰῶν τε καὶ αἰγῶν καὶ βοῶν φίλων ἀγέλην κεκτῆσθαι. ἀτάρ, ἔφη, πότερον τῇ τύχῃ ἐπιτρέπεις, ἐάν τίς σοι φίλος ὥσπερ μυῖα πρόσπτηται, ἢ καὶ αὐτή τι μηχανᾷ;
>
> 'If anyone gets friendly with me and wants to be generous, that's how I get my living.'—'Good heavens, Theodote,' said Socrates, 'it's a splendid asset to have a flock of friends—much better than having a flock of sheep and goats and cattle. But tell me, do you leave it to chance whether a friend wings his way towards you, like a fly, or do you devise something yourself?'[97]

To Theodote, as we have seen in the previous section, the vocabulary of φιλία and "treating well" (εὖ ποιεῖν), is part of a vocabulary of self-presentation, that defines her as an autonomous partner in a reciprocal relationship (and not merely a commodified body). Socrates reacts by taking Theodote's euphemistic φιλία-talk at face-value: the conversation develops into a dialogue on φιλία.

That is, a dialogue on φιλία as an *art* or skill: Socrates is interested if there is a *knack* (μηχανή) to attracting φίλοι. In valuing "a flock of friends" (φίλων ἀγέλην) over a flock of livestock (οἰῶν τε καὶ αἰγῶν καὶ βοῶν),[98] Socrates introduces the animal imagery leading up to the hunting metaphor that will feature

97 *Mem.* III.xi.5–6.

98 To have (κεκτῆσθαι) a flock of friends (φίλων ἀγέλην) is a greater boon (κτῆμα) than live-

in the rest of the dialogue: the next question is whether friends are acquired by mere chance, τύχῃ, like a fly (μυῖα) that accidentally lands on one, or by some knack (μηχανή).[99] From this point onwards, the dynamics of the conversation flips: Theodote, evidently displaying an active involvement in the conversation, starts to ask questions herself—or rather, she starts answering questions with counter-questions: "How could I find a device (μηχανή) for catching friends?" (xi.6), "Do you advise me to weave a trap?" (xi.7), "Should I implement the techniques of hare-hunting in the pursuit of friends?" (xi.9). Weaving a web of suggestive questions, Socrates is gradually turning into an advisor.

With the image of the accidental fly we make a shift from domesticated animals to the first hunting metaphor. Socrates suggests that Theodote's "knack" (μηχανή) is more appropriate (προσηκόντως) than the methods employed by spiders (φάλαγγες). It is in the description of spiders' behavior that the element of hunting becomes explicit: spiders, too, hunt (θηρῶσι) for a living, using a fine net (ἀράχνια λεπτὰ ὑφηνάμεναι; θήρατρον) to indiscriminately catch whatever flies into it[100]—obviously not a method suited to catch friends, for friends are elected, not caught indiscriminately, as Socrates will expound in xi.10–11.

Let us pause for a moment to register something odd. A spider weaving a web is not exactly a prototypical case of hunting: there is no heroic pursuit, no fleeing quarry to enhance the prestige of the catch, no tactics—merely good preparation and patience.[101] As we will see, the example is cleverly chosen to facilitate a crucial shift in the dialogue.

Socrates and Theodote quickly dismiss the image of the spider: friends are the most valuable prey (τὸ πλείστου ἄξιον ἄγρευμα) and hence cannot be caught without skill (οὐ ἀτέχνως), for even relatively low-value prey (τὸ μικροῦ ἄξιον), as for instance hares, require many skills (πολλὰ τεχνάζουσιν). An elaborate description of hare-hunting follows (finally hunters and prey that are actually *moving*!), with a specification of the three types of hounds that are trained for

---

stock. On Xenophon's manipulation of κτῆμα-vocabulary, see also Chapter Five Section 2.4.

99 A similar shift takes place in Socrates' dialogue with Critoboulus (*Mem.* II.vi.5–8): the moment the conversation turns to the topic of hunting friends, Critoboulus is "activated" and takes on the role over interrogator.

100 *Mem.* III.xi.6.

101 Rather, the image of the hunting spider seems to belong to a discourse of victimization (see also Section 2.3 below). In I.iii.8–15, the only conversation in the *Memorabilia* that features Xenophon as a character, Socrates, mock-enraged with Critoboulus for kissing Alcibiades' pretty son, compares a kiss with "a bite of a poisonous spider, that renders the victim a slave to his passions."

hare-hunting: one type especially adapted to hunt them at night, another pack of hounds trained for tracking them by scent, and a third pack to catch them in pursuit. In case the prey still escapes (ἀποφεύγουσι), it will be driven into nets.[102] Now *this* is hunting as an art!

Of course, in this context, hunting is merely a metaphor. But metaphors are Trojan horses, and one of the implications shuffled into the conversation is that Theodote's occupation, her dealing with "friends", is an art, a τέχνη, a transferrable skill with a clear method and an identifiable object. As such, the dialogue with Theodote is a natural follow-up on Socrates' conversations with Parrhasius the painter, Cleiton the sculptor and Pistias the armorer[103]—a series of inquiries after the principles behind their respective τέχναι.

Moreover the hunting metaphor is one with a rich history in Greek erotic literature and for obvious reasons: it vividly captures the essence of erotic pursuit, in which the subject of seduction and courting (usually an *erastes*) is pictured as a hunter who pursues (διώκειν), and the object of courting (usually an *eromenos*) is imagined as quarry that flees (φεύγειν).[104] This hunting metaphor underscores the fundamental asymmetry in erotic pursuit:[105] seduction is imagined as involving an active party that takes the initiatives and a passive party that is expressly not supposed to initiate contact but that does have room to consent to advances or decline them.[106]

---

102 *Mem.* III.xi.7–9. The type of hunting described here, with night hunting and the use of nets and traps, is discussed in great detail by Xenophon in his *Cynegeticus*, including the type of dogs necessary for the different aspects of or phases in the hunt (III–IV), the equipment that should be used (VI.1), feeding and care (VI.2), breeding (VII.1–4), naming (VII.5) and training (VII.6–12). It should be noted that this type of hunting is introduced in the *Cynegeticus* as an individual type of hunting, where the hunter-landowner hunts for his own benefit and because of leisure; this type is discouraged and forbidden in Plato's *Laws*, who favors the civic form of hunting. L'Allier (2012), 494–495. For the implications, see Section 2.4 below. On the individualistic type of hunting, see also also Schnapp (1997), 56–63. On the aristocratic connotations of the activity of hunting, and its connection with aristocratic warfare (specifically ambush), Schnapp (1997), 156–159; cf. Barringer (2001), 10–69.

103 *Mem.* III.viii–x.

104 E.g. Pl. *Symp.* 184a–b, Sappho 1.21, Thgn. 1287–1294, 1299–1304, 1355; Anacreon 417, Pindarus fr. 127, Meleagros 116, Rhianos 5.1. Cf. Barringer (2001), 70–124; Schnapp (1997); Koch-Harnack (1983); Dover (1978), 84ff.; Hupperts (2000), 43, 119ff. The metaphor is also common in Socratic literature: e.g. Pl. *Prot.* 309a (Socrates pursuing Alcibiades), *Phdr.* 241, *Symp.* 182e.

105 Dover (1978), 84.

106 The passive party is expected to play out this freedom of response: as hunting is a sport, a challenging quarry raises the value of the capture, the hare being a notorious example for being swift and cunning—qualities that emphatically come to the fore in Socrates'

Of course, metaphors are dangerous, and Socrates has to make plain that there is a crucial difference between hunting lovers and hunting quarry: friends cannot be caught and kept with violence (βία) (for that would not be seduction!).[107] This too is a theme prominent in popular Attic culture: vase paintings of pederastic courtship depict subject and object of pursuit face to face, exchanging animal gifts, i.e. hunting game (frequently a hare),[108] evoking the metaphor of courting as hunting while at the same time redeeming the metaphor from its aggressive elements by incorporating it in a χάρις-economy. The object of courtship is "hunted" with gifts, i.e. "seduced", *not* coerced with violence.[109] One can refuse a gift ("flee") and choose not to reciprocate if one is not willing to enter into a relationship with the giver—entirely in the spirit of erotic χάρις.

But what about φιλία? Hunting a lover is metaphorical protocol, hunting a client seems feasible, but can we hunt for friends as well? Or does Socrates' hunting metaphor undermine Theodote's carefully cultivated self-presentation as an expert in φιλία, does Socrates tear down her verbal veil?

2.2 Mem. *II.vi: Hunting "Friends"*

The metaphor of *friend*-hunting, as distinct from erotic hunting, recurs elsewhere in Socratic literature, where the friendships involved invariably seem to have a sexual component to them.[110] Does this mean that in these contexts φιλία serves as a euphemism for erotic pursuit, or are the hunting methods discussed universally applicable to all types of φιλία-relationships *including* erotic ones?

φιλία or ἔρως—does the difference even matter? *Is* there a difference? This is a contested matter, placed on the philological agenda by the so-called Pohlenz-

---

description of the hare hunt. Cf. Dover (1978), 87. In the *Cynegeticus* (V.33), the mere sight of the hare and its flight is said to be so charming that it makes one forget the person one covets.

107 III.xi.11. Cf. *Mem.* II.vi.9ff. where for similar reasons even hare-hunting is dismissed as a method suited to catch friends.

108 Barringer (2001), 70ff.; Dover (1978), 92; Hupperts (2000), 119ff.

109 This image is made explicit in Plato's *Sophist* 222d where *erastai* are said to hunt their *eromenoi* using gifts as hunting weapons.

110 Pl. *Lys.* 206a, Xen. *Symp.* IV.63, Xen. *Cyr.* VIII.ii.2 (φιλίαν θηρεύειν). See Tamiolaki (2014) for a systematic comparison of the use of the hunting metaphor in Pl. *Lys.* and Xen. *Mem.* II.vi. Cf. Huss (1999), 315: "Das typische Motiv der Freundesjagd, das sexuell konnotiert sein kann oder nicht (…)." Xenophon's engagement with the topic of friend hunting probably depends on Aeschines of Sphettos' treatment of the issue. Gigon (1956), 156.

Von Arnim-controversy.[111] Triggered by a discussion on the relation between Plato's *Symposium* and *Lysis*, Pohlenz approached φιλία and ἔρως as kindred phenomena,[112] while to Von Arnim the two terms designated "two fundamentally different dispositions of the souls and relations between men": φιλία, according to Von Arnim, is "perfect friendship" free from desire and hence incompatible with ἔρως.[113] There is, of course, a world of positions conceivable between "kindred" and "incompatible": Grube, for instance, suggested a genus-species relation (with φιλία as genus, ἔρως as species),[114] Hyland a hierarchical relationship of φιλία—ἔρως—ἐπιθυμία, with increasing degrees of reason,[115] Dirlmeier a disposition—emotion distinction (with φιλία as disposition, ἕξις, and ἔρως as emotion or affect, πάθος).[116]

Roughly, it may be said that φιλία denotes a reciprocal relation and the internalized disposition that goes with it.[117] ἔρως is a unidirectional force, emanating from a subject of ἐρᾶν to its object, a force that *may* be reciprocated but does not need to be.[118] φιλία and ἔρως may coexist when two people, involved in a

---

111 See Bolotin (1979), 201–226 for a critical discussion of the Pohlenz-Von Arnim-controversy. Cf. Levin (1971).

112 Pohlenz (1916), 254: "weil der φιλία das Moment des Strebens und Begehrens immanent sei"; 59: "[D]ass er (sc. Plato) die φιλία vom ἔρως nicht ganz absondern will, dass auch ihr das Moment des Begehrens innewohnt, sagt er ausdrücklich 221b." cf. Pohlenz (1913).

113 Von Arnim (1914), 62: "Diese vollkommene (…) Freundschaft" and, referring to the same phenomenon "mit der reinen, von allem Begehren der Bedürftigkeit freien Liebe, die allein im höchsten und eigentlichsten Sinne φιλία gennant zu werden verdient." This applies primarily to the conception of φιλία in Plato's *Lysis*. Von Arnim is followed in this by Von Wilamowitz (1920), II, 68 who finds Plato's juxtaposition of φιλία and ἔρως misguided as according to him the two are "zwei grundverschiedene Verhältnisse".

114 Grube (1958), 92 n. 1. Grube's analysis applies only to the Pl. *Symp*. and *Lys*.

115 Hyland (1968). See Cummins (1981) for the fundamental objection against Hyland's methodology of expecting a rigid (or even technical) and stable use of vocabulary in Plato's dialogues.

116 Dirlmeier (1931), 58–71. On the fundamentally asymmetrical nature of the ἔρως lexical field, and on the way in which Xenophon's Socrates articulates a form of erotic mutuality as a spiritual mutual affection, see also Pentassuglio (2018), who rightly stresses that whereas Plato reforms the role of the ἐρώμενος, Xenophon transforms the role of the ἐραστής. Tamiolaki (2014) argues that in Xenophon, ἔρως does not play a central role in the discussion of friendship. On παιδικός ἔρως in Xenophon, see Chernyakhovskaya (014), 166–177 who nuances the traditional view that Xenophon objected against homoerotic love.

117 On the semantics of ΦΙΛ-terminology, see Chapter One.

118 Davidson (2007), 23; cf. Ludwig (2002), 1–24. Note that ἔρως does not specifically designate *sexual* desire. To be sure, ἔρως is all about desire and longing, about a subject of ἐρᾶν being oriented towards an object of ἔρως, but sexual aspects are not implied: it can be directed towards food, singing and dancing, to making love as well as war, to weeping. For specifically sexual desires and pleasures terms such as τὰ ἀφροδισία could be used. *Pace* Dover

long-term reciprocal bond (φιλία), find their desire (ἔρως) reciprocated. But in general, the bulk of social life is made of reciprocal bonds that go without desire and the bulk of love poetry is made of desire that is not reciprocated.

There is no reason to presume that the term φιλία precludes relationships with erotic motives and desires: one of the three types of friendship distinguished by Aristotle, the φιλία διὰ τὸ ἡδύ, clearly includes pederastic relationships (and presumably other erotic relations as well). Another illuminating case can be found in Plato's *Lysis*, the very origin of the semantic controversy.[119] Overtly a dialogue about φιλία, the very setting of the dialogue suggests an erotic subtext simmering with desire: Hippothales is staged as a suitor of young Lysis in competition with Socrates (the dialogue starts with a discussion between the two *erastai* about the strategies and etiquette involved in approaching the *erômenos*); moreover, near the end of his argumentation, Socrates establishes an explicit connection between φιλία, ἐπιθυμία and ἔρως: they all have the οἰκεῖον, that what is akin, as their object.[120] Nevertheless, the examples of φίλος, the dialogue's central term, move smoothly "pals" (Lysis and Menexenos) and "would-be lovers" (Hippothales desiring Lysis) to "parents and children",[121] presuming a continuity between different manifestations of φιλία that would be precluded by a purely euphemistic reading.[122] Even if the immediate pretext for the conversation is an interest in erotic seduction, Plato's *Lysis* really *is* about φιλία—not as a euphemism for or a domestication of a raunchy topic, but as a more abstract and fundamental denominator of the topic at interest. The preconditions for such discursive shifts inhere in the semantics of φιλία:[123] neither the noun φιλία nor φίλος dictates a specific relationship *type* nor the presence of specific emotions (although φιλία-bonds may be perfectly compatible with sentiments of love and attachment); φιλία merely

(1989), 49–50, who defines ἔρως as "strong sexual desire" in contexts of *contrast with* φιλία. Cf. Ludwig (2002), 7–8, also on "a tendency of recent scholarship (…) to reduce the meaning of *eros* in all instances to sexual desire."

119 On this episode, see Hindley (2010 [1999]); Tamiolaki (2014) for a systematic comparison of the treatment of φιλία in Pl. *Lys.* and Xen. *Mem.* II.vi.; Dorion (2011: 193) for an argument against assuming a direct dependency of *Mem.* II.vi. from *Lysis.*

120 Pl. *Lys.* 221e. Cf. Tamiolaki (2014), 3§7.

121 Moreover, parts of the argumentation about the proper object of φιλία in the *Lysis* resemble argumentation about the proper object of ἔρως in the *Symposium*. This has instigated the Pohlenz-Von Arnim-controversy. See n. 112 and n. 113 above.

122 In the *Lysis*, Plato moves smoothly from φίλος as a social category to internalized φιλεῖν and back, and from personal φίλος to impersonal φίλον, displaying an interest in an abstraction from and generalization of the interpersonal. Tamiolaki (2014).

123 Chapter One Section 2.

characterizes a particular aspect of relationships,[124] i.e. its long-term reciprocal dimension, be it within the family, in business, politics or in erotics.

A similar discursive phenomenon occurs in *Mem.* II.vi where we find the metaphor of hunting applied to friends. The conversation between Socrates and young Critoboulus, well embedded in a series of conversations about φιλία, revolves around the selection and acquisition of φίλοι. Especially from II.vi.30 onwards, the reader is led to suspect that Critoboulus may have a very particular "friend with benefits" in mind, a boy he wishes to seduce to become his ἐρώμενος/παιδικά: there is talk of finding friends "good in soul and beautiful in body",[125] of "not applying one's hands on prospective friends"[126] (but, instead, acquiring them in the right way), of "applying one's lips to theirs".[127] As a matter of fact, Socrates may have been responsible for steering the conversation into this direction: in vi.21, Socrates kicks off a lengthy discussion of restraint, moderation and moral goodness in general by reflecting on τὰ φιλικά (dispositions or marks of φιλία)—a neologism coined in parallel with τὰ πολεμικά (II.vi.1: directly contrasted to τὰ φιλικά), τὰ θηρατικά (II.vi.33) and its implicit Platonic subtext τὰ ἐρωτικά.[128] It is plausible, as Melina Tamiolaki suggests, that Xenophon coined the phrase to mark a contrast with the Platonic τὰ ἐρωτικά;[129] but it is also important to bear in mind that the new phrase, while replacing its counterpart τὰ ἐρωτικά, simultaneously *evokes* the very term it intends to replace. Is Socrates being a euphemistizing tease here, using *double entendre* to provoke Critoboulus, or does he use euphemism to teach young Critoboulus a veiled lesson? Or is Socrates genuinely committed to generalize the topic of his discussion to a concept that encompasses *all* kinds of reciprocal relations? Generalizations can be used both as euphemizing abstractions ("I have *needs*") and as philosophical move—to keep open both interpretative possibilities seems to be a characteristic of Xenophon's Socrates. The tension becomes even more amplified at the end of Socrates' speech, where the focus shifts to Critoboulus' concrete issues:

---

124 Here I disagree with the semantic thesis of Konstan (1997), 53ff., who claims that the noun φίλος denotes a distinct social category, analogous to our "friend". See Introduction Section 2.

125 II.vi.30: ἐπὶ τοὺς ἀγαθοὺς τὰς ψυχὰς καὶ ἐπὶ τοὺς καλοὺς τὰ σώματα.

126 II.vi.32: οὐ προσοίσοντος τὰς χεῖρας.

127 II.vi.32: τὸ στόμα πρὸς στόμα προσοίσεις.

128 E.g. Pl. *Symp.* 198d1, 201d8, 209e6.

129 Tamiolaki (2014), 2§10: "It seems then that for Xenophon, *philia* is treated conventionally, like ... 'business as usual.'"

[Text 12]

> ἀλλὰ θαρρῶν, ἔφη, ὦ Κριτόβουλε, πειρῶ ἀγαθὸς γίγνεσθαι, καὶ τοιοῦτος γενόμενος θηρᾶν ἐπιχείρει τοὺς καλούς τε κἀγαθούς. ἴσως δ' ἄν τί σοι κἀγὼ συλλαβεῖν εἰς τὴν τῶν καλῶν τε κἀγαθῶν θήραν ἔχοιμι διὰ τὸ ἐρωτικὸς εἶναι· δεινῶς γάρ, ὧν ἂν ἐπιθυμήσω ἀνθρώπων, ὅλος ὥρμημαι ἐπὶ τὸ φιλῶν τε αὐτοὺς ἀντιφιλεῖσθαι ὑπ' αὐτῶν καὶ ποθῶν ἀντιποθεῖσθαι, καὶ ἐπιθυμῶν|$_{29}$ συνεῖναι καὶ ἀντεπιθυμεῖσθαι τῆς συνουσίας. ὁρῶ δὲ καὶ σοὶ τούτων δεῆσον, ὅταν ἐπιθυμήσῃς φιλίαν πρός τινας ποιεῖσθαι· μὴ οὖν ἀποκρύπτου με οἷς ἂν βούλῃ φίλος γενέσθαι· διὰ γὰρ τὸ ἐπιμελεῖσθαι τοῦ ἀρέσαι τῷ ἀρέσκοντί |$_{30}$ μοι οὐκ ἀπείρως οἶμαι ἔχειν πρὸς θήραν ἀνθρώπων.

> "Don't lose heart, Critobulus, but try to make yourself a good man, and when you have succeeded, *you can set about hunting for truly good people*. Perhaps even I myself might be able to lend you a hand in the search *on account of my experience in erôs*. When I *take a fancy to* anyone, it's extraordinary how completely I throw myself *into getting them to reciprocate my friendship, passion or craving for their society, as the case may be*. I can see that you will feel the same need *when you set your heart on making friends with people*. Well, don't keep me in the dark about your aspirations; thanks to my efforts to please those who please me, I think I'm not without experience *in capturing people*."[130]

The topic of the hunt is resumed: Socrates offers assistance in "the hunt for the noble gentlemen (εἰς τὴν τῶν καλῶν τε κἀγαθῶν θήραν)"[131] on account of his being an "expert in erotics" (διὰ τὸ ἐρωτικὸς εἶναι).[132] This expertise is explained (γάρ) in terms that stretch the possibilities of ambiguity and *double entendre*: there is talk of Socrates having desires for (ἐπιθυμήσω) persons, of his straining his every nerve to have his friendship (φιλῶν), his longing (ποθῶν) and his desire *for their company* (ἐπιθυμῶν συνεῖναι) reciprocated (ἀντιφιλεῖσθαι ὑπ' αὐτῶν, ἀντιποθεῖσθαι, ἀντεπιθυμεῖσθαι τῆς συνουσίας), of his observing in Critoboulus too a desire *for friendship* (ἐπιθυμήσῃς φιλίαν). The entire semantic field of erotics,

---

130 *Mem.* II.vi.28–29.

131 The term *kalokagathai* has aristocratic connotations. See Chapter Five. Cf. Bourriot (1995), Bevilacqua (2010), 187–196. Tamiolaki (2014) explores the political implications of Socratic theories of φιλία in both Pl. *Lys.* and Xen. *Mem.*

132 According to Tamiolaki (2014) this is an element of irony in this self-description at the expense of Critoboulos. "The irony undermines rather than enhances Socrates' erotic activity and opinions about love affairs."?

desire, longing and craving is activated and defused at the same time: Socrates manages to simultaneously evoke the possibility of a narrow erotic interpretation in which the conversation revolves around the hunt for a lover, *and*, by systematically qualifying the verb ἐπιθυμέω with a direct object, to make sure that the conversation can still be understood as one on the topic of φιλία[133]—the general theme of his preceding speech *and* of the preceding chapters of *Memorabilia* Book II.[134]

The point is that Socrates and Critoboulus are not playing the same game. Although *both* may be indulging in euphemistic speech, it is different sorts of euphemizing they are after.[135] To Critoboulus, the terms φιλία and φίλος may function as a thin cover, a vague denominator, for more overtly erotic vocabulary—perhaps as a face-saving device to alleviate some of the connotations of ἔρως (one-sided, aggressive, invasive unsettling, symptomatic for a lack of self-control),[136] or rather as part of the sort of cultivated innuendo and allusiveness that make up the charm and witty intimacy of a symposiastic setting.[137] In terms of Cognitive Theory of Metaphor, it is only the tar-

---

133 Even when the direct object is itself deliberately ambiguous, such as συνουσία. Cf. Chapter Five Section 1.2.

134 In terms of the Cognitive Theory of Metaphor (applied by Crespo Fernández (2008) to euphemisms as well, see n. 27 below), Socrates is making use of the potential of *bidirectionality* of euphemisms and metaphors. Crespo Fernández (2008), 101: "[U]sing metaphors with a lexicalized sexual meaning in discourse does not only involve a projection from the source domain onto the target domain, since the target domain may also be projected onto the source domain. As in *come*, the tabooed conceptual traits have progressively become an integral part in the reference of the word, the sexual taboo will be activated, either consciously or not, in the interpretation of the term."

135 Crespo Fernández (2008), 100, on comparable "asymmetric" metaphors or euphemisms, where the hearer is made to interpret a word metaphorically whereas the speaker has no (ostensive) metaphorical intention.

136 Davidson (2007), 23ff.; Faraone (1999) 29 and 29 n. 121.

137 Although II.vi seems to take place in a spatial vacuum (there are no indications as to where we should imagine that this conversation is taking place), its tone and thematics seems to evoke the aristocratic symposium. On the interpretative intimacy required and presupposed by euphemizing speech see Crespo Fernández (2008), 105. Henderson (1991) explains the workings of sexual euphemism in Old Comedy as "block[ing] the emotional force of the reference and mak[ing] it impossible for the mind to focus on anything but vague impressions." (54–55). This is an underappreciation of the comic force of sexual euphemisms that tend to be funny because of their potential to turn into dysphemisms: once the euphemisms are lexicalized the audience *knows exactly* what is being referred to. Cf. Crespo Fernández (2008: 98) and Chamizo Domiguez & Sánchez Benedito (2000: 68–70) for a distinction of three types of euphemisms according to their degree of lexicalization: (1) lexicalized, when the figurative meaning (target) is regarded as the normal or literal meaning (source); (2) semi-lexicalized, when the substitute (source) is associ-

get domain (ἔρως, "the *real* topic") that matters.[138] To Socrates, both source and target domain matter, because the target domain (erotic encounters) is nothing but a specific subcategory of the source domain (reciprocity). That is, Socrates deliberately leaves open the option of taking the φιλία vocabulary at face value, inquiring the implications and propounding guidelines that pertain to examples in the field of politics as well as business. Socrates is concerned with universally applicable rules of conduct that go for all kinds of φιλία-relationships, including those with an erotic interest without being confined to them. These universally applicable rules of φιλία are elaborated on in vi.22–27 revolve around ἐγκράτεια, self-restraint and the control over short-term appetites.[139] The universal rule that goes for the *hunt* on friends is mentioned at the beginning of T12: it is only by becoming ἀγαθός oneself that one can hunt for the καλοί κἀγαθοί.

Similarly, in the case of Theodote's friend-hunt, Theodote's use of φιλία-terminology may very well be euphemistic like her use of χάρις-vocabulary, so central to her self-fashioning as a hetaera: Theodote wants us to regard her contacts with her "visitors" as relationships with φίλοι, partners in long-term reciprocal relationships with whom she exchanges favors, including sexual ones, on a voluntary basis. But to Socrates there are no euphemisms, no pleasant names for underlying realities that turn out to be different;[140] if Theodote's chooses to name her visitors φίλοι, then that is what they *are*, not only what they are named. Hence, in the rest of the dialogue we see Socrates playing along the language game while at the same time challenging this conceptualization of Theodote's contacts in terms of φιλία, by testing the applicability of the terminology on the situation.

Understanding Socrates' choice of words as mere euphemisms would be missing the point: this is a dialogue that investigates the nature of reciprocity, of φιλία, not of unilateral ἔρως. Rather, it is Theodote's use of euphemisms that

---

ated with the taboo (target); (3) creative, when there is a novel mapping of a euphemistic phrasing (source) and the taboo referred to (target)—this is a mapping that is only accessible in its phraseological context.

138 Within the Cognitive Theory of Metaphor, metaphors are understood as cognitive, or conceptual, tools: one conceptual domain (the source domain, from which we draw metaphorical expressions) is mapped onto a target domain (the conceptual domain that is the *explanandum*). Through mapping, we come to an understanding of the target domain *in terms of* and *with the structure of* the source domain. The locus classicus is Lakoff & Johnson (1980). See Crespo Fernández (2008) for the application of Cognitive Theory of Metaphor on euphemism.

139 Hindley (2010 [1999]), 90–91: "The point is, once again, self-restraint, not abstinence."

140 Cf. Chapter Two, Section 1.

allows Socrates to "misrecognize" what she is actually talking about and to instigate a conversation about reciprocity.

2.3 *Who is Hunting Whom?*

The hunt is open, the games have begun. Still, there remains one thing to be explained: Theodote is the hunter, not the hare. Socrates' remarkable choice of the spider as the first image of the hunter has facilitated the surprising analogy in which Theodote is the hunter instead of the passive object of seduction.

This too has an analogue in popular conceptions: lovers often fashion themselves as victims of their whimsical objects of desire. They emphasize how they choose to "enslave themselves" to their boyfriends or how their boy-lovers exert erotic power over them[141]—a pre-emptive pose that counters any charge that the lover abuses his superior position and that moreover protects the boys from the charge of slavish surrender.[142] Often this paradoxical use of the hunting metaphor figures the victim "caught by the nets of desire"[143]—which reminds us of the opening of the dialogue where Socrates analyzes Theodote's ἐπίδειξις as more profitable to her than to the spectator, because her sight has the power to arouse ἐπιθυμία and πόθος in the spectator.

The metaphor of chasing game into hunting-nets (δίκτυα) pictures those who are supposed to be the subject of seduction, Theodote's "friends", themselves as prey hunted down by desire or love. With hindsight, this sheds lights on Socrates' remarkable choice for the spider as an image of the hunter: the image expresses the crippling and entangling effect of attraction on the topic of desire.[144] Both images belong in the victimizing discourse of the suffering

141 The most notorious example is the Cydias fragment quoted in Pl. *Charm.* 155d–e in a context that suggests a similar role reversal: Charmides is the predator, Socrates the prey. For the motif of victimization, cf. Pausanias in Pl. *Symp.* 183a, Xen. *Mem.* I.ii.11; the pederastic poems in "Theognis" Book II, e.g. lines 1235–1238, 1305–1310, 1337–1340, 1341–1350, 1357–1360. Fisher (2001), 45; Golden (1984) and (1990), 58–59. This counterdiscourse of victimization is not the dominant theme in Attic visual and literary culture; as such, it has escaped notice of Koch-Harnack (1983), Dover (1978) and Huss (1999). It does nonetheless have precedents, most notably in Plato's *Charmides*, but also in visual culture. See Barringer (2001), 70ff.

142 Fisher (2001), 45. The commonplace of the thankless boy in Greek elegy reflects precisely the fact that an object of seduction is supposed to be free to decline and that the boy has a possibility of *not* returning the favors of his seducer at the price of having a reputation of thanklessness. See Davidson (2007), 38ff.

143 E.g. Ibycus fr. 2, Soph. *fr.* 932. Moreover, the image of *erôtes* as archers reflects the idea of pretty boys that "wound" their senior lovers. Cf. Goldhill (1998), 117 n. 34.

144 In *Mem.* I.iii.8–15 (the only conversation in the *Mem.* that features Xenophon as a character), Socrates, mock-enraged with Critoboulus for kissing Alcibiades' pretty son, compares

lover, but Socrates' framing of the spider as a hunter gives an initial impetus to the role reversal that puts Theodote in the role of active hunter.[145]

In making Theodote the hunter, Socrates is testing the integrity of her language. He endows her with the very agency implied by the autonomy that she herself claimed by using the vocabulary of long-term relationships, the terminology of χάρις, φιλία and εὖ ποιεῖν—a vocabulary that is somewhat at odds with other aspects of her self-presentation: her position as object of the gaze as well as her role as object of πείθειν. This traditional and passive position is compromised by Socrates' re-interpretation of the situation and his paradoxical use of the hunting metaphor.

2.4 *The Hunting Sophist: A Didactic Turn*

So what exactly is Theodote's hunt *for*? What is it about? At the end of the dialogue, Theodote suggests that she is ready to visit Socrates instead of the other way around and Socrates has succeeded in reversing the roles: he has emerged as the "strange object of desire by demonstrating his mastery over the position of the desiring subject."[146] But what was at stake in the first place?

Let us briefly go back to the beginning of the episode where Theodote is introduced to Socrates by an informant who claims that her beauty is "beyond description" (κρεῖττον λόγου) (xi.1).[147] To someone like Socrates the suggestion that Theodote's κάλλος "beats λόγος", beats reason, is, of course, an outright provocation and a philosophical challenge.[148] The dialogue is staged as a battle between beauty and λόγος, celebrating the supremacy of philosophical dialectics over physical beauty.[149]

---

a kiss with a bite of a poisonous tarantula, that renders the victim a slave to his maddening passions. On this passage see Pangle (2018), 60 ff.

145 In applying the hunting metaphor on Theodote's situation, Socrates possibly cashes in on a tendency in the ancient Greek world to represent courtesans along the same lines as a male *erastes*. Not only do courtesans possess an economic autonomy that comes very close to that of the typical Athenian male, in New Comedy they are also frequently represented as aggressively hunting out their lovers—an easy target of ridicule, of course, for little could be so degrading as courtesans past their prime being forced to desperately chase "seducers". Fantham (1986), 47–48; Faraone (1999), 156 ff.

146 Goldhill (1998), 121–122.

147 Pangle (2018) points out that the expression "beating λόγος" applies to the ugly as well as to the beautiful (n. 91): Thucydides (2.50) uses the expression for describing the plague.

148 Cf. the sophistic catch phrase: ποιεῖν τὸν ἥττω λόγον κρείττω. E.g. DK 80a21 (Ar. *Rhet.* II.xxiv (1402a13–28)) Cf. Narcy (2004), 215. There is more at stake than "the classic problem of ecphrasis and beauty": how can what is greater than *logos* be described adequately. Goldhill (1998), 114.

149 The fact that Socrates repeats the expression (III.xi.1: οὐ γὰρ δὴ ἀκούσασί γε τὸ λόγου

Moreover, Theodote's posing for her admirers is an ἐπίδειξις, a demonstration—the buzz-word appropriated by the sophists for their art/knack of rhetorical display, rhetorical demonstration.[150] The emphatic, and rather laborious, re-evaluation of Theodote's ἐπίδειξις in terms of "benefit" (ὠφελιμωτέρα, ὠφελήσεται) harks back to Xenophon's recurrent claim that the city in general and Socrates' direct companions in particular have benefited (ὠφελεῖσθαι) from Socrates' company,[151] in contrast to sophistic demonstration that (it seems to be implied) benefits the sophist more than the pupil.

When Theodote asks Socrates how to apply the methods of hare-hunting to the enterprise of acquiring friends, Socrates suggests that the hunting dogs be substituted by "someone who will track and find rich men with good taste (τοὺς φιλοκάλους καὶ πλουσίους)". This evokes an alternative use of the image of the "man-hunter". The sophist. The hunter is not only a popular image of the

---

κρεῖττον ἔστι καταμαθεῖν) points out that it is this challenge to λόγος that triggers his fascination—as Chernyakhovskaya (2014: 183) points out. For similar readings of the phrase κρεῖττον λόγου, see Azoulay (2004a: 372–375), Danzig (2010: 173) "Translating overly literally, this expression implies that the power of her beauty is greater than her power of reason", O'Connor (2011: 61), Narcy (2004: 215), and Gray (1998), 145: "The point of Socrates' analysis of her attractions is of course that they are after all not beyond speech." According to Narcy (2004), 221 this reflects a competition between Socrates and Theodote over Alcibiades. An alternative interpretation is to take Socrates as a caricature of Theodote, as Pangle (2018) proposes.

150 For the sophistic appropriation of rhetorical ἐπίδειξις as their trademark specialty, see Pl. *Euthyd.* 274a10–b1, Pl. *Hipp.Mj.* 282c6–d5; cf. Pernot (2015), 12. However, the sophists do not have a monopoly on ἐπίδειξις, as some of the Hippocratic treatises (which may or may not have belonged to the same intellectual milieu as the sophists) also qualify as such. See Demont 1993, Jouanna 1984, Thomas (2000). An obvious example of sophistic epideixis within Xenophon's oeuvre would be The Heracles Parable in *Mem.* II.i.21 ff., introduced with the verb ἐπιδείκνυται. It should be noted that it is particularly the middle voice vorms (ἐπιδείκνυσθαι) that are used to denote the typical oratorical exhibition or show-off, whereas the verb forms used to describe Theodote's activity are in the active voice (xi.1: ἐπιδευκνύειν, xi.2: ἐπέδειξεν). Nevertheless, the allusive connection between Theodote's display and the sophists' exhibitionism is suggested by the abstract noun ἡ ἐπίδειξις (xi.2). Cf. Thomas (2000), 202.

151 E.g. *Mem.* I.i.4, I.ii.2, I.ii.60–61, I.vii.5, II.iv.1, II.v.1, II.vi.1, II.vii.1, III.i.1, III.vi.1, III.viii.1, III.x.1, IV.i.1, IV.iv.1, IV.vii.1. In *Mem.* I.iii.1, after the first two chapters that constitute a more explicit defense of Socrates, Xenophon opens the rest of his *Memorabilia* with a clear mission statement: Ὡς δὲ δὴ καὶ ὠφελεῖν ἐδόκει μοι τοὺς συνόντας τὰ μὲν ἔργῳ δεικνύων ἑαυτὸν οἷος ἦν, τὰ δὲ καὶ διαλεγόμενος, τούτων δὴ γράψω ὁπόσα ἂν διαμνημονεύσω. ("I said above that in my opinion he actually benefited his associates, partly by practical example and partly by his conversation. I shall record as many instances as I can recall."). *See also*: Dorion (2006), Nehamas (1998), 110–111, Tamiolaki (2014), Humble (2018), 592–594.

lover, the ἐραστής, chasing his beloved, but also a stock-image of the sophist, the man-hunter, in search of new pupils from whom to extort massive fees.[152]

A well-known example we find in Plato's *Sophist* where the Eleatic Stranger and Theaetetus attempt to "hunt down", i.e. to define, the elusive nature of the sophist (222d–223a). One of the candidate definitions is the sophist as a man-hunter: within the class of "the hunt on private persons", there is the subdivision called ἐρωτικὴ τέχνη, the afore-mentioned branch of hunting-by-gift-giving (δωροφορικόν). The sophist, on the other hand, is characterized as the class of "hunt on private persons" that involves pay (μισθός) in cash (νόμισμα)—the branch of hunt labeled μισθαρνητικόν, "involving pay". Note that on closer look, the underlying exchange patterns are different for the gift-giving man-hunt and its fee-taking counterpart: within the art of erotics, it is the hunter, the active lover, who hunts *with* gifts; by contrast, the sophists hunt young men *for the sake of* pay. Lovers are givers, sophists are takers. Both erotics and sophistry are classified as types of man-hunting, but they are demarcated from one another by the same ideological dividing line that distinguishes the world of χάρις, gift-giving and seduction from the sordid world of commerce and coercion. The two worlds both dictate their own distinct ethics of reciprocity and norms of exchange.

The same dividing line recurs in the closing chapter of Xenophon's *Cynegeticus*:[153]

---

152 Delatte (1933), 160–161. In Pl. *Symp.* 203d ἔρως is imagined as a hunter (θηρευτής) and philosopher. For the notoriously exorbitant high fees charged by sophists see Blank (1985).

153 On this last chapter, and Xenophon's "defensive attack on the sophists" (Hobden & Tuplin 2012: 12), where "the writer, in his most rhetorical passage, says in effect that he despises rhetoric as practiced in his days" (Marchant 1968: XLI), see L'Allier (2012), esp. 477: "The violence of Xenophon's words against the sophists can be explained by the fact that the work could itself easily be labelled as sophistic", 486: "From Xenophon's point of view, *Cynegeticus* is a philosophical text with a sophistical structure." There is a marked difference in tone between this passage from the *Cynegeticus*, voiced by the persona of Xenophon, and the *Memorabilia* where we hear the character Socrates speak. Xenophon is unambiguously wholesale in his dismissal of the sophists as educators, denying them any σοφία whatsoever; Xenophon's Socrates, by contrast, criticizes the sophists for their commercialism but does nonetheless acknowledge that they do possess σοφία. Cf. Dorion (2012), 462 n. 14. Moreover, the term φιλοσοφία, used quite blandly by Xenophon's Socrates, acquires a more explicit and emphatic positive appraisal as well as a more thoroughly theorized status in the *Cynegeticus*. L'Allier (2012), 486. It should be noted that Xenophon's invective in the *Cynegeticus* is directed at the sophists of his own day, not to those from the generation that Socrates interacted with, such as Prodicus and Antiphon. Cf. Hobden & Tuplin (2012), 12.

[Text 13]

οἱ σοφισταὶ δ' ἐπὶ τῷ ἐξαπατᾶν λέγουσι καὶ γράφουσιν ἐπὶ τῷ ἑαυτῶν **κέρδει**, καὶ οὐδένα οὐδὲν **ὠφελοῦσιν**· οὐδὲ γὰρ σοφὸς αὐτῶν ἐγένετο οὐδεὶς οὐδ' ἔστιν, ἀλλὰ καὶ ἀρκεῖ ἑκάστῳ σοφιστὴν κληθῆναι, ὅ ἐστιν ὄνειδος παρά γε εὖ φρονοῦσι. τὰ μὲν οὖν τῶν σοφιστῶν παραγγέλματα παραινῶ φυλάττεσθαι, τὰ δὲ τῶν φιλοσόφων ἐνθυμήματα μὴ ἀτιμάζειν· οἱ μὲν γὰρ σοφισταὶ **πλουσίους καὶ νέους θηρῶνται, οἱ δὲ φιλόσοφοι πᾶσι κοινοὶ καὶ φίλοι**· τύχας δὲ ἀνδρῶν οὔτε τιμῶσιν οὔτε ἀτιμάζουσι.

The Sophists speak and write to deceive people for their own *profit* and *do* nothing *useful* for anyone; for none of them ever was or is wise, but it is enough for each of them to be called a Sophist, which is a term of abuse among well-thinking persons. Accordingly I advise my readers to be on their guard against the precepts of the Sophists, but not to scorn the arguments of the philosophers; for the Sophists *hunt rich young men, while the philosophers are available and amiable to everyone*; they neither value nor despise men's fortunes.[154]

The sophist is depicted as hunting rich young men, operating in a commercial sphere of high fees and deception (ἐξαπατᾶν), and with self-interest, not the willingness to be beneficial, as motivation (ἐπὶ τῳ ἑαυτῶν κέρδει), a sphere strictly demarcated from the gentle world of the philosophers, who make themselves available and beneficial to everyone and who operate on the basis of long-term φιλία ties. The motivation behind the "hunt" is crucial: a few paragraphs further on (*Cyn.* XIII.12), the contrast shifts to one between the zero-sum practice of "friend-hunt", driven by self-interest (φιλοκερδεία) and at the expense of the friend (ἐπ' ἀνδρὸς βλάβῃ), and the hunt for wild animals that contributes to the common good.[155] As we have seen in Socrates' debate with

154 *Cyn.* XIII.8–9; *transl.* Phillips & Willcock (1999).

155 In *Mem.* II.vi, a more positive image of friend-hunting emerges: Socrates makes an effort to adjust the hunting metaphor, originating from the more violent and invasive sphere of ἔρως, to the benign sphere of φιλία, which by its very nature is incompatible with violence (βία) and deceit (ἀπάτη). In *Cyn.* Xenophon is facing other difficulties. Here he attempts to promote the individualistic hunter as an ideal citizen. This requires a reform of traditional "civic" hunting ideology that privileges the aristocratic group hunt and an argument that the individual hunter too can be useful to the city (*Cyn.* XII). This also presumes a less tight relation between the individual hunter and the sophist then the one forged by Plato in his *Sophist*. Hence, to Xenophon, the intention to be beneficial to the city and to fellow-

Antiphon the sophist,[156] the opposition between sophist and philosopher is organized along the same lines as the opposition between the zero-sum world of commerce and the world of χάρις—the same ideological opposition that holds between the occupation of the prostitute and the art of the courtesan.

When we compare the Antiphon-debate with the Theodote-episode, Socrates emerges as a practitioner of an art that poses identity problems to him that are very similar to Theodote's: how to demarcate his activities from seemingly isomorphous sophistic education. The discursive strategy Socrates chooses resembles the courtesan's: to appropriate the vocabulary of long-term relationships and claim that his activities are embedded in a different type of relationship than the practice of his near-siblings, in a way that does not contradict the subject matter. For, as Socrates elsewhere suggests, there is a tension between being a teacher in virtue and charging fees,[157] very similar to the conceptual contradiction between being seductive and accepting pay.

But there are differences. Theodote is a friend-hunter who, at the beginning of the dialogue, turns out to extract benefit herself from ἐπίδειξις rather than benefiting her friends. Socrates is invited to become her co-hunter (συνθηρατής) of friends[158]—a metaphorical matchmaker or procurer, as he elsewhere boasts to be. In Xenophon's *Symposium* for instance, he acts as a matchmaker for Hermogenes and Callias,[159] and his success in flattering Callias is applauded by Hermogenes:

[Text 14]

> καὶ ὁ Ἑρμογένης εἶπε· Νὴ τὴν Ἥραν, ἔφη, ὦ Σώκρατες, ἄλλα τέ σου πολλὰ ἄγαμαι καὶ ὅτι νῦν ἅμα χαριζόμενος Καλλίᾳ καὶ παιδεύεις αὐτὸν οἷόνπερ χρὴ εἶναι.
>
> 'I swear, Socrates,' said Hermogenes, 'the thing I admire most in you—and there are many others—is that, at the same time as *paying* Callias *a compliment*, you *instruct* him in how he ought to behave.'[160]

citizens becomes a leading characteristic of the Good Individualistic Hunter—and of the philosopher. L'Allier (2012), 494–495.

156 See Chapter Five.

157 E.g. I.ii.5–7. See Chapter Five Section 4.

158 III.xi.15: καὶ ἡ Θεοδότη, Τί οὖν οὐ σύ μοι, ἔφη, ὦ Σώκρατες, ἐγένου συνθηρατὴς τῶν φίλων; ("Theodote said, "Why don't you help me in my hunt for friends, Socrates?"").

159 *Symp.* III.10, IV.56–64.

160 *Symp.* VIII.12.

Here, quite exceptionally, the verb χαρίζεσθαι is used with reference not to the *erômenos*, but to the third party, the matchmaker Socrates, who not only gratifies the *erastes*' desire for the boy[161] as well as the boy's desire for compliments,[162] but also attains a didactic goal (παιδεύεις).[163]

Contrary to Theodote, Socrates does live up to the vocabulary of φιλία and χάρις, as his philosophical education[164] does not take the shape of sophistic ἐπίδειξις, the ostentatious demonstration of rhetorical skill that makes one wonder who is doing a favor to whom. He is not the hunter profiting from his prey, but the co-hunter who may be capable of helping the hunter Theodote realize her true goals.

3 Desire Management

3.1 *Beneath the Veil of Words*

So how *does* friend hunting exactly work? Socrates' suggestion remains in the realm of metaphor: obviously Theodote needs a human hound to track down men of wealth and good taste and drive them into her nets (τὰ σὰ δίκτυα),[165] the close-enfolding nets of her body (εὖ περιπλεκόμενον, τὸ σῶμα) and her soul inside:

[Text 15]

> Ἔν μὲν δήπου, ἔφη, καὶ μάλα εὖ περιπλεκόμενον, τὸ σῶμα· ἐν δὲ τούτῳ ψυχήν, ᾗ καταμανθάνεις καὶ ὡς ἂν ἐμβλέπουσα χαρίζοιο καὶ ὅ τι ἂν λέγουσα εὐφραίνοις, καὶ ὅτι δεῖ τὸν μὲν ἐπιμελόμενον ἀσμένως ὑποδέχεσθαι, τὸν δὲ τρυφῶντα ἀποκλείειν, καὶ ἀρρωστήσαντός γε φίλου φροντιστικῶς ἐπισκέψασθαι καὶ καλόν τι πράξαντος σφόδρα συνησθῆναι καὶ τῷ σφόδρα σοῦ φροντίζοντι ὅλῃ τῇ ψυχῇ κεχαρίσθαι· φιλεῖν γε μὴν εὖ οἶδ' ὅτι ἐπίστασαι οὐ μόνον μαλακῶς, ἀλλὰ καὶ εὐνοϊκῶς· καὶ ὅτι ἀρεστοί σοί εἰσιν οἱ φίλοι, οἶδ' ὅτι οὐ λόγῳ ἀλλ' ἔργῳ ἀναπείθεις.

161 Thomsen (2002), 155 ff.

162 Huss (1999), 376–377.

163 For Socrates as a διδάσκαλος, cf. Xen. *Mem.* III.viii.8, IV.1, IV.ii.1, IV.vii.2, *Ap.* XX f.

164 Tamiolaki (2014), 3§17 on Xenophon's Socrates as the master of friendship (as opposed to his Platonic counterpart who disavows any expertise).

165 *Mem.* III.xi.9.

> 'One, certainly,' said Socrates, 'which is *very close-enfolding*: your body. And in it is your mind, which teaches you *how to look charming* and talk gaily, and tells you that you must give a warm welcome to an attentive lover, but bolt the door against a selfish one; that, if a *lover* falls ill, you must look after him *devotedly*; that, if he has a stroke of luck, you must share his pleasure enthusiastically; and that, if he *cares* for you deeply, you must be gratifying to him wholeheartedly. As for *loving*, I am sure that you know how to love not only *passively*, but *with real affection*; and you *convince* your *lovers* that *you are fond of them*, I know, *not by words but by deeds*.'[166]

It is easy to get the dialectics of body (τὸ σῶμα) and soul (ἡ ψυχή) described here wrong: the passage reads as an unproblematic adherence to a body-soul dualism, contrasting love of body and love of ψυχή, and therefore propagating a sublimation of ἔρως from the realm of the body to the soul.[167] However, as Clifford Hindley points out, Xenophon's Socrates wields a light and functional notion of the "soul": "The ψυχή is that which orders a person's life as a whole, and it may cover both the directing mind and the personality which results."[168] Hence, the point is not that the ψυχή should redirect Theodote's hunt; rather it actively supports and facilitates the hunt. The transition evoked in the passage is not from the physical to the spiritual, but from short-term attraction instigated by physical beauty alone to long-term commitment grounded in behavior, no sublimation but complementation:[169] if Theodote *really* aspires to capture friends, she not only needs to be selective, but she has to be told by her soul how to really gratify (χαρίζεσθαι)—i.e. what *real* χάρις is. As χάρις and φιλία are reciprocal endeavors, here we see it is *Theodote* who is told to look (ἐμβλέπουσα, presumably "looking in the face", "with eye-contact") while gratifying a friend—another indication that the roles are being reversed.[170] Moreover, *real* χάρις entails the display of a range of emotions and dispositions: to be cheerful (εὐφραίνοις) when talking, to be well-pleased (ἀσμένως) when welcom-

166 *Mem.* III.xi.10; *transl. adapted.*

167 On the history of the notion "love of ψυχή" and its relation to Socratic thought, see Guthrie (1971: 147–164).

168 Hindley (2010 [1999]), 88.

169 Cf. Hindley (2010 [1999]), 88 on *Mem.* IV.i.12: "When Sokrates is said to "love the soul", what he loves are not insubstantial wraiths, but "people whose minds dispose them to virtue.""

170 Already noted by Goldhill (1998), 118. A socially correct object of the gaze is not supposed to return the look, but to modestly casts his or her eyes down (which reinforces his/her status as object). Cf. Gilhuly (2009), 1–5 ff. on the symposiasts gazing at Autolycus in Xen. *Symp.* I.8–10.

ing a respectful lover, to look after an ill friend thoughtfully (φροντιστικῶς), to empathize with him when he is lucky (συνησθῆναι).[171] In other words: when the friend cares for her deeply (τῷ σφόδρα σοῦ φροντίζοντι) she ought to be devoted to him with her entire soul (ὅλῃ τῇ ψυχῇ κεχαρίσθαι). Note that with its perfective verbal aspect, κεχαρίσθαι characterizes a disposition ("to be devoted") rather than a single (euphemized) act ("to gratify")—again a move from performance to intentionality.

Here we see Socrates draw a systematic distinction between *real* φιλία and *real* χάρις on the one hand and its counterfeit, the isomorphous practice of the prostitute who only uses the vocabulary of reciprocity, as Anaxilas' sphynx does: a hetaera may *look* like a friend, but underneath the superficial (lexical) resemblances of the true φίλος there is a range of internalized dispositions, emotions and virtues. Again: Socrates is not propagating abstinence or sublimation; the point of the body-soul-dualism is that the soul, as the seat of intentions, makes the difference between seemingly identical engagements.

This dialectics of inside and outside is played out in the pun on the close-folding (περιπλεκόμενον) hunting-net that is Theodote's body. The term operates on several levels. There is, of course, the weaving metaphor, fitting nicely in the imagery of both the spider's web and the hunting-nets employed in hare-hunting. There is a move, a transition, from the outside (Theodote's body) to the inside (her soul):[172] a *real* friend not only gratifies her/his friend with the body, but with a whole repertory of internalized dispositions, emotions and virtues—factors that may not always be visible, because the body is "veiling" them well (τὸ σῶμα is εὖ περιπλεκόμενον), but that in the end make all the difference between a counterfeit friend and a real one. (Here, we see a very literal case of the demarcation strategy that we have encountered in Chapters One to Four, to internalize the criteria that distinguish φιλία-exchanges from isomorphous exchanges: on the level of the body, prostitute/hetaera and the real friend may seem to gratify the friend; but *real* gratification in real friendship requires a different attitude of the soul.) And there is a meta-discursive level: the weaving metaphor applies to Theodote's euphemistic veil of words.[173] This use has a

171 Cf. "Anybody can symphatize with the sufferings of a friend, but it requires a very fine nature—it requires, in fact, that nature of a true Individualist—to sympathize with a friend's success." Oscar Wilde (1891).

172 Davidson (1997), 130 suggests that the image of Theodote's body as a "net", or a "veil", hints at the innermost part of the female body, i.e. the vagina. In this context, I find it somewhat far-fetched, as there is a clear opposition between body and soul made here.

173 Goldhill (1998), 118.

parallel in *Against Timarchus*, where Aeschines claims that Timarchus' promiscuous erotic track record not only reveals that he has been living ἡταιρηκώς, as somebody's boy-lover,[174] but also as a prostitute (πεπορνευμένος). Aeschines consistently makes a show of his hesitation to discuss coarse subject matter such as prostitution,[175] beating around the bush and making an ostentatious fuss about having to utter the very word "prostitution":

[Text 16]

> (…) οὐκέτι δήπου φαίνεται μόνον ἡταιρηκώς, ἀλλὰ καὶ—μὰ τὸν Διόνυσον οὐκ οἶδ' ὅπως δυνήσομαι **περιπλέκειν** ὅλην τὴν ἡμέραν—καὶ πεπορνευμένος·
>
> (…) he will seem to you no longer *to have been an escort*; no—and by Dionysos I do not know how I can keep *wrapping it up* all day long—to have prostituted himself.[176]

With the pathos of the prude, Aeschines exclaims that he cannot keep being euphemistic: he "knows not how he can keep on veiling (περιπλέκειν) all day long". As a prosecutor, he is impelled to be explicit about subject matter that civilized people prefer to talk about in less vulgar expressions—e.g. Misgolas' testimony that is delicate (οὐκ ἀπαίδευτον) and hence omits the act that dare not speak its name, the thing itself (αὐτὸ μὲν γὰρ τοὔνομα τοῦ ἔργου).[177] Aeschines reduces the difference between prostitution and Timarchus' allegedly more honorable encounters with Misgolas to a mere difference in *names*, a lexical distinction merely motivated by matters of politeness, cultivation, and style—not truth.[178] But the wrapping can be undone and the thing itself revealed for what it is. Similarly, Socrates' use seems to hint at a reality underneath the verbal veil of χάρις- and φιλία-terminology: the transaction that is *really* going on, the *true* nature of the hetaera.

---

174 The verb ἑταιρεῖν (and the deverbative noun ἑταίρησις) are not used of a *hetaera* but predominantly of a boy "who played a homosexual role analogous to that of a hetaira." Dover (1978), 21. Cf. Aesch. 1.51ff.

175 E.g. in 1.38 he excuses himself for being this explicit (σαφῶς εἴποιμι) because the subject matter (Timarchus' behavior) necessitates him to do so.

176 Aesch. 1.52; *transl.* Fisher (2001).

177 1.45.

178 In other contexts too, the image of "veiling" and weaving webs of words stand in opposition to speaking plainly and straight-forwardly. Cf. Eur. *Phoen.* 494–496: περιπλοκὰς λόγων. In Antiphanes fr. 75.1 K-A the expression περιπλοκὰς λίαν ἐρωτᾷς is opposed to σαφῶς; in Straton fr. 35 K-A περιπλοκὰς λέγεις is opposed to speaking ἁπλῶς and σαφέστερον.

As for caring (φιλεῖν), Socrates continues, a *real* friend knows how to do so not only "gently" (μαλακῶς, perhaps "passively"),[179] but also with display of good intent, εὐνοϊκῶς, (like one ought to do with parents and neighbors, see Section One).[180] Moreover, she needs to convince (ἀναπείθεις) her friends that they satisfy her (ἀρεστοί σοί εἰσιν), in word and deed: *she* needs to πείθειν her friends as much as they do her, and not so much in word but in deed (οὐ λόγῳ ἀλλ' ἔργῳ), i.e. not lexically by using the vocabulary of φιλία and χάρις, but actively and actually.

Theodote is playing naïve, in a show of coquetry and ostensible shock over Socrates' *demasqué*, swearing that she does not *contrive* (μηχανῶμαι) any of these things:

[Text 17]

> Μὰ τὸν Δί', ἔφη ἡ Θεοδότη, ἐγὼ τούτων οὐδὲν μηχανῶμαι.—Καὶ μήν, ἔφη, πολὺ διαφέρει τὸ κατὰ φύσιν τε καὶ ὀρθῶς ἀνθρώπῳ προσφέρεσθαι. καὶ γὰρ δὴ βίᾳ μὲν οὔτ' ἂν ἕλοις οὔτε κατάσχοις φίλον, εὐεργεσίᾳ δὲ καὶ ἡδονῇ τὸ θηρίον τοῦτο ἁλώσιμόν τε καὶ παραμόνιμόν ἐστιν.
>
> 'Honestly,' said Theodote, 'I don't *use any of these methods*.' 'Then again,' said Socrates, 'it's much better to keep one's human relationships *natural and right*. You can't capture or keep a friend by force; but by showing the creature kindness and giving it pleasure, you can both catch it and keep it by you.'[181]

Theodote pretends to be appalled because Socrates speaks way too explicitly and systematically about what it takes to be a good friend. She resents rulification, the idea that friendship can be described this methodically (e.g. μηχανῶμαι). Socrates adds that it makes all the difference when it is done naturally (perhaps "casually") and correctly (κατὰ φύσιν τε καὶ ὀρθῶς), as violence may

179 In homo-erotic contexts, μαλακός refers to effeminate boys or effeminate behavior, associated with submission to penetration. In general μαλακία is associated with femininity (Hdt. 7.153.4, Ar. *EN* 1150b15), as the opposite of masculine behavior (e.g. Eur. *Suppl.* 882–885). Aristotle defines μαλακία, juxtaposed with *akolasia* and *truphê*, as "a failure to resist or be strong in the face of things that most men are able to resist" (*EN* 1150b1–2), and as opposed to *karteria* (*EN* 1116a14, 1150a31–b19). To Xenophon, μαλακία is close to *habrotês* (*Symp.* VIII.8). Cf. Kurke (1997). Cf. Huart (1968) 373–376 and Hunt (2010), 122 ff. on μαλακία in the context of politics and battle.

180 On the importance of εὔνοια in Xenophon's conception of φιλία, see Section 5 below.

181 *Mem.* III.xi.11.

suffice for one-off catches; but to catch *and* hold on to an animal (τὸ θηρίον) requires unorthodox hunting techniques: longer term investments in relationships by means of benefits (εὐεργεσίᾳ) and pleasure (ἡδονῇ).[182]

3.2 *Playing Hard to Get: The Dietetics of χάρις*

What follows is a Socratic demonstration of the knack of controlling other people's desires (III.xi.12–14), in a way that still remains "natural and correct":

[Text 18]

> Δεῖ τοίνυν, ἔφη, πρῶτον μὲν τοὺς φροντίζοντάς σου τοιαῦτα ἀξιοῦν, οἷα ποιοῦσιν αὐτοῖς μικρότατα μελήσει, ἔπειτα δὲ αὐτὴν ἀμείβεσθαι χαριζομένην τὸν αὐτὸν τρόπον· οὕτω γὰρ ἂν **μάλιστα φίλοι γίγνοιντο καὶ πλεῖστον χρόνον φιλοῖεν καὶ μέγιστα εὐεργετοῖεν. χαρίζοιο δ' ἂν μάλιστα, εἰ δεομένοις δωροῖο τὰ παρὰ σεαυτῆς**· ὁρᾷς γὰρ ὅτι καὶ τῶν βρωμάτων τὰ ἥδιστα, ἐὰν μέν τις προσφέρῃ πρὶν ἐπιθυμεῖν, ἀηδῆ φαίνεται, κεκορεσμένοις δὲ καὶ βδελυγμίαν παρέχει, ἐὰν δέ τις προσφέρῃ λιμὸν ἐμποιήσας, κἂν φαυλότερα ᾖ, πάνυ ἡδέα φαίνεται.

> 'So in the first place,' said Socrates, 'when people care for you, you should make only such demands of them as they can satisfy with a minimum of trouble. Then, you should *repay their favours in kind*. In this way they are likely *to become most attached to you, to go on loving you for the longest time*, and *to be most generous to you*. And you are likely *to give them most pleasure if you bestow what you have to give only when they ask for it*. You can see that even the most delightful dishes seem disagreeable if they are served before the appetite is ready, and if one is satiated, they actually cause disgust; but even inferior food seems quite attractive if it is served after hunger has been aroused.'[183]

χάρις is slimmed down to a minimalistic notion: gratification, χαρίζεσθαι,[184] is reduced to requital (ἀμείβεσθαι); it entail *first* asking something from friends

---

182 Note that Socrates does not make a categorical distinction between catching an animal (τὸ θηρίον) and catching a human prey; as we shall see in the next chapter, to Xenophon the underlying principle is the same for all long-term bonds.

183 *Mem.* III.xi.12–13.

184 The euphemistic quality of both χάρις and χαρίζεσθαι is best recorded, as one may expect, in comic sources. The verb χαρίζεσθαι ("being nice to") can be used bluntly to refer to the granting of sexual favors. E.g. Aristoph., *Ach.* 883 f., *Eq.* 1368, *Eq.* 517. In such comic contexts, χάρις tends to acquire very concrete reference, coming to stand for "penis" or "vagina". Henderson (1991), 160; see also n. 50 and n. 137 above.

and then making similar immediate returns (ἀμείβεσθαι χαριζομένην τὸν αὐτὸν τρόπον); only giving when asked to (δεομένοις δωροῖο τὰ παρὰ σεαυτῆς)—with the explanation that this way they become most friendly (μάλιστα φίλοι γίγνοιντο) and keep on being friends as long as possible (πλεῖστον χρόνον φιλοῖεν) and become the greatest well-doers (μέγιστα εὐεργετοῖεν).[185] This mode of thinking sounds uncannily like a hetaera's course in Customers' Relations—not like the art of friendship at all.

Moreover, Socrates, comparing friendship to hunger and "favors" to food, advises Theodote to keep her prospective friends hungry by postponing gratification:

[Text 19]

> Πῶς οὖν ἄν, ἔφη, ἐγὼ λιμὸν ἐμποιεῖν τῶν παρ' ἐμοὶ δυναίμην;—Εἰ νὴ Δί', ἔφη, πρῶτον μὲν τοῖς κεκορεσμένοις μήτε προσφέροις μήτε ὑπομιμνήσκοις, ἕως ἂν τῆς πλησμονῆς παυσάμενοι πάλιν δέωνται, ἔπειτα τοὺς δεομένους ὑπομιμνήσκοις ὡς κοσμιωτάτῃ τε ὁμιλίᾳ καὶ τῷ φαίνεσθαι βουλομένη χαρίζεσθαι καὶ διαφεύγουσα, ἕως ἂν ὡς μάλιστα δεηθῶσι· τηνικαῦτα γὰρ πολὺ διαφέρει τὰ αὐτὰ δῶρα ἢ πρὶν ἐπιθυμῆσαι διδόναι.
>
> 'Very well,' said she, 'how am I to arouse hunger for what I have to give?' 'Why, surely,' said Socrates, 'if, when your admirers are satiated, you neither offer nor hint at your favours, until the satisfaction has passed and they *feel the want* again; and next, when they most feel want, if you drop hints by a combination of the most modest behavior and obviously wanting to *gratify* them, and by obviously holding *back* until their *need* is as great as possible—*for the same favours are much better then than before the desire for them is aroused.*'[186]

At first sight the latent analogy between sexual desire and hunger may bring to mind modern parallels: the conceptual metaphor SEX IS EATING is a common metaphor underlying colloquial expressions ranging from "to eat one's meal", "to have *appetites*" to "that woman is a little *cookie*". However, the conceptual mapping is different. In modern idiom, the metaphor serves to either euphem-

185 Goldhill (1998), 119: "*Charis* is now to be constructed on an equal (minimal) and reciprocal basis. (…) The economics of gratification appear here to aim at a stable state, where need and satisfaction coincide."

186 *Mem.* III.xi.14.

ize copulation or to dysphemize, and objectify, women-as-sex-objects.[187] To Xenophon's Socrates, the desire-hunger analogy does not so much bring up the idea of consumption, but rather serves to bring out the dietetics of consumption, the principles of Socratic hedonism, according to which true pleasure comes from consuming what one needs and when one needs it.[188] This dietetics not only applies to the maximization of one's own desires, but also to the arousing of desire in others. Socrates explicitly incites Theodote to manipulate other people's desires and, by implication, exploit their lack of self-control: to wait until they feel the want (ἕως δέωνται), and when they become aware of the want (τοὺς δεομένους) and to behave as a model of propriety (ὡς κοσμιωτάτη) and to make a show of reluctance to yield (διαφεύγουσα), until their need is as great as can be (ἕως ἂν ὡς μάλιστα δεηθῶσι), because then the same gifts (τὰ αὐτὰ δῶρα) mean much more than when they are offered before they are desired (πρὶν ἐπιθυμῆσαι).

Here, Socrates' talk about gratification and gifts has dropped to a level of euphemism: the explicit ὁμιλίᾳ and ἐπιθυμῆσαι,[189] the vocabulary of hunt/seduction (διαφεύγουσα—now Theodote is the prey!), the talk about "giving the things of yourself" (δωροῖο τὰ παρὰ σεαυτῆς) make plain that Socrates' use of the terminology of χάρις, gift-giving and φίλοι are a case of *double entendre*, with unambiguously erotic referents, innuendos: as in the Anaxilas fragment (T9), "wanting" or "needing" (δέομαι) unambiguously refers to sexual needs. The use of χάρις-vocabulary has shrunk to mock politeness and a clever show of sophistication. Similarly, the rules of χαρίζεσθαι propagated here coincide with the rules of the market: it is all about satisfactions of needs and wants (cf. the vocabulary of δέομαι), how to satisfy customers in the short run, while making sure they will be needy again in the long run; how to reciprocate in the same coin; how to cash in on frequent customers. Is this a cynical strategy?

187 In fact, a cluster of metaphors is at play in modern English idiom: WOMEN ARE DESSERTS, SEX IS EATING, THE OBJECT OF SEX IS FOOD and SEXUAL DESIRE IS HUNGER. See Crespo Fernández (2008), 98–99.

188 In the Prodicean parable of Heracles at the Crossroads (*Mem.* II.i), Virtue scoffs at the promises made by Vice, who, according to Virtue, does not know true pleasure for she "eats before she's hungry and drinks before she's thirsty" (*Mem.* II.i.30). On Socratic hedonism and desire, see Thomsen (2002).

189 The combination with ὡς κοσμιωτάτη effectively de-euphemizes ὁμιλίᾳ.

4 The Secrets of Love Magic

At this point, we should keep the analogy between Socrates and Theodote in mind: they both hunt. As a matter of fact, Theodote's invitation to Socrates to become her συνθηρατής, her fellow-hunter, seals the identification.[190] Theodote's ἐπίδειξις arouses desire by her carefully dosed exposure, her showing only "as much of herself as decency allows"; she refrains from the extreme exposure characteristic of the brothel prostitute. In the same way, Socrates has not shot his bolt like a sophist does in his ostentatious display of rhetorical skills, his ἐπίδειξις; rather, he teases his prospective pupils by gradual exposition, by hinting at the knowledge and wisdom he possesses and shares with his companions, and by carefully holding back information at the moment Theodote's curiosity is aroused.

Socrates' exposition of the method of friend-hunting is self-reflexive. Theodote is told to be selective in the friends she welcomes: she should give a warm welcome to the eager suitor (τὸν ἐπιμελόμενον), but shut the door on a spoiled brat. In the same way, Socrates is said to select his friends on basis of their receptivity: the prospective pupil is not only recognized by his quickness to learn and his ability to remember what he has learned, but also by his desire (ἐπιθυμεῖν) to acquire wisdom.[191]

Theodote shows herself an eager suitor, for she indicates that she desires Socrates' company, although it has not yet occurred to her that the tables are turned, as she suggests that Socrates may become her co-hunter and invites him to her place. Socrates immediately replies, with a *leçon par l'exemple*. Posing as

---

190 Thomsen (2002), 130: "[T]he *syn-*, the *fellow-*, is Theodote's clever addition: You, Socrates, must immediately become my fellow-pimp (…) *and my fellow courtesan*."

191 E.g. Xen. *Mem.* I.vi.13–14; Chapter Five, Section 1. Cf. the Euthydemus-episode in *Mem.* IV.ii, where the desire to learn is not yet evident in the pupil. Socrates manages to seduce Euthydemus, who initially stands aloof watching from the outside how Socrates converses with his companions, into a conversation (as he also did with Theodote). This initial seduction works as a first selection procedure that selects those people who are susceptible enough to subject them to testing, ἐλέγχειν, a Socratic procedure in which the claims to wisdom are refuted and, if the victim is susceptible to what Socrates has to offer, arouses the desire to know. So too did Euthydemus who, enthusiastic in his pursuit of knowledge and wisdom, is extremely eager to spend as much time with Socrates as possible, "never leaving" Socrates again. See Tarrant (2002) for the contention that Socratic ἔλεγχος is primarily applied to persons rather than propositions. For the distinction between different types of Socratic elenchus, see: Johnson (2005). Cf. Dorion (2000); Slings (1999); Morrison (1994). Fürst (1996), 69–77 on Plato's conception of φιλία as the ideal setting for ἔλεγχος (mostly in the *Gorgias*).

a busy hetaera, he turns her down,[192] playing hard to get and manages to make her eager to come to him, giving clues as to how she is supposed to seduce him: by means of love magic.

4.1 *Socrates the Co-hunter*

Socrates' self-representation as an ἐρώμενος or an object of desire is of course a well-known theme in Socratic literature, where often the objective of role reversals is to make the younger companion take an active role in the quest for virtue and wisdom.[193] In Xenophon's Socratic works too, we see the elevating effects of beauty on those who pursue her. Critoboulus, in his speech in the *Symposium*, makes the rather bold claim that his beauty will benefit (ὠφελήσει) people (IV.17), for it is the beautiful beloved that "inspires" virtues into his lover, making him more generous, strenuous, heroic, modest and self-restrained (IV.15). Again, we see the mechanisms of χάρις at work: in the world of seduction, where coercion is out of the question, playing hard to get makes a pursuer outdo himself in terms of generosity and self-restraint—just like the quarry that gives the huntsman a good run enhances the physical shape of the hunter.

In a dialogue aiming to alter misconceptions of reciprocity there is an obvious objective in Socrates' posing as an object of desire: to invite and provoke Theodote to break out of her one-sided conception of φιλία, in which there is a clear distinction between an active partner who initiates contact and a passive reactive partner, and to live up to her vocabulary of reciprocity by taking initiatives and making investments herself.

But there is more to it than sheer role reversal as things get increasingly unsettling towards the end of the dialogue where the hunting image becomes even more complicated. For after Socrates' elaborate exposition of the art of

192 According to Strauss, this is the only instance of Socrates refusing to "be together" with someone who desired his company. Strauss (1972), 89.

193 Cf. Edmonds (2000), 271; Halperin (1990b); Reece (1988), 69–70. The most notable example occurs in Plato's *Symposium*, where Alcibiades accuses Socrates of "deceit" (ἀπάτη) as he "pretended to be an ἐραστής, but turned out to be rather the object of desire" (Pl. *Symp*. 217–218) and at the end of the *Charmides* where the desirable young Charmides has turned into the pursuing party, desiring the company of Socrates, his midwife. Cf. Reece (1988), 69–70. Plato's paradoxical identification of Socrates as a desirable ἐρώμενος serves to transform prevailing conceptions of beauty into another notion of beauty, a beauty that is philosophically functional and that coincides with the good, serving as a midwife to the thoughts of the young men in Socrates' company, that directs the gaze of the lover to its real object, the beauty of the Forms. Edmonds (2000), Halperin (1990b), Reece (1988), Thomsen (2002), Narcy (2004).

desire management (xi.12–14), Theodote invites Socrates to become her co-hunter (συνθηρατής) of friends[194]—presumably harking back to Socrates' interpretation of the hunting metaphor (xi.9): the methods of the hare-hunt are applicable to friend-hunting when for the hounds we substitute "someone who will track and find men of wealth and good taste and drive them into Theodote's nets". In other words, Socrates is offered a career-change to become a professional pimp—a proposition that is less of an anomaly than may appear at first sight for it is in line with Socrates' recurrent assimilation with women of the working class,[195] such as a midwife,[196] a matchmaker[197] and a procuress.[198] This is a productive class of metaphors expressive of the educational processes of protreptics, counseling and coaching an apprentice philosopher[199] as each of these professions is given a metaphorical twist by Socrates: a midwife that assists young minds in giving birth to wisdom, a go-between that matches a student with the right teacher, a pimp that makes people mutually useful to one another.[200]

With wit Socrates outflirts Theodote:

194 Xen. *Mem.* III.xi.15: καὶ ἡ Θεοδότη, Τί οὖν οὐ σύ μοι, ἔφη, ὦ Σώκρατες, ἐγένου συνθηρατὴς τῶν φίλων; (Theodote said, "Why don't you help me in my hunt for friends, Socrates?")

195 As this episode is the only one in Xenophon's *Memorabilia* picturing Socrates in conversation with a woman, a woman moreover implicated in what we might label "commercial sex", it is tempting to regard Theodote as a counterpart of Aspasia or Diotima—those articulate female personalities in the other Socratic authors who were notorious for their erotic expertise. E.g. Tilg (2004), 205: "Theodote repräsentiert die gefährliche Seite Aspasias. Sokrates bewahrt ihr gegenüber jedoch überlegen seine Selbstbeherrschung und macht es damit besser als Perikles. Das Motiv Perikles-Aspasia wird als negativer Vergleichspunkt für eine apologetische Demonstration angeschlagen, aus der Sokrates als moralisch-politisches Vorbild für das öffentliche Leben hervorgeht." Cf. Halperin (1990b), Ehlers (1966). Henry (1995), 49, finds this implausible on the grounds that this would invert the (alleged) pupil/teacher relation between Aspasia and the historical Socrates; however, the historicity of the Aspasia-Socrates relation seems to me too uncertain, while a paradoxical inversion of such a relation may not be problatic or ruled out in the type of fan fiction surrounding Socrates.

196 E.g. Pl. *Theaet.* 149 ff.

197 E.g. Pl. *Theaet.* 151bff.; Xen. *Symp.* IV.64 (Socrates as μαστροπός). Cf. Henry (1995), 48, for the contention that the Xenophontic Socrates goes less far than his Platonic counterpart in appropriating "a role culturally defined as feminine."

198 E.g. Xen. *Symp.* III.10, IV.56–64.

199 Cf. Thomsen (2002).

200 Thomsen (2002).

[Text 20]

> Ἐάν γε νὴ Δί', ἔφη, πείθῃς με σύ.—Πῶς οὖν ἄν, ἔφη, πείσαιμί σε;—Ζητήσεις, ἔφη, τοῦτο αὐτὴ καὶ μηχανήσει, ἐάν τί μου δέῃ.

> 'I will, believe me,' said Socrates, 'if you *persuade* me.'—'How can I *persuade* you?'—'You'll look to that yourself,' he said, 'and *you'll find a way*, if you *need* any help from me.'[201]

As we have seen, "wanting" or "needing" (δέομαι) can refer to sexual needs and sexual requests:[202] here it is Theodote who desires (δέῃ) and who is to seduce (πείθειν) Socrates, and it is Socrates who is to gratify (χαρίζεσθαι) Theodote. Moreover, in assuring Theodote that she'll "sure think of some device (μηχανήσει)", referring back to the discussion of the "skill" (μηχανή) required to catch friends (III.xi.5), (a skill that Theodote denies to be using (xi.11)), Socrates implicitly invites her to bring the preceding exposition on methods of friend-hunting into practice—*on him*. In other words: he is willing to help Theodote provided that she makes him her friend. But how?

As Theodote begs Socrates to come (εἴσιθι) and see her often, Socrates alludes to his ἀπραγμοσύνη:

[Text 21]

> Ἀλλ', ὦ Θεοδότη, ἔφη, οὐ πάνυ μοι ῥᾴδιόν ἐστι σχολάσαι· καὶ γὰρ ἴδια πράγματα πολλὰ καὶ δημόσια παρέχει μοι ἀσχολίαν· εἰσὶ δὲ καὶ φίλαι μοι, αἳ οὔτε ἡμέρας οὔτε νυκτὸς ἀφ' αὑτῶν ἐάσουσί με ἀπιέναι, φίλτρα τε μανθάνουσαι παρ' ἐμοῦ καὶ ἐπῳδάς.—Ἐπίστασαι γάρ, ἔφη, καὶ ταῦτα, ὦ Σώκρατες;—Ἀλλὰ διὰ τί οἴει, ἔφη, Ἀπολλόδωρόν τε τόνδε καὶ Ἀντισθένη οὐδέποτέ μου ἀπολείπεσθαι; διὰ τί δὲ καὶ Κέβητα καὶ Σιμίαν Θήβηθεν παραγίγνεσθαι; εὖ ἴσθι ὅτι ταῦτα οὐκ ἄνευ πολλῶν φίλτρων τε καὶ ἐπῳδῶν καὶ ἰύγγων ἐστί.—Χρῆσον τοίνυν μοι, ἔφη, τὴν ἴυγγα, ἵνα ἐπὶ σοὶ πρῶτον ἕλκω αὐτήν.—Ἀλλὰ μὰ Δί', ἔφη, οὐκ αὐτὸς ἕλκεσθαι πρὸς σὲ βούλομαι, ἀλλὰ σὲ πρὸς ἐμὲ πορεύεσθαι.—Ἀλλὰ πορεύσομαι, ἔφη· μόνον ὑποδέχου.—Ἀλλ' ὑποδέξομαί σε, ἔφη, ἂν μή τις φιλωτέρα σου ἔνδον ᾖ.

> 'Well, Theodote, (…) it's not very easy for me to find the time for it. I have a great deal of private and public business that keeps me occupied; and

201 *Mem.* III.xi.15.

202 Goldhill (1998), 120.

> I have some *girlfriends* too, who will never let me leave them by day or night, because *they are learning from me about love potions and incantations.*' 'Do you really know about them too, Socrates?' she asked. 'Why do you suppose that Apollodorus here and Antisthenes never leave me? And that Cebes and Simmias come to visit me from Thebes? *You may be sure that these things don't happen without a lot of love potions, incantations and iunx spells.*' 'Lend me *your magic wheel*, then, so that I may spin it first for you.' 'Certainly not,' he said, '*I don't want to be drawn to you; I want you to come to me.*' 'Very well, I will,' she declared, 'Only mind you let me in.' 'Yes, I'll let you in,' said Socrates, 'unless I have *someone* with me *that I like better.*'[203]

The role reversal seems complete: Theodote will come to Socrates (πορεύσομαι), practically begs him to receive her (ὑποδέχου), and Socrates manages to outbid Theodote by claiming the positions of the object of seduction—but only by representing himself as some sort of old maiden surrounded by girls who crave for his presence, for he teaches them the tricks and dodges of love-magic and he may or may not have time to receive Theodote as he may be occupied ("have someone ἔνδον").[204] Socrates appears to have turned into an overage courtesan, a crone, with a full-time job entertaining girlfriends or in instructing and passing on experience to younger colleagues.

It is important to get the tone and atmosphere of the encounter right. Socrates is no stranger to "ironic self-deprecation"[205] and there are obvious Xenophontic parallels to Socrates' coquetry and his playing "busy". A notorious one is the *Symposium*, where Socrates mock turns down Antisthenes, saying he is "engaged in other business" (ἄλλα πράττω)—an intervention framed by the authorial voice as "bantering" (ἐπισκώψας) and "pretend-coquetry" (ὡς δὴ θρυπτόμενος),[206] in conformity with the lighter mood (παιδιή) associated with the

203 *Mem.* III.xi.16–18; *transl. adapted.*

204 This could be an allusion to a standard phrase for a *hetaera* being "occupied". Cf. Lucian, *Dialogi meretricii*, 12.1: ἔνδον ἕτερος; Ruhnken (1772), 235: "est enim propria meretricum, amatores excludentium formula, ἔνδον ἕτερος." Cf. Santoni (1989), 292: "l'espressione abituale con cui un'etera mandava via uncliente, dicendo appunto che c'era in casa qualcun altro."

205 Faraone (2006), 218.

206 Xen. *Symp.* VIII.4 (Καὶ ὁ Σωκράτης ἐπισκώψας ὡς δὴ θρυπτόμενος εἶπε· Μὴ νῦν μοι ἐν τῷ παρόντι ὄχλον πάρεχε· ὡς γὰρ ὁρᾷς, ἄλλα πράττω.), with Huss (1999), 365, on θρύπτεσθαι as "zögerlich-ablehnend", hesitatingly, or coyly, declining. θρύπτεσθαι is qualified by a narratorial ὡς δή ("ironisch-distanziert", Huss ad loc., "ironical", Denniston (1950), 230), that not

symposiastic setting.[207] The symposiastic quality of the Theodote episode too has been pointed out by several scholars,[208] and Socrates' quasi-erotic banter should be appreciated as such.

Still, in T21 things seem to be pushed to an awkward extreme. While most interpretations concede that the girl-friends (φίλαι) mentioned refer to the companions present at the conversation,[209] several commentators have expressed discomfort over the turn the dialogue is taking, attempting ironical, satirical and allegorical readings of this passage, reading the φίλαι, for instance, as an allegory for Socrates' ἡδοναί.[210] Other readings have sought to understand the "dearer girl inside" (τις φιλωτέρα) as representing Socrates' soul (ψυχή), dearer than Theodote and therefore capable of self-restraint.[211]

There is a middle course between assuming a deeper-level allegorical reading on the one hand and dismissing these paragraphs as a touch of Socratic irony or satire on the other. Bear in mind that up till now Socrates has been walking the tightrope of *double entendre*, being *faux*-naively aware of how *Theodote* understands his talk about "friend-hunt" and "friends with benefits" as euphemisms, while at the same time taking care that his recommendations and principles of friendship can still, and in a more fundamental manner, be understood in a literal way.[212]

---

only marks the *as if*-ness of Socrates' coyness (ὡς), but also the fact that he is playing a socially recognizable role (δή, "obviously").

207 Cf. the work's programmatic introduction: not only the serious acts of great and good men (τῶν καλῶν κἀγαθῶν ἀνδρῶν ἔργα τὰ μετὰ σπουδῆς πραττόμενα) deserve mention, but also "what they do in their lighter moods" (τὰ ἐν ταῖς παιδιαῖς) (Xen. *Symp.* 1.1). Cf. Huss (1999), ad loc.

208 E.g. Chernyakhovskaya (2014), 191 n. 96.

209 Vlastos (1991), 30: "These 'girlfriends' are philosophers, depressingly male and middle-aged"; Goldhill (1998), 121–123: "Socrates' mastery (over desire) makes all his pupils his female friends. (…) Socrates' triumph over the *hetaera* is won at the cost of the bizarre representation of him with his girlfriends." Cf. Tredennick & Waterfield (1990), 170 n. 2., Azoulay (2004), 406, Tilg (2004), 406, Faraone (2006), 218, Danzig (2010), 174, Bevilacqua (2010), 572, Dorion & Bandini (2011), 388, O'Connor (2011), 62, One scholar thinks that Socrates (who "did in fact have an eye for women") refers to other hetaeras, Lind (1997), 289.

210 Chernyakhovskaya (2014), 188.

211 According to Narcy (2004), 217, the final line cannot be taken literally (it is hardly conceivable that Socrates' companions visit Socrates at home, for he spends his time in public space) and hence must refer to Socrates' ψυχή, the "dearer friend inside", who is κυρία over the body, along the same lines as Alcibiades' comparison of Socrates with beautiful figurines inside a Pan-figurine (ἔνδοθεν δὲ ἀνοιχθείς) that refer to Socrates' σωφροσύνη in Pl. *Symp.* 216d6–7.

212 Cf. Huss (1999) on Socratic "double-speak" in the *Symposium*: "Sokrates liebt es auch,

There is certainly an element of comedy in the gender reversal presupposed by the designator φίλαι, "girlfriends", to refer to a pack of Socratic apprentice philosophers—as there an element of delightful self-deprecation in Socrates "comparing his own knack for attracting young men and keeping them by his side with the ability of a courtesan to do the same".[213] However, while this final scene makes the comparison of Socrates with Theodote (that had been looming over the conversation from the moment Socrates took on the challenge of confronting something "stronger than λόγος") beyond obvious, the comparison simultaneously suggests *difference*. While to Theodote "friends" may have been a pure euphemism, Socrates' companions *are* genuine friends. Here is where the love magic comes in: there is a way to make sense of the motive of love magic without playing it down as an element of local color belonging to the world of courtesans that was not Socrates' patch to begin with—especially when we realize that the love magic-metaphor recurs in a couple of episodes elsewhere in the *Memorabilia*.

4.2 Mem. *II.iii and II.vi: Love Magic*

Love magic does indeed belong to the world of the courtesan who has obvious interests in attracting new wealthy visitors. ἴυγξ-spells, most commonly used by courtesans, for instance, incite uncontrollable lust in the victim.[214] But Socrates, significantly, does not only mention erotic spells, but also φίλτρα that are not typically spells inducing desire and *attracting* people, but are regarded as more beneficial charms that, as the terminology suggests, induce φιλία:[215] they *bind* people. As such, φίλτρα are generally used by individuals who wish to repair or heal marriages or other pre-existing relationships.[216]

There are two other episodes in which Socrates mentions φίλτρα in the *Memorabilia*. Both revolve around φιλία: in the Chaerecrates-episode (II.iii), the case under scrutiny is a disturbed φιλία-relationship between two brothers that needs to be healed; in the Critoboulus-episode (II.vi),[217] the question at stake

Begriffe zweideutig zu gebrauchen, das eine im Scherz zu sagen und doch das andere im Ernst zu meinen." (65). Cf. Joël (1901), 716.

213 Faraone (2006), 218.

214 Jason applied ἴυγξ-spells to Medea who all of a sudden found herself set aflame with *erôs* and *pothos* for him. Pind. *Pyth.* 4.213–219; cf. Faraone (1999), 7; Faraone (1993).

215 For the instrumental character of the suffix –τρον see Frisk, s.v. φίλος.

216 A prototypical (but unfortunate) example is Deianeira who mistakenly kills Heracles in the belief that she is saving her marriage with a φίλτρον. Soph. *Trach.* 577; cf. Armoni (2001), 33 ff. Faraone (1999), 7; Faraone (1994). Faraone (2006), 218, also points out that aging courtesans desparate to keep their customers close also use φίλτρα.

217 For an analysis of the friend-hunt and the love magic-metaphor in II.vi see Neitzel (1981).

is very similar to the one in the Theodote-episode, i.e. how to hunt friends and initiate friendships.[218] In both cases, the φίλτρον-terminology is clearly brought in as a metaphor, and in both cases, Socrates evokes and activates the etymological relation between φίλτρα and φιλία, suggesting that φίλτρα are means to initiate and sustain φιλία.

Let us first take a look at an occurrence of the φίλτρα-metaphor in a context that discusses a pre-existing relationship: the Chaerecrates-episode.[219] Here, Socrates is mediating in a quarrel between the young man and his older brother Chaerephon, urging the younger brother to restore their φιλία-relationship and turn his brother into an asset instead of a liability (a ζημία). Chaerecrates, in his desperation, asks Socrates for a φίλτρον to make his brother well-disposed towards him. In a school-book example of Socratic midwifery, Socrates makes Chaerecrates aware of his latent knowledge of φίλτρα:

[Text 22]

> Λέγε δή μοι, ἔφη, εἴ τινα τῶν γνωρίμων βούλοιο κατεργάσασθαι, ὁπότε θύοι, καλεῖν σε ἐπὶ δεῖπνον, τί ἂν ποιοίης;—Δῆλον ὅτι κατάρχοιμ' ἂν τοῦ αὐτός, ὅτε θύοιμι, καλεῖν ἐκεῖνον.—Εἰ δὲ βούλοιο τῶν φίλων τινὰ προτρέψασθαι, ὁπότε ἀποδημοίης, ἐπιμελεῖσθαι τῶν σῶν, τί ἂν ποιοίης;—Δῆλον ὅτι πρότερος ἂν ἐγχειροίην ἐπιμελεῖσθαι τῶν ἐκείνου, ὁπότε ἀποδημοίη.—Εἰ δὲ βούλοιο ξένον ποιῆσαι ὑποδέχεσθαι σεαυτόν, ὁπότε ἔλθοις εἰς τὴν ἐκείνου, τί ἂν ποιοίης;—Δῆλον ὅτι καὶ τοῦτον πρότερος ὑποδεχοίμην ἄν, ὁπότε ἔλθοι Ἀθήναζε· καὶ εἴ γε βουλοίμην αὐτὸν προθυμεῖσθαι διαπράττειν μοι ἐφ' ἃ ἥκοιμι, δῆλον ὅτι καὶ τοῦτο δέοι ἂν πρότερον αὐτὸν ἐκείνῳ ποιεῖν.—**Πάντ' ἄρα σύγε τὰ ἐν ἀνθρώποις φίλτρα ἐπιστάμενος πάλαι ἀπεκρύπτου.**
>
> 'Tell me, then,' said Socrates, 'if you wanted to prevail upon one your acquaintances to invite you to dinner whenever he was holding a celebration, what would you do?' 'Obviously I should begin by inviting him when I was celebrating.' 'And if you wanted to induce one of your friends to take care of your property when you were away from home, what would you do?' 'Obviously I should first try to take care of his when he was away.' 'And if you wanted to make a foreigner give you hospitality when you visited your country, what would you do?' 'Obviously I should first give him

ἐπῳδαί also have a prominent role in Plato's *Phd.* (77e–78a) and *Charm.* in the context of seduction and σωφροσύνη (e.g. 176b). See McPherran (2004), Delatte (1933), 153.

218 See Section 2.2 above.

219 On the Chaerecrates-episode, see also Section 5 below; Cf. Chapter Five Section 4.

> hospitality when he came to Athens. And if I wanted him to be eager to achieve the object of my visit for me, obviously I should have first to do the same for him.' '*So you know all the magic spells that influence human conduct, and have kept your knowledge dark all this time*!'[220]

The love-charm turns out to be a simple but universal principle:[221] make the first move. Active Partnership, taking initiatives, is an imperative in all kinds of reciprocal relationships that involve long-term interests as investment in a relationship is what binds the partner. Hence, there is little more to these φίλτρα than making the first move in doing good to the other.

A similar use of the φίλτρον-metaphor, now in the context of a relationship that is yet to be initiated, is to be found in the Critoboulus-episode (*Mem.* II.vi), a dialogue that, like the Theodote-episode, elaborately deals with the process of selecting and acquiring φίλοι in the context of a hunting metaphor (II.vi.9–11): hunting friends requires techniques different from hunting wild animals, for pursuit (κατὰ πόδας), deceit (ἀπάτῃ) and force (βίᾳ) only breed enmity, not friendship:

[Text 23]

> **Φίλοι δὲ πῶς; ἔφη.—Εἶναι μέν τινάς φασιν ἐπῳδάς, ἃς οἱ ἐπιστάμενοι ἐπᾴδοντες οἷς ἂν βούλωνται φίλους αὐτοὺς ποιοῦνται· εἶναι δὲ καὶ φίλτρα, οἷς οἱ ἐπιστάμενοι πρὸς οὓς ἂν βούλωνται χρώμενοι φιλοῦνται ὑπ' αὐτῶν.**
>
> 'But how are friends made?' asked Critobulus. 'They say that there are *incantations* which those who *know* them can use *to win the friendship* of anyone that they like; and *drugs* too, which can be used by those who *understand* them to make them loved by anyone that they *like*.'[222]

Friends are caught with incantations (ἐπῳδαί) and love charms (φίλτρα): with incantations one *makes* them one's friends (φίλους αὐτοὺς ποιοῦνται), with charms one secures that the friendship is reciprocal (φιλοῦνται ὑπ' αὐτῶν).

Socrates' example of incantations, ἐπῳδαί, is the song of the Sirens who know the art of tempting by praising (II.vi.11) and who κατεῖχον their victims—so too

220 *Mem.* II.iii.11–14.

221 Cf. Gigon (1956), 134: "Das scheinbar so geheimnisvoll abgelegene Zaubermittel ist in Wirklichkeit eine völlig durchsichtige, ja banale ethisch-gesellschaftliche Regel."

222 *Mem.* II.vi.10–11.

do ἐπῳδαί have a binding force.[223] The Sirens find their real-life Athenian counterpart in Pericles who knew how to make the citizens φιλεῖν him by putting them under his verbal spells, i.e. by praising them (II.vi.12).[224] (Here it is tempting to think of the Pericles in the *epitaphios*, exhorting the Athenian citizens to fix their eyes on the polis day by day (τὴν τῆς πόλεως δύναμιν καθ' ἡμέραν ἔργῳ θεωμένους) and to become "her lovers" (ἐραστὰς γιγνομένους αὐτῆς), i.e. active investors in the collective ἔρανος-fund constituting the citystate of Athens.)[225]

The other half of the pair, the φίλτρα, is represented by Themistocles who made the polis φιλεῖν him by attaching something good to the polis (περιάψας τι ἀγαθόν)—presumably the fortifications and ships deployed to protect the city of Athens. The section on love magic is wrapped up by Critoboulus:

[Text 24]

> Δοκεῖς μοι λέγειν, ὦ Σώκρατες, ὡς, εἰ μέλλοιμεν ἀγαθόν τινα κτήσασθαι φίλον, αὐτοὺς ἡμᾶς ἀγαθοὺς δεῖ γενέσθαι λέγειν τε καὶ πράττειν.
>
> 'I suppose you mean, Socrates, that if it were our intention to secure a good friend, *we ought to make ourselves good both in word and deed.*'[226]

In order to make a good man one's friend, one must become (γενέσθαι) a good friend oneself, i.e. good in speaking and acting (λέγειν τε καὶ πράττειν): incantations (ἐπῳδαί) are a metaphor for initiating φιλία by *saying* things, charms (φίλτρα) for securing reciprocal φιλία by *doing* things.[227]

The image that emerges from other uses in the *Memorabilia*, is that the φίλτρον-metaphor expresses the social maxim that, unlike short-term interpersonal encounters, long-term relationships require investments and a willing-

223 On the various metaphorical roles of the Sirens, see Chernyakhovskaya (2014), 188–189 n. 87.

224 Xenophon's Socrates insists on the importance of *praising* the potential φίλος (although the praise needs to have a basis in reality, *Mem.* II.vi.33–39), whereas Plato's Socrates urges the *erastês* to not praise his *erômenos* but to humble him instead (*Lys.* 210e). See Tamiolaki (2014), 3§15.

225 Cf. Tamiolaki (2014), 4§14. For the interpretation of the Thucydidean passage, Sara Monoson (1994).

226 *Mem.* II.vi.14.

227 Neitzel (1981). The image of the "incantations" surfaces in Plato's oeuvre as well, as a metaphor for Socratic dialectics; see Dorion (2011), 200–201. In Xenophon, "incantations", i.e. expressions of praise, are meant first and foremost to lure someone into a φιλία-relation, not so much into a particular epistemic state. The hunt is primarily for the friend, not for truth—although one may be implied by the other.

ness to make the first move. A φίλτρον, a means to initiate and sustain φιλία, turns out to be some kind of a model-gift, a blow-up representation of what gifts do: they bind people by creating and strengthening ties of goodwill and gratitude.

4.3 *Playing Hard to Get vs. Love Magic*

The word/deed-pair, evoked by the images of the ἐπῳδαί and the φίλτρα, is reminiscent of Socrates' guidelines to Theodote that insist that she needs to convince (ἀναπείθεις) her friends not so much in word but in deed (οὐ λόγῳ ἀλλ' ἔργῳ) (T15). This reminds us of the fact that Socrates and Theodote are still merely *talking* about φιλία. It is the power of Socrates' λόγος that, for now, seems to be stronger than Theodote's beauty as he seems to have incited the urge in Theodote to come and seduce him. His incantations, ἐπῳδαί, seem to have worked. But how about the φίλτρα?

As we have seen, the φίλτρον-metaphor evokes a key-principle of Socrates' philosophy of friendship in the *Memorabilia*: Active, or pro-active, Partnership: taking the leap of faith by "paying it forward", by taking initiatives in benefiting the other.[228] As such, it propagates a radically different notion of χαρίζεσθαι and gift-giving than the rules of Playing Hard to Get: Active Partnership is about giving first, *not* asking first; it is about defeating the other in well-doing, *not* gaining as much as possible from a well-doer. Hence, Socrates' propagation of Playing Hard to Get turns out to be a *reductio ad absurdum* of Theodote's parlance—enough as a teaser to make the other active, but not the very substance of friendship that consists in being active oneself.

By playing along the language game so essential to her self-definition, Socrates guides Theodote to the somewhat unsettling understanding that she may not be able to imbue words like χάρις and φιλία with real meaning, that she may not yet be the friend she would like to believe she is. In her trade, the language of χάρις, the ideologically crucial but thin dividing line between seduction and self-commodification, dissolves into a euphemistic cover-up for commercial intercourse, in which she is passively waiting for her "friends" to come along, in which χαρίζεσθαι is reduced to delivery-on-pay and χάρις is narrowed down to transactions on a *quid pro quo*-basis. Despite her use of the language of long-term reciprocity, her φιλία remains a unilateral matter, with an active party that initiates contact and a passive party that responds: she makes a living out of friends who do her good, but her way of reciprocating is mere "requital" on a *quid pro quo*-basis, a travesty of the principle of χάρις. If Theodote were

228 Tamiolaki (2014), 3§18, describes the same principle as "strong agency".

genuinely interested in long-term relationships instead of one-off catches, she would do all those things that real φίλοι do: to visit a sick friend, to congratulate a lucky friend, to dedicate herself with heart and soul to an eager suitor. Just like the other professional craftsmen whom Socrates confronts with their lack of a genuine understanding of the essence of their τέχνη, Theodote comes to realize she still has a lot to learn—from the old and experienced courtesan Socrates.

Socrates has a better understanding of the Art of Friendship, Theodote's τέχνη, as he has proved himself a better *friend*. His friendships, with Cebes, Simmias, Antisthenes and Apollodorus, have been shown to be lasting, living up to the ethics of reciprocity implied by the terminology of χάρις and φιλία. To Socrates' companions, already engaged in bonds of φιλία with Socrates, this is a clear clue, for they know from previous encounters what φίλτρα represent: he expects his prospective friends to be actively engaged in their joint enterprise, their quest for wisdom, and demands active participation and initiatives. To Theodote, Socrates' mentioning of love magic is a Siren's song, a teaser, hinting at wisdom and knowledge of the Socratic Art of Friendship beyond the rules of Playing Hard to Get and protreptic towards philosophy, Socrates' true preoccupation, "the other love",[229] the dearer friend perhaps (τις φιλωτέρα). Theodote is willing to visit him but still expects some guarantee that he will be there for her. Socrates' jesting answer is also revealing of the nature of χάρις: when it comes to seduction and friendship, there is no such guarantee. One has to be prepared to take a shot in the dark.[230]

It is this principle of Active Partnership that is being articulated and shaped in this dialogue, through a series of terminological inquiries and paradoxical metaphors: the demolition of the "euphemistic" use of χάρις-vocabulary, the imagery of hunting, the semantic field of desire and seduction and the metaphor of magic charms. All these fields prescribe a clear-cut divisions of roles, between a pursuing and acting partner and a passive partner undergoing pursuit and treatment. All these fields are reformed by Socrates to underscore the point that all moral dealings with fellow persons require active partnership.

229 For philosophy as Socrates "other love", cf. Pl. *Gorg*. 481d3–4.

230 This may be a case of *amplification*, the technique of elaborating by repetition and, according to Gray (1998) one of the structuring rhetorical principles of the *Memorabilia*. The intended audience of the metaphor would, then, be dual: Socrates' companions (with whom Socrates communicates over Theodote's head) and Xenophon's readership.

5 The Socratic Principle: Pay It Forward

To recapitulate what we have so far: we have seen how Xenophon consistently evokes the discourse of erotics and seduction while at the same time transforming it. Love magic and hunting both recurrently feature as metaphors for the acquisition of φίλοι—*and for retaining them*. As commentators have recognized, the latter topic, the retention of friends, is a preoccupation typical for Xenophon.[231]

This points to another defining feature of this dialogue. Xenophon consistently preserves some "plausible deniability" as to how applicable the language of φιλία really is in a situation that seems to lend itself better for description in terms of ἔρως and seduction. This ambiguity is functional: it makes the point that there is something seductive about making friends and, conversely, that there is something genuinely reciprocal about seduction. The mapping works both ways.

If the mapping works both ways, both scenario's (erotic seduction and friendship) allow for a role-division. An erotic scenario may be characterized by an active pursuing lover and the reactive object of his desire—a well-known scenario. But how does one distinguish roles in a φιλία-relationship? Although Socrates uses the dialogue to teach Theodote the lesson that seduction and erotics presuppose a form of *true* reciprocity, to *us* the same dialogue reveals something different: that reciprocity presupposes a fundamental asymmetry, an inequality between donor and recipient, giver and receiver, between active[232] and passive partners.

What does this "activity" or "strong agency" consist of in the case of reciprocal bonds of solidarity, such as φιλία? It is here that the notion of Active Partnership comes in: an active friend is a friend who takes initiatives instead of merely responding to prior benefaction. A true friend knows how to "pay it forward", a form of activity that results in a form of moral inequality that can only be countered by a new inequality and asymmetry brought about by a counter-initiative.

5.1 *Active Partnership and ἐγκράτεια*

The principle of Active Partnership and the imperative to Pay it Forward are recurring themes in Xenophon's oeuvre and it is inextricably bound up with de doctrine of proper use and the Socrates' programmatic orientation to the long-

231 Tamiolaki (2014), 4§10.

232 Cf. Tamiolaki's notion of friends with "strong agency" (2014).

term good. We have seen its consistent manifestations throughout Xenophon's Socratic works. In the Antiphon episode we have seen how the beauty/wisdom-analogy[233] (PROSTITUTE : VIRTUOUS BOY-LOVER = SOPHIST : GENTLEMAN CITIZEN) is employed to disambiguate Socratic interactions with sophistic education: the prostitute and the sophist both operate in a world of short-lived interactions and disembedded transactions of commodified values, whereas beauty and wisdom are most properly "used" in the context of long-term relationships between φίλοι. We have also seen how this analogy casts Socrates not only in the role of the gentleman citizen, but also in a role analogous to the ἐρώμενος, the passive partner in an erotic encounter—a paradoxical self-presentation that serves the didactic purpose of provoking a conversation partner to take on an active role. While this is a procedure well-known from other Socratic authors,[234] in Xenophon's Socratic works this protreptic manoeuvre concerns not only a matter of method (preparing a conversation partner for an active role in the dialectical process), but also substantive: it has a bearing on the very matter and contents of Socratic ethics.

An example we have already encountered is the mother, the paradigmatic φίλος who practices the imperative of Active Partnership to the extreme:[235] a mother makes maximum investments in an insecure future by nurturing a child who does not know her yet, is not aware of her generosity and is not capable to guarantee that he will ever reciprocate the favor. Note that these are all qualitative considerations that explain the irredeemable magnitude of a mother's χάρις: this χάρις is not a reaction to a preceding gift or favor, but unconditional as there are no expectations of return in the short run and only very insecure ones in the remote future.

Although the case of the mother is an extreme example, other relationships work along similar lines:

[Text 25]

> Οὐκοῦν, ἔφη ὁ Σωκράτης, καὶ τῷ γείτονι βούλῃ σὺ ἀρέσκειν, ἵνα σοι καὶ πῦρ ἐναύῃ, ὅταν τούτου δέῃ, καὶ ἀγαθοῦ τέ σοι γίγνηται συλλήπτωρ καί, ἄν τι σφαλλόμενος τύχῃς, εὐνοϊκῶς ἐγγύθεν βοηθῇ σοι;—"Εγωγε, ἔφη.—Τί δέ; συνοδοιπόρον ἢ σύμπλουν, ἢ εἴ τῳ ἄλλῳ ἐντυγχάνοις, οὐδὲν ἄν σοι διαφέροι φίλον ἢ ἐχθρὸν γενέσθαι, ἢ καὶ τῆς παρὰ τούτων εὐνοίας οἴει δεῖν ἐπιμελεῖσθαι;—"Εγωγε, ἔφη.

233 πόρνος : σώφρων ἐρώμενος = σοφιστής : καλος κἀγαθὸς πολίτης. Xen. *Mem.* I.vi.13.
234 Most notably Plato, see n. 193 and n. 197 above.
235 See Chapter Three Section 4.

> Well then, said Socrates, do you want to be pleasant to your neighbor, so that he may give you a light for your fire when you need it, and both contribute to your success and give you prompt and *friendly help* if you meet with any misfortune?—Yes, I do.—Take the case of a fellow traveler or fellow voyager, or anyone else you might meet: would it make no difference to you whether he became your friend or your enemy? Do you think you ought to concern yourself with *the goodwill* of people like these?—I do think so.[236]

The rhetoric of the passage has a familiar ring by now: it echoes Prodicus' Virtue in II.i and it prepares for Chaerecrates' φίλτρον in II.iii: if you want your neighbor to help you in times of need, display good intent (εὔνοια) and offer help (εὐνοϊκῶς βοηθεῖν) to him first; if you attach value to the goodwill (εὔνοια) of your travel companions and shipmates, be attentive (ἐπιμελεῖσθαι) to them. The common denominator is the notion of Active Partnership: if you want a good neighbor, *be* a good neighbor; if you want a friend, *be* a friend. Taking the lead breeds εὔνοια, precisely because it signifies εὔνοια itself. See that you make the first move (II.iii.14: πρότερος εὖ ποιεῖν)—as Socrates also urges Chaerecrates to towards his brother Chaerephon.[237] Taking initiatives is, it is suggested, an imperative in all kinds of reciprocal relationships.

In the context of the conflict between Chaerecrates and Chaerephon, Socrates expects this strategy to work, because Chaerephon is φιλότιμος, a man of honor:

[Text 26]

> οὐχ ὁρᾷς ὡς φιλότιμός ἐστι καὶ ἐλευθέριος; τὰ μὲν γὰρ πονηρὰ ἀνθρώπια οὐκ ἂν ἄλλως μᾶλλον ἕλοις ἢ εἰ δοίης τι, τοὺς δὲ καλοὺς κἀγαθοὺς ἀνθρώπους προσφιλῶς χρώμενος μάλιστ' ἂν κατεργάσαιο. καὶ ὁ Χαιρεκράτης εἶπεν· Ἐὰν οὖν ἐμοῦ ταῦτα ποιοῦντος ἐκεῖνος μηδὲν βελτίων γίγνηται;—Τί γὰρ ἄλλο, ἔφη ὁ Σωκράτης, ἢ κινδυνεύσεις ἐπιδεῖξαι σὺ μὲν χρηστός τε καὶ φιλάδελφος εἶναι, ἐκεῖνος δὲ φαῦλός τε καὶ οὐκ ἄξιος εὐεργεσίας; ἀλλ' οὐδὲν οἶμαι τούτων ἔσεσθαι· νομίζω γὰρ αὐτόν, ἐπειδὰν αἴσθηταί σε προκαλούμενον ἑαυτὸν εἰς τὸν ἀγῶνα τοῦτον, πάνυ φιλονικήσειν ὅπως περιγένηταί σου καὶ λόγῳ καὶ ἔργῳ εὖ ποιῶν.

---

236 *Mem.* II.ii.12.

237 *Mem.* II.iii.14. See Section 4.2 above. Cf. Chapter Three Section 4.4 and Chapter Five Section 3.2. This appears to be a motive under Minor Socratics such as Aristippus of Cyrene and Euclides of Megara. See p. 182 n. 214.

> Don't you see what a noble and generous nature he has? Low types of humanity are most likely to be won over by a gift; but the best way to influence truly good people is by *courtesy*. Chaerecrates said, Supposing that I do what you recommend, and he shows no improvement?—In that case, said Socrates, you will simply run the risk of demonstrating that you are *a good and affectionate brother*, and he is a bad one who doesn't deserve to be treated kindly. But I don't want to suppose that anything of the sort will happen. I think that when he once realizes that you are challenging him to this kind of contest, *he will be very keen to outdo you in kindness both spoken and practical.*[238]

There is a moral prestige to being an Active Partner. Socrates predicts that treating Chaerephon kindly (προσφιλῶς χρώμενος) will provoke a *combat de générosité*, framing the offering of service and counter-service in terms that recall athletic competition (φιλονικήσειν) and superiority (περιγενήται).[239] Once more this is a metaphor that takes a Socratic twist. First of all, it dispels Chaerecrates' worry that taking the initiative to restore their φιλία by doing good to Chaerephon is a waste of generosity. The competition metaphor enables Chaerecrates to reframe this issue: worst case scenario is that Chaerecrates will have displayed himself as "a good person loyal to his brother" (χρηστός τε καὶ φιλάδελφος), which is not a waste at all—a reflection of the well-known Socratic principle that it is always better to be harmed than to harm someone else.[240] The metaphor of competition, φιλονικία, and the vocabulary of φιλοτιμία, prestige, turn generosity into something that one can excel in, as the *real*

---

238 *Mem.* II.iii.16–17; Azoulay (2004), 142: Dans les *Mémorables*, Socrate donne une tournure éthique à ce principe. Il précise ainsi que le répertoire des faveurs doit s'adapter à la vertu du récipiendaire: « On ne saurait mieux prendre un misérable qu'avec des présents; mais pour un homme vertueux, c'est surtout avec de bons procédés qu'on le gagne ». Le philosophe opère donc une distinction entre dons substantiels et attentions symboliques qui recoupe une séparation morale et politique entre leurs destinataires. »

239 The dismissal of gift-giving (as merely a means to seduce baser men) may strike us as odd as it all of a sudden introduces a distinction between immaterial services (to which the imperative paying it forward applies) and material gifts that are coveted by κακοί. In part, this dismissal can be understood as material gifts are more easily commodified than immaterial favors: it takes a gentleman to appreciate a friendly disposition. Another aspect of this dismissal may be the fact that the phenomenon of δωροδοκία, bribery, is an available paradigm for "befriending" people.

240 E.g. Pl. *Gorg.* 508e.

competition underlying apparent material risks, gains and losses. There are higher values at stake.

Moreover, the competition metaphor makes palpable that a φιλία-bond extends beyond the dynamics of a one-off interaction: it indicates that in well-functioning reciprocal relationships, where *both* partners are virtuous gentlemen, there will be an *ongoing* competition of generosity. The imperative of Active Partnership does not only express a strategy for *initiating* φιλία, but also reflects a rule of conduct to *sustain* an existing φιλία-relationship. In a healthy reciprocal relationship *both* partners alternately take initiatives in conferring benefits on the other. Within such a relationship, favors and gifts are never regarded as a mere reaction to "antecedent graces"; rather, each event in the never-ending chain of reciprocity is viewed as a *new* manifestation of generosity that strengthens the bond between the partners, that moves up the standards and that amplifies the expectations on both sides.[241] Equality between partners is not so much a point of departure in φιλία, it is not a given, but a *result* of an evenly matched competition: if one of the partners "wins", the resulting φιλία-relationship will be asymmetrical, i.e. between a morally superior party and an inferior party who is irredeemably indebted; if both persist to challenge each other, the result will be a balanced bond, of rather a balanc*ing* see-saw like dynamic.[242]

Hence, the principle of Active Partnership is the core the Socratic doctrine of Proper Use: ὀρθὴ χρῆσις, the right way of dealing with the people who matter, and the correct use of the world around us.[243] As such, the principle of Active Partnership and Socrates' philosophy of friendship are an integral part of the larger didactic program of the *Memorabilia*, that revolves around self-mastery, physical endurance and self-sufficiency. It is expressed in Prodicus' myth of Heracles that drove home the point that you have to sow before you can reap and to benefit your friends before you will be appreciated,[244] you have

---

241 For a comparable (though not identical) idea, cf. Godelier (1996), 44 on the implicit logic of gifts "which create debts that are not cancelled by a counter-gift. For the object which returns to its original owner *is not given back,* but is *given again.*" Godelier discusses the fringe case of a (numerically) identical object returning to the initial donor. In an Active Partnership, each participant presents an act as an initiative, an act of *active* χάρις—i.e as an act of "giving again" instead of "giving back".

242 According to Azoulay (2004), the example of the two brothers is the only instance of φιλία in Xenophon's oeuvre that does not, at some point, slide into asymmetrical bonds. See Chapter Seven Section 2.3 for Aristotle's conception of asymmetrical φιλία-bonds.

243 See Chapter Five Section 2.

244 *Mem.* II.i.28: εἴτε ὑπὸ φίλων ἐθέλεις ἀγαπᾶσθαι, τοὺς φίλους εὐεργετητέον (…) εἴτε γῆν βούλει σοι καρποὺς ἀφθόνους φέρειν, τὴν γῆν θεραπευτέον. See Chapter Five Section 3.2.

to toil before you can know true happiness and self-fulfillment (in contrast to the dietetics or Vice who eats before she's hungry and drinks before she's thirsty).[245]

The foundational principle of self-mastery, ἐγκράτεια, presupposes an opposition between long-term goods and short-term interests: it stipulates a repression of the impulses of short-term appetites that may yield satisfaction in the short run but that pose a threat to the realization of long-term goods.[246] ἐγκράτεια is the precondition for the development of virtue in an individual,[247] for virtue is the result of practice,[248] requiring a complete mastery of body and soul.[249] But what is more, since ἐγκράτεια is the ability to suspend the desire for immediate gratification and to reflect upon what is *really* useful, it is also the prerequisite for proper use, for initiating and sustaining relationships that are genuinely beneficial to both partners: for Active Partnership.

5.2 *Misrecognition: Indebtedness Engineering*

Socratic morality, as most versions of virtue ethics, is ultimately ethical individualism:[250] it directs an individual towards the development of *his own* virtue. This means that Socrates' education is intended to help the conversation partner develop his self-restraint by envisioning the long-term good and by stimulating him to be an Active Partner towards others—active, that is, not necessarily an equal one. As he tells Chaerecrates: equality between partners may happen when the other too is eager to win the battle of generosity. But equality is *not* the moral goal of φιλία. The goal is to win. As long as you adhere to the principle of Active Partnership, you will be the moral winner to which the other, when not equal, is irredeemably indebted.

---

245 *Mem.* II.i.30: πρὶν ἐπιθυμῆσαι πάντων ἐμπίπλασαι, πρὶν μὲν πεινῆν ἐσθίουσα, πρὶν δὲ διψῆν πίνουσα. See Section 3.2 above.

246 *Mem.* I.ii.14, I.iii.5–14, I.v.1, I.v.6, I.vi.8, II.i, III.xiv, IV.5.9, IV.viii.11. According to Dorion (2006), ἐγκράτεια, together with the concepts of καρτερία and αὐτάρκεια, forms the core of Socratic ethics in the *Memorabilia*. Dorion (2006). See however Edmunds (2018) who argues that there is no such "triad". Cf. p. 316 n. 219.

247 *Mem.* I.v.4–5; Dorion (2006).

248 ἄσκησις; *Mem.* I.ii.19–23, II.i.20, II.i.28, II.vi.39, III.iii.6, III.v.14, III.ix.1–3.

249 *See* Dorion (2006) for an overview of the functions of ἐγκράτεια in Socrates' moral philosophy in the *Memorabilia*.

250 Annas (2007), 205, on ethical egoism: "The egoism in question here is ethical egoism, the theory that holds that my own good is the ethical standard for what it is right for me to do, the dispositions I should have, and so on." "Ethical individualism", or "ethical egoism", is not to be confused with the descriptive "egoism" that features in the egoism/altruism opposition. See Chapter Five, Section 3; cf. Annas (2007) for a discussion of the misguided charge of egoism directed at virtue ethics in general.

Here is where things get a bit dark to our taste. Take for instance the "story of the dog" (ὁ τοῦ κυνὸς λόγος),[251] recounted by Socrates in one of his expositions on φιλία, a story dating back to the time when animals could talk. One day a sheep came up to her master and said: "I do not understand your conduct. We sheep provide you with wool and lambs and cheese, but you give us nothing except what we get from the earth. But to the dog, who provides you with nothing of this kind, you give a share of your own food." The dog overheard the conversation and said: "Quite right, too. For I am the one who keeps you from being stolen by men and carried off by wolves. If I did not watch over you, you wouldn't even be able to graze in the first place for fear of being killed." In the light of his argument the sheep conceded the dog his privileges.

To be slightly more precise: this is a fable told by Socrates to Aristarchus—the same Aristarchus who was advised by Socrates to start a wool-manufacturing workplace with the female relatives that were under his care.[252] The workplace is a success and the χάρις within the family is restored. After a while, however, the women have started to complain that Aristarchus is the only member of the household who eats the bread of idleness. Socrates advises him to tell the women the story of the dog, for Aristarchus is their watch-dog (φύλαξ) and keeper (ἐπιμελητής);[253] without him they would not have been capable to live and work in safety and comfort. Aristarchus is advised to assert his position as top dog, as Active Partner, towards his relatives and to make plain that he was the original donor of the primordial gift: without him, the women would have had no life and work in the first place. There certainly *is* χάρις in the exchange, but the women should not mistake mutual cooperation for equivalence or equality: they are in a position of irredeemable debt, no matter how much they contribute to the household. The prestige of his Active Partnership has been translated into a position of preference (προτιμᾶσθαι),[254] a more static condition of inequality. The animals, the dog, sheep and wolves, are therefore not

---

251 *Mem.* II.vii.13–14.

252 *Mem.* II.vii. Chapter Two Section 4.1. Cf. Bandini-Dorion (2011a) for the Aesopean quality of this story; Van Dijk (1997), 337, for the generic features (e.g. the introductory formula ὅτε φωνήεντα ἦν τὰ ζῷα, and the epimythium καὶ σὺ οὖν) that make the story recognizable as a fable.

253 Van Dijk (1997), 338, for the verbal parallels that establish the comparison between the fable and Aristarchus' situation. Note that the "master" from Socrates' Story of the Dog is eclipsed when the story is applied to Aristarchus' situation: the dog has replaced the master. Cf. Van Dijk (1997), 338–339; Zafiropoulos (2001).

254 *Mem.* II.vii.14.

merely part of the furniture that comes with the language of fable. The animal kingdom is a hierarchical place: it has leaders and followers, kings and subordinates, it assumes fundamental differences, natural inequalities inscribed into its long-term order that do not require constitutional justification.[255]

We have seen several other examples how in and through Active Partnership, power relations are initiated, reinforced and legitimated. Piety is distinct from the art of traffic, precisely because no human χάρις can be a sufficient return for the good done to us by the gods.[256] How, then, should one gratify the gods?[257] By following the law of the cities (νόμῳ πόλεως) which is universal (πανταχοῦ): to please the gods with sacrifices according to power (κατὰ δύναμιν ἱεροῖς θεοὺς ἀρέσκεσθαι).[258] Similarly, a son can never disavow his father like a father can disavow his son, for adequate compensation can never be rendered to parents.[259] It is impossible to honor one's parents according to merit (κατ' ἀξίαν), for a mother is the φίλος par excellence,[260] whom one can only reciprocate to according to ability and to whom one will always remain indebted[261]—even when (and here the Lamprocles story takes a nasty twist) she is quite unreasonable and one should, like actors in a tragedy, learn to listen to her without being annoyed.[262] Benefactors give more than their beneficiaries can ever return and hence gain τιμή; the beneficiaries only reciprocate κατὰ τὴν δύναμιν.[263] Unlike commercial transactions, χάρις- and gift exchanges, precisely *because* they do not aim at immediate equivalence, allow for more flexibility—an elasticity that can turn into situations of permanent indebtedness and asymmetries.[264] Active Partnership that is not adequately answered with a "competing" active initiative by the other partner congeals into a position of superiority.[265]

255 Cf. Azoulay (2004), 307. The *locus classicus* of the use of fable to express the givenness of inequalities is the Fable of the Hawk and the Nightingale in Hes, *O&D* 20–211.

256 *Mem.* IV.iii.15: ἐκεῖνο δὲ ἀθυμῶ, ὅτι μοι δοκεῖ τὰς τῶν θεῶν εὐεργεσίας οὐδ' ἂν εἷς ποτε ἀνθρώπων ἀξίαις χάρισιν ἀμείβεσθαι. Cf. Chapter Two Section 1.2.

257 *Mem.* IV.iii.16: πῶς ἂν τοῖς θεοῖς χαρίζοιτο.

258 *Mem.* IV.iii.16. See also *Mem.* I.iii.3 for the notion of the Hesiodic (*O&D* 336) καδδύναμιν, "according to one's power". Cf. Theophrastus, *On Piety*, fr. 12.42–48 (Pötcher).

259 E.g. Ar. *EN* VIII.xiv (1163b14–22). See Chapter Three Section 5 (Alcestis).

260 E.g. *Mem.* II.ii. See Chapter Three Section 4.

261 E.g. Ar. *EN* IX.i (1164b6).

262 *Mem.* II.ii.8–9.

263 E.g. Ar. *EN* VIII.xiv (1163b12–15).

264 A similar asymmetry is described in the "isomorphism of sex and power" postulated by Foucault (1984).

265 These elements of hierarchy and inequality are missed by Gray (2011), 291–329, who reads Azoulay's interpretation of Xenophontic friendship in terms exploitation. However,

The phenomenon is profusely observed in the anthropological and sociological record. A mundane (and rather grim) example is offered in Korn & Mc Corkle's[266] description of the practice of inmates in American prisons to force other inmates to accept cigarettes: they place gifts of cigarettes in the cells of inmates they have selected for personal domination. If these intended victims fail to find the donor and make them take back the "gifts" they are understood to be the personal property of the donor. Individuals can bring others under their sway by enforcing obligations through gifts, up to the point where it becomes "symbolic violence" to a recipient who is put under a threat to reciprocate the impossible.[267] The mutually reinforcing processes of reciprocal exchange and hierarchy formation is well documented in the anthropological field, as e.g. in Whyte's study about hierarchies in slums and gangs, where the ability to reciprocate has immediate consequences for the hierarchical structure of the group: a leader must always be able to reciprocate; followers have subordinate positions in the hierarchy because they are not equally capable of discharging obligations.[268]

Azoulay does not discuss exploitation *per se*, but instead analyzes an undeniable (historical and linguistic) reality in the work of Xenophon, i.e. unequal relationships.

266 Korn & Mc Corkle (1954).

267 The notion of "symbolic violence", i.e. "giving as a way of possessing", is coined by Bourdieu (1977), 5–7, 192 ff. Two basic types of power management based on reciprocal relationships may be distinguished: the "big man" and the "chief" (Sahlins (1972), 208 ff.; Van Wees (1998), 42–43). The "big man" is emblematic for personal power is achieved through reciprocity (that serves as a "starting mechanism"), where individuals become leaders by impairing the other's capacity to discharge debts. The more one frustrates the other's attempt towards equal reciprocation, the more permanent the control one can exert on the flow of goods. Power develops from control over a single transaction, to repeated asymmetry in control, to permanent control over the flow of goods, to control over *people*—as in patron-clients relationships. The "chief" represents institutional, ascribed, power is upheld by reciprocity and redistribution: the party in control collects "gifts" of tribute and labor and generously redistributes these resources to his people, e.g. in feasts.

268 Whyte (1964), 257–258: "Not all the corner boys live up to their obligations equally well, and this factor partly accounts for the differentiation in status among them. The man with a low status may violate his obligations without much change in his position. His fellows know that he has failed to discharge certain obligations in the past, and his position reflects his past performances. On the other hand, the leader is depended upon by all the members to meet his personal obligations. He cannot fail to do so without causing confusion and endangering his position. (...) The leader spends more money on his followers than they on him. The farther down in the structure one looks, the fewer are the financial relations which tend to obligate the leader to a follower. This does not mean that the leader has more money than others or even that he necessarily spends more—though he must always be a free spender. It means that the financial relations must be explained in social terms."

This concurs with the convincing large-scale analysis of χάρις in Xenophon by Vincent Azoulay.[269] Azoulay argues how in Xenophon's oeuvre friendships are more often unequal than not,[270] and how the vocabulary of φιλία serves to mask the real workings of χάρις and to euphemize the relations of dependency between leaders and followers or leaders and allies. This results in a picture of Xenophon's analysis of power that is reminiscent of Weber's notion of "charismatic authority": the type of leadership that is legitimized by the charismatic qualities of the leader, his "gift of grace", and that incites personal devotion in followers who are bound to the leader by personal acts of grace.[271] Xenophon's understanding of power too, in Azoulay's analysis, revolves around χάρις, the gift of grace, and the exchange of mutual of favors that slides (by "*glissement*") from horizontal reciprocity between equals into lopsided, or vertical, exchanges between a superior donor who secures power over the recipient.[272] The indiscriminate labelling of all these χάρις-reciprocities as φιλία-bonds obfuscates the power play of domination and dependence.[273]

However, as the examples cited above show, it is not so much the vocabulary of friendship that euphemizes power-relations: it is true that φιλία-vocabulary is silent about hierarchy and applicable to equal and unequal bonds alike—but that does not mean that φιλία-vocabulary *imply* equality where there is none.[274] Certainly Xenophon does not seem to presuppose such equality: his prime example of the ultimate φίλος is the mother of Lamprocles (*Mem.* II.ii), the most superior φίλος, imposing the most irredeemable debt of motherhood on her son, a model that sets the standard for all the discussions on φιλία to follow. In general, the asymmetry in the friendships discussed by Xenophon's Socrates are blatantly obvious and hardly disguised or veiled.[275] Rather than being euphemized, power and hierarchy in φιλία are being *legitimized*—by

269 Azoulay (2004). It is lamentable that this excellent work of scholarship has received so few responses in Anglo-Saxon scholarship. The discussion in Gray (2006) does not do justice to the subtlety and the well-documented nature of the argument.

270 Azoulay (2004), 291ff.

271 Weber (1978: 1111–1157) distinguishes three types of legitimate domination: tradition, legal rationality and charisma.

272 Azoulay (2004). Cf. Bourdieu (1980) who sees the difference between symmetrical and asymmetrical reciprocity as only a gradual change "which is the base of political authority" (210).

273 Azoulay (2004), 298.

274 This is an assumption found in many studies on Classical φιλία and that recurs in Azoulay's idea that Xenophon's philosophy of friendship is a forerunner of Hellenistic unequal friendships. See Chapter One Section 1.

275 This may be a characteristic of Xenophon's Socratic works. Other mechanisms may prevail in historiographic works.

Active Partnership: the act of χάρις that establishes graceful indebtedness, by the grandeur of quantitative lavishness and the grace of qualitative superiority that befalls the one who takes initiative, who gives before being asked, who actively engages with the needs of the friend.

6 Concluding Remarks: Language Games at the Market Frontier

So what *was* at stake in Socrates' conversation with the most beautiful woman in Athens? As I have argued, it is crucial to understand *Mem.* III.xi as a dialogue on φιλία, on friendship, or reciprocal solidarity. This we should take at face value. Yes, the language of φιλία and χάρις does lend itself to erotic interpretations and euphemistic use. And yes, the setting of the dialogue certainly triggers such an understanding of the dialogue's subject matter. But this does not mean that *Mem.* III.xi is a conversation that merely pretends to be about friendship while "really" only discussing "friends with benefits".

It may be for Theodote. For a hetaera, the language of χάρις and φιλία is a crucial discursive means of self-definition, of keeping oneself at the right side of the "Market Frontier", of the "emotion work" required in the trade of "selling" one's body. But while Theodote only uses the *language* of χάρις and φιλία to signal a relational embedding of her "benefactions", Socrates points out that the demarcation between genuine φιλία and its travesty is not just a verbal one: the defining feature of true φιλία is Active Partnership, competitive generosity instead of exploitative encounters, active benefaction instead of passive requital.

As the Antiphon-episode did, the encounter with Theodote displays awareness of the fact that things may *look* the same on the outside, while being radically distinct in quality. It also betrays an awareness of the many ways in which such a contrast, this "invisible difference", may be construed: there is euphemism (making things different by giving them different names), there is perception, or a form of "seeing as" (making things different by interpreting them differently), and there is quality (making things different by defining them by valuing the intentions and emotions associated with them). To Xenophon's Socrates, the difference between isomorphous exchanges of benefactions lies not in the *names* that we use for them ("prostitution" vs. "friendship") but in the *quality* of acts of giving: is the giving unsolicited, does it exhibit initiative, does it come with the right internalized dispositions, are you feeling what you *should* feel?

What, then, is the philosophical significance of this episode? As I have argued, *Mem.* III.xi is not only a negative demonstration that Theodote does not really understand her own τέχνη, the Art of Friendship. It also contains, however allusive, a positive argument as to what *does* constitute true φιλία: the principle of Active Partnership. Active Partnership is a **precondition** for philosophical dialectics: Socrates is playing hard to get, to incite initiative and agency in Theodote. It provides the **setting** of philosophical dialectics, of friends sharing virtues and sharing friends becoming virtuous. And it is the very **substance** of philosophical ethics. To Socrates, the sophist, the businessman and the hetaera suffer from the same flaw, as they, having a false conception of the good, can only interact with fellow-humans on the degrading basis of mutual passivity. As the genuine good can only be acquired by an active shaping of the self, and virtue is to be attained in interaction with the world, virtue comes down to the capacity to relate properly to the world around us: to the gods, the community and to other individuals. The proper way to "deal with" other individuals requires Active Partnership: actively investing in a reciprocal relationship. Active Partnership is what demarcates long-term exchanges from seemingly isomorphous short-term transactions. Active Partnership requires internalized dispositions, attitudes and emotions—goodwill, trust, generosity, empathy in good and bad times, the willingness to take initiative—or, in Socrates' terms a ψυχή that actively supports what the body is overtly doing. In Xenophon's oeuvre, the sophist, the businessman and the hetaera are represented as passive. They do not actively select their exchange partners, their "gratifying" is reduced to mere requital and they are not δωροφορικόν but μισθαρνητικόν: they do not *give* gifts, but they *receive* payment.

This suggests an interesting difference between Plato and Xenophon with respect to Socrates' erotic doctrine. In Plato's dialogues it is ἔρως that is made philosophically productive, as it represents a principle of motion. When sublimated from the physical realm, ἔρως is the driving force of philosophy, facilitating protreptics and the ascending movement of the soul towards the beauty of the forms. In Xenophon's *Memorabilia* the operative term is φιλία: Socrates appropriates the terminology of the long-term order, as the very *contents* of his philosophical conversations are all about the question how an individual can become virtuous by learning to relate to the long-term order, his family, friends, the polis and the gods. At the same time, φιλία is also the very medium of Socratic education as his philosophical enterprise of developing virtue takes place within the context of reciprocal friendships in which both partners are actively engaged—a bilateral relationship that benefits both partners. The sophist is merely a pale imitation of a teacher, operating with the wrong notion of reciprocity and hence revealing his defective ἐγκράτεια, because mastery of one's appetites and impulses is not only the prerequisite of commitment in a long-term relationship but also the very precondition for the development of virtue. In contrast, Socrates' understanding of the reciprocal obligations and expectations that go with true φιλία qualifies him not only as a better friend than Theodote, but also as a better teacher than the sophist.

Here we may get to the true target of this episode. Although in general Xenophon's Socrates does not display the same obsession with definitional rigor and semantic precision as his Platonic counterpart, he *is* invested in normative linguistics, i.e. in the correct use of ethical terminology, and he *is* averse to the lexical window-dressing that characterizes the self-presentation of the hetaera—but not *only* the hetaera. Perhaps the Theodote episode is more than an exotic oddity in the series of Socratic conversations, resonating in a more general vain the language games played out at the Market Frontier.

James Fredal makes a case for reading the sophistic practice of charging fees for wisdom and instruction in public speaking as a conscious and deliberate "economic innovation" with a certain kind of performative quality.[276] By putting a concrete and precise price on their teachings, turning authoritative discourse from a gift into a "commodity for sale in an open market economy",[277] the sophists engaged in a form of demystification: they made the mechanisms of reciprocity at work in aristocratic gift-exchange visible, they unveil the *méconnaissance*, the economic veil of ignorance, making explicit the "fiduciary basis of trade in authoritative discourse".[278] It is attractive to interpret this performative demystification, as Fredal does, against the backdrop of the νόμος-φύσις debate, the intellectual trend of making explicit the conventional, and fundamentally political, basis of valuation and judgment. Fredal suggests an analogy between Protagoras' practice of charging fees and his open avowal to being a sophist: Protagoras "prefers to measure and claim for himself the value of his wisdom rather than misrecognizing it under the cloak of gentlemanly kindness and friendship achieved through gift giving".[279] Just like notions of justice and religion may be invented to serve particular stakeholders, the long-term values associated with aristocratic gift exchange, such as Active Partnership, may legitimize existing power relations.

Fredal's interpretation is appealing for sophists like Plato's Protagoras and may likewise work for Xenophon's Antiphon: his almost theatrical market men-

276 Fredal (2008).

277 Fredal (2008), 158.

278 Fredal (2008), 166; cf. 157–158: "[T]he sophistic innovation stripped "trade in wisdom" from its elite mystification, revealing what it had always been: a concealed pursuit for "advantage"."

279 Fredal (2008), 165.

tality could be read as a performative act as well.[280] However, it may not work for all sophists (nor for the sophists as a group) and it runs counter to a striking aspect in the *representation* of sophists. Especially in Plato's generic portrayal of the sophists, the sophists are prone to fashion themselves as participants in a χάρις-economy:

[Text 27]

> καὶ γὰρ οἱ σοφισταί, τἆλλα σοφοὶ ὄντες, τοῦτο ἄτοπον ἐργάζονται πρᾶγμα· φάσκοντες γὰρ ἀρετῆς διδάσκαλοι εἶναι πολλάκις κατηγοροῦσιν τῶν μαθητῶν ὡς ἀδικοῦσι σφᾶς [αὐτούς], **τούς τε μισθοὺς ἀποστεροῦντες καὶ ἄλλην χάριν οὐκ ἀποδιδόντες**, εὖ παθόντες ὑπ' αὐτῶν.
>
> For all their cleverness in other respects, there's an anomaly in the sophists' affairs: they claim to be teachers of virtue, but they often accuse their pupils of wronging them, their benefactors, *by withholding their gratitude in some form, and especially by not paying fees.*[281]

Note that the χάρις-economy is not imagined as an *alternative* for μισθός-payment: rather it is presented in close juxtaposition with monetary payment (**τούς τε μισθοὺς ἀποστεροῦντες καὶ ἄλλην χάριν οὐκ ἀποδιδόντες**), *subsuming* μισθός (**καὶ ἄλλην χάριν**). This points to a broader tendency in Plato's work where sophists, despite the fact that they charge money for their lessons, are prone to represent their relations with their students as more than a purely commercial transaction. Above and beyond the objectifiable compensations, there is an "additional" χάρις, material or symbolical, that adds a moral or social dimension to the exchange at hand: sophists will help you if you pay money and put down χάριτες,[282] and they convince the young to pay money (χρήματα διδόντας) for their associations and be grateful in addition (χάριν προσειδέναι).[283]

280 See Chapter Five Section 1.

281 Pl. *Gorg.* 519c3–d1; *transl.* Waterfield (1994). Cf. Chapter Five Section 4.2 (T34).

282 Pl. *Crat.* 391b10: χρήματα ἐκείνοις τελοῦντα καὶ χάριτας κατατιθέμενον. Here the plural suggests that χάριτες should be taken to be material manifestations of χάρις; however, material or not, the χάριτες are mentioned separately from χρήματα, which suggests an additional reward outside a payment that is agreed upon in advance. Cf. Socrates on the appropriate response to those who try to help him escape: Pl. *Crit.* 48d (χρήματα τελοῦντες (…) καὶ χάριτας).

283 Pl. *Apol.* 19e–20a. Cf. a passage in the Platonic *Theages* where the young men who are persuaded by sophists are said to "pay down beside a large sum of money as fee, and to

The formulations ironically echo sophistic self-presentation: whereas Xenophon's Antiphon prides himself on a successful no-nonsense business-model, Plato's sophists prefer to see themselves as benefactors and their teaching practice as civic service.[284] Within such a self-presentation χάρις-terminology is instrumental in obfuscating the mercenary nature of their *modus operandi*, and in upgrading it: immaterial χάρις is an additional asset, above and beyond the payment of a teacher.[285] A professional teacher is more than a business man, mercenary or prostitute. He is a visionary helper and benefactor of the community—that is, until Plato's Socrates exposes this χάρις-talk as a mere euphemism for monetary compensation.[286] Just like Xenophon's Theodote.

The language of long-term reciprocity, of χάρις and φιλία, proves to be a battleground for a variety of language games. It is a discursive device shared by

---

be grateful in addition" (προσκατατιθέντας ἀργύριον πάνυ πολὺ μισθόν, καὶ χάριν πρὸς τούτοις εἰδέναι; 127a6–7).

284 Similarly Isocrates reports how the parents of his students not only pay him (χρήματα διδόασιν), but also react very positively (χαίρουσιν) to their children's education. Is. 15.241. The verb χαίρειν may evoke the χάρις-rhetoric in the rest of the speech where Isocrates consistently characterizes his education as a form of civic service. Cf. Too (1995: 109–110), (2008: 6–7). The χάρις-terminology serves to characterize the exchange between teacher and pupil as not entirely commercial or socially detached; the education offered by Isocrates not only involves long-term bonds between teacher and the students' parents but also participates in the long-term social order of the city. Cf. Blank (2014) The juxtaposition of payment and gratitude occurs frequently as a colloquialism. King Oedipus promises anyone who will inform him about the identity of the killer of Laius by "paying him gain and storing up gratitude besides" (κέρδος τελῶ 'γὼ χἠ χάρις προσκείσεται). Soph. *OT* 232. The preverb πρόσ- conveys the idea of gratitude above material reward; the simplex verb κεῖσθαι contains a metaphor from deposits of money. E.g. Aristoph. *Ran*. 624, Soph. *Ant*. 485, Pind. *Isthm*. 5.18. κείμενα as deposits: Hdt. 6.86, Thuc. 1.129. Cf. Jebb (1887), ad loc., referring to Pl. *Ep*. 346c as an example. For the metaphor of friends as deposits of wealth, see Section 1 above.

285 This may also be the background to the recurring idea that some sophists offer *more* than what they are paid for. Plato represents Hippias as the sophist who earns exorbitant amounts of money from his teachings. In *Hipp. Maj*. 281b–c, the sophist's practice is emphatically *not* represented as a *quid pro quo*-matter. Rather, Hippias has the capacity to confer private (ἰδίᾳ) and public (δημοσίᾳ) benefits (ὠφελεῖν, εὐεργετεῖν) that *exceed* (ἔτι πλείω) the amount of money that he receives (πολλὰ χρήματα). Cf. also Pl. *Prot*. 328b. Although Blank (1985: 7) categorizes these remarks as an instance of the idea that "a sophist must give his customer his money's worth" (cf. Xen. *Mem*. III.i.11); this is, by implication, true, but the rhetorical gist of the passage is that *Hippias*' practice is emphatically *not* represented as a *quid pro quo*-matter. Plato's propensity to see χάρις merely as euphemism for *quid pro quo*-exchanges may also explain why he does not think of reciprocity as a viable alternative to market trade (as noted by Danzig & Schaps (2001)): to him, personal reciprocity is in the end only an informal variety of market trade or barter—not a qualitatively and morally distinct one.

286 E.g. Pl. *Rep*. 1.338b1–9; see Chapter Four Section 2.5.

sophists, hetaeras *and* Socrates to position themselves on the right side of the Market Frontier, a verbal veil and an act of *méconnaissance* used to cover up underlying short-term monetary interests and power play. It may also be the object of demystification: by sophists, who aim to expose and delegitimize the aristocratic discourse of gift exchange; by Plato's Socrates, who exposes the sophists' posh χάρις-and-civic-service-talk as lexical window-dressing; and by Xenophon's Socrates, who exposes Athens' most beautiful woman as a dressed-up prostitute and a sophist in disguise.

CHAPTER 7

Relational Economics: Aristotle on Value and Equivalence

> διὸ καὶ Χαρίτων ἱερὸν ἐμποδὼν ποιοῦνται, ἵν' ἀνταπόδοσις ᾖ· τοῦτο γὰρ ἴδιον χάριτος; ἀνθυπηρετῆσαι γὰρ δεῖ τῷ χαρισαμένῳ, καὶ πάλιν αὐτὸν ἄρξαι χαριζόμενον.
>
> That is why cities erect the temple of the Graces in a conspicuous place, in order that there might be a return for what is given. For this is the special characteristic of gratitude, since we should not only do a service in return for someone who has done us a favor but, on another occasion, start by doing a favor too.
>
> ARISTOTLE, *EN* V.V (1132a3–5)

∴

When is a relationship "strictly business", when do we call it "economical"? In the 1950s and 1960s, economic anthropology developed a set of conceptual tools that became influential for the comparative study of economies. One defining distinction was made by Karl Polanyi in an article where he reflected upon the "two root meanings of 'economic' ":[1]

[Text 1]

> The substantive meaning of economic derives from man's dependence for his living upon nature and his fellows. It refers to the interchange with his natural and social environment, in so far as this results in supplying him with the means of material want satisfaction. The formal meaning of economic derives from the logical character of the means-ends relationship, as apparent in such words as "economical" or "economizing". It refers to

1 Polanyi (1957).

 | DOI:10.1163/9789004416147_008

> a definite situation of choice, namely, that between the different uses of means induced by an insufficiency of those means.[2]

In its formal meaning, economics prescribes a set of rules "referring to choice between the alternative uses of insufficient means". Formalistic economics is ultimately premised on a principle of scarcity and rational action, "rational" being defined in a cognitive-instrumental way. "Economic" in this formal sense is, according to Polanyi's argument, only applicable to an economy of a specific type, i.e. a system of price-making markets, where all goods and services (including the "fictive commodities" land, labor and capital) are purchasable and where all income is derived from these.[3] Only (Western) market capitalist economies that are primarily integrated through exchange on price-setting markets can be analyzed within the framework of formal economics. Other economies, where economic activities are "embedded" in social processes, can only be described in terms of substantive economics.[4]

The anthropological formalism/substantivism-distinction has been taken up in the study of the ancient economy, where formalists approach the ancient economy as a functionally segregated and independent sphere of activity (with a profit-maximizing, want-satisfying logic),[5] whereas substantivists maintain that the ancient economy was socially embedded,[6] insisting that in Greek οἰκονομία means "household management" and is conceptually unrelated to the modern sense of "economy" that implies a disembedded realm with its own distinct logic and rationality.[7]

---

2 Polanyi (1957), 243.

3 Firth (1970) and followers consider the postulates of marginalist economics of universal application. In the 1970s the formalist/substantivist-debate witnessed a second wave including formalist anthropologists working with formal decision-making models, and substantivist anthropologists working with the concept of "mode of production", the articulation of different modes of production and issues of "transition" to capitalist economies.

4 On Polanyi's twin notions "disembedded" and "embedded", see also Chapter One Section 3.1.

5 E.g. Cohen (1991), Loomis (1998), Harris (2002). See Chapter One Section 3.1.

6 Finley (1985), 17–23, 155, 160; (1965), 11–33; (1970), 3–25. Cf. Weber (1968), 311–398, Hasebroek (1933), 97–105, Will (1954), 7–22, Pearson (1957), 3–11, Lowry (1979), 65–86, Millett (1983), 36–52, Millett (1991), 59, 218–230, Morris (1994), 351–366. For a critique on Polanyi's logic of "embedding" and "disembedding" as rooted in a stage theory of history, see Bresson (2016), 2–30.

7 Substantivist approaches traditionally attribute a limited role of money in the ancient Greek economy (e.g. Finley (1985), (1965), (1970), who insists on the "cellular self-sufficiency" of the ancient household), and tend to downplay the impact of monetization on the disembedding of the economy. E.g. Von Reden (1995)'s argument that the Athenian money-economy was an "embedded money economy". Cf. Davies (1998), 240.

It is granted that it is misguided to imagine that ancient markets ever reached the level of disembeddedness of the modern capitalist market economy in industrialized societies.[8] It is equally misguided to understand developments in economic history in terms of a unidirectional movement along a scale from embeddedness towards disembeddedness.[9] Moreover, as anthropologists point out, "pure" disembedded economic relations have seldom been observed in any culture:[10] everywhere access to land, labor, energy and knowledge expresses and defines political and social relations. Within the confines of these limiting conditions and qualifications, the substantivism/formalism-discussion is an extremely complex one on many levels, and whose outcome depends to a large extent on what exactly is being studied: performance or structure,[11] reality or representation.[12]

The previous chapters have suggested an additional consideration on the issue of representation. Market exchange in ancient Athens was, in reality, guided by and embedded in social and political values and norms: in practice, instead of balanced prices, social proximity or distance remained determining factors in pricing.[13] On a market too, φίλοι tended to get a better deal than total strangers, because friendship reduces the dangers of deceit, excessive pricing and violence (i.e. friendship reduces "transaction costs").[14] Nevertheless,

---

8 See Bohannan & Dalton (1962), 1–20 for an argument that the principle of market exchange is to be distinguished from the marketplace.

9 Silver (1995), 196.

10 E.g. Narotzky (2001), 4070.

11 North (1981), 3, defines "performance" as the "typical concerns of economists", i.e. quantitative accounts of production, distribution of costs and benefits, the stability of production etc.; "structure" is those characteristics of a society which are believed to be the basic determinants of performance, such as political and economic institutions, technology, demography and ideology. Morris, Saller & Scheidel (2007) note a tendency for historians of Greek economy to focus more on structure than on performance whereas historians of Roman economy have shifted their attention to performance the last few decades.

12 E.g. Kurke (1999), (2002) for an argument that elitist tradition represses the political dimension of coinage by misrepresenting coinage and the agora as *only* an economic instrument and an economic space, i.e. by conceiving of the public sphere as the domain of *only* disembedded economics. See however the criticism of Figueira (2000), who objects that Kurke uses the terminology too impressionistically by practically conflating "embedded" with "socialized" and "disembedded" with "individualistic" or "deracinated".

13 Möller (2008), 370. Cf. Millett (1991) on credit mechanisms among friends.

14 The term "transaction cost" was originally coined by Coase (1988 [1937]). Cost-free transactions are imaginary: market transactions always cost something in terms of time and effort to find and evaluate the relevant information and to effectuate the deal. These costs can efficiently be lowered by bringing transactions into a rule-bounded system where par-

ancient sources tend to treat retail sellers and shopkeepers as men acting outside the norms of φιλία, with a different and distinct mentality—especially so in situations of isomorphism.

The conceptual construction and representation of the market and commerce that we find in some of our sources, as being detached from social relations, seems to emerge specifically in contexts of isomorphism, where sophists are compared to philosophers, prostitutes to courtesans, mercenaries to faithful servants. It is in these contexts, in which commercial transactions are compared to socially stronger ties such as φιλία, that moral and political dichotomies come into play. As we have seen, these contexts invite a construction of φιλία as a morally privileged subjective other-regarding bond where goods circulate as invaluable and priceless gifts of self-negation. This construction works both ways. As contexts of isomorphism promote a demarcation of φιλία-reciprocities from commercial transactions, the market in turn is constructed as typically disembedded and a-social, featuring socially disengaged characters such as mercenaries, prostitutes, sophists and petty retail traders. Isomorphism breeds a Hostile Worlds view.

1 Aristotle Discovers the Economy?

So: how disembedded does it get in ancient economic reflection? We started our argument in Chapter Two with the civic significance that Aristotle attributed to the shrine for the Χάριτες. It serves as a perpetual reminder to people to "know the χάρις": not only in the reactive sense of reciprocating a good turn, but also in the proactive sense of initiating reciprocity. The placing of the shrine is significant. Topographically, because it is possible that Aristotle is here referring to a shrine on the Athenian Agora.[15] This seems to suggest that the Age of Grace is not long gone at all: χάρις is alive and kicking, dwelling on the market, of all places (the place of double dealing and deceit!), adorning even those relationships of sordid commerce. But the placing of the shrine is also significant in a discursive sense: Aristotle's mention of the Graces directly precedes one of the most controversial statements in the history of economics:

ticipants can trust on procedures. Cf. Ober (2008) for an application of the concept to institutions and procedures in democratic Athens.

15 See Chapter Two, n. 15.

[Text 2]

As builder to shoemaker, shoes to a house.[16]

This proposition, from Aristotle's discussion of reciprocal justice in the *Nicomachean Ethics*, has often been hailed as a starting point of Western economic reflection.[17] It is here that Aristotle is supposed to have "discovered the economy" as a more or less autonomous phenomenon,[18] to offer a precursor of a labor theory of value,[19] or, conversely, a utilitarian or market-theory of value that assigns value on the basis of laws of supply and demand.[20] However, the same proposition has also been treated with contempt as "pedestrian" and "trivial",[21] or as essentially defective, or metaphysically problematic.[22]

What all these interpretations take for granted is the idea that in this proposition Aristotle, in however seminal form or defective way, is describing a realm of human activity that is "economic", disembedded, extricated from social, political and religious concerns. The growing disjunction between what we may dub "market exchanges" and φιλία-exchanges that we have seen in the previous chapters seems to culminate here in Aristotle's analysis of justice in exchange.

1.1 *The Argument*

In this chapter, it is this assumption that will be subjected to scrutiny: does Aristotle offer an account of disembedded exchanges? The answer will be a simple: no.

First, it will be argued that chapter v.v of the *Nicomachean Ethics* does not offer a theory of price formation (Section 2). Secondly, it will be argued that although Aristotle does acknowledge that market exchanges, such as between a builder and a shoemaker, involve a form of abstraction, this does by no means

16 Ar. *EN* v.v (1133a22–24).

17 Ross (1954), xiv: "This analysis, one of the earliest efforts in political economy, has been generally recognized as an important example of Aristotle's analytic genius." Soudek, 45: "One of Aristotle's most challenging contributions to the development of economic thought is his theory of exchange."

18 Polanyi (1968 [1957]).

19 E.g. Williams (1972), Soudek (1952), Spengler (1955).

20 E.g. Hardie (1968), Barker (1906), Van Johnson (1939), Von Leyden (1985).

21 Schumpeter (1954), 57: "we find (if such a thing may be said without offense of so great a figure) decorous, pedestrian, slightly mediocre, and more than slightly pompous common sense."

22 Meikle (1995); Castoriadis (1978).

imply that Aristotle recognized market exchanges as a separate realm free from social, political and moral concerns. The tendency among commentators is to focus on notions of "value" in Aristotle; I will make a case that Aristotelian "economics" is best understood in terms of relations. Along these lines, it will be argued that Aristotle's chapter on reciprocal justice is better read as a reflection on a specific type of interpersonal relationship than on the nature of economic value (Section 3).

Aristotle's analysis of the ratio between shoemaker, builder and their products is explicitly presented as a model with limited applicability, only valid in regard to a specific type of interpersonal relationships. It will be argued that this relation type is the elusive category of "political friendship", a phenomenon that is often mistakenly understood as a "political emotion"[23] or interpreted as "civic friendship", a detached and mercantile civic bond in a community of "calculating bankers and accountants".[24] Although πολιτικὴ φιλία *is* a utilitarian bond, what makes it "political" is that it has reference to the ultimate aims of the project of the polis (Section 4).

My interpretation of the Shoemaker/Builder proportion builds on the analyses of, amongst others, Scott Meikle, Gabriel Danzig and Jill Frank.[25] I concur with Meikle in reading the proportion as expressive of the tautological truth of the market (Section 2); with Danzig in reading the equation as a way not to calculate prices, but to legitimate existing prices/valuations (Section 3); with Frank in emphasizing the close connection of χρεία and χρῆσις, and in approaching χρεία as an underdetermined category (Section 3.3). Over and above this I argue that the shoemaker/builder-relation is best understood by reference to what it is *not*: an unequal exchange relationship (Section 2.3) and an exchange of incommensurables (Sections 3.4 and 3.5).

Aristotle's chapter on reciprocal justice gains more significance when read against his theory of friendship. Although *EN* v.v does not offer a theory of price formation, it does offer a theory of value: to Aristotle, value, together with equivalence, is a relation phenomenon, and his conceptualization of it is to an important degree informed by his ideas about the ties that bind people. Political Friendship refers to only one specific subset of human interactions, and Aristotle is careful not to confuse the value structures of distinct relationship types: only in some situations do we behave as shoemaker and builder.[26]

23 Arendt (1958), Barber (1984), Balot (2006), Cooper (1990).

24 Interpretation of Hobbesian friendship in Yack (1993), 110, 127.

25 Meikle (1995), Danzig (2000), Frank (2005).

26 This is only one instance of Aristotle's device of "focalization", made explicit in his ubiq-

2 Equivalence

2.1 *A Friend in Need*

Aristotle's conceptual response to the isomorphism of different kinds of exchange relations is one of radical reorganization. Whereas 5th- and 4th-century moral discourse was preoccupied with preserving the boundaries between *philia* and other forms of mutual exchange, Aristotle lumps together any and all relations of cooperative consensual exchange,[27] ranging from the generalized reciprocity among near kin to the detached one-off transaction taking place on the market, on the ground that both categories are eventually premised on the same motivation: need.[28] As we have seen, to Aristotle, owing to their basis, utility friendships constitute an inferior form of friendship. Need makes bonds intrinsically weak: they are easily dissolved, and consequently not friendships in the fullest sense of the word.[29] They are liable to disappointments and complaints,[30] and they cease to exist once the underlying needs, the rationale of their existence, are satisfied.[31]

Aristotle's demarcation of a class of Utility Friendship is the ultimate consequence of the commonplace in Greek moral reflection that what draws individuals together and sustains their bond is some form of deficiency, a "lack of" or "need for" something. This notion from folk psychology is adopted in the work of moral philosophers in the Classical Age,[32] most notably by Plato, who in his *Symposium* makes desire (ἔρως) successively the desire to become

---

uitous employment of the operator *qua* (ᾗ), and expounded at length and authoritatively by De Rijk (2002), chapter 2.7.

27 1131a3–6: ἑκούσια μὲν τὰ τοιάδε οἷον πρᾶσις ὠνὴ δανεισμὸς ἐγγύη χρῆσις παρακαταθήκη μίσθωσις. ("Voluntary exchanges are selling, buying, lending with interest, pledging, giving free use of something, depositing, and hiring out."). Note that these are all one-sided allocations.

28 For the range of relationships that falls under Utility Friendship, see Chapter Four Section 3.

29 At some points in Aristotle's ethical writings, Utility Friendship is dismissed as "only resembling true friendships". E.g. *EN* 1156a16–17, friendship only in an "analogical sense" (*EN* 1157a25–30) as opposed to virtue friendship that are friendships πρώτως καὶ κυρίως (*EN* 1157a29–30). Friendships for the cause of utility tend to be instable and dissolve quickly (*EN* 1157a24–26), as the rationale of their existence is cancelled as soon as the partners' needs are fulfilled. Cf. Pangle (2003), 39–40. The class of utility friendships encompasses all types of relationships regulated by a notion of reciprocal utility (*EN* 1162b22–31).

30 *EN* 1157b19.

31 *EN* 1262b16.

32 On the Cyrenaic, and possibly Socratic, origins of this notion, see Chapter Five Section 2.3.2.

whole again,[33] the desire that originates in a lack,[34] and the son of Resource and Poverty (Πενία), destined to be "always in need" (πένης ἀεί; ἀεὶ ἐνδείᾳ).[35] Similarly, in the *Lysis*, where the ultimate grounds of φιλία are investigated, Plato's Socrates offers an "archaeology of desire", according to which φιλία finds its source in desire that presupposes need,[36] for the object of desire is that which a thing lacks (οὐ ἂν ἐνδεὲς ᾖ).[37] To Plato's Socrates, this "archaeology of desire" explains the ultimate grounds of φιλία and ἔρως—of everything that drives people to one another and binds them together. φιλία typically is a cohesive force sustaining bonds between individuals,[38] which explains our propensity to live together in communities.[39]

At the same time, the conception of φιλία as a bond based on deficiency and need raises some serious moral problems. One of the issues that remain unresolved in Plato's *Lysis* is the unsettling implication that individuals who possess wisdom, i.e. persons whose character does not lack anything, cease to need friends.[40] Along similar lines, in the *Euthyphro*, Socrates demonstrates how the reduction of piety to commerce (prayer and sacrifice are exchanged in return for benefits from the gods) yields the absurd implication that the gods need

33 The speech of Aristophanes: Pl. *Symp.* 189c2–193d6.

34 The *elenchus* of Agathon: Pl. *Symp.* 199c3–201c7. Aristotle reacts against the notion that ἔρως always expresses a lack of something "that we do not *have*" (e.g. Pl. *Symp.* 200d2: κεκτῆσθαι) in insisting that happiness is not a κτῆμα (e.g. Ar. *EN* IX.ix 1169b28–30).

35 The myth of Diotima: Pl. *Symp.* 203a8–204c6.

36 Pl. *Lys.* 210c5–d4.

37 To this, Socrates adds that the origin of need is loss, for that which one lacks is something one is deprived of. Pl., *Lysis* 221d–222a. Cf. Price (1989), 9–14. This conceptual analysis of φιλία is akin to the analysis of ἔρως in *Symp.* 199c3–201c7; Penner & Rowe (2005), 157–172, 300–306.

38 Not only between individual humans, but, by means of metaphorical extension, also between humans and gods, between all living things, or, in the guise of a cosmic principle, even between physical elements. E.g. Empedocles for whom φιλία and its opposite νεῖκος represent the general and universal cohesion and repulsion between the elements (DK 31 B17, B30, B33, B116); Heraclitus who explains the dynamics of the phenomenal world in terms of the attraction of opposites (DK 22B8, B80). Cf. Pl. *Lys.* 215e; Ar. *EN* VIII.i (1155b1–6), *EE* VII. (1235a13–16).

39 E.g. the myth of Protagoras in Pl., *Prot.* 320c–323c. Because of its cohesive capacity, the term φιλία is often used to refer to the force that keeps entire communities of co-dependent individuals together. E.g. Pl. *Alc.* 1.126b–c; *Gorg.* 508a, *Prot.* 322c, *Rep.* 351d, *Clit.* 409e, *Leg.* III.693b1–5, III.701d7–9, Ar. *EN* VIII.i (1155a23), *EE* VII.x (1242a8), *Pol.* I.ii (1252b27–1253a3).

40 Pl. *Lysis* 215b. This puzzle is the consequence of seeing not only happiness and wisdom, but also friends, as "possessions", κτήματα, items that one can κτᾶσθαι. E.g. 211e2–3, 212a5. Cf. Smith-Pangle (2003), 20–36; Joosse (2011).

anything.[41] This outcome, that friendship is dispensable for gods or individuals who have reached completion or moral perfection, obviously flies in the face of the popular intuition that friendship has an intrinsic moral value.

It is for reasons such as these that for Aristotle lack and need, in short deficiency, cannot be a basis for a morally perfect friendship.[42] Whereas to Plato's Socrates relationships based on deficiency are paradigmatic of interpersonal relationships, Aristotle treats Utility Friendship, the kind of friendship based on need, as seriously defective, and as friendship "only incidentally" and not in the fullest sense;[43] only φιλία based on virtue deserves the name of friendship "in its primary and proper sense".[44] The other types are quickly dismissed as "friendships" only in an analogical sense (καθ' ὁμοιότητα),[45] since they fail to offer a solid base for a long-term relationship. As noted above, especially friendships for the sake of utility tend to be instable and dissolve quickly.[46] In terms of the analysis of exchange, Aristotle's classification has two important consequences. First, it lumps together the entire range of voluntary reciprocal exchanges of utilities into the single category of Utility Friendships (which gives a clear field/ clears the field? weet niet wat idiomatisch for reductionism). Secondly, it solves some of the traditional puzzles of isomorphism, such as the status of teachings in virtue, by denying that these encounters are reciprocal exchanges at all.[47] Whereas the sophists make wisdom a commodity for sale, to

41 Pl. *Euth.* 14c3–15c10. See Chapter Two on the role of χάρις in the argumentation. Cf. Xen. *Mem.* I.vi.10, *Cyr.* VIII.iii.40 on the contention that gods have no needs.

42 On Aristotle's conception of perfect friendship (τελεία φιλία) and his classification of friendship as a solution of the problems prompted by Plato's conception, see Gauthier-Jolif (1959) II, 675 ff., Smith-Pangle (2003), 20–36, Whiting (2006).

43 *EN* VIII.iii (1156a16–17). Cf. Smith-Pangle (2003), pp. 39–40.

44 *EN* VIII.v (1157a29–30): καὶ πρώτως μὲν καὶ κυρίως.

45 *EN* VIII.v (1157a25–30). Although applying the logical terminology καθ' αὑτό and κατὰ συμβεβηκός, Aristotle is evasive about the nature of the similarity between the three εἴδη in *EN* VIII.iii (1156a11 ff.). The analysis in *EE* applies ordinal ranking (πρώτη φιλία vs. δεύτεραι φιλίαι) and makes use of "focal predication" (πρὸς ἕν) to explain the relation between the friendship types. See Owen (1960) on focal analysis in Aristotle; Price (1989), 131–161 on its application in *EE*. Fortenbaugh (1975) for the criticism that the focal relationship in *EE* between the varieties of friendship should proceed through the φιλητά but fails to do so and hence lapses into homonymy. Cf. Gartner (unpublished) for a construction of focal predication between the three φιλητά in *EE*. Pakaluk (1998b) for the egalitarian implication that the focal predication construction in *EE* broadens the application of the term φιλία as opposed to the restrictive tendencies in *EN*. Owen (1960) maintains that the treatment in *EN* also involves focal analysis; Annas (1977) argues that focal analysis is absent in the Nicomachean account of friendship.

46 See Chapter Five Section 2.3.2.

47 See also Chapter Five.

Aristotle wisdom, virtue and happiness are not possessions (κτήματα) that can be objects of exchange, but activities that are realized in Virtue Friendships.[48] Those who attempt to sell wisdom make a category mistake, for the "coin" of Virtue Friendships, the good, cannot be changed into the legal tender of utility: there is no common measure to the good (an activity) and the useful (an object). Aristotle preemptively elevates an exchange that is potentially isomorphous with a commercial transaction above the category of Utility Friendships.

In the light of this dismissal of relationships based on need,[49] it is somewhat surprising to see Aristotle affirm that it is utility friendship that safeguards solidarity and social cohesion within the polis. This crucial bond that keeps together the polis is a particular subtype of utility friendship: πολιτικὴ φιλία, "friendship of the citizen (*polites*)", often translated as either "political friendship" or "civic friendship". It has been supposed that this πολιτικὴ φιλία is a moral or social emotion indispensable for the coherence of a political community,[50] as, for instance, generalized "mutual respect",[51] or "empathy"[52] or

48 In *EN* I.viii (1098b32–1099a7) it is argued that the chief good (τὸ ἄριστον) is located not in the possession (κτῆσις) of excellence but in its use (χρῆσις), i.e. in its ἐνεργεία: διαφέρει δὲ ἴσως οὐ μικρὸν ἐν κτήσει ἢ χρήσει τὸ ἄριστον ὑπολαμβάνειν, καὶ ἐν ἕξει ἢ ἐνεργείᾳ. This suggests not only that dealing with property is an instance of excellence, but also that there is an *analogy* between property and virtue. Cf. Frank (2005), 70: "It is by understanding property as a verb and not strictly as a noun, as an activity of use and not strictly as a fungible thing, that we see that property is bound to, is indeed a site of, virtue. And it is by understanding virtue as a verb and not strictly as a noun, as an activity and not strictly as a thing, that we see virtue as a kind of property."

49 Aristotle does acknowledge that Utility Friendship is the paradigmatic model of friendship in popular morality. Cf. *EN* 1157a26: οἱ ἄνθρωποι λέγουσι φίλους ...

50 Aristotle's πολιτικὴ φιλία is one of the grounds why Aristotle is often drawn into the controversy between contractarianism and communitarianism as a proponent of the latter, e.g. by MacIntyre (1981) and Arendt (see n. 51 below). For a diametrically opposed vision on political cohesion in pagan antiquity, see, e.g.: Wolin, *Politics and Vision*, (1960), 56: "[I]t required the Christian notion of *agape* before there could be an idea of love as a force fusing together a community."

51 Arendt (1958), 218: "Yet what love is in its own, narrowly circumscribed sphere, respect is in the larger domain of human affairs. Respect, not unlike the Aristotelian *philia politike*, is a kind of "friendship" without intimacy and without closeness; it is a regard for the person from the distance which the space of the world puts between us, and this regard is independent of qualities which we may admire or of achievements which we may highly esteem." Cf. Arendt (1958), 53–54, 218. See Beiner (1983), 119 for the observation that Arendt's understanding of political friendship is "Kantian rather than Aristotelian".

52 Cf. Barber (1984), 188–189, who also draws an explicit contrast between "contract and friendship", between "an incorporated economic association (limited liability) and civil community."

"sympathy" that breeds consensus,[53] or as "a certain measure of mutual goodwill and trust".[54] At the other end of the spectrum, Aristotle's notion of political friendship has prompted mercantile interpretations of his ideal polis as a community of calculating bankers and accountants.[55] However, as will be argued, the phenomenon that Aristotle has in mind is far more concrete: more formalistic than the notions of mutual respect, empathy or goodwill that are implied in such a translation as "political friendliness", but more substantively moral than is implied by such a translation as "civil friendship". Political friendship is what happens on the market, when buyers do nothing more than paying the price set for the object of their purchase. The stock example of political friends are the shoemaker and builder, to whom we shall now turn.

2.2 *The Shoemaker-Builder-Ratio*

The passage on "the reciprocal (variety of justice)" in book v of Aristotle's *Nicomachean Ethics* is notoriously obscure.[56] First of all, it is important to keep in mind that Aristotle's notion of "the reciprocal" or "reciprocity" (common translations) and the modern-day anthropological concept are *faux amis*: "reciprocity" is a conventional translation of a term coined by Aristotle himself, τὸ ἀντιπεπονθός, which literally means "that which is affected-in-return", "that which is acted-on-in-return".[57]

Reciprocal justice is,[58] according to Aristotle, operative in all "associations that involve exchange" (ἐν ταῖς κοινωνίαις ταῖς ἀλλακτικαῖς). His examples are:

53 Balot (2006), 257: "While justice is indeed the key to establishing political stability, it cannot be identified or exemplified in particular cases—from the distribution of offices to court judgments—unless it is informed by the citizens' sympathetic relationship with one another. Citizens must be bound, for Aristotle, by a relationship of civic friendship (*philia*). Civic friendship builds consensus and thereby makes the criteria of justice more obvious."

54 Cooper (1990), 235: "Where civic friendship characterizes a population there exists, as a recognized and accepted norm, a certain measure of mutual goodwill, and also mutual trust, among the people making up the population." See Annas (1990) for detailed and sound criticism of Cooper's position.

55 See n. 24 above.

56 Finley (1970), 33: "not one of Aristotle's more transparent discussions."; Joachim (1995), 150: "in the end unintelligible to me." Cf. For an overview of similar reactions, see Meikle (1995), 7.

57 The modern convention of rendering ἀντιπεπονθός as "reciprocity" originates from the Latin translation by Guilielmo du Val (1629), who renders ἀντιπεπονθός as *perpessio mutua et reciproca*. Initially, the term was translated with the calque *contrapassum* (Robert Grosseteste), *repassio, retaliatio* (Feliciano, Averroès). Cf. Theocarakis (2008), Kaye (1998).

58 There is debate over the question whether in Aristotle's treatment of justice "reciprocity" is introduced as a third subdivision of particular justice alongside the other two, distribu-

- a builder and a shoemaker exchanging a house and shoes (1133a6–10, a22–24);
- two physicians who do not become partners to an exchange (1133a16);
- a physician and a farmer who do become partners to an exchange (1133a17);
- a shoemaker and a farmer (1133a31–1133b6);

—inhabitants of a society with some elementary form of division of labor which is complemented by exchange. Aristotle seems to be articulating a form of exchange that is in a sense "disembedded": an exchange taking place between socially disengaged actors (there is no indication that the shoemaker and builder know each other personally, although it is, of course, a priori likely, among a limited population, that the lines are short!), whose motivation is not primarily moral, social or political in nature.

Within these exchanges, currency plays a central role.[59] As currency is only valid within the confines of the political community,[60] the polis, this means that shoemaker, builder, farmer and doctor are inhabitants of the same political unit, which in turn implies that the exchange partners conduct exchange *in their quality as* members of the same political unit. Here, Aristotle's obscure notion of "political friendship" (πολιτικὴ φιλία) comes in: citizens who engage in exchanges are "political friends". Elsewhere in the *Nicomachean Ethics*, typologically similar stock examples (shoemaker and weaver this time) are given as examples of "political friendship":

[Text 3]

> Ἐν πάσαις δὲ ταῖς ἀνομοιοειδέσι φιλίαις τὸ ἀνάλογον ἰσάζει καὶ σῴζει τὴν φιλίαν, καθάπερ εἴρηται, οἷον καὶ ἐν τῇ πολιτικῇ τῷ σκυτοτόμῳ ἀντὶ τῶν ὑποδη-

---

tive and corrective justice, (Irrera (2005), Judson (1997), Scaltsas (1995), Gauthier & Jolif (1970)), as a subcategory of corrective justice Vinogradoff (1908)), i.e. corrective justice in the case of voluntary exchanges (Danzig (2000)), not as a form of particular justice, but of universal justice (Ritchie (1894)), or not as a form of justice at all (Gauthier & Jolif 1970, Meikle (1995)). Here, I follow the argument of Danzig (2000), who convincingly argues that in Aristotle's classification of justice reciprocity *is* a form of justice (1132b32, 1134a24), and more precisely: the variety of corrective justice (διορθορτικόν) concerned with voluntary transactions. Aristotle's authorial comment, that τὸ ἀντιπεπονθός "does not fit the case either of the just in the distributive sense or of that in the rectificatory" (1132b23–24), only applies to rectificatory justice in cases of *involuntary* transactions.

59 1133b21–26.

60 Aristotle insists on the fact that νόμισμα merely has conventional value (e.g. *Pol.* 1257b10–17). The link between validity and political community is made more explicit in the pseudo-Platonic *Eryxias*, where the point is developed that the currency (νόμισμα) of one society may be useless (ἀχρεῖον) in another if it is not χρήσιμον (400e).

μάτων ἀμοιβὴ γίνεται κατ' ἀξίαν, καὶ τῷ ὑφάντῃ καὶ τοῖς λοιποῖς. ἐνταῦθα μὲν οὖν πεπόρισται κοινὸν μέτρον τὸ νόμισμα, καὶ πρὸς τοῦτο δὴ πάντα ἀναφέρεται καὶ τούτῳ μετρεῖται·

"In all friendships based on dissimilarity, what is proportionate equalizes and preserves the friendship, as has been said, just as *in political friendship* too the shoemaker gets a return for his shoes according to their value, and similarly with the weaver and all the rest. *Here, then, currency has been made available as a common measure*, and everything else is referred to and measured by this."[61]

Within relations of "political friendship",[62] coin money serves as a common measure (κοινὸν μέτρον) of value, facilitating "equalization" and safeguarding the friendship. While this oblique reference to the phenomenon of political friendship (the *only* reference within the *EN*)[63] presents some serious complications in its own right,[64] it may also shed light on one of the main interpretative problems of Aristotle's treatment of reciprocity, the famous equation:

---

61 Ar. *EN* IX.i (1163b32–64a2); *all translations of EN are by* Broadie & Rowe (2002); *here adapted.*

62 That φιλία is implied in ἐν τῇ πολιτικῇ is corroborated by the parallel phrase ἐν δὲ τῇ ἐρωτικῇ a few lines later (a3) that without doubt refers to erotic friendships.

63 See section 2.3 below.

64 As Pakaluk (1998), 149–150 points out, the most natural referent of the term would be the discussion of friendship based upon types of constitution in VIII.10–12; however, it is clear, that these are not the type of friendships discussed here. Moreover, Aristotle here seems to suggest rather surprisingly that political friendship and the examples he mentions are instances of friendships that are "non-uniform" or "dissimilar" (ἀνομοιοειδής), bonds between friends who have different motivations for appreciating one another and engaging in friendship (as e.g. in an erotical relationship in which one partner appreciates the pleasure of the encounter whereas the other appreciates the utility that his partner has to offer). The exchange between shoemaker and weaver is an example of two partners who merely have different products to offer, but that does not make the relationship non-uniform. I follow Pakaluk's reading of the passage, in taking political friendship as a *contrastive* example: unlike political friendships that are uniform (ὁμοειδής) in nature and hence have a common measure, relationships that are non-uniform, as e.g. the erotical relationship, often lead to quarrels because there is no common measure in the first place. The example of the shoemaker and the weaver refers back (καθάπερ εἴρηται) to the previous chapters (VIII.14 and 15) that deal with equal *and* unequal friendships that operate on the basis of proportionality; hence it is introduced to draw a contrast with non-uniform friendships. Pakaluk (1998), 149–150. Cf. Meikle (1995), 129–146.

[Text 4]

> As builder to shoemaker, shoes to a house. (A : B = D : C)[65]

In the standard commentaries, the builder-to-shoemaker-ratio has been understood as expressing an exchange between two persons who are *un*equal: in social status or worth,[66] in the quality of the labor that they produce[67] or by the different degree of skill involved.[68] Moreover, since in most of these interpretations it is not easy to see how these qualitative inequalities can get a quantified expression in this proportion, other interpreters have chosen for quantitative ratio's, suggesting that shoemaker and builder stand for the labor time they invest in producing their products—reading Aristotle as a precursor of a labor theory of value.[69] Karl Marx in the end dismissed this possibility, because Aristotle in his view lacked a concept of abstract labor, i.e. some sort of abstract notion that makes the labor of a builder commensurable with the labor of a shoemaker.[70]

Before the precise substance of this equation—Aristotle's notion of need and his underlying conception of value—can be discussed, it is necessary to settle the question as to how the equation is to be read in the first place. Reciprocity, according to Aristotle, proceeds through proportionate requital (τὴν ἀντίδοσιν τὴν κατ' ἀναλογίαν), and this proportionate requital is brought about by "diagonal coupling" (ἡ κατὰ διάμετρον σύζευξις):

[Text 5]

> ποιεῖ δὲ τὴν ἀντίδοσιν τὴν κατ' ἀναλογίαν ἡ κατὰ διάμετρον σύζευξις. οἰκοδόμος ἐφ' ᾧ α, σκυτοτόμος ἐφ' ᾧ β, οἰκία ἐφ' ᾧ γ, ὑπόδημα ἐφ' ᾧ δ. δεῖ οὖν λαμβάνειν τὸν οἰκοδόμον παρὰ τοῦ σκυτοτόμου τὸ ἐκείνου ἔργον, καὶ αὐτὸν ἐκείνῳ

65 Ar. *EN* v.v (1133a22–24).

66 Williams (1972), Rackham (1926).

67 Grant (1874), ii, 120.

68 Soudek (1952), Spengler (1955).

69 E.g. Danzig (2000), who argues that although Aristotle does not propound a labor-theory of value here, he does set out a status-theory of the value of labor: the labor of some professions is worth more than the labor of others. Aristotle, according to Danzig, does not attempt to rectify the market-place, but to justify its apparent *in*equalities by arguing that paying the existing prices of houses and shoes is in accordance with justice.

70 Castoriadis (1978) takes this line of criticism further and in a sense less far. He has a perfectly articulate conception—of human *in*equality by claiming that Aristotle lacked a full-blown conception of human equality. Cf. Seaford (2012).

> μεταδιδόναι τὸ αὑτοῦ. ἐὰν οὖν πρῶτον ᾖ τὸ κατὰ τὴν ἀναλογίαν ἴσον, εἶτα τὸ ἀντιπεπονθὸς γένηται, ἔσται τὸ λεγόμενον. εἰ δὲ μή, οὐκ ἴσον, οὐδὲ συμμένει· οὐθὲν γὰρ κωλύει **κρεῖττον εἶναι** τὸ θατέρου ἔργον ἢ τὸ θατέρου· δεῖ οὖν ταῦτα ἰσασθῆναι.
>
> What brings about *proportional requital* is the coupling of diametrical opposites. Let A be a builder, B a shoemaker, C a house, D a shoe: then what is required is that the builder should receive from the shoemaker what the shoemaker has produced, and that he himself should give the shoemaker a share in his own product. If, then, there is first of all equality in proportional terms, and reciprocal exchange occurs after that, the requirement stated will be fulfilled, if not, there is no equality, and there is nothing to keep the parties together; for the product of the one may well be *superior* to that of the other. So these need to be equalized.[71]

In accordance with "diagonal coupling"—nothing more than the simple fact that A and B will trade their products with each other (the builder is not after a house, but wants to have shoes, and the shoemaker wants a house)—a process of equalization (ἰσασθῆναι) takes place. The concepts of "making equal" and of "equal" itself, which are central to Aristotle's understanding of justice (τὸ δίκαιον), have been laid out in a previous chapter (v.iii). Seeing that justice is a form of equality, distributive justice involves at least four terms: two persons to whom the distribution in view is just, and two things distributed:

[Text 6]

> ἀνάγκη ἄρα τὸ δίκαιον ἐν ἐλαχίστοις εἶναι τέτταρσιν· οἷς τε γὰρ δίκαιον τυγχάνει ὄν, δύο ἐστί, καὶ ἐν οἷς, τὰ πράγματα, δύο. καὶ ἡ αὐτὴ ἔσται ἰσότης, οἷς καὶ ἐν οἷς· ὡς γὰρ ἐκεῖνα ἔχει, τὰ ἐν οἷς, οὕτω κἀκεῖνα ἔχει· εἰ γὰρ μὴ ἴσοι, οὐκ ἴσα ἕξουσιν, ἀλλ' ἐντεῦθεν αἱ μάχαι καὶ τὰ ἐγκλήματα, ὅταν ἢ μὴ ἴσα ἴσοι ἢ μὴ ἴσοι ἴσα ἔχωσι καὶ νέμωνται.
>
> "Necessarily, then, the just involves at least four terms: the parties to whom justice is done are two, and so are the objects justly distributed. Also, the equality between the persons will be the same as that between the things, in so far as the second pair, the things, stand to each other in

71 Ar. *EN* v.v (1133a6–13); *translation adapted*.

> the same relationship as the first; for if people are not equal to each other, they will not have equal shares—and it is here that the battles and accusations start, when either equals get shares that are not equal or people that are not equal have and are assigned shares that are."[72]

The options are: either the two persons are equals (ἴσοι), and then the things exchanged need to be equal (ἴσα) (as is the case with corrective justice: an eye for an eye, tit for tat); or the two persons are not equal, and then the things exchanged should not be equal either (as is the case in some forms of distributive justice, where e.g. people who have contributed more get more).

In the case of exchange between shoemaker and builder (T3), it is said explicitly that "the work of one" may be "superior" (κρεῖττον),[73] than the work of the other—a house, for instance, may "beat" a pair of shoes, i.e. it is worth more than a pair of shoes—in which case "they (i.e. the products of both partners (note the neuter ταῦτα), D and C in terms of the equation) have to be equalized". As reciprocity is a form of justice,[74] equality is stipulated, and as the products of exchange need to be "equalized" (ἰσασθῆναι), the *partners* are assumed to be equal as well.[75]

How exactly are exchange *partners* equalized?[76] Aristotle proceeds to make the observation that exchange usually takes place between two partners who are different in an important sense, as they have different things to offer:

---

72 Ar. *EN* v.iii (1131a20–24); *translation adapted.*

73 1133a12–13. In a similar discussion in the *Magna Moralia* (1194a18 and 25), the expression κρεῖττον εἶναι is not used; instead derivatives of ἄξιος are used to express notions of value. Cf. Meikle (1995), 10–11, who shows how translations of κρεῖττον with "better than" or "superior to" have led commentators to suppose that Aristotle either had a form of social inequality in mind or implied judgment on the quality of the products. Note also that Aristotle takes for granted that one product may be "more" or "superior" (κρεῖττον) to another. This corroborates the approach taken by Danzig (2000), 148, that the equation in v.v does not serve to calculate prices, but to legitimate already existing prices. On the different nature of the example in *MM*, that does not offer a genuine four-term exchange but stipulates equivalences between different exchange relationships, see Danzig (2000), 399 n. 1.

74 1132b29: τὸ τοιοῦτον δίκαιον. See discussion above in n. 42.

75 As is explicitly corroborated in 1133a19–20: ἀλλὰ τούτους δεῖ ἰσασθῆναι. τούτους is a masculine plural.

76 Cf. 1133b4–5: οὕτως ἴσοι καὶ κοινωνοί ("in this way they are equal and partners"). It is important to note that Aristotle insists that the equality in question is a *premise*, a point of departure, *before* exchange has taken place. (1133b1–3).

[Text 7]

ἔστι δὲ τοῦτο καὶ ἐπὶ τῶν ἄλλων τεχνῶν· ἀνῃροῦντο γὰρ ἄν, εἰ μὴ ⟨ὃ⟩ ἐποίει τὸ ποιοῦν καὶ ὅσον καὶ οἷον, καὶ τὸ πάσχον ἔπασχε τοῦτο καὶ τοσοῦτον καὶ τοιοῦτον. οὐ γὰρ ἐκ δύο ἰατρῶν γίνεται κοινωνία, ἀλλ' ἐξ ἰατροῦ καὶ γεωργοῦ, καὶ ὅλως ἑτέρων καὶ οὐκ ἴσων· ἀλλὰ τούτους δεῖ ἰσασθῆναι.

(...) For it is not two doctors that enter into a partnership, but rather a doctor and a farmer, and in general people *who are of different kinds and not equals; but then they have to be* made *equals*.[77]

Here, the inequality clearly refers to different and unequal *persons* (ἑτέρων καὶ οὐκ ἴσων, genitive case agreeing with the "physician and farmer"), and "they" who have to be equalized clearly refers to the persons as well (τούτους, masculine accusative). The persons need to be *made* equal, implying that whether or not shoemaker and builder are unequal, for the purposes of exchange they are "made equal", or understood as equal.

Equalization presupposes the ability to compare, i.e. products of exchange, too, need to be comparable:

[Text 8]

διὸ πάντα συμβλητὰ δεῖ πως εἶναι, ὧν ἐστὶν ἀλλαγή. ἐφ' ὃ τὸ νόμισμ' ἐλήλυθε, καὶ γίνεταί πως μέσον· πάντα γὰρ μετρεῖ, ὥστε καὶ τὴν ὑπεροχὴν καὶ τὴν ἔλλειψιν, πόσα ἄττα δὴ ὑποδήματ' ἴσον οἰκίᾳ ἢ τροφῇ.

Hence everything that is exchanged must be somehow comparable. *This is the role that money has been introduced to fill*, so that it becomes in a way *intermediate*; for it measures everything, and thus also measures excess and deficiency—so just how many shoes it takes to match a house, or board.[78]

Money is introduced as a middle term, enabling one to calibrate scales and weigh things that in the natural world are very different, such as shoes and houses, and thus it is in money that we can express "excess and deficiency" (τὴν ὑπεροχὴν καὶ τὴν ἔλλειψιν), i.e. that a house is worth so-and-so much more

77 Ar. *EN* v.v (1133a17–19); *transl. adapted.*

78 Ar. *EN* v.v (1133a19–22); *transl. adapted.*

than a shoe, and hence to calculate the number (πόσα ἄττα) of shoes that are needed to make the objects exchanged equal (ἴσον).

[Text 9]

> δεῖ τοίνυν ὅπερ οἰκοδόμος πρὸς σκυτοτόμον, τοσαδὶ ὑποδήματα πρὸς οἰκίαν ἢ τροφήν. εἰ γὰρ μὴ τοῦτο, οὐκ ἔσται ἀλλαγὴ οὐδὲ κοινωνία. τοῦτο δ', εἰ μὴ ἴσα εἴη πως, οὐκ ἔσται.
>
> So it ought to be that as builder is to shoemaker, thus so and so many pairs of shoes are to a house or board. For without this (*sc.* equalization), there will be no exchange nor any communal association; and there will be equalization only if the things in question are somehow equal.[79]

Hence, the proportion A : B = D : C can be reformulated as follows: no matter how unequal and heterogeneous builders and shoemakers may be, for purposes of exchange they are "equalized", i.e.: they are treated as equals *qua* transactors, in their quality as transactors: A : B = 1 : 1.[80] To make the exchange products equal as well, the D : C must also be 1 : 1, which comes down to determining how many shoes it takes to compensate for a house: *x*D : C.[81] In other words: the analogy does not provide a method for calculating values of objects; it does not express a theory of value and price-formation. It simply expresses the truism that on the market the value, worth or status of *persons* are bracketed off as temporarily irrelevant.[82] All that matters is the equivalence between the *objects*.

---

79 Ar. *EN.* v.v (1133a23–24); *transl. adapted.*

80 Here the difference between "equal" in the sense of "equivalent" and "equal" in the sense of "identical" is crucial. Aristotle's claims that "τὸ ἀντιπεπονθός does not fit the case either of the just in distributive sense or of that in the rectificatory" (1132b23–24) and that "in commercial associations parties are bound together by a form of the just that is like this, i.e. what is reciprocal on proportional terms (τὸ ἀντιπεπονθὸς κατ' ἀναλογίαν), not in terms of numerical equality (καὶ μὴ κατ' ἰσότητα)." Because the objects of exchange are not identical, strict numerical equality (1 house for 1 shoe) is not fair; proportional exchange entails "*making* equal", i.e. establishing how many shoes are equivalent to a house. Meikle (1995), 10.

81 Meikle (1995), following Heath (1949), 274–275.

82 Heath (1949), 275: "The fact is that the relative "worth" of *A* and *B* has really nothing to do with the particular transaction." Hence, the equality and justice involved look much like corrective justice, with two important differences: (1) it is not injuries that are exchanged, but useful products between two voluntary partners; (2) the objects exchanged are not identical, but equivalent. This is in fact in line with the interpretation of Danzig (2000),

2.3 *Political Friendship*

One obvious objection against this reading is that the analogy becomes trivial and the mathematics becomes obsolete or even pointless.[83] However, the analogy should be read as deliberately trivial.[84] It describes the way commercial exchanges work: they aim at equivalence, and therefore they need money as a common measure. Trading goods on the market requires, according to Aristotle, a fictitious equality between transactors: it requires abstraction from them as full-fledged persons. Does abstraction imply disembedding? It is here that the notion of Political Friendship again becomes relevant: shoemaker and builder are to be treated as equals *qua* transactors as they have exchanges in their quality as political friends.

As mentioned above, there is only one oblique reference to πολιτικὴ φιλία in *NE*. It is, however, possible to corroborate and elucidate both this reference and the account of reciprocal justice in V.v, by looking at the more extensive treatment of political friendship in de *Eudemian Ethics*. The precise relation between the two Aristotelian ethical treatises is a point of contention:[85] there is no firm consensus about the authorship of the *EE*,[86] the date of its composition (before or after *NE*),[87] and its independent value as a source for Aristotle's

who interprets "reciprocity" as corrective justice in case of voluntary exchanges. However, to Danzig it is essential that the proportion revolves around the justification of *in*equalities.

83 Lowry (1987), 194: "Meaningless". Cf. Heath (1949). Meikle (1995), 114: "There is no serious mathematics involved in these things."

84 Danzig (2000), 400 points out that there are analogous cases where Aristotle only stipulates principles operative in certain situations, without offering a full-blown theoretical solution or mathematical calculation. A case in point is Aristotle's discussion of distributive justice, where it is argued that distributions ought to be made "in accordance with the deserts of the people", but where no explanation is offered who deserves more or by how much.

85 The relation between *EN* and *EE* is for several reasons more complicated than the relation between *EN* and the *Politics* (that explicitly refers back to *EN*, e.g. in *Pol.* II.2 1161a30–31).

86 Unlike nineteenth-century scholarship has it (most notably Schleiermacher (1835) and Spengel (1841)), the general opinion currently is that *EE* is authentic (Rowe (1971), Kenny (2017; cf. 1992, Appendix 1), Dirlmeier (1979)); Schofield (1998) and Pakaluk (1998) regard *EE* as Aristotelian in character, but, on grounds of its marked "egalitarianism", attribute its authorship to a student of Aristotle; see Pakaluk (1998) for a some interesting speculations on this matter.

87 *EE*'s precise relation to *EN* remains obscure, as some argue that *EN* is a revision of *EE* (Rowe (1971)), whereas others date *EE* later than *EN* (Kenny (2017; cf. 1992, Appendix 1); Pakaluk (1998)). The origin of the so-called "common books", i.e. the books assigned by manuscript tradition to both treatises (*EN* 5, 6, 7 and *EE*, 4, 5, 6), is a separate question. Kenny, for instance, argues that although the *EE* is later, the common books originate from *EE* and were only inserted in *EN* later in the manuscript tradition.

moral philosophy.[88] As the *EE* is a long way from having been studied as extensively as the *EN*, the jury is still out on the comparative value of both treatises. Hence I take it to be methodologically sound to suspend judgment on the question which treatise is a more authoritative testimony to Aristotle's ethical thought.[89] What will be offered in the following analysis of πολιτικὴ φιλία serves incidentally as an argument for compatibility: it will be argued that the evidence from *EE* is largely compatible with that from *EN* (and the *Politics*), and hence may be used to complement the accounts of political friendship, concord and community offered in *EN* and *Politics*.

Political Friendship, a subtype of Utility Friendship,[90] operates "in the fullest degree" on the principle of utility,[91] i.e. up to the extreme that this "friendship" is immediately dissolvable.[92] Friendships between citizens *as citizens* are based on utility and, as in the case of two cities that cooperate on the basis of a treaty,[93] operate as ready-made transactions: they dissolve the moment common advantage disappears. As we have seen in Chapter Four, this one-off character is typical for the "legal" variety of Utility Friendship:

[Text 10]

> ἔστι δὲ τῆς χρησίμου φιλίας εἴδη δύο, ἡ μὲν νομικὴ ἡ δ' ἠθική. βλέπει δ' ἡ μὲν πολιτικὴ εἰς τὸ ἴσον καὶ εἰς τὸ πρᾶγμα, ὥσπερ οἱ πωλοῦντες καὶ οἱ ὠνούμενοι.

---

88 Moreover, among those who presume that *EE* is later than *EN* judgment is still divided over the question which of the two ethics has a stronger claim to be the definitive statement of Aristotle's moral philosophy.

89 I follow Kenny (2017) in this. Moreover, the *general* relation between the two compositions need not always imply that on a local level subject matter that only occurs in one of the two is either an innovation or superseded by the other (later) version; other explanations are conceivable for such "local divergences" (e.g. a topic may have become *less relevant* in the later composition but its treatment may in itself be sound or consistent with other works of Aristotle).

90 *EE* VII.x (1242b22): ἡ δὲ πολιτικὴ ἐστι μὲν κατὰ τὸ χρήσιμον.

91 *EE* VII.x (1242a7–9): ἡ δὲ πολιτικὴ συνέστηκε μὲν κατὰ τὸ χρήσιμον καὶ μάλιστα. *Pace* Irwin (1990), 94 who argues that political friendship is a special case of virtue-based friendship.

92 *EE* VII.x (1242b24–27): καὶ ὥσπερ αἱ πόλεις ἀλλήλαις φίλαι, οὕτω καὶ οἱ πολῖται, καὶ ὁμοίως "οὐκέτι γιγνώσκουσιν Ἀθηναῖοι Μεγαρῆας", καὶ οἱ πολῖται, ὅταν μὴ χρήσιμοι ἀλλήλοις, ἀλλ' ἐκ χειρὸς εἰς χεῖρα ἡ φιλία· "[F]ellow-citizens are one another's friends in the same way as different cities are, and "Athens no longer knoweth Megara," nor similarly do citizens know one another, when they are not useful to one another; their friendship is a ready-money transaction."

93 *EE* VII.x (1242b24–25): καὶ ὥσπερ αἱ πόλεις ἀλλήλαις φίλαι Bergk, *Fr. Eleg.*, Adespota 6. The scope of the analogy in *EE* is the easy dissolvability of the relationship. It does *not* imply that relations between cities are also political friendships.

> διὸ εἴρηται "μισθὸς ἀνδρὶ φίλῳ." ὅταν μὲν οὖν καθ' ὁμολογίαν ⟨ᾖ⟩ ἡ πολιτικὴ αὕτη φιλία, [καὶ] νομική· ὅταν δ' ἐπιτρέπωσιν αὐτοῖς, ἠθικὴ βούλεται εἶναι φιλία καὶ ἑταιρική.
>
> But Utility Friendship is of two kinds, the merely legal and the moral. Political friendship *looks to equality and to the object*, as buyers and sellers do—hence the saying "Unto a friend his wages". When, therefore, it is based on a definite agreement, then this political friendship is a (merely) legal one; but when they trust each other for repayment, it tends towards being a moral friendship, that between comrades.[94]

Political friendship represents the extreme variety of Utility Friendship that is law-based and that seeks exact equivalences within exchanges without any delay of return and without any quantitative vagueness,[95] "like buyers and sellers do":[96] it operates on stated terms[97] and on the basis of a contract,[98] as well as of observing equality and equivalence (εἰς τὸ ἴσον, κατ' ἴσα, κατ' ἰσότητα).[99]

This characterization of Political Friendship is consistent with my interpretation of the shoemaker-builder-ratio: in a Political Friendship, we abstract from full-fledged persons, we approach them as citizens in the abstract, who, in their quality as transactors, are treated as equals.[100] No matter how unequal or heterogeneous builders and shoemakers may be in real life, these differences

94 Ar. *EE* VII.x (1242b31–37). See also Chapter Four Section 3.2 (T21).

95 Cf. *EN* VIII.xiii 1162b21–a24. See Chapter Four.

96 ὥσπερ does not need to imply that the buyer/seller-case is merely an *analogy* for political friendships; it may also introduce an example ("as in the case of …").

97 The full Hesiod quotation alluded to includes the notion of stated terms: μισθὸς δ' ανδρὶ φίλῳ εἰρημένος ἄρκιος ἔστω. (Hes. *O&D* 371).

98 *EE* VII.10 (1243a32–33): "Political friendship, then, **looks at the agreement and to the thing** (εἰς τὴν ὁμολογίαν καὶ εἰς τὸ πρᾶγμα), but moral friendship at the intention (εἰς τὴν προαίρεσιν)." Law-based utility friendships are contrasted with the character-based (ἠθική) variety of utility friendship that is based on intention (*EE* 1243b10; cf. b2–3) and trust (1242b40–43a2), and is more companionable and likely to be lasting (1243a2–6).

99 *EE* 1242a9–11, b21–22, 27–31, 33. The importance in equality is in implication of the transient nature of political friendships (1242a9–10). The focus on equality in political friendship is in line with the more "egalitarian" outlook of the *EE* noticed by Pakaluk (1998) and Schofield (1998). At the beginning of VII.4 (1239a4–5) it is stated that whereas friend*ships* may be both hierarchical and egalitarian, only those who are engaged in an equality friendship are *friends*.

100 Inamura (2015) focuses on the political implications of this notional equality as a basis for Aristotle's conception of the civic relationship as the "exchange of the roles of governing and being governed".

are deemed irrelevant for purposes of arriving at a fair transaction: the transactors are equal, hence the objects of transactions must also be equivalent.

2.4 *Unequal Exchanges*

Still, the proportion A : B = D : C, i.e. 1 : 1 = 1 : 1, remains quite trivial. The proportion becomes only meaningful as a contrastive model against which other types of exchanges, *un*equal exchanges, can be understood. Elsewhere in the *Nicomachean Ethics*, Aristotle takes quite a bit of trouble to analyse such unequal exchanges, i.e. unequal Utility Friendships. Like Political Friendships, these friendships consist in the exchange of utilities; however, they are unequal: one of the partners is "superior" with respect to utility, i.e., one of the partners is richer.[101] Like unequal friendships in general, unequal Utility Friendships often give rise to quarrels and problems, because such friends tend to disagree on the terms of their interactions and have different conceptions and expectations as to what is fair:

[Text 11]

> Διαφέρονται δὲ καὶ ἐν ταῖς καθ' ὑπεροχὴν φιλίαις· **ἀξιοῖ γὰρ ἑκάτερος πλέον ἔχειν**, ὅταν δὲ τοῦτο γίνηται, **διαλύεται** ἡ φιλία. οἴεται γὰρ ὅ τε βελτίων προσήκειν αὑτῷ πλέον ἔχειν· τῷ γὰρ ἀγαθῷ νέμεσθαι πλέον· ὁμοίως δὲ καὶ ὁ ὠφελιμώτερος· **ἀχρεῖον** γὰρ ὄντα οὔ φασι δεῖν ἴσον ἔχειν· λειτουργίαν τε γὰρ γίνεσθαι καὶ οὐ φιλίαν, εἰ μὴ κατ' ἀξίαν τῶν ἔργων ἔσται τὰ ἐκ τῆς φιλίας. οἴονται γάρ, **καθάπερ ἐν χρημάτων κοινωνίᾳ πλεῖον λαμβάνουσιν οἱ συμβαλλόμενοι πλεῖον, οὕτω δεῖν καὶ ἐν τῇ φιλίᾳ**. ὁ δ' ἐνδεὴς καὶ ὁ χείρων ἀνάπαλιν· φίλου γὰρ ἀγαθοῦ εἶναι τὸ ἐπαρκεῖν τοῖς ἐνδεέσιν· τί γάρ, φασίν, ὄφελος σπουδαίῳ ἢ δυνάστῃ φίλον εἶναι, μηδέν γε μέλλοντα ἀπολαύειν;
>
> People quarrel in friendships based on superiority too; for each of the two parties ***thinks he should have more***, and when this happens, the friendship is *dissolved*. For if one of the parties is superior, he thinks it appropriate for him to have more because it is appropriate for good people to be assigned more; and similarly if one of the parties is in a position to bestow the greater benefits (sc. he will claim a greater share), for they say that if someone is *useless* he shouldn't have an equal share, because it turns into a kind of charity instead of friendship, if what results from the friendship

101 It is this notion of τιμή that eventually makes Aristotle's category of *unequal* friendships (as distinct from non-uniform friendships) untenable, as the value of τιμή cannot be explained with reference to utility alone. See Section 3.5 below.

> is not going to accord with the value of what the parties have done. *They think that it should be the same in a friendship as in a financial partnership, where those who contribute more get more.* But the person in need, or the inferior character, takes the converse position: that helping out the ones who are in need is the mark of a good friend; for what, they say, is the use of being friends with a good or a powerful person if one is not going to get anything out of them?[102]

The problem is stated in general terms: friendships based on superiority (καθ' ὑπεροχήν) are vulnerable to disagreements, because each party thinks he is entitled to get the bigger share (ἀξιοῖ ἑκάτερος πλέον ἔχειν). The first example is an unequal Virtue Friendship, with one friend being superior with regard to Virtue, i.e. being "better" (βελτίων), thinking it appropriate to be allotted the larger share (νέμεσθαι πλέον) on account of this virtue (τῷ ἀγαθῷ).

The second example involves inequality in Utility: the "more useful" (ὁ ὠφελιμώτερος) friend, i.e. the wealthier friend, reasons on the basis of performance? (κατ' ἀξίαν τῶν ἔργων) and believes he is entitled to the bigger share: he has been more useful (having contributed more) than the other, whom he perceives as "useless" (ἀχρεῖος):[103]

[Text 12]

Justice according to the superior friend, on the basis of merit:

A	:	B	=	D	:	C
rich	:	poor	=	more	:	less

This, however, is the logic of a "business partnership" (καθάπερ ἐν χρημάτων κοινωνίᾳ), the type of venture where contributing more also means getting more of the reward or yield. Conversely, the less wealthy, inferior friend reasons on the basis of need: being less wealthy, he *needs* more, and therefore is entitled to a larger share:

---

102 Ar. *EN* VIII.xiv (1163a25–35); *transl. adapted.*

103 The poetic adjective ἀχρεῖος of course activates the etymological connection with the vocabulary of utility (of being χρήσιμος): an ἀχρεῖος friend is "useless" in the literal sense of "being inferior with respect to utility". However, the poetic register also evokes *moral* connotations: an ἀχρήϊος ἀνήρ (Hes. *O&D* 297) is a morally inferior person. Cf. Soph. fr. 667, where the ἀχρεῖοι are opposed to the εὐγενεῖς.

[Text 13]

Justice according to the inferior friend, on the basis of need:

A	:	B	=	D	:	C
rich	:	poor	=	less	:	more

This, according to Aristotle (who adopts the slightly contemptuous focalization of the superior friend here), is the logic of "pure charity" (λειτουργία). In the end, both are right in expecting the larger share—i.e.: a larger share in different things:

[Text 14]

> ἔοικε δ' οὖν ἑκάτερος ὀρθῶς ἀξιοῦν, καὶ δεῖν ἑκατέρῳ πλέον νέμειν ἐκ τῆς φιλίας, οὐ τοῦ αὐτοῦ δέ, ἀλλὰ τῷ μὲν ὑπερέχοντι τιμῆς τῷ δ' ἐνδεεῖ κέρδους· τῆς μὲν γὰρ ἀρετῆς καὶ τῆς εὐεργεσίας ἡ τιμὴ γέρας, τῆς δ' ἐνδείας ἐπικουρία τὸ κέρδος.
>
> Now it seems that the expectations of each of the two sides are correct, and that each should be assigned a larger yield out of the friendship, only not of the same thing: *the superior person should get more honour, the needy one more in the way of gain*; for excellence and beneficence, *have honour as their choice compensation*, whereas material gain/ profit is what aids one in need/ assistance for the needy.[104]

On grounds of need, the inferior friend is to receive material gain (τὸ κέρδος), the value of which can be expressed in monetary terms, because its measure is need. On grounds of merit, the superior friend is to receive the larger share, a share of social value or esteem (τιμή),[105] the "reward of excellence and beneficence" (τῆς ἀρετῆς καὶ τῆς εὐεργεσίας γέρας). This deal can only provide a solution on the assumption that τιμή is of a different order than the material compensation that the needy friend receives, yet has the potency to compensate for material loss. We shall revert to the nature of τιμή towards the end of the chapter in Section 3.5.

---

104 Ar. *EN* VIII.xiv (1163b1–5).

105 On τιμή, see Blok (2017), chapter 4, Cairns (1993), Van 't Wout (2010), 250 and (2011), 432. τιμή is a form of social capital: status, esteem and deference. In the Archaic and Classical Period τιμή tends to manifest itself in concrete and visible form.

This is how unequal exchanges work: if the objects exchanged are not equal, the exchange will create, enhance and perpetuate inequality between the subjects of exchange. Aristotle's discussion of unequal utility friendship provides a meaningful contrast to exchanges such as between shoemaker and builder that are axiomatically based on equality between transactors *qua* transactors. On the market, we exchange things *as if* our persons do not need to be taken into the equation; we only look at the objects and try to establish equality between the/ose. This of course only replicates the question as to how equality between objects can be attained. If the analogy was never meant to provide a theory of price-formation, how does Aristotle's theory of value work? Indeed, is there any such theory?

3 Value and Values

3.1 *The Measure of Things*

Aristotle is quick to qualify his claim that it is currency (νόμισμα) that makes everything commensurable.[106]

At first sight, as we saw in T6, currency may seem a plausible common measure, "the unit (ἑνί τινι) with which everything is measured".[107] The concepts of "unit" (ἕν) and "measure" (μέτρον) are to be understood from Aristotle's more extensive discussion of commensurability and measure in his *Metaphysics*. In this context, "measure" is defined as "that by which quantity is known";[108] quantity "is known either by a one or by a number",[109] "one" being "the first measure of a kind, and above all of quantity".[110] Whatever the precise nature of the measure, it needs to be "homogeneous with the thing measured"[111] (e.g. the measure of a length is length, of an articulate sound sound, of weight a weight etc.), and the measure must be something "predicable of things alike".[112] If currency is a

106 Throughout his discussion of the role of money as "the measure of everything", Aristotle not only interacts with Plato's conception of χρεία as the origin of human communities, but also with Protagoras' famous Man Measure-statement. Van Berkel (2012).

107 In the discussion of liberality at the beginning of book IV, χρήματα ("material wealth") is defined as "all the things the value of which is measured by currency" (*NE* IV.i 1119b26 χρήματα λέγομεν πάντα ὅσων ἡ ἀξία νομίσματι μετρεῖται).

108 Ar. *Met.* X.i 1052b20: μέτρον γάρ ἐστιν ᾧ τὸ ποσὸν γιγνώσκεται.

109 Ar. *Met.* X.i 1052b20–21: γιγνώσκεται δὲ ἢ ἑνὶ ἢ ἀριθμῷ τὸ ποσὸν ᾗ ποσόν. Note the implication that (as is well known) "one" is not seen as a number in antiquity. Cf. Klein (1968).

110 Ar. *Met.* X.i 1052b18–19: μάλιστα δὲ τὸ μέτρῳ εἶναι πρώτῳ ἑκάστου γένους καὶ κυριώτατα τοῦ ποσοῦ:

111 Ar. *Met.* X.i 1053a25: Ἀεὶ δὲ συγγενὲς ὁ μέτρον.

112 Ar. *Met.* XIV.i 1088a8–9: δεῖ δὲ ἀεὶ τὸ αὐτό τι ὑπάρχειν πᾶσι τὸ μέτρον. A similar point is made

measure that measures everything, this implies that currency is, in some way, homogeneous with everything and predicable of everything:[113] everything has its price.

On second thoughts, realizing that establishing a measure "cannot itself create commensurability",[114] Aristotle concedes that "truth be told" (τῇ μὲν ἀληθείᾳ),[115] money is a mere substitute (ὑπάλλαγμα) for something else:

[Text 15]

> δεῖ ἄρα ἑνί τινι πάντα μετρεῖσθαι, ὥσπερ ἐλέχθη πρότερον. τοῦτο δ' ἐστὶ τῇ μὲν ἀληθείᾳ ἡ χρεία, ἣ πάντα συνέχει· εἰ γὰρ μηθὲν δέοιντο ἢ μὴ ὁμοίως, ἢ οὐκ ἔσται ἀλλαγὴ ἢ οὐχ ἡ αὐτή· οἷον δ' ὑπάλλαγμα τῆς χρείας τὸ νόμισμα γέγονε κατὰ συνθήκην· καὶ διὰ τοῦτο τοὔνομα ἔχει νόμισμα, ὅτι οὐ φύσει ἀλλὰ νόμῳ ἐστί, καὶ ἐφ' ἡμῖν μεταβαλεῖν καὶ ποιῆσαι ἄχρηστον.
>
> *Everything, in that case, must be measured by some one thing*, as was said before. *In truth this one thing is need, which holds everything together*; for if people did not need things, or if they do not need them in the same, then either there will be no exchange, or the exchange will be a different one. But as a kind of substitute for need, convention has brought currency into existence—and it is called currency because of this, i.e. because it exists not by nature but by custom, and because it is in our power to change it and render it useless.[116]

Money is a conventional proxy (it functions κατὰ συνθήκην)[117] of need (χρεία),[118] being whatever it is by custom (νόμῳ), not by nature, as it is in our power (ἐφ'

in *Phys.* VI.ii 232b. Aristotle thereby dismisses Protagoras' Man Measure-statement as trivial.

113 Cf. Pack (2010), 11.

114 Meikle (1995), 22.

115 The expression τῇ ἀληθείᾳ is more emphatic than τῷ ὄντι and occurs only in Aristotle's ethical works. Cf. 1133b19. Dirlmeier (1979), ad loc.

116 Ar. *EN* V.5 (1133a24–31); *transl. adapted.*

117 The same expression κατὰ συνθήκην is used by Aristotle in *De Interpretatione* to describe the signification of nouns: a noun is sound signifying by convention (κατὰ συνθήκην) (*De Int.* 16a19); it signifies by convention (κατὰ συνθήκην), because no noun is by nature (φύσει) significant, but only when it has become a symbol (σύμβολον) (*De Int.* 16a26–28). For the comparison between language and money, see also Cratinus fr. 239 (K-A), Plut. *Lyc.* 19, *Mor.* 406b. Cf. Shell (1982), Seaford (2004), 8, 293–296.

118 It has been noted that Aristotle here, in his account of need as the basis of exchange, refers

ἡμῖν) to change its nature and make it useless (ἄχρηστον): i.e. money only has its value (of being useful) indirectly by virtue of being a conventional representation of something else.[119] It is need (χρεία) that "holds everything together" (πάντα συνέχει).

Here, Aristotle seems to be trying to have his cake and eat it: need (χρεία) is a plausible feature for all things exchanged to have in common—it is a commensurating property—but it lacks a unit and is not easy to quantify.[120] Money provides units and facilitates quantification. The solution Aristotle attempts to offer is to regard money as the conventional representation of need: need provides commensurability, money provides a measure.[121] This raises some questions: what exactly is "need"? And how exactly is the quality of need related to the quantitative measure that money provides?

3.2 *Need*

Aristotle's theory of value has often been approached as a precursor of subjective utilitarianism. It is in line with this neoclassical economic interpretation that χρεία is translated as "demand": a subjective value, i.e. "felt utility".[122] However, recent interpretations have expressed fundamental objections against this allegedly anachronistic interpretation of χρεία.

Lindsay Judson, for instance, objects to a conflation of χρεία with "demand", arguing that χρεία refers to objective needs as opposed to subjective wants.[123] The key to his argument is the wording of T13, where Aristotle motivates the claim that in reality it is χρεία that holds everything together, with the explanatory remark that "if people did not need things (εἰ γὰρ μηθὲν δέοιντο) there will

---

to Plato's discussion of societal development in *Rep.* II (χρεία *Rep.* 369c2, 372a2; ἀλλαγή 371b8, cf. *Leg.* 742a2). E.g. Dirlmeier (1979) ad loc.

119 Cf. *Pol.* I.9 1257b16. This is reminiscent of the type of anecdote as the one told about Diogenes the Cynic who allegedly defaced the currency to demonstrate that the value of money is merely based on νόμος (D.L. 6.71). Cf. Seaford (2004), 7–8; 136–124.

120 Judson (1997) argues that quantification of need is impossible on the grounds that the strength of a need is not a measurable quantity.

121 Most commentators agree that this solution is not satisfactory. Meikle (1995).

122 E.g. Hardie (1980), 196; Barker (1906), 384 glosses "demand" in terms of desire or satisfaction ("as Aristotle himself tells us, value depends on demand, on felt utility"). Cf. Van Johnson (1939) (an item has value "only insofar as it fulfils a human want"), Von Leyden (1985), 14–15.

123 See Mourelatos (1970), 652 and Schein (1998), 295 for the notion that XPH-terminology refer to "subjective, internally based needs, requirements, and constraints" as opposed to δεῖ and cognates that tend to refer to external, objective constraint or causal necessity. Cf. Redard (1953), 56, Benardete (1965), Liddel (2007), 159, Barrett (1964). On the semantics of XPH-terminology, see Chapter Five Section 2.

not be an exchange or a different one".[124] This paraphrase of χρεία in terms of δέομαι ("to need, to be in lack of") suggests that Aristotle uses χρεία to refer to objective needs, not subjective wants.[125] On this interpretation, there *is* a basis for comparing relative values of commodities: objectively determined human need. Expressing relations between goods and people (a need has goods as its object and at the same time is a feature of the person who is in need),[126] need is what makes it possible to attribute value to houses and shoes. However, whereas it is possible to establish *relatively* that a person in objective terms needs a certain object more than another object, the absolute *strength* of need is in the end not a measurable quantity.[127]

To Scott Meikle, the most serious objection against a conflation of χρεία with "demand" or "utility" is the implication that χρεία would genuinely make products commensurable. Modern "demand" constitutes a homogeneous measure of value,[128] whereas in Aristotelian theory, use value and utility are defined by the heterogeneity of the ends that they are directed at[129]—a heterogeneity that in the end rules out genuine commensurability. To Meikle, the problem boils down to the question as to how use value (the value of a shoe as a shoe) is related to exchange value (the value of a shoe as an exchange object)—the central question in neoclassical economics. According to Meikle, Aristotle is himself aware that he is incapable of solving this problem, because there is a metaphysical gap between use value (the qualitative dimension in which you *need* an object) and exchange value (the quantitative dimension in which you *exchange* the object). There can be no properly quantitative relationship between different qualities.[130] Hence, Aristotle fails to provide a genuine basis for the calculation of the relative values of commodities, and admits defeat:

---

124 I.e. not an exchange based on mutually equal χρεία, but, for instance, an unequal utility friendship where the partners do not have χρεία "to the same extent" (ὁμοίως).

125 Similarly, as Dirlmeier (1979) and others have noted, this chapter interacts with Plato's *Republic* (369b5 ff.), where the origins of social communities, and of exchange, are explained in terms of the χρεῖαι, such as supply of food, shelter and clothing—examples of objective needs as opposed to subjective wants. Judson (1997), 159–160.

126 Judson (1997), 168. Judson argues that χρεία is a feature in respect of which the *subjects* of exchange vary and hence reads the equation as an inverse proportion.

127 Judson (1997), 173.

128 Either as cardinal utility (calculable in terms of expected utility) or as ordinal utility (aggregated preferences). Hausman & McPherson (1996). Meikle (1995), 28–42.

129 Meikle (1995), 190; cf. Frank (2005), 86–92, Mei (2009).

130 Meikle (1995), 15–21.

[Text 16]

> τῇ μὲν οὖν ἀληθείᾳ ἀδύνατον τὰ τοσοῦτον διαφέροντα σύμμετρα γενέσθαι, πρὸς δὲ τὴν χρείαν ἐνδέχεται ἱκανῶς.
>
> *Strictly speaking, of course, it is impossible that things so different* (*in kind*) *should become commensurable*, but with an eye to people's need (for them) a sufficient degree of commensurability can be achieved.[131]

Both Meikle and Judson reject a subjectivist interpretation of χρεία. It may be conceded that they are right in objecting against an understanding of Aristotelian χρεία in anachronistic terms of "demand": demand, a consumer's eagerness to acquire a product, is notionally a homogeneous quality (it only allows for "less" or "more") that is indeed alien to Aristotle's heterogeneous concepts of use and utility. However, as Gabriel Danzig aptly points out,[132] an objective interpretation of χρεία is just as much at odds with Aristotle's use of the term. In the same passage T13 that Judson refers to, for instance, Aristotle establishes a direct relationship between χρεία and all *actual* instances of exchange, saying that "when there is no need, there will be no exchange". On an objective interpretation of need, this would rule out all cases in which people have exchanges in order to obtain products that they merely *want*, without genuinely and objectively *needing* them—which is absurd. χρεία must also include all the subjective motivations that lead to actual exchanges.

Both Meikle and Judson have to admit that, on an "objective" interpretation of χρεία, Aristotle's project of quantification of values fails. But whereas Judson suspects that Aristotle may not have been aware of the problem of commensurability,[133] Meikle argues that Aristotle was acutely aware of the metaphysical failure of his project of finding a commensurating property that provides the link between use value and exchange value.

While in general offering a groundbreaking analysis of a much-contested passage, Meikle's reading occasionally suffers under a metaphysical overload.[134] His analysis relies on a conception of use-value that originates with

131 Ar. *EN* V.v (1133b18–20); *transl. adapted.*

132 Danzig (2000), 414.

133 Judson (1997), 173 proposes three possible interpretations of the impasse: (1) Aristotle recognized the problem of measurement of need; (2) Aristotle fell into the trap of inferring the existence of a calculus of needs (he over-mathematized his account); (3) Aristotle did not see the problem; the hybrid role he assigned to money obscures the underlying problem that need is not easily measured or quantified.

134 See Mei (2009), 526–527, on the anachronistic nature of "use" value vs. "exchange" value.

Adam Smith, according to whom use value is, in the end, an un-economic category, as well as with Karl Marx, according to whom use value is an irreducible value that naturally belongs to the object and cannot be expressed in quantity. Both Smith and Marx hold that comparative valuation of goods distorts their use-value. It is important to realize that Aristotle nowhere speaks of "use value" or "exchange value"—rather of objects *having* certain kinds of uses or *being* exchanged: things allow for a "proper" use or a use for the sake of exchange,[135] but *both* are viewed as instances of "use" by Aristotle. As we will see in the next section, Aristotle allows for cases in which exchange too constitutes "good use".

One of the most valuable aspects of Meikle's analysis is his attempt to dissociate currency (νόμισμα), that provides a unit to express commensurability, from the χρεία, that "holds everything together":

[Text 17]

> εἰ δ' οὕτω μὴ ἦν ἀντιπεπονθέναι, οὐκ ἂν ἦν κοινωνία. ὅτι δ' ἡ χρεία συνέχει ὥσπερ ἕν τι ὄν, δηλοῖ ὅτι ὅταν μὴ ἐν χρείᾳ ὦσιν ἀλλήλων, ἢ ἀμφότεροι ἢ ἅτερος, οὐκ ἀλλάττονται (…)
>
> If reciprocity could not be achieved in this way, there would be no sharing (in activity) between the parties. *That it is need that holds them together, turning them as it were into a single thing*, is shown by the fact that when the parties involved are not in need of each other—either both for each other, or one of the two for the other—they make no exchange (…).[136]

Need "holds together", because if partners do not need each other and each other's products, they simply will not arrive at an exchange. The problem is the phrase "being as it were a single thing": it is not made explicit *what* is held together by need. Rackham translates the phrase as "by serving as a single standard", implying that it is the *objects* that are held together: need holds things together because it is a single and homogeneous standard of value. Meikle[137] thinks this implausible on linguistic grounds: "one single thing" (ἕν τι ὄν) is singular neuter, whereas "need" (χρεία) is feminine. This argument is not compelling: subject and predicate do not necessarily have to agree in gender.

Mei argues that in *Politics* I, Aristotle does not envisage an opposition between "use" and "exchange".

135 Ar. *Pol.* I.ix (1257a6–13): οἰκεία χρῆσις vs. ἀλλαγῆς ἕνεκεν.

136 Ar. *EN* V.v (1133b5–8); *transl. adapted.*

137 Meikle (1995), 33.

However, Meikle's is right to point out that, whereas many translators supply objects of exchange as the direct object of "holds together", Aristotle elsewhere uses the verb "holding together" (συνέχει) to refer to people or actors;[138] in the present context too, it seems more natural to read "need holds *them*, i.e. people conducting an exchange, together". Without need there would be no partnership between the transactors.

On this reading, the phrase "being as it were a single thing" does not refer to the ontological status of χρεία, the subject of "holds together", but to the *result* of holding together: needs holds people together by making them a single thing, a cooperative partnership—for the time of the exchange.[139] Hence, Aristotle does not so much fail to solve the problem of commensurability by means of the notion of χρεία. Rather, it seems that χρεία was never meant to provide a common measure. Need, χρεία, simply holds people together, by providing the reason for exchange in the first place;[140] money merely, by force of convention, gives expression to the fact that we need each other.

Of course, this only takes the metaphysical edge off of the problem without solving the problem of value itself: how do we determine the amount of χρεία that an object has? The question is: is this really Aristotle's problem? Is Aristotle interested in offering a theory of value or price-formation? It rather seems that Aristotle's analysis presupposes that prices are already fixed; it merely shows how paying the price is performing an act of justice.[141] Aristotle demonstrates

138 *EN* 1155a23 (φιλία keeps together cities), *EN* 1132b30 (reciprocity keeps together associations). Meikle (1995), 34.

139 Aristotle's notion of κοινωνία ("community", "association" or "communality") can occur on more than one level. κοινωνία is a generic term for any community of interest, any social group emerging out of social interaction, ranging from commercial partners to fellow travellers, from the *oikos* to the polis—wherever individuals hold something in common (κοινόν). κοινωνία between travelers: *EN* VIII.9 (1159b28), *Pol.* I.5 (1263a17); between commercial partners: *EN* V.5 (1133b5–6, b14–16); VIII.14 (1163a31). The polis as a κοινωνία: *Pol.* I.1 (1252a1–7); *Hist. An.* I.1 (488a7–14). See Kraut (2002), 353–356. Cf. Yack (1993), 27–33.

140 This accords with Aristotle's account of the origin of communities. e.g. Ar. *EE* VII.10 (1242a7–9): διὰ γὰρ τὸ μὴ αὐταρκεῖν δοκοῦσι συνελθεῖν, ἐπεὶ συνῆλθόν γ' ἂν καὶ τοῦ συζῆν χάριν. "for people seem to have gathered due to their lack of adequate livelihood since they would have done so in any case for the sake of living together."

141 Danzig (2000). However, I differ with Danzig on the reading of the analogy: whereas he argues that the analogy serves as a justification of existing inequalities, I read the analogy as a stipulation of the conditions of exchange in a market situation. See above. Cf. Judson (1997), who points out that Aristotle's concern is an *ethical* concern: to establish the basis of fairness in exchange. Roll (1954), 35 formulates a similar point, but in negative, or disappointed, wording: "what begins with the promise of being a theory of value ends up with a mere statement of the accounting function of money."

how principles of justice are operative even in such ephemeral interactions as between shoemaker and builder.

3.3 *Need, Use, Utility*

In general, it is unlikely that Aristotle would regard χρεία as a homogeneous substance. Elsewhere in the *Nicomachean Ethics*, in the discussion of the virtue of liberality,[142] the logical connection between the meaning of the various nouns and verbs deriving from the XPH-root is made explicit:

[Text 18]

> ὧν δ' ἐστὶ χρεία, ἔστι τούτοις χρῆσθαι καὶ εὖ καὶ κακῶς· ὁ πλοῦτος δ' ἐστὶ τῶν χρησίμων· ἑκάστῳ δ' ἄριστα χρῆται ὁ ἔχων τὴν περὶ τοῦτο ἀρετήν· καὶ πλούτῳ δὴ χρήσεται ἄριστα ὁ ἔχων τὴν περὶ τὰ χρήματα ἀρετήν· οὗτος δ' ἐστὶν ὁ ἐλευθέριος. χρῆσις δ' εἶναι δοκεῖ χρημάτων δαπάνη καὶ δόσις· ἡ δὲ λῆψις καὶ ἡ φυλακὴ κτῆσις μᾶλλον.
>
> Things for which there is *need/use* (χρεία) can be *used* (χρῆσθαι) both well and badly; wealth is something that *has a use* (τῶν χρησίμων); and each thing is *used* (χρῆται) best by the person possessing the excellence relating to that thing: wealth, then, too, *will be used* (χρήσεται) best by the person possessing the excellence relating to *money* (τὰ χρήματα), and this is the open-handed person. *The using* (χρῆσις) *of money* (χρημάτων) *seems to consist in spending and giving; receiving and guarding it seems rather to constitute possession.*[143]

Here, in a passage reminiscent of Xenophon's *Oeconomicus*,[144] Aristotle maps out the different modalities of use by activating the etymological connection between several lexemes of the XPH-root. It is argued that the best use (χρῆσις) of resources (τῶν χρησίμων), is in accordance with the particular excellence that pertains to money (χρήματα): liberality (ἐλευθεριότης), characterized by the observance of the mean in relation to wealth, especially in the act of giving (δόσις).[145] There is a direct and logical connection between objects of need

142 For Aristotle's conception of liberality, see Swanson (1994).

143 Ar. *EN* IV.i (1120a4–9).

144 See Chapter Five Section 2.4. A similar sentiment is expressed by Democritus (68B282): χρημάτων χρῆσις ξὺν νόωι μὲν χρήσιμον εἰς τὸ ἐλευθέριον εἶναι καὶ δημωφελέα, ξὺν ἀνοίηι δὲ χορηγίη ξυνή.

145 *EN* IV.1 (1119b22): Λέγωμεν δ' ἑξῆς περὶ ἐλευθεριότητος. δοκεῖ δὴ εἶναι ἡ περὶ χρήματα μεσότης· ἐπαινεῖται γὰρ ὁ ἐλευθέριος οὐκ ἐν τοῖς πολεμικοῖς, οὐδ' ἐν οἷς ὁ σώφρων, οὐδ' αὖ ἐν ταῖς κρίσεσιν, ἀλλὰ περὶ δόσιν χρημάτων καὶ λῆψιν, μᾶλλον δ' ἐν τῇ δόσει.

(χρεία), objects that have a use (χρήσιμα), the activity of use (χρῆσθαι, χρῆσις) and money (χρήματα). What you need is what is useful for you.

What is particularly striking here is that using money (and "things of which there is a need" in general) is seen as something that can be done well (or "best", ἄριστα) and, by implication, less well, or indeed badly: it constitutes a virtue (ἀρετή). As virtues are dispositions to act in a certain way according to Aristotle,[146] use is an activity as well. Activities are defined by their ends (their use *to/toward p*).[147] Therefore, from an ethical point of view, there is a difference between *good* use and *bad* use, *good* needs and *bad* needs, *good* utilities and *bad* utilities, *good* utility friends and *bad* utility friends—depending on the goal or end that is realized in the activity of use.[148] The end of building is to produce a house; the end of shoemaking is to produce shoes; the end of playing tennis is the game itself. These are all heterogeneous goals and they can never be made commensurable by Aristotle's lights.[149]

The notion of a "good" use of wealth (πλοῦτος) is further articulated in the context of definitions of ownership (things being οἰκεῖα) and possession (κτῆσις) in the *Rhetoric*. Here, it becomes clear that Aristotle envisages a parallelism between virtue and wealth, since in both cases use (χρῆσθαι) is better than merely possessing (κτᾶσθαι):[150]

[Text 19]

> πλούτου δὲ μέρη νομίσματος πλῆθος ⟨καὶ⟩ γῆς, χωρίων κτῆσις, ἔτι δὲ ἐπίπλων κτῆσις καὶ βοσκημάτων καὶ ἀνδραπόδων πλήθει καὶ μεγέθει καὶ κάλλει διαφερόντων, ταῦτα δὲ πάντα ⟨οἰκεῖα⟩ καὶ ἀσφαλῆ καὶ ἐλευθέρια καὶ χρήσιμα. ἔστιν δὲ χρήσιμα μὲν μᾶλλον τὰ κάρπιμα, ἐλευθέρια δὲ τὰ πρὸς ἀπόλαυσιν (κάρπιμα δὲ λέγω ἀφ' ὧν αἱ πρόσοδοι, ἀπολαυστικὰ δὲ ἀφ' ὧν μηδὲν παρὰ τὴν χρῆσιν

146 *EN* I.8 (1098b32–1099a7).

147 *EN* III.5ii (1115b22); *Met.* Θ (1050a22–24).

148 For the notion of proper use (ὀρθὴ χρῆσις), see Chapter Five Section 2.

149 In this sense, Marx was right in saying that Aristotle lacks the notion of abstract labor, some common substance that makes the labor of builder and shoemaker commensurable.

150 In *EN* I.8 (1098b32–1099a7) it is argued that the chief good (τὸ ἄριστον) is located not in the possession (κτῆσις) of excellence but in its use (χρῆσις), i.e. in its ἐνεργεία: διαφέρει δὲ ἴσως οὐ μικρὸν ἐν κτήσει ἢ χρήσει τὸ ἄριστον ὑπολαμβάνειν, καὶ ἐν ἕξει ἢ ἐνεργείᾳ. This suggests that not only that dealing with property is an instance of excellence, but also that there is an *analogy* between property and virtue. Cf. *EE* II.i 1219b1–3. See Frank (2005), 70 ff. on the analogy between property and virtue, followed by Mei (2009), who stresses the element of interpretation or deliberation as decisive in the ethics of "use" in Aristotle.

> γίγνεται ὅ τι καὶ ἄξιον). ὅρος δὲ ἀσφαλείας μὲν τὸ ἐνταῦθα καὶ οὕτω κεκτῆσθαι ὥστ' ἐφ' αὑτῷ εἶναι τὴν χρῆσιν αὐτῶν, τοῦ δὲ οἰκεῖα εἶναι ἢ μὴ ὅταν ἐφ' αὑτῷ ᾖ ἀπαλλοτριῶσαι· λέγω δὲ ἀπαλλοτρίωσιν δόσιν καὶ πρᾶσιν. ὅλως δὲ τὸ πλουτεῖν ἐστιν ἐν τῷ χρῆσθαι μᾶλλον ἢ ἐν τῷ κεκτῆσθαι· καὶ γὰρ ἡ ἐνέργειά ἐστι τῶν τοιούτων καὶ ἡ χρῆσις πλοῦτος.
>
> The parts of *wealth* are abundance of cash ⟨and⟩ land, possession of tracts distinguished and also possession of implements and slaves and cattle distinguished by number and size and beauty; and all these things [should be] privately owned and securely held and freely employed and useful. Things that are productive are more useful, but things for enjoyment are [more] freely employed; and by productive I mean what produces income, by enjoyable that from which there is no gain beyond the use of it, or none worth mentioning. The mark of security is the possession of property in such a place and in such a way that use of it lies with the owner; being one's own (or not) depends on who has the the right of alienation, and by alienation I mean gift and sale. All in all, wealth consists more in use than in possession; for it is the actualization and use of such goods that constitutes wealth.[151]

In order to fully qualify as "wealthy", a number of conditions are to be met: one's properties must be numerous, large and beautiful, secure (ἀσφαλῆ),[152] liberal (ἐλευθέρια) and useful (χρήσιμα), and used rather than merely owned. The condition "liberal and useful" (καὶ ἐλευθέρια καὶ χρήσιμα) is to be understood as disjunctive:[153] the two conditions are defined in a way that makes them mutually exclusive. Useful are those properties that generate revenues (τὰ κάρπιμα ... ἀφ' ὧν αἱ πρόσοδοι), whereas liberal properties are those "for enjoyment" (τὰ πρὸς ἀπόλαυσιν)[154] in that they are employed in intrinsically valuable activities

151 Ar. *Rhet.* 1.5.7 (1361a12–25); *transl.* Kennedy (2007), *adapt.*

152 Miller (1995), 312 notes that the criteria that properties are οἰκεῖα and ἀσφαλῆ are also central in the modern Anglo-American concept of property rights. He does *not*, as Frank (2005) 54n3 has it, *assimilate* Aristotle's concept of property to the modern Anglo-American concept of property rights.

153 Miller (1991), 245 n. 2; (1995), 312. On "liberal", ἐλευθέριος, as referring to "behavior and qualities appropriate to a free person" (Alpern 1983: 312–313), see also Chapter Four Section 3.3.

154 In *EN* 1095b17–1096a11 where the three kinds of lives are distinguished, the ἀπολαυστικός is the life that has ἡδονή (i.e. the gratification of appetites and desires) as its sole object—as opposed to the πρακτικός or πολιτικός that has ἀρετή as its τέλος and the θεωρητικός that has θεωρία as its object. Here, in T19, ἀπόλαυσις may be used for "enjoyment" in a more general sense to serve the opposition with the "use" of properties as a means to an ulterior end. But Cope & Sandys (1877), 1:82: "ἀπόλαυσις is properly 'sensual enjoyment'".

(ἀφ' ὧν μηδὲν παρὰ τὴν χρῆσιν γίγνεται). The definition of security (ἀσφαλεία) is that it is up to the owner (ἐφ' αὑτῷ) how and where a possession is to be used (τὴν χρῆσιν); and, finally, the definition of a possession being one's own (οἰκεῖα εἶναι ἢ μή)[155] is that it is up to the owner (ἐφ' αὑτῷ) to "alienate" it (ἀπαλλοτριῶσαι), i.e. dispose of it by giving away or selling (δόσιν καὶ πρᾶσιν).[156] More in general, Aristotle adds, being wealthy consists in the use (ἐν τῷ χρῆσθαι) rather than the possession (ἐν τῷ κεκτῆσθαι) of property, for wealth lies in the actualization (ἡ ἐνέργεια) and use (ἡ χρῆσις) of properties: *genuine* wealth is to a set of possessions as ἐνέργεια is to δύναμις.[157]

Hence, there are two ways of using (χρῆσθαι) one's property:[158] as χρήσιμα, as means to generate revenues; or in a liberal fashion, by use (χρῆσις) for the sake of the very act of using, i.e. as an intrinsically valuable activity.[159] In other words: property is both tool and practice, "both an external good and a characterological good".[160] The two ways of alienation that Aristotle distinguishes, giving away and selling, correspond to the two distinct "uses" of property: sell-

---

155 See Grimaldi (1980) for a reading that follows the manuscripts with regard to the location of ἢ μή. Spengel transposes ἢ μή to follow ἀπαλλοτριῶσαι.

156 Kraut (2002), 322–323 points out that the right of alienation of property is qualified in Aristotle's *Politics* where citizens in the best city do not have the freedom to sell or give away their private allotments of land. This would imply that the plots of land allocated to each citizen are not "owned" by them in the sense of T19. Moreover, an individuals' freedom to acquire, sell, or transfer goods may be restricted by laws. However, to the present discussion these restrictions to private property are not relevant. The salient point is that Aristotle makes allowances, however qualified and restricted, for private property with an appeal to the possibility of the exercise of virtue.

157 Cf. the discussion of wealth in *Pol.* I.9 (1257b8 ff.), where money is denied to be *true* wealth—not only because its value is conventional (and sometimes "mere nonsense", ὁτὲ δὲ πάλιν λῆρος), but also because the accumulation of money is unnatural: accumulation means not applying it to one's own use (πρὸς χρῆσιν) or towards realizing the good life (πρὸς τὸ εὖ ζῆν). Cf. Meikle (1996) and (1994).

158 This distinction is not the same as the distinction drawn in *Pol.* I.9 (1257a5–14) where it is argued that property is essentially dual. Cf. Meikle (1995), 48–50, Frank (2005), 54–111. In *Pol.* I.9 Aristotle distinguishes between "uses of property" in terms of the value structure of the *objects* of exchange, i.e. between "natural use" and "use in exchange" (a distinction that, according to Meikle (1995), 9–2, gives rise to a metaphysical rift between qualitative and quantitative value). The two uses of property distinguished in *Rhet.* I.v oppose activity and object: the exercise of virtue is a type of use the value of which inheres in the *activity* of use. This is categorically different from the type of use in both "natural use" and "use in exchange" (which is parasitic upon natural use) where value derives from (either the quantitative or the qualitative) characteristics of the *object* of use.

159 Socrates insists on a similar understanding of wealth in the *Euthydemus* (280a–e). Cf. Frank (2005), 70.

160 Frank (2005), 71.

ing property serves the ulterior end of generating income; "giving away" is a use of property that is intrinsically valuable.

Hence, both giving away and spending or selling are more proper manifestations of wealth than mere possession, because they both are cases of the *use* of wealth. The *good* use of wealth is using it in a way that makes the use an intrinsically valuable activity: in giving it to someone, rather than spending or selling it as a means to an ulterior end. In Aristotle's view, actions are defined by their ends.[161] As wealth is most properly activity (ἐνέργεια), and as the right to alienation (both in selling and in giving) is a defining criterion of ownership, property is not only a necessary condition for the practice of the virtue of liberality, but is itself the very ite where the practice of virtue takes place.[162]

This yields a conception of "need" that is fundamentally different from a utilitarian concept of "demand" in terms of subjective need. As Jill Frank points out, if "subjective need" is the measure of an exchange, than exchange is fair when both parties derive an equal amount of pleasure from the exchange.[163] Utility is conflated with pleasure, use is reduced to maximization of pleasure. In Aristotle's view, as we have seen, both "utility" and "use" are underdetermined: "use" can be good or bad, depending on the question whether virtue is realized in the act of using; similarly, utility is a derivative category of value, because something seems useful "through which some good or pleasure comes about".[164] In similar fashion, χρεία can encompass objective needs, i.e. preconditions for mere survival *and* for living the good live by realizing virtues, as well as subjective wants, that may actually be ill-understood needs directed towards the mere satisfaction of pleasure.

3.4 *The Limits of Commensurability*

Whereas Aristotle does not offer a theory of price-formation in his *Nicomachean Ethics*, he does offer a theory of value. The key is in the notorious passage where Aristotle seems to deny the possibility of genuine commensurability:

[Text 20; cf. Text 16]

> τὸ δὴ νόμισμα ὥσπερ μέτρον σύμμετρα ποιῆσαν ἰσάζει· οὔτε γὰρ ἂν μὴ οὔσης ἀλλαγῆς κοινωνία ἦν, οὔτ' ἀλλαγὴ ἰσότητος μὴ οὔσης, οὔτ' ἰσότης μὴ οὔσης

161 *EN* III.5ii (1115b22); *Met.* Θ (1050a22–24).

162 Frank (2005), 69.

163 Frank (2005), 87.

164 *EN* VIII.ii (1155b19–21): δόξειε δ' ἂν χρήσιμον εἶναι δι' οὗ γίνεται ἀγαθόν τι ἢ ἡδονή, ὥστε φιλητὰ ἂν εἴη τἀγαθόν τε καὶ τὸ ἡδὺ ὡς τέλη. "but that would seem to be useful through which some good or pleasure comes about, so that it will be the good and the pleasant that are lovable as ends."

> συμμετρίας. τῇ μὲν οὖν ἀληθείᾳ ἀδύνατον τὰ τοσοῦτον διαφέροντα σύμμετρα γενέσθαι, πρὸς δὲ τὴν χρείαν ἐνδέχεται ἱκανῶς.
>
> Currency, then, acts like a measure, making things commensurable and so equalizing them; for there would be no association if there were no exchange, no exchange without equality, and no equality without commensurability. Strictly speaking, it is impossible that things so different in kind should become commensurable, but with a view to people's needs a sufficient degree of commensurability can be achieved.[165]

The crucial sentence is that stating the contrast between the *stricto sensu* (τῇ ἀληθείᾳ) impossibility of things being commensurable, and the commensurability that can be achieved in sufficient degree (ἱκανῶς), "with a view to need" (πρὸς τὴν χρείαν). The phrase πρὸς τὴν χρείαν is sometimes understood as a qualification implying a contrast with full-fledged theoretical commensurability, and is accordingly translated as "for practical purposes"[166] or "for ordinary use":[167] theoretically there is no commensurability, but there is as much of a semblance of commensurability as will do in real life. Especially the "in a sufficient degree" recalls a famous line from the beginning of the *Ethics* where Aristotle states that in ethical and political matters precision must not be sought to the same degree as in mathematics.[168]

As some commentators point out, the sentence should be taken even more literally:[169] the phrase restricts the possibility of commensurability to the domain of χρεία. Whereas metaphysically commensurability between things as heterogeneous as shoes, beds, corn-licenses and wine is impossible, with a view to χρεία there is "a sufficient degree" of *faux*-commensurability.[170] This statement, then, still amounts to Aristotle admitting defeat.[171]

What is insufficiently appreciated, however, is that the πρὸς τὴν χρείαν-phrase also serves as a restrictive expression in contrast to other types of

165 Ar. *EN* v.v (1133b16–21); *transl. adapted.*

166 Rackham (1926).

167 Danzig (2000), 415 n. 42, who adduces parallels to this use of χρεία from *An. Pr.* 24b15 and *Cael.* 269b21.

168 *EN* I.iii (1094b12–28). This Aristotelian proviso makes it less likely that Aristotle inadvertedly over-mathematizes his account of need. *Pace* Judson (1997).

169 Judson (1997), 171; Meikle (1995), 35.

170 Meikle (1995), 31: "[Aristotle's] search for an explanation of commensurability ended with the admission of frustration (…)."

171 Danzig (2000), 399–400 aptly observes that Aristotle himself does not at all seem troubled by this "failure".

exchanges: money only works in the domain of need. Shoes and beds are never *really* commensurable, only, to a certain extent, with respect to the dimension of "need". This is an important restriction in Aristotle's ethics, because the realm of "need" (χρεία) is the realm of "the useful" (τὸ χρήσιμον; also, τὸ ὠφέλιμον, τὸ συμφέρον), which is a different category of value than "the good" or "the pleasant".[172]

The limitative purport of "with a view to people's needs" gains significance if we look at the discussion of non-uniform friendships where people try to do the impossible: exchanging the good for the useful. In exchanges of non-uniform friendship, friends operate with different measures of value. An example is the exchange of philosophy for money—an exchange that yields the risk of quarrels between student and pupil because of the lack of a common measure between knowledge and money:

[Text 21]

> πολλὰ ἐγκλήματα γίνεται ἐν ταῖς φιλίαις τοῖς μὴ κατ' εὐθυωρίαν, καὶ τὸ δίκαιον ἰδεῖν οὐ ῥᾴδιον. **χαλεπὸν γὰρ μετρῆσαι ἑνὶ τῷδε τὸ μὴ κατ' εὐθυωρίαν**, οἷον συμβαίνει ἐπὶ τῶν ἐρωτικῶν. ὃ μὲν γὰρ διώκει ὡς τὸν ἡδὺν ἐπὶ τὸ συζῆν, ὃ δ' ἐκεῖνον ἐνίοτε ὡς χρήσιμον· ὅταν δὲ παύσηται τοῦ ἐρᾶν, ἄλλου γινομένου ἄλλος γίνεται, καὶ τότε λογίζονται παντί τινος, καὶ ὡς Πύθων καὶ Παμμένης διεφέροντο **καὶ ὡς διδάσκαλος καὶ μαθητής (ἐπιστήμη γὰρ καὶ χρήματα οὐχ ἑνὶ μετρεῖται)** (…).
>
> In friendships not based on direct reciprocity many causes for recrimination occur, and it is not easy to see what is just; *for it is difficult to measure by one given thing relations that are not directly reciprocal.* An example is what it happens in love affairs, for here one party pursues the other as an agreeable person to live with, but the other sometimes the one as being useful, and when the lover ceases to love, one having changed the other changes too, and then they calculate the quid pro quo, and quarrel as Pytho and Pammenes used, *and as teacher and pupil do in general* (*for knowledge and money have no common measure*) (…).[173]

172 See *EN* II.iii (1104b30–32). Cf. *EN* VIII.ii (1155b17–19).

173 Ar. *EE* VII.x (1243b15–22); *transl.* Rackham (1971), *adapted.*

In non-uniform friendships,[174] i.e. friendships that are "not aligned" or "not on the same line",[175] there is no common measure, no "this one thing" (ἑνὶ τῷδε), with reference to which values can be measured and relations can be evaluated: knowledge (ἐπιστήμη) and money (χρήματα) are not measured "by one" (ἑνί). This is made clear even more explicitly in the case of philosophy, because philosophy is the activity of realizing human potential by performing virtues—a different realm from that of money, which only measures need:

[Text 22]

> ἐν οἷς δὲ μὴ γίνεται διομολογία τῆς ὑπουργίας, οἱ μὲν δι' αὑτοὺς προϊέμενοι εἴρηται ὅτι ἀνέγκλητοι (τοιαύτη γὰρ ἡ κατ' ἀρετὴν φιλία), **τὴν ἀμοιβήν τε ποιητέον κατὰ τὴν προαίρεσιν (αὕτη γὰρ τοῦ φίλου καὶ τῆς ἀρετῆς)**· οὕτω δ' ἔοικε καὶ τοῖς φιλοσοφίας κοινωνήσασιν· **οὐ γὰρ πρὸς χρήμαθ' ἡ ἀξία μετρεῖται, τιμή τ' ἰσόρροπος οὐκ ἂν γένοιτο, ἀλλ' ἴσως ἱκανόν, καθάπερ καὶ πρὸς θεοὺς καὶ πρὸς γονεῖς, τὸ ἐνδεχόμενον.**
>
> but where there is no agreement about services to be rendered, those who take the initiative in giving for their friends' own sake, as has been said, make no accusations, since this is what friendschip according to excellence is like, *and the return for it should be made with respect to the giver's disposition to give, since this is the mark both of his being a friend and of his excellence*—and this too, it seems, is how a person should make a return to those who have imparted philosophy to him, *since the value of this is not measured in relation to money, and honour will not balance it in the scales, though presumably it will suffice to do what is possible, just as in relation to gods and to parents.*[176]

---

174 This resembles the economic notion of "isolated exchange": two parties exchange in primary reliance upon their own subjective preferences without reference to alternative market opportunities. In modern economics isolated exchange is fundamentally distinct from market exchange that presupposes an informed market where individuals deduce their transactions from a market price, i.e. a sense of an on-going pattern of exchange among more individuals. Cf. Lowry (1987), 185–189. Cf. Pakaluk (1998), 155 (although he presumes that even in non-uniform exchanges the parties have a notion of market price at their disposal).

175 The expression μὴ κατ' εὐθυωρίαν is remarkable here. As Bonitz' index indicates, the phrase predominantly occurs in Aristotle's physical works (with the exception of *Rhet.* II.2 1379a11 and *Met.* II 994a2).

176 *EN* IX.ii (1164a33–64b5); *transl. adapted.*

Aristotle takes friendship centered around philosophy to be an instance of friendship based on virtue (ἀρετή), which is logically less liable to conflict.[177] Here it is explicitly stated that virtue friendships involve an exchange of goods that does not allow measurement along the lines that money does. The value of philosophy cannot be measured in terms of money (οὐ πρὸς χρήμαθ' ἡ ἀξία μετρεῖται) and cannot be balanced by deference or esteem (τιμὴ ἰσόρροπος οὐκ ἂν γένοιτο), because in the context of a virtue friendship purposive choice (προαίρεσις) comes to be the measure of friendship and virtue:

[Text 23]

> ἐν δὲ ταῖς κατ' ἀρετὴν ἐγκλήματα μὲν οὐκ ἔστιν, μέτρῳ δ' ἔοικεν ἡ τοῦ δράσαντος προαίρεσις· τῆς ἀρετῆς γὰρ καὶ τοῦ ἤθους ἐν τῇ προαιρέσει τὸ κύριον.
>
> However, in friendship based on excellence there are no accusations, and *it looks as if the measure is the decision of the doer*; for the determinant of *excellence* and *character* lies in *this* decision.[178]

In virtue friendships, the measure is the "intention of the doer".[179] The metaphor of a "measure" (μέτρον) highlights the contrast with the constitution of utility friendships, where the measure of benefaction equals the utility or benefit to the recipient and, it is suggested, is easy to quantify. In the case of virtue friendships, where the measure is purposive choice, it is harder to imagine such quantification; the notion of "measure" is presumably applied more metaphorically as the standard for the moral quality of virtuous action towards friends: the quality of a virtuous action depends on the moral decision-choice that precedes it (a favor is only a favor if it is intended as such by an agent who

---

177 In *EN* VIII.xiii (1162b6–13) it is stated that virtue friends will not quarrel if they act virtuously. See previous section.

178 *EN* VIII.xiv (1163a21–22); *transl. adapted.*

179 We should keep in mind that virtue friendships are, in the end, not structured as reciprocal exchanges. For the notion that virtue friendship is based on προαίρεσις, see also *EE* VII.x (1243b9–10, 1243b2–3), *EN* VIII.v (1157b30–31). Moral virtue is defined by Aristotle as a ἕξις προαιρητική: *EN* II.vi (1106b36–a2), *EE* II.x (1227b5–11), acting in accordance to virtue as "the distinguishing mark" (ἴδιον) of the morally virtuous man: *Rhet.* I.ix (1367b22–23) for abiding to one's προαίρεσις means being ἐγκρατής and failing to do so is ἀκράτεια: *EN* VII.i (1145b8–17). On the concept of προαίρεσις and its central place in Aristotle's ethics, see Chamberlain (1984) and Mele (1981); see especially Wiggins (1978–1979) on problems of προαίρεσις in relation to commensurability; Irwin (1992) for the relation of προαίρεσις to other concepts designating intentional mental states such as βούλησις.

understands its consequences), somewhat on the analogy of the value of a useful action that depends on the quantity of its usefulness.[180]

Hence the goods of utility friendship are fundamentally incommensurable with those of virtue friendship—*even* when in both cases the same objects are involved. From the point of view of the virtue friend, the act of giving a gift is the performance of a virtue; the value of this act does not coincide with the value of the object exchanged, but it is to be measured by the quality of the choice or intention. From the point of view of the utility friend, the value of the gift is the value of the object itself, because that is what he needs, and within utility friendship need is what measures the goods. *Even* the act of giving money cannot be measured in terms of its monetary value: the value of the act of giving someone 100 euros is not the 100 euros itself, it is the moral quality of the decision to use money to perform a virtue. In these situations, there is no proportionate analogy.

Philosophy, like virtue, is an activity, not an external object, and its value cannot be measured in terms of money but only of intention and purposive choice. This yields a contrast with the mercantile practice of the sophists, evoked by the examples of Protagoras and the sophists in the preceding passage, who do exchange "wisdom" for money.[181] For sophists, who are engaged in this non-uniform exchange of wisdom for money, there are two options: either letting the customer fix the value of what is given ("wisdom"), as Protagoras did,[182] or fixing the price in advance, when the customer is still unaware of the true value of the sophist's wisdom.[183]

Therefore, Aristotle's reservations with regard to the scope of the commensurability that can be provided by money should not so much be read as a reflection on the metaphysical gap between useful value and exchange value, or on a failure to conceive of the category of abstract labor—but as the statement of a theory of value in which "needs" are a qualitatively different category

180 Pakaluk (1998a), 153 on *EN* IX.i (1164a33–36): "That he (Aristotle) brings in again the principle of compensation according to choice shows that he regards it as an important idea, yet he has said little to explain it."

181 *EN* IX.ii (1164b23–34). On the monetization of education and wisdom, see Chapter Five.

182 *EN* IX.ii 1164a22–28; cf. *EE* VII.x 1242b34. See also Pl. *Prot.* 328b–c for a variant where the pupil may dispute the μισθός by going to a temple and swearing to what he believes to be the worth (ἀξία) of the instruction—subjective valuation after the fact, as in Aristotle's report. In Aristotle's discussion of sophistic practice vs philosophical approaches to the valuation of wisdom, Protagoras' Man Measure Statement is, again, evoked by the emphatic use of the central term μέτρον. Here, the idea that man is the measure of all χρήματα is trivialized as to mean "the customer is always right".

183 See Johnstone (2011), 19, for a reading of this passage against the background of pricing practices in 4th-century Greece.

from "the good", circulating in different types of relationships. The laborious analogy of shoemaker and builder, only justifies equivalences in the realm of needs. Aristotle does not admit defeat; he upholds incommensurability.[184]

3.5 *Social Valuation and Symbolic Economy*

At various points of the discussion, we have seen the central role of τιμή, social valuation or esteem. In unequal utility exchanges, both parties get the larger share out of the exchange, but of different things: more κέρδος for the inferior friend, more τιμή, the γέρας of beneficence, for the superior one.[185] In virtue friendships, the value of philosophy cannot be measured by money, nor can it be counterbalanced by τιμή.[186] In both cases, it is stressed that τιμή is a reward of a different order.

However, Aristotle is nowhere unequivocally clear about the nature and value structure of τιμή.[187] The evidence suggests a pervading awareness of incommensurability: although τιμή does involve (it is possible to bestow more (πλέον νέμειν) of it, and hence also less), it is not to be measured by the same standard as utilities, as it circulates in a symbolic economy whose constituents are not entirely reducible to the realm of need and utility.

In book IV, τιμή is characterized as the prize (ἆθλον) of excellence (τῆς ἀρετῆς):[188] a *reward* for excellence but not a compensation, since it is fundamentally insufficient:

[Text 24]

> καὶ ἐπὶ μὲν ταῖς μεγάλαις καὶ ὑπὸ τῶν σπουδαίων μετρίως ἡσθήσεται, ὡς τῶν οἰκείων τυγχάνων ἢ καὶ ἐλαττόνων· ἀρετῆς γὰρ παντελοῦς οὐκ ἂν γένοιτο ἀξία τιμή, οὐ μὴν ἀλλ' ἀποδέξεταί γε τῷ μὴ ἔχειν αὐτοὺς μείζω αὐτῷ ἀπονέμειν (.)

184 See Nussbaum (2001), 294–297 for the idea that to Aristotle, the ontological incommensurability of goods and moral values contributes to the preciousness of life, as well as to the fragility of the good life. Cf. Pack (2010), 14 n. 25: "Aristotle is the philosopher of heterogeneity." This contrasts with neoclassic economic theory that stresses homogeneity through utility and cost/benefit analysis. Simmel (1950), 414.

185 T14 (*EN* VIII.xiv 1163b1–5). See Section 2.4.

186 T22 (*EN* IX.ii 1164a33–64b5). See Section 3.4.

187 In the context of a utility friendship, it remains unclear whether τιμή functions as a useful good or a surrogate useful good or as an entity that is ultimately incommensurable with utility. Cf. Pakaluk (1998a), on Aristotle's discussion of unequal friendships in VIII.xiv: "The whole matter is unclear, and the difficulties are compounded by his never distinguishing explicitly the function of honour described here, and its very different function described in VIII.vii–viii." (148).

188 *EN* IV.iii (1123b35–1124a1): τῆς ἀρετῆς γὰρ ἆθλον ἡ τιμή, καὶ ἀπονέμεται τοῖς ἀγαθοῖς.

> "[I]n the case of great honours, accorded to him by people of excellence, he will be moderately pleased, on the grounds that he is (only) getting what accrues to him, or actually less than that—*for there could be no honor worthy of complete excellence*. All the same, he will accept it in so far as they have nothing larger to mete out to him."[189]

There cannot possibly be τιμή that is equivalent to real virtue.[190] Hence, not only is τιμή not to be measured with reference to utility; it is also an incommensurate and insufficient compensation for virtue. The moral quality of a virtuous act can never be reduced to an equivalence with τιμή: people who act virtuously just do not do so *in order to* obtain τιμή.

If we think back to Aristotle's categorization of φιλία into three kinds corresponding to the three categories of value—the useful, the pleasant, the good—we recall that only utilities are proper objects of exchange. The good, as Aristotle defines it, is not a κτῆμα that can be exchanged, but an activity that friends can share in. Attempts to exchange the good, e.g. wisdom, for money, are destined to fail because it conflicts with the ontological structure of the good (sophists who attempt to do so reveal their merchandise to be counterfeit),[191] and is bound to cause conflicts because it is impossible to reach consensus over the value of incommensurable goods: it is a non-uniform friendship. How then does Aristotle's discussion of τιμή, as a return for virtue, in unequal friendships fit in?

The answer is that Aristotle acknowledges that exchanges can have a moral moment, without implying that this moral aspect is an exchange object itself, exchangeable with utility: the superior partner who displays virtue (e.g. the virtue of beneficence, of liberality) receives τιμή, which is a *token* (σημεῖον) of hisreputation for doing good (εὐεργετικῆς εὐδοξίας):

[Text 25]

> τιμὴ δ' ἐστὶν μὲν σημεῖον εὐεργετικῆς εὐδοξίας· (…) μέρη δὲ τιμῆς θυσίαι, μνῆμαι ἐν μέτροις καὶ ἄνευ μέτρων, γέρα, τεμένη, προεδρίαι, τάφοι, εἰκόνες, τροφαὶ δημόσιαι, τὰ βαρβαρικά, οἷον προσκυνήσεις καὶ ἐκστάσεις, δῶρα τὰ παρ' ἑκάστοις τίμια. καὶ γὰρ τὸ δῶρόν ἐστι κτήματος δόσις καὶ τιμῆς σημεῖον, διὸ καὶ οἱ

189 *EN* IV.iii (1242a4–9); *transl. adapted.*

190 T14.

191 Cf. Ar. *Soph. El.* 165a for the prototypical definition of the sophist's trade as counterfeit. Cf. Blank (2014), 379 n. 4, See also Chapter Five Section 1.1.

> φιλοχρήματοι καὶ οἱ φιλότιμοι ἐφίενται αὐτῶν· ἀμφοτέροις γὰρ ἔχει ὧν δέονται· καὶ γὰρ κτῆμά ἐστιν οὗ ἐφίενται οἱ φιλοχρήματοι, καὶ τιμὴν ἔχει οὗ οἱ φιλότιμοι.
>
> Honor is a *sign of a reputation for doing good*; (...) the constituents of honor are sacrifices, memorial inscriptions in verse or prose, receipt of special awards, grants of land, front seats at festivals, burial at the public expense, statues, free food in the state dining room; and such practices found among barbarians as prostation and rights of precedence and gifts that are held in honor in each society; *for a gift too is a grant of a possession and sign of honor*, which is why gifts are desired both by the ambitious and by those who are fond of money: they are craved by the latter as a possession and by the former as an honor; so that they furnish both with what they want.[192]

Significantly, the gift, which is an example of τιμή, is here defined as consisting of both a material part (the allocation of property, κτήματος δόσις) and a symbolic part: it is a token of deference (τιμῆς σημεῖον). If we bear in mind the inequality implied in the relation between benefactor and beneficiary, it becomes clear that τιμή is meant to compensate for the asymmetry between exchange objects.[193] The surplus value is paid out in τιμή. This is how unequal utility friendships work: because the objects exchanged are unequal (the partners are unequal with respect to utility) the partners become unequal in terms of τιμή: in terms of social standing. This is a moralizing account of the way power works—as opposed to equal utility friendships where the respective status of the exchange partners is irrelevant to the fairness in the exchange.

Hence, in unequal friendships, inequality can be taken account of (ἀνταποδοτέον) in terms of τιμή:

[Text 26]

> οὕτω δὴ καὶ τοῖς ἀνίσοις ὁμιλητέον, καὶ τῷ εἰς χρήματα ὠφελουμένῳ ἢ εἰς ἀρετὴν τιμὴν ἀνταποδοτέον, ἀποδιδόντα τὰ ἐνδεχόμενα. τὸ δυνατὸν γὰρ ἡ φιλία ἐπιζητεῖ, οὐ τὸ κατ' ἀξίαν·

192 *Rhet.* I.v.ix (1361a27–b2); *transl.* Kennedy (2007), *adapt.*

193 On a communal level too, Aristotle thinks that benefactors cannot be accorded communal money *and* τιμή at the same time (*EN* VIII.xiv (1163b5–12)): τιμή is not an "extra" on top of monetary compensation, but is granted to the person who "comes worse off" (ἐλαττομένῳ) in terms of money.

> This, then, is the way a person should have dealings with unequals too, and if he is being helped in terms of money or towards excellence he should *give honour in return, paying back what he can*. For friendship looks for what is possible, not for strict equivalence with merit (...).[194]

τιμή serves as a compensation for both money and virtue that the inferior friend cannot match according to desert (κατ' ἀξίαν). However, this construction, the complementarity of money and deference, preserves a sense of "equivalence" (ἀνταποδοτέον (T26); ἐπανισοῖ, "establish equality" in the lines immediately preceding T26)[195] that is in a way misleading, since τιμή is not quantifiable along the same lines as monetary recompense.

The value of τιμή cannot be measured by need, as τιμή circulates in a symbolic economy of prizes (γέρας, ἆθλον) and tokens (σημεῖον) as a reward for excellence (ἀρετή) without ever being capable of fully compensating for this ἀρετή. τιμή is the symbolic currency that, from Aristotle's perspective, marks a divide between utility and virtue as incommensurable quantities. Although Aristotle does use terminology that involves quantity and equivalence, he also takes care to preserve the boundaries between these different types of capital by insisting on their incommensurability: there is a distinct measure of value for ἀρετή; value expressions in terms of monetary value are carefully avoided, and τιμή and material gain are complementary, hence distinct.

Beneath Aristotle's approach to exchange relations lies his conception of the proper use of utilities, as we have seen in Section 3.3: utilities can be used in two ways, by spending them as a means to the acquisition of revenues, and by the intrinsically valuable activity of giving. Aristotle dismisses the idea that virtue and wisdom could/ can ever become goods on a free market. Instead, he applauds the exercise of virtue through beneficence and liberality—i.e. by fostering unequal utility friendships. Hence, his discussion of τιμή can ultimately be read as a legitimization of asymmetrical power relationships: because τιμή can never be a sufficient return for the virtue of liberality and beneficence, the debt of the inferior partner is irredeemable. By insisting that, in unequal exchange friendships, partners should reciprocate on the basis of capacity rather than equivalence, "Aristotle paves the way for the obligation between

194 *EN* VIII.xiv (1163b12–15); *transl. adapted.*

195 Cf. *EN* V.ii (1130b30–1131a9) where τιμή is one of the objects of distributive justice. Its juxtaposition with χρήματα, as well as its collocation with notions of "sharing" (ἐν ταῖς διανομαῖς) and "parts" (ἄνισον καὶ ἴσον) suggest quantifiability and, hence, commensurability; at the same time the juxtaposition with χρήματα implies that τιμή is not reducible to material assets.

patron and client and a redefinition of friendship along these lines in the post-classical period."[196]

4 The Politics of Need

4.1 *Holding the City Together*

Need does not provide a common measure, but simply "holds people together", in the sense that need, by providing a motivation for exchange, brings together shoemaker and builder so as to constitute a successful transaction. However, Aristotle suggests that need also "holds people together" on a larger scale and on a more general level:[197]

[Text 27]

> ἡ δὲ πολιτικὴ συνέστηκε μὲν κατὰ τὸ χρήσιμον καὶ μάλιστα. διὰ γὰρ τὸ μὴ αὐταρκεῖν δοκοῦσι συνελθεῖν, ἐπεὶ συνῆλθόν γ' ἂν καὶ τοῦ συζῆν χάριν.
>
> Political friendship on the other hand is constituted in the fullest degree on the principle of utility, for they are deemed to have got together for lack of self-sufficiency, when in fact they would have got together merely for the sake of living together.[198]

[Text 28]

> διόπερ τὸ ἴσον τὸ ἀντιπεπονθὸς σῴζει τὰς πόλεις, ὥσπερ ἐν τοῖς Ἠθικοῖς εἴρηται πρότερον.
>
> That is why equal reciprocation preserves city-states, as we have said earlier in the *Ethics*.[199]

---

196 Schroeder (1997), 45. See also Chapter Four Section 3.5.

197 See Judson (1997), 159, for the argument that this chapter interacts with Plato, *Republic* 369b5 ff., where the origins of communities (including the exchange of goods) is explained in terms of χρεία. Phrases like the "first and greatest of the χρεῖαι" (being food; the second is shelter, the third clothing) support an interpretation of χρεία as objective need (what X is *in want of*), instead of subjective want. This is compelling for the Platonic, essentialistic, understanding of χρεία, but does not in itself preclude a different notion of χρεία in Aristotle's ethics.

198 *EE* VII.X (1242a6–9); *transl. adapted.*

199 *Pol.* II.ii (1161a30–31); *transl.* Reeve (1998), *adapted.*

Political friendship holds the city together.[200] Need not only motivates two exchange partners to cooperate (T27); the existence of political communities such as the polis finds its origins in man's lack of autarky. The fundamental rationale of the existence of the polis is to secure an adequate livelihood[201] for living the good life:[202]

[Text 29]

> ἡ δ' ἐκ πλειόνων κωμῶν κοινωνία τέλειος πόλις, ἤδη πάσης ἔχουσα πέρας τῆς αὐταρκείας ὡς ἔπος εἰπεῖν, γινομένη μὲν τοῦ ζῆν ἕνεκεν, οὖσα δὲ τοῦ εὖ ζῆν. (…) ἔτι τὸ οὗ ἕνεκα καὶ τὸ τέλος βέλτιστον· ἡ δ' αὐτάρκεια καὶ τέλος καὶ βέλτιστον. ἐκ τούτων οὖν φανερὸν ὅτι τῶν φύσει ἡ πόλις ἐστί, καὶ ὅτι ὁ ἄνθρωπος φύσει πολιτικὸν ζῷον (…).
>
> A complete community constituted out of several villages, once it reaches as it were the limit of all-round self-sufficience, is a city-state; It comes to be for the sake of living, but it exists for the sake of the living well. (…) Moreover that for the sake of which something exists, that is to say, its send, is best, and self-sufficiency is both end and what is best. It is evident from these considerations, then, that a city-state among the things that exist by nature, that a human being is by nature an animal fit for living in a city-state. (…).[203]

In the process of the agglomeration of several villages,[204] a natural limit is attained the moment a polis is formed: a polis is the basic unity that reaches the "critical mass" required to enable its citizens not only to secure an economically sufficient standard of living, but also thereby to attain to a certain quality

---

200 In *EN* 1132b33a the formulation is τῷ ἀντιποιεῖν γὰρ ἀνάλογον συμμένει ἡ πόλις. Although it is tempting to imagine a conceptual difference between ἀντιποεῖν and ἀντιπάσχειν (the one more conducive to the active exercise of virtue, the other more corrective in nature), it is not clear to me if Aristotle makes such a difference. Interestingly, the author of the *Magna Moralia* states that it is the use of *nomisma* to facilitate exchange that holds together the *koinonia* of the polis (1194a23–25).

201 Cf. M. Schofield (1998), 42.

202 Aristotle distinguishes two kinds of self-sufficiency in the city: (1) "simple self-sufficiency" (being ἁπλῶς αὐτάρκης, *Pol.* 1328b18; 1275b21), with regard to living (*Pol.* 1328b17: πρὸς ζωὴν αὔταρκες), i.e. with regard to necessary things (ἐν τοῖς (…) ἀναγκαίοις αὐτάρκης, *Pol.* 1326b4–5; cf. 1321b17); (2) self-sufficiency with regard to the good life (αὐτάρκες (sc. the πλῆθος of which a polis consists) πρὸς τὸ εὖ ζῆν; 1256b32). Cf. Mayhew (1997), 40–48.

203 *Pol.* I.ii (1252b27–1253a3); *transl.* Reeve (1998), *adapted.*

204 *Pol.* 1252b16–1253a3; Cf. 1280b40–1281a1.

of life. The polis is the first community that allows citizens to rise above the struggle to merely survive and to aspire to live *a good life*,[205] as the polis is the smallest community that can provide for the material as well as immaterial preconditions of a good life.[206]

Hence, it is the *polis* that reaches the limit of self-sufficiency (αὐταρκεία)—not its citizens. The citizens are fundamentally dependent upon each other, as they form a community based on a division of labor and its correlate: exchange.[207] It is this exchange, the logical consequence of the division of labor in a polis, that Aristotle hails in his conception of a πολιτικὴ φιλία, the exchange relationship[208] between shoemakers, builders, farmers and doctors who exchange their products *because of* need (χρεία) and in accordance with proportionate reciprocity. As we have seen, this exchange need not be restricted to economic exchanges in our modern sense, but includes any exchange based on need and in accordance with reciprocity that underwrite the purposes of the polis.

Because of the size of the political community, such individual citizens may not know each other personally;[209] moreover, as the encounters may be brief and singular, they are conducted as one-off transactions on a *quid pro quo*-basis, satisfying the needs (χρεία) of two partners who briefly cooperate on a basis of utility (τὸ χρήσιμον) in ties that may be immediately dissolved once the joint goal is achieved—while *still*, on a systemic level, keeping the polis together because, by contributing to meeting the material and immaterial conditions of the adequate livelihood required for a good life they are the "realizations and expressions of political association".[210]

---

205 The 'good life' requires and incorporates adequate livelihood, but is itself something over and above the satisfaction of these economic needs. Cf. 1278b15 ff., 1280a31 ff., 1280b29 ff. 1291a22 ff., 1326b2 ff., *EN* 1297b14–16.

206 In *Pol.* III.vi (1278b1–29), there are three distinct motivations for human beings to form cities: (1) they desire to live together for its own sake (τὸ συζῆν), cf. *EE* 1242a7–9; (2) they come together for the sake of mere life (τὸ ζῆν αὐτό); (3) they are drawn together by the common good (τὸ κοινῇ συμφέρον) to the extent they can partake of noble living (τὸ ζῆν καλῶς). By (1) Aristotle denies that need is a sufficient condition to bring people together (cf. *EE* 1242a7–9); by (3) Aristotle reasserts that τὸ συμφέρον is, in the end, to be understood in terms of the noble.

207 Exchange is a fundamental condition of polis life where "one man is a carpenter, another a farmer, another a shoemaker, and so on." *Pol.* 1280b20 ff. Cf. Plato on division of labor in *Rep.* 369b–371e. Cf. Meikle (1995), 12 n. 7.

208 *Pol.* 1261a32; *EN* 1132b31. Schofield (1998), 42: "the friendship characteristic of citizens as such."

209 Irrera (2005), 581. But they *do* have direct contact with one another and know each other inasmuch as they have a common enterprise.

210 Schofield (1998), 42 ff. Hence, the polis has logical priority over its citizens as "does the

4.2 *Reciprocal Justice is Paying the Price*

Because political friendships always contain an implicit reference to the polis they form (they cannot be viewed in abstraction from the final end of the polis), there is a fundamental difference between a commercial transaction between a shoemaker and builder from the same polis, and one between a shoemaker and builder from two different communities.[211] This difference resides in the fact that between individuals from different cities there is no common system of court and magistrates that has jurisdiction over both; more fundamentally, there is no shared morality and shared understanding of values.[212]

This means that even in the minimal case where all that the shoemaker and the builder do is paying each other the fixed prices of their products, i.e. following the law, still the shoemaker and the builder contribute to the realization of the goals and aims of the polis.[213] A true polis is well-conducted, having *euno-*

whole over the parts". *Pol.* 1253a18–29. This approach may reconcile some of the diverging interpretations of πολιτικὴ φιλία. Cooper (1990) recognizes that Aristotle treats πολιτικὴ φιλία as a utility friendship, in 235 n. 18 he insists that πολιτικὴ φιλία is not a *personal* friendship. In reaction to this interpretation, Annas (1990) expresses scepticism as to the possibility of *all* citizens of a πόλις have some form of friendship with one another, because to Aristotle friendship is a personal relation that requires intimacy and shared activities. But Schofield (1998) makes political friendship too contingent, by assuming that the political association of which they are a realization is solely aimed at economic survival, at mere living, instead of the "good life".

211 This is indicated in *Pol.* III.9 where Aristotle makes clear that the bonds linking fellow citizens are not those that link individuals from different cities. People do not form cities on the basis of economic needs alone, i.e. for the sake of mere living (*Pol.* 1280a25–31), nor for the sake of defense, exchange or mutual utility (1280a33–b5). Cf. Cooper (1990), 229; Irrera (2005), 581.

212 In *Pol.* I.1 (1253a7–15) Aristotle argues that man's nature as a "social animal" (πολιτικὸν ζῷον) is revealed by the gift of speech that enables him to communicate not only pleasure and pain but also their conceptions about the long-term good and the common good. Price (1989), 194: "Understanding values needs a language; implementing them needs a city." Cf. Cooper (1990), 241. Thomas Hobbes too acknowledges the uniqueness of human being because of his capacity to communicate advantage and harm, just and unjust, but regards this capacity as a source of conflict and disorder, unique to human life, (T. Hobbes, *Leviathan*, [London 1968], 96, 100, 189–190), as "the trumpet of war and sedition" (*Of Man and Citizen*, [Garden City 1972], 168–169). Cf. Yack (1985).

213 Danzig (2000), 424: "Aristotle's insight is that what appears to be merely buying and selling is really an expression of social relations." Some commentators suggest that the tension between the utilitarian character of political friendship and the insistence of the moral objects of the polis can be reconciled by assuming a development of political friendship towards the ἠθικὴ variety of utility friendships. E.g. Cooper (1990), Alpern (1983), Price (1989), 195–199. Yack (1993), 116–118 objects, pointing out that Aristotle is highly critical of the character-based variety of utility friendships, deeming it unnatural and the cause of conflict (*EE* 1242a–b); see also Chapter Four Section 3. Whereas I

mia (proper organization),[214] and true *eunomia* implies a certain quality of a city's laws: they are more than mere contracts and protectors of the just claims individuals make against others;[215] they serve the purposes of the good life, aiming to bring about happiness for every citizen.[216] As happiness consists in an activity (i.e. the practice of ethical virtue)[217] within a system of justice and laws,[218] the task of the lawgiver is to secure the preconditions for every citizen to practise virtue.[219] Hence, the lawgiver must be concerned with education,[220] by promoting leisure[221] and a habituation[222] in practising intrinsically valuable activities.[223] Moral habituation, in turn, requires a legal system.[224] On a minimal scenario, the citizens have not yet internalized the laws they live by,[225] and

---

do not find Yack's objection fatal, I also disagree with Cooper e.a.: when "converted" into character-based utility friendships, political friendships cease to be (mere) relations typical for living in a polis and turn into "thicker" more personal relationships. Whereas from the point of view of the development of virtue Aristotle would certainly applaud that, such insistence on "conversion" does not do justice to the import of πολιτικὴ φιλία in its own right as underwriting the purposes of the polis. See Frank (2005), 151 for a different tack: "Advocates of use friendship as a model of political concord meet these objections by claiming that even if use friends do not themselves live the good life, their friendships nevertheless promote it." Schofield (1998), 49 points out that the corresponding passages in *EN* (1162b16, 1163a6) "lacks both the cynical tone struck in these quotations and their suggestion that ethical friendship is generally doomed to collapse into political."

214 *eunomia* is the end of political science. *EN* III.v (1112b14), *EE* I.v (1216b18).

215 The protection of such claims may be a necessary condition for the existence of the polis, but not its final cause. This minimalist theory of law that Aristotle is arguing against, here ascribed to Lycophron, has a parallel in Hippias' conception of law in Xen. *Mem.* IV.iv.13 and in Glaucon's explanation of the origin of justice on behalf of Thrasymachus in Plato, *Rep.* 358e3–359b1.

216 *Pol.* VII.ii (1324a23–25), VII.ix (1329a23–34).

217 *EN* I.x (1101a14–16), *EE* II.vii (1219a38–39, b1–2), *Pol.* VII.i (1323b21–23), VII.viii (1328a37–38), VII.ix (1328b35–36; 1329a22–23), VII.xiii (1332a21–25).

218 *Pol.* I.ii (1253a31–39).

219 *EN* I.xiii (1102a7–10), II.i (1103b3–6), X.ix (1179a35–b4); *Pol.* VII.xiii (1332a28–38).

220 *Pol.* VII.xiv (1333a11–16).

221 Higher activities of the soul are characterized by leisure. *EN* X.vii (1177b4–26). Leisure consists in intrinsically valuable activity. *EN* X.vii (1177b16–26); *Pol.* VIII.iii (1338a1–6).

222 *Pol.* VII.xiii (1332b10–11).

223 *Pol.* VII.xiv (1333a37–39), VII.iii (1325b20), VII.xv (1334a34–40).

224 Parents lack the compelling force of laws which is indispensable for habituation. *EN* X.ix (1179b23–1180a5).

225 Modern theorists have taken the distinction between contract and friendship as disjunctive. E.g. Barber (1984), 188–189 who draws an explicit contrast between "contract and friendship", between "an incorporated economic association (limited liability) and civil community." Aristotle regards the difference not in terms of a disjunction but in terms

behave in accordance with justice by abiding the laws out of a sense of personal advantage; at the other extreme, the moral habituation by abiding laws has resulted in an intrinsic disposition that supports their law-abidingness.[226] In both cases, the cooperative activities between fellow citizens are regulated by principles that aim at improving their moral quality. In a true polis, even the exchange between a shoemaker and a builder who are fellow-citizens is imagined to be conducted by laws designed to make citizens excellent—laws that differ fundamentally from covenants and treaties between communities.

Hence political friendships are not "political" in the sense that they are friendships between "politicians" within a distinct political realm;[227] nor are they "civic friendships" in the sense that they display a basic love, respect, sympathy or empathy between fellow citizens, although these emotions may very well result from and contribute to what friendship of the polis *is*: it consists in exchanges between fellow citizens in their quality as political animals—i.e. animals who not only like to live together,[228] but who need a community in order to realize their full potential.[229] These exchanges would not have been possible on a smaller scale than that of the polis, for only on the scale of the polis can division of labor be organized to such an extent that individual citizens have the means and the leisure to fulfill themselves.

5 Concluding Remarks

When Aristotle states that φιλία "keeps cities together", it is πολιτικὴ φιλία that he has in mind: the bond between two citizens who engage in exchange on the basis of proportional reciprocity in order to satisfy their needs. This need, χρεία, draws together both (1) the cooperative partnership of two citizens, by providing them with a common measure that enables them to exchange *and*, in a logically prior sense, (2) the cooperative community of the polis, by being the very reason for humans to get together. On the individual level, these utility friendships yield inferior bonds that are inherently weak, unreliable and easily dissolved—bound to cause disappointments and disagreements. On a

---

of different stages in the extent of virtue internalization and hence as a difference in the ethical development of citizens. See also Chapter Four Section 3.

226 Cf. Irrera (2005), 582.

227 Schofield (2002), 37, warns against the temptation to envision an idea of "the state as an authority from which we expect legal and institutional systems designed to ensure the fair treatment of any persons".

228 *EE* 1242a7–9; *Pol.* III.6 (1278b18–29).

229 Cf. *Historia Animalium* I.1 (488a7–488a14).

systemic level, however, political friendships produce the ties and joints that bind the polis as a whole together into a basic unit of livelihood and self-sufficiency. It is only in the context of these equal relations based on need that money can function as a representation of need. In all other relationships—in unequal utility friendships, pleasure friendships, virtue friendships—it is ultimately misguided to strive for equivalence and to use money as a measure of value.

However, the human interactions that Aristotle labels "political friendship" are only one subcategory of relationship types: only those that are based on need and that are ephemeral, taking place between citizens who do not know each other personally. Within these interactions, the partners of exchange are treated as equals *as if* their social status and worth are not relevant: they only need to look at the objects and establish equivalence between these. Hence, in a qualified sense, we may say that Aristotle articulates, and therefore conceptually "discovers", a distinct sphere in which human interactions and choices need not be guided by social and moral concerns. Nevertheless, even the ephemeral interactions taking place in this distinct sphere are fundamentally embedded in the political project of the polis and are therefore not free from moral and political considerations. Political friendships, between builder and shoemaker, sustain and legitimate the long-term order of the polis.

Epilogue: Hostile Worlds

> The economist (...) keeps the motivations of human beings pure, simple and hardheaded, and not messed up by such things as goodwill or moral sentiments. (...). [T]here is (...) something quite extraordinary in the fact that economics has in fact evolved in this way, characterizing human motivation in such spectacularly narrow terms. One reason why this is extraordinary is that economics is supposed to be concerned with real people. It is hard to believe that real people could be completely unaffected by the reach of the self-examination induced by the Socratic question, "how should one live?"
>
> AMARTYA SEN (1987)

•••

> Methodological individualism starts with an ultimate unanalyzable factor, the rational being sovereign over his own choices. This starting point gets in the way of any attempt to relate the structure of individual goals to the goals of an organized social environment.
>
> MARY T. DOUGLAS (1990)

∴

Who is the protagonist of the ancient economy? Is it the Homo Economicus, the rational individual maximizing his interests, the brainchild of John Stuart Mill, and the driving force of economic progress?[1] Or is it rather, as Max Weber insisted, the Homo Politicus, the status-maximizing head of the self-sufficient atomistic household?[2]

This is not the place to bring the long-superseded primitivism/modernism controversy back on an agenda far beyond the scope of this book.[3] This is just to

1 Mill (1844), Essay v, Ch. 3.

2 Weber (1968).

3 The "primitivist vs. modernist"-debate, also called the Bücher-Meyer-controversy centers around the question whether the ancient economy was similar to modern economies, despite differences in size and complexity. The "primitivists" (Bücher (1906), Weber (1968), Hasebroek (1931)) hold that the ancient economy was a closed household economy in which

 | DOI:10.1163/9789004416147_009

point out how the Homo Economicus and the Homo Politicus are conceptually similar. They are both individuals, embodiments of methodological individualism: the idea that the individual person is the building block of any reality accessible to social theory, and that statements about a social system must be reducible to statements about individuals and their properties and relations. The individual has logical primacy; relations are derivative and a function of individuals.

Of course, it would be hyperbolic to argue that ancient social theory did not bother about the individual. It would indeed be blatantly false. We have seen in this book how ancient moral systems are characterized by "ethical individualism" or "ethical egoism": they are eudaemonistic systems that hold that one's own good (that is: one's *genuine* good) is the ethical standard, the criterion for doing the right thing.[4]

However, we have also seen that in 4th-century moral discourse, notions such as use, wealth, value and equivalence, are understood as relational phenomena.[5] Moreover, I have tried to show how the relational counterpart to the Homo Economicus, the Purely Economic Transaction or the Perfectly Disembedded Exchange, is a fictional notion that has emerged from situations of isomorphism: ancient sources that treat retail sellers, shopkeepers, sophists and prostitutes as people acting outside the norms of φιλία, with a distinct mentality, tend to do so in situations of isomorphism. In other words, I have tried to make the case that for a deeper understanding of ancient economic thinking and social theory something can be gained by shifting the focus from conceptions and evaluations of the individual to the ways in which interpersonal relations and interactions are conceived.

The relational perspective is also crucial for understanding the workings of χάρις, the successful interaction as experienced from the inside;[6] for the semantics of ΦΙΛ-lexemes, that are first and foremost expressive of relations of solidarity;[7] for conceptions of virtue, beauty and wisdom, that arise out of and are enjoyed in friendly interactions[8]—*and* for the conception of emotions.

---

money was of little economic relevance. The modernists (Meyer (1899)) maintain that 5th-century Athens did know industrial production, international commerce and large-scale monetary exchange. The discussions are summarized in Schaps (2004), 18–26, Cartledge (2002), Andreau (2002), Von Reden (2010), 9–12; Engen (2010), 6–9, 20–35, Bresson (2016), 1–30.

4 Chapters Five and Six.

5 Chapters Five and Seven.

6 Chapter Two.

7 Chapter One.

8 Chapter Five and Six.

I have argued that in ancient Greek social theory, emotions are not seen as the causal basis, but as a natural consequence of a φιλία-bond. They are not understood as spontaneous givens, but as qualities emerging out of a successful interaction or a well-functioning relationship of mutual solidarity. Emotions are produced by relations and interpreted in terms of relations, rather than the other way around. You don't make people your φίλοι because you feel in a certain way towards them, but you feel this way because they are your φίλοι, because you share a φιλία-bond with them. In 5th- and 4th-century social theory, certain emotions too are best approached as relational phenomena.[9]

A follow-up question: if helping friends makes one a good friend, who is the best friend of all? Xenophon would say that among the human candidates the ultimate super-φίλος would be the mother, the greatest benefactor of all, donor of a χάρις so great that the recipient has "to know χάρις" irredeemably and endlessly.[10] For Aristotle, the best φίλος would be the philosopher with whom one engages in activities that exercise the virtues of both friends. The Aristotelian runner-up would be the benefactor who gives without any expectations of return. Our three candidates, again, share a common feature: they almost cease to be reciprocal. Xenophon's supreme active friend is the friend who, by giving so much that she cannot be compensated, almost places herself outside reciprocal φιλία.[11] Aristotle's perfect friends are not interested in the give and take of reciprocity, but only in exercising virtues—the virtues of pursuing wisdom, courage, and liberality (the virtue of *giving*). Aristotle's benefactor is the donor of a gift so perfect that it ceases to be potentially reciprocal. We here see a drive towards the asymmetrical, the irredeemable, the hierarchical and the no-longer-reciprocal—in short, towards the type of φιλία that dominated Hellenistic friendship theory. And we see here a foreshadowing of the Great Rift: that between the one-sided perfect gift and the reciprocal credit that always betrays ulterior motives.[12]

This great rift that has turned the gift into a selfless, one-sided allocation may be seen as the ultimate consequence of a Hostile Worlds Thesis—i.e. of a cultural reaction to the isomorphism of φιλία-reciprocity and market exchange. We have seen that reductionism, the Nothing-But approach, was a culturally available response to situations of isomorphism: in comic dismissals of χάρις

9 Chapters One and Two.
10 Chapter Three and Six.
11 Chapter Six.
12 Chapter Four.

as mere politeness, a euphemism or hypocrisy;[13] in the absurd idea that children are credit instruments;[14] in the idea that gifts are fake, merely credit in disguise.[15]

We have also seen how the Hostile Worlds thesis is more dominant in 5th- and 4th-century social theory: on a lexical level, in the use of the language of χάρις,[16] in conceptions of the parent-child bond, where thicker conceptions of obligation are articulated against the push of a Nothing-But worldview,[17] in the conception of the Debtor Paradigm of Obligation,[18] in the quest for the utility of friends[19] and in the valuation of pro-active friendship.[20]

My thesis has been that 5th- and 4th-century social theory witnessed the conceptual articulation of both φιλία-reciprocity and market exchange in a mutually dependent way. In this double trend, the potential isomorphism of χάρις-exchange or φιλία-reciprocity and market transactions has given rise to an understanding of friendly reciprocity that puts a premium on displaying and perceiving the subjective elements of reciprocal exchange: the dispositions, intentions, emotions and moral orientations that come with the give-and-take of friendship. These come to be seen as distinctive features of φιλία and χάρις-reciprocity. On the other hand, we have seen the articulation of the disembedded transaction—that, however, in the end, is understood by Aristotle as a form of φιλία after all: embedded in the long-term order of the polis.

This suggests that the scholarly debate on the nature of φιλία in the Classical Period is in an important sense misguided in its use of analytical distinctions, such as that between objective duties and subjective obligations, between instrumental relations and elective affinities, between self-interest and other-regarding behavior. If we aim to understand the Greek understandings of personal relationships, these oppositions are not suited as neutral tools for descriptive purposes; rather, they are themselves objects of inquiry, as they can be studied as social strategies and cultural constructs, arising from specific contextual conditions, such as the need to demarcate relationship types, to morally privilege one type over the other, or to legitimize a certain conduct and existing relations.

13 Chapter Two.
14 Chapter Three.
15 Chapter Four.
16 Chapter Two.
17 Chapter Three.
18 Chapter Four.
19 Chapter Five.
20 Chapter Six.

Bibliography

Aarts, J., "Coins, Money and Exchange in the Roman World. A Cultural-Economic Perspective", in: *Archaeological Dialogues* 12.1 (2005), 1–28

Adeleye, G., "The purpose of the *dokimasia*," *Greek, Roman, and Byzantine Studies* 24 (1983), 295–306

Adkins, A.W.H., *Merit and Responsibility: a study in Greek values*, Oxford 1960

Adkins, A.W.H., "Friendship and self-sufficiency in Homer and Aristotle", *Classical Quarterly* 13 (1963), 30–45

Agamben, G., *The Use of Bodies*, Stanford 2015

Alessandri, S., "κίβδηλος: Due passi nel lessico monetale (e dintorni)", *Atti della Accademia Peloritana dei Pericolanti* 72 (1998), 5–32

Alexander, J.C., *Fin de Siècle Social Theory. Relativism, Reductionism, and the Problem of Reason*, London & New York 1995

Alexiou, M., *The Ritual Lament in Greek Tradition*, Cambridge 1974

Allan, D.J., *The Philosophy of Aristotle*, Oxford 1970

Allen, D., "Greek tragedy and law", in: M. Gagarin & D.J. Cohen (eds.), *The Cambridge Companion to Ancient Greek Law*, Cambridge 2005, 374–393

Allison, J.W., "*Axiosis*, the new *arete*: a Periclean metaphor for friendship", *Classical Quarterly* N.S. 51.1 (2001), 53–64

Alpern, K.D., "Aristotle on the friendships of utility of pleasure", *Journal of the History of Philosophy* 21.3 (1983), 303–315

Alphen, E. van, M. Bal & C. Smith (eds.), *The Rhetoric of Sincerity*, Stanford 2009

Anderlini, L., & H. Sabourian, "Some note on the economics of barter, money and credit", in: C. Humphrey & S. Hugh-Jones (eds.), *Barter, Exchange and Value: an anthropological apprach*, Cambridge 1992, 75–106

Anderson, E., *Value in Ethics and Economics*, Cambridge 1993

Andreau, J., "Market, fairs and monetary loans: cultural history and economic history in Roman italy and Hellenistic Greece", in; P. Cartledge, E.E. Cohen & L. Foxhall (eds.), *Money, labour and land: approaches to the economies of ancient Greece*, London 2002, 113–129

Annas, J., "Plato and Aristotle on friendship and altruism", *Mind* 86 (1977), 532–554.

Annas, J., *An Introduction to Plato's Republic*, Oxford 1981

Annas, J., "The Hellenistic Version Of Aristotle's Ethics", *The Monist* 73.1 (1990), 80–96

Annas, J., *The Morality of Happiness*, Oxford 1993

Annas, J., "Virtue Ethics and the Charge of Egoism", in: P. Bloomfield (ed.), *Morality and Self-Interest*, Oxford 2007, 205–221

Antonucci, T.C., "Personal characteristics, social support, and social behavior", in: R.H.

Binstock, E. Shanas (eds.), *Handbook of Aging and the Social Sciences*, New York 1985, 94–128

Apelt, O., *Zur Eudemischen Ethik*, Weimar 1894

Appadurai, A., "Gratitude as a Social Mode in South India", *Ethos* 13.3 (1985), 236–245

Appadurai, A. (ed.), *The Social Life of Things. Commodities in Cultural Perspective*, Cambridge 1986, 64–91

Arendt, H., The Modern Concept of History. *The Review of Politics*, 20.4 (1958), 570–590

Armoni, C.A., *Liebestränke und Giftmord: Die Gestalt der Deianeira in den Trachiniaei des Sophokles. Mit einer Discussion über das Verständnis von φάρμακα bzw. φίλτρα in der klassischen Zeit*, Göttingen 2001

Arnaoutoglou, I., "Between *koinon* and *idion*: legal and social dimensions of religious associations in ancient Athens", in: P. Cartledge, P.C. Millett & S. von Reden (eds.), *Kosmos: Essays in Order, Conflict and Community in Classical Athens*, Cambridge 1998, 68–83

Arnott, W.G. (trans.), *Menander. Samia Sikyonioi, Synaristosai, Phasma, Unidentified Fragments*, Cambridge MA 2000

Asheri, D., A.B. Lloyd & A. Corcella, *A Commentary on Herodotus I: Books I–IV*, Oxford & New York 2007

Atwood, M., *Payback: Debt and the Shadow Side of Wealth*. Sydney 2008

Auhagen, U., *Die Hetäre in der griechischen und römische Komödie*, München 2009

Austin, J.L., *How to Do Things with Words*, Oxford 1962

Azoulay, V., *Xénophon et les Grâces du Pouvoir. De la* charis *au* charisme, Paris 2004a

Azoulay, V., "Exchange as entrapment: mercenary Xenophon?", in: R.L. Fox (ed.), *The Long March. Xenophon and the Ten Thousand*, New Haven & London 2004b, 289–304

Badhwar, N.K., "Why it is wrong to be always guided by the best: consequentialism and friendship", *Ethics* 101.3 (1991), 483–504

Badhwar, N.K., "Introduction", in: (id), *Friendship. A Philosophical Reader*, New York 1993

Bähre, E., "Reluctant solidarity. Death, urban povery and neighbourly assistance in South Africa", *Ethnography* 8.1 (2007), 33–59

Bähre, E., "Liberation and redistribution: social grants, commercial insurance, and religious riches in South Africa", *Comparative Studies in Society and History* 53.2 (2011), 371–392

Bal, M., *Narratology. Introduction to the Theory of Narrative*, Toronto/ Buffalo/ London 1997 [1985]

Balot, R.K., *Greed and Injustice in Classical Athens*, Princeton 2001

Balot, R.K., *Greek political thought*, Malden, MA 2006

Bammer, A., "Bronzen aus dem Artemision von Ephesos", in: O. Brinna & E. Friedrich (eds.), *Echo. Beiträge zur Archäologie des mediterranen und alpinen Raumes: Johannes B. Trentini zum 80. Geburtstag*, Innsbruck 1990, 21–35

Bammer, A., "Les sanctuaires des VIIIe et VIIe siècles à l'Artémision d'Éphèse", *Revue Archéologique* (1991), 63–84

Baracchi, C., "Beyond comedy and tragedy of authority: the invisible father in Plato's *Republic*," *Philosophy and Rhetoric* 34.2 (2001), 151–176

Barbon, N., *A Discourse upon Trade*, London 1690

Barker, E., *Political Thought of Plato and Aristotle*, London 1906

Barrett, W.S., *Euripides, "Hippolytos"*, Oxford 1964

Barringer, J.M., *The Hunt in Ancient Greece*, Baltimore & London 2001

Bartels, M.L., *Plato's Pragmatic Project: A Reading of Plato's Laws*, Leiden 2014

Basore, J. (transl.), *Moral essays*, Cambridge, MA & London 1928

Bassi, K., "The semantics of manliness in Ancient Greece", in: R.M. Rosen & I. Sluiter (eds.), *Andreia. Studies in Manliness and Courage in Classical Antiquity*, Leiden & Boston 2003, 25–98.

Bearman, P., "Generalized Exchange", *The American Journal of Sociology* 102.5 (1997), 1383–1415

Beekes, R., *Etymological Dictionary of Greek*, Leiden 2010

Beiner, R.S., *Political judgment*, London 1983

Belfiore, E., "Harming Friends", C. Gill, N. Postlethwaite & R. Seaford (eds.), *Reciprocity in Ancient Greece*, Oxford 1998

Belfiore, E., *Murder among Friends: Violation of* Philia *in Greek Tragedy*, New York/Oxford 2000

Benardete, S., "XPH and ΔEI in Plato and Others", *Glotta* 43 (1965), 285–298

Benveniste, E., "Gifts and Exchange in the Indo-European Vocabulary", *Problems in General Linguistics*, Coral Gables 1971

Benveniste, E., *Indo-European Language and Society*, London 1973

Benveniste, E., "Actif et moyen dans le verbe", *Journal De Psychologie Normale Et Pathologique* 43 (1950), 121–129

Berger, F. "Gratitude", *Ethics* 85 (1975), 298–309

Berlin, I., *The Hedgehog and the Fox: an Essay on Tolstoy's View of History*, London 1957

Bernstein, E., "The meaning of the purchase: desire, demand and the commerce of sex," *Ethnography* 2.3 (2001), 389–420

Berranger, D., *Recherches sur l'histoire et la prosopographie de Paros à l'époque archaïque*, Clermont-Ferrand 1992

Bett, R., "The Sophists and Relativism," *Phronesis* 34 (1989), 139–169

Bevilacqua, F., *Memorabili di Senofonte* (introduzione, nota bibliografica, testo critico, nota critica, traduzione e commento a cura di F. Bevilacqua), Torino 2010

Bicchieri, C., "Decision and game theory", in: E. Craig (ed.), *Routledge Encyclopedia of Philosophy*, London 1998, Retr. October 09, 2008, from https://www.rep.routledge.com/articles/thematic/decision-and-game-theory/v-1

Biernat, P., "Sacrifice in *Euthyphro* 14a–15b," *Classical Philology* 113.1 (2018), 330–340

Blank, D.L., "Socratic vs Sophists on Payment for Teaching", *Classical Antiquity* 4.1 (1985), 1–49

Blank, T., "Philosophy as *Leitourgia*. Sophists, Fees and the Civic Role of *paideia*", in: F. Carlà & M. Gori (eds.), *Gift Giving and the Embedded Economy in the Ancient World*, Heidelberg 2014, 377–402

Blaydes, F.H.M., *Analecta Comica Graeca*, Halle (Saale) 1905

Blok, J.H., "Interior designs. Approaches to the mind in the Greco-Roman world", *Psychoanalytische Perspectieven* 20.2 (2002), 155–170

Blok, J.H., "Perikles' citizenship law: a new perspective", *Historia* 58.2 (2009), 141–170

Blok, J.H., *Citizenship in Classical Athens*, Cambridge 2017

Blum, L.A., *Friendship, Altruism, and Morality*, London & New York 1980

Blum, L.A., "Altruism", in: L.C. Becker & C.B. Becker (eds.), *Encyclopedia of Ethics*, New York 1992, 35–39

Blundell, M.W., *Helping Friends and Harming Enemies. A Study in Sophocles and Greek Ethics*, Cambridge 1989

Blustein, J., *Parents and Children*, Oxford 1982

Bogaert, R., "La banque à Athènes au IVe s. av. J.C.", *Museum Helveticum* 43 (1986), 19–49

Bohannan, P. & G. Dalton (eds.), *Markets in Africa*, Chicago 1962, 1–26

Bolkestein, H., *Wohltätigkeit und Armenpflege im vorchristlichen Altertum: ein Beitrag zum Problem 'Moral und Gesellschaft'*, Groningen 1967 [1939]

Bolmarcich, S., "Communal values in ancient diplomacy", in: R.M. Rosen & I. Sluiter, *Valuing Others in Classical Antiquity*, Leiden 2010, 113–136

Bolotin, D., *Plato's Dialogue on Friendship: An Interpretation of the Lysis, with a New Translation*, Ithaca 1979

Bourdieu, P., *Outline of a Theory of Practice*, Cambridge 1977

Bourdieu, P., *The Logic of Practice*, transl. by Richard Nice, Stanford 1990 [1980]

Bourdieu, P., "Marginalia—Some additional notes on the gift", in: A.D. Schrift (ed.), *The Logic of the Gift: Toward an Ethic of Generosity*, London 1997

Bourdieu, P., *Practical Reason: On the Theory of Action*, Stanford 1998

Bourriot, F., *Kalos kagathos kalokagathia: d'un terme de propagande de sophistes à une notion sociale et philosophique: étude d'histoire athénienne*, Hildesheim 1995

Bowen, A. (transl.), *Xenophon: Symposium*, Warminster 1998

Brandt, R., "The Concepts of Duty and Obligation", *Mind* 73 (1974), 374–393

Bravo, B., "Remarques sur les assises sociales, les formes d'organisation et la terminologie du commerce maritime à l'époque archaïque", *Dialogues d'Histoire Ancienne* 3 (1977), 1–59

Bremer, J.-M., "The Reciprocity of Giving and Thanksgiving in Greek Worship", in: C. Gill, N. Postlethwaite & R. Seaford (eds.), *Reciprocity in Ancient Greece*, Oxford 1998, 127–137

Bresson, A., "Aristotle and foreign trade", in: E.M. Harris, D.M. Lewis & M. Woolmer (eds.), *The Ancient Greek Economy. Markets, Households and City-States*, Cambridge 2016, 41–65

Bresson, A., *The Making of the Ancient Greek Economy. Institutions, Markets, and Growth in the City-States*, translated by S. Rendall, Princeton & Oxford 2016

Broadie, S. & C. Rowe (transl.), *Nicomachean Ethics/ Aristotle*, Oxford 2002

Buccioni, E., "Revisiting the Controversial Nature of Persuasion in Plato's Laws." *Polis: The Journal for Ancient Greek Political Thought* 24.2 (2007), 262–283

Bücher, K., *Die Entstehung der Volkswirtschaft*, Tübingen 1906

Buffière, W., *Eros Adolescent. La Pédérastie dans la Grèce Antique*, Paris 1980

Bundy, E.L., *Studia Pindaria, I–II: The Eleventh Olympian Ode; The First Isthmian Ode*, Berkeley 1962

Burke, P., "Strengths and Weaknesses of the History of Mentalities," *History of European Ideas* 7.5 (1986), 439–451

Burkert, W., *Griechische Religion der archaischen und klassischen Epoche*, Stuttgart 1977

Burnet, J., *The Ethics of Aristotle*, London 1900

Butler, J., *Fifteen sermons preached at the Rolls Chapel*, London 1726

Buxton, R.G.A., Persuasion in Greek tragedy: A study of Peitho. Cambridge 1982

Cairns, D., *Aidôs. The Psychology and Ethics of Honour and Shame in Ancient Greek Literature*, Oxford 1993

Calame, C., "Entre rapports de parenté et relations civiques: Aphrodite l'hétaïre au banquet politique des hétairoi", in: F. Thélamon (ed.), *Aux Sources de la Puissance: Sociabilité et Parenté. Actes du Colloque de Rouen, 12–13 Novembre 1987*, Rouen 1989

Cambron-Goulet, M., "The criticism—and the practice—of literacy in the ancient philosophical tradition", in: E. Minchin (ed.), *Orality, Literacy and Performance in the Ancient World*, Leiden 2012, 201–226

Camp, J. McK., *The Athenian Agora. Excavations in the Heart of Classical Athens*, London 1986

Card, C., "Gratitude and obligation", *American Philosophical Quarterly* 25.2 (1988), 115–127

Carey, C., "Legal space in Classical Athens", *G&R* 41 (1994), 172–186

Carey, C., *Aeschines*, Texas 2000

Carlà, F. & M. Gori (eds.), *Gift Giving and the "Embedded" Economy in the Ancient World*, Heidelberg 2014

Carrier, J.G., "Gifts, Commodities, and Social Relations: A Maussian View of Exchange", *Sociological Forum* 6.1 (1991), 119–136

Carrier, J.G., *Gifts and Commodities: Exchange and Western Capitalism Since 1700*, London & New York 1995

Carruthers, B.G. & W.E. Espeland, "Money, meaning, and morality", *American Behavioral Scientist* 41.10 (1998), 1384–408

Carson, A., *Economy of the Unlost (Reading Simonides of Keos with Paul Celan)* Princeton 1999

Carsten, J., "Cooking Money: Gender and the Symbolic Transformation of Means of Exchange in a Malay Fishing Community", in: J. Parry. & M. Bloch (eds.), *Money and the Morality of Exchange*, Cambridge 1989, 117–141

Carsten, J., *After Kinship*, Cambridge 2004

Cartledge, P., *Agesilaos and the crisis of Sparta*, London 1987

Cartledge, P., *Aristophanes and his Theatre of the Absurd*, Bristol 1990

Cartledge, P., "The Economy (Economies) of Ancient Greece", *Dialogos* 5 (1998), 4–24

Cartledge, P., "The Political Economy of Greek Slavery", in: P. Cartledge, E.E. Cohen & L. Foxhall (ed.), *Money, Labour and Land: Approaches to the Economies of Ancient Greece*, London 2002, 156–166

Castoriadis, C., "From Marx to Aristotle, from Aristotle to us", *Social Research* 45.4 (1978), 667–738

Chadwick, J., *Lexicographica Graeca: Contributions to the Lexicography of Ancient Greece* Oxford 1996

Chamberlain, C., "The meaning of prohairesis in Aristotle's *Ethics*", *TAPA* 114 (1984), 147–157

Chamizo Dominguez, P.J. & F. Sánchez Benedito, *Lo que nunca se aprendió en clase, eufemismos y disfemismos en el lenguaje erótico inglés*, Grenada 2000

Chantraine, P., *Dictionnaire étymologique de la langue grecque: histoire des mots*, Paris 1968–1980

Chernyakhovskaya, O., *Sokrates bei Xenophon. Moral—Politik—Religion*, Tübingen 2014

Chernyakhovskaya, O., "Mechanisms of Pleasure according to Xenophon's Socrates", in: G. Danzig, D. Johnson & D. Morrison (eds.), *Plato and Xenophon: comparative studies*, Leiden & Boston 2018, 318–339

Christ, M.R., "Liturgy avoidance and antidosis in Classical Athens", *TAPA* 120 (1990), 147–169

Christ, M.R., *The Bad Citizen in Classical Athens*, Cambridge 2006

Citti, V., "Una coppia nominale in Lisia", in: M. Moggi & G. Cordiano (eds.), *Schiavi e dipendenti nell'ambito dell' "oikos" e della "familia"*, Pisa 1997, 91–96

Classen, C.J., "Xenophons Darstellung der Sophistik und der Sophisten", *Hermes* 112 (1984), 154–167

Coase, R.H., *The Firm, the Market and the Law*, Chicago 1988 [1937]

Codere, H., "Exchange and Display", *IESS* 239–245

Cohen, D.J., *Theft in Athenian Law*, München 1983

Cohen, E.E., *Athenian economy and society: a banking perspective*, Princeton 1992

Cohen, E.E., *The Athenian Nation*, Princeton 2000

Cohen, E.E., "Introduction", in: P. Cartledge, E.E. Cohen & L. Foxhall (ed.), *Money, labour and land: approaches to the economies of ancient Greece*, London 2002a, 1–7

Cohen, E.E., "An unprofitable masculinity", in: P. Cartledge, E.E. Cohen & L. Foxhall (ed.), *Money, labour and land: approaches to the economies of ancient Greece*, London 2002b, 100–112

Cohen, E.E., "Free and unfree sexual work: an economic analysis of Athenia prostitution", in: C.A. Faraone & L. MacClure (eds.), *Prostitutes and courtesans in the ancient world*, Madison WI 2006

Collard, C., *Supplices/Euripides*, Groningen 1975.

Conacher, D.J. (ed.), *Alcestis/Euripides*, Warminster 1988

Connor, W.R., *The New Politicians of Fifth-century Athens*, Princeton 1971

Cook, A.B., *Zeus: a Study in Ancient Religion*, Cambridge 1914–1940: Part II: Zeus god of the dark sky (thunder and lightning), 1925

Cooper, J.M., "Aristotle on the forms of friendship", *Review of Metaphysics* 30 (1977a), 619–648

Cooper, J.M., "Friendship and the Good in Aristotle", *The Philosophical Review* 86.3 (1977b), 290–315

Cooper, J.M., "Political animals and civic friendship", in: G. Patzig, *Aristoteles' Politik: Akten des XI. Symposium Aristotelicum: Friedrichshafen/Bodensee, 25.8–3.9.1987*, Göttingen 1990, 220–241

Cooper, J.M., "An Aristotelian Theory of the Emotions", in: A. Oksenberg Rorty (ed.), *Essays on Aristotle's "Rhetoric"*, Berkeley & Los Angeles 1996, 238–257

Cooper, J.M. (ed.), *Plato. Complete Works*, Indianapolis/Cambridge 1997

Cope, E.M., & J.E. Sandys, *The Rhetoric of Aristotle*, Cambridge 1877

Corey, D., "The case against teaching virtue for pay: Socrates and the sophists", *History of Political Thought* XXIII.2 (2002), 189–210

Corey, D., *The Sophists in Plato's Dialogues*, New York 2015

Courbin, P., "Obéloi d'Argolide et d'ailleurs", in: R. Hägg (ed.), *The Greek Renaissance of the Eigth Century BC: Tradition and Innovation*, Stockholm 1983

Cox, C.A., *Household Interests. Property, Marriage Strategies, and Family Dynamics in Ancient Athens*, Princeton 1998

Cozzo, A., *Kerdos. Semantica, Ideologie e società nella Grecia antica*, Roma 1988

Craig, E., "Monism", in E. Craig (ed.), *Routledge Encyclopedia of Philosophy*, London (1998)

Crespo-Fernández, E., "Sex-related euphemism and dysphemism: an analysis in terms of conceptual metaphor theory," *Atlantis* 30.2 (2008), 95–110

Cross, R. & A. Woosley, *Plato's Republic: A philosophical commentary*, London & New York 1964

Crump, T., *The Phenomenon of Money*, London 1981

Crump, T., "Money and Number: the Trojan Horse of Language," *Man* n.s. 13.4 (1978), 503–518

Cummins, W.J., "*Eros, epithumia* and *philia* in Plato", *Apeiron* 15 (1981), 10–18

Cuomo, S., *Ancient Mathematics*, London 2001

Dalton, G., "Barter", *Journal of Economic Issues* 16.1 (1982), 181–190

Daneš, J., "The political thought of the Suppliant women", *Graeco-Latina Brunensia* 16.2 (2011), 17–30

Danzig, G., "The Political Character of Aristotelian Reciprocity", *Classical Philology* 95.4 (2000), 399–424

Danzig, G., "Why Socrates was not a farmer: Xenophon's *Oeconomicus* as a philosophical dialogue", G&R Ser. 2 50.1 (2003), 57–76

Danzig, G., "Big Boys And Little Boys: Justice And Law In Xenophon's Cyropaedia and Memorabilia," *Polis: The Journal for Ancient Greek Political Thought* 26.2 (2009), 271–295

Danzig, G., *Apologizing for Socrates: How Plato and Xenophon created our Socrates*, Lanham MD 2010

Danzig, G., Johnson, D., & Morrison, D. (eds.), *Plato and Xenophon: Comparative studies*, Leiden & Boston 2018

Danzig, G., & D.M. Schaps, "The Economy: what Plato saw and what he wanted", in: F. Lisi (ed.), *Plato's Laws and its Historical Significance*, Sankt Augustin 2001, 143–148

Davidson, J.N., *Courtesans & Fishcakes. The Consuming Passions of Classical Athens*, London 1997

Davidson, J.N., *The Greeks and Greek Love. A Radical Reappraisal of Homosexuality in Ancient Greece*, London 2007

Davies, J.K., "Ancient Economies: Models and Muddles", in: H. Parkins & C. Smith (eds.), *Trade, Traders and the Ancient City*, London & New York 1998, 221–252

Davis, J., *Exchange*, Minneapolis 1992

Day, J.W., "Interactive offerings: early Greek dedicatory epigrams and ritual," *HSCP* 96 (1994), 37–74

Day, J.W., "Epigram and reader: generic force as (re-)activation of ritual," in: M. Depew & D. Obbink (eds.), *Matrices of Genre: Authors, Canons, and Society*, Cambridge 2000, 37–57, 248–254

Day, J.W., *Archaic Greek Epigram and Dedication: Representation and Reperformance*, Cambridge 2010

De Jong, I.J.F., *Narrators and Focalizers. The Presentation of the Story in the Iliad*, Amsterdam 1987a

De Jong, I.J.F., "Beiträge aus dem Hamburger Thesaurus Graecae Linguae I: Homeric κέρδος and ὄφελος", *MH* 44 (1987b), 79–81

De Jong, I.J.F., *A Narratological Commentary on the Odyssey*, Cambridge 2001

Delatte, A., *Le troisiéme livre des* Souvenirs Socratiques *de Xénophon*, Paris 1933, 148–161

Demont, P. "La formule de Protagoras: l'homme est mesure de toutes choses", in: P. Demont (ed.), *Problèmes de la morale antique*, Amiens 1993, 39–59

Denniston, J.D., *The Greek Particles*, Oxford 1950 [1934]

De Rijk, L.M., *Aristotle: Semantics and Ontology. Part* 1, Leiden 2002

De Saussure, F., *Course in General Linguistics*, New York 1966

Derrida, J., "The Time of the King", in: A. Schrift, *The Logic of the Gift: Toward an Ethic of Generosity*, London 1997

Desmond, W.D., *The Greek Praise of Poverty. Origins of Ancient Cynicism*, Indiana 2006

De Ste. Croix, G.E.M., "Greek and Roman accounting", in: A.C. Littleton & B.S. Yamey (eds.), *Studies in the History of Accounting*, London 1956, 14–74

Dickey, E., *Greek Forms of Address. From Herodotus to Lucian*, Oxford 1996

Diggle, J., *Characters/Theophrastus*, Cambridge 2004

Dindorf, L. & T. Thalheim (eds.), *Xenophontis Scripta Minora*, Leipzig 1910

Dirlmeier, F., *PHILOS und PHILIA im vorhellenistischen Griechentum*, München 1931

Dirlmeier, F. (ed.), *Aristoteles, Eudemische Ethik, übersetzt und kommentiert*, Berlin 1969

Dirlmeier, F. (ed.), *Nikomachische Ethik/Aristoteles*, Darmstadt 1979

Dodd, N., *The Sociology of Money*, Cambridge 1994

Dodds, R.T., *The Greeks and the Irrational*, Berkeley 1951

Donlan, W., *The Aristocratic Ideal in ancient Greece. Attitudes of Superiority from Homer to the end of the fifth century B.C.*, Lawrence 1980

Donlan, W., "Scale, Value and Function in the Homeric Economy", *American Journal of Ancient History* 6 (1981), 101–107

Donlan, W., "Pistos Philos Hetairos", in: Th.J. Figueira & G. Nagy (ed.), *Theognis of Megara. Poetry and the Polis*, Baltimore & London 1985 (a), 223–244

Donlan, W., "The social groups of Dark Age Greece", *CP* 80 (1985 (b)), 293–308

Dorion, L.-A., "Euthydème et Dionysodore sont-ils des Mégariques?", in: T. More Robinson & L. Brisson (eds.), *Plato: Euthydemus, Lysis, Charmides. Proceedings of the V Symposium Platonicum*, Sankt Augustin 2000, 35–30

Dorion, L.-A., "*Akrasia* et *enkrateia* dans les *Mémorables* de Xénophon", *Dialogue* XLII (2003), 645–672

Dorion, L.-A., "Xenophon's Socrates", in: S. Ahbel-Rappe. & R. Kamtekar (eds.), *A Companion To Socrates*, Malden MA, 2006, 93–109

Dorion, L.-A., "The Strausian Exegesis of Xenophon: The Paradigmatic Case of Memorabilia IV 4", in: Gray, V.J. (ed.), Xenophon, Oxford & New York 2010, 283–323

Dorion, L.-A., "The Nature and Status of sophia in the Memorabilia", in: Hobden, F. & C. Tuplin, *Xenophon: Ethical Principles and Historical Enquiry*, Leiden 2012, 455–475

Dorion, L.-A. & M. Bandini, *Xénophon: Mémorables, tome 2, 1re partie: Livres II–III*, Paris 2011a

Douglas, A.X., *The Philosophy of Debt*, London 2015

Douglas, M.T., "Converging on Autonomy: Anthropology and Institutional Economics", in: O.E. Williamson (ed.), *Organization Theory: from Chester Barnard to the Present and Beyond*, Oxford 1990, 95–115

Dover, K.J., *Aristophanes' Clouds*, Oxford 1968

Dover, K.J., *Greek Popular Morality in the Time of Plato and Aristotle*, Berkeley & Los Angeles, 1974

Dover, K.J., *Greek Homosexuality*, Cambridge MA 1989 [1978]

Dowd, K., "The invisible hand and the evolution of the monetary system", in: J. Smithin (ed.), *What is Money?*, London 2000, 139–156

Dubischar, M., *Die Agonszenen Bei Euripides: Untersuchungen Zu Ausgewählten Dramen*, Stuttgart 2001

Du Boulay, J., *Portrait of a Greek mountain village*, Oxford 1974

Due, B., *The Cyropaedia. Xenophon's aims and methods*, Aarhus & Copenhagen 1989

Dunbar, N. (comm.), *Aristophanes' Birds*, Oxford 1995

Duncan, R., "*Philia* in the *Gorgias*", *Apeiron* 8.1 (1974), 23–25

Durkheim, E., *On the Division of Labor in Society*, New York 1933

Du Val, G., *Aristotelis Opera omnia quae extant, graecè & latinè: Veterum ac recentiorum interpretum*, Paris 1629

Dyson, M., "Alceestis' children and the character of Admetus", *JHS* 108.1 (1988), 13–23

Ebeling, H., *Lexicum homericum*, Hildesheim 1963

Edmonds III, R.G., "Socrates the beautiful: role reversal and midwifery in Plato's *Symposium*", *TAPA* 130 (2000), 261–285

Edmunds, L., "Xenophon's Triad of Socratic Virtues and the Poverty of Socrates", in: G. Danzig, D. Johnson & D. Morrison (eds.), *Plato and Xenophon: comparative studies*, Leiden & Boston 2018, 252–276

Ehlers, B., *Eine vorplatonische Deutung des sokratischen Eros. Der Dialog* Aspasia *des Sokratikers Aischines*, München 1966

Eisenstadt, S.N., & L. Roniger, *Patrons, clients and friends. Interpersonal relations and the structure of trust in society*, Cambridge 1984

Ekeh, P.P., *Social Exchange Theory: The Two Traditions*, Cambridge Mass 1974

Emmons, R.A., "The psychology of gratitude: an introduction", in: R.A. Emmons & M.E. McCullough (eds.), *Psychology of Gratitude*, Oxford NY, 2004, 3–16

Engberg-Pedersen, T., *The Stoic Theory of oikeiosis*, Aarhus 1990

Engen, D.T., *Honor and Profit: Athenian Trade Policy and the Economy and Society of Greece, 415–307 B.C.E.*, Michigan 2010

English, J., "What do grown children owe their parents?", in: O. O'Neill & W. Ruddick (eds.), *Having children. Philosophical and legal reflections on parenthood*, Oxford 1979

Evelyn-White, H.G. (trans.), *Hesiod; the Homeric Hymns and Homerica*, New York & London 1914

Evens, T.M.S., "Bourdieu and the Logic of Practice: is all Giving Indian-Giving or is "Generalized Materialism" not Enough?", *Sociological Theory* 17.1 (1999), 3–31

Fantham, E., "Sex, Status and Survival in Hellenistic Athens: A Study of Women in New Comedy", *Phoenix* 29.1 (1975), 44–74

Fantham, E., "ΖΗΛΟΤΥΠΙΑ: A Brief Excursion into Sex, Violence, and Literary History," *Phoenix*, 40.1 (1987) 45–57

Faraguna, M., "All origini dell Oikonomia: Dall'anonimo di giamblico ad Aristotele", *Atti Della Accademia Nazionale Dei Lincei* v (1994), 551–589

Faraone, C.A., "The Wheel, the Whip and Other Implements of Torture: Erotic Magic in Pindar Pythian 4.213–19," *The Classical Journal* 89.1 (1993), 1–19

Faraone, C.A., "Deianeira's Mistake and the Demise of Heracles: Erotic Magic in Sophocles' Trachiniae," *Helios 21.2* (1994) 115–135

Faraone, C.A., *Ancient Greek Love Magic*, Cambridge MA & London 1999

Farenga, V., "La tirannide greca e la strategia numismatica", *Mondo classico: percorsi possibili*, Ravenna 1985, 39–49

Ferrari, G. "Socrates in the Republic", in: *Plato's 'Republic': A Critical Guide* Cambridge 2010

Festugière, A.J., "ΑΝΘ' "ΩΝ. La formule 'en échange de quoi' dans la prière grecque hellénistique", *Revue des sciences philosophiques et théologiques* 60 (1976), 369–418

Figueira, T.J., "Coins, Bodies, Games, and Gold (Review)", *AJPh* 121.4 (2000), 642–646

Figueira, T.J., "Economic Thought and Economic Fact in the Works of Xenophon", in: C. Tuplin & F. Hobden (eds.), *Xenophon: Ethical Principles and Historical Enquiry*, Leiden 2012, 665–688

Finkelstein, M.I. (= Finley), "Ἔμπορος, Ναύκληρος, and Κάπηλος: a prolegomena to the study of Athenian trade", *CPh.* 30.4 (1935), 320–336

Finley, M.I., "Classical Greece." in: *Deuxième conference internationale d'histoire economique, Aix-en-Provence 1962, Vol. 1: Trade and Politics in the Ancient World*, Paris 1965, 11–35

Finley, M.I., "Aristotle and economic analysis", *Past & Present* 47 (1970), 3–25

Finley, M.I., *The Ancient Economy* [1973], London 1985a

Finley, M.I., *Studies in Land and Credit in Ancient Athens*, New Brunswick 1985b

Firth, R., *Themes in Economic Anthropology*, Oxford 1970

Fisher, N.R.E., *Social Values in Classical Athens*, London 1976

Fisher, N.R.E. (trans. & comm.), *Aeschines/Against Timarchus*, Oxford & NY 2001

Fitzgerald, J.T. (ed.), Friendship, Flattery, and Frankness of Speech: Studies on Friendship in the New Testament World, Brill 1996

Forster, E.M., *A passage to India*, 1924, 254

Fortenbaugh, W.W., "Aristotle's analysis of friendship: function and analogy, resemblance and focal meaning", *Phronesis* 20 (1975), 51–62

Foucault, M., *The History of Sexuality: 2: The Use of Pleasure*, London 1984

Foxhall, L., "Household, Gender and Property in Classical Athens", *CQ* 39.1 (1989), 22–44

Foxhall, L., "Pandora unbound: a feminist critique of Foucault's History of Sexuality", in: N. Lindesfarne-Tapper & A. Cornwall (eds.), Dislocating Masculinity: comparative ethnographies, London 1994, 133–146

Foxhall, L., "The politics of affection: emotional attachments in Athenian society", in: P. Cartledge, P.C. Millett & S. von Reden (eds.), *Kosmos: essays in order, conflict and community in classical Athens*, Cambridge 1998, 52–67

Foxhall, L., *Olive Cultivation in Ancient Greece. Seeking the Ancient Economy*, Oxford 2007

Fraenkel, E., *Beobachtungen zu Aristophanes*, Rome 1984

Fragoulaki, M., *Kinship in Thucydides. Intercommunal Ties & Historical Narrative*, Oxford 2013

Frank, J., *A Democracy of Distinction: Aristotle and the Work of Politics*, Chicago 2005

Fredal, J., "Why shouldn't the sophists charge fees?", *Rhetoric Society Quarterly* 38.2 (2008), 148–170

Frede, D., "Mixed Feelings in Aristotle's Rhetoric", in: A. Oksenberg Rorty (ed.), *Essays on Aristotle's Rhetoric*, Berkeley & Los Angeles 1996, 258–285

Freese, J.H. (trans.), *Aristotle: The Art of Rhetoric*, Cambridge MA & London 1975

Frisk, H., *Griechisches etymologisches Wörterbuch*, Heidelberg 1970

Fritzsche, A.T., Epistula critica de locis quibusdam Ethicorum Eudemeorum, Leipzig 1849

Fürst, A., *Streit unter Freunden. Ideal und Realität in der Freundschaftslehre der Antike*, Stuttgart 1996

Furtwängler, A.E., "Neue Beobachtungen zur frühesten Münzprägung", *Schweizerische Numismatische Rundschau* 65 (1986), 153–165

Gagarin, M., *Antiphon the Athenian. Oratory, Law, and Justice in the Age of the Sophists*, Austin, 2002

Gallant, T.W., "Agricultural systems, land tenure, and the reforms of Solon", *ABSA* 77 (1982), 111–124

Gallant, T.W., *Risk and Survival in Ancient Greece. Reconstructing the Rural Domestic Economy*, Cambridge 1991, 143–169

Garland, R., *The Greek Way of Life: From Conception to Old Age*, Ithaca 1990

Gartner, C., "*Philia* in Aristotle's *Eudemian Ethics*", paper read on 10 November 2011 in the *Forum Antiquum Lecture Series* at Leiden University (unpublished).

Gauthier, R.A. & J.Y. Jolif (eds.), *L'éthique à Nicomaque/Aristote*, Louvain 1959

Geertz, C., *The Interpretation of Culture*, New York 1973

Geertz, C., "'From the native's point of view': on the nature of anthropological understanding", *Bulletin of the American Academy of Arts and Sciences* 28.1 (1974), 26–45

Gerber, D.E. (trans.), *Greek Elegiac Poetry: from the seventh to the fifth centuries* B.C. *Vol. I*, London & Cambridge MA 1999

Gernet, L., *Anthropologie de la Grèce antique*, Paris 1968

Gernet, L., "'Value' in Greek myth", in: R.L. Gordon (ed.), *Myth, religion and society*, Cambridge 1981, 111–146, 251–254

Gerrans, P., "Tacit knowledge, rule following and Pierre Bourdieu's philosophy of social science", *Anthropological Theory* 5.1 (2005)

Gianotti, G.F., *Per una poetica pindarica*, Torino 1975

Gigon, O., *Kommentar zum Ersten Buch von Xenophons Memorabilia*, Basel 1953

Gigon, O., *Kommentar zum zweiten Buch von Xenophons Memorabilien*, Basel 1956

Gilhuly, K., *The Feminine Matrix of Sex and Gender in Classical Athens*, Cambridge 2009

Gill, C., *Personality in Greek Epic, Tragedy, and Philosophy*, Oxford 1996

Gill, C., "Altruism or Reciprocity in Greek Ethical Philosophy?", in: C. Gill, C., N. Postlethwaite & R. Seaford (eds.), *Reciprocity in Ancient Greece*, Oxford (1998), 303–328

Glidden, D.K., "The *Lysis* on loving one's own", *CQ* 31.1 (1981), 39–59

Glotz, G., *La solidarité de la famille dans le droit criminel en Grèce*, Paris 1904

Godelier, M., *Horizon, trajets marxistes en anthropologie*, Paris 1977

Godelier, M., *L'Énigme du Don*, Paris 1996

Golden, L., "Euripides' Alcestis: Structure and Theme", *The Classical Journal* 66.2 (1970), 116–125

Golden, M., "Slavery and homosexuality in Athens", *Phoenix* 38 (1984), 308–324

Golden, M., *Children and Childhood in Classical Athens*, Baltimore 1990

Goldfarb, B., "The Conflict of Obligations in Euripides' "Alcestis"", *Greek, Roman and Byzantine Studies* 33.2 (1992), 109–126

Goldhill, S., *Language, Sexuality, Narrative: The* Oresteia, Cambridge 1984

Goldhill, S., *Reading Greek Tragedy*, Cambridge 1986

Goldhill, S., "The Great Dionysia and civic ideology", in: J.J. Winkler & F.I. Zeitlin (eds.), *Nothing to do with Dionysos? Athenian drama in its social context*, Princeton 1990, 97–129

Goldhill, S., *The Poet's Voice. Essays in Poetics and Greek Literature*, Cambridge 1991

Goldhill, S., "The seductions of the gaze: Socrates and his girlfriends", in: P. Cartledge, P.C. Millett & S. von Reden (eds.), *Kosmos: essays in order, conflict and community in classical Athens*, Cambridge 1998, 105–124

Gomme, A.W. & F.H. Sandbach, *Menander: A Commentary*, Oxford 1973

Gonzalez, F.J., "Plato's *Lysis*: an Enactment of Philosophical Kinship," *AncPhil* 15 (1995), 69–90

Gonzalez, F.J., "Socrates on Loving One's Own." *CP* 95.4 (2000), 279–398

Goodwin, W.W., *Syntax of the Moods and Tenses of the Greek Verb*, London 1897

Gottesman, "The beggar and the clod: the mythic notion of property in ancient Greece", *TAPA* 140 (2010), 287–322

Gould, S.J., *The Hedgehog, the Fox, and the Magister's Pox*, Cambridge Mass 2003

Gouldner, A.W., "The Norm of Reciprocity: A Preliminary Statement", *American Sociological Review* 25.2 (1960), 161–178

Graeber, D., *Toward an anthropological theory of value: The false coin of our own dreams*, New York 2001

Graeber, D., "Value: Anthropological Theories of Value", in: J.G. Carrier (ed.), *A handbook of economic anthropology*, Cheltenham, 2005

Graeber, D., *Debt. The First 5000 Years*, New York 2011

Gramm, W.S., "Economic metaphors: ideology, rhetoric, and theory", in: J.S. Mio & A.N. Katz (eds.), *Metaphor: Implications and Applications*, New Jersey 1996

Grant, A., *The ethics of Aristotle: illustrated with essays and notes by Sir Alexander Grant* 3d ed., rev. and partly rewritten., London 1874

Grant, J.N., "The father-son relationship and the ending of Menander's *Samia*," *Phoenix* 40.2 (1986), 172–184

Gray, V.J. (ed.), The Framing Of Socrates: The Literary Interpretation Of Xenophon's Memorabilia, Stuttgart 1998

Gray, V.J., "Xenophon Et Les Graces Du Pouvoir: De La Charis Au Charisme," *Classical Review* 56.1 (2006), 43–45

Gray, V.J. (ed. & comm.), *Xenophon on Government*, Cambridge 2007

Gray, V.J., *Xenophon's Mirror of Princes: Reading the Reflections*, New York 2011

Gray, R.T., "Buying into signs: money and semiosis in eighteenth-century German language theory", *The German Quarterly* 69.1 (1996), 1–14

Gregory, C.A., *Gifts and Commodities*, London 1982

Grierson, P., "The origins of money", *Research in Economic Anthropology* 1 (1978), 1–35

Griffin, M., "*De beneficiis* and Roman society", *The Journal of Roman Studies* 93 (2003), 92–113

Grimaldi, W., *Aristotle, Rhetoric: A commentary*, New York 1980

Grube, G.M.A., *Plato's Thought*, London 1958

Gummere, R.M. (trans.), *Ad Lucilium epistulae morales*, London 1917

Guthrie, W.K.C., *The Sophists*, Cambridge 2005

Hadot, P., *Philosophy as a Way of Life. Spiritual Exercises from Socrates to Foucault*, Cambridge MA 1995

Halperin, D.M., "Platonic eros and what men call love", *AncPhil* 5.2 (1985), 161–204

Halperin, D.M., "The Democratic Body: Prostitution and Citizenship in Classical Athens", in: *One Hundred Years of Homosexuality and Other Essays on Greek Love*, New York/London 1990a, 88–112

Halperin, D.M., "Why is Diotima a Woman?", in: *One Hundred Years of Homosexuality and Other Essays on Greek Love*, New York/London 1990b, 113–152

Halperin, D.M., "Questions of Evidence: Commentary on Koehl, DeVries, and Williams", in: M. Duberman (ed.), *Queer Representations: Reading Lives, Reading Cultures*, New York & London 1997a, 39–54

Halperin, D.M., *Saint Foucault: towards a gay hagiography*, Oxford 1997b

Hammond, M. & P.J. Rhodes (trans.), *The Peloponnesian war*, Oxford 2009

Hangard, J., *Monetaire en daarmee verwante meforen: studiën over het metaforisch ge-*

bruik van de terminologie van muntwezen, onderzoek en bewerking van edele metalen en zegelwezen in de Griekse literatuur tot Aristoteles, Groningen 1963

Hanink, J., "Epithaphioi mythoi and tragedy as encomium of Athens," *TC* 5.2 (2013), 289–317

Hardie, W.F.R, *Aristotle's Ethical Theory*, Oxford 1968

Harris, E.M., "Paul Millett: Lending and Borrowing in Ancient Athens", *The Classical Review* 43.1 (1993), 102–107.

Harris, E.M., "Workshop, marketplace and household: the nature of technical specialization in classical Athens and its influence on economy and society", in: P. Cartledge, E.E. Cohen & L. Foxhall (ed.), *Money, labour and land: approaches to the economies of ancient Greece*, London 2002, 67–99

Harris, E.M., "The legal foundations of economic growth in ancient Greece: the role of property records", in: E.M. Harris, D.M. Lewis & M. Woolmer (eds.), *The Ancient Greek Economy. Markets, Households and City-States*, Cambridge 2016, 116–148

Harris, E.M. & D.M. Lewis & M. Woolmer (eds.), *The Ancient Greek Economy. Markets, Households and City-states*, Cambridge 2016

Harris, E.M. & D.M. Lewis & M. Woolmer, "Introduction: markets in Classical and Hellenistic Greece," in: E.M. Harris, D.M. Lewis & M. Woolmer (eds.), *The Ancient Greek Economy. Markets, Households and City-States*, Cambridge 2016, 1–40

Harris, M., "History and significance of the emic/etic distinction", *Ann. Rev. Anthropol.* 5 (1976), 329–350

Harrison, E.B., "Charis, Charites", *LIMC* III, 191–203

Hart, K., "Heads or Tails? Two Sides of the Coin", *Man* 21 (1986), 637–656

Hart, K., "Money is always personal and impersonal", *Anthropology Today* 23.5 (2007), 12–16

Harvey, D., "Painted ladies: fact, fiction, and fantasy", in: J. Christiansen & T. Melander (eds.), *Proceedings of the 3rd Symposium on Ancient Greek and Related Pottery*, Copenhagen 1988, 242–254

Hasebroek, J., *Griechische Wirtschafts- und Gesellschaftsgeschite*, Tübingen 1931

Hasebroek, J., *Trade and Politics in Ancient Greece*, transl. by L.M. Fraser and D.C. MacGregor. London 1933. (Originally published as *Staat und Handel im alten Griechenland* [Tübingen, 1928].)

Hausman, D.M. & S. MacPherson, *Economic analysis and moral philosophy*, Cambridge 1996

Heath, M., *The Poetics of Greek Tragedy*, Stanford 1987

Heath, T.L., *Mathematics in Aristotle*, Oxford 1949

Hedrick, C.W., The Decrees Of The Demotionidai, Atlanta, GA 1990

Heisenberg, W., "Über den anschaulichen Inhalt der quantentheoretischen Kinematik und Mechanik", *Zeitschrift für Physik* 43 (1927)

Heller, A., *A Theory of Feelings*, Assen 1979

Helm, B, "Friendship", *Stanford Encyclopedia of Philosophy*, 17/5/2005

Helmbold, W.C., Plutarch's Moralia: in sixteen volumes. Vol. VI: 439a–523b, London & Cambridge, MA 1939

Hénaff, M. (*transl. by* J.-L. Morhange), *The Price of Truth. Gift, Money and Philosophy*, Stanford 2010

Henderson, J., *The Maculate Muse: Obscene Language in Attic Comedy*, New York 1991

Henry, M., *Prisoner of History: Aspasia of Miletus and Her Biographical Tradition*, Oxford 1995

Herman, G., *Ritualised friendship and the Greek city*, Cambridge 1987

Hewitt, J.S., "The Terminology of 'Gratitude' in Greek", *CPh* XXII (1927), 142–161

Heyd, D., "Supererogatory promises. A comment on Kawal's "promising and supererogation"", *Philosophia* 32.1–4 (2005), 399–403

Hicks, R.D. (trans.), *Lives of the Eminent Philosophers / Diogenes Laertius. 2 vols.*, London & Cambridge MA 1970–1972

Hickson-Hahn, F.V., "The politics of thanksgiving", in: C.F. Konrad (ed.), *Augusto Augurio: Rerum Humanarum et Divinarum Commentationes in Honorem Jerzy Linderski*, Stuttgart 2004, 31–51

Hindley, C., "*SOPHRON EROS*: Xenophon's Ethical Erotics", in: C.J. Tuplin (ed.), *Xenophon and his world*, Stuttgart 2004, 125–146

Hindley, C., "Xenophon on Male Love," in: Gray, V.J., *Xenophon*, Oxford & New York 2010 [1999]

Hirschman, A.O., *The Passions and the Interests: Political Arguments for Capitalism before its Triumph*, Princeton 1977

Hobbes, *Leviathan*, London 1968

Hobbes, *Man and Citizen*, New York 1972

Hobbes, *The Elements of Law, Natural and Politic. Part I: Human Nature*, Oxford 1999 [1650]

Hobden, F. & C. Tuplin (eds.), *Xenophon: Ethical Principles and Historical Enquiry*, Leiden 2012

Hochschild, A.R., "The commodity frontier", in: J. Alexander, G. Marx & C. Williams (eds.), *Self, Social Structure, and Beliefs: Essays in Sociology*, Berkeley & Los Angeles 2004, 38–56

Hochschild, A.R., "Emotional life on the market frontier," *Annual Review of Sociology* 37 (2011), 21–33

Hoey, A., "The name on the coin: metaphor, metonymy, and money", *Diacritics* 18.2 (1988), 26–37

Hoigard, C. & L. Finstad, *Backstreets: Prostitution, Money and Love*, University Park 1992

Hooker, J.T., "Χάρις and ἀρετή in Thucydides", *Hermes* 102.2 (1974), 164–169

Hooker, J.T., "Homeric *philos*", *Glotta* LXV (1987), 44–65

Hooker, J.T., "Homer, Patroclus, Achilles", *SO* LXIV (1989), 30–35

Hopper, R.J., *Trade and Industry in Classical Greece*, London 1979

Hornblower, S., *A commentary on Thucydides. Vol. I: Books I–III.*, Oxford 1991

Horsmann, G., "Athens Weg zur eigenen Währung: der Zusammenhang der metrologischen Reform Solons mit der Timokratischen", *Historia* 49 (2000), 259–277

Howgego, C., *Ancient History from Coins*, London & New York 1995

Huart, P., *Le Vocabulaire de l'Analyse Psychologique dans l'Oeuvre de Thucydide*, Paris 1968

Hudson-Williams, T., *The Elegies of Theognis and other Elegies included in the Theognidean Sylloge*, London 1910

Hughes, G.J., *Aristotle on Ethics*, London & New York 2001

Humble, N., "Xenophon's Philosophical Approach to Writing: Socratic Elements in the Non-Socratic works", in: A. Stavru & C. Moore (eds.), *Socrates and the Socratic Dialogue*, Leiden & Boston 2018

Hume, D., *A Treatise of Human Nature. 2 vols.*, New York 1959 [1739]

Hummel, P., "Philos. Motivation et démotivation étymologiques", *IG* 34 (1987), 36–41

Humphrey, C., "Barter and Economic Disintegration", *Man* N.S. 20.1 (1985), 48–72

Humphrey, C. & S. Hugh-Jones, *Barter, Exchange and Value. An Anthropological Approach*, Cambridge 1992

Hunt, P.A., *War, Peace, and Alliance in Demosthenes' Athens*, Cambridge NY 2010

Hunter, V.J., *Policing Athens. Social Control in the Attic Lawsuits, 420–320 B.C.*, Princeton 1994

Hupperts, C., *Eros Dikaios. Deel 1 Homoseksualiteit bij de Grieken in de 6e–4e eeuw: Gedrag en Moraal*, Amsterdam 2000, p. 39

Hurka, T., "Value and friendship: a more subtle view", *Utilitas* 18.3 (2006), 232–242

Huss, B., *Xenophons Symposion. Ein Kommentar*, Stuttgart & Leipzig 1999

Hutter, H., *Politics as Friendship: the Origins of Classical Notions of Politics in the Theory and Practice of Friendship*, Waterloo 1978

Hwang, K.-K., "Filial Piety and Loyalty: Two Types of Social Identification in Confucianism", *Asian Journal of Social Psychology* 2 (1999), 163–183

Hyland, D.A., "Ἔρως, Ἐπιθυμία, and Φιλία in Plato", *Phronesis* 13 (1968), 32–46

Iakov, D., "Der Redenstreit in Euripides' *Alkestis* und der Charakter des Stückes", *Hermes* 127.3 (1999), 274–285

Iakov, D., *Εὐριπίδης, Ἄλκηστη. Ἑρμηνευτική ἔκδοση*, Athens 2012

Inamura, K., *Justice and Reciprocity in Aristotle's Political Philosophy*, Cambridge 2015

Ingham, G., "Babylonian madness: on the sociological and historical "origins" of money", in: J. Smithin (ed.), *What is Money?*, London 2000, 16–41

Ingham, G., *The Nature of Money*, Cambridge 2004

Inwood, B., "Politics and paradox in Seneca's *De Beneficiis*", in: A. Laks & M. Schofield (eds.), *Justice and Generosity*, Cambridge 1995, 241–265

Inwood, B., *Reading Seneca Stoic philosophy at Rome*. Oxford & New York 2005

Irigaray, L., *This Sex which is Not One*, Ithaca 1977

Irrera, E., "Between advantage and virtue: Aristotle's theory of political friendship", *History of Political Thought* 26.4 (2005), 565–585

Irwin, T.H., Plato's Moral Theory: the Early and Middle Dialogues, Oxford 1977

Irwin, T.H., (trans.), *Nicomachean Ethics*, Indianopolis 1985

Irwin, T.H., *Aristotle's First Principles*, Oxford 1990

Irwin, T.H., "Who discovered the will?", *Philosophical Perspectives* 6 (1992), 453–473

Irwin, T.H., *Plato's Ethics*, Oxford 1995

Isaac, B.L., "Karl Polanyi", in: J. Carrier (ed.), *A Handbook of Economic Anthropology*, Cheltenham & Northampton 2005, 14–25

Jebb, R.C. (ed.), *Sophocles: the Plays and Fragments. Part I: The Oedipus Tyrannus*, Cambridge 1887

Joachim, H.H., *Aristotle, the "Nicomachean Ethics"*, Oxford 1951

Joël, K., *Der echte und der Xenophontische Sokrates*, Berlin 1901

Johnson, D.M., "Xenophon's Socrates on Law and Justice", *APh* 23 (2003), 255–281

Johnson, D.M., "Xenophon at his most Socratic (*Memorabilia* 4.2)", *OSAPh* XXIX (2005), 39–73

Johnson, D.M., "Strauss on Xenophon", in: F. Hobden & C. Tuplin (eds.), *Xenophon: Ethical Principles and Historical Enquiry*, Leiden & Boston 2012, 123–159

Johnstone, S., "Virtuous toil, vicious work: Xenophon on Aristocratic style", *CPh* 89 (1994), 219–240

Johnstone, S., *A History of Trust in Ancient Greece*, Chicago & London 2011

Jonkers, G., *Moeten. Griekse Hulpwerkwoorden van Modaliteit*, Amsterdam 1981 (unpublished MA-thesis at VU University Amsterdam)

Joosse, L.A., "Why a Philosopher Needs Others. Platonic and Stoic Models of Friendship and Self-Understanding," PhD thesis, Utrecht University 2011

Jouanna, J., "Rhétorique et Médecine dans la collection Hippocratique," *Revue Des Études Grecques*, 97.460, (1984), 26–44.

Judson, L., "Aristotle on fair exchange", *OSAPh* 15 (1997): 147–175

Juffras, D., "Sophocles' *Electra* 973–985 and Tyrannicide," *TAPA* 121 (1991), 99–108

Jursa, M., *Aspects of the Economic History of Babylonia in the First Millennium* BC*: Economic Geography, Economic Mentalities, Agriculture, the Use of Money and the Problem of Economic Growth*, Münster 2010

Kahn, C.H., "Aristotle and Altruism", *Mind* 90 (1981), 20–40

Kallet-Marx, L., *Money, Expense and Naval Power in Thucydides' History* 1–5.24, Berkeley & Los Angeles & Oxford 1993

Kallet, L., "The Athenian Economy", in: L.J. Samons II (ed.), *The Cambridge Companion to the Age of Pericles*, Cambridge 2007, 70–95

Kant, I., *Grundlegung zur Metaphysik der Sitten*, Riga 1797

Kaulbach, F. (ed.), *Immanuel Kants "Grundlegung zur Metaphysik der Sitten". Interpretation und Kommentar*, Darmstadt 1988

Kawall, J., "Promising and supererogation", *Philosophia* 32.1–4 (2005), 389–398

Kaye, J., *Economy and nature in the fourteenth century: money, market exchange, and the emergence of scientific thought*, Cambridge 1998

Keister, L.A., "Financial markets, money, and banking", *Annual Review of Sociology* 28 (2002), 39–61

Keller, S., "Four Theories Of Filial Duty", *The Philosophical Quarterly*, 56 (2006), 254–274

Kelly, J.D., "Fiji Indians and 'commoditization of labor'", *American Ethnologist* 19.1 (1992), 97–120

Kennedy, G.A. (trans.), *On Rhetoric: a Theory of Civic Discourse*, New York 2007 [1991]

Kenny, A., *The Aristotelian Ethics: a Study of the Relationship between the Eudemian and Nicomaechan Ethics of Aristotle*, Oxford 2017

Kenny, A., *Aristotle on the Perfect Life*, Oxford 1992

Kerferd, G.B., *The Sophistic Movement*, New York 1981

Kierkegaard, S., *Über den Begriff der Ironie mit ständiger Rücksicht auf Sokrates*, Düsseldorf & Köln 1961 [1841]

Kim, H.S., "Archaic coinage as evidence for the use of money", in: A. Meadows & K. Shipton (eds.), *Money and its uses in the ancient Greek world*, Oxford 2001

Kim, H.S., "Small change and the moneyed economy", in: P. Cartledge, E.E. Cohen & L. Foxhall (ed.), *Money, labour and land: approaches to the economies of ancient Greece*, London 2002, 44–51

Klamer, A. & T.C. Leonard, "So what's an economic metaphor?", in: P. Mirowski (ed.), *Natural images in Economic Thought: Markets Read in Tooth and Claw*, Cambridge 1994, 20–54

Klein, P. & G. Selgin, "Menger's theory of money: some empirical evidence", in: J. Smithin (ed.), *What is Money?*, London 2000, 217–251

Klein, J., *Greek Mathematical Thought and the Origin of Algebra*, (transl. by E. Brann), Cambridge MA, 1968

Koch-Harnack, G., *Knabenliebe und Tiergeschenke. Ihre Bedeutung im päderastischen Erziehungssystem Athens*, Berlin 1983

Konstan, D., "Greek friendship", *AJP* 117.1 (1996), 71–94

Konstan, D., *Friendship in the classical world*, Cambridge 1997

Konstan, D., "Reciprocity and Friendship", in: C. Gill, N. Postlethwaite & R. Seaford (eds.), *Reciprocity in Ancient Greece*, Oxford 1998

Konstan, D., "Altruism", *TAPA* 130 (2000a), 1–17

Konstan, D., "οἰκία δ' ἐστί τις φιλία: Love and the Greek family," *Syllecta Classica* 11 (2000b), 106–126

Konstan, D., *The Emotions of the Ancient Greeks. Studies in Aristotle and Classical Literature*, Toronto/ Buffalo/ London 2006

Konstan, D., "'Can't Buy Me Love': The Economy of Gifts in Amorous Relations", in: M. Satlow (ed.), *The Gift in Antiquity*, Malden Mass 2013, 960196

Konstan, D., *In the Orbit of Love: Affection in Ancient Greece and Rome*, Oxford 2018

Kopytoff, "The cultural biography of things: commoditisaton as process", in: A. Appadurai (ed.), *The Social Life of Things: Commodities in Cultural Perspective*, Cambridge 1986, 64–91

Korn, R. & L.W. McCorkle, "Resocialization within walls", *Annals of the American Academy of Political and Social Science* 293 (1954), 88–98

Korver, J., *De terminologie van het crediet-wezen in het Grieksch*, Amsterdam 1934

Kovacs, D. (trans.), *Euripides: Children of Heracles, Hippolytus, Andromache, Hecabe*, Cambridge MA 1995

Kovacs, D. (trans.), *Euripides: Suppliant Women, Electra, Heracles, Trojan Women*, Cambridge MA 1998

Kovacs, D. (trans.), *Euripides: Cyclops, Alcestis, Medea*, Cambridge MA 2001

Kraay, C.M., "Hoards, small change and the origin of coinage", *JHS* 84 (1964), 76–91

Kraay, C.M., *Greek Coins*, London 1966

Kränzlein, A., *Eigentum und Besitz im griechischen Recht des fünften und vierten Jahrhunderts v. Chr.*, Berlin 1963

Kraut, R., *Aristotle on the Human Good*, Princeton 1989

Kraut, R., *Aristotle: Political Philosophy*, Oxford 2002

Kretschmer, P., "Griechisch φίλος", *Indogermanische Forschungen* 45 (1927), 267–271

Kroll, J.H., "From Wappenmünzen to gorgoneia to owls", *The American Numismatic Society Museum Notes* 26 (1981), 1–32

Kroll, J.H., "Silver in Solon's Laws", in: R. Ashton & S. Hurter (eds.), *Studies in Greek Numismatics in Memory of Martin Jessop Price*, London 1998, 535–544

Kühner, R., *Xenophons Memorabilien*, Leipzig 1882

Kühner, R. & B. Gerth e.a., *Ausführliche Grammatik der griechischen Sprache. 3 vol.*, Hannover 1890–1965

Kundera, M., *The Unbearable Lightness of Being*, London 1984

Kurke, L., "*Kapêleia* and Deceit", *AJPh* 110 (1989), 535–544

Kurke, L., *The Traffic in Praise*, Ithaca & London 1991

Kurke, L., "Inventing the *hetaira*: sex, politics, and discursive conflict in Archaic Greece", *Classical Antiquity* 16.1 (1997), 106–154

Kurke, L., *Coins, bodies, games, and gold: the politics of meaning in archaic Greece*, Princeton 1999

Kurke, L., "Money and mythic history: the contestation of transactional orders in the fifth century BC", in: W. Scheidel & S. von Reden (eds.), *The Ancient Economy*, New York 2002

Kurke, L., "'Counterfeit oracles' and 'legal tender': the politics of oracular consultation in Herodotus", *CW* 102.4 (2009), 417–438

L'Allier, L., "Why did Xenophon write the Last Chapter of the *Cynegeticus*", in: C. Tuplin

& F. Hobden (eds.), *Xenophon: Ethical Principles and Historical Enquiry*, Leiden 2012, 477–498

Lacey, W.K., *The Family in Classical Greece*, London 1968

Lakoff, G., "The contemporary theory of metaphor", in: A. Ortony (ed.), *Metaphor and Thought*, Cambridge 1993, 202–351

Lakoff, G. & M. Johnson, *Metaphors we live by*, Chicago 1980

Lakoff, R.T., *The Language War*, Berkeley & Los Angeles 2000

Lamb, W.R.M., *Plato: Laches; Protagoras; Meno; Euthydemus*, London & Cambridge, MA 1924

Langacker, R.W., *Foundations of Cognitive Grammar II: Descriptive Application*, Stanford 1991

Lanni, A., "Social Norms in the Courts of Ancient Athens", *Journal of Legal Analysis* 1.2 (2009), 691–736

Lapavitsas, C., "The social relations of money as a universal equivalent: a response to Ingham", *Economy and Society* 34.3 (2005), 389–403

Lape, S., *Reproducing Athens. Menander's Comedy, Democratic Culture, and the Hellenistic City*, Princeton & Oxford 2004

Lardinois, A., "Wisdom in Context: the Use of Gnomic Statements in Archaic Greek Poetry", Ph.D. diss. Princeton University 1995

Larson, J., *Greek Nymphs: Myth, Cult, Lore*, Oxford 2001

Larson, J., *Understanding Greek Religion*, London 2007

Lasch, C., *Haven in a Heartless World: The Family Besieged*, New York 1977

Latacz, J., *Zum Wortfeld Freude in der Sprache Homers*, Heidelberg 1966

Latacz, J., *Homers Ilias: Gesammtkommentar auf der Grundlage der Ausgabe von Ameis-Hentze-Cauer (1868–1913)*, München 2000

Laum, B., *Heiliges Geld*, Tübingen 1924

Lea, S.E.G. & P. Webley, "Money as tool, money as drug: the biological psychology of a strong incentive", *Behavioral and Brain Sciences* 29.2 (2006), 161–209

Lefèvre, E., "Die Frage nach dem ΒΙΟΣ ΕΥΔΑΙΜΩΝ. Die Begegnung zwischen Kyros und Kroisos bei Xenophon", *Hermes* 99 (1971), 283–296

Leighton, S.R., "Aristotle and the Emotions", in: A. Oksenberg Rorty (ed.), *Essays on Aristotle's "Rhetoric"*, Berkeley & Los Angeles 1996, 206–237

Le Rider, G., *La naissance de la monnaie*, Paris 2001

Lévi-Strauss, C., *The Elementary Structures of Kinship*, Boston 1969

Levin, D.N., "Some observations concerning Plato's *Lysis*", in: J.P. Anton & G.L. Justas (eds.), *Essays in Ancient Greek Philosophy*, Albany NY 1971

Levine, D.B., "Symposium and the polis", in: T.J. Figueira & G. Nagy (eds.), *Theognis of Megara. Poetry and the Polis*, 1985, 176–196

Lewis, S., *News and Society in the Greek Polis*, Chapel Hill 1996

Liddel, P., *Civic Obligation and Individual Liberty in Ancient Athens*, Oxford 2007

Lind, L.R. "Socrates and the Ladies." *Classical and Modern Literature: A Quarterly* 17.4 (1997), 287–292

LiPuma, E., "The meaning of money in the age of modernity", in: D. Akin & J. Robbins (eds.), *Money and Modernity: State and Local Currencies in Melanesia*, Pittsburgh 1999, 192–213

Lloyd, M., *The Agon in Euripides*, Oxford 1992

Lloyd-Jones, H. (trans.), *Sophocles. Vol. 1*, London & Cambridge MA 1994

Locke, J., *An Essay concerning Human Understanding*, edited by A.C. Fraser, Oxford 1894

Loomis, W.T., *Wages, Welfare Costs and Inflation in Classical Athens*, Michigan 1998

Loraux, N., *The Invention of Athens. The Funeral Oration in the Classical City*, Cambridge MA 2006

Love, J., *Antiquity and Capitalism*, London 1991

Löw, O., *ΧΑΡΙΣ*, Cambridge 1908

Loomis, W.T., *Wages, Welfare Costs and Inflation in Classical Athens*, Ann Arbor 1998

Loraux, N., *The Invention of Athens. The Funeral Oration in the Classical City*, translated by A. Sheridan, New York (2006 [1981])

Lowry, S.T., "Recent Literature on Ancient Greek Economic Thought." *Journal of Economic Literature* 17 (1979), 65–86

Lowry, S.T., *The Archaeology of Economic Ideas: the Classical Greek Tradition*, Durham 1987

Lowry, S.T., "The economic and jurisprudential ideas of the Ancient Greeks: our heritage from hellenic thought", in: S.T. Lowry & B. Gordon (eds.), *Ancient and Medieval Economic Ideas and Concepts of Social Justice*, Leiden 1998, 11–38

Ludwig, P.W., *Eros and Polis. Desire and Community in Greek Political Theory*, Cambridge 2002

Luschnig, C.A.E. & H. Roisman, *Euripides' Alcestis*, Norman 2003

Lyons, D.J., "Dangerous gifts: ideologies of marriage and exchange in ancient Greece", *ClAnt* 22.1 (2003), 93–134

Lyons, J., *Structural Semantics: an Analysis of Part of the Vocabulary of Plato*, London 1963

Lyons, J., *Introduction to Theoretical Linguistics*, Cambridge 1968

Lyons, J., *Linguistic Semantics: an Introduction*, Cambridge 1995

MacCormack, G., "Reciprocity", *Man* NS 11.1 (1976), 89–103

MacDowell, D.M., *The Law in Classical Athens*, Ithaca, 1978

MacDowell, D.M., *Demosthenes the Orator*, Oxford 2009

MacFarlane, A., "The Root of All Evil", in: D. Parkin (ed.), *The Anthropology of Evil*, Oxford 1985

MacIntyre, A., "Egoism and altruism", in: P. Edwards (ed.), *The Encyclopedia of Philosophy* II, New York 1972, 462–466

MacLachlan, B., *The Age of Grace.* Charis *in early Greek poetry*, Princeton 1993

Macve, R.H., "Some glosses on Ste. Croix's Greek and Roman accounting", *History of Political Thought* VI (1985), 233–264

Maier, G., *Eranos als Kreditinstitut*, Erlangen 1969

Malinowski, B., *Argonauts of the Western Pacific. An Account of Native Enterprise and Adventure in the Archipelagoes of Melanesian New Guinea*, London 1922

Mannebach, E. (ed.), *Aristippi et Cyrenaicorum Fragmenta*, Leiden & Köln 1961

Marchant, E.C. & O.J. Todd, (transl.) *Xenophon: In seven volumes. 4: Memorabilia and Oeconomicus*, Cambridge MA & London 1968

Mastronarde, D.J., *Medea*, Cambridge 2002

Maurer, B., "The anthropology of money", *Annual Review of Anthropology* 35 (2006), 15–36

Marx, K., *Das Kapital*, Vol. 1 [1867], Berlin 1962

Mayhew, R., *Aristotle's Criticism of Plato's Republic*, Maryland 1997

Mayhew, R., *Prodicus the Sophist: Texts, Translations, and Commentary*, Oxford 2011

McClure, L., *Courtesans at Table: Gender and Greek Literary Culture in Athnaeus*, New York 2003

McPherran, M.L., "Justice and Pollution in the Euthyphro," *Apeiron* 35.2 (2002), 105–130.

McPherran, M.L., "Socrates and Zalmoxis on drugs: charms and purification", *Apeiron* 37.1 (2004), 12–33

McPherran, M.L., "The Gods and Piety of Plato's Republic", in: G.X. Santas, *The Blackwell Guide to Plato's Republic*, Oxford 2006

Mei, T.S., "The preeminence of use: reevaluating the relation between use and exchange in Aristotle's economic thought", *Journal of the History of Philosophy* 47.4 (2009), 523–548

Meikle, S., "Aristotle on money", *Phronesis* 39.1 (1994), 26–44

Meikle, S., *Aristotle's Economic Thought*, Oxford 1995

Meikle, S., "Aristotle on business", *CQ* 46.1 (1996), 138–151

Meineke, A. (ed.), *Fragmenta Comicorum Graecorum*, Berlin 1970

Mele, A.R., "Choice and virtue in the 'Nicomachean Ethics'", *Journal of the History of Philosophy* 19.4 (1981), 405–423

Menger, C., "Geld", in: F.A. Hayek (ed.), *Schriften über Geld und Währungspolitik*, Tübingen 1909, 1–116

Merkelbach & West, *Fragmenta Hesiodea*, Oxford 1967

Mette, H.J., "Schauen und Staunen", *Glotta* 39 (1960), 49–71

Mette, H.J., "Moschion, ὁ κόσμιος," *Hermes* 97.4 (1969), 432–439

Meyer, E. *Die wirtschaftliche Entwicklung des Altertums*, Jena 1895

Mikalson, J.D., *Religion in Hellenistic Athens*, Berkeley 1998

Mikalson, J.D., *Greek Popular Religion in Greek Philosophy*, Oxford 2010

Mill, J.S., *Principles of Political Economy with some of their applications to social philosophy*, London 1848

Miller, C.R., "Blood Money: Death, Sacrifice, and Money in Plato's Republic," *Political Theory* 45.2 (2017), 216–239

Miller, W. (trans.), *De officiis*, Cambridge MA & London 1913

Miller, W. (trans.), *Xenophon: Cyropaedia. 2 vols.*, London & Cambridge MA 1914

Millett, P., "Maritime Loans and the Structure of Credit in Fourth-Century Athens", in: P. Garnsey, K. Hopkins & C.R. Whittaker (eds.), *Trade in the Ancient Economy*, Berkeley & Los Angeles 1983, 36–52

Millett, P., "Hesiod and his world", *PCPhS* CCX (1984), 84–115

Millett, P., *Lending and Borrowing in Ancient Athens*, Cambridge 1991a

Millett, P., "Sale, Credit and Exchange in Athenian Law and Society", in: P. Cartledge, P.C. Millett & S.C. Todd (eds.), *Nomos*, Cambridge 1991b, 167–194

Millett, P., "The Rhetoric of Reciprocity in Classical Athens", in: Gill, Chr., N. Postlethwaite & R. Seaford (eds.), *Reciprocity in Ancient Greece*, Oxford 1998a

Millett, P., "Encounters in the Agora", in: P. Cartledge, P. Millett & S. von Reden (eds.), *Kosmos: essays in order, conflict, and community in classical Athens*, Cambridge/New York 1998b, 37–51

Mirowski, P., "Refusing the gift", in: S. Cullenberg & J. Amariglio (eds.), *Postmodernism, Economics and Knowledge*, New York 2001, 431–458.

Mirowski, P., *Science Bought and Sold. Essays in the Economics of Science*, Chicago 2002

Mitchell, L.G., *Greeks Bearing Gifts. The Public Use of Private Relationships in the Greek World, 435–323 BC*, Cambridge 1997

Möller, A., "Classical Greece: Distribution", in: W. Scheidel, I. Morris & R.P. Saller (eds.), *The Cambridge Economic History of the Greco-Roman World*, Cambridge 2007, 362–384

Molm, L.D., J.L. Collett & D.R. Schaefer, "Building Solidarity through Generalized Exchange: a Theory of Reciprocity," *American Journal of Sociology* 13.1 (2007), 205–242

Monroe, K.R., "Altruism and self-interest", in: N.J. Smelser & P.B. Baltes (eds.), *International Encyclopedia of the Social & Behavioral Sciences*, Amsterdam/Paris/NY etc. 2001, 415–418

Mooring, J.A., B. Van Leeuwen & R.J. van der Spek, "Introducing coinage: comparing the Greek world, the Near East, and China," in: R.J. van der Spek & B. van Leeuwen (eds.), *Money, Currency and Crisis. In Search of Trust, 2000 BC to AD 2000*, Abingdon 2018, 132–148

Morris, I., "Gift and commodity in Archaic Greece", *Man* 21.1 (1986a), 1–17

Morris, I., "The use and abuse of Homer", *Class. Ant.* 5.1 (1986b), 81–138

Morris, I., "Circulation, deposition and the formation of the Greek Iron Age", *Man* 24 (1989), 502–519

Morris, I., "Lending and Borrowing in Ancient Athens", *Classical Philology*, 88.4 (1993), 340–346

Morris, I., "The community against the market in classical Athens", in: C.M. Duncan & D.W. Tandy (eds.), *From Political Economy to Anthropology: situating Economic Fife in Past Societies*, Montreal & New York 1994a, 52–79

Morris, I., "The Athenian economy twenty years after 'The ancient economy'", *CPh* 89 (1994b), 351–366

Morris, I., "Hard Surfaces", in: P. Cartledge, E.E. Cohen & L. Foxhall (ed.), *Money, labour and land: approaches to the economies of ancient Greece*, London 2002, 8–43

Morris, I., R.P. Saller & W. Scheidel, "Introduction", in: I. Morris, R.P. Saller & W. Scheidel (eds.), *The Cambridge Economic History of the Greco-Roman World*, Cambridge 2007

Morrison, D.R., "Xenophon's Socrates as Teacher", in: P. vander Waerd (ed.), *The Socratic Movement*, New York 1994, 181–208

Morrison, D.R., "Xenophon's Socrates on the Just and the Lawful", *Ancient Philosophy* 15.2 (1995), 329–347

Morrison, D.R., "Xenophon's Socrates as Teacher", in: V. Gray (ed.), *Xenophon*, Oxford & New York 2010, 195–227

Morrison, D.R., *The Cambridge Companion to Socrates*, Cambridge 2010

Morrow, G.R., *Plato's Cretan City: A Historical Interpretation of the Laws*, Princeton 1960

Mossman, J., "Women's voices in Sophocles", in: A. Markantonatos (ed.), *Brill's Companion to Sophocles*, Leiden & Boston (2012), 491–506

Mourelatos, A.P.D., *The Route of Parmenides. A Study of Word, Image, and Argument in the Fragments*, New Haven 1970

Moussy, C., *Gratia et sa famille*, Paris 1966

Müller, A., *Versuch einer neuen Theorie des Geldes, mit besondere Rücksicht auf Grossbritannien*, Leipzig 1816

Mueller, M., "The language of reciprocity in Euripides' *Medea*", *AJPh* 122.4 (2001), 471–504

Murray, A.T. (trans.), *The Odyssey Books 1–12/ Homer*, London & Cambridge MA, 1995

Nadon, C., *Xenophon's prince. Republic and empire in the* Cyropaedia, Berkeley & Los Angeles London, 2011

Naerebout, F.G., "Moving Events: Dance at Public Events in the Ancient Greek World", in: E. Stavrianopoulou (ed.), *Ritual and Communication in the Graeco-Roman World* (*Kernos suppl. 16*), Liège 2006, 37–67.

Nagel, T., *The Possibility of Altruism*. Oxford 1970

Nagle, D.B., *The Household as the Foundation of Aristotle's Polis*, Cambridge 2006

Nagy, G., "Theognis and Megara. A poet's vision of his city", in: T.J. Figueira & G. Nagy (eds.), *Theognis of Megara. Poetry and the polis*, Baltimore 1985, 22–81

Narcy, M., "La meilleure amie de Socrate. Xénophon, *Mémorables*, III 11", *Études Philosophiques* (2004), 213–234

Narotzky, S., "Economic Anthropology", in: N.J. Smelser & P.B. Baltes (eds.), *International Encyclopedia of the Social & Behavioral Sciences*, NY 2001, 4069–4073

Narotzky, S. & P. Moreno, "Reciprocity's dark side. Negative reciprocity, morality and social reproduction", *Anthropological Theory* 2.3 (2002), 281–305

Nehamas, A., *The Art of Living. Socratic Reflections from Plato to Foucault*, Berkeley/Los Angeles/London 1998

Neitzel, H., "Freundesjagd—zur Interpretation von Xenophon, Mem. 2,6,13f.", *Würzburger Jahrbücher für die Altertumswissenschaft* 7 (1981), 51–61

Nestle, W., "Die Horen des Prodikos", *Hermes* 71 (1936), 151–157

Neumann, J. von, "Zur Theorie der Gesellschaftspiele", *Mathematische Annalen* 100 (1928), 295–320

Neumann, J. von & O. Morgenstern, *Theory of Games and Economic Behavior*, Princeton 1944

Nietzsche, F., *On the Genealogy of Morals*, Essay 1, Sections 4–5, in: *Basic Writings of Nietzsche*, transl. Walter Kaufmann (New York, 1968), 498–501

Nietzsche, F., *Nachgelassene Fragmente 1885–1887*, Kritische Studienausgabe Herausgegeben von Giorgio Colli und Mazzino Montinari, München 1967–1977

Nightingale, A.W., *Genres in Dialogue: Plato and the Construct of Philosophy*, Cambridge 1995

North, D.C., *Structure and Change in Economic History*, New York 1981

Noutsopoulos, T., "The role of money in Plato's *Republic*, Book 1," *Historical Materialism* 23.2 (2015), 131–156

Nussbaum, M.C., *The Fragility of Goodness. Luck and Ethics in Greek Tragedy and Philosophy*, Cambridge 1986

Nussbaum, M.C., "Whether from Reason or Prejudice: Taking Money for Bodily Services," *The Journal of Legal Studies*, 27.s2 (1998), 693–723

Nussbaum, M.C., *The Upheavals of Thought: The Intelligence of Emotions*, Cambridge 2001

Ober, J., *Mass and Elite in Democratic Athens. Rhetoric, Ideology, and the Power of the People*, Princeton 1989,

Ober, J., *Democracy and Knowledge Innovation and Learning in Classical Athens*, Princeton 2008

O'Connor, D.K., "The Erotic Self-Sufficiency of Socrates: A Reading of Xenophon's *Memorabilia*", in: P. vander Waerd (ed.), *The Socratic Movement*, New York 1994, 151–180

O'Connor, D.K., "Xenophon and the Enviable Life of Socrates", in: D. Morrison (ed.), *The Cambridge Companion to Socrates*, Cambridge 2010, 48–74

Oksenberg Rorty, A., *Essays on Aristotle's "Rhetoric"*, Berkeley 1996

Ormand, K., *Exchange and the Maiden: Marriage in Sophoclean Tragedy*, Austin 1999

Osborne, R., "Pride and prejudice, sense and subsistence: exchange and society in the Greek city", in: J. Rich & A. Wallace-Hadrill, *City and country in the Ancient World*, London/New York 1991, 119–145

Osborne, R., "Pots, trade and the archaic Greek economy", *Antiquity* 70 (1996), 31–44

Osborne, R., *Greece in the Making. 1200–479 BC*, London 1996

Osborne, R., "Archaic Greece", in: W. Scheidel, I. Morris & R.P. Saller (eds.), *The Cambridge Economic History of the Greco-Roman World*, Cambridge 2007, 277–301

Osborne, R., "Sophocles and contemporary politics", in: K. Ormand (ed.), *A Companion to Sophocles*, Chicester 2012, 270–286

Osborne, R. & S.E. Alcock, *Placing the gods: sanctuaries and sacred space in ancient Greece*, Oxford 1994

Owen, G.E.L., "Logic and metaphysic in some earlier works of Aristotle", in: I. Düring & G.E.L. Owen (eds.), *Aristotle and Plato in the Mid-fourth Century. Papers of the Symposium Aristotelicum held at Oxford in August 1957*, Göteborg 1960, 163–190

Pack, S.J., *Aristotle, Adam Smith and Karl Marx. On Some Fundamental Issues in 21st Century Political Economy*, Cheltenham & Northampton 2010

Padilla, M.W., "Gifts of humiliation: charis and tragic experience in *Alcestis*", *AJPh* 121.2 (2000), 179–211

Pakaluk, M., *Aristotle. Nicomachean Ethics Book VIII and IX*, Oxford 1998a

Pakaluk, M., "The egalitarianism of the Eudemian Ethics", *CQ* n.s. 48.2 (1998b), 411–432

Panessa, G., "La philia nelle relazioni interstatali del mondo greco", in: N. Giuseppe & T. Gerhard (eds.), *Symposium 1988: Vorträge zur griechischen und hellenistischen Rechtsgeschichte: Siena—Pisa, 6–8 Juni 1988*, Köln 1990

Pangle, T.H., *The Socratic Way of Life: Xenophon's* Memorabilia, Chicago 2018

Parker, L., *Alcestis*, Oxford 2007

Parker, R.C.T., "Pleasing Thighs", in: C. Gill, N. Postlethwaite & R. Seaford (eds.), *Reciprocity in Ancient Greece*, Oxford 1998, 105–126

Parry, J. & M. Bloch (eds.), *Money and the Morality of Exchange*, Cambridge 1989

Parry, J. & M. Bloch, "Introduction: Money and the morality of exchange", in: J. Parry & M. Bloch (eds.), *Money and the Morality of Exchange*, Cambridge 1989, 1–32

Parry, J., "The Gift, the Indian Gift, and the 'Indian Gift'", *Man* N.S. 21.3 (1986), 453–473

Peacock, M.S., "Review Article: the origins of money in ancient Greece: the political economy of coinage and exchange", *Cambridge Journal of Economics* 30 (2006), 637–650

Pearson, H.W., "The Secular Debate on Economic Primitivism", in: K. Polanyi, C.M. Arensberg & H.W. Pearson (eds.), *Trade and Market in the Early Empires*, Glencoe Ill. 1957, 3–11

Pearson, L., *Popular Ethics in Ancient Greece*, Stanford 1962

Peek, W., "Attische Epigramme", *Mnemosyne*, 4.1 (1936), 1–16

Peek, W., *Griechische Vers-Inschriften*, Berlin 1955

Peels, S., *Hosios: A Semantic Study of Greek Piety*, Leiden 2016

Pelling, C., "Conclusion", in: C. Pelling, *Greek Tragedy and the Historian*, Oxford 1997, 213–235

Pendrick, G.J., *Antiphon the Sophist: the Fragments*, Cambridge 2002

Penner, T. & C. Rowe, *Plato's* Lysis, Cambridge 2005

Pentassuglio, F., "Socrates Erotikos: Mutuality, Role Reversal, and Erotic Paideia in Xenophon's and Plato's Symposia", in: G. Danzig, D. Johnsen & D. Morrison (eds.), *Plato and Xenophon: comparative studies*, Leiden & Boston 2018, 365–390

Pernot, L., *Epideictic Rhetoric*, Austin 2015

Perrotta, C., *Consumption as an Investment: Routledge studies in the history of economics 71*, London 2004

Peschel, I., *Die Hetäre bei Symposion und Komos in der attisch-rotfigurigen Vasenmalerei des 6.–4. Jh. v. Chr.*, Frankfurt 1987

Philipp, G.B., "Kritzeleien eines erleichterten Lehrers auf einem hölzernen Buchdeckel", *Gymnasium* 85 (1978), 151–159

Phillips, A.A. & M.M. Willcock (eds.), *Xenophon & Arian/ On Hunting (ΚΥΝΗΓΕΤΙΚΟΣ)*, Warminster 1999

Picard, O., "Philippe II et la monnayage des cités grecques", *REG* 103 (1990), 1–15

Pirenne-Delforge, V., "Les Charites à Athènes et dans l'île de Cos," *Kernos* 9 (1996), 195–214

Pitt-Rivers, J., "Postscript: the place of grace in anthropology", in: J.G. Peristinay & J. Pitt-Rivers (eds.), *Honour and Grace in Anthropology*, Cambridge 1992, 215–246

Pohlenz, M., *Aus Platos Werdezeit*, Berlin 1913

Pohlenz, M., "Review of Hans von Arnim, *Plato's Jugenddialoge und die Entstehungszeit des Phaidros*", *Göttingische Gelehrte Anzeigen* 178 (1916), 241–272

Pokorny, J., *Indogermanisches etymologisches Wörterbuch*, Bern 1959

Polanyi, K., *The Great Transformation*, New York 1944

Polanyi, K., "Aristotle discovers the economy", in: K. Polanyi, C.M. Arensberg & H.W. Pearson (eds.), *Trade and Market in the Early Empires*, Glencoe Ill. 1957b, 64–94

Polanyi, K., "The Economy as Instituted Process", in: K. Polanyi, C.M. Arensberg & H.W. Pearson (eds.), *Trade and Market in the Early Empires*, Glencoe Ill. 1957c, 243–269

Polanyi, K., *Primitive, Archaic, and Modern Economies: Essays of Karl Polanyi*, ed. G. Dalton, New York 1968 [1957]

Pomeroy, S.B., *Xenophon* Oeconomicus. *A social and historical commentary*, Oxford 1994

Pomeroy, S.B., *Families in Classical and Hellenistic Greece: Representations and Realities*, Oxford 1997

Porzig, W., *Die Namen für Satzinhalte im Griechischen und im Indogermanischen*, Berlin 1942

Price, M.J., "Thoughts on the beginnings of coinage", in: C.N.L. Brooke, B.H.I.H. Stewart e.a. (eds.), *Studies in Numismatic Method*, Cambridge 1983, 1–10

Price, A.W., *Love and Friendship in Plato and Aristotle*, Oxford 1989

Prichard, H.A., *Moral Obligation and Duty and Interest: Essays and Lectures*, Oxford 1968

Pulleyn, S., *Prayer in Greek Religion*, Oxford 1997

Quincey, J.H., "Greek expression of thanks", *JHS* 86 (1966), 133–158

Qviller, B., "The dynamics of the Homeric society", *SO* LVI (1981), 109–155

Rabinowitz, N.S., *Anxiety Veiled: Euripides and the Traffic in Women*, Ithaca 1993

Raccanelli, R., *L'amicitia nelle commedie di Plauto: un' indagine antropologica*, Bari 1998

Rackham, H., *The Nicomachean ethics*, London 1926

Rackham, H. (trans.), *The Athenian Constitution; The Eudemian Ethics; On Virtues and Vices / Aristotle*, London & Cambridge MA & London 1971

Rademaker, A.M., *Sophrosyne and the rhetoric of self-restraint. polysemy & persuasive use of an ancient Greek value term*, Leiden 2005

Ramsøy, O., "Friendship", in: D.L. Sills (ed.), *International Encyclopedia of the Social Sciences* 6 (1968), 12–17

Rauh, N.K. & P. Butler, *The Sacred Bonds Of Commerce: Religion, Economy, And Trade Society At Hellenistic Roman Delos, 166–87 B.C.*, Amsterdam 1993

Rédard, G., *Recherches sur χρή, χρῆσθαι. Étude Sémantique*, Paris 1953

Redfield, J.R., "Notes on the Greek Wedding", *Arethusa* 15 (1982), 181–201

Reece, A., "Drama, narrative, and Socratic *erôs* in Plato's *Charmides*", *Interpretation* 26 (1998), 65–76

Reeve, C.D.C. (transl.), *Politics*, Indianapolis 1998

Reeve, C.D.C. (transl.), *Nicomachean ethics*, Indianapolis 2014

Reinhold, M., "The Generation Gap in Antiquity", *TAPA* 114 (1970), 347–365

Rhodes, P.J., *A Commentary on the Aristotelian Athenaion Politeia*, Oxford 1981

Rhodes, P.J., "The Athenian code of laws, 410–399 B.C.", *JHS* 111 (1991), 87–100

Rhodes, P.J., "The reforms and laws of Solon: an optimistic view", in: J.H. Blok & A.P.M.H. Lardinois (eds.), *Solon of Athens. New historical and philological appraches*, Leiden 2006, 248–260

Ricardo, D., *On the Principles of Political Economy, and Taxation*, London 1817

Ricoeur, P., *Freud and Philosophy: an Essay on Interpretation*, Yale 1970

Risch, E., *Wortbildung der homerischen Sprache*, Berlin 1937

Risseeuw, C., R. Palriwala & K. Ganesh, *Care, Culture and Citizenship. Revisiting the Politics of the Dutch Welfare State*, Amsterdam 2005

Risseeuw, C. & M. Van Raalte, *Conceptualizing Friendship in Time and Place*, Amsterdam 2017

Ritchie, D.G., "Aristotle's subdivision of "particular justice"", *CR* 8 (1894), 185–192

Robb, K., *Literacy and Paideia in Ancient Greece*, New York 1994

Robbiano, C., *Becoming Being. On Parmenides' Transformative Philosophy*, Sankt Augustin 2006

Robbins, J. & D. Akin, "An introduction to Melanesian currencies: agency, identity, and social reproduction", in: D. Akin & J. Robbins (eds.), *Money and Modernity: State and Local Currencies in Melanesia*, Pittsburgh 1999, 1–40

Robertson, B.G., "The scrutiny of new citizens at Athens", in: V. Hunter & J. Edmonson (eds.), *Law and Social Status in Classical Athens*, Oxford 2000, 149–174

Robinson, D., "Homeric *philos*. Love of Life and Limbs, and Friendship with one's *thumos*", in: E.M. Craik (ed.), *'Owls to Athens'. Esaays on Classical Subjects presented to Sir Kenneth Dover*, Oxford 1990, 97–108

Rocchi, M., "Contributi allo studio delle Charites, I.", *StudClas* 18 (1979), 5–16

Roisman, H.M., "*Kerdion* in the *Iliad*: profit and trickiness", *TAPA* 120 (1990), 23–35

Roll, E., *A History of Economic Thought*, London, 1954

Rosch, E., "Cognitive representation of semantic categories", *Journal of Experimental Psychology* 104.3 (1975), 192–223

Rosen, S., *Plato's Republic*. Yale 2005

Rosen, R.M. & I. Sluiter (eds.), *Andreia: studies in manliness and courage in classical antiquity*, Leiden 2003

Rosen, R.M. & I. Sluiter, *Free Speech in Classical Antiquity*, Leiden 2004

Rosen, R.M. & I. Sluiter, *Valuing Others in Classical Antiquity*, Leiden 2010

Roskam, G., "Plutarch against Epicurus on Affection for Offspring. A Reading of *De Amore Prolis*", in: G. Roskam & L. van der Stockt (eds.), *Virtues for the People. Aspects of Plutarchan Ethics*, Leuven 2011, 175–204

Rosenzweig, R., *Worshipping Aphrodite. Art and Cult in Classical Athens*, Ann Arbor 2004

Ross, W.D., *Aristotle*, London 1923

Ross, W.D. (trans.), *The Nicomachean Ethics of Aristotle*, Oxford 1925

Ross, W.D. (trans. & intr.), *The Nicomachean Ethics of Aristotle*, London 1954

Rowe, C.J., *The Eudemian and Nicomachean Ethics: A Study in the Development of Aristotle's Thought*, Cambridge 1971

Rubinstein, L., *Adoption in IV. Century Athens*, Copenhagen 1993

Rubinstein, L., *Litigation and Cooperation: Supporting Speakers in the Courts of Classical Athens*, Stuttgart 2000

Rudebusch, G., "Neutralism in Book I of the Republic", in: D. Cairns, F. Hermann, & T. Penner (eds.), *Pursuing the Good: Ethics and Metaphysics in Plato's Republic*, Edinburgh 2007, 76–92

Ruhnken, D., *Xenophontis Memorabilium Socratis dictorum*, Leiden 1772

Ruiyao, L., "Shanghai says people who fail to visit parents will have credit status lowered," *Caixin Online* April 11, 2016

Sahlins, M., *Stone Age Economics*, London 1972

Samons, L.J., *Empire of the Owl: Athenian Imperial Finance*, Stuttgart 2000.

Santoni, A., *Senofonte. Memorabili: introduzione, traduzione e note*, Milano 1989

Sara Monoson, S., "Citizen as *Erastes*: Erotic Imagery and the Idea of Reciprocity in the Periclean Funeral Oration", *Political Theory* 22 (1994), 253–276

Saunders, T.J. (transl.), *Aristotle: The Politics*, London 1981

Saunders, T.J. (transl.), *Plato: The Laws*, London 2005

Sayer, A., "Bourdieu, Smith and Disinterested Judgement.", *The Sociological Review*, 47(3), 1999, 403–431

Scafuro, A.C., "Identifying Solonian Laws", in: J. Blok & A.P.M.H. Lardinois (eds.), *Solon of Athens. New Historical and Philological Approaches*, Leiden & Boston 2006, 175–196

Scafuro, A.C., *Demosthenes, Speeches 39–49*, Austin 2011

Scaltsas, T., "Reciprocal justice in Aristotle's *Nicomachean Ethics*", *Archiv f. Gesch. d. Philosophie* 77 (1995), 248–262

Scanlon, T.M., *What we owe to each other*, Cambridge (Mass)/London 1998

Schaps, D.M., *Economic Rights of Women in Ancient Greece*, Edinburgh 1979

Schaps, D.M., "The Monetization of the Marketplace in Athens", in: J. Andreau, P. Briant & R. Descat (eds.), *Économie Antique. Prix et formation des prix dans les économies antiques. Entretiens d'Archéologie et d'Histoire* 3, Saint-Bertrand-de-Comminges 1997

Schaps, D.M., "Socrates and the Socratics: when wealth becomes a problem", *CW* 96.2 (2003), 131–157

Schaps, D.M., *The Invention of Coinage and the Monetization of Ancient Greece*, Ann Arbor 2004

Scheid-Tissinier, E., *Les usages du don chez Homère. Vocabulaire et pratiques*, Nancy 1994

Schein, S.L., "Φιλία in Euripides' *Alcestis*", in: *Mètis. Anthropologie des mondes grecs anciens* 3.1–2 (1988), 179–206

Schein, S.L., "Verbal adjectives in Sophocles: necessity and morality", *CP* 93.4 (1998), 293–307

Schiappa, E., *Protagoras and logos: a study in Greek philosophy and rhetoric*, Columbia 2003

Schieffelin, E.L., "Reciprocity and the construction of reality", *Man* NS 15.3 (1980), 502–517

Schleiermacher, F., "Über die ethischen Werke des Aristoteles", in: *Samtliche Werke*, Berlin 1835

Schmidt, J.H.H., *Synonymik der griechischen Sprache*, Amsterdam 1969 [1879]

Schmoll, H., *Die griechischen Verba auf -ίζω*, Tübingen 1955

Schnapp, A., *Le chasseur et la cité: chasse et érotique en Grèce ancienne*, Paris 1997

Schofield, M., "Political friendship and the ideology of reciprocity", in: P. Cartledge, P. Millett & S. von Reden (eds.), *Kosmos: essays in order, conflict, and community in classical Athens*, Cambridge/New York 1998, 37–51

Schofield, M., *Plato. Political Philosophy*, Oxford 2006

Schriefl, A., *Platons Kritik an Geld und Reichtum*, Berlin & Boston 2013

Schriefl, A., "Plato on the Incompatibility of Wealth and Justice: the Property Arrangements in the *Republic*," *History of Political Thought* XXXIX.2 (2018), 193–215

Schroeder, F.M., "Friendship in Aristotle and some Peripatetic philosophers", in: J.T. Fitzgerald (ed.), *Greco-Roman Perspectives on Friendship*, Atlanta 1997, 35–57

Schumpeter, E.B. & Schumpeter, J.A., *History of economic analysis*, New York 1954

Schwarz, B. & G. Trommsdorff e.a., "Reciprocity in Intergenerational Support: A Comparison of Chinese and German Adult Daughters", *Journal of Family Issues* 31.2 (2010), 234–256

Schwarzenberg, E., *Die Grazien*, Bonn 1966

Schwarzenbach, S.A., *On Civic Friendship. Including Women in the State*, New York & Chicester 2009

Scodel, R., "Αδμητου λογος and the Alcestis", in: *Harvard Studies in Classical Philology* 83 (1979), 51–62

Scott, M., "*Philos, Philotês* and *Xenia*", *Act. Cl.* 22 (1969), 1–14

Scott, M., "*Charis* in Homer and the Homeric Hymns", *Act.Cl.* 26 (1983), 1–14

Scott, M., "*Charis* from Hesiod to Pindar", *Act. Cl.* 27 (1984), 1–13

Seaford, R., "Dionysus as destroyer of the household: Homer, tragedy, and the polis", in: T.H. Carpentier & C.A. Faraone (eds.), *Masks of Dionysus*, Ithaca N.Y. 1993, 115–146

Seaford, R., *Reciprocity and Ritual: Homer and Tragedy in the Developing City State*, Oxford 1994

Seaford, R., "Tragic money", *JHS* 118 (1998) 119–139

Seaford, R., *Money and the Early Greek Mind*, Cambridge 2004

Seaford, R., "Money and the genesis of the Wester subject", *Historical Materialism* 20.1 (2012), 78–102

Searle, J.R., *Speech Acts. An Essay in the Philosophy of Language*, Cambridge 1969

Sedláček, T., *Economics of Good and Evil: The Quest for Economic Meaning from Gilgamesh to Wall Street*, Oxford 2011

Selle, H., *Theognis und die Theognidea*, Berlin 2008

Sen, A., *On Ethics and Economics*, Oxford 1987

Shell, M., *The Economy of Literature*, Baltimore 1978

Shell, M., *Money, Language, and Thought: Literary and Philosophic Economiesfrom the Medieval to the Modern Era*, Berkley 1982

Sheppard, D., *Plato's* Republic. *An Edinburgh philosophical guide*, Edinburgh 2009

Shipton, K., "The private banks in fourth-century B.C. Athens: a reappraisal", *CQ* 47 (1997), 396–422

Silver, A., "Friendship in commercial society: eighteenth-century social theory and modern sociology", *AJS* 95.6 (1990), 1474–1504

Silver, A., "'Two Different Sorts of Commerce.' Friendship and Strangership in Civil Society", in: J. Weintraub & K. Kumar (eds.), *Public and Private in Thought and Practice. Perspectives on a Grand Dichotomy*, Chicago & London (1997), 43–74

Silver, M., *Economic Structures of Antiquity*, London 1995

Simmel, G., *Philosophie des Geldes*, Leipzig 1907

Simmel, G., *Philosophische Kultur. Gesammelte Essais*, Leipzig 1919

Simmel, G., "Faithfulness and Gratitude", in: K. Wolff, *The Sociology of Georg Simmel*, New York 1950 [1908]

Simmel, G., *The Philosophy of Money*, London 1978 [1900]

Skidelsky, R. & Skidelsky, E., *How much is Enough? The Love of Money, and the Case for the Good Life*, London 2012

Skultety, S.C., "Currency, Trade and Commerce in Plato's Laws", *History of Political Thought*, 27(2), 189–205

Skinner, B.F., *Science and Human Behavior*, New York 1953

Slings, S., *Plato: Clitophon*, Cambridge 1999

Sluiter, I. & R.M. Rosen, "General Introduction", in: R.M. Rosen & I. Sluiter (eds.), *Andreia: Studies in Manliness and Courage in Classical Antiquity*, Leiden 2003

Sluiter, I. & R.M. Rosen, "Chapter One. General Introduction", in: R. Rosen & I. Sluiter (eds.), *Valuing Others in Antiquity*, Leiden 2010, 1–15.

Sluiter, I., "Deliberation, Free Speech and the Marketplace of Ideas", in: T. van Haaften (ed.), *Bending Opinion. Essays on Persuasion in the Public Domain* (*Rhetoric in society*), Leiden 2011, 25–47

Smith, A., *The Theory of Moral Sentiments*, Indianapolis 1982 [1759]

Smith, A., *An Inquiry into the Nature and Causes of the Wealth of Nations*, Indianapolis 1976 [1776]

Smith, A., *Lectures on Jurisprudence*, Indianopolis 1978 [1763]

Smith-Pangle, L., *Aristotle and the Philosophy of Friendship*, Cambridge 2003

Snell, B., *Die Entdeckung des* Geistes. *The Discovery of the Mind. The Greek Origins of European Thought*, Oxford 1953

Snodgrass, A.M., *The Dark Age of Greece*, Edinburgh 1971

Snodgrass, A.M., "Archaology and the study of the Greek city", R.J. Murray & A. Wallace-Hadrill, *City and the country in the ancient world*, London 1991, 1–23

Snoek, J.A.M., *Initiations: a Methodological Approach to the Application of Classification and Definition Theory in the Study of Ritual*, Pijnacker 1987

Sober, E. & D.S. Wilson, *Unto Others: The Evolution and Psychology of Unselfish Behavior*, Cambridge 1998

Sohn-Rethel, A., *Geistige und körperliche Arbeit. Zur Theorie der gesellschaftlichen Synthesis*, Frankfurt 1973

Solomon, J. (ed.), *Ethica Eudemia*, Oxford 1915

Sommerstein, A.H., *The Comedies of Aristophanes 11: Wealth*, Warminster 2001

Sommerstein, A.H., *Menander: Samia*, Cambridge 2013

Soudek, J., "Aristotle's theory of exchange: an inquiry into the origin of economic analysis", *Proceedings of the American Philosophical Society* 96.1 (1952), 45–75

Spengler, J.J., "Aristotle on economic imputation and related matters", *Southern Economic Journal* 21 (1955), 371–389

Springborg, P., "Politics, primordialism, and orientalism: Marx, Aristotle, and the myth of Gemeinschaft", *American Political Science Review* 80 (1986), 185–211

Stallybrass, P. & A. White, *The Politics and Poetics of Transgression*, London 1986

Stanley, P.V., "The function of trade in Homeric society", *MBAH* 2 (1986), 5–14

Stanley, P.V., *Ancient Greek Market Regulations and Controls*, Berkeley 1976

Stein, M., *Definition und Schilderung in Theophrasts Charakteren*, Stuttgart 1992

Steiner, D.T., "Moving images: fifth-century victory monuments and the athlete's allure", *Class. Ant.* 17.1 (1998), 123–150

Steiner, D.T., *The Tyrant's Writ*, Princeton 1994

Steinmetz, P., *Charaktere II: Kommentar und Übersetzung*, München 1962

Stenzel, J., *Philosophie der Sprache*, Oldenbourgh 1934

Stern-Gillet, S., *Aristotle's Philosophy of Friendship*, Albany, NY 1995

Stevens, J.A., "Friendship and profit in Xenophon's *Oeconomicus*", in: P.A. van der Waart (ed.), *The Socratic movement*, Ithaca 1994, 209–237

Stevenson, T.R., "The Ideal Benefactor and the Father Analogy in Greek and Roman Thought", *CQ* n.s. 42.2 (1992), 421–436

Stocker, M., "Values and Purposes: the Limits of Teleology and the Ends of Friendship", *The Journal of Philosophy* LXXVIII.12 (1981), 747–765

Storey, I.C., *Euripides: Suppliant women*, London 2008

Strathern, M., *Women in between: female Roles in male World*, London 1972

Strathern, M., *The Gender of the Gift: Problems with Women and Problems with Society in Melanesia*, Berkeley 1990

Strathern, M., "Qualifed value: the perspective of gift exchange", in: C. Humphrey & S. Hugh-Jones (eds.), *Barter, Exchange and Value: an Anthropological Approach*, Cambridge 1992, 169–191

Strauss, B.S., *Fathers and Sons in Athens. Ideology and Society in the Era of the Peloponnesian War*, London 1993

Strauss, L., "The Spirit of Sparta or the Taste of Xenophon." *Social Research* 6.4 (1939), 502–536

Strauss, L., *Xenophon's Socrates*, Ithaca and London 1972

Striker, G., "Emotions in context: Aristotle's treatment of the passions in the *Rhetoric* and his moral psychology", in: A. Oksenberg Rorty (ed.), *Essays on Aristotle's Rhetoric*, Berkeley & Los Angeles 1996, 286–302

Strøm, I., "Obeloi of pre- or proto-monetary value in the Greek sanctuaries", in: T. Linders & B. Alroth (eds.), *Economics of Cult in the Ancient Greek World*, Uppsala 1992, 41–51

Strubbe, J.H.M., "Epigrams and Consolation Decrees for Deceased Youths," *L'antiquité classique* 67 (1998), 45–75

Suttles, G., "Friendship as a social institution", in: G.J. McCall (eds.), *Social Relations*, Chicago 1970, 95–135

Swanson, J.A., "Aristotle on liberality: Its relation to justice and its public and private practice," *Polity*, 27.1 (1994), 3–23

Taillardat, J., "φιλότης, πίστις et foedus", *REG* 95 (1982), 1–14

Tamiolaki, M., "Plato and Xenophon on Friendship. A Comparative Study (Plato Lysis and Xenophon Conversations of Socrates 2.6)", *CHS Research Bulletin* 2.2 (2014)

Tamiolaki, M., "Socrates' attitude towards politics in Xenophon and Plato", G. Danzig, D. Johnsen & D. Morrison (eds.), *Plato and Xenophon: comparative studies*, Leiden 2018

Tandy, D.W., *Warriors into Traders: the Power of the Market in Early Greece*, Berkeley 1997

Tannen, D., "What's in a frame? Surface evidence for underlying expectations", in: R.O. Freedle (ed.), *New Directions in Discourse Processing*, Norwood N.J. 1979

Tarrant, H., "*Elenchos* and *Exetasis*: Capturing the Purpose of Socratic Interrogation", in: G.A. Scott (ed.), *Does Socrates have a Method? Rethinking the Elenchus in Plato's Dialogues and Beyond*, Pennsylvania 2002, 61–77

Tarrant, H., "Socratic synousia: a post-Platonic myth?", *Journal of the History of Philosophy* 43.2 (2005), 131–155

Taussig, M., *The Devil and Commodity Fetishism in South America*, Chapel Hill 1980

Tell, H., "Wisdom for Sale? The Sophists and Money", *Classical Philology* 104 (2009), 13–33

Tell, H., *Plato's Counterfeit Sophists*, Washington DC 2011

Theocarakis, N.J., "*Antipeponthos* and reciprocity: the concept of equivalent exchange from Aristotle to Turgot", *International Review of Economics* 55 (2008), 29–44

Thomas, R., *Herodotus in Context* Cambridge 2000

Thomas, R., "Writing, law, and written law", in: M. Gagarin & D.J. Cohen (eds.), *The Cambridge Companion to Ancient Greek Law*, Cambridge 2005

Thomsen, O., "Socrates and Love", *CM* 52 (2002), 117–178

Thomson, G., *Studies in Ancient Greek society*, vol. II: *the First Philosophers*, London 1955

Thornton, B.S., *Eros: The Myth of Ancient Greek Sexuality*, Boulder 1997

Thury, E.M., "Euripides' *Alcestis* and the Athenian Generation Gap", *Arethusa* 21.2 (1988), 197–214

Tilg, S., "Die naive Hetäre und die grosse Politik (Xenophon, *Memorabilia* 3,11)", *MH* LXI (2004), 193–206

Titmuss, R.M., *The Gift Relationship: from Human Blood to Social Policy*, Harmondsworth 1970

Todd, S.C., *The Shape of the Athenian Law*, Oxford 1993

Todd, S.C. (trans.), *Lysias*, Austin 2000

Todd, S.C., "Lysias against Nikomachos: the fate of the expert in Athenian law", in: L. Foxhall & A.D.E. Lewis (eds.), *Greek Law in its Political Setting: Justification not Justice*, Oxford 1996, 101–131

Too, Y.L., *The Rhetoric of Identity in Isocrates: Text, Power, Pedagogy*, Cambridge 1995

Too, Y.L., *A Commentary on Isocrates' Antiodisis*, Oxford 2008

Tooby, J. & Cosmides, L., "Friendship and the Banker's Paradox: Other pathways to the evolution of adaptations for altruism", in: W.G. Runciman, J. Maynard Smith, & R.I.M. Dunbar (eds.), *Evolution of Social Behaviour Patterns in Primates and Man. Proceedings of the British Academy, 88*, Oxford 1996, 119–143

Toren, C., "Drinking Cash: the Purification of Money through Ceremonial Exchange in Fiji", in: J. Parry & M. Bloch (eds.), *Money and the Morality of Exchange*, Cambridge 1989, 142–164

Tredennick, H. & W. Waterfield (trans.), *Conversations of Socrates*, London 1990

Tsutsui, T., N. Muramatsu & S. Higashino, "Changes in Perceived Filial Obligation Norms among Coresident Family Caregivers in Japan", *The Gerontologist* 54.5 (2014), 797–807

Tullock, G., "Competing monies", *Journal of Money, Credit and Banking*, 7 (1975), 491–497

Uehara, E., "Reciprocity Reconsidered: Gouldner's 'Moral Norm of Reciprocity' and Social Support", *Journal of Social and Personal Relationships* 12.4 (1995), 483–502

Van Alphen, E., M. Bal & C.E. Smith, *The Rhetoric of Sincerity*, Stanford 2009

Van Berkel, T.A., "Pricing the invaluable: Socrates and the value of friendship", in: R. Rosen & I. Sluiter (eds.), *Valuing Others in Antiquity*, Leiden 2010, 249–278

Van Berkel, T.A., "Made to measure: Protagoras' metron," in: J.M. van Ophuijsen, M. van Raalte, P. Stork (eds.), *Protagoras of Abdera. The Man, his Measure*, Leiden 2013, 37–68

Van Berkel, T.A., "Friendship after Money: the Case of Classical Greece," in: C. Risseeuw & M. van Raalte (eds.), *Conceptualizing Friendship in Tme and Place*, Leiden 2017, 75–97

Van Berkel, T.A., "Socratic Economics and the Psychology of Money", in: G. Danzig, D. Johnson & D. Morrison (eds.), *Plato and Xenophon: Comparative Studies*, Leiden 2018, 391–432

Van Dijk, G.-J., *AINOI, ΛΟΓΟΙ, ΜΥΘΟΙ. Fables in Archaic, Classical, and Hellenistic Literature*, Leiden & New York 1997

Van der Mije, S.R., "Achilles' god-given strength", *Mnem.* 40.3–4 (1987), 241–267

Van Emde Boas, E., *Language and Character in Euripides'* Electra, Oxford 2017

Van Johnson, V., "Aristotle's Theory of Value", *The American Journal of Philology*, 60.4 (1939), 445–451

Van Raalte, M., "Socratic παρρησία and its afterlife in Plato's *Laws*", in: I. Sluiter & R.M. Rosen (eds.), *Free Speech in Classical Antiquity*, Leiden 2004, 279–312

Van Straten, F.T., "Gifts for the Gods", in: H.S. Versnel (ed.), *Faith, Hope and Worship*, Leiden 1981, 65–151, 285–311

Vander Waerdt, P.A., "Socrates in the Clouds", in: Vander Waerdt, P.A. (ed.), *The Socratic Movement*, Ithaca & London 1994, 48–86

Van 't Wout, P.E., "Solon's law on stasis: promoting active neutrality", *CQ* 60.2 (2010a), 289–301

Van 't Wout, P.E., "Visiblity and social evaluation in Athenian litigation", in: R.M. Rosen & I. Sluiter (eds.), *Valuing Others in Classical Antiquity*, Leiden 2010b, 249–277

Van Wees, H., *Status Warriors. War, Violence and Society in Homer and History*, Amsterdam 1992

Van Wees, H., "The law of gratitude: reciprocity in anthropological theory", in: C. Gill, N. Postlethwaite & R. Seaford, *Reciprocity in Ancient Greece*, Oxford 1998

Van Wees, H., "Mass and elite in Solon's Athens: the property classes revisited", in: J.H. Blok & A.P.M.H. Lardinois (eds.), *Solon of Athens. New Historical and Philological Approaches*, Leiden 2006, 351–389

Veligianni, C., "ΧΑΡΙΣ in den attischen Ehrendekreten der Klassischen Zeit und die Ergänzung in *IG* I^3 101, Z. 35–37, 51–52," *AHB* 3 (1989), 36–401.

Veligianni, C., *Wertbegriffe in den attischen Ehrendekreten der Klassischen Zeit*, Stuttgart 1997

Verdenius, W.J., "Pindar's fourteenth Olympian Ode", *Mnem.* 32.1/2 (1979), 12–38

Verdenius, W.J., *A commentary on Hesiod: Works and Days, vv. 1–382*, Leiden 1985

Vérilhac, A.-M., *ΠΑΙΔΕΣ ΑΩΡΟΙ: Poésie funéraire*, 1978

Vernant, J.-P., *Mythe et société en Grèce ancienne*, Paris 1974

Versnel, H.S., "Religious Mentality in Ancient Prayer", in: H.S. Versnel (ed.), *Faith, Hope and Worship: Studies in Greek and Roman Religion*, Leiden 1981, 1–64

Versnel, H.S., "Some reflections on the relationship magic-religion", *Numen* 38.2 (1991), 177–197

Vinogradoff, P., *Aristotle on Legal Redress*, Harvard 1908

Vlastos, G., "The Individual as an Object of Love in Plato", *Platonic Studies*, Princeton 1973, 3–42

Vlastos, G., "Socratic Irony", *Socrates. Ironist and Moral Philosopher*, Cambridge 1991, 21–44

Vohs, K.D., et. al., "The Psychological Consequences of Money", *Science* 314 (2006), 1154–1156

Vondeling, J., *Eranos*, Groningen 1961

Von Arnim, H., *Platos Jugenddialoge und die Entstehungszeit des Phaidros*, Leipzig 1914

Von Gierke, O., *Deutsches Privatrecht, vol. 2: Schuldrecht*, Munich-Leipzig 1917

Von Leyden, W., *Aristotelian Equality and Justice: His Political Argument*, New York 1985

Von Reden, S., "Deceptive readings: poetry and its value reconsidered", *CQ n.s.* 45.1 (1995), 30–50

Von Reden, S., "Money, law and exchange: coinage in the Greek polis", *JHS* 117 (1997) 154–176

Von Reden, S., *Exchange in Ancient Greece*, London 2003 [1995]

Von Reden, S., *Money in Classical Antiquity*, Cambridge 2010

Von Reden, S., *Antike Wirtschaft*, Berlin & Boston 2015

Von Wilamowitz-Moellendorff, U., *Platon*, Berlin 1920

Voss, J.F., J. Kennet, J. Wiley & T.Y.E. Schooler, "Experts at degate: the use of metahpor in the U.S. Senate debate on the Gulf Crisis", *Metaphor and Symbolic Activity* 7.3 & 4 (1992), 197–214

Wagner-Hasel, B., "Egoistic Exchange and Altruistic Gift", in: G. Algazi, V. Groebner & B. Jussen (eds.), *Negotiating the Gift. Pre-Modern Figurations of Exchange*, Göttingen 2003, 141–171

Walcot, P., *Greek Peasants, Ancient and Modern. A Comparison of Social and Moral Values*, Manchester 1970

Waterfield, R. (trans.), *Plato/ Republic*, Oxford 1993

Waterfield, R. (trans.), *Plato Gorgias*, Oxford & New York 1994

Waterfield, R. (trans.), *The Histories / Herodotus*, Oxford 1998

Webb, S.H., *The Gifting God. A Trinitarian Ethics of Excess*, Oxford 1996

Weber, M., *Economy and Society*, New York 1968

Weber, M., *Wirtschaft und Gesellschaft*, Tübingen 1972 [1922]

Wehrli, F., *Motivstudien zur griechischen Komödie*, Zürich 1936

Weiner, A.B., "Reproduction: a replacement for reciprocity", *American Ethnologist* 7.1 (1980), 71–85

Weiner, A.B., *Inalienable Possessions. The Paradox of Keeping-While-Giving*, Berkeley & Los Angeles 1992

Weissenberger, M., "Vater-Sohn-Beziehung und Komödienhandlung in Menander's 'Samia'," *Hermes* 119.4 (1991), 415–434

West, M.L., *Theogony*, Oxford 1966

West, M.L., *Hesiod. Works and Days. Ed. with prolegomena and commentary*, Oxford 1978

White, E.B. & K.S. White, *A Subtreasury of American Humor*, New York 1941

Whitehead, D., "Cardinal virtues: the language of public approbation in democratic Athens," *Classica et Mediaevalia* 44 (1993), 37–75

Whiting, J., "The Nicomachean Account of *Philia*", in: R. Kraut (ed.), *The Blackwell Guide to Aristotle's Nicomachean Ethics*, Malden MA 2006

Whyte, W.F., *Street Corner Society. The Social Structure of an Italian Slum*, Chicago & London, 1943

Wiggins, D., "Weakness of will, commensurability, and the objects of deliberation and desire", *Proceedings of the Aristotelian Society* n.s. 79 (1978–1979), 251–277

Wilde, O., "The Soul of Man under Socialism," *Fortnightly Review* 49 (1891), 292

Wilk, R.R. & L.C. Cliggett, *Economies and Cultures. Foundations of Economic Anthropology* (2nd edition), Colorado 2007

Will, E., "De l'Aspect éthique des origines grecques de la monnaie", *RH* 212 (1954), 209–231

Williams, B., *Problems of the Self*, Cambridge 1977

Wilson, D.F., *Ransom, Revenge, and Heroic Identity in the* Iliad, Cambridge/New York 2002

Winkler, J.J., *The Constraints of Desire: The Anthropology of Sex and Gender in Ancient Greece*, New York & London 1990

Wiseman, J.P., "Friendship: bonds and binds in a voluntary relationship", *Journal of Social and Personal Relationship* 3.2 (1986), 191–211

Wohl, V., *Intimate Commerce. Exchange, Gender and Subjectivity in Greek Tragedy*, Austin 1998

Wohl, V., *Law's Cosmos: Juridical Discourse in Athenian Forensic Oratory*, Cambridge 2010

Wolin, S.S., *Politics and Vision: Continuity and Innovation in Western Political Thought*, London 1960

Wong, E., "A Chinese virtue is now the law," *New York Times* July 2, 2013.

Worthington, I., *A Historical Commentary on Dinarchus: Rhetoric and Conspirace in Later Fourth-Century Athens*, Michigan 1992

Wray, R., "Modern money", in: J. Smithin (ed.), *What is Money*?, London 2000, 42–67

Wray, R., *Credit and State Theories of Money: The Contributions of A. Mitchell Innes*, Cheltenham UK & Northampton US 2004

Wray, R., *The Athenian Agora III: Litery and Epigraphical Testimonia*, Princeton 1957

Wycherley, R.E., *The Athenian Agora III. Literary and Epigraphical Testimonia*, Princeton 1957

Wyse, W., *The Speeches of Isaeus with Critical and Explanatory Notes*, Cambridge 1904

Yack, B., "Community and Conflict in Aristotle's Political Philosophy," *The Review of Politics* 47.1 (1985), 92–112

Yack, B., *The Problems of a Political Animal: Community, Justice, and Conflict in Aristotelian Political Thought*, Berkeley & Los Angeles 1993

Yamagishi, T. & K.S. Cook, "Generalized Exchange and Social Dilemmas," *Social Psychology Quarterly* 56.4 (1993), 235–248

Yan, Y., "The gift and gift economy," J.G. Carrier (ed.), *A Handbook of Economic Anthropology*, Cheltenham/Northampton 2005, 246–261

Yunis, H.E., *A New Creed. Fundamental Religious Beliefs in the Athenian Polis and Euripidean Drama*, Göttingen 1988

Yunis, H.E., *On the Crown/Demosthenes*, Cambridge 2001

Zafiropoulos, C.A., *Ethics in Aesop's Fables: The 'Augustana' Collection*, Leiden 2001

Zeitlin, F.I., *Playing the Other: Gender and Society in Classical Greek Literature*, Chicago 1996

Zelizer, V.A., *Pricing the Priceless Child: The Changing Social Value of Children*, New York 1985

Zelizer, V.A., *The Purchase of Intimacy*, Princeton 2005

Zhang, Z. & G. Danan e.a., "Coresidence With Elderly Parents in Contemporary China: The Role of Filial Piety, Reciprocity, Socioeconomic Resources, and Parental Needs" *Journal of Cross-Cultural Gerontology* 29.3 (2014), 259–276

Zheng, G., S. Shi & H. Tang, "Population Development and the Value of Children in the People's Republic of China", in: G. Trommsdorff & B. Nauck (eds.), *The Value of Children in Cross-Cultural Perspective: Case Studies from Eight Societies*, Lengerich 2005, 239–282

Index of Modern Authors

Index of Names and Subjects

Index of Greek Terminology

Index of Ancient Sources

List of Key Passages

Chapter 3

Chapter 4

Chapter 5

Chapter 6

Chapter 7